English Result

Intermediate Teacher's Book

Annie McDonald & Mark Hancock

with Rachel Godfrey

OXFORD

UNIVERSITY PRESS

Contents

Introduction

Welcome to **English Result**! We've focused on making each lesson motivating, attractive, and memorable. We've planned the course to be complete and success-oriented. We treat language as a practical, action-oriented tool for communication. We've made the course transparent and easy to follow, with a clear lesson and unit structure. We hope you enjoy it!

Motivating

English Result is designed to motivate. We believe that quality of learning depends on quality of attention, and students will only pay attention if they are motivated. Student motivation may be extrinsic (they study the subject for external rewards) or intrinsic (they like the subject for its own sake), or a mix of these.

Adult and young adult students often have very good extrinsic reasons for learning English – for work, exams, study, or travel, for example. However, this alone does not guarantee that they will be successful; especially considering that many will have tried to learn English before with disappointing results. We've often heard frustrated students say things like, 'I've studied English for six years and I still can't speak it!'. These students need a fresh new approach, including course material which is intrinsically appealing.

We've written **English Result** with this in mind, by creating material which will act like a magnet to attract student attention. In our experience, texts and tasks are likely to work as 'attention magnets' if they have one or more of the following properties:

– curiosity
– entertainment
– challenge
– enjoyment
– space for personalization
– space for choice and control

For this reason, we have consciously tried to make sure that at least one of these properties is central to each lesson.

Once the students' attention has been attracted, their motivation needs to be sustained during the lesson and through the course. They need to feel that they are making progress and achieving something worthwhile. This achievement is motivating in itself. We aim to cultivate achievement motivation in a number of ways:

– By providing engaging lessons which begin by stating a practical communicative objective (**How to ...**) and provide all the necessary input for the students to achieve that objective.

– By providing tasks which are clear, focused, challenging, do-able, personalisable, and which offer choices.

– By providing assessment tools for both learner and teacher which are transparent and allow the students to check their own progress against the independent, internationally recognized student attainment levels in the CEFR (the **Common European Framework of Reference**). For more information, go to www.oup.com/elt/teacher/result.

Attractive and memorable

English Result is designed for maximum visual impact. The entire left-hand page of the main lessons consists of a striking combination of picture and text. These 'impact pages' are designed to attract the students' attention. They are the kinds of pages that would probably spark the curiosity of any person thumbing through the book, even someone *not* studying English. These pages are addressed to the reader-as-person, rather than the reader-as-student-of-English, and their impact is not diluted by instructions, explanations, or exercises. The impact page forms the 'centre of gravity' of the lesson, helping to give each lesson a distinct and memorable character.

We believe that variety from lesson to lesson is crucial to maintaining the students' interest, so the impact pages include a wide mix of genres such as the following:

– magazine articles
– comedy sketches
– mystery stories
– games
– puzzles
– personality tests
– general knowledge quizzes
– poems
– art

There is always a strong visual component on the impact pages. We feel that images are very valuable in language learning for a number of reasons:

– In language teaching, a picture is like a text where the students provide the words. As a result, a picture can provide content for a lesson but at the same time leave the students with an active role in constructing the language.

– A picture can provide a very clear context for new language. Often, this context would be impossible to describe in words at the student's level of English.

– Pictures are level-flexible. The more language you know, the more you can say about the picture.

– Pictures are attention magnets.

Success-oriented

English Result is designed for success.

- **Optimum level of challenge:** The course is based on realistic expectations of what the students should be able to achieve in a lesson. For example, we do not expect students to be able to discuss issues in fluent English when they have only been prepared to produce a few basic exchanges. The course is challenging enough to keep a student of this level alert, but not so difficult that they get lost and lose their sense of control. In this way, students are positioned right at the edge of their competence and are pushing it forward.

- **Positive approach:** The course takes a positive approach to learning and progress by helping both the student and teacher to focus on what students CAN do rather than what they can't. Language learning is a complex process and we do not expect that, at the end of a lesson, a student will be able to produce a flawless performance in a communicative task. Instead, we take a positive approach to learning by helping teachers and students focus on elements of communication which are successful, rather than viewing an utterance as something to be corrected. In this way, students can see how far they've come and not only how far they've got to go.

- **Support:** In **English Result Intermediate**, students are given plenty of support in all skills. In speaking, for example, new words and phrases are often modelled on the audio component to help with pronunciation. Students are also introduced to communication strategies and different techniques they can use to deal with difficulties they might experience in conversations, for example, how to correct a misunderstanding. Students are given the opportunity to prepare and plan before freer communicative tasks. Often, students' attention is focused on how to do a particular reading or listening task, so that they are empowered to use appropriate and effective strategies for the task at hand. All of this kind of scaffolding means that students are not simply 'thrown in at the deep end', and success is more than just a matter of luck.

- **Realistic learning load:** The language presented in **English Result Intermediate** is tightly graded and controlled so as not to overwhelm the learner. The grammar and vocabulary input is informed by publications related to the Common European Framework of Reference, based on what is most useful and frequent. In this way, students are not adrift in an endless sea of new language – they are in a pool, and they have a good chance of reaching the other side.

- **Recycling:** New language is continually recycled from lesson to lesson and across the course. In addition to this implicit recycling, there is explicit recycling in the E lessons and Review lessons at the end of every unit. The E lessons are designed to put some of the new language from the unit into action in the context of a carefully staged and supported writing task. The Review lessons give students a chance to revisit all the new grammar and vocabulary in the unit.

- **Feedback on progress:** English Result comes with a comprehensive set of assessment material so that students can test their new skills on a regular basis and get reliable feedback on what they're doing well and what they need to do more work on.

Action-oriented and practical

English Result encourages students to see language in terms of what they can do with it, rather than as a body of knowledge. Often, students view language as just a list of words and grammar structures and they end up in the frustrating position where they know a lot about the language but they still can't speak it. In our experience, most students would like to imagine themselves coming out of a course being able to say, 'I can use English', rather than, 'I know the past tense of irregular verbs in English.' To help move towards this, we have tried to show how the new language is used to create meaning and to communicate:

- The **How to** titles of all the lessons indicate a practical purpose for the language in the lesson, showing the students that they are not simply learning new vocabulary and structures 'because they are there'.

- New grammar and vocabulary are presented within the flow of a lesson, as part of an overall practical objective, and not just for their own sake.

- The **Can do** bar at the end of each lesson reminds students that they are learning practical abilities, not passive knowledge.

Complete

The **English Result Intermediate** syllabus is closely informed by Council of Europe publications and includes a comprehensive coverage of the various competences outlined in them. A strong A2 student who has worked successfully through **English Result Intermediate** should be able to place themselves at or above B1 for listening, reading, spoken interaction, spoken production, and writing at the end of the course. For more information, go to www.oup.com/elt/teacher/result

- **Communicative tasks:** The **English Result Intermediate** lesson themes are functional in nature, and are based on activities described as being appropriate for a B1-level learner. In this way, the student can easily see the use of the language they are learning, and it is pitched to their level to provide an optimum degree of challenge.

- **Skills:** In addition to the traditional four skills of listening, reading, speaking, and writing, **English Result** follows the CEFR by regarding the speaking skill as comprising both spoken interaction (conversation) as a skill in its own right, and spoken production (for example, giving a short self-introduction) as a separate skill. This helps to ensure that the students experience a balanced range of speaker roles so that they really can come away from the course being able to 'speak English'.

- **Strategies:** **English Result** pays explicit attention to the various strategies students can use to overcome difficulties in communicative situations, such as asking for clarification or listening and identifying clues to meaning. In this way, students will be empowered and not left helpless whenever they hit a communication problem.

- **Language competence:** **English Result** has clearly identifiable grammar, vocabulary, and pronunciation strands, which are highlighted at the top of each lesson page as well as in the contents pages. In addition, attention is paid to sociolinguistic competence (namely aspects of culture such as appropriate ways of addressing people) and pragmatic competence (for example being able to make and respond to suggestions appropriately or using linkers to join ideas together). This gives students a full picture of what the language is and how it works.

Clear unit structure

All 12 units of **English Result Intermediate** have the same six-lesson structure:

- Lessons A–D each consist of two pages: the impact page on the left and the lesson page on the right.
- Lesson E is one page, reviewing the language in the unit and building up to a written output task.
- Each unit ends with a one-page Review lesson, providing extra practice of the grammar and vocabulary covered in the unit.

This clear structure means that you know where you are at a glance, making the course clear and easy-to-use.

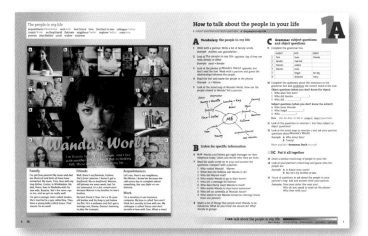

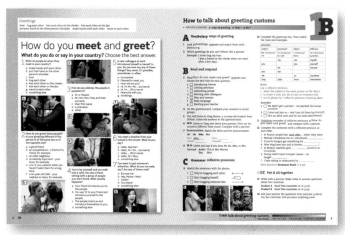

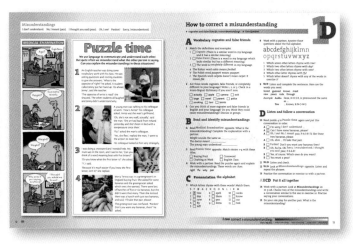

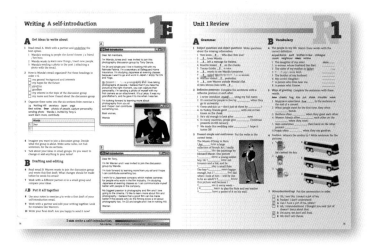

How English Result works

How to ...

The **How to** provides a clear focus and makes the practical learning outcome absolutely transparent to the student.

Left-hand impact page

Every A to D lesson includes a whole page of visual stimulation to keep motivation high.

Many different genres, from news articles to adverts, cartoon strips to mystery stories, quizzes to games, help to provide variety and keep the material fresh.

Visual help

Images are used extensively to make texts and new language more accessible and memorable for the students.

Greetings

bow hug each other kiss each other on the cheeks kiss each other on the lips
put your hand on the other person's shoulder shake hands with each other wave to each other

How do you **meet** and **greet**?

What do you do or say in your country? Choose the best answer.

1 What do people do when they meet in your country?
   a shake hands with each other
   b put their hand on the other person's shoulder
   c bow
   d hug each other
   e kiss each other on the cheeks
   f kiss each other on the lips
   g wave to each other
   h *something else*

2 How do you greet these people? Is your greeting different if the person is of the same sex or of the opposite sex?
   a a good friend
   b an acquaintance – a friend of a friend, for example
   c an older neighbour
   d somebody important – your boss, for example
   e one of your parents when you haven't seen them for a long time
   f a six-year-old child – your nephew or niece, for example

3 How do you address the people in question 2?
   a Sir or Madam
   b Mr / Ms / Mrs / Miss and their surname
   c their first name
   d a nickname
   e *other*

4 You're by yourself and you walk into a café. You see a friend sitting with a group of people you don't know. What usually happens?
   a Your friend introduces you to the people.
   b You say 'hi' to your friend and introduce yourself to the people.
   c The people stand up and introduce themselves to you.
   d *something else*

5 A new colleague at work introduces himself or herself to you. Do you ever say any of these things? Say *never*, *it's possible*, *sometimes*, or *often*.
   a Enchanted.
   b Pleased to meet you.
   c How old are you?
   d Hi, I'm Mr / Ms ... (surname)
   e Hi, I'm ... (first name)
   f Peace be with you.
   g Greetings.

6 You meet a teacher from your school in the street. What do you say?
   a Hello, teacher!
   b Hello, Mr / Ms ... (surname)
   c Hello, ... (first name)
   d Hello, Sir / Miss.
   e *something else*

7 You want to get someone's attention. What do you normally say? Are any of these rude?
   a Excuse me!
   b Hey, Mister / Miss!
   c Listen!
   d You there!
   e *something else*

8 1B

GVP bar

The grammar, vocabulary, and pronunciation content of each lesson is clearly signposted so teachers and students know what to expect.

Vocabulary

The vocabulary input is manageable and relevant – high-frequency, useful language that is of immediate practical value.

Students are given the opportunity to expand their vocabulary in areas which are relevant for them. This helps them to talk about their own life and circumstances.

Vocabulary is constantly recycled across lessons, helping students to fix it in their minds.

Reading and listening skills

Receptive skills, sub-skills, and strategies appropriate for a student aspiring to reach level B1 are made explicit in the section headings. Teachers and students know what they are practising and why.

Both audio and textual materials are true to their genre. For example, casual conversation contains features of natural speech such as hesitation. Scripted dialogues contain authentic sound effects so students are exposed to the contrasting varieties of spoken English they might expect to hear both in the media and on the street.

Pronunciation

Pronunciation sections flow naturally from the **How to**, grammar, or vocabulary of each lesson, helping students see how pronunciation fits into the wider picture.

Equal weight is given to segmental features such as sounds and to supra-segmental features such as sentence stress. In this way, students get balanced practice of English pronunciation both receptively and productively.

Pronunciation exercises take a meaning-based approach wherever possible, so that students can see how pronunciation can change meaning.

Grammar bank

The **Grammar Bank** at the back of the book provides clear reference notes plus extra exercises for students who need more controlled practice.

Productive Skills

The **Put it all together** section at the end of every A–D lesson gives students the chance to put new language into action in a speaking or interaction activity. This provides an opportunity for freer oral practice of the new language.

The students are given plenty of support and preparation for these activities to help give them the best possible chance of success.

The **Put it all together** section at the end of every E lesson is a piece of written work that has been carefully prepared, step-by-step, throughout the whole lesson. In this way, students have plenty of ideas, strategies, and appropriate language before they start writing. Students are also shown stages involved in the writing process.

Grammar sections

Students always see new grammar in context before it is actively presented to them. This shows the grammar in action and demonstrates how it contributes to meaning, before they focus on the form.

Students are encouraged to work out rules and patterns of language for themselves so that the presentation is more memorable.

Reflection

The **Can do** bar at the end of each lesson reminds students what the lesson has been about and invites them to reflect on how much they have learnt. This helps them to self-assess their achievement realistically and positively.

How to talk about greeting customs

1B

g reflexive pronouns   v ways of greeting   ✓ *Miss* /ɪ/ or *Ms* /z/

A Vocabulary **ways of greeting**

1 Look at **Greetings** opposite and match them with photos a–g.

2 Which greetings do you use? When? Tell a partner.
Examples I never hug my boss.
I kiss a friend on the cheeks when we meet after a few days.

B Read and respond

3 Read **How do you meet and greet?** opposite and choose the best title for each question.
a ☐ Introducing friends
b ☐ Getting attention
c ☐ Addressing people
d ☐ Meeting new colleagues
e ☐ Men and women
f ☑ Body language
g ☐ Meeting your teacher

4 Do the questionnaire. Compare your answers in small groups.

5 You will listen to Greg Brown, a 20-year-old student from Britain. Guess his answers to the questionnaire.

6 1B.1▶ Listen to Greg and check your guesses. How are his answers different from yours? Compare with a partner.

7 **Pronunciation** Match the titles and the pronunciation.
Mr Ms ~~Miss~~ Mrs
/mɪs/ _Miss_   /mɪz/ _____
/ˈmɪsɪz/ _____   /ˈmɪstə(r)/ _____

8 1B.2▶ Listen and say if you hear *Mr, Ms, Miss,* or *Mrs*.
Example **Audio** This is Mrs Mirren.
You Mrs!

C Grammar **reflexive pronouns**

9 Match the sentences with the photos.
1 ☐ They're hugging each other. ⟵——⟶
2 ☐ She's hugging herself. ⟸
3 ☐ She's hugging someone else. ——⟶

10 Complete the grammar box. Then match the rules and examples.

pronouns			
subject	possessive	object	reflexive
She introduced me.	He introduced his wife.	I introduced them.	We introduced ourselves.
	my	me	myself
you		you	yourself
	his		himself
she	her		
we		us	ourselves
they	their	them	themselves

Rules
Use a reflexive pronoun:
1 when the subject is the same person as the object.
2 to make it clear you did it and not someone else.
3 in the phrase *by* + reflexive pronoun, meaning *alone*.

Examples
a ☐ We didn't get a painter – we painted the house ourselves.
b ☐ Come and join us – don't just sit there by yourself!
c ☐ He's an adult now and he can look after himself.

11 Underline examples of reflexive pronouns in **How do you meet and greet?** and compare with a partner.

12 Complete the sentences with a reflexive pronoun or *each other*.
1 In France, people kiss _each other_ when they meet.
2 Nobody introduced me so I introduced _____.
3 If you're hungry, get something for _____.
4 How long have you and Jo known _____?
5 In Britain, relatives give _____ presents at Christmas.
6 Danny didn't have trumpet classes – he taught _____.
7 I hate eating in restaurants by _____.

More practice? **Grammar Bank** ≫ p.136.

ABC Put it all together

13 Work with a partner. Make notes to answer questions about two countries.
Student A Read **Two countries** on ≫ p.126.
Student B Read **Two countries** on ≫ p.133.

14 Ask your partner the questions from exercise 13 about his / her countries. Did you learn anything new?

I can talk about greeting customs. ▮▮▮▮▮▮▮▮
Tick ✓ the line.   with a lot of help   with some help   on my own   very easily

9

What else does English Result offer?

Student's Book

Workbook
with MultiROM

Workbook
with Answer Key Booklet
and MultiROM

Teacher's Book
with DVD

Class Audio CDs

For students: extra practice material www.oup.com/elt/result
For teachers: extra resources www.oup.com/elt/teacher/result

Teacher's Book

The **English Result** Teacher's Book has been designed as a resource:
- for planning before the lesson
- for quick reference during the lesson
- for step-by-step guidance during a lesson

The Teacher's Book is interleaved with the Student's Book so that the teaching notes are on the page facing the corresponding classroom material. This, together with strong section headings, clear answer keys, and colour-coded extra activities, makes for easy navigation and fast cross-referencing.

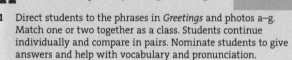

A Vocabulary ways of greeting

1   Direct students to the phrases in *Greetings* and photos a–g. Match one or two together as a class. Students continue individually and compare in pairs. Nominate students to give answers and help with vocabulary and pronunciation.

> a shaking hands, hands on shoulder
> b kiss each other on the cheeks
> c kiss each other on the lips
> d hug each other   e shake hands with each other
> f bow   g wave to each other

Extra help
Call out a photo letter, for the class to say the phrase from *Greetings*. Monitor and drill pronunciation, encouraging students to link words together and say the phrases with natural rhythm. Students continue in pairs or small groups.

What's in it?

The teacher's notes for each lesson are in three main sections:

- **Orientation** This gives you all the background information about the language and content of the lesson so that you can see 'the bigger picture'.

- **Step-by-step lesson notes** These guide you through the lesson.

- **Assessment guide** At the end of the lesson, this helps you assess student performance so that you and your students can see how far they've come.

Orientation

These notes appear in the first column of a set of notes for each lesson, and provide you with a variety of lesson-appropriate information: the context of situation, the language focus of the lesson, and what will happen in the *Put it all together*. The section ends with practical preparation ideas and warmer suggestions.

- **Context notes** This is a an overview of what the students will mainly focus on during the lesson, along with a brief summary of the input material to help you quickly 'tune in' to the material.

- **Language focus** This is an 'at-a-glance' boxed summary of main language areas of the lesson (grammar, vocabulary and phrases, pronunciation and discourse), along with an indicator of language points being previewed, recycled or which should be treated for recognition purposes only. This helps you distinguish between areas of language which need greater attention and language which is incidental to a particular lesson.

- **Language notes** These notes give extra information about aspects of the new language that often confuse students, such as structures which may be different in their own language, or false friends. In this way, you'll be prepared for those 'difficult' questions.

- **Culture notes** These are brief notes on aspects of everyday culture such as different politeness conventions or conversational norms. You can use this information to help your students become more inter-culturally aware. For more information, go to www.oup.com/elt/teacher/result.

- **End-product notes** These notes provide a summary of the final task: what students will be doing, what materials they can look back to for support, and how they will work together to do it. This means you know in advance what the whole lesson is building towards.

- **Preparation notes** These notes tell you what you can do before the lesson to make it run more smoothly, such as asking students to bring dictionaries or thinking about classroom organization for particular activities. This helps to ensure you're not caught unprepared.

- **Warmer notes** The **Warmer** section provides topic-opener activities for you to get your students thinking and talking about the topic and to introduce the **How to ...**, the communicative task focus and aim of the lesson.

Step-by-step lesson notes

Numbered exercise notes

These notes accompany the exercises in the Student's Book, following the same numbering system for ease of navigation. The notes include:

- Advice on **classroom management**, for example how students should be grouped.
- **Teaching techniques**, for example, learner training. When dealing with reading and listening activities, it is often helpful to give students the opportunity to think about different ways of doing a task. The lesson notes in the Teacher's Book offer suggestions to help you raise students' awareness to different strategies they could use and to help them become more effective and successful language learners.
- Tips on when and how to give **feedback** on students' performance, and what aspects of their performance to focus on. The notes also advise you where *not* to expect accuracy or correct error. For more information go to www.oup.com/elt/teacher/result.
- **Text orientation** for the listening and reading sections in each lesson, we provide a mini-orientation to the topic of a text, a summary of the sub-skills being developed, and supplementary information on the genre of a written text or the qualities of a listening text.

Extras

These notes are in colour so that you can distinguish them from the procedural notes. They include:

- **Language notes** on typical problem areas in the focus language.
- **Teaching tips** to give you extra ideas for dealing with different teaching points.
- **Extra help** for dealing with students who are having difficulty.
- **Extra activities** in case you have extra time and would like to give more practice.
- **Extra plus**: ideas to provide more challenge for those students who need it.
- **Early finishers**: extra activities for mixed ability classes or where some students finish earlier than others.
- **Answer keys**: These have been designed to be quickly located for ease of use during the lesson.

Student performance

At the end of each lesson, you will find an **assessment checklist** to help you to assess and give feedback on student performance, and to focus student attention on specific criteria when they are deciding where to place themselves on the **Can do** bar.

Student performance

Students should be able to exchange factual information.

You can use this checklist to monitor and give feedback or to assess students' performance.

Content	Do students answer the questions? exercise 4
Grammar	Do students use subject and object pronouns accurately? exercise 10
Vocabulary	Do students use a variety of greetings phrases? exercise 4

I can **talk about greeting customs.**

Students tick *on my own* if they have answered the questions using their notes. They tick *with some help* if they have read a couple of sentences from *Pairwork, Two countries*.

- **Balanced** The list gives you a menu of criteria by which to judge performance, for example, content, grammar (accuracy and range), fluency, interaction, or coherence. The criteria are systematically varied from lesson to lesson so that your assessment and feedback is balanced and not dominated by only one aspect, such as grammatical accuracy, for example.
- **Practical** When you assess student performance, it is impossible to focus on all aspects at once. For this reason, there are only a few criteria specified in each assessment checklist, in order to make the task more manageable. In addition, for each criterion, a very concrete and specific feature is specified for you to listen out for, helping to make your assessment more focused and objective rather than impressionistic. This also helps give your students informative feedback.
- **Appropriate** The task checklists in **English Result Intermediate** are based on the scales at B1 in the Common European Framework of Reference. This means you can be confident that the assessment criteria are relevant and appropriate to the students' level.
- **Transparent** The assessment checklists are transparent for both teacher and student alike. They make it easy for you to explain and for students to understand exactly what they're doing well and what could be improved. A final note in the Student Performance section gives more advice on helping students self-assess on the **Can do** bar at the bottom of the page. For more information, go to www.oup.com/elt/teacher/result.

Notes for Review lessons

The Review lessons in the Student's Book provide a set of familiar, free-standing exercises which students can use to review the main grammar and vocabulary in a unit. The accompanying Teacher's Book notes provide a wealth of extra activities and exercise types to help tailor the material to your students' needs. For further information, go to www.oup.com/elt/teacher/result.

The **Review** lessons can be used in a variety of different ways. For example:

- You can have a quiet class, to allow students to work at their own pace, and make yourself available to attend individual questions.
- Students could work through all the exercises in pairs or small groups.
- Students could chose which exercises they want to do.
- You could also use the **Review** activities at an appropriate point in your lesson to give students further controlled practice.
- You could set the **Review** exercises as homework, possibly asking students to choose two or three exercises, and give students parts of the answer key for them to self-correct.

In each set of Teacher's Book **Review** lesson notes, you will find:

- A Review Lesson **Warmer**, with an exercise or activity based on ten key phrases from the unit.
- **Warm-up activities** for each exercise: suggestions for optional short (often whole-class) activities which get students thinking about a language point before they do the exercise.
- **Set-up notes** for each exercise: practical advice and answer keys.
- **Follow-up notes** for each exercise: suggestions for optional activities which usually have a more student-centred focus.
- **Early finishers**: suggestions for further activities which students can do individually, often giving them the opportunity for personal reflection on their work on the unit as a whole.

Also in the Teacher's Book

Unit Tests

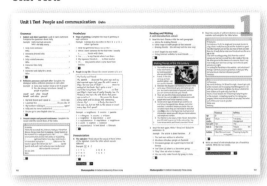

- One photocopiable Test per Student's Book unit (see p.162)
- Each Test includes Grammar, Vocabulary, Pronunciation Awareness, and Reading and Writing sections.
- Easy to administer with clear instructions and examples for students and marking guidelines for teachers.

DVD

Key features:

- 30 minutes of classroom footage and author commentary to show you how the material works in the classroom.
- Accompanying teacher training worksheets www.oup.com/elt/teacher/result.

Other components

Workbook

- One page of grammar, vocabulary, and pronunciation practice exercises for each Student's Book lesson (with **Can do** self-assessment).
- Two pages of **Skills practice** every unit to develop students' reading, writing, and listening skills.
- **Self check tests** for every unit to help students reflect on their learning and measure their progress.

MultiROM

- **Student's MultiROM** with interactive listening, vocabulary, and pronunciation practice plus downloadable study documents.

Website

The **Result Website** provides extra interactive and downloadable materials, including:

- Listening tests
- Speaking tests
- CEFR support
- English Result Portfolio
- Worksheets to accompany the DVD
- Extra practice for students

Teacher's site: www.oup.com/elt/teacher/result
Student's site: www.oup.com/elt/result

Assessment in English Result

English Result contains a coherent, comprehensive, flexible, and reliable set of assessment materials for both teachers and students. These materials can be found in various components in **English Result**: the Student's Book, Workbook, Workbook MultiROM, Teacher's Book, and Website.

We take a broad view of assessment and provide a set of resources we think will be useful for both teachers and students. We believe that one of the main purposes of assessment is to show what has been achieved, and so, in keeping with the key values of the course, we have provided material to help you to provide reliable feedback and to credit students for what they are able to do. In other words, as well as providing traditional tests, we also offer assessment materials which are success-oriented and informative. We hope the result will be a positive impact on motivation and learning.

For teachers: We provide a set of traditional tests which comprehensively assess language and skills on a unit-by-unit basis, and which are easy to administer and mark. To help teachers feel that they are being fair and consistent in their assessment, we also provide clear answer keys with suggestions on how to allocate marks and what to focus on when assessing the writing and speaking skills. For more information, go to www.oup.com/elt/teacher/result.

For students: We provide a range of materials which will encourage students to reflect on their progress in relation to their personal learning needs and current learning goals. Our aim is to help teachers to help students to take greater responsibility for their own learning. At the end of the course, students who want to will be able to see how their progress in **English Result Intermediate** relates to the Council of Europe 'Can do' descriptions in relation to level B1 for Listening, Reading, Spoken Interaction, Spoken Production, and Writing.

Assessment for teachers

Put it all together tasks

In the Teacher's Book lesson notes, we provide a general description of the type of activities students do in the **Put it all together** section in each lesson. We also offer some task-specific criteria to help you focus on particular aspects of students' language. The checklists offer different criteria on a lesson-by-lesson basis, and using these will help you become more confident in using a range of criteria for speaking and writing tasks. If you want to use the criteria to give your students a mark for their performance, you should also add an overall evaluation of how well you felt students performed the task.

Unit tests

The **Unit Tests** give students the chance to show how much they can do. On pp.162–185 of the Teacher's Book, there are photocopiable **Unit tests**. There are three sections, testing Grammar, Vocabulary, and Pronunciation Awareness, and a further two sections with Reading Comprehension and Writing tasks. There are 60 marks in total for this part of the test, divided equally between language and skills. Overall, each test takes about 55 minutes, and is easy to administer, with clear instructions and examples which demonstrate to students what they have to do. The listening and speaking tests, with 20 marks allocated to each skill, can be found on www.oup.com/elt/teacher/result.

All the questions and activities are based on the material students have covered in the corresponding Student's Book unit. The grammar and vocabulary content of a unit test is closely linked to the unit's Review Lesson, with a range of testing questions designed to help to build students' confidence before they embark on more specific exam training courses, for example if they plan to sit internationally recognized language examinations.

We have designed the speaking tests so that you can choose to focus on either spoken interaction or spoken production, testing students in groups of two or three. There are role cards for students, with clear instructions for each part of the test. There are also step-by-step instructions, and user-friendly assessment criteria to help you award marks for your students' spoken performance reliably and with confidence.

Samples of the **Unit Tests** and answer keys were trialled in different countries, and we looked carefully at how the students answered questions and what the teachers had to say about the material. The insights we gained informed development of the tests and the answer keys.

The answer keys

The **Unit Test** answer keys on pp.000–000 of the Teacher's Book include guidance on how to deal with students' mistakes in relation to the testing focus of particular questions. For example, in order to help you be sure you are responding to students' answers objectively and consistently, we suggest that it is best if no half marks are awarded. In a reading comprehension test, for example, we advise that an answer which shows a student has understood a text should not be penalized for spelling mistakes. This isn't to say that accurate spelling isn't important – students will be required to demonstrate this in another part of the test.

In the answer keys, we also include assessment criteria to help you assess students' writing and speaking skills, plus advice on how to distribute marks for the different areas. The task-specific assessment criteria have been anchored to B1 descriptions of ability in the CEFR, and they follow a similar format to the assessment checklists in the Teacher's Book notes. You could use information you collect to diagnose and build up a picture of strengths and weaknesses on a class basis or for individual feedback. By showing students how you assess, you can help them develop criteria to evaluate their own work and identify areas needing further attention.

Assessment for students

The Can do bar

At the end of each lesson in the Student's Book, students are invited to reflect on their performance in the task and mark their self-assessment on the **Can do** bar at the bottom of the page. The bar is worded to encourage a positive outlook and is a simple learner-training device. With regular use, it should:

- engage students in the learning process
- make the link between their own learning experiences and progress
- help students identify their personal learning goals
- develop the ability to become more realistic in their self-assessment
- increase student motivation

The Teacher's Book lesson notes offer some assessment criteria which you could use to help students reflect on their performance before they mark the **Can do** bar. There is also a brief description of the abilities of a student who might be considered to be at one of the middle positions on the scale – *with some help* or *on my own*. The other positions, *with a lot of help* and *very easily*, can be described relative to the middle positions.

Students can return to their initial self-assessment and review their position on the bar after they have worked with other **English Result** materials, for example the Workbook. Students can transfer their self-assessment to the Biography in the **English Result Portfolio Practice Book** at regular intervals. Later, these can be transferred to the Passport, which has descriptions of ability in the five skills based on the CEFR. Thus, the bar acts as a personalized record of both achievement during the lesson, and progress over the course.

The Self Check Tests

In addition to on-going self-assessment using the **Can do** bars at the end of each lesson, students are given the opportunity to think about their progress by using the Self Check Tests after each unit of the Workbook. Students are given an answer key, and encouraged to use the tests as a do-it-yourself diagnostic tool.

The questions are based on grammar, vocabulary, and pronunciation awareness. Once students have checked their answers, they are encouraged to reflect on their performance and self-assess their achievements. The notes which follow the Self Check activities help students reflect on language and skills achievement. Using these, students can determine personal study objectives and are given information which guides them to corresponding Student's Book, Workbook, and MultiROM activities for further practice.

The Portfolio Practice Book

The **English Result** Portfolio Practice Book is based on the principles behind Council of Europe accredited models. It is for students who want to keep records of their work, to record and reflect on their learning experiences, to monitor their progress and to see how their learning progresses during the course.

Students reflect on their ability to perform communicative tasks they practise at the end of each lesson. Later, they will be guided on to use this information for more global self-assessment using skill-specific descriptions for levels A2, A2+, B1, and B1+. These provide students with a stepping stone to CEFR level descriptions in an officially accredited European Language Passport.

Teacher's notes explain the purpose of the different sections in the portfolio, and how to integrate them with the course. For more information, go to www.oup.com/elt/teacher/result.

2   **Contents**

4   **Contents**

Contents 5

The people in my life

acquaintance /əˈkweɪntəns/ aunt /ɑːnt/ best friend boss (brother)-in-law colleague /ˈkɒliːg/
cousin /ˈkʌzn/ ex-(boyfriend) flatmate neighbour /ˈneɪbə/ nephew /ˈnefjuː/ niece /niːs/
parents step-(father) uncle widow widower

Wanda's World

I'm Wanda Jones. I'm 24, single, and I live with another girl in a small flat in Notting Hill. These are the people in my life …

Family

I've got four parents! My mum and dad are divorced and both of them have remarried. My mum, Tina, lives with my step-father, Costas, in Wimbledon. My dad, Harry, lives in Marbella with his new wife, Roxette. She's the same age as me, and we get on really well!

I've got a younger sister called Sandra. She's married to a guy called Ray. They have a young baby called Grace. That means I'm an aunt!

Friends

Well, there's my flatmate, Fatima. She's from Lebanon. I haven't got a boyfriend. My ex-boyfriend, Warren, still phones me every week, but I'm not interested. It's a bit complicated because Warren is my brother-in-law's brother.

My best friend is Stan. He's a 54-year-old barber and his shop is just below my flat. He's a widower and he's got a teenage son, Danny. Danny's learning to play the trumpet.

Acquaintances

Let's see, there's our neighbour, Mrs Mirren. I know her because she calls every day to complain about something. Her cats fight on our balcony.

Work

I'm a secretary in an insurance company. My boss is called Tom and I think he's secretly in love with me. My colleague is called Tracey and she's secretly in love with Tom. What a mess!

How to **talk about the people in your life**

Orientation

Context

In this lesson, students practise talking about their family, friends and neighbours.

The DVD box illustration, *Wanda's World*, shows various people in Wanda's life.

In *The people in my life*, the phonetic transcriptions show the pronunciation of words which is not always obvious from the spelling.

Language

Focus grammar	subject and object questions (present and past): *Who loves Wanda?, Who does Wanda love?, Who visited Wanda?, Who did Warren visit?*
Preview language	address forms: *Mr, Mrs*
Focus words	people and relationships: *acquaintance, cousin, colleague, (brother)-in-law, ex-(boyfriend), niece, nephew, step-(father), widow, widower*
Recognition vocabulary	words: *balcony, baggage, complicated, remarried, secretly, secretary, trumpet* phrases: *related to ..., What a mess!*
Recycled language	words: *aunt, boss, boyfriend, complain, divorced, flatmate, friend, married, neighbour, parents, teenage, uncle* grammar: *present simple, personal pronouns, possessive 's*

Language note

This lesson includes vocabulary for family members. Students whose native language marks gender distinction (like Spanish) often feel that English isn't as rich as their own language. On the other hand, it might seem strange that one English word describes several different relations. In Italian, for example, *nipote* is nephew, niece, grandson and granddaughter.

End product

In *Put it all together,* students ask and answer questions about people in their life. Their conversation is based on mind maps similar to the one in exercise 5.

Preparation

Take some mono or bilingual dictionaries to class to show or remind students how transcriptions can help them with pronunciation for exercise 2. Look at the mind map in exercise 5 so you can monitor and help students understand how it works.

Warmer

Write the following words at random on the board: *what, how, sister, many, where, why, name, live, from, old, brothers*. Students use the words to make questions for you to answer. Put students into pairs to ask and answer similar questions and to make a note of their partner's answers. Write *His / Her name is ...* on the board and invite students to introduce their partner using their notes. Ask one or two follow-up questions, using the people and relationships vocabulary above (see *Recycled language*). Encourage students to ask follow-up questions.

Write *How to talk about the people in your life* on the board.

A **Vocabulary** the people in my life

1 Set a short time limit for students, in pairs, to add family words to the list. Elicit suggestions around the class.

2 Direct students to *The people in my life* on **» p.6**. Do one or two examples as a class before students continue individually. Elicit answers around the class and check vocabulary as necessary.

Point out the phonetic transcriptions and model and drill pronunciation if necessary. Show how the words in brackets are generative, e.g. *step*-father or *step*-mother.

> **female:** aunt, niece, widow [Sobrina]
> **male:** uncle, nephew, step-(father), ex-(boyfriend), widower, [Viudo]
> (brother)-in-law [cuñado]
> **either:** flatmate, neighbour, colleague, acquaintance, [conocido]
> best friend, boss, parents, cousin [primo]

3 Direct students to the photos in *Wanda's World* on **» p.6**. Point out that photo h, in the middle, is Wanda. Read the instructions and check students understand the activity. Say the letter of one or two pictures and elicit guesses about each person's relationship to Wanda. Students continue in pairs. Monitor for correct pronunciation of *people* words and *'s* for possession. Ask for suggestions, but do not give answers at this stage.

4 Read the instructions and direct students to *Wanda's World* on **» p.6**. Do the example as a class to demonstrate the activity. Encourage students to look quickly through the text to find *Fatima* and any information about her which will help them identify her *(she's Wanda's flatmate and she looks Lebanese)*.

Monitor and help as necessary as they continue the activity. Ask for volunteers to name each of the people in the photos and to explain why. Check new vocabulary.

> b Mrs Mirren c Stan d Tom e Ray f Grace g Sandra
> h Wanda i Tina j Costas k Danny l Harry m Roxette
> n Tracey o Warren

5 Direct students to the mind map. Point to *me* in the centre and ask *Who?* (*Wanda.*) Say *Harry* and elicit *Harry is Wanda's father.* Repeat with *Roxette* and point out the word *family*. Explain that the words *family*, *friends*, *work*, *acquaintances* have the names of people in that category around them. Point out that the category words in the mind map are the same as the subtitles in *Wanda's World*.

If necessary, do one or two more examples with the class, before students continue in pairs. As you go over the answers, see what students remember about the different people.

> Tina: mother Costas: step-father Sandra: sister
> Ray: brother-in-law Grace: niece Tom and Tracey: colleagues

Extra help

Students take turns to point to a person in *Wanda's World*. Their partner says the relationship between the person and Wanda. Monitor and give pronunciation practice as necessary.

Extra activity

Introduce strategies for remembering vocabulary. Give students two minutes to study the words in *The people in my life*. Books closed. Students write the words they can remember. Ask students how they studied the words, e.g. by drawing a mind map, grouping words in topics. Encourage students to experiment with a different strategy for the lesson vocabulary for homework.

B Listen for specific information

In this section, students listen to short recorded voice-mail messages and focus on key words.

6 1A.1 Ask students why listening to phone messages is difficult. *(Because there are no visual clues.)* Elicit the type of information people usually include in a voice-mail message (name of person speaking, the time, the main points of the message, when the person will phone again). Ask *How do you listen to a voice-mail message? To every word or to key words? (Key words.)* Read the instructions and play the audio. Students compare answers in pairs. Play the audio a second time if necessary, pausing after each message to elicit the answer.

> 1 Mrs Mirren (Margaret) 2 Mr Robbins (Tom) 3 Warren
> 4 Sandra 5 Fatima's mum 6 Wanda's dad (Harry) 7 Fatima
> 8 Wanda's mum (Tina)

Extra help

Say the following sentences for students to say true or false.
1 Mrs Mirren was angry because Wanda's visitor was noisy. (T)
2 Mr Robbins wants Wanda to arrive later tomorrow. (F)
3 Warren met the woman in the next flat for coffee. (F)
4 Sandra and Ray are inviting Wanda to a concert. (F)
5 Fatima's mum called Fatima but she didn't answer. (T)
6 Wanda's dad wants Wanda to meet Roxette at the airport. (T)
7 Fatima hasn't got her keys to the flat. (T)
8 Wanda's mum wants to have dinner at Wanda's flat. (F)

7 Ask students to read questions 1–9 and check vocabulary. Direct students to audio script 1A.1 on >> p.150. Students compare answers in pairs, before you check as a class. Monitor and note how well students understand the difference between *subject* and *object* questions. Do not go into details at this point since this is the grammar focus of the next section.

> 2 work later 3 Wanda 4 Sandra
> 5 Fatima's mum 6 Roxette 7 Fatima 8 Tina
> 9 Mr Robbins, Warren, Sandra, Roxette, Fatima, Tina

8 Go through the instructions and check students understand the activity. Set a short time limit for students to write their list and decide what Wanda should do tomorrow. Put students into groups to discuss their ideas. Monitor, make a note of some suggestions and contribute to the discussions. Nominate students to make a suggestion and a reason why. Take a class vote on what Wanda should do tomorrow.

C Grammar subject questions and object questions

9 Write *Tom loves ...* from the grammar box on the board and elicit the answer for the blank *(Wanda)*. Ask students which word is the *verb* and label it. Ask about the *subject* and *object* of the verb and label them. Direct students to the grammar box. Point out the column headings for each part of the sentence. Go through items 2–6 as a class.

> 2 Ray 3 Wanda 4 Wanda 5 Fatima 6 Tina

10 Circle the verb in *Tom loves Wanda* on the board. To illustrate why we ask questions about the subject or object of a verb, say the sentence twice. First, mumble the word *Tom* and elicit the question *Who loves Wanda?*. Say the sentence again, this time mumbling the word *Wanda* to elicit *Who does Tom love?* Write both questions on the board and highlight the difference in form. Go through items 1–6 as a class. Elicit the rule.

> 2 marry 3 Warren visit 5 her key 6 divorced Harry
> **Rule:** Use *do*, *does*, *did* in **object** questions.

11 Go through the instructions and do one or two items from exercise 7 as a class. Monitor and help as necessary as students continue individually. Check answers as a class.

> 1 subject 2 object 3 object 4 subject 5 subject 6 object
> 7 subject 8 subject 9 subject

12 Read the instructions and do one or two examples with the class. Put students into pairs to take turns to ask and answer questions using the mind map. Monitor and give positive feedback for accurate question formation. Make a note of any problem areas to go over as a class at the end of the activity.

Extra help

Transformation drill: Object questions. Say sentences about the people in *Wanda's World*, mumbling the object of the verb, e.g. **T** *Wanda lives with mmm.* **SS** *Who does Fatima live with?* etc.

Extra plus

In pairs, students take turns to make statements about the people in *Wanda's World* on >> p.6, mumbling the subject or the object. Partners ask about information that wasn't clear.

ABC Put it all together

13 Go through the instruction and direct students to *The people in my life* on >> p.6 for ideas. Monitor and help students as they draw their own mind maps.

14 Students ask and answer about each other's family in pairs. Ask students to note who the people are.

15 Read the instructions and go through the examples. Remind students to use both subject and object questions as in exercise 10.

Student performance

Students should be able to ask and answer about factual personal information.

You can use this checklist to monitor and give feedback or to assess students' performance.

Content	Do students ask several questions about the people? exercise 12
Vocabulary	Do students use three or more family words? exercise 5
Pronunciation	Do students pronounce family words clearly enough to be understood? exercise 5

I can **talk about the people in my life.**

Direct students to the self-assessment bar. Ask them to find more examples in their book (at the end of each lesson). Explain that marking the bar after each lesson will help them see how they are making progress and to decide if they need extra practice.

Copy the bar onto the board, and guide students towards a general idea of what the different positions mean here, e.g. students tick *very easily* if they asked three questions about each person without looking at their notes; *on my own* if they looked at their notes occasionally; *with some help* if they looked at their notes before asking every question; *with a lot of help* if they read the example questions in exercise 15. Monitor and help students mark their position. Encourage them to think about what they can rather than can't do.

Early finishers

Students tick vocabulary in *The people in my life* they plan to study for homework.

Additional material

www.oup.com/elt/result for extra practice activities
www.oup.com/elt/teacher/result for extra teacher resources

How to talk about the people in your life

G subject questions and object questions   v the people in my life

A Vocabulary the people in my life

1 Work with a partner. Write a list of family words.
   Example mother, son, grandfather …

2 Look at **The people in my life** opposite. Say if they are
   male, female, or either. *Walquera*
   Example aunt = female

3 Look at the photos in **Wanda's World** opposite, but
   don't read the text. Work with a partner and guess the
   relationships between the people.

4 Read the text and name the people in the photos.
   Example a = Fatima

5 Look at the mind map of Wanda's World. How are the
   people related to Wanda? Tell a partner.

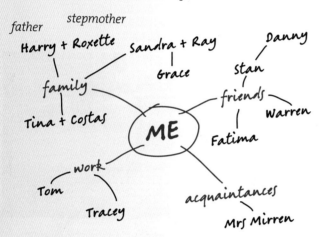

B Listen for specific information

6 **1A.1▶** Wanda and Fatima got eight messages on their
   telephone today. Listen and decide who they are from.

7 Read the audio script on **>> p.150** and answer the
   questions. Compare with a partner.
   1 Who visited Wanda? *Warren*
   2 What does Mr Robbins ask Wanda to do?
   3 Who did Warren visit?
   4 Who wants Wanda to go to their house?
   5 Who left a message for Fatima?
   6 Who does Harry want Wanda to meet?
   7 Who wants Wanda to stay home tomorrow?
   8 Who left an umbrella at Wanda's house?
   9 Who wants to see Wanda tomorrow evening? (more
      than one person!)

8 Make a list of things that people want Wanda to do
   tomorrow. What do you think she should do? Why?
   Decide in groups.

C Grammar subject questions and object questions

9 Complete the grammar box.

	subject	verb	object
1	Tom	loves	Wanda.
2	Sandra	married	
3	Warren	visited	
4	Warren	loves	
5		forgot	her key.
6		divorced	Harry.

10 Complete the questions about the sentences in the
    grammar box and underline the correct word in the rule.
    Object questions (when you don't know the object)
    1 Who does Tom love?
    2 Who did Sandra *marry* ?
    3 Who did *Wanda Warren visit* ?
    Subject questions (when you don't know the subject)
    4 Who loves Wanda?
    5 Who forgot _____?
    6 Who _____?

    Rule Use *do, does,* or *did* in subject/object questions.

11 Look at the questions in exercise 7. Are they subject or
    object questions?

12 Look at the mind map in exercise 5 and ask your partner
    questions about **Wanda's World**.
    Example A Who loves Tom?
              B Tracey!

    More practice? **Grammar Bank >> p.136.**

ABC Put it all together

13 Draw a similar mind map of people in your life.

14 Look at your partner's mind map and guess who the
    people are.
    Example A Is Adam your uncle?
              B No, he's my brother-in-law.

15 Think of questions to ask about the people in your
    partner's map. Ask and answer with your partner.
    Examples Does your sister live near you?
              Who do you speak to most on the phone?
              Who lives with you?

I can talk about the people in my life. ▬▬▬▬▬

Greetings

bow   hug each other   kiss each other on the cheeks   kiss each other on the lips
put your hand on the other person's shoulder   shake hands with each other   wave to each other

How do you **meet** and **greet**?

What do you do or say in your country? Choose the best answer.

1 What do people do when they meet in your country?

a shake hands with each other
b put their hand on the other person's shoulder
c bow
d hug each other
e kiss each other on the cheeks
f kiss each other on the lips
g wave to each other
h *something else*

2 How do you greet these people? Is your greeting different if the person is of the same sex or of the opposite sex?

a a good friend
b an acquaintance – a friend of a friend, for example
c an older neighbour
d somebody important – your boss, for example
e one of your parents when you haven't seen them for a long time
f a six-year-old child – your nephew or niece, for example

3 How do you address the people in question 2?

a Sir or Madam
b Mr / Ms / Mrs / Miss and their surname
c their first name
d a nickname
e *other*

4 You're by yourself and you walk into a café. You see a friend sitting with a group of people you don't know. What usually happens?

a Your friend introduces you to the people.
b You say 'hi' to your friend and introduce yourself to the people.
c The people stand up and introduce themselves to you.
d *something else*

5 A new colleague at work introduces himself or herself to you. Do you ever say any of these things? Say *never*, *it's possible*, *sometimes*, or *often*.

a Enchanted.
b Pleased to meet you.
c How old are you?
d Hi, I'm Mr / Ms … (surname)
e Hi, I'm … (first name)
f Peace be with you.
g Greetings.

6 You meet a teacher from your school in the street. What do you say?

a Hello, teacher!
b Hello, Mr / Ms … (surname)
c Hello, … (first name)
d Hello, Sir / Miss.
e *something else*

7 You want to get someone's attention. What do you normally say? Are any of these rude?

a Excuse me!
b Hey, Mister / Miss!
c Listen!
d You there!
e *something else*

How to talk about greeting customs

Orientation

Context

In this lesson, students talk about different ways of greeting and addressing other people.

The photos decorating the quiz show various ways of greeting. The quiz questions, in *How do you meet and greet?* invite readers to think about greeting customs in their own country.

Greetings gives phrases to describe different ways of greeting.

Culture note

There are many different meeting and greeting conventions, including 'body language', e.g. touching and eye contact. Students need to be aware of possible differences, and be able to explain these if necessary.

Language

Focus grammar	reflexive pronouns: *myself, yourself, him / herself, ourselves, yourselves, themselves; each other*
Preview grammar	present simple and present continuous
Focus words	ways of greeting: *bow, hug, introduce, kiss, shake hands, wave*
Focus phrases	greetings: *Pleased to meet you., Hi. I'm ..., Hello.*
Recognition vocabulary	*body language, get someone's attention, greet, meet, rude*
Recycled language	words: *acquaintance, cheek, colleague, first name, hand, head, lips, madam, Miss, Mr, Mrs, Ms, neighbour, nephew, nickname, niece, shoulder, sir, surname* grammar: *subject, possessive, and object pronouns*
Pronunciation	*Miss* /mɪs/ *Ms* /mɪz/ *Mrs* /ˈmɪsɪz/ *Mr* /ˈmɪstə(r)/ *Miss* /s/ or *Ms* /z/ 1B.2

Language notes

The pronunciation of *Ms* can be /mɪz/ or /məz/ in Britain. In the USA, it is always /mɪz/.

Some intransitive verbs in English are reflexive in other languages, e.g. in Spanish *relax* is *relajarse* (*se* = reflexive morpheme); in Italian *fall asleep* is *addormentarsi* (*si* = reflexive morpheme). Students sometimes transfer this to English.

End product

In *Put it all together*, students find out about greeting customs in other countries using their notes. In *Pairwork* on >> **p.126** and **p.133** they have information about customs in two countries.

Preparation

Read the *Teaching tip* for exercise 4. Look at *Pairwork 1B* to help students with exercise 13.

Warmer

Ask students about places they have visited and how people greet each other. Encourage students to tell stories about meeting people from a different culture for the first time, and how they felt and reacted. Direct students to the photos on >> **p.8**. In small groups, students guess the nationality or regional origin of the people (*a European b French c Turkish d Pakistani / Afghani e African-American f Japanese g Japanese*).

Write *How to talk about greeting customs* on the board.

A Vocabulary ways of greeting

1 Direct students to the phrases in *Greetings* and photos a–g. Match one or two together as a class. Students continue individually and compare in pairs. Nominate students to give answers and help with vocabulary and pronunciation.

> a shaking hands, hands on shoulder
> b kiss each other on the cheeks
> c kiss each other on the lips
> d hug each other   e shake hands with each other
> f bow   g wave to each other

Extra help

Call out a photo letter, for the class to say the phrase from *Greetings*. Monitor and drill pronunciation, encouraging students to link words together and say the phrases with natural rhythm. Students continue in pairs or small groups.

2 Go through the instructions and examples. Elicit or write examples of people on the board, e.g. *neighbours, family members, colleagues at work*. Put students into pairs to continue the activity and monitor and join in with conversations. Ask volunteers to tell the class and review vocabulary as necessary.

B Read and respond

In this section, students read for gist and detail to do a questionnaire.

3 Read the instructions and check students understand *meet and greet*. Ask students to read titles a–g and check vocabulary as necessary. Do the first item as a class. Ask students questions about how they read, e.g. *Did you need to understand every word? (No.) Did you read slowly? (No.) Which words and phrases helped you? (hands, shoulder, hug, etc.)* Tell students to ignore any new vocabulary for the moment.

Monitor and help as necessary as students continue individually. Go over answers as a class, eliciting or pointing out key words.

> 2 e (same/opposite sex)   3 c (address, Sir, Madam)
> 4 a (café, friends, say hi)   5 d (colleague, work)   6 g (teacher)
> 7 b (attention, Excuse me!)

4 Go through the instructions and explain that students answer about what people do in *their* country. Monitor and explain any new vocabulary as students continue individually.

Put students into small groups to compare similarities and differences. Monitor and listen for interesting answers, especially for differences between students with the same cultural background. Encourage students to justify answers. Go through each question as a class and ask for volunteers to share information or any interesting facts. Do not overcorrect for accuracy, but help students get their ideas across.

Teaching tip

After you have finished exercises 3 and 4, ask students how they read in their own language. Ask *When do you read to get a general idea of what a text is about? (To see if it is interesting.)* and *When do you read carefully? (To find specific information.)* Advise students to use the same ways of reading in a foreign language to help them become better readers.

5 Tell students they will listen to a young British student, Greg, answering the quiz questions. Go through each question in turn and elicit suggestions of what he might say. Encourage students to explain why, based on their own experiences in Britain, meeting British people in different places or watching films. Do not comment on answers at this stage.

6 1B.1 Read the instructions. Tell students that there is more than one answer to some of the questions and play the audio. Play it a second time, pausing to give students time to make a note of the answers before they compare in pairs. Go over answers as a class, encouraging students to comment on anything they found surprising.

> 1 a, b, d, e, f, g   2 a kisses a woman on the cheek, shakes a man's hand; b, c, d say hello, or good morning; e hugs father, kisses mother; f hugs or touches head   3 c   4 a   5 b, c (but only to a child), e   6 c   7 a (all the others are rude)

7 Copy the titles onto the board. Review meaning by asking *male* or *female*, *married* or *single* for each one. Go through the example with the class and put students in pairs to continue. Check answers, drilling pronunciation of each word as necessary.

> /mɪz/ = Ms   /ˈmɪsɪz/ = Mrs   /ˈmɪstə(r)/ = Mr

8 1B.2 Go through the instructions with the class. Play and pause the audio for students to follow the example. Continue with the audio, pausing after each sentence. Nominate several students to give each answer and monitor for correct pronunciation. Give extra pronunciation practice as necessary.

> 1 Mrs   2 Mr   3 Miss   4 Ms   5 Mr   6 Ms   7 Mrs   8 Miss

Extra help
To help students distinguish between *Miss* and *Ms*, point out the /s/ and /z/ difference and do a minimal pair drill. Students test each other.
To help students distinguish between *Mrs* and *Mr*, point out the difference between the final syllable and do a minimal pair drill. Students test each other.

Extra activity
Write the following scenarios on the board: best friends meeting after six months; colleagues arriving at work; a shop assistant and customer; new neighbours; teacher and student meeting outside school; teenage friends meeting at the cinema. Students compare what they would say in these situations.

C Grammar reflexive pronouns

9 Direct students to photos a–c and do the activity as a class.

> a hugging each other   b hugging herself
> c hugging someone else

10 Direct students to the grammar box. Go through the column headings and identify the different types of pronouns in the example sentences. Complete the box as a class.

> **subject:** I, he   **possessive:** your, our
> **object:** him, her   **reflexive:** herself

Direct students to read the rules and the examples. Check vocabulary as necessary. Monitor and help as students match the sentences and the rules. Go over answers as a class.

> **Rules:** 1 c (The subject of *is* and *look after* is the same).
> 2 a (People usually or often get painters to paint their houses. Here the speaker wants to emphasize that they, not somebody else, painted the house)
> 3 b

11 Set a short time limit of about three minutes for students to find and underline examples in *How do you meet and greet?* Check answers as a class.

> Question 1 each other   Question 4 yourself, themselves
> Question 5 him/herself

12 Go through the instructions and ask students to read sentences 1–7. Check vocabulary. Do the example as a class, pointing out that *each other* can be used for two people or many. Monitor and make a note of any difficulties as students continue individually. Ask for volunteers to give answers and elicit or explain why the reflexive pronoun is used, referring to the rules in exercise 10 as appropriate.

> 2 myself   3 yourself   4 each other   5 each other   6 himself
> 7 myself

Extra help
Cue-response drill. Say a couple of sentences for students to continue with the appropriate reflexive pronoun. *T I didn't go to the hairdresser's. I cut it …* **SS** *… myself.* **T** *I took my car to the garage. I couldn't repair it …* **SS** *… myself.* **T** *We didn't buy this pie. We made it …* **SS** *ourselves.* etc.

ABC Put it all together

13 Go through the instructions and put students into A/B pairs. As turn to >> **p.126** and Bs to >> **p.133**. Check students understand the activity. Monitor and help them find the answers to the three questions, checking students are making short notes to answer the questions for both countries.

14 Read the instructions before students do the activity. At the end, ask around the class about any new information students have learnt about greeting customs in the four countries. Ask further general questions, e.g. *Do they say this to everyone? Do they do this with men and women?*

Student performance
Students should be able to exchange factual information.

You can use this checklist to monitor and give feedback or to assess students' performance.

Content	Do students answer the questions? exercise 4
Grammar	Do students use subject and object pronouns accurately? exercise 10
Vocabulary	Do students use a variety of greetings phrases? exercise 4

I can **talk about greeting customs.**

Students tick *on my own* if they have answered the questions using their notes. They tick *with some help* if they have read a couple of sentences from *Pairwork, Two countries*.

Early finishers
Students repeat the activity without using their notes.

Additional material

www.oup.com/elt/result for extra practice activities
www.oup.com/elt/teacher/result for extra teacher resources

How to talk about greeting customs

G reflexive pronouns   **V** ways of greeting   **P** *Miss* /s/ or *Ms* /z/

A Vocabulary ways of greeting

1 Look at **Greetings** opposite and match them with photos a–g.

2 Which greetings do you use? When? Tell a partner.
Examples I never hug my boss.
      I kiss a friend on the cheeks when we meet after a few days.

B Read and respond

3 Read **How do you meet and greet?** opposite and choose the best title for each question.
   a ☐ Introducing friends
   b ☐ Getting attention
   c ☐ Addressing people
   d ☐ Meeting new colleagues
   e ☐ Men and women
   f ☐1 Body language
   g ☐ Meeting your teacher

4 Do the questionnaire. Compare your answers in small groups.

5 You will listen to Greg Brown, a 20-year-old student from Britain. Guess his answers to the questionnaire.

6 **1B.1▶** Listen to Greg and check your guesses. How are his answers different from yours? Compare with a partner.

7 **Pronunciation** Match the titles and the pronunciation.

Mr Ms ~~Miss~~ Mrs

/mɪs/ *Miss*   /mɪz/ _____
/ˈmɪsɪz/ _____   /ˈmɪstə(r)/ _____

8 **1B.2▶** Listen and say if you hear *Mr, Ms, Miss,* or *Mrs.*
Example **Audio** This is Mrs Mirren.
      You   Mrs!

C Grammar reflexive pronouns

9 Match the sentences with the photos.
   1 ☐ They're hugging each other.   ⟷
   2 ☐ She's hugging herself.   ↰
   3 ☐ She's hugging someone else.   →

10 Complete the grammar box. Then match the rules and examples.

pronouns			
subject	possessive	object	reflexive
She introduced me.	*He introduced his wife.*	*I introduced them.*	*We introduced ourselves.*
	my	me	myself
you		you	yourself
	his		himself
she	her		
we		us	ourselves
they	their	them	themselves

Rules
Use a reflexive pronoun:
1 when the subject is the same person as the object.
2 to make it clear you did it and not someone else.
3 in the phrase *by* + reflexive pronoun, meaning *alone.*

Examples
a ☐ We didn't get a painter – we painted the house ourselves.
b ☐ Come and join us – don't just sit there by yourself!
c ☐ He's an adult now and he can look after himself.

11 Underline examples of reflexive pronouns in **How do you meet and greet?** and compare with a partner.

12 Complete the sentences with a reflexive pronoun or *each other.*
   1 In France, people kiss *each other* when they meet.
   2 Nobody introduced me so I introduced _____.
   3 If you're hungry, get something for _____.
   4 How long have you and Jo known _____?
   5 In Britain, relatives give _____ presents at Christmas.
   6 Danny didn't have trumpet classes – he taught _____.
   7 I hate eating in restaurants by _____.

More practice? **Grammar Bank** ≫ p.136.

ABC Put it all together

13 Work with a partner. Make notes to answer questions about two countries.
   Student A Read **Two countries** on ≫ p.126.
   Student B Read **Two countries** on ≫ p.133.

14 Ask your partner the questions from exercise 13 about his/her countries. Did you learn anything new?

I can talk about greeting customs.

Tick ✓ the line. with a lot of help with some help on my own very easily

Las Meninas

In 1656, Diego Velázquez painted *Las Meninas,* one of the most famous works in the history of Western art. Today, the painting is on display in the Prado Museum in Madrid. Thousands of people visit the museum every day, and most of them want to see this masterpiece by Velázquez before they leave.

When you look at the picture, the first thing you see is five-year-old Princess Margarita ⑥. She's standing in the middle of a group of girls and she's looking directly at you. The girls are wearing expensive dresses with very wide skirts. Margarita's dress is white and shines brightly in the light from a window on the right. The two girls on either side of the princess are her maids of honour, Maria and Isabel. Maria ☐ is kneeling and offering Margarita a drink. Isabel ☐ is standing to the right of Margarita and she's looking in our direction.

Apart from her maids of honour, little Margarita also has two dwarfs to keep her company. Their names are Nicolas ☐ and Maribarbola ☐. You can see them at the front on the right. A dog is lying in front of them and Nicolas is trying to wake it up with his foot.

Behind Isabel, the maid of honour, we can see Marcela ☐, the woman who looks after the princess. She's saying something to the princess's bodyguard ☐. At the back of the room, through the doorway, we can see José Nieto ☐. He looks after the palace buildings. He's going up the stairs, or perhaps he's coming down, it isn't clear. He's looking towards us.

Finally, on the left of the scene is the painter himself, Diego Velázquez ☐. He's working on an enormous painting, but we can't see what it is. Is he painting the whole scene in a mirror, or is he painting something else? We will never know.

Position

at the back (of the room)
in the middle (of …)
at the front (of …)
on the left (of …)
on the right (of …)

in front (of the girl)
to the left (of …)
to the right (of …)
behind (the girl)

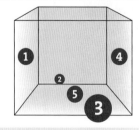

How to explain who people are

Orientation

Context

In this lesson, students will practise using the present simple and continuous to talk about what is happening in a picture.

Las Meninas (The Maids of Honour), is a painting by Diego Velázquez and was painted in 1656. At first sight, it looks as if the painter is painting the viewer. However, in the mirror to the left of the painter, we see the King and Queen. This suggests that they are standing where the viewer is, and Velázquez is painting them.

Position illustrates the meaning of absolute and relative prepositional phrases.

Culture note

People send different signals to each other during conversations. For example, they indicate they are listening, they understand a speaker, they want to respond to a question, or are surprised by something. Students often 'import' words and phrases from their first language when they have conversations in English. They can sound more fluent and gain time to think if they use conversation markers in English (see *Discourse* below).

Language

Focus grammar	present simple and continuous: *I'm studying art history so I spend ...*
Focus phrases	prepositions of position: (absolute) *at the back, in the middle, at the front, on the left/right;* (relative) *behind, in front, to the left/right*
Recognition vocabulary	*bodyguard, directly, kneeling, maids-of-honour, notice, on either side, shines, wide*
Recycled language	verbs: *believe, look at, stand, study, want, watch, work*
Discourse	conversation markers: *oh, ok, right, uh huh?, Well*

Language note

A place in which art is displayed is called a *gallery* in English, but might be called a *museum* in other languages. In English, a *museum* usually refers to is a place where historical artefacts are displayed.

End product

In *Put it all together*, students ask and answer questions to identify people in a photo. They have the same photo, but the names of different people are given.

Preparation

Collect extra pictures or photos which contain several people if you would like to do the *Extra plus* activity after exercise 6. Familiarize yourself with the photos in *Pairwork 1C* for exercise 15.

Warmer

Ask *When did you last go to an art gallery? Who with? What did you see? Did you talk about the paintings? Were you given a catalogue? Was it useful? Why? Why not?*

Direct students to the picture on >> p.10 and give them two minutes to look at it. Books closed. Ask *What can you remember about the picture?* Elicit ideas. Write notes on the board before students look at the picture again to see what they remembered.

Write *How to explain who people are* on the board.

A Read an art catalogue description

In this section, students skim a catalogue before reading carefully for detail.

1 Read the questions and put students into pairs to discuss the painting. Ask for volunteers to tell the class. Help them express their ideas but do not overcorrect for accuracy.

> **artist:** Diego Velázquez
> **place:** Madrid, palace of Spanish King Philip IV   **time:** 1656

2 Read the instructions and the two questions, checking vocabulary. Ask *How are you going to read the text to answer the questions? Quickly for the general idea, slowly and understand every word, or quickly to find some key words and then slowly for detail? (Quickly then slowly.)* Students continue individually. Remind them not to worry about new vocabulary at this point.

> 1 Margarita
> 2 The painter is Velázquez. He's painting the King and Queen (the people in the mirror) or the person/viewer in the art gallery who is looking at the scene (nobody knows).

3 Read the instructions and direct students to the painting. Do one or two examples as a class to demonstrate the activity. Students continue individually and compare in pairs. Ask volunteers for answers and check the class agrees before giving feedback. Students write the numbers in the text.

> 1 Diego Velázquez   2 José Nieto   3 Marcela
> 4 princess's bodyguard   5 Maria (Maid of honour)
> 7 Isabel (Maid of honour)   8 Maribarbola   9 Nicolas
> Not mentioned: the people in the mirror.

B Vocabulary position

4 Direct students to *Position* on >> p.10. Use the names of different students in your class to show the difference between the phrases in the two illustrations, e.g. *Pablo is at the back of the room. Pablo is in front of Maria.* Students complete the activity in pairs. Monitor and check students use the preposition *of* where necessary.

> absolute position (the room): 1 on the left of   2 at the back of
> 3 at the front of   4 on the right of   5 in the middle of
> relative position (the girl): 6 to the left of   7 behind
> 8 in front of   9 to the right of

Extra help

Call the number of a dot for students to call out the position as a class. Make sure students say the complete phrase, e.g. *on the left of the room.* Drill pronunciation as necessary, encouraging them to run the words together. Students continue in pairs.

5 Go through the instructions and do items 1 and 2 together as a class. For item 1, draw a simple diagram of a bus on the board to illustrate the difference between *at the front* and *in front*, and *at the back* and *behind*. For item 2, draw a road with two lanes on the board and a cross in the left-hand lane. Use the diagram to show the difference in meaning between *on the right* and *to the right*.

Explain that the phrases in items 1 and 2 are followed by *of* /əv/. Direct students to *Position* and ask *Which phrase is the odd one out? (behind* because it isn't followed by *of.)*

6 Direct students to *Las Meninas* and go through the example as a class. Do a couple more examples if necessary, before students continue in pairs. Monitor and give positive feedback for correct sentences and fluent use of *Position* phrases.

Extra help

Students draw a plan of their classroom, and put themselves in the middle. They place other students in different positions. In pairs, students describe where people are seated. Their partner makes a new seating plan. At the end of the activity, students compare plans.

Extra plus

Put students into small groups and distribute your own pictures (see *Preparation*). They write three sentences to describe the position of the people. Put two groups together to swap pictures and write three sentences about their new picture. Groups compare sentences and see if they agree.

C Grammar present simple and continuous

7 Read the instructions and direct students to *Las Meninas* on **>> p.10** to answer the question (*José Nieto*). Ask students to explain why, and elicit some examples of sentences in the present simple and continuous from the text. Write them in two columns on the board. Check that students understand the difference between the verbs *see, watch, notice,* and *look*. Monitor and review the form of both tenses if necessary.

8 Direct students to the grammar box and rules. Read statements a–e and check understanding. Do one or two examples as a class before students continue individually. Monitor and help as necessary. Check answers as a class.

> 1 e   2 b   3 b   4 c   5 c   6 d   7 d   8 a   9 a

9 Read the instructions. Tell students to look at the picture and do the first item together as a class. Put students into pairs to continue and monitor and help as necessary. Nominate students to give answers. Ask the class to say which rule each answer illustrates.

> 1 's touching   (a/d)   2 's holding/think (d/a)
> 3 's painting/paints (d/b)   4 spend/'re helping (b/d)
> 5 are talking/work (d/c)   6 like/'m writing (a/e)

Extra help

Books closed. Say some true or false sentences about people in the picture. Students repeat the sentence as a class only if it is factually correct. Students continue the activity in pairs.

10 Go through the instructions. Ask for volunteers to give one example for rules a–e before students continue individually. Monitor and help as necessary.

Put students into pairs to tell their partner. Make a note of any language problems to go over at the end of the section. Ask for volunteers to tell the class about their partner.

11 Put students into different pairs. Explain the activity and direct students to the example. Remind students to pronounce the third person *s* and to use *to be* for the present continuous. Ask for volunteers to tell the class about their partner.

Extra plus

Students work in small groups. They take turns to say true/false sentences about themselves using the present simple and continuous. The others guess which sentences are true.

D Listen for detail

In this section, students listen for specific information and to conversation markers in context.

12 1C.1 Explain that students will hear two people in the Prado Museum, Madrid, talking about *Las Meninas*. Read the instructions and give or elicit general ideas about what people looking at the picture might talk about. Play the audio for students to identify the two parts of the painting they talk about. Ask students to locate the parts of the picture as you check answers.

> the King and Queen; the painter's red cross

13 Students read questions 1–5 before listening again. Remind students to listen very carefully for detail. Play the audio. Ask students to compare answers in pairs and give them the option of listening again before going over the answers.

> 1 in the room (standing where the speakers are)   2 the princess and the other people in the picture   3 on the painter's jacket   4 the king   5 the king (some people say)

14 Read the instructions and information with the class. Check vocabulary. Direct students to audio script 1C.1 on **>> p.150** and do the first item together. Explain that students should find the word and then look at what people say afterwards to help them find the answers. Put students into pairs to compare answers before going through the activity as a class.

> 2 c   3 a

Extra help

Divide the class in half to read the conversation aloud. They then swap roles.

ABCD Put it all together

15 Put students into pairs and direct them to *Pairwork* photos on **>> p.126** and **>> p.133**. Go through the instructions and tell students they have the same photos, but different people are named. Nominate or ask for volunteers to read the example dialogue to demonstrate the activity. At the end of the activity, ask students to show each other their photos.

Student performance

Students should be able to give short descriptions of people and actions.

You can use this checklist to monitor and give feedback or to assess students' performance.

Interaction	Do students use conversation markers? exercise 14
Grammar	Do students use the present simple and continuous appropriately? exercise 11
Vocabulary	Do students use different expressions for position? exercise 6

I can explain who people are.

Students tick *on my own* if they have given enough information for their partner to identify most of the people in the photo. They tick *with some help* if their partner has had to ask another question about one or two of the people.

Early finishers

In pairs, students look again at *Las Meninas* on **>> p.10**. They imagine they are in an art gallery and have a conversation about it.

Additional material

www.oup.com/elt/result for extra practice activities
www.oup.com/elt/teacher/result for extra teacher resources

How to explain who people are

G present simple and continuous   v position

A Read an art catalogue description

1 Look at the painting opposite with a partner. Do you know anything about this painting? Do you like it?

2 Read **Las Meninas** opposite and answer the questions.
   1 Who's the little girl in the white dress?
   2 Who's the painter and what is he painting?

3 Write the numbers of the people in **Las Meninas** in the text. Which people in the picture are *not* mentioned?

B Vocabulary position

4 Look at the phrases in **Position** opposite. Match them with the numbers in the diagrams.

5 Underline the correct words.
   1 The driver sits at the front/in front of a bus and the passengers sit at the back of/behind the driver.
   2 In Britain, cars drive on the left/to the left of the road. If you want to pass a slow lorry, you have to pass on the right/to the right of it.

6 Test a partner about the people in the painting.
   Example A Where's Marcela?
            B She's to the left of the bodyguard.

C Grammar present simple and continuous

7 Read this text. Which man in the painting is it about?

I'm studying¹ art history so I spend a lot of time in the Prado. Sometimes I watch² the visitors. When they see Las Meninas, they usually look³ at the princess first. But later, they usually notice this man. He works⁴ in the palace – he checks⁵ that all the palace rooms are clean and in order. At this moment, he's standing⁶ on the stairs and he's looking⁷ into the room. Perhaps he wants⁸ to look at the painting. Some historians believe⁹ he was a relative of the artist.

8 Match the verbs in red in exercise 7 with the rules in the grammar box.

Use present simple for ...	Use present continuous for ...
a verbs which describe states.* *I like art.*	d actions happening at this moment. *She's looking at the princess.*
b an action which happens often. *Tourists always visit the Prado.*	e actions happing these days, but perhaps not at this moment. *I'm learning to paint.*
c permanent or long-term facts. *He lives in Madrid.*	

* State verbs include: *believe, know, like, see, understand, want*, etc.

9 Work with a partner. Put the verbs in the present simple or the present continuous.
   1 Nicolas _wants_ to wake the dog – he _____ it with his foot. want/touch
   2 José Nieto _____ something in his hand – I _____ it's a book. hold/think
   3 Diego _____ a picture. He _____ a lot of pictures of the royal family. paint/paint
   4 Maria and Isabel _____ a lot of time with the princess. They _____ her now. spend/help
   5 Marcela and the bodyguard _____ about something. They _____ for the king. talk/work
   6 I _____ Las Meninas – I _____ an essay about it for my class. like/write

10 Write a sentence about you for each of the rules a–e in exercise 8. Then tell a partner.
   Example rule a – I like European films.

11 Change partners. Talk about your first partner.
   Example Magda wants something to eat.
   More practice? **Grammar Bank** >> p.136.

D Listen for detail

12 **1C.1▶** You will hear a tourist, Barbara, and a guide talking about **Las Meninas**. What two parts of the painting do they talk about?

13 Listen again and answer the questions.
   1 Where are King Phillip and Queen Mariana?
   2 Who is looking at them?
   3 Where is the red cross?
   4 Who gave it to the painter?
   5 Who painted it?

14 Read the audio script on >> p.150. Underline the words in red below and match them with their meanings.
   1 [b] oh   a to show you're going to answer a
   2 [ ] uh huh?   question.
   3 [ ] well   b to show surprise, or that the
                      information is new to you.
                    c to show that you're following what
                      the person is saying.

ABCD Put it all together

15 Work with a partner. Look at a photo and ask and say who the people are. Then compare your information.
   Student A Look at **Family photo** on >> p.126.
   Student B Look at **Family photo** on >> p.133.

I can explain who people are. ▬▬▬▬▬▬▬▬▬▬▬▬▬▬▬▬▬▬
Tick ✓ the line.   with a lot of help   with some help   on my own   very easily

Misunderstandings

I don't understand.   No, I meant (pair).   I thought you said (pear).   Oh, I see!   Pardon?   Sorry, I misunderstood.

MEDICAL EXAMINATION

Age? Eighteen.

Height? One metre seventy.

Weight? Weight?

Why aren't you saying anything? I thought you asked me to wait ...

Puzzle time

We use language to communicate and understand each other.
But quite often we *misunderstand* what the other person is saying.
Can you explain the misunderstandings in these situations?

1 An English teacher was doing some vocabulary work with his class. He was asking questions and inviting students to give the answers. 'What is the opposite of right?' he asked. A student called Jenny put her hand up. 'Go ahead, Jenny', said the teacher.

'The opposite of write is read!' she shouted. The other students all laughed and Jenny didn't understand why.

2

A young man was talking to his colleague at work. 'How's Anita?' his colleague asked. Anita was the man's girlfriend.

'Oh, she's not very well, actually', said the man. 'She arrived back from Ireland yesterday and she's been in bed with a temperature since then.'

'Flu?' asked the man's colleague.

'Yes, she flew', replied the man, 'I went to the airport to meet her.'

His colleague looked at him very strangely.

3 I was doing a crossword and I needed help. My mum was in the room, and I said to her, 'Can you think of a word meaning boat with five letters?'

'Do you know what the first letter is?' she asked.

'Y', I said.

'Because it's much easier if you know the first letter, isn't it?' she replied.

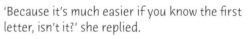

4

Maria Teresa was in a greengrocer's in England buying fruit. She asked for some bananas and the greengrocer asked which ones she wanted. There were lots of bunches of five or six bananas, but she didn't want that many. Then she noticed there was a bunch with just two bananas, and said, 'I'll take that pair, please'.

The greengrocer was confused. 'Pardon? Don't you want any bananas, then?' he asked.

How to correct a misunderstanding

Orientation

Context

In this lesson, students will practise using phrases to resolve misunderstandings.

In the cartoon strip, *Medical Examination*, a doctor is taking the personal details of an army recruit. A misunderstanding arises when the recruit interprets *weight* as *wait*.

In *Puzzle time* there are four different situations in which communication breaks down. There are some useful phrases for dealing with such situations in *Misunderstandings*.

Culture note

Misunderstandings can occur when similar words exist in different languages, especially when a word in one language has a false friend (a similar word with a different meaning) in another language. When misunderstandings do occur, politeness conventions in English require that the person who doesn't understand (rather than the person who has perhaps been unclear or made a mistake) apologizes and so indirectly asks for clarification.

Language

Focus phrases	misunderstandings: *I don't understand., I meant ..., I thought you said ..., Oh, I see!, Pardon?, Sorry, I misunderstood.*
Preview grammar	past simple and past continuous
Recognition vocabulary	*actually, bunch, carpet, chatting, cognates, confused, false friends, file, flu / flew, height, pear / pair, rhyme, recruit, strangely, weight*
Recycled language	words: *ask, colleague, girlfriend, greengrocer, say* phrases: *sounds the same as, the opposite of*
Pronunciation	letters of the alphabet 1D.1

End product

In *Put it all together*, students write two conversations using the information in *Pairwork* >> p. 126 and based on exercise 10. Students practise the role play in small groups.

Preparation

Think of examples of cognates and false friends in English and the language(s) of your students for exercise 3. Check *Misunderstandings* in *Pairwork* >> p.126 so you can help students with exercise 14. Take a few monolingual dictionaries to class.

Warmer

Write *misunderstanding* on the board and elicit or explain the meaning. Ask students if they have ever had a cross-cultural misunderstanding which happened because of language differences (either in their own country or in a country where a different language is spoken). Ask volunteers to tell their stories and help them get their ideas across. Ask *What's the best thing you can do in these situations?* Put students into small groups to discuss. Ask a spokesperson from each group to tell the class and take a vote on the best suggestions.

Write *How to correct a misunderstanding* on the board.

A Vocabulary cognates and false friends

1 Read the instructions and definitions 1–3 with the class. Go through examples a–c and ask *Which definition?* Elicit other examples from your students' first language, or other languages they know.

> 1 b   2 c   3 a

2 Read the instructions and check students understand the activity. Distribute monolingual dictionaries if you have them. Do one or two examples as a class, asking volunteers to say 1, 2, or 3. Monitor and comment on students' answers as they continue the activity individually. Ask for volunteers to tell the class about the similarities and differences between words in their language and English.

> Students' answers will depend on their first language background. Some examples for Spanish speakers include: smoking 1, 2 (*smoking* is used as a gerund, but as a noun it means *smoking jacket* in English); large 2 (*largo* in Spanish means *long* in English).

3 Go through the instructions and give examples for your students' language(s) if you can. Put students into small groups to discuss their ideas. Monitor and help as necessary, and draw the discussion to a close when students have run out of ideas. Ask for a volunteer from each group to summarize their ideas.

B Read and identify misunderstandings

In this section, students read short narratives for detail.

4 Read the instructions and check vocabulary as necessary. Direct students to the pictures in *Medical Examination* on >> p.12 and ask about the people, place and situation to set the context. Put students into pairs to continue the activity. Ask for volunteers to give answers. Write *weight* and *wait* /weɪt/ on the board to show that both words are pronounced the same. Students can look up both words in the dictionary.

> *Weight* sounds the same as *wait*. The doctor meant *weight*. The young man understood *wait*.

5 Go through the instructions and check vocabulary in the titles. Direct students to *Puzzle time* and ask how they are going to read the stories. *Word for word or quickly for the general idea? (Quickly.)* Explain that you will deal with any new vocabulary later. Set a short time limit before students continue individually. Take a class vote for the best title for each story and nominate individual students to justify their answers.

> 1 English Class   2 Chatting at Work   3 Crossword
> 4 Buying Fruit

6 Go through the instructions and demonstrate the activity using the first story. Tell students to read *English Class* again and decide which word caused the problem. (right, *it sounds the same as* write.) Ask why the others in the class laughed (the student gave the wrong answer). Students continue in pairs. Encourage them to use dictionaries to help. Monitor and help as necessary. Ask for volunteers to give answers.

> 1 The teacher asked about the opposite of the word *right* and expected the answer *left*. The student thought about the word *write* and gave the answer *read*.

2 The man's colleague wanted to know if Anita had *flu* but, because *flu* sounds the same as *flew*, (the past tense of *to fly*) the man thought his colleague was asking about how Anita had travelled.

3 The mother thought the child was asking the question *Why?* rather than telling her that the letter *Y* is the first letter of the word.

4 Maria Teresa used the word *pair* meaning 'two of something' but the greengrocer thought she had changed her mind and wanted some *pears*.

C Pronunciation the alphabet

7 Go through the instructions and the example to check students understand the activity. Ask students to read words 1–13 and check vocabulary. Monitor and help with pronunciation as necessary, while students continue individually. Nominate students to give the answers. Monitor for correct pronunciation.

2 A   3 Q   4 I   5 F   6 L   7 M   8 N   9 S   10 X   11 O
12 R   13 Z

Extra help

Students choose the names of three people from the unit and spell them for a partner. The partner writes the names and says what they can remember about the people.

8 Go through the instructions and point out that, for this exercise, students work with the full alphabet. Do one or two examples to check students understand the activity before they continue in pairs. Ask for answers around the class and give extra pronunciation practice as necessary.

1 c, d, e, g, p, t, v   2 j, k   3 u, w   4 y   5 h

9 1D.1 Read the instructions and check students understand the meaning and pronunciation of the words. Drill pronunciation as necessary. Read the example and play the audio for students to follow. Continue with the audio, pausing after each item for students to respond as a class. Monitor for accurate pronunciation of the letters of the alphabet.

Repeat the activity if necessary and nominate individual students to spell the words.

2 peace   3 guessed   4 through   5 rode   6 meat
7 new   8 bored

Extra help

Students use audio script 1D.1 on >> p.150 and repeat the activity in pairs.

D Listen and follow a conversation

In this section, students listen for detail to follow the order of a conversation in which a misunderstanding occurs.

10 Tell students that the conversation is what Maria Teresa and the greengrocer *actually* said in *Buying Fruit* on >> p.12. Tell students to look at the things both A and B say. Ask *Who misunderstands? (B.) Who explains the misunderstanding? (A.)*

Direct students to the example to show where the conversation starts. Students sequence the conversation individually and compare in pairs. Do not give answers at this stage.

11 1D.2 Remind students that they will listen for key words to check their answers. Play the audio. Direct students to audio script 1D.2 on >> p.150 to check their answers.

12 1D.3 Direct students to *Misunderstandings* on >> p.12 again. Go through each one in turn. Point out how both speakers in audio script 1D.2 apologize for their misunderstanding, repeat what they thought the speaker had said, and spell words to help clarify. Play the audio, pausing for students to repeat after each one. Monitor and encourage students to mimic intonation to sound sincere. Give positive feedback.

13 In pairs, students practise reading the dialogue. Encourage students to smile as they speak as it will help them sound friendlier. Monitor and encourage them to look less and less at their book so they become more confident and independent. Remember to praise students when they produce accurate sentences. Check students swap roles. Nominate or ask for two volunteers to read the conversation to the class. Ask the class if they sounded friendly.

Extra activity

In pairs, students write one or two conversations for two of the misunderstandings in *Puzzle time*. They continue the conversation so the misunderstanding is resolved. Pairs rehearse their conversations and choose one to act out for another pair.

ABCD Put it all together

14 Put students into pairs and direct each pair to *Misunderstandings* on >> p.126. Go through the instructions and point out that pairs should choose two of the situations. Encourage students to use *Misunderstandings* on >> p.12 and the dialogue in exercise 10 and to spell words if necessary to help. Monitor and help as necessary. Check students swap roles as they practise saying the conversations.

15 Put students into groups of four to do the role play. Ask for volunteers to tell the class about their misunderstandings at the end of the activity.

Student performance

Students should be able to give short explanations or reformulations.

You can use this checklist to monitor and give feedback or to assess students' performance.

Interaction	Do students repeat back what their partner says to confirm understanding? exercise 13 Do students apologize before asking for repetition or clarification? exercise 13
Pronunciation	Do students pronounce the letters of the alphabet clearly? exercise 9

I can **correct a misunderstanding.**

Students tick *on my own* if they have role played one of the conversations without looking at their notes. They tick *with some help* if they have looked at their notes occasionally when role playing both conversations.

Early finishers

Pairs write a conversation for another misunderstanding in exercise 15 and repeat the activity.

Additional material

www.oup.com/elt/result for extra practice activities
www.oup.com/elt/teacher/result for extra teacher resources

How to correct a misunderstanding

v cognates and false friends; misunderstandings   P the alphabet

A Vocabulary cognates and false friends

1 Match the definitions and examples.
1 ☐ Cognate (There is a similar word in my language and it has a similar meaning.)
2 ☐ False friend (There is a word in my language which looks similar but has a different meaning.)
3 ☐ The word is completely different in my language.

a The Italian word *calcio* means *football*.
b The Polish word *paszport* means *passport*.
c The Spanish word *carpeta* doesn't mean *carpet*. It means *file*.

2 Are these words cognates, false friends, or completely different in your language? Write 1, 2, or 3. Check in a mono-lingual dictionary if you aren't sure.

☐ actually ☐ apple ☐ camera ☐ exit
☐ large ☐ novel ☐ parent ☐ police
☐ smoking ☐ taxi ☐ tennis

3 Can you think of more cognates and false friends in English and your language? Do you think they could cause misunderstandings? Discuss in groups.

B Read and identify misunderstandings

4 Read **Medical Examination** opposite. What is the misunderstanding? Complete the explanation with a partner.
Weight sounds the same as _____.
The doctor meant _____.
The young man understood _____.

5 Read **Puzzle time** opposite. Match stories 1–4 with these titles.
☐ Buying Fruit   ☐ Crossword
☐ Chatting at Work ☐ English Class

6 Work with a partner. Read the puzzles again and explain the misunderstandings. These words are clues.

right flu why pair

C Pronunciation the alphabet

7 Which letters rhyme with these words? Match them.
S F B̶ A Z X Q O N L I R M
1 [B] tree   6 ☐ spell   10 ☐ necks
2 ☐ day   7 ☐ them   11 ☐ know
3 ☐ new   8 ☐ pen   12 ☐ car
4 ☐ fly   9 ☐ dress   13 ☐ bed
5 ☐ Jeff

8 Work with a partner. Answer these questions about the full alphabet.

abcdefghijklmn
opqrstuvwxyz

1 Which seven other letters rhyme with *tree*?
2 Which two other letters rhyme with *day*?
3 Which two other letters rhyme with *new*?
4 Which other letter rhymes with *fly*?
5 Which letter doesn't rhyme with any of the words in exercise 7?

9 **1D.1▶** Listen and complete the sentences. Here are the words you need.

bored guessed knows meat
new peace rode through

Example **Audio** Nose, N-O-S-E, is pronounced the same as …
          You   … knows; K-N-O-W-S

D Listen and follow a conversation

10 Read puzzle 4 in **Puzzle time** again and put this conversation in order.
A ☐ I'm sorry, I don't understand …
A [1] Can I have some bananas, please?
A ☐ Oh, I see! No, I meant pair, P-A-I-R! I'd like those two bananas, please.
A ☐ Oh, ehm … I'll take that pair.
B ☐ Pardon? Don't you want any bananas then?
B ☐ Oh, ha ha. OK. Sorry, I misunderstood. I thought you said pear, P-E-A-R!
B ☐ Yes, of course. Which ones do you want?
B ☐ You want a pear?

11 **1D.2▶** Listen and check.

12 **1D.3▶** Look at **Misunderstandings** opposite. Listen and repeat the phrases.

13 Practise the conversation in exercise 10 with a partner.

ABCD Put it all together

14 Work with a partner. Look at **Misunderstandings** on ⟫ p.126. Choose two of the misunderstandings and write a conversation similar to the one in exercise 10. Practise saying your conversations.

15 Do your role play for another pair. What is the misunderstanding?

Writing A self-introduction

A Get ideas to write about

1 Read email A. Work with a partner and <u>underline</u> the best option.
   1 Wanda's writing to people she doesn't know / a friend / her boss.
   2 Wanda wants to learn new things / meet new people.
   3 Wanda's sending a photo in the post / attaching a photo with the email.

2 How is Wanda's email organized? Put these headings in order 1–6.
   - [ ] my general background and interests
   - [ ] my hopes for the future
   - [1] greeting
   - [ ] goodbye
   - [ ] my interest in the topic of the discussion group
   - [ ] my name and how I heard about the discussion group

3 Organize these notes into the six sections from exercise 2.
   24 Notting Hill secretary Japan yoga
   Best wishes ~~Dear~~ photos of people, capture personality
   sending photo Wanda J, invited by Tony G
   want learn more, contribute

	Wanda
1	*Dear*
2	
3	

4 Imagine you want to join a discussion group. Decide what the group is about. Write some notes, not full sentences, for the six sections.

5 Talk about your ideas in small groups. Do you want to change or add anything to your notes?

B Drafting and editing

6 Read email B. Warren wants to join the discussion group and wrote this first draft. What changes should he make before he sends his email?

7 Work with a different partner or in a small group and compare your ideas.

AB Put it all together

8 Use your notes in exercise 4 to write a first draft of your self-introduction email.

9 Work with a partner and edit your writing together. Look for mistakes like Warren's.

10 Write your final draft. Are you happy to send it now?

A

✉ Self-introduction _ □ ✕

Dear list members,

I'm Wanda Jones and I was invited to join this photography discussion group by Tony Garcia.

I'm 24 and single and I live in Notting Hill with my flatmate Fatima. I'm a secretary at Safeguard Home Insurance. I'm studying Japanese at evening classes because I want to go and work in Japan. I enjoy Tai Chi and Yoga.

My biggest passion is photography and I love taking photographs of people. I believe that if you take the picture at the right moment, you can capture their personality. I'm sending a photo of myself with my first camera as an attachment. It's a Leica. It was my grandfather's, and he gave it to me when I was ten.

I'm looking forward to learning more about photography from you all and I hope I can contribute something too.

Best wishes,

Wanda

B

✉ Self-introduction _ □ ✕

Dear Mr Tony,

I'm Mr Warren and I was invited to join the discussion group by Wanda.

I'm look forward to learning more from you all and I hope I can contribute something too.

I work for a Japanese company which makes cameras for people who work in the film industry. I'm studying Japanese at evening classes so I can communicate myself better with people in the company.

My biggest passion is photography and film and I love going to the cinema. I'd like to learn more about film and photography. I believe that a good film can be made better if the people who do the filming know a lot about photography too. I'm 22 and single and I live in notting Hill.

Warren

I can write a self-introduction.

Tick ✓ the line.   with a lot of help   with some help   on my own   very easily

Orientation

Context and Language

In this lesson, students write a self-introduction to list members on an email discussion group. This is usually written in a formal style.

Recycled language	words: *attachment, boss, flatmate, grandfather, photography, personality, secretary, single, yoga* phrases: *Best wishes, Dear Mr ..., I'm looking forward to ...* grammar: *pronouns; present simple and present continuous*
Recognition language	words: *capture, contribute, passion* phrases: *discussion group, list members, general background*

End product

In *Put it all together*, students write a self-introduction email of about 80–90 words based on examples in the lesson. They peer review and edit their writing, before producing a second draft.

Warmer

Ask students what types of things people write and why. Write ideas on the board and add *a self-introduction email* if necessary. Elicit ideas on the differences between the types of texts and their purposes. Do not overcorrect for accuracy at this stage.

Write *How to write a self-introduction* on the board.

A Get ideas to write about

In this section, students think about the audience and purpose of a text. They analyse the organization of an email introduction.

1 Direct students to the photo and ask what they can see. Ask them to read sentences 1–3 and check vocabulary. Students continue the activity. Check answers.

> 1 people she doesn't know   2 learn new things
> 3 attaching a photo with the email

Teaching tip

When you check vocabulary, encourage students to guess the meaning of the word first and elicit ideas. Ask them how they guessed, for example, by thinking about the topic of the text and sentence, the position of the word in the sentence, etc.

Extra activity

Ask some true/false questions to check students understand the text e.g. *Wanda works at Safeguard Home Insurance. (T) Wanda's working in Japan. (F)*

2 Ask students to read items 1-6 and check vocabulary. Read the instructions and go through the activity with the whole class. Ask about Wanda's email at the end of the activity, e.g. *Does it contain the information you would expect to find? (Yes.)*

> 2 my name and how ...   3 my general background ...
> 4 my interest in ...   5 my hopes for ...   6 goodbye

3 Go through the instructions and check students understand the activity. Draw a table on the board, with rows numbered 1–6 to represent the points in exercise 2. Ask students to read the items, and point out that they are written in note form, e.g. initials for names of people. Choose one or two items from the words and phrases and write them in the appropriate rows on the board. Ask students to copy the table and put them into pairs to complete the activity. Monitor and help as necessary.

> 2 Wanda J, invited by Tony G   3 24, Notting Hill, secretary, Japan, yoga   4 photos of people, capture personality, sending photo   5 want learn more, contribute   6 Best wishes

4 Read through the instructions. Ask students to draw another table with rows numbered 1–6. Encourage them to write their ideas as they come to mind. Monitor and help, checking students are writing in note-form and give positive feedback where appropriate.

5 Put students into small groups to take turns to explain what they will write about. Encourage them to use the language of suggestions and responses, e.g. *Why don't you ...?, That's a good idea!* Check students amend their notes as they go along.

B Drafting and editing

In this section, students proofread a first draft of an email.

6 Direct students to email B and ask them to read it quickly. Ask *Was it easy to follow? Does it say what you expected to read? Is it formal or informal? Is it accurate?* Point out that an email to join a discussion group would be quite formal.

Go through the instructions and do one or two examples. Remind students to look at organization, address forms, grammar, and vocabulary. Students continue individually.

7 Students compare answers in pairs or small groups. Ask for volunteers to explain the changes they would make and why.

> **names:** Mr Tony – Mr Garcia; Mr Warren – Warren; Wanda – Wanda Jones
> **grammar:** I'm look forward to – I'm looking forward to
> **vocabulary:** communicate myself better – communicate better
> **organization:** change the paragraph order – Warren's second paragraph should come before the closing; I'm 22 and ... should start paragraph 3

AB Put it all together

8 Read the instructions and direct students to the notes they made in exercise 4. Remind them to think about who they are writing to and why. Monitor and help as necessary.

9 Students edit their work in pairs. Monitor and encourage a collaborative working atmosphere.

10 Ask students to write a final draft, and to review it before handing it in.

Student performance

Students should be able to write a short, well-organized self-introduction email.

You can use this checklist to monitor and give feedback or to assess students' performance.

Content	Have students covered the points a reader would expect?
Organization	Have students used a greeting and said goodbye? Have students organized their ideas logically?

I can **write a self-introduction email.**

Students tick *on my own* if they have produced a second draft which has few mistakes. They can tick *with some help* if their second draft needs further revision.

Early finishers

Students plan, write, and review a first draft reply from a list member to Wanda's email.

Additional material

www.oup.com/elt/result for extra practice activities
www.oup.com/elt/teacher/result for extra teacher resources

Warmer

Remember who

Read out or write sentences 1–10 below on the board from Unit 1. In small groups, students write down who said or wrote them. Students look through the unit to check their answers at the end.

1 I'm 24 and single.   2 I called at your flat today but you were out. 3 Could you work a bit later tomorrow evening?   4 In Britain, shaking hands is quite common.   5 Who are those two people? 6 Which ones do you want?   7 Why don't you come round for dinner tomorrow night?   8 I never introduce myself with Mr and my surname.   9 That's the king and queen.   10 I thought you asked me to wait.

1 Wanda   2 Warren   3 Mr Robbins   4 Greg (Brown)
5 Barbara   6 the greengrocer   7 Tina   8 Greg Brown
9 the museum guide   10 the recruit

A Grammar

1   Subject questions and object questions 1A exercise 10

Warm-up: Say one or two sentences from the exercise, mumbling the missing word to elicit a question from the students. Review the grammar box on **>> p.7** if necessary.

Set-up: Direct students to the example. Ask *What's the tense of the first sentence in? (Present simple.) And the second? (Present simple.)*

2 Who loves Wanda?
3 Who left a message for Fatima?
4 Who did Roxette kiss on the cheeks?
5 Who does Tracy think is nice?
6 Who wants to see Wanda tomorrow?
7 Who called Wanda (to invite her to dinner)?
8 Who did Warren visit yesterday?
9 Who saw Warren outside Wanda's flat?
10 Who does Mrs Mirren live with?

Follow-up: Put students into pairs to ask questions about the people in their answers to the *Warmer*. Give them time to write questions and monitor and check for accuracy.

2   Reflexive pronouns 1B exercise 12

Warm-up: Say one or two reflexive pronouns from the grammar box on **>> p.9** and elicit others around the class.

Set-up: Go through the instructions and example as a class.

2 themselves   3 yourself   4 each other   5 himself
6 each other   7 ourselves

Follow-up: Students write three similar sentences and swap with a partner.

3   Present simple and continuous 1C exercise 9

Warm-up: Direct students to the painting and elicit five words they think might appear in the text. Write them on the board and ask students to read the text to see if they were right.

Set-up: Check vocabulary in the text as necessary.

2 like   3 shows   4 's wearing   5 's playing   6 seems   7 feel
8 know   9 see   10 'm learning   11 has

Follow-up: Students use the photos in *Pairwork* on **>> p.126** and **>> p.133**. In pairs, they describe a person for a partner to guess who it is.

B Vocabulary

4   The people in my life 1A exercises 2, 3

Warm-up: Draw three columns on the board: *male, female,* or *either*. Add one example for each. Books closed. Set a time limit of about 90 seconds for students, in pairs, to suggest words for each column. Write them on the board. Check understanding.

Set-up: Read the instruction. Do the example as a class to check students understand.

2 widow   3 aunt   4 colleague   5 brother-in-law   6 cousin
7 neighbour   8 acquaintance

Follow-up: Students write the names of six people in their lives. They work with a partner and ask each other about the people. Monitor and give extra pronunciation practice if necessary.

5   Ways of greeting 1B exercise 1

Warm-up: Books closed. Write the title for the exercise on the board and elicit different ways of greeting.

Set-up: Check students remember the words in the word pool. Do the example as a class.

2 shake   3 hug   4 kiss, cheeks   5 put, shoulder   6 wave

Follow-up: Put students into groups of four. Ask each pair to mime ways of greeting, for the others to guess the phrases.

6   Position 1C exercise 4

Warm-up: Write the name of a student on the board and ask *Where is he/she?* Elicit answers around the class. Monitor for accuracy and correct if necessary.

Set-up: Go through the instructions with the class.

2 in front of   3 to the right of   4 at the back of
5 at the front of   6 in the middle of

Follow-up: In pairs, students copy the diagram from *Position* on **>> p.10** and write nine numbers in different places. They exchange diagrams with another pair who write phrases describing the position of the number. Pairs check each other's answers.

7   Misunderstandings 1D exercise 10

Warm-up: Write these words on the board: *understand, I, don't, meant, thought, you, sorry, said, see, pardon, misunderstood, oh.* Students make *Misunderstandings* phrases and check on **>> p. 12.**

Set-up: Ask students to read the sentences quickly and to explain the misunderstanding. *(A wants a pot of tea, B thought A wanted a pot of cheese.)*

3 A Pardon? ...   4 B We don't sell ...   5 A Oh, I see ...
6 B Ah, I misunderstood ...

Follow-up: Students write a jumbled conversation for a situation in *Misunderstandings* on **>> p.126**. They swap exercises and then correct each other's answers at the end.

Early finishers

Students review the unit and choose ten words they want to remember for the next class. They draw three columns and write the words in the first column. They write a translation in the second and an example sentence in the third.

Unit 1 Review

R1

A Grammar

1 Subject questions and object questions Write questions about the missing information.

1 Tom loves __?__. *Who does Tom love?*
2 __?__ loves Wanda.
3 __?__ left a message for Fatima.
4 Roxette kissed __?__ on the cheeks.
5 Tracey thinks __?__ is nice.
6 __?__ wants to see Wanda tomorrow.
7 __?__ called Wanda to invite her to dinner.
8 Warren visited __?__ yesterday.
9 __?__ saw Warren outside Wanda's flat.
10 Mrs Mirren lives with __?__.

2 Reflexive pronouns Complete the sentences with a reflexive pronoun or *each other*.

1 I never introduce *myself* using my full name.
2 It's normal for people to live by _____ when they go to university.
3 Come and join us – don't just sit there by _____!
4 In Turkey, friends greet _____ with one or two kisses on the cheek.
5 He's old enough to look after _____ now.
6 In many countries, people give _____ Christmas presents on 6th January.
7 We made this wedding cake _____. I hope it tastes OK!

3 Present simple and continuous Put the verbs in the correct tense.

The Musée d'Orsay in Paris
¹ *has* have a large collection of French Art. I really
² _____ like the paintings by Edouard Manet. One picture
³ _____ show a young soldier boy. He ⁴ _____ wear red trousers and a hat, and he
⁵ _____ play a small flute. The boy ⁶ _____ seem happy enough, but I ⁷ _____ feel sad when I look at him – will he live to be an adult? I ⁸ _____ know this picture well because I
⁹ _____ see it every week – I ¹⁰ _____ learn to play the flute and my teacher ¹¹ _____ have a poster of it on his wall.

B Vocabulary

4 The people in my life Match these words with the correct definition.

acquaintance aunt brother-in-law colleague cousin neighbour ~~niece~~ widow

1 The daughter of my sister. _*niece*_
2 A women whose husband has died. _____
3 The sister of my mother or father. _____
4 Somebody I work with. _____
5 The brother of my husband. _____
6 My uncle's daughter. _____
7 A person who lives near me. _____
8 A person who I know. _____

5 Ways of greeting Complete the sentences with these words.

~~bow~~ cheeks hug kiss put shake shoulder wave

1 Musicians sometimes *bow* to the audience at the end of a concert.
2 When people meet for the first time, they often _____ hands.
3 Brothers often _____ when they greet each other.
4 Women friends often _____ each other on the _____ when they meet.
5 Men sometimes _____ their hand on the other person's _____.
6 People often _____ when they say goodbye.

6 Position Where's the smiley 😊? Write sentences for the pictures.

1 *He's behind the box.*
2
3
4
5
6

7 Misunderstandings Put the conversation in order.

- [ ] A Oh, I see! No, I meant a pot of tea.
- [ ] A Pardon? I don't understand.
- [1] A Can I have a pot of tea, please?
- [ ] B Ah, I misunderstood. I thought you said 'pot of cheese'! Sorry about that.
- [2] B I'm sorry, we don't sell food.
- [ ] B We don't sell cheese.

People and places

This is a young man called Tariq from Morocco in North Africa. He and his family are Muslims and they live in the Atlas mountain region. In this picture, we see him in front of the white walls of the village mosque. He's wearing the traditional blue cloth of his people.

age and gender	young man
nationality	Moroccan
religion	
ethnic background	Berber
(part of) continent	
country	
region	
environment	mountains, desert

1 a Huli man

2 an Aymara woman

3 a young Berber man

4 a young Wodaabe man

5 a Maasai woman

6 a Maori man

7 a Mayan girl

8 a Yanomami girl

9 an Inuit man

10 a Bedouin boy

How to talk about your background

Orientation

Context

In this lesson, students will practise talking about themselves, their ethnic background and places they are from.

People and places describes the person in photo 3 and gives a list of types of information about people.

The captioned photos show indigenous people from different parts of the world.

Language

Focus grammar	*the* before geographical names
Focus words	people and places: *environment, ethnic background, gender, group, nationality, (part of) continent, region, religion*
Recognition vocabulary	ethnic backgrounds: *Aymara, Bedouin, Berber, Inuit,* etc. countries, regions, continents: *Bolivia, Central America, the Middle East,* etc. religions: *Christian, Muslim,* etc. people: *beads, cloth, decorated, fur coat, headscarf, necklace, mud, spear, tattoos, tribe* places: *mountain ranges, oceans and seas, island groups* other: *a working class family*
Recycled language	words: *ceremony, city, country, desert, festival, island, lake, mountains, traditional* capital letters for countries and places grammar: *present simple and continuous*
Pronunciation	spelling and pronunciation: *c* and *g* /s/, /k/, /dz/, /g/ **2A.3**

End product

In *Put it all together,* students work in small groups and use their notes to give a short factual presentation about themselves and their background. Their presentation is based on audio script 2A.3 on >> **p.151.**

Preparation

Think of three famous people your students will know if you plan to do the *Warmer.* Use the categories in *People and places* on >> **p.16** and make a note of their details. Take dictionaries to class.

Warmer

Put students into small groups. Read your descriptions of famous people and ask students to guess who they are. Tell students that each group can ask you questions or to repeat parts of the information. See if students can tell you anything more about the person or place they are from.

Write *How to talk about your background* on the board.

A Vocabulary people and places

1 Go through the instructions and ask students for one example for the first two columns to check they understand the titles. Students continue in pairs. Monitor and help as necessary, checking students are using capital letters.

> **religious groups:** Christian, Muslim, Jewish
> **regions/parts of continents:** Central America, the Middle East, the South Pacific, East Africa
> **countries:** Guatemala, Tanzania

2 Set a time limit of about three minutes for students to add more examples to each column. Encourage students to use their dictionaries to check any spelling they are unsure of. Ask around the class for suggestions.

3 Direct students to *People and places* on >> **p.16** and tell them to read the text to answer the question *(photo 3).* Ask students to complete the information in the box. Monitor and help, encouraging students to use the captions under the photo.

Go over answers as a class, checking students understand the category words. Drill the words and phrases.

> **religion:** Muslim
> **(part of) continent:** North Africa
> **country:** Morocco   **region:** Atlas Mountains

Extra activity

Books closed. Use the captions to review indefinite articles *a/ an.* Describe the people for students as a class to call out *a* or *an,* e.g. **T** *Aymara woman* **SS** *an* **T** *Berber man* **SS** *a* etc.

4 Go through the instructions and the example. Point out that *maybe* is used to indicate that the speaker is guessing. Do one or two photos together as a class and put students into pairs to continue. Set a short time limit to keep the pace and monitor and help as necessary. Ask for suggestions around the class and tell students to make brief notes by the photos. Do not comment on suggestions at this stage as the activity prepares students for the listening section that follows.

B Listen for key words

In this section, students listen for key words in short description texts.

5 2A.1 Read the title of the section and ask students when they would listen for key words and phrases in real life. *(To find out specific information, e.g. listening to a voice-mail message.)* Tell students that key words and phrases are usually stressed and so are easier to understand.

Go through the instructions and play the audio for students to underline key words as they listen and to answer the question *(photo 2).* Remind them not to worry about correct spelling, especially of place names. After the listening, point out that, by understanding a few key words, students were able to understand who was being described.

> **key words:** woman, Lake Titicaca, Bolivia, (black) hat, (cloth) bag, Aymara

Teaching tip

Drawing students' attention to using the same strategies that they would use in their L1 helps build confidence and increase motivation. It will also help students to become more self-reliant eventually.

6 2A.2 Tell students they will listen for key words in nine short descriptions. Go through the instructions and play the audio. Pause after each description and elicit the photo number. Ask students to put a tick by their guesses in exercise 4, but do not comment on this at the moment.

> a 3　b 4　c 10　d 5　e 6　f 7　g 8　h 1　i 9

7 Play the audio again for students to find one piece of extra information for each photo. Direct students to audio script 2A.2 on >> p.151 to check their answers and the notes they made in exercise 4.

Extra help

Ask students to underline two new words in each description in the audio script. In pairs, they look at photos 1–10 to see if they can guess the meaning before checking in a dictionary.

C Grammar *the* before geographical names

8 Direct students to the headings of the two columns in the grammar box. Check vocabulary. In pairs, students write the names of the places in the box. Ask for volunteers to give answers and point out the exceptions below the box.

> **use *the* before:** mountain ranges – the Alps; rivers – the Nile; oceans and seas – the Atlantic; island groups – the Canary Islands; deserts – the Arabian Desert; some countries – the United States; some regions – the Far East
> **don't use *the* before:** single mountains – Mount Everest; countries – India; continents – Asia; single islands – North Island; cities – London; lakes – Lake Victoria

9 Go through the instructions. Use the example to demonstrate that students should use 'environment' words like *lake* or *mountain* and the information in the grammar box to help them work out the answer. Monitor and help as students continue individually. Nominate students to give answers.

> 2 The/the　3 –/–　4 –/–　5 –/the　6 –/the　7 –/the

Extra help

Books closed. Choose five geographical names from exercise 8 and make anagrams. Put students into pairs and set a time limit for them to write the names on a piece of paper. Pairs swap pieces of paper and correct each other's answers.

Extra plus

Give students time to study the vocabulary in exercise 8. In pairs, students take turns to test a partner. Student A says a category. Student B says a place.

D Spelling and pronunciation *c* and *g*

10 Read the title of the section. Ask students if spelling in English always represents pronunciation. *(No.)* Tell students that the pronunciation of the two letters changes, depending on which letters it comes before. Go through the information in the box and point out the exceptions. Do the activity as a class.

> the letter *c* before *e, i, y*: city, place
> before any other letter: country, Africa
> the letter *g* usually: gender, religion
> before any other letter: background, group

11 Read the instructions. Ask students to read the text and check any vocabulary. Point out the use of the present simple tense for states and repeated habits. Put students into pairs to decide how the letters in green are pronounced. Monitor and help as necessary.

12 2A.3 Play the audio, pausing as necessary for students to check their answers.

Extra activity

Students take turns reading the text and checking each other's pronunciation. Monitor and give positive feedback for intelligible pronunciation.

13 Go through the instructions. Books closed. Put students into pairs to take turns to make statements about Gerry. Elicit suggestions around the class and monitor pronunciation and accurate use of the present simple tense. Give extra practice as necessary.

Extra plus

Ask students to find the words *and* and *because* in the text. In pairs, students see how many sentences they can make about Gerry using the conjunctions.

ABCD Put it all together

14 Read the instructions and check students understand the categories. If your students come from the same place, encourage them to add more personal details. For example, for interests, students could add places they have visited and people they have met. Monitor and help as necessary, directing students to the text in exercise 11 for ideas. Give students time to rehearse, mumbling presentations to themselves before doing exercise 15.

15 Put students into small groups. Tell them to make a note of similarities between themselves and others as they listen to the presentations. At the end of the activity, ask for volunteers to report any similarities to the class.

Student performance

Students should be able to give a short, factual presentation.

You can use this checklist to monitor and give feedback or to assess students' performance.

Content	Do students talk about most of the topics in *People and places*? exercise 4
Grammar	Do students use the present simple tense appropriately? exercise 13
Pronunciation	Do students mostly pronounce *c* and *g* clearly? exercise 13

I can talk about my background.

Students tick *on my own* if they have given their presentation using their notes. They tick *with some help* if they have looked at the text in exercise 11 occasionally for ideas.

Early finishers

Students choose two different categories from exercise 14 and repeat exercise 15.

Additional material

www.oup.com/elt/result for extra practice activities
www.oup.com/elt/teacher/result for extra teacher resources

How to talk about your background

G *the* before geographical names   V people and places   P spelling and pronunciation *c* and *g*

A Vocabulary people and places

1 Work with a partner and match these names with the three categories.

~~Bolivia~~ Christian Guatemala Muslim
Central America the Middle East the South Pacific
Jewish Tanzania East Africa

religious groups	regions / parts of continents	countries
		Bolivia

2 Add more names to the three categories.

3 Look at the information in **People and places** opposite. Which photo is it about? Complete the information.

4 Work with a partner. Guess at least two pieces of **People and places** information for the other people.

Example Well, in photo 1 there's a young man, maybe 17 years old …

B Listen for key words

5 **2A.1▶** Listen and read this text. Which photo is it about? Underline the words which helped you.

This picture shows a woman standing beside Lake Titicaca in Bolivia. She's wearing a traditional black hat and carrying a brightly coloured cloth bag. The Aymara people have their own language, called Aymara.

6 **2A.2▶** Listen to these descriptions and match them with the photos. Were your guesses correct in exercise 4?

7 Listen again. Find one extra piece of information for each photo. Compare with a partner.

C Grammar *the* before geographical names

8 Write these names in the grammar box.

Asia the Alps the Arabian Desert India the Atlantic
North Island the Canary Islands London the Nile
~~Polynesia~~ the United States the Far East Lake Victoria
Mount Everest

use *the* before …	don't use *the* before …
mountain ranges –	regions – *Polynesia*
rivers –	single mountains –
oceans and seas –	countries –
island groups –	continents –
deserts –	single islands –
some countries* –	cities –
some regions* –	lakes –

*Examples the United Kingdom, the Czech Republic; the Middle East

9 Write *the* or nothing in the gaps.

1 _____ Lake Titicaca is in __*the*__ Andes mountains.
2 _____ Atlas Mountains are north of _____ Sahara Desert.
3 _____ Baffin Island is in _____ Canada.
4 _____ Lake Victoria is in _____ Africa.
5 _____ Jordan is in _____ Middle East.
6 _____ Polynesia is in _____ Pacific Ocean.
7 _____ Britain is also called _____ United Kingdom.

More practice? **Grammar Bank** >> p.137.

D Spelling and pronunciation *c* and *g*

10 Add these words to the rule box.

Africa background city country
gender group place religion

spelling rule	the letter *c* =		the letter *g* usually =
Before *e, i, y*	/s/		/dʒ/ *
		the Pacific /pəˈsɪfɪk/	age /eɪdʒ/
Before any other letter or at the end of a word	/k/		/g/
		the Arctic /ˈɑːktɪk/	Mongolia /mɒŋˈgəʊliə/

*Except *give, get, begin, together*

11 Read this text. How are the letters in green pronounced? Say them with a partner.

My name's Gerry. I'm 19 and I work in a garage. I'm from a village near Galway in the west of Ireland. I speak English and Gaelic. I'm not religious but my parents are Catholic. I come from a working class family. I've got cousins in America because my aunt Celia married an American man and moved to the USA. They live in Georgia. I enjoy motor racing and I write articles for a car magazine.

12 **2A.3▶** Listen and check.

13 Work with a partner. Close your book. What do you remember about Gerry?

ABCD Put it all together

14 Write notes about yourself and your background. Choose at least five of the topics below.

name age home region country job religion
family background ethnic background interests

15 Work in groups. Tell the others in your group about your background. Use your notes to help you.

I can talk about my background.

Tick ✓ the line.   with a lot of help   with some help   on my own   very easily

Chinese tourists hurry to Britain to find shoes, fog, and the 'big stupid clock'

Britain receives crowds of Chinese tourists after Beijing changes visa rules.

A bus with a large group of Chinese tourists stopped outside the Clarks shoe shop in the Bicester Village Shopping Park near Oxford. 'I've never
05 seen anything like it', said one of the shop assistants, 'They were queuing right out of the door.' The tourists wanted to buy shoes for their family back home and some of them bought six pairs. Many of them came
10 with paper cut-outs of their relatives' feet – a clever idea, as you can never be sure that shoes sizes are accurate.

In the past, only business people and students could get visas to visit the UK, and
15 people hardly ever visited as tourists. But the visa rules have changed. Now, Chinese tourists are allowed to travel to Britain in groups. Also, the Chinese economy is strong and airlines are introducing more
20 direct flights from China to Britain. This is all good news for British tourism.

But what do the Chinese expect to find when they come here? According to Calum MacLeod of the Great Britain-
25 China Centre, they sometimes have old-fashioned ideas of Britain. They think of Charles Dickens's book Oliver Twist and the famous London fog. 'When I tell people I live in London, they often ask me
30 how bad the fog is,' says MacLeod.

'They are interested in the UK's history and traditions,' says MacLeod. Lai Gaik Ung Polain, a tour guide, agrees. 'We usually take them to see the famous tourist attractions in London
35 and the south east of the country such as Buckingham Palace and the Houses of Parliament, and they always want to see Big Ben.' In Chinese, they call it Da Ben Zhong, meaning 'Big stupid clock'. But they are quite often interested in less well-known sights too, such as Winston Churchill's home or Karl Marx's grave.

But they don't only want to go sightseeing while they are in Britain. 'We always take our groups

In Chinese, Big Ben is called 'Big Stupid Clock'

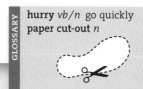

Karl Marx's grave is also popular

50 to Soho to eat Chinese food', says Polain. Most tourists enjoy food from home when they are abroad. Shopping is important, too. Chinese tourists rarely stay in Britain for more than a few days before continuing to another European country. They often buy presents for family
55 and friends. Apart from Clarks, well-known British goods such as Burberry raincoats are also popular. You can buy many of these goods in China, but people usually prefer to buy them in the country of origin if they can.

60 People in the British tourism business are very pleased. They are comparing it to twenty years ago, when tourists suddenly started coming from Japan.

GLOSSARY

hurry vb/n go quickly
paper cut-out n

expect vb to think or believe that something will happen
tradition n a custom; a habit which has continued for a long time
attraction n an interesting thing for tourists to see

How to talk about tourism

Orientation

Context

In this lesson, students practise talking about aspects of tourism in their country or region.

The headline in the article on >> **p.18** describes what Chinese tourists tend to buy in Britain (shoes), what they expect the weather to be like (foggy, based on Britain at the time of Charles Dickens) and mentions 'the big stupid clock' (which comes from the Chinese for Big Ben, *Da Ben Zhong*).

The accompanying photos show Chinese tourists and tourist sights they tend to visit.

Glossary explains some key vocabulary.

Culture note

Stereotypes are often based on *perceived* rather than *real* behaviours of groups of people. These ideas tend to be applied to nationalities or groups as a whole, whether they are true or not. Research has shown there is often no correlation between perceived cultural characteristics and individual identities.

Language

Focus grammar	adverbs of frequency
Focus words	adverbs of frequency: *always, usually, often, quite often, sometimes, rarely, hardly ever, never*
Recognition vocabulary	words: *crowds, old-fashioned, paper cut-out, stereotypes, tourism, well-known, visa* phrases: *country of origin, hurry up*
Recycled language	words: *abroad, attraction, expect, foggy, sight, sightseeing, souvenirs, tour guide, tradition* phrases: *I think..., I don't think ..., maybe ...* grammar: *present simple*

Language note

Adverbs of frequency can be placed in initial, mid, or end position in a sentence, depending on the type. In this lesson, they occur in mid-position, before the verb or part of the verb. Variations will be studied later in the course.

End product

In *Put it all together,* students describe typical or famous things about their country or a region of their country. They rehearse the presentation before giving it from memory. The presentation is based on audio script 2B.2.

Preparation

Think about classroom organization for exercise 15.

Warmer

Put students into teams and ask for the name of the following places in London. *1 The home of the royal family? (Buckingham Palace) 2 An old palace and prison where the Crown Jewels are kept? (The Tower of London) 3 Where Charles and Di were married? (St Paul's Cathedral) 4 Where the government sits? (the Houses of Parliament) 5 A famous clock? (Big Ben) 6 Where people party on New Year's Eve? (Trafalgar Square) 7 A ferris wheel with a view of London? (The London Eye) 8 Where you can see models of famous people? (Madame Tussauds)*

Write *How to talk about tourism* on the board.

A Read a newspaper article

In this section, students scan a newspaper article before reading for detail and interpreting information.

1 Go through the instructions and check vocabulary. Monitor and help as students continue the activity individually. Put students into pairs to compare ideas. Elicit suggestions around the class and write suggestions on the board. Students can refer to these if they need help for exercise 17.

2 In pairs, students make a similar list for Britain. Put pairs of students together to compare lists and ask volunteers to give suggestions. Encourage students to add comments and exchange opinions as you talk about each topic.

3 Direct students to *Chinese tourists ... on* >> **p.18**. Ask them to look at the picture and headline and guess what the article is about. Elicit ideas, but do not comment at this stage. Read the instructions and ask students how they are going to read. *(Look quickly to find examples of the words in exercise 1.)* Set a time limit of about three minutes to encourage students to scan the text, ignoring new vocabulary at this point. Ask volunteers for examples.

> **books:** Oliver Twist   **clothes:** raincoats, shoes
> **famous people:** Winston Churchill, Karl Marx
> **food:** Chinese food   **geography:** the south east, abroad
> **places that tourists visit:** Buckingham Palace, the Houses of Parliament, Big Ben
> **souvenirs:** not mentioned   **weather:** fog

4 Go through the instructions and ask who *they* in item 1 refers to *(Chinese tourists)*. Point out the glossary at the end of the article. Do the example with the class to demonstrate the activity. Ask students to read items 2–6 and check vocabulary as necessary. Monitor and help as students continue individually, making a note of any problems with word order. Do not correct mistakes at this point as this is the focus of the next section. Go over answers as a class and check any new vocabulary.

> 2 usually   3 always   4 quite often   5 always   6 rarely

Teaching tip

Review the different reading strategies students have used. Point out that before we read newspaper articles, we normally use pictures and skim and scan to get the general idea of content, before reading in detail. Reflect on how these stages have helped students gain an understanding of the newspaper article and comment on their success.

5 Read questions 1–5 as a class and check vocabulary. Ask students to read the text again and answer the questions. Monitor and help as necessary. Nominate students to give answers and use the line numbers to help the class locate relevant information. Do not overcorrect for accuracy, but help students get their ideas across.

> 1 Shoes sizes are often different in different countries.
> 2 Visa rules have changed; the Chinese economy is strong; there are more direct flights.
> 3 They think England is the still the same as it was when Charles Dickens was writing.
> 4 The text mentions 'less well-known sights'.
> 5 They like to buy famous makes, e.g. Burberry raincoats in the country of origin.

Extra activity

Put students into groups to talk about stereotyping. Ask *Do you think that all Chinese tourists buy exactly the same things? What do people from your country do when they go on holiday? Do they all go to the same place? Do they all do the same things?* (See *Culture note*.) Ask students to decide if the article stereotypes Chinese tourists. *(Not really, it uses words and phrases like: some of them, hardly ever, sometimes, often, usually, quite often, rarely.)*

6   Put students into pairs to answer the question. If they have been to Britain or are studying in Britain, they can talk about what they have done or did. Monitor and help as necessary as students discuss the topic. Ask for volunteers to tell the class, and encourage students to comment on each other's ideas.

B Grammar adverbs of frequency

7   Go through the instructions and direct students to the last column in the box. Ask them to read the phrases. Check understanding and elicit or explain that the final words in each line rhyme and that the completed text is a poem about tourists in Britain in general (not the Chinese tourists in the article). Students do the activity individually before comparing in pairs. Do not go over answers at this point as they will listen to check in exercise 8.

8   2B.1 Play the audio for students to listen and check answers.

> usually   often   sometimes   never

9   Play the audio a second time for students to mumble along with the recording. Tap out the rhythm if necessary to encourage students to keep time.

Extra help

Students read alternate lines, in pairs or small groups.

10   Go through the instructions and do the activity as a class.

> 1 before   2 after   3 after

11   Read the instructions and sentences 1–6 as a class and check vocabulary. Monitor and help as necessary before students compare their ideas in pairs. Go through each item as a class, asking for volunteers to explain their sentences.

Extra plus

Students write a short verse about visitors to their country using exercise 7 as a model.

C Listen for detail

In this section, students listen intensively to short descriptions of four countries.

12   2B.2 Go through the instructions and ask students to read and listen to the first clue. Play the audio and pause at the end of the first clue. Ask students which words give them clues about the country *(mountains, famous, Eiger, Matterhorn)*.

Go through the example conversation as a class, pointing out the use of *I think, maybe,* and *I don't think* as phrases to introduce opinion. Continue with the audio, pausing after the next two clues for the first country. Give students time to exchange ideas and elicit suggestions after each one. Play the audio and continue with the activity. Elicit and confirm answers at the end of each set of three clues.

> 1 Switzerland   2 Holland   3 Russia   4 Brazil

Teaching tip

At the end of the activity, point out that sometimes the main topic is not clear at the beginning of spoken or recorded texts. Explain that it's a good idea to think about the general idea first, and to continue listening to confirm an idea.

13   Direct students to the topic words in exercise 1. Tell students to listen again and write the topic words for each country. Go over answers as a class or direct students to audio script 2B.2 on >> p.151 to check answers in pairs.

> 1 geography, food, souvenirs   2 food, places tourists visit, famous people   3 geography, famous people, places tourists visit   4 food, places tourists visit, famous people

14   Read the instructions and example to demonstrate the activity. Monitor and help as students continue in pairs, checking they are using note-making strategies from Unit 1.

15   Put students into groups of four and remind them to use frequency adverbs when they describe their countries. Encourage students to repeat words and phrases to check they have understood correctly. Monitor and make a note of any problems with uses of frequency adverbs to go over as a class at the end. Give praise when students give interesting clues.

Extra activity

Students repeat the activity with a different pair.

ABC Put it all together

16   Go through the instructions. If you have a monolingual class, ask students to choose a region of their country. Tell students to think of three or more clues and monitor and help as necessary, checking students are writing notes rather than full sentences.

17   Put students into pairs to do the activity. Tell the students who are listening to make a note of the topics in exercise 1 as their partner gives information. Students tell each other which topics they talked about at the end and see if they were correct.

Student performance

Students should be able to give a short factual presentation from memory.

You can use this checklist to monitor and give feedback or to assess students' performance.

Content	Do students talk about three or more different topics? exercise 15
Interaction	Do students ask for repetition or clarification if necessary? exercise 15
Grammar	Do students mostly use adverbs of frequency in the correct position? exercise 11

I can talk about tourism.

Students tick *on my own* if they have given two or more clues without using their notes. They tick *with some help* if they have looked at the board once or twice for ideas.

Early finishers

In pairs, students repeat exercise 17 without their notes. Partners make a note of how many frequency adverbs they used.

As a follow-up project, students could do some Internet research to find out more about another place.

Additional material

www.oup.com/elt/result for extra practice activities
www.oup.com/elt/teacher/result for extra teacher resources

How to talk about tourism

G adverbs of frequency   P adverbs of frequency

A   Read a newspaper article

1   Think of at least one example of each of these things which are famous or typical of your country. Compare your list with a partner.
   books   clothes   famous people   food   geography
   places that tourists visit   souvenirs   weather

2   What things do you think are typical of Britain? Make a list with your partner. Compare with another pair.

3   Read **Chinese tourists ...** opposite. Find examples of the things in exercise 1.

4   Change one or two words in each sentence to make it correct. Compare with a partner.
   1   They ~~always~~ have old-fashioned ideas about Britain.   *sometimes*
   2   The tour guides sometimes take them to see the usual sights.
   3   They hardly ever want to see Big Ben.
   4   They are never interested in less well-known sights.
   5   The tour guides sometimes take them to Soho to eat Chinese food.
   6   They usually stay in Britain for more than a few days.

5   Answer the questions with a partner.
   1   Why do you think the tourists have paper cut-outs of their relatives' feet?
   2   Why are more tourists coming from China now? Find three reasons in the text.
   3   Why do the tourists think that London is foggy?
   4   How do we know that these tourists are more interested in history than typical visitors to London?
   5   Why is shopping important to these Chinese tourists while they're in Britain?

6   Would you do the same things these Chinese tourists do? Tell a partner.

B   Grammar adverbs of frequency

7   Put these adverbs of frequency in order to complete the rhyme.
   sometimes   usually   never   often

They	always	like the city lights
They	_____	go to see the sights
They	_____	go to see Big Ben
They	quite often	visit 'Number Ten'
They	_____	take a photo there
They	rarely	miss Trafalgar Square
The action	hardly ever	stops
They		want to miss the shops

8   **2B.1▶** Listen and check your answers.

9   **Pronunciation** Say the rhyme. Try to keep to the rhythm.

10   Read the sentences in exercises 4 and 7 and answer the questions.
   Do the adverbs of frequency come before or after ...
   1   a main verb?
   2   the auxiliary verb *be*?
   3   the subject of the verb?

11   Add adverbs of frequency to these sentences to make them true. Compare your ideas with a partner.
   1   Tourists visit my home town. *Tourists hardly ever visit my home town. They usually prefer to go to the coast.*
   2   I go abroad on my holidays.
   3   I eat Chinese food.
   4   Tourists are interested in the history of my country.
   5   Foreigners have old-fashioned ideas of my country.
   6   I visit the usual tourist sights in my own country.

   More practice? **Grammar Bank >>** p.137.

C   Listen for detail

12   **2B.2▶** You will hear a quiz about typical images of four countries. For each country there are three clues. After each clue, work with a partner and discuss which countries you think it could be.
   Audio First clue – When people think of this country, they usually think of mountains ...
   Example   A I think this is in Europe – maybe Austria?
                  B Yeah, it could be, or Switzerland. But I don't think it's in South America.

13   Listen again. What type of information do you hear about each country? Choose from the topics in exercise 1.
   Example   Country 1: geography ...

14   Work with a partner. Think of three countries and make a list of typical images of them. Use the topics in exercise 1 to help you.
   Example   Eiffel Tower, The Louvre ...

15   Work with another pair of students. Give them clues about your three countries. Use the clues in exercise 12 as an example. Try to guess the other pair's countries.

ABC   Put it all together

16   Think about *your* country or region (or a country you know). Make notes about some of the topics in exercise 1.

17   Tell your partner about your country. Listen and say which topics from exercise 1 they tell you about.

I can talk about tourism.
Tick ✓ the line.   with a lot of help   with some help   on my own   very easily

Pieces in a Museum

1 _____ ~ Zambia

This item is made of wood and it looks like the letter T. It has a round leg and a curved piece across the top. The leg is wider at the bottom than at the top. It is used as a pillow. It is also used for sitting on, like a stool. There is a piece of rope tied around the top part of the leg. This is used for carrying the headrest around with you on your belt. These headrests are still used today.

2 _____ ~ USA

This item is a kind of glove made of leather. It has tubes for the four fingers and thumb, but they are tied together. There is a wide piece of leather connecting the thumb and first finger. Baseball players use this glove for catching the ball, because the ball is hard and moves fast.

3 _____ ~ Ireland

This item has a wooden handle. At each end of the handle, there are metal plates. There are a lot of curved wires connected to the metal plates. The whole thing looks like a capital D. It was used in the kitchen for mashing vegetables, especially potatoes. Modern potato mashers usually have a different shape.

4 _____ ~ England

This item is a ball made of green glass in a net connected to a piece of rope. Fishermen used these balls for keeping fishing nets near the surface of the water. The glass balls contain air so they don't go under the water. Modern fishing floats are usually made of plastic instead of glass.

5 _____ ~ Brazil

This is a round container made of dried gourd. The top part is covered with silver, and there is a metal tube inside the container. The container is a cup for drinking 'maté', a kind of tea. The metal tube is used as a straw for drinking the tea from under the tea leaves.

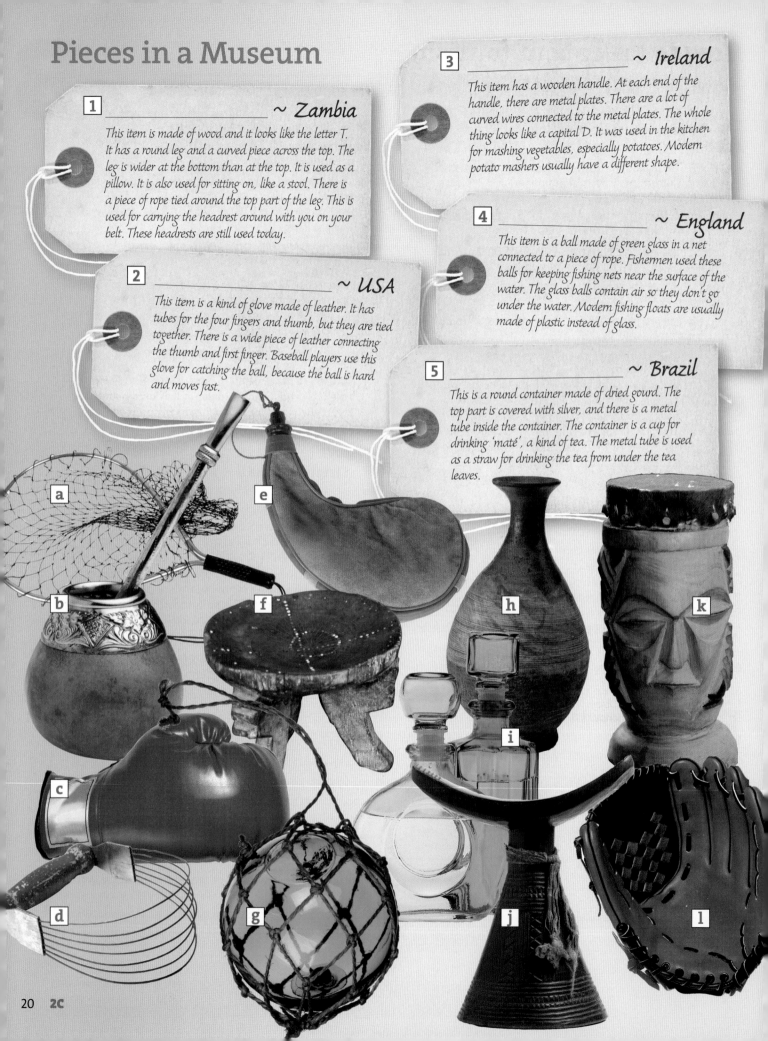

a

b

c

d

e

f

g

h

i

j

k

l

How to describe objects

Orientation

Context
In this lesson, students will practise describing objects they don't know the words for.

The museum catalogue describes five artefacts from different countries. The names of the articles have been removed.

Photos a–l show different objects from around the world.

Language

Focus words	material: *leather, rope* shape and size: *curved, flat, long, narrow, round, wide* parts of an object: *handle, side, top (part)*
Focus phrases	statements: *a kind of, covered with, It's ... used as, looks like, made of, used for* questions: *What does it look like?, What's it used for?, Where's it from?*, etc.
Recognition vocabulary	words: *animal skin, baseball glove, dish, dried gourd, drum, fishing floats, hollow, maté cup and straw, metal plates, potato masher, silver, surface, tube, wooden headrest* phrases: *instead of*
Recycled language	words: *cardboard, china, cloth, container, glass, metal, plastic, square, thin, wood* phrases: *it's made of ..., it's got ..., it's used for ...* grammar: *wh- question forms*
Pronunciation	stress of prepositions: What's it used for? /fɔː/ It's used for cutting fruit. /fə/ **2C.1**

Language note
Short grammar words (articles, conjunctions, and prepositions) like *a, the, and, or, to, of* are usually unstressed. This lesson focuses on the unstressed forms of *for, of, from,* and *as* when they occur at the end of a sentence.

End product
In *Put it all together*, students work in groups, using the photos in *Pairwork* on **>> p.127** to ask questions and identify an object. They have rehearsed a similar conversation in exercise 15.

Preparation
Read the *Teaching tip* after exercise 5. Familiarize yourself with the information in *Pairwork*, Object A **>> p.126** and Object B on **>> p.133** for exercise 14. Take dictionaries to class.

Warmer
Choose an item from photos a–l on **>> p.20**. Tell students that you lost one of these objects when you were moving house recently and they have to guess which one it was. Put them into two or three teams to prepare five yes/no questions to ask you about the object. Give students these categories to think about before they start: *material, shape and size, parts of the object*. Tell them they can only guess after they have asked all their questions. Teams take turns to ask questions and guess the object.

Write *How to describe objects* on the board.

A Read for detail

In this section, students read short descriptions for gist and detail.

1 Read through the instructions and examples and check vocabulary as necessary. Put students into pairs and set a two- or three-minute time limit for them to continue. Draw three columns on the board and elicit suggestions. Write the words on the board and check any new vocabulary as necessary.

> **Suggested answers**
> **material:** cloth, plastic, glass, cardboard, china
> **shape and size:** square thin, round
> **parts of an object:** leg, top, bottom

2 Go through the instructions with the class and direct students to photos a–l on **>> p.20**. Elicit or give the following phrases *It's made of ..., It's got ..., It's used for ...* and write them on the board. Do one or two examples together to demonstrate the activity.

Go through each item in turn, eliciting suggestions and helping students to get their ideas across. Do not expect students to name the objects in the same way they are given in the answer key. Help students get the general idea across.

> a fishing net   b drinking gourd with straw   c boxing glove
> d antique potato masher   e leather wine drinking pouch
> f wooden African three-legged stool   g glass fishing floats
> h ceramic vase   i glass perfume bottles
> j wooden African headrest   k wooden African drum
> l baseball glove

3 Read the instructions and titles with the class. Encourage students to use words or parts of words they know in the titles and texts to do the activity. Direct students to text 1 in *Pieces in a museum* on **>> p.20** and do the first item as a class to demonstrate the activity. Students continue individually and compare in pairs. Ask for volunteers to give answers and to explain which words (or parts) helped them find the answers.

> 1 Wooden Headrest   2 Baseball Glove   3 Potato Masher
> 4 Fishing Floats   5 Maté Cup and Straw

4 Tell students to find one photo (a–l) to match with each text on **>> p.20**. Nominate students to give answers. Refer to the information in the texts to help students understand any mistakes.

> 1 j   2 l   3 d   4 g   5 b

5 To demonstrate the activity, write the word *tubes* on the board ask students to find it in text 2 on **>> p. 20**. Ask students to read the first two sentences carefully to underline clues which would give them an idea of the meaning of the word. *(Clues: kind of glove, leather, four fingers and thumb.)* Ask students to repeat the activity with a different word before checking the meaning in a dictionary.

Teaching tip
Put students into pairs or small groups to tell a partner about the word they chose, how they guessed the meaning and if they were (more or less) correct. Students may be aware of some strategies for guessing the meaning of words. By giving students the opportunity to exchange ideas, they might learn other ways of guessing that are suitable for words in different contexts, e.g. using parts of words, looking at language either side of an unknown word for clues or to see if the word is part of a phrase.

B Vocabulary phrases for describing objects

6 Go through the instructions and the example as a class. Ask students to read sentences 2–6 and check vocabulary. Tell students that they might find more than one possible answer (especially if they use their imaginations!). Monitor and help as necessary as students continue individually. Nominate students to give answers.

> **Suggested answers**
> 2 b, e   3 e, h, i   4 k   5 c, l   6 f, j

7 Tell students they will find the phrases in green in more than one text. Monitor and help as necessary, showing students that sometimes they will have to look across a couple of words to find the phrase, e.g. in text 2 (**use** this glove **for**).

> 1 made of: text 1, 4 (twice), 5   2 used for: text 1 (twice), 2, 4
> 3 used as: text 1, 5   4 covered with: text 5
> 5 kind of: text 2, 5   6 looks like: 1, 3

8 Read through the instructions and the example as a class to demonstrate the activity. Check students understand the word *pillow*. Direct students to photos a–l to see if they can identify the object (*g*).

Ask students to read items 2–4 and check vocabulary before they continue in pairs. Monitor and help as necessary. Ask for volunteers to explain the difference between the pairs of sentences. Point out or elicit that the phrases *used as, looks like, made of,* and *used for* are very useful when you can't think of or don't know the exact words or name of something.

> 2 b It isn't a glove, but it looks similar.   3 a Only the outside is made of leather.   3 b The whole object is made of leather.
> 4 a It isn't a water carrier but it can contain water.

9 2C.1 Draw two columns on the board. Write the title and copy the first example from each column. Read the instructions. Play the audio and underline the stressed prepositions in each column as students listen.

Play the audio a second time, pausing after each sentence for students to repeat. Monitor and nominate individual students to say sentences, giving extra practice as necessary.

Extra help
Choose some items in the classroom and ask students to ask you questions using the questions in the first column in the box in exercise 9. Students repeat the activity in pairs.

10 Put students into pairs and nominate one pair to read the example. Direct students to the photos on >> p.20 and the phrases in exercise 9. Remind them to pronounce the preposition appropriately. Give positive feedback on pronunciation.

Extra activity
In pairs, students take turns to say five sentences about the items on >> p.20. Their partner guesses the item. They look at the sentences in exercise 6 to help with ideas.

C Listen to a description of an object

In this section, students predict words they expect to hear in a conversation before listening to check predictions and noting detail.

11 Read the instructions and direct students to photo b on >> p.20. In pairs, students write six words they expect to hear.

Extra help
Elicit suggestions around the class. Write them on the board and ask the class to vote on the best six words.

12 2C.2 Go through the instructions and play the audio. Play the audio a second time if necessary.

13 Ask students to read questions 1–5 and check vocabulary. Ask students to answer the questions from memory and compare answers in pairs. Play the audio again if necessary.

Nominate students to give answers. At the end, ask *In which other country do people use these cups? (Brazil.) Do you think they have the same problems? Why? Why not?*

> 1 the south of Brazil   2 mixing sugar
> 3 you get the (tea) leaves in your mouth
> 4 it will fall over (so you don't put it down)
> 5 put more hot water in the cup.

14 Go through the instructions and direct As to *Object A* on >> **p.126** and Bs to *Object B* on >> **p.133**. Monitor and help students make notes to answer the questions as necessary.

15 Go through the instructions and put students in pairs to take turns and do the activity. Remind them they can repeat what they think their partner said to check they have understood correctly. Ask students to point out the object at the end of each turn.

Extra plus
Students write a paragraph similar to *Object A* on >> **p.126** and *Object B* on >> **p.133** to describe one of the objects on >> **p.20**. They read the description for the class to guess the object.

ABC Put it all together

16 Direct students to *Guess the Objects* on >> **p.127**. Go through the instructions and put students into small groups. Give them a short period of time to choose three or four objects and think about the answers to the questions in exercise 14. Students continue, guessing the object from the labelled photos.

Student performance
Students should be able to give short factual descriptions.

You can use this checklist to monitor and give feedback or to assess students' performance.

Interaction	Do students answer their partner's questions appropriately? exercise 14
Fluency	Do students mostly answer questions without a lot of hesitation? exercise 10
Vocabulary	Do students use different size and shape words to answer questions? exercise 2

I can describe objects.
Students tick *on my own* if they have answered questions to describe their object using their notes. They tick *with some help* if they have looked at the phrases in the box in exercise 9 a few times for help.

Early finishers
Students think of objects which are typical of a place they know (either their country or a region of their country, or another country they know). They make notes and describe and explain what they are used for. Others in the group decide which objects are the strangest, most useful, or most interesting.

Additional material

www.oup.com/elt/result for extra practice activities
www.oup.com/elt/teacher/result for extra teacher resources

How to describe objects

v words and phrases for describing objects   P stress of prepositions

2C

A Read for detail

1 Work with a partner. Think of as many words as you can to continue these lists.

material *wood, leather, metal ...*
shape and size *wide, flat, long ...*
parts of an object *top, side, handle ...*

2 Look at the photos opposite. Say or guess what the things are with a partner. Try to use some of your words from exercise 1 to describe them.

3 Read **Pieces in a Museum** opposite and match texts 1–5 with these titles.
- [ ] Fishing Floats
- [ ] Baseball Glove
- [ ] Maté Cup and Straw
- [ ] Potato Masher
- [ ] Wooden Headrest

4 Match texts 1–5 with five things in photos a–l.

5 Choose one new word from each text. Guess the general meaning, then check in your dictionary.

B Vocabulary phrases for describing objects

6 What is *it*? Match the sentences with photos a–l.
1 It's made of wood. *f, j, k*
2 It's used for drinking wine from.
3 It could be used as a water container.
4 The top of it is covered with animal skin.
5 It's a kind of glove.
6 The top part of it looks like a dish.

7 Underline examples of the phrases in green in exercise 6 in **Pieces in a Museum**.

8 What is the difference in meaning? Decide with a partner.
1 a It's a pillow.
  b It's used as a pillow.
Example b = It isn't a pillow, but you can rest your head on it.
2 a It's a glove.
  b It looks like a glove.
3 a It's covered with leather.
  b It's made of leather.
4 a It's used for carrying water.
  b It's a water carrier.

9 Pronunciation 2C.1▶ Listen and repeat. Notice how the preposition sounds different in A and B.

A end of sentence (stressed)	B middle of sentence (unstressed)
What's it used for? /fɔː/	It's used for cutting fruit. /fə/ It's used for opening tins.* /fər/
What's it made of? /ɒv/	It's made of metal. /əv/
Where's it from? /frɒm/	It's from Africa. /frəm/
What's it used as? /æz/	It's used as a stool. /əz/

*Pronounce the r in *for* if the next word starts with a vowel sound.

10 Work with a partner. Point and ask about the objects in the photos in **Pieces in a Museum**.
Example A What's this made of?
        B It's made of wood.

C Listen to a description of an object

11 You will hear a conversation between two friends, Elaine and Nilson. Nilson is from Brazil and he tells Elaine about photo b opposite. Work with a partner and write six words you think you will hear in the conversation.
Example cup ...

12 2C.2▶ Listen to the conversation and tick ✓ the words you wrote in exercise 11 if you hear them.

13 Answer the questions.
1 Where in Brazil do they use these maté cups?
2 What did Elaine first think the metal straw was for?
3 What happens if you drink maté directly from the cup?
4 What happens if you put the cup directly on a table?
5 What do people do when they've finished the drink?

14 Work in pairs. Write notes to answer the questions.
Student A Look at **Object A** on >> p.126.
Student B Look at **Object B** on >> p.133.

1 Where is it from?
2 What's it used for?
3 What's it made of?
4 What does it look like?

15 Ask about your partner's object. Use the questions from exercise 14. Do you know what the object is?

ABC Put it all together

16 Work in groups. Look at **Guess the objects** on >> p.127. Take turns to choose an object. The other students ask questions to guess which object it is.

I can describe objects.
Tick ✓ the line.   with a lot of help   with some help   on my own   very easily

21

Culture Shock

Part 1

A couple of years ago I worked in Japan for a while. During the first week, I didn't go out much because I had a terrible cold. In the second week, I was feeling a bit better, and when some work colleagues invited me out, I said 'yes'. We went to
05 a restaurant in the evening, and my new friends explained to me how to use chopsticks. It was difficult at first, but after some practice, I was using them really well and I didn't need to ask for a fork. It was my first time outside Britain, and I was eating Japanese-style like a native. I was feeling
10 quite pleased with myself. Then the problems started.

Part 2

My cold was not quite finished and my nose was still running a little. I took out a tissue, turned away from the table and quietly blew my nose. I noticed a person at the next table was looking at me strangely. When I turned to my friends again, they looked
15 away. Something was wrong. Anyway, the moment passed and the conversation started again. The person I knew best in the group was sitting next to me, and a bit later I quietly asked him if there was something wrong. He explained to me that in Japan, people don't blow their noses in public – especially at
20 the table. Oops! That was my first mistake of the evening.

The next time I needed to blow my nose, I decided to leave the table and go to the toilet. I didn't know where to put my chopsticks, so I stuck them in my bowl of rice. My friend said 'No, don't do that. Just leave them on the table.' Later, I discovered that leaving your
25 chopsticks in your rice means death in Japanese culture! That was my second mistake of the evening, and I wanted it to be the last.

When I returned from the toilet, it was nearly time to leave. I noticed there were some little bowls of tea with lemon next to everybody's place on the table. It was hot, and I started
30 drinking it before it got cold. Then I noticed some of my friends were covering their mouths and looking at each other. They were trying not to laugh. 'What's wrong?' I asked the friend next to me. 'That's not for drinking,' he explained, 'it's for washing your fingers.' That was it – mistake number three!
35 For a moment, I didn't know whether to laugh or cry. But in the end I started laughing, and little by little everybody else started laughing. Finally, we were all crying with laughter.

Simon Kerrigan *Leicester*

Time expressions

Time period	Relating two times	Putting events in order
-|------------|-	-•------------•-	-•-------•-------•-
in the evening during the first week for a moment for a while	before it got cold after some practice a couple of years ago a bit later when I returned	my first time at first the second week then the next time in the end finally

How to tell an anecdote

Orientation

Context

In this lesson, students will practise telling anecdotes using the past simple and past continuous.

The small photos illustrate the main events in the story *Culture Shock*. The writer, Simon Kerrigan, describes cultural mistakes he made in a restaurant with his friends in Japan.

The illustrations in *Time expressions* are grouped according to three general uses: referring to periods of time, relating two events or situations according to time, and sequencing events.

Language

Focus grammar	past simple and past continuous
Focus phrases	time phrases: *a bit later, a couple of years ago, after some practice, before it got cold, during the first week, for a moment/while, in the evening, when I returned*
Recognition vocabulary	words: *chopsticks, culture shock, tissue* phrases: *blow my/your nose, bowl of rice, feeling pleased with myself, in public, my nose was running, Japanese-style*
Recycled language	words: *shoulders, beard* grammar: *past continuous to describe a longer action in progress, regular and irregular past participles (asked, invited, started, went, knew, etc.)*
Discourse	time sequencers: *first time, then, next time, in the end, finally* conversation markers: *well, oh, uh huh, anyway, you know, mmm*

Language notes

In *English Result Pre-intermediate*, students were introduced to the past simple and past continuous when a shorter action interrupts a longer one. Here, the past continuous is also used to set the scene or context of a story.

Speakers of some languages use *during* to express how long something took, rather than when it happened, e.g. they might say *We went to France during two weeks*.

End product

In *Put it all together*, students tell a partner an anecdote using their notes. Students use conversation markers in audio script **2D.1**, both as speakers and listeners.

Preparation

Choose five countries your students know about if you plan to use the *Warmer* (see below). Take recorders to class if you want to record the final activity. Take dictionaries to class.

Warmer

Write the names of five countries on the board, e.g. Alaska, France, Greece, Barbados and Australia. Pair the countries at random and ask students for similarities and differences between them.

Tell students to imagine a person from one country went on holiday to one of the other places. See if they can think of any interesting stories the tourists might have to tell when they get back home.

Write *How to tell an anecdote* on the board.

A Read an anecdote

In this section, students skim the first part of a text for specific information. They predict the content of the second part, before reading to confirm.

1 Go through the instructions and the example. Put students into pairs and monitor and join in with the conversations. Nominate individuals to tell the class about their experiences and help students get their ideas across.

2 Read the instructions. Ask students how they are going to read the text to find the answers. *Quickly or slowly? (Quickly and then slowly when they find words connected with the idea.)* Go over answers as a class and help students with any new vocabulary.

> **bad thing:** had a cold   **good thing:** learnt to use chopsticks quickly

3 Direct students to the photos and tell them to cover part 2 of the story. Ask them what they can see in each photo and write useful vocabulary on the board, e.g. *chopsticks, bowl*.

In pairs, students guess how they think the story will continue. Monitor and encourage them to justify their ideas as they discuss in pairs. Ask volunteers to explain how they think the story will continue and why. Take a vote on the best idea.

4 Direct students to part 2 of *Culture Shock* on **>> p.22**. Read the questions and check students understand. Give students a few minutes to talk about the first question before nominating a few students to share their answers with the class.

Direct students to the photos one at a time and elicit the events.

> a drinking tea   b something funny   c a person blowing their nose   d leaving chopsticks in bowl of rice   e a finger-rinsing bowl

5 Read questions 1–2 and check vocabulary. Monitor and help as necessary as students discuss the questions in pairs.

Ask for volunteers to give their opinions. Monitor for the use of the past simple and past continuous and make a note of any problems. Do not correct for accuracy at this point as the grammar is studied in the next section.

B Grammar past simple and past continuous

6 Direct students to the first box and write the sentences on the board. Underline the verbs and ask students to identify the past simple and past continuous. Label both tenses.

Ask questions to focus on the different meaning of both tenses, e.g. *Which verb tense tells us about the situation at the beginning of the story? (Past continuous.)* Elicit or explain that dots indicate the context of the story (what was happening at the beginning) and the arrows indicate the events of the story (which are told in the past simple). Elicit more examples of events in the story and monitor for correct use of the past simple, e.g. *he blew his nose at the table, he went to the toilet*.

Direct students to the second box and copy the sentence on the board. Ask *Which action is in progress? (Friends covering their mouths.) What happened? (He noticed.)* Elicit or explain that in the second box, they indicate the longer action. Go through rules 1–4 as a class.

> 1 context   2 events   3 longer   4 shorter

7 Direct students to Part 1 of *Culture Shock* on **>> p.22** and ask them to find and underline examples of the past simple and past continuous. Elicit answers as a class and monitor for accuracy. Review regular and irregular past participles and form as necessary. Ask students to continue with Part 2 of the text individually. Students compare answers in pairs.

8 Go through the instructions and do items 1–3 in the first sentence to demonstrate the activity. Ask students to read the text and check vocabulary as necessary. Remind students that they can find and check the past tense and participles of regular and irregular verbs in their dictionaries. Put students into pairs to continue and monitor and help as necessary. To check answers, read the text aloud and pause at the verb part for students to call out the answers as a class.

> 1 was sitting   2 was reading   3 got   4 was wearing   5 stood
> 6 sat   7 noticed   8 had   9 saw   10 said   11 had   12 got
> 13 was going   14 came   15 was running

C Vocabulary time expressions

9 Direct students to *Time expressions* on **>> p.22** to find and underline the expressions in *Culture Shock*. If necessary, write the title of each group of expressions and copy the diagrams on the board. Check students understand the meaning of the phrases using sentences in the text, e.g. *a couple of years ago* links *now* (when the writer wrote the text) to an unspecified time in the past.

10 Go through the instructions and check students understand the activity. Ask students to read the sentences and check any vocabulary. Read the first few sentences to the class and elicit suitable time phrases (there is more than one possibility). Students complete the activity in pairs. Monitor and help as necessary. Tell students to take turns reading their story.

D Listen to an anecdote

In this section, students listen to a short narrative for specific information and to identify conversation markers used by both the speaker and listener.

11 2D.1 Go through the instructions. Read the example and check students understand the activity. Ask students to read the story again in exercise 10 and to make notes as they listen. Play the audio. Students compare in pairs and listen a second time if necessary. Direct students to audio script 2D.1 on **>> p.151** to check answers.

Elicit or point out that the extra facts help the listener because they make it easier to understand and more interesting.

12 Read the instructions and the words before the box. Ask *What do they mean?* and elicit or explain that these are words and phrases people use in conversation. Ask students to guess who said them and compare in pairs.

13 Direct students to audio script 2D.1 on **>> p.151** to check their answers.

> **story teller:** well, anyway (three times), you know (twice)
> **listener:** oh (Oh yeah? – twice, Oh no – once), uh huh, mmm

14 Do the activity as a class. Read the instructions and options a–c. Ask students to say which option is best. Elicit or explain why the other options are wrong.

> b I'm interested.

ABCD Put it all together

15 Go through the instructions and explain to students that their stories can be about everyday events, e.g. problems with an umbrella on a rainy day or bumping into somebody they haven't seen for a long time. Encourage students to check that their notes have answered the questions and remind them to use phrases from *Time expressions* on **>> p.22**. Give students time to rehearse telling their stories from their notes.

16 Put students into pairs to tell their anecdote and to show they are interested listeners. Check students swap roles.

Student performance
Students should be able to tell a short narrative.

You can use this checklist to monitor and give feedback or to assess students' performance.

Content	Do students include extra details? exercise 11
Coherence	Do students use time expressions to relate events? exercise 10
Interaction	Do students show they are interested listeners? exercise 14

I can **tell an anecdote.**

Students tick *on my own* if they have told the story using their notes. They tick *with some help* if they have looked at *Time expressions* once or twice.

Additional material

www.oup.com/elt/result for extra practice activities
www.oup.com/elt/teacher/result for extra teacher resources

How to tell an anecdote

G past simple and past continuous V time expressions

A Read an anecdote

1 Compare the place you live and somewhere in another country or region you've visited. What differences did you notice? Tell a partner.

Example I visited Palermo last year. The buses were a different colour and the water tasted different.

2 Read **Culture Shock** part 1 opposite. Find one good and bad thing about Simon's first couple of weeks in Japan.

3 Look at the photos and cover part 2. Work with a partner and guess how the story will continue.

4 Read **Culture Shock** part 2. Were your guesses in exercise 3 correct? What events do the photos show?

5 Work with a partner and discuss these questions.

1 Which of Simon's mistakes do you think was the worst? Put them in order.

2 What do you think Simon learnt from this experience?

B Grammar past simple and past continuous

6 Read the grammar boxes. Underline the correct words in the rules below.

the context of the story	the events of the story
I was feeling quite pleased with myself. Then the problems started.	

a shorter action *in the middle of...*	I noticed ...
a longer action	some of my friends were covering their mouths.

Rules

1 Use the past continuous for the context/events of the story.

2 Use the past simple for the context/events of the story.

3 Use the past continuous for a shorter/longer action.

4 Use the past simple for a shorter/longer action.

7 Underline examples of the past simple and past continuous in **Culture Shock**.

8 Work with a partner. Decide which is the best tense for the verbs – past simple or past continuous.

I sit[1] on a busy underground train one day, and I read[2] a newspaper when an old woman get[3] on. She wear[4] dark glasses and a hat. I stand[5] up to offer her my seat. When she sit[6] down, I notice[7] she have[8] big shoulders. Then I see[9] she had a beard. She say[10] 'Thank you' and she have[11] a man's voice! I get[12] off at the next stop, and while I go[13] up the stairs, the 'old woman' come[14] past me. A police officer run[15] after her. Or him!

More practice? **Grammar Bank** >> p.137.

C Vocabulary time expressions

9 Look at the phrases in **Time expressions** opposite. Find and underline them in **Culture Shock**.

10 Work with a partner. Add one time expression to each sentence in the story below. Practise telling the story.

I lived in Spain.
I didn't go out because I had a cold.
I was feeling better.
Some friends invited me out to eat.
We met at ten and went to a bar.
My friends ate the 'tapas', or bar snacks, but I didn't eat because I wanted to be hungry for dinner.
I asked, 'When are we going to have dinner?' My friends laughed and said, 'The tapas WERE the dinner!'
I went to bed hungry.

D Listen to an anecdote

11 2D.1▶ Listen to Linda telling a friend the story in exercise 10. What extra facts do you hear?

Example Linda was studying Spanish.

12 Do you remember (or can you guess) who says these words and noises – Linda or the listener? Put them in the correct box. Compare with a partner.

well oh uh huh ~~anyway~~ you know mmm

story teller words	listener words and noises
anyway	

13 Look at the audio script on >> p.151 and check.

14 What do the listener words and noises mean?

a I'm not listening.

b I'm interested.

c I've heard this story before.

ABCD Put it all together

15 Think of an anecdote of something that happened to you or someone you know. Make notes about it. Here are some ideas and questions to help you.

an evening out   a bad journey   an interesting experience   a visit to another country

Where did it happen?
How did it start?
Who were you with?
How did you feel?

16 Tell your anecdote to a partner. Listen to your partner's story and make listening noises to show you're interested.

 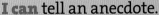

Writing An intercultural experience

A Vocabulary review

1 Are these words and phrases used to talk about people, places, or things?

bowl Christian colleagues container East Africa
ethnic background fork gender glove handle
leather Muslim region The Middle East tour guide
tourist attraction weather

2 Can you remember any other words? Compare your ideas with a partner.

B Read and understand a narrative

3 Read the story and choose the best title.
1 Going on Holiday
2 A Different Way of Doing Things
3 The British Cup of Tea

Last year I went abroad for the first time – to Britain. In Brazil, when we think of Britain, we often think of pubs as typical places, so I decided to find one. It wasn't difficult! As I was walking along the street in Notting Hill, I found a traditional pub selling home-made food and traditional English beer.

I went inside and sat down at a table. I waited for a few minutes, but nobody came to serve me. While I was waiting, I noticed that there wasn't any table service and people went to the bar themselves. I went and asked for a cup of tea. The barman filled a small pot with hot water, put a tea bag in it, and then put the pot and a cup on a tray. I asked for some milk and sugar and he pointed to a small table in a corner of the room. I picked up the tray, took it to my table, and then went to get the milk and sugar.

Suddenly I heard the barman shouting 'Excuse me, excuse me!' I turned to look at him, and he said 'That's one pound fifty, please!' Then I understood that you have to pay when you get your drink. I felt really stupid, but I'll know what to do if I go there again.

Monica Ribeira Santos Brazil

4 Read the story again. Work with a partner and decide if the sentences are *true* or *false*. If there is no information in the text, write *doesn't say*.
1 It was raining.   *Doesn't say*
2 Monica has travelled in foreign countries a lot.
3 She went to the pub at lunchtime.
4 The first thing she did was sit down at a table.
5 She watched other people.
6 The barman gave her some milk and sugar.
7 In English pubs, you don't pay for your drinks when you leave.

C Organize your writing: paragraphs

5 Look at Monica's story. Underline the correct option.
1 There are two/three/four paragraphs in her description.
2 Each paragraph has one sentence/more than one sentence.
3 Paragraph 1 tells the reader about the result of the main event/the context/the main event.
4 Paragraph 2 tells the reader about the result of the main event/the context/the main event.
5 Paragraph 3 tells the reader about the result of the main event/the context/the main event.

6 What does Monica include in her paragraphs? Tick ✓ the information.

Paragraph 1 (context)	when and where I went ✓
	the place
	the people
	what I knew about the place before I went
	what sights I saw

Paragraph 2 (event)	where I was when the event happened
	what I did/said
	what the weather was like
	what other people did/said

Paragraph 3 (result)	what happened in the end
	what things are for
	what I learned

D Get ideas to write about

7 Work in small groups. Talk about intercultural experiences similar to Monica's story. The story can be about you, somebody you know, or a character in a film. Choose the best story and write notes next to some of the headings in exercise 6.

8 Use your notes and tell your story to a partner from another group. Do you need to add more information?

ABCD Put it all together

9 Use your notes in exercise 7 to write a description of an intercultural experience. Remember to use paragraphs.

10 Check your writing.

11 Read your partner's description. Have they used paragraphs? Are the context, main event, and result clear? Is any information missing?

I can write a description of an intercultural experience.

Tick ✓ the line.   with a lot of help   with some help   on my own   very easily

Orientation

Context and Language

In this lesson, students write a story to describe an intercultural mistake, either personal or about someone else.

New language	words: *barman, beer, pub* phrases: *table service*
Recycled language	words: *abroad, Christian, colleagues, container, corner, ethnic background, fork, gender, glove, handle, leather, pointed, pot, region, tea bag, traditional, tray* phrases: *home-made food, pick up* time expressions: *last year, suddenly, then, while* grammar: *past simple and continuous*

End product

In *Put it all together*, students write a narrative of about 90 words with three paragraphs. They follow the organization in exercise 6. Students review each other's writing for organization and detail.

Warmer

Write *Intercultural experience* and *Britain* and *Brazil*. Put students into small groups to discuss what people from both countries might find strange or different if they went to the other country. Ask a spokesperson from each group to tell the class their ideas.

Write *How to write a description of an intercultural experience* on the board.

A Vocabulary review

1   Draw three columns on the board: *people, places, things*. Elicit an example for each. Set a short time limit for students to copy the table and classify the words. Check answers.

> **people:** Christian, colleagues, ethnic background, Muslim, gender   **places:** East Africa, region, The Middle East, tour guide, tourist attraction   **things:** container, fork, glove, handle, leather, weather

2   Students add three more words to each column. Monitor and direct students to earlier lessons for ideas. Ask each student to choose a word and to say which column it belongs in.

B Read and understand a narrative

In this section, students read a narrative for gist and detail.

3   Read the instructions, stressing that students should choose the *best* title. Set a short time limit of about three minutes. Take a vote on each title and nominate a student to explain their answer. Help students get their ideas across.

> 2 A Different Way of Doing Things. Option 1 doesn't cover the event itself, and option 3 only refers to part of the story.

4   Go through the instructions and example. Ask students to read sentences 1–7 and check vocabulary. Monitor and help as students continue individually. Check answers, asking students to explain why a statement is false.

> 2 False. (The story is about her first visit abroad.)   3 Doesn't say.   4 True.   5 Doesn't say.   6 False. (He pointed to the table in the corner of the room.)   7 True.

C Organize your writing: paragraphs

In this section, students analyse paragraph structure in a narrative in exercise 3.

5   Go through the exercise with the class, referring back to Monica's story in exercise 3 to check students understand.

> 1 three (Draw students' attention to what a paragraph looks like.)
> 2 more than one   3 the context (Ask students for examples of information that Monica mentions: the time and place.)
> 4 the main event (Ask for a volunteer to tell the story.)
> 5 the result of the main event (Ask for a volunteer to say what the result was: Monica learned what to do in the future.)

6   Direct students to the three sections and check vocabulary. Ask students to read the story again and identify the information Monica included.

> **Para 1:** the place, what I knew about the place before I went
> **Para 2:** what I did/said, what other people did/said
> **Para 3:** what happened in the end, what I learned

D Get ideas to write about

7   Put students into small groups to exchange stories. Direct them to the topics in exercise 1, and suggest they look again at the objects in lesson 2C to help with ideas. Once students have chosen the best story, they use their ideas to make notes next to the headings in exercise 6. They can write their ideas as a mind map.

8   Pair students so they are working with a student from another group. They tell their stories and, as they listen, make a note of any details they want to know more about. Students answer their partner's questions and make notes to include more information about a topic.

ABCD Put it all together

9   Students write their story of about 90 words. Remind them to use the past simple, past continuous, and time expressions.

10   Ask students to review their writing for detail and organization. Suggest they make a note of any changes around the text.

11   Students swap stories and think about any extra detail they want to know. Encourage a collaborative atmosphere and ask students to thank each other after they have given feedback.

Student performance

Students should be able to produce a short, logically paragraphed narrative.

You can use this checklist to monitor and give feedback or to assess students' performance.

Content	Have students included enough detail?
Organization	Have students followed the paragraph structure in exercise 6?
Grammar	Have students used the past simple and past continuous appropriately?

I can write a description of an intercultural experience.

Students tick *on my own* if their partner has answered *yes* to the questions in exercise 11. They tick *with some help* if they need to change the organization or add more information.

Early finishers

Students write a second draft of their story for display.

Additional material

www.oup.com/elt/result for extra practice activities
www.oup.com/elt/teacher/result for extra teacher resources

Warmer

Remember where

Ask students to write the name of the place from lessons A–D. Read sentences 1–10 below, for students to answer in pairs or small groups.

1 Chinese tourists go there. 2 People from this country call Big Ben 'the big stupid clock'. 3 People who live in this country use a dried gourd with a straw to drink from. 4 People from this country sit and sleep on the same things. 5 The Maasai people live in this country. 6 In this country, people don't blow their noses in public. 7 The Aymara people live in this country. 8 You can find the Louvre in this city. 9 There are lots of canals in this city. 10 They have 'tapas' in this country.

> 1 London   2 China   3 Brazil   4 Zambia   5 Kenya   6 Japan
> 7 Bolivia   8 Paris   9 Amsterdam   10 Spain

A Grammar

1   *the* before geographical names 2A exercise 8

Warm-up: Draw two columns on the board and label them *countries* and *rivers*. Put students into small teams and set a two-minute time limit for them to think of as many words as they can for each column. Go over suggestions and ask *The* or *nothing?* (*the* for rivers, for most countries.) Ask about other geographical names, e.g. mountain ranges, single mountains, deserts, cities, etc. Students revise the grammar box on **>> p.17**, exercise 8 if necessary.

Set-up: Do the first sentence as a class.

> 2 –/–/–   3 –/the/the   4 –/ the   5 –/the/–   6 –/–/–/the

Follow-up: Students write four similar sentences about places they know well. They swap with a partner.

2   Adverbs of frequency 2B exercise 7

Warm-up: Books closed. Write the words from the first item on the board for students to make the sentence.

Set-up: Ask students to underline the verbs in items 2–7.

> 2 My parents never go to the cinema.
> 3 Tourists hardly ever visit my town.
> 4 I usually read the news on the Internet.
> 5 We sometimes go to the mountains at the weekend.
> 6 My father quite often sings in the shower.
> 7 It rarely rains in the Atacama Desert.

Follow-up: Students mingle to see if they can find a person who has written the same information for two or more items.

3   Past simple and past continuous 2D exercise 6

Warm-up: Write the following words on the board for students to make two sentences: *started, myself, I, then, problems, with, the quite, was, pleased, feeling.* Tell students to check their answer on **>> p.23**, exercise 6.

Set-up: Direct students to the pictures and ask students to say two verbs in the past tense for each one.

> 2 Someone knocked on the door while we were having dinner.
> 3 The light broke while I was reading.
> 4 A fish bit my toe while I was swimming.
> 5 We were watching TV when a thief came in through the window.
> 6 I was driving when a dog ran across the road.
> 7 I was standing at the bus stop when somebody stole my money.

Follow-up: In pairs, students write three pairs of verbs for another pair to make sentences using the past simple and past continuous.

B Vocabulary

4   People and places 2A exercise 1

Warm-up: Say the place names on **>> p.17**, exercise 8 for students to classify.

Set-up: Read the instructions and point out that there are two of each of the things in the list.

> **nationalities:** French, Moroccan   **religions:** Christian, Muslim
> **continents:** Europe, Asia   **countries:** Argentina, Bolivia
> **regions:** The Middle East, North Africa
> **types of environment:** mountain, desert

Follow-up: In pairs, students write the anagrams of three places they know. They swap with another pair, who find the names and say what type of places they are.

5   Words and phrases for describing objects 2C exercise 6

Warm-up: Write *sporran* and *samovar* on the board. Ask students to use the phrases in the exercise to describe each one.

Set up: Ask students to read sentences 1–7 and check vocabulary. Suggest students underline the nouns to make it easier for them to think about which phrase to use.

> 2 covered with   3 used for   4 used as   5 looks like
> 6 made of   7 kind of

Follow-up: Students work in groups of four. Each one chooses an object from **>> p.20** for the others to ask questions to find out what it is.

6   Time expressions 2D exercise 10

Warm-up: Draw three columns on the board. Label them *time period, relating two times,* and *putting events in order.* In pairs, students think of phrases to write in each column. Direct students to *Time expressions* on **>> p.22** to check their answers.

Set-up: Ask students to read the story and say what happened on the holiday. Go through the first item together and remind students to look at the words before and after the blank to help them find the answer.

> 2 while   3 first   4 after   5 later   6 evening   7 then   8 when
> 9 finally   10 end

Follow-up: In small groups, students take turns to tell each other about their week. They count and see who can use most time expressions.

Early finishers

Students write sentences about personal possessions, using each of the phrases in exercise 5. They underline the prepositions which are unstressed at the end of the sentence (see **>> p.21**, exercise 9).

Unit 2 Review

A Grammar

1 **the before geographical names** Write *the* or nothing in the gaps.

1 *The* River Nile flows through many countries in _____ Africa.
2 _____ Brazil and _____ Argentina are two large countries in _____ South America.
3 _____ New York is on _____ Atlantic Ocean side of _____ United States.
4 _____ Mauritania is in _____ Sahara Desert.
5 _____ Lake Titicaca is in _____ Andes mountains, on the border between Peru and _____ Bolivia.
6 _____ Mount Everest is between _____ Nepal and _____ Tibet and is in _____ Himalayas.

2 **Adverbs of frequency** Put the words in order to make sentences. Then change the sentences to make them true for you.

1 late bed always I to go *I always go to bed late.*
2 cinema go My never parents the to
3 ever hardly my Tourists town visit
4 I Internet news on read the the usually
5 at go mountains sometimes the the to We weekend
6 father in My often quite shower sings the
7 Atacama Desert in It rains rarely the

3 **Past simple and past continuous** Write sentences about the pictures. Use the words given.

I/when the phone
I was having a shower when the phone rang.

Someone/while we

The light/while I

A fish/while I

We/when a thief

I/when a dog

I/when someone

B Vocabulary

4 **People and places** Find two examples of each of the things in the list.

nationalities religions ~~ethnic backgrounds~~ continents
countries regions types of environment

C	S	E	A	R	G	E	N	T	I	N	A	T
M	O	U	N	T	A	I	N	W	G	O	B	O
A	V	F	M	A	O	R	I	E	C	R	O	F
B	E	D	O	U	I	N	R	R	B	T	L	D
O	C	H	R	I	S	T	I	A	N	H	I	E
E	U	R	O	P	E	L	K	F	N	A	V	D
Q	U	I	C	H	D	L	I	I	P	F	I	E
H	W	I	C	O	Y	J	A	M	U	R	A	S
U	E	D	A	A	I	E	P	S	K	I	D	E
F	R	E	N	C	H	E	I	A	I	C	S	R
T	H	E	M	I	D	D	L	E	E	A	S	T

5 **Words and phrases for describing objects** Complete the sentences with these phrases.

~~made of~~ made of used for used as
covered with kind of looks like

1 Her belt was *made of* leather.
2 The table top was _____ plastic to protect it.
3 This box was _____ keeping jewellery in.
4 At one time, these knives were _____ money.
5 It _____ a book, but in fact it's a box.
6 The brush handle is _____ wood.
7 A stool is a _____ chair with no backrest.

6 **Time expressions** Complete the text with these words.

after ~~ago~~ end evening finally
first later then when while

A few years ¹*ago*, I was camping in Scotland. I put up my tent next to the river and then sat outside for a ²_____. At ³_____, everything was fine, but ⁴_____ a while, lots of flies came out so I went inside the tent to escape. A bit ⁵_____ in the ⁶_____, I decided to make dinner on my small gas cooker. I put some powdered soup in a pan and ⁷_____ added some water. I heated it and ⁸_____ it was ready, I started to eat. However, I forgot to switch off the gas. It burnt a hole in the tent, and all the flies came in. I hid inside my sleeping bag but I couldn't breathe and ⁹_____ I had to put my head out. The flies started biting me again. In the ¹⁰_____, I had to pack up and leave that place.

Bernadette

20 years ago

The things I remember most about my first school are the smell of boiled vegetables in the canteen, the noise of games and fights in the playground, and Bernadette. Bernadette used to sit at the front of the class, and she was perfect. She was the teacher's pet, and she always got the correct answers. She was top of the class and got A grades in all her subjects. I used to love her, secretly.

Bernadette was good at everything. She used to sing well in assembly. She played the clarinet and never made mistakes. She was the captain of the hockey team. She ran around the playing field faster than anyone and she didn't use to get tired or sweat like the rest of us. She was too good to be true. I used to smile at her. I stood by doors and waited for her to pass. I wanted her to see me, but she never even looked. Was I invisible? Did she think she was too good for me? That's what I thought at the time.

But now I know I was completely wrong. I was looking on the Internet a couple of weeks ago and I typed in Bernadette's name, just out of interest. Eventually, I found her email address and I wrote a message to her. I didn't get a reply immediately and I thought that was the end of the story. However, a couple of days later, Bernadette made contact. After exchanging a couple of emails, we decided to meet for coffee. I was really curious to know what she was like now, this girl of my childhood dreams. But when we finally met, she looked completely different from how I remembered. I couldn't believe that I used to fancy her.

We talked a little about what we'd done since leaving school and our lives now. She's married with two kids and has a part-time job in a supermarket. Then we started talking about school, and we laughed together over our memories of those days. I was enjoying the conversation and I confessed that I used to love her. I thought she would laugh, but instead, she said something which completely changed the way I see my schooldays. She said, 'I used to love you too, but I didn't say anything because I was too shy.'

Now

How to talk about your schooldays

Orientation

Context

In this lesson, students will practise using *used to* to talk about memories of school.

In *Bernadette*, the writer recounts primary school memories and a girl he secretly loved. When he was older, he traced the girl, Bernadette, through an Internet site, and met her for coffee.

Glossary gives the meaning of some key words.

The two photos show typical British primary schools twenty years ago and today.

There is also a song about Bernadette on the audio, 3A.1.

Language

Focus grammar	used to: *I used to sing., I didn't use to sing., Did you use to sing?*
Focus words	school subjects: *Chemistry, Geography, History, Languages, Maths, Physics*, etc. things in the classroom: *blackboard, chair, desk, noticeboard* events in the school day and year: *assembly, break, classes* places in school: *canteen, playground, hall*
Recognition vocabulary	words: *clarinet, confessed, curious, exchange, fancy, fights, grades, heater, invisible, memories, perfect, pupils, shy, sweat, uniform* phrases: *correct answers, fall in love, make contact, teacher's pet, too good to be true, top of the class*
Recycled language	grammar: *regular and irregular past participles* time phrases: *every day, when we were ... , last Saturday, today*, etc. pronunciation: /juːz/ and /juːzd/
Pronunciation	rhythm: ●●/●●●/●●●● 3A.2

Language note

The verb *used to* only exists in the past. The question is usually made using the auxiliary *do Did you use to sing?*, rather than *Used you to sing?* In this structure, *use* is pronounced /juːs/ and *used* /juːst/. This contrasts with the pronunciation of *use* as a main verb in the present and past tense /juːz/ and /juːzd/.

End product

In *Put it all together*, students tell each other (in pairs or small groups) about three or more school memories using their notes. They can use audio script 3A.3 for help.

Warmer

Write *Schools today are better than twenty years ago.* on the board. Put students into small groups and set a time limit of about three minutes for students to talk about how schools have changed. Take a vote on who agrees with the statement and encourage students to give reasons for their opinion. Monitor for the use of irregular past participles and write them on the board as you go along. Ask if students are still in contact with friends from their last school.

Write *How to talk about your schooldays* on the board.

A Read a short story

In this section, students read a story for gist and detail.

1   Go through the instructions and check students understand the opinions. Put students into pairs to discuss them. Monitor and encourage students to give examples to justify their opinions. Respond to interesting comments and make contributions. Ask for volunteers or nominate students to share their ideas with the class.

2   Put students into pairs and read the instructions. Encourage students to use their dictionaries to find new words. Go through each category as a class and check students understand any new vocabulary.

> school subjects: *Geography, Chemistry, Physics, Languages*, etc.
> things in the classroom: *desk, chair, noticeboard*, etc.
> events in the school day: *classes, assembly*, etc.
> places in school: *classrooms, canteen, hall, staffroom*, etc.

3   Direct students to *Bernadette* on >> **p.26**. Read the instructions and descriptions a–c with the class, checking students understand vocabulary. Point out that they should choose the best option to describe the text, and be prepared to say why other options are not appropriate. Tell students that you will deal with any new vocabulary later.

Take a class vote to see which description is the most popular. Nominate or ask for volunteers to say why they chose their description and why they didn't choose one of the others. Help students get their ideas across but do not overcorrect for accuracy at this point.

> b is the best option. Option a isn't appropriate because the writer didn't know Bernadette's feelings until he met up with her later. Option c isn't appropriate because the writer doesn't make a comparison between the strength of his love for Bernadette and other loves.

4   Ask students to read questions 1–5 and check vocabulary. Monitor and help as necessary as students answer them in pairs. Nominate students to give answers.

> 1 He mentions the canteen, playground, class, playing field.
> 2 She was good at everything (all school subjects, music, sports).
> 3 She ignored him (never looked at him).
> 4 No, he doesn't (when he met her, he couldn't believe that he used to fancy her).
> 5 She said she used to love him too.

Extra activity

Encourage students to think about and try out different ways of guessing the meanings of words in a text. Write these phrases on the board and ask students to find the words: *the teacher's favourite student; a sport; an adjective for something that people can't see; finally or in the end; feel attracted; tell a secret.* In pairs, students complete the activity. Go over the answers, asking different students to explain how they guessed each one. Point out that students could use these different ways of guessing before they check in a dictionary.

B Grammar *used to*

5 Write the sentence *He used to fancy her.* on the board. Underline *used to* and ask students to find other examples of *used to* in the text.

> used to sit (line 4)   used to love (line 8)   used to sing (line 9)
> didn't use to get tired or sweat (lines 12–13)   used to smile
> (line 14)   used to fancy (line 29)   used to love (lines 35, 39)

6 Go through the instructions and do the exercise as a class.

> 1 b   2 a

7 Read the instructions and ask students to answer the questions individually before comparing in pairs.

> Correct rules: 2, 4

8 Direct students to the grammar box and elicit answers as a class. Write the sentences on the board for students to copy.

> + She used to sing   – She didn't use to sing.   ? Did he use to love her?

9 Go through the instructions and remind students that they can't use *used to* if the action only happened once and it's still true now. Do the example as a class. Ask students to read sentences 2–6 and check vocabulary. Monitor and help as students continue individually. Check answers, asking students if it is possible (not) to use *used to* for each item and ask them to explain why.

> 3 She didn't use to speak to me when we were at school.
> 4 Not possible. *last Saturday* indicated that the action happened once.
> 5 Did you use to fancy anybody in your class?
> 6 Not possible. The action only happened once.

10 Direct students to the pictures on **>> p.26** and ask students where the schools are. *(Britain.)* Go through the instructions and example. Put students into pairs to find differences and set a short time limit of about three minutes. Elicit suggestions.

> **differences:** uniforms, school bags, desks, classroom furniture

C Pronunciation rhythm

11 3A.1 Read the instructions and check students understand the activity. Give students time to reread the story before the listening. Play the audio, pausing at the end of each verse for students to make notes. Ask students to compare with a partner and play the audio a second time if necessary.

> **not mentioned:** vegetable smells in the canteen; games and fights in the playground; Bernadette didn't use to get tired; he used to stand by doors; what they did when they met recently

12 Go through the instructions and check students understand what is meant by rhythm. Copy the pronunciation box on the board and use the examples to illustrate each of the patterns. Monitor and help as necessary as students work individually. Ask students to compare their answers in pairs.

13 3A.2 Play the audio, pausing after each item for students to listen, check and repeat. Ask for volunteers to give more examples of *used to* phrases for the middle column. Monitor for correct pronunciation of the unstressed *to* /tə/.

> 1 last week   2 get it wrong, teacher's pet, make mistakes
> 3 front of the class

14 Direct students to audio script 3A.2 on **>> p.151**. Do the activity as a whole class, divide the class into A/B and ask students to say alternative lines of the verse. Tap along with the audio to help students maintain the rhythm.

Extra activity
Put students into pairs to say the verse or sing the song and monitor each other's pronunciation.

D Listen for general meaning

In this section, students listen to descriptions for gist and detail.

15 3A.3 Go through the instructions and ask students how they are going to listen. *For every word or general ideas? (General ideas.)* Play the audio. Check answers and elicit reasons.

> **Antonia:** No. (She used to sit and look out of the window, she used to hate Maths, used to get extra homework.)
> **Jeremy:** Not really. (He used to hate going outside in the rain for the breaks, and the school uniform. He used to enjoy the school trips.)

16 Read the instructions and check vocabulary. Elicit suggestions around the class and write them on the board. Ask students if they agree with the suggestions, and put a question mark by any they aren't sure of. Play the audio a second time if necessary for students to listen and check.

> subjects (worst), teachers, the building, special events, the classroom, clothes

17 Read the instructions and put students into pairs to complete the activity. Monitor and check for accurate use of *used to*. Play the audio for students to listen again and check. Direct students to audio script 3A.3 on **>> p.151–52** if necessary.

ABCD Put it all together

18 Go through the instructions and direct students to exercise 2. Monitor and help with ideas as necessary.

19 Put students into pairs or small groups to do the activity. As groups finish, ask which school sounds best and why.

Student performance
Students should be able to give a short factual description.

You can use this checklist to monitor and give feedback or to assess students' performance.

Content	Do students talk about three or more topics? exercise 17
Vocabulary	Do students have enough vocabulary to talk about the topics? exercises 2, 4
Pronunciation	Do students pronounce *used to* reasonably clearly? exercise 14

I can talk about my schooldays.
Students tick *on my own* if they have done the activity using their notes. They tick *with some help* if they have used their notes and looked once or twice at the grammar box for extra help.

Early finishers
Students choose one topic they didn't talk about in exercise 19 and repeat the activity.

Additional material

www.oup.com/elt/result for extra practice activities
www.oup.com/elt/teacher/result for extra teacher resources

How to **talk about your schooldays**

A Read a short story

1 Do you agree with these opinions? Compare with a partner.
  1 Schooldays are the happiest days of your life.
  2 I'd love to meet my old school friends again now.

2 Add more words to these lists with a partner.
  School subjects *History, Maths ...*
  Things in the classroom *blackboard ...*
  Events in the school day and year *break ...*
  Places in school *playground ...*

3 Read **Bernadette** opposite. Choose the best description.
  a Our memories of school are better than the reality.
  b One piece of information can change your memories.
  c Our first love is the strongest.

4 Answer the questions with a partner.
  1 What places in the school does the writer mention?
  2 What was Bernadette good at?
  3 How did Bernadette treat the writer?
  4 Does the writer still love Bernadette?
  5 How did Bernadette surprise the writer?

B Grammar *used to*

5 Underline examples of *used to* in **Bernadette**.

6 Read sentences 1 and 2. Are a and b *true* or *false*?
  1 Bernadette used to sit at the front of the class.
    a She sat at the front once.
    b She probably sat at the front every day.
  2 I used to love her.
    a I don't love her any more.
    b I still love her today.

7 What is the difference between *used to* and past simple? Tick ✓ the correct rules and ~~cross out~~ the wrong rules.
  Rules We can choose *used to* instead of past simple to ...
  1 talk about single actions in the past.
  2 talk about repeated actions in the past.
  3 talk about a state in the past which is still true now.
  4 talk about a state in the past which isn't true now.

8 Complete the grammar box.

+		He used to love her.
−		He didn't use to love her.
?	Did she use to sing?	

9 Can you choose *used to* in these sentences? If you can, write the *used to* sentence.
  1 I <u>took</u> the bus to school every day.
    I used to take the bus to school every day.
  2 Bernadette <u>ate</u> an apple in the break one day.
    (*used to* not possible)
  3 She <u>didn't speak</u> to me when we were at school.
  4 I <u>met</u> Bernadette last Saturday.
  5 Did you <u>fancy</u> anybody in your class?
  6 How did you <u>find</u> Bernadette's email address?

10 Work with a partner. Look at the pictures of the classroom opposite. How was it different 20 years ago?
  Example The walls didn't use to be white. They used to be yellow.
  More practice? **Grammar Bank** >> p.138.

C Pronunciation rhythm

11 **3A.1▶** Listen to a song about the **Bernadette** story. What information from the story is *not* mentioned in the song?

12 Write these phrases in the box.
  front of the class get it wrong teacher's pet
  last week make mistakes

1 ●●	2 ●●●	3 ●●●●
first time	used to sit	sit at the front

13 **3A.2▶** Listen, check, and repeat.

14 Practise saying the song lyric on >> p.151. Keep the rhythm.

D Listen for general meaning

15 **3A.3▶** Listen to Antonia and Jeremy talking about their memories of school. Do you think they liked school?

16 Listen again. Tick ✓ the topics they talk about.
  ☐ subjects (best and worst) ☐ teachers and pupils
  ☐ the building ☐ clubs and extra activities
  ☐ special events ☐ the classroom ☐ clothes

17 Work with a partner. Try to remember what they said about each topic. Then listen again and check.

ABCD Put it all together

18 Choose three or more of the topics in exercise 16 and write notes about your memories of school.

19 Work in pairs or groups. Talk about your school memories. Which school sounds the best?

I can talk about my schooldays.

Tick ✓ the line. with a lot of help with some help on my own very easily

Dictionary entries

achieve /əˈtʃiːv/ *verb* [T] to complete sth by hard work and skill: *He has worked hard and achieved a lot this year.*

achievement /əˈtʃiːvmənt/ *noun* [C, U] sth good you have completed successfully through hard work and skill: *Winning the first prize was one of her greatest achievements.*

fail /feɪl/ *verb* [I, T] not to be successful in sth e.g. a test or exam: *I've failed my driving test three times.*

give up sth to stop trying to do sth, perhaps because it is too difficult: *He started flute lessons but it was too difficult so he gave up in the end.*

keep doing sth to continue doing sth or repeat an action many times: *If you keep trying, you will succeed in the end.*

manage /ˈmænɪdʒ/ *verb* [I, T] to do sth successfully or deal with sth difficult: *Did you manage to reach the top of the mountain?*

pass /pɑːs/ *verb* [I, T] to get the necessary result in an exam or test: *She passed her Maths exam with a grade A.*

succeed /səkˈsiːd/ *verb* [I] to achieve what you want to do: *He's finally succeeded in completing the puzzle.*

success /səkˈses/ *noun* [U] the fact that you have achieved what you wanted to do: *The project was a great success.*

successful /səkˈsesfl/ *adj* having achieved what you wanted to do: *The diet was successful and I lost five kilos.*

World's oldest primary pupil arrives in New York

Kimani Ng'ang'a from Kenya, aged 85, is the world's oldest primary school pupil. He has arrived in New York this week to speak at the United Nations about the importance of free primary education.

Kimani started at primary school last year, when the Kenyan government introduced free primary education. He didn't go to school as a child because his family couldn't pay the fees.

A successful student

Kimani is a successful student. He is only in the second year but he has achieved a lot since he started. He has managed to become head boy of the school this year. He gives help and advice to the teachers and other pupils in the school. The head teacher is very pleased with Kimani's achievements – 'When Kimani started school, he couldn't hold a pen. Now he has learnt to write a few words in Swahili.'

The Swahili and Kikuyu languages, and Maths are Kimani's

Kimani's classmates are the same age as his great-grandchildren.

favourite subjects, and he also enjoys Science. He says English is very difficult but he will keep trying. He says he has learnt a lot from the other pupils. 'They teach me games,' he says, 'and I tell them stories of the colonial days.'

It's never too late …

Kenya used to be a British colony, and in the 1950s, Kimani fought for independence with the Mau Mau rebels. He wants to learn Maths to count his compensation money, he says. He also wants to learn to read the bible. 'You are never too old to learn,' he told reporters.

It's a record!

Recently, Kimani has achieved a place in the Guinness Book of Records as the world's oldest primary school pupil. He has 30 great-grandchildren. Two of them are in the same school as him, but they are in higher years.

Kimani waited a long time for his first day at school, but he never gave up and finally he succeeded. He wants to tell world leaders that all children should be able to go to school. 'To me, freedom means going to school and learning,' he told reporters. But he has other plans for his visit to New York, too. 'I would also like to marry a rich American woman,' he said. We wish him every success.

Kimani says, 'To me, freedom means going to school and learning.'

GLOSSARY **rebel** *n* a person who fights against the government of their country
compensation *n* money given to pay for damage or suffering

28   **3B**

How to talk about your achievements

Orientation

Context
In this lesson, students will practise talking about recent and past achievements.

The text is about an 85-year-old African man, Kimani Ng'ang'a who is famous because he is the world's oldest primary school pupil. He appears in the Guinness Book of Records.
Glossary gives the meaning of some key words.

The pictures show Kimani's classmates and Kimani on a school bus.

Dictionary entries lists the key vocabulary of the lesson, showing how pronunciation, form, and meaning are given in dictionaries.

Language

Focus grammar	present perfect and past simple: *She achieved ..., She's achieved ...*
Preview grammar	gerund and infinitive: *he managed to pass, he succeeded in getting*, etc.
Focus words	achievement words: *achieve, achievement, fail, manage, pass, succeed, success, successful* phrases: *give up sth, keep doing sth*
Focus phrases	time phrases: *a few minutes ago, in 2002, in the last few minutes, last week, since you started, this week/year, today, when ..., yesterday*
Recognition vocabulary	*colonial, colony, compensation, fees, fought, freedom, independence, rebels, the bible*
Recycled language	words: *Maths, pupils, Science, since, subjects* definition phrases: *the noun/adjective of, the opposite of* grammar: *regular and irregular past tense and participles*

Language note
Students are introduced to nouns made from verbs, e.g. *succeed – success*. In the examples in this lesson, the stress does not change. This is shown in *Dictionary entries* on **>> p.28**.

End product
In *Put it all together*, students have a conversation about various achievements in their lives.

Preparation
Look at how the words in *Dictionary entries* are recorded in dictionaries your students use.

Warmer
Write the following activities on the board: *make a cup of coffee, climb a mountain, learn to play an instrument, use a mobile phone*. Ask students to rank them according to how difficult they are. Students compare lists in pairs and then small groups.

Ask for volunteers from each group to tell the class and compare any differences. Encourage students to give an explanation. Do not overcorrect for accuracy but help students get their ideas across.

Ask or tell students about the *Guinness Book of Records* (in which world records of different types of activities are kept). Ask which of the activities on the board might be an entry.

Write *How to talk about your achievements* on the board.

A Vocabulary achievement words

1 Go through the instructions and examples with the class. Put students into pairs to continue the activity. Monitor and comment on interesting achievements. Ask for volunteers to share their achievements with the class.

2 Go through the instructions and items 1–6 as a class, checking vocabulary. Direct students to *Dictionary entries* on **>> p.28** and do the first item together as a class. Talk students through the entry for *achievement* and check they understand the following features: pronunciation, word class, the countability code, the abbreviations *sth*, and the example sentence showing how the word can be used.

Monitor and help as students continue individually. Go over answers as a class. Check any information in the entries that students are unsure of.

> 2 pass   3 give up   4 success   5 successful   6 manage

Extra activity
Ask students to look up the same words in their dictionaries and compare how the information is recorded, e.g. in some dictionaries the phrasal verb *give up* might be a separate entry, in others it might be included under the entry for *give*.

3 Go through the instructions as a class. Ask students to read sentences 1–5. Check vocabulary and do the first item as a class, pointing out how the example sentence in *Dictionary entries* illustrates that the word *manage* is followed by *to* + infinitive. Monitor and help as necessary. Students compare answers in pairs before checking answers.

> 2 He succeeded in passing his exams.
> 3 He never gave up trying.
> 4 His teachers are pleased with his achievements.
> 5 He has been successful in learning to write.

Teaching tip
Use the dictionary entries to show students that the position of the stress in the following verbs and nouns does not change: *achieve – achievement, success – successful*. This will prepare them for lesson 3D, in which they look at nouns and adjectives in which stress does change across word classes.

B Read a newspaper article

In this section, students anticipate the content of a newspaper article from pictures. They read for gist to check and for detailed understanding.

4 Direct students to the photos and ask what the article might be about. Elicit ideas around the class and help students get their ideas across. Do not comment on the accuracy of the guesses for the moment. Write notes of different ideas on the board.

5 Ask students to read the article quickly, ignoring new vocabulary, to check their guesses. Go through the points on the board to see how much the class guessed correctly and give positive feedback when they were correct. Elicit the following key information as you go along: *the name of the man: Kimani, age: 85, nationality: Kenyan, famous because: the oldest primary school pupil in the world*.

6 Go through the first item as a class. Ask students to read items 2–6 and check vocabulary. Tell students to make a note of why a sentence is false and monitor and help as necessary.

> 2 True.   3 False. (The children teach him games.)
> 4 False. (He wants to learn to read it.)   5 True.
> 6 False. (He wants to marry a rich woman.)

7 Read through the instructions and questions 1–3, checking vocabulary. Put students into pairs to discuss the questions. Monitor and encourage students to give detailed answers. Elicit answers and explanations around the class.

> 1 He believes in the importance of free education – his parents wanted him to go to school but they couldn't afford to pay.
> 2 He has achieved so much.
> 3 Because it means all children can go to school and learn.

Extra activity
Ask students to find nouns with the following meanings in the text: *a student at school (pupil); the noun from the adjective important (importance); the money you pay for services (fees); the boss of a school (head teacher); a country which is ruled by a foreign government (colony); the children of grandchildren (great-grandchildren); the noun from the adjective free (freedom).* Go over answers as a class and ask students to say which parts of the text helped them guess.

C Grammar present perfect and past simple

8 Direct students to the grammar box and copy the sentences at the top of each column onto the board. Underline the verb forms. Ask about each tense, the name and how it is formed. Ask for examples of negative and question forms, reminding students of how the different auxiliary (*be* and *have*) is used for each tense. Go through the sentences in each column eliciting the missing words to complete the sentences in the box.

> **past simple:** I **didn't** study   I **visited**   ... **did** you learn ...?
> **present perfect: Have** you achieved ...?   **I've** phoned ...
> ... **have** you learnt ...?

9 Read the instructions. Go through each of the time phrases in the grammar box in exercise 8, one column at a time. Ask students to respond as a class, calling out if the expressions refer to finished or unfinished time. Write *finished* above the first sentence on the board, and *unfinished* above the second. Go through the rules together.

> **Rules:** past simple – finished time   present perfect – unfinished time

Extra help
Say the time phrases. Students say *finished* or *unfinished* as a class without looking at their books. Students test a partner.

10 Read the instructions and do the first item as a class. Point out that if students focus on the action at the end of the sentence, then this will help them decide on the correct tense. Ask students to read sentences 2–4 and check vocabulary. Point out the difference between *when* and *since* in sentences 3 and 4.

Monitor and help. Direct students to the grammar box as necessary as they continue individually. Check answers as a class by nominating individual students.

> 2 had   3 didn't achieve   4 hasn't achieved

Extra help
Say a time phrase from the grammar box. Students, in teams, make a sentence. Give two points for each correct answer.

Extra plus
In pairs, students say a time phrase from the box for a partner to make a sentence.

Extra activity
Students write two questions, using the past simple and present perfect and an appropriate time phrase from the box in exercise 8. They mingle and ask others to find two people who gave the same answer for each question.

11 Read the information and the instructions. Go through the example as a class, checking students understand. Direct students' attention to *in the last few minutes* and *in my/your life*. Elicit verbs to describe the types of events that we usually talk about for the different times (*in the last few minutes: phone, lose, called, made some tea* etc. *in my life: been to a place* etc.) so students sense the difference between a simple recent event which is important now and a life experience. Go through the examples and rules together as a class.

> a 1, 4   b 2, 3

12 Ask students to draw two columns: *experiences* and *recent events*. Ask them to think of three examples for each category. Monitor and help as necessary with ideas and suggestions. Put students into pairs to exchange information and monitor and make a note of any persistent errors. Ask for volunteers to tell the class about their experiences and recent events. Go over any language problems at the end.

Extra help
Students change partners and repeat the activity.

Extra plus
Students change partners and repeat the activity from memory.

ABC Put it all together

13 Go through the instructions and the example conversation. Point out how A's second question continues the topic. Ask for volunteers to have the example conversation, encouraging them to continue for a couple more turns. Students complete the activity in pairs.

Student performance
Students should be able to develop a topic of conversation.

You can use this checklist to monitor and give feedback or to assess students' performance.

Content	Do students talk about different topics? exercise 12
Grammar	Do students use a variety of tenses? exercise 12
Vocabulary	Do students use achievement words correctly? exercise 3

I can **talk about my achievements.**
Students tick *on my own* if they have done the activity using their notes. They tick *with some help* if they have used their notes and looked once or twice at the grammar box for extra help.

Early finishers
Students choose a different time period and repeat the activity. They compete to see who can ask the most questions.

Additional material

www.oup.com/elt/result for extra practice activities
www.oup.com/elt/teacher/result for extra teacher resources

How to **talk about your achievements**

G present perfect and past simple   V achievement words; time phrases

A   **Vocabulary** achievement words

1 Think of interesting things you've done in your life, or things you'd like to do. Tell a partner.

Examples I've learned to drive.
          I'd like to climb Mount Everest.

2 Look at **Dictionary entries** opposite. Find these words.
1 the noun of *achieve*   *achievement*
2 the opposite of *fail*
3 the opposite of *keep trying*
4 the noun of *succeed*
5 the adjective of *succeed*
6 a verb meaning *to be able to do sth difficult*

3 Write a second sentence with the same meaning, using the word in blue. Use **Dictionary entries** to help.
1 He succeeded in getting a place. managed
   He managed to get a place.
2 He managed to pass his exams. succeeded
   He succeeded in ...
3 He kept trying. gave up
   He never ...
4 The teachers are pleased with what he's achieved.
   achievements
   His teachers ...
5 He has succeeded in learning to write. successful
   He has been ...

B   **Read a newspaper article**

4 Look at the photos in **World's oldest primary pupil ...** opposite. Guess what the article is about. Compare with a partner.

5 Read the article. Were your guesses correct?

6 Read the article again. Write *true* or *false*.
1 Kimani's parents wanted him to go to school.   *True*
2 Kimani couldn't write before he started school.
3 Kimani teaches the children games.
4 He has learnt to read the bible.
5 There are no primary school students in the world older than Kimani.
6 He has married a rich woman.

7 Discuss these questions with a partner.
1 Why was Kimani invited to speak in New York?
2 Why is Kimani's teacher pleased with his achievements?
3 Why is free primary education important to Kimani?

C   **Grammar** present perfect and past simple

8 Write the missing words in the grammar box.

past simple	present perfect
Kimani arrived in New York yesterday.	Kimani has arrived in New York today.
I _____ study much last week.	I haven't studied much this week.
Did you achieve much last year?	_____ you achieved much this year?
I _____ Kenya in 2002.	I've visited Kenya once in my life.
She phoned a few minutes ago.	_____ phoned three times in the last few minutes.
What _____ you learn when you started?	What _____ you learnt since you started?

9 Look at the time expressions in blue in exercise 8. Do they refer to a finished time or unfinished time? Underline the correct words in the rules.

Rules Use the past simple / present perfect for past actions which happened in a finished time.
Use the past simple / present perfect for past actions which happened in an unfinished time.

10 Put the verb in the past simple or present perfect.
1 They *'ve had* a very successful year this year.   have
2 They _____ a very successful year last year.   have
3 She _____ much when she was at university.
   not achieve
4 She _____ much since she started university.
   not achieve

11 Match the time phrases with the sentences. Then match the sentences with *a* and *b* in the grammar rule.

in the last few minutes   in my/your life

1 I've never been to Africa.   *in my life*
2 Your mum's just phoned.
3 Oh no, I've lost my passport!
4 Have you ever broken your leg?

Rule We often use the present perfect ...
a [1] to talk about experiences in life.
b [ ] to give news about recent events.

12 Use the rules in exercise 11 and make three true sentences about you. Tell a partner.
More practice? **Grammar Bank** >> p.138.

ABC   Put it all together

13 Write notes about your achievements. Use some time phrases from exercise 8. Discuss with a partner.
Example A What have you done this year?
          B I've learnt some new songs on the guitar.
          A Oh really? What songs have you learnt?

I can talk about my achievements.

Tick ✓ the line.   with a lot of help   with some help   on my own   very easily

29

Teen Dream

1

Mum Daniel Peter Marston! Just look at the time! Where have you been? This isn't a hotel, you know!

2

Daniel I wish my mum understood me!

3

M You look tired, Danny. Don't get up. Shall I wake you up when the football starts?
D What? Eh … yeah, thanks Mum.

4

Emma Mum – Danny's left the bathroom floor wet!
M I'm sure that's not true, Emma. Don't make up stories about your brother. Hurry up Danny, the football's about to start. Don't tidy up. I'll put away your clothes if you like.

5

M I'll turn on the telly for you. Just sit down, take your trainers off, and put your feet up. Help yourself to crisps.

6

M Lunch is on the table, Danny!
D Oh, Mum! I'm watching The Simpsons!
M Oh, sorry! Would you like me to bring your lunch on a tray?
D Yes, please.

7

M Don't worry about the dishes, Danny. I'll wash up today. Why don't you turn up your music – it's very nice! Is everything alright?
D No. I'm fed up!

8

M Why don't you try something new? Take up the electric guitar. Get a tattoo.
D Alright! I'll invite 30 friends for a party next Friday. We'll put on heavy metal music, turn it up really loud, and dance on the furniture. Is that OK?

9

M Oh, that sounds great! I'm looking forward to it already!
D Aargh! I can't stand it! You're too NICE! You're my mum – you're supposed to shout at me and tell me off! If you carry on like this, I'll grow up SPOILT!

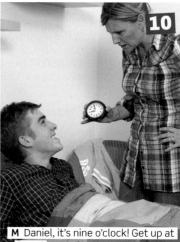

10

M Daniel, it's nine o'clock! Get up at once!
D Oh! Good morning, Mum! I love you!

Hospitality phrases

- ☐ Don't worry about the dog.
- ☐ Help yourself to some of these biscuits.
- ☐ I'll take your coat if you like.
- ☐ Do you need anything, or is everything alright?
- ☐ Just leave your bag on the sofa.
- ☐ Shall I change the channel for you?
- ☐ Why don't you watch TV for a bit?
- ☐ Would you like me to make you a cup of tea?

How to offer hospitality

Orientation

Context

In this lesson, students will practise using offers and suggestions as hospitality phrases to make a guest feel welcome.

The photo story is about a teenage boy who dreams of an ideal life, one in which his mother does the opposite of what she would normally. For example, instead of telling him to get up, she suggests he stays in bed and that she'll come and wake him when the football starts. His mother even defends him when his sister complains about the state he's left the bathroom in.

Hospitality phrases gives some key phrases for suggestions and offers.

Culture note

Greeting rituals are different for people of different ages and in different cultures.

Language

Focus grammar	phrasal verbs: *make a story up, make up a story, make it up*
Focus phrases	phrasal verbs: *carry on, fed up, grow up, make up, put away, put on, take off, take up, tell off, tidy up, turn on, turn up, wake up* hospitality phrases: *Don't worry about ..., Help yourself to ..., I'll ... if you like., Is everything alright?, Shall I ...?, Why don't you ...?, Would you like me to ...?*
Recognition language	words: *the dishes, spoilt, tattoo, telly, tray* phrases: *heavy metal music, supposed to*
Recycled language	*angry, bathroom, clean, furniture, happy, housework, parents, pleased, should, surprised, teenagers, unhappy*

Language note

There are some phrasal verbs in which the noun or pronoun cannot be placed before the particle, e.g. *look after the baby* not *look the baby after*. These are studied later in the course. Other phrasal verbs are normally intransitive (don't take an object), e.g. *hurry up*. Dictionaries show how phrasal verbs are used.

End product

In *Put it all together*, students take turns to role play being a host and a visitor to a friend's house. The role play is based on audio script 3C.2. Students are given time to prepare.

Preparation

Familiarize yourself with the *Pairwork* activity on >> **p.127** for exercise 14, *Put it all together*.

Warmer

Tell students to imagine they are having a guest to stay for the weekend. Put them into small groups and allocate a different type of guest to each group, e.g. a five-year old cousin, an uncle, a grandparent, a good friend. Ask students to write a list of things to do to make the guest feel welcome. One student from each group reads their list and the class guesses the guest.

Write *How to offer hospitality* on the board.

A Read a photo story

In this section, students use visuals to guess the general content of a story before reading for detail.

1   Go through the instructions and statements 1–3 in both sections. Check any vocabulary. Put students in pairs to discuss the statements and monitor and help as necessary.

Ask about each statement in turn. Ask for a show of hands to show who agrees and disagrees with the statements, and encourage students to say why/why not. See if students can add to the list.

2   Direct students to *Teen Dream* on >> **p.30**. Ask students to look quickly at the pictures and encourage them to explain the title. *(Danny's a teenager who has a dream.)*

> At the beginning he looks happy, but this starts to change during his dream.

3   Go through the vocabulary and ask students to match each word/phrase with a picture to explain how Danny feels in each situation. Do the activity as a class if students don't know or can't remember the vocabulary.

> 1 fed up/unhappy   2 angry   3 surprised   4 happy/surprised
> 5 happy/surprised   6 happy/surprised   7 unhappy/fed up
> 8 happy/pleased   9 unhappy/angry   10 happy/pleased

Extra help

Write the phrasal verb *fed up* on the board. Ask students which word is a verb and which word is a preposition. Focus on the meaning. Tell students that, although *fed* is the past of *feed*, when it's used with the preposition it has a completely different meaning.

4   3C.1 Go through the instructions and sentences 1–6. Ask students to find the sentences in the photo story. Ask students to identify the phrasal verb in each sentence and write them on the board. Play the audio, pausing after the first item to demonstrate the activity. Point out the difference in word order. Continue with the audio, and pause after each item for students to make notes. Play the audio a second time if necessary, before going over answers as a class.

> 2 I'll put your clothes away.   3 I'll turn the telly on.
> 4 Take off your trainers.   5 ... turn your music up?
> 6 We'll put heavy metal music on.

Extra activity

Ask students to give examples of what Danny's mum does in the dream which are the opposite of what she would normally do, e.g. she says he can stay in bed late. She defends him to his sister; tells him not to tidy up; offers to put his clothes away; offers to turn the TV on for him; tells him to take his shoes off and put his feet up; offers him some crisps; offers to bring his lunch on a tray; tells him to leave the dishes; suggests he turns his music up, take up electric guitar get a tattoo; she's happy for him to have 30 friends around for a party.

Extra plus

Ask students to find three ways Danny's mum refers to him and see if students can suggest why. *(Daniel Peter Marston, Danny, Danny Marston. She uses the longer versions of his name when she is angry with him. The shortest form is friendlier.)*

B Grammar and vocabulary phrasal verbs

5 Go through the instructions and point out that the two words together are called phrasal verbs. Explain that all the phrasal verbs are in the story. Ask students to find the first one in the text and do the example as a class. Read meanings 2–6 to check vocabulary before students continue individually. Monitor and help as necessary. Ask students to compare in pairs before nominating students to give answers.

> 2 turn on   3 put away   4 take off   5 turn up   6 put on

6 Go through the examples and do the activity as a class. Ask students to find the nouns and corresponding pronouns *it* and *them* in the two sets of sentences. Ask students for examples of particles in the sentences *(up, off)*. Elicit the rules.

> He took **them** off. He took off **his shoes**.
> **Rules: Nouns** can go before OR after the particle.
> Don't put **pronouns** after the particle.

7 Go through the instructions and the example as a class. Ask students to read sentences 1–5 and check vocabulary before students continue individually. Monitor and refer students back to the text and exercise 5 for help if necessary. Ask for volunteers to give answers.

> 2 ✓   3 ✓   4 ✗ turn it up   5 ✗ take them off

8 Read the instructions and do the first item as a class, showing or eliciting from students that they should look at the pictures to find the topic (in the example, picture 3) and then read the photo story to find the phrasal verb. Monitor and help students as necessary as they continue individually. Nominate students to give answers.

> 2 wake up   3 hurry up   4 take up   5 tell off   6 carry on
> 7 grow up

9 Go through the instructions and ask students to read sentences 1–6 to check vocabulary. Do item 1 as a class, telling students that the other words in the sentence will give them clues about which verb to use and what tense it should be in, present or past. Monitor and check for common mistakes to go over at the end of the section. Ask students to compare in pairs before you nominate individuals to give answers.

> 1 grow up   2 wake up   3 made it up   4 told me off
> 5 take your jacket off   6 carry on

Extra activity
Ask students to use three phrasal verbs and to make three sentences about themselves, two true and one false. They tell a partner, who guesses which sentence is false.

C Listen for detail

In this section, students listen to a conversation and identify hospitality phrases as they hear them.

10 3C.2 Read the instructions to the class. Play the audio. Ask for volunteers to give the answers and see if the class agrees.

> Jessica. She wants to see Danny.

11 Go through the instructions and direct students to *Hospitality phrases* on >> p.30. Play the audio. Ask students to compare in pairs and play the audio a second time if necessary.

> 1 I'll take your coat if you like.   2 Just leave your bag on the sofa.   3 Would you like me to make you a cup of tea?
> 4 Why don't you watch TV for a bit?   5 Shall I change the channel for you?   6 Help yourself to some of these biscuits.
> 7 Don't worry about the dog.   8 Do you need anything, or is everything alright?

Extra activity
Jumble the words in some of the hospitality phrases Danny's mum uses for students to make the phrases, e.g. *if take coat I'll your like you. (I'll take your coat if you like.)*

Extra plus
Books closed. Write the following words on the board: *Don't, Help, I'll, Shall, Why, Would.* Students write *Hospitality phrases* they would like somebody to say to them when they get home.

12 3C.3 Play the audio, pausing for students to repeat each sentence. Monitor for intonation and check students use an 'inviting' tone. Encourage students to run words together to sound more fluent.

13 Direct students to audio script 3C.2 on >> p.152. Ask students to find the hospitality phrases and decide if Danny's mum is making a suggestion or offering to do something to check they understand meaning.

Divide the class into A/B halves and read the conversation as a class. Ask students to smile as they read so they sound friendly. Put students into pairs to practise the conversation and check they swap roles. Monitor and give positive feedback for friendly-sounding conversations.

ABC Put it all together

14 Put students into pairs and direct them to *Pairwork* on >> p.127. Monitor and help as necessary as students plan what they will say to their guest.

15 Ask for two volunteers to read the example and point out that B thanks A for the offer. Tell students to include 'small talk', e.g. *How was your journey?* to make the conversation sound natural.

Put students in pairs to do the role play and check they swap roles. Remind students to smile and sound friendly.

Student performance
Students should be able to make offers and suggestions.

You can use this checklist to monitor and give feedback or to assess students' performance.

Interaction	Do students use and respond to hospitality phrases appropriately? exercise 13
Fluency	Do students use hospitality phrases without a lot of hesitation? exercise 13
Accuracy	Do students mostly say hospitality phrases accurately? exercise 13

I can **offer hospitality.**
Students tick *on my own* if they have done the role play mainly from memory. They can tick *with some help* if they have looked occasionally at *Hospitality phrases* on >> p.30.

Early finishers
Students swap partners and repeat the activity.

Additional material

www.oup.com/elt/result for extra practice activities
www.oup.com/elt/teacher/result for extra teacher resources

How to offer hospitality

G phrasal verbs   V phrasal verbs; hospitality phrases

A Read a photo story

1   Do you agree with these statements? Discuss with a partner.

Teenagers should …
1   tidy their rooms.
2   pay for their clothes.
3   clean the bathroom.

Parents should …
1   do everything for their teenage sons and daughters.
2   ask teenagers to help in the house.
3   pay teenagers to do housework.

2   Read **Teen Dream** opposite. Is Danny happy about the situation in his dream?

3   How do you think Danny feels in each picture? Why? Discuss with a partner. Use these words.

angry   fed up   happy
pleased   surprised   unhappy

4   3C.1▶ Listen to **Teen Dream** and find the differences in the six sentences.
1   Don't make up stories.   *Don't make stories up.*
2   I'll put away your clothes.
3   I'll turn on the telly.
4   Take your trainers off.
5   Why don't you turn up your music?
6   We'll put on heavy metal music.

B Grammar and vocabulary phrasal verbs

5   Match the phrasal verbs with their meanings.

~~make up~~   put away   put on   take off   turn on   turn up

1   invent a story   *make up*
2   start a machine
3   put things you aren't using in their correct place
4   remove something you're wearing
5   increase the volume, for example on a TV or radio
6   play a CD or DVD

6   Complete the examples and <u>underline</u> the correct words in the rules. Compare with a partner.

I made a story up. ✓   I made it up. ✓
I made up a story. ✓   I ~~made up it~~. ✗

He took his shoes off. ✓   He took _____ off. ✓
He took off _____. ✓ ~~He took off them.~~ ✗

Rules
Nouns/Pronouns can go before OR after the particle.
Don't put **nouns/pronouns** after the particle.

7   Tick ✓ the correct sentences and correct the wrong ones.
1   I washed the dishes and put away them.
    ✗ *… and put them away.*
2   He had a shower and put his best clothes on.
3   After we got off the plane, we turned on our mobile phones.
4   I can't hear the TV – can you turn up it, please?
5   Don't go to bed in your socks – take off them!

8   Find phrasal verbs in **Teen Dream** with these meanings.
1   leave your bed   *get up*
2   stop sleeping
3   be quick
4   start a new hobby
5   speak angrily to somebody
6   continue
7   become an adult

9   Work with a partner. Complete the sentences with phrasal verbs from **Teen Dream**.
1   When I _____, I want to be a doctor.
2   Be quiet! You'll _____ the baby!
3   The story isn't true – you _____ it _____!
4   I didn't do my homework and the teacher _____ me _____.
5   If you're hot, _____ your jacket _____.
6   You should _____ until the job's finished.

More practice? **Grammar Bank** >> p.138.

C Listen for detail

10 3C.2▶ A visitor calls at Danny's house. Listen. What is her name and who does she want to see?

11 Listen again. Put the **Hospitality phrases** opposite in the order you hear them. Compare with a partner.

12 3C.3▶ Listen and repeat.

13 Look at audio script **3C.2**▶ on >> p.152. Practise the conversation with a partner.

ABC Put it all together

14 Work with a partner. Read **Hospitality role play** on >> p.127 and decide what you are going to say.

15 Do the role plays. Take turns to be host and visitor.
    Example   **A** Hello, come in! I'll take your coat if you like.
                B Oh, thank you. It's a bit wet, I'm afraid …

>START

A You are a 16-year-old in Britain and you have just finished your GCSE exams at a state secondary school. Your exam results weren't bad. What do you do?

1 You leave school. ❯ *Go to Q.*

2 You carry on at school for two more years to get your 'A' levels. ❯ *Go to B.*

B Your 'A' level results are quite good and you decide to go to university. Your parents want you to go into medicine but you prefer literature and languages. What do you do?

1 Apply for a place to study medicine. ❯ *Go to P.*

2 Follow your interests. Apply for a place to study modern languages. ❯ *Go to C.*

C In your third year of modern languages, you go to Berlin on an Erasmus programme. You love Germany and you start going out with a person you meet there. What do you do?

1 Quit university, stay in Germany, stay with your partner, and look for a job. ❯ *Go to F.*

2 Go back to Britain to finish your degree. ❯ *Go to O.*

D You hate the work and it isn't well-paid. You quit the job. ❯ *Go to Q.*

E After two years, you lose your job. ❯ *Go to Q.*

F You don't get on with your partner and you decide to leave. You return to Britain and look for a job. ❯ *Go to L.*

G You study to become an electrician. What do you do when you qualify?

1 You get a job in a local company. ❯ *Go to K.*

2 You go self-employed. ❯ *Go to J.*

H Finally, you are a 'doctor', but not a medical doctor as your parents wanted! You spend your days in tutorials and giving lectures.

Are you happy with this?

I You graduate and you become a doctor. You don't like the job at first, but after a while it isn't so bad, and you are well-paid. You've got a big house, a nice car, and a safe job.

Are you happy with this?

J Your electrical business grows. You have a lot of people working for you. You can earn a lot in a good year. You have a nice home and good holidays, but you never know if the business will do well next year.

Are you happy with this?

K Your job isn't well-paid, but it isn't bad. You get on well with your colleagues. You like the work. It's close to home and you can walk to work. You don't have to take work home with you, so your free time is really free.

Are you happy with this?

L You teach German in a private secondary school. You're never going to be rich, but it's a secure job. You get a bit of extra money by teaching evening classes in a further education college.

Are you happy with this?

M In the end, you get a job in an international advertising agency. The money's great, life is fast, and you travel a lot. The job's very competitive, but it isn't secure.

Are you happy with this?

N You get a place to study medicine. But after a few months, you hate it. You feel sick every time you watch an operation. What do you do?

1 Carry on with the course. ❯ *Go to I.*

2 Apply for a place to do modern languages instead. ❯ *Go to C.*

3 Leave university. ❯ *Go to Q.*

O You get a BA degree in German language and literature. What do you do next?

1 Get a job as a teacher. ❯ *Go to L.*

2 Go back to Germany to live with the person you met there. ❯ *Go to F.*

3 Stay at university to do a master's and then a doctorate. ❯ *Go to H.*

P Your 'A' levels aren't good enough to do medicine. What do you do?

1 Take your 'A' levels again. ❯ *Go to N.*

2 Apply for a place to study modern languages. ❯ *Go to C.*

3 Go to a further education college to get technical qualifications. ❯ *Go to G.*

Q What do you do next?

1 Sign on at the job centre. ❯ *Go to S.*

2 Go to a further education college to get technical qualifications. ❯ *Go to G.*

3 Go to an advertising agency and do in-service training in the photography department. ❯ *Go to R.*

R You do well in the job, but you can't go further without getting more qualifications. What do you do?

1 Do 'A' levels and apply for a place to study medicine at university. ❯ *Go to N.*

2 Carry on in the same job. ❯ *Go to K.*

3 Do a course in marketing and publicity at night school. ❯ *Go to M.*

S You sign on at the job centre and they offer you three jobs. Which one do you take?

1 Telephone sales operator for an Internet service provider. ❯ *Go to D.*

2 Assistant in an old-people's home. ❯ *Go to R.*

3 A secretary in an advertising agency. ❯ *Go to E.*

How to talk about your education and career

Orientation

Context

In this lesson, students will practise using education words to talk about a real or imagined education and career, starting in their own country

The magazine article, *Leaving School*, is designed as a maze. It charts the possibilities of a 16-year-old person who has studied in Britain. There are several points at which a decision has to be made, and the reader is directed to a new stage in their career after they have made a choice.

Culture note

Qualifications in different countries and education systems may have similar names, but the duration of courses and the level of certificates might be different. In Britain, GCSEs are qualifications in different subjects, taken at the end of compulsory secondary education. There is no school-leaving exam. 'A' levels are usually taken after a further two years of study and are required for university entrance.

Language

Focus words	qualifications and education: *'A' level, chemistry, degree (BA or BSc), department, doctorate, education, faculty, GCSE, Masters, night school, photography, publicity, professor, qualification, technology*
Focus phrases	education: *evening class/night school, school teacher/ university professor*
Recognition vocabulary	words: *application, competitive, current, electrician, equivalent, Erasmus, graduate, lectures, programme, place, quit, self-employed, tutorials, well-paid* phrases: *advertising agency, in-service training, job centre, old-people's home, sign on, secure job, telephone sales operator*
Recycled language	education: *career, classes, college, economics, further education, history, secondary school, subject, teacher, university* grammar: *past simple tense*
Pronunciation	word endings which can affect stress: *-tion, -ogy, aphy, -ity* 3D.1

Language notes

In the field of education, students often find that there are both cognates and false friends between their language and English, e.g. *Masters, career professor, doctorate, college.*

The suffix *–tion* changes the meaning of a verb. The noun describes the process or result of the action, e.g. *education* is the process or result of the action *to educate*. The suffix *-ogy* is used for the study of something.

End product

In *Put it all together*, students tell a partner about their real or imagined education and career using their notes. This is based on audio script 3D.2 and exercise 14.

Warmer

Write these stages of education on the board: *primary school, secondary school, university.* Ask students to write the usual ages of people who go to them. Ask for volunteers to give examples and elicit extra information about other educational institutions, what people study, and how old they are.

Write *How to talk about your education and career* on the board.

A Vocabulary education

1   Read the question and put students into pairs to compare notes. If your students are from the same country, ask them to listen carefully and check the information is factually correct.

Extra help

If students need more ideas, write these cues on the board: *leave schools, end of school exam, certificate, exam to go to university, free schools.* Name a topic and ask for volunteers to tell the class about their country.

2   Go through the names of British qualifications and elicit or give the full form for abbreviations (*'A' = advanced, GCSE = General Certificate of Secondary Education, BA = Bachelor of Arts, BSc = Bachelor of Science*). Students complete the activity in pairs. Go over the answers as a class. Ask students about the equivalents in their country and if any words are cognates or false friends.

> 2 'A' level   3 degree   4 Masters   5 doctorate

3   Read the instructions, the words and the first item with the class. Ask students to read items 2–8 and check vocabulary. Encourage students to use their dictionary to check their answers at the end. Students continue individually and compare in pairs. Check answers as a class and point out collocations, e.g. *night school* and *evening classes*. Ask students if they have these words in their language, and if they mean the same (cognates) or something different (false friends).

> 2 faculty   3 college   4 classes   5 school   6 professor
 7 teacher   8 school

B Read and make decisions

In this section, students read a maze and make decisions at each point which directs them to the next part of the text.

4   Direct students to text A in *Leaving School* on >> **p.32**. Ask students to read the text and elicit one advantage and disadvantage of the two options. Put students into pairs to continue and monitor and help as necessary.

> **Suggested answers**
 Option 1: leaving something you're not good at/don't like, can get a job, be independent
 Option 2: with further qualifications you might have better job opportunities, it gives you time to decide what you want to do next

5   Read the instructions and check students understand the activity. Tell them to imagine that their education took place in Britain. Monitor and help as necessary. Encourage students to guess new vocabulary. Tell students to write letters of their route with their notes.

6   Put students into pairs to compare what happens to them in the end. Ask for a show of hands to see which students are happy and which aren't. Ask students to explain why. Help students get their meaning across but do not overcorrect for accuracy.

Extra activity

Tell students to find five new words in the texts they read and guess their meaning before checking in a dictionary.

C Pronunciation word endings which can affect stress

7 Read the section title and ask students if suffixes are used to change types of words in their language. Ask for examples and see if students can explain how they are used. Go through the information in the first box as a class. Write the verb and noun in the first example on the board and copy the stress pattern. Point out how the stress moves position in the noun. Model and drill both words for pronunciation. Repeat with the second set of words. Write the next two words on the board and elicit or ask for volunteers to say the nouns with the stress pattern indicated in the box.

Go through the second box in the same way, this time pointing out the different word endings and that the words in the first column are both nouns and adjectives. Ask students to spell the words.

8 3D.1 Play the audio, pausing for students to repeat and copy the stress pattern. Play the audio a second time if necessary.

Extra activity
Students work in pairs and test a partner. They choose a word from the first column of each box for a partner to say a noun.

9 Go through the instructions together as a class. Direct students to the first box and elicit the answer. Repeat for the examples in the second box.

> 1 -tion   2 -ogy, -aphy, -ity

10 Go through the instructions and elicit one or two more examples for each word ending. Tell students that they can think of any words, not only words about education. Put students in pairs and encourage them to use a dictionary to check any words they think might exist in English. Ask for suggestions around the class.

> **Suggested answers**
> **-tion:** action, attention, calculation, communication, connect – connection
> **-ogy:** psychology, sociology, theology
> **-aphy:** biology, geography
> **-ity:** activity, university

Extra activity
Encourage students to copy the tables and stress patterns. They can add more words as they study the course.

D Listen and make notes

In this section, students listen to a short monologue for key information and detail.

11 3D.2 Read the instructions and the two questions. Play the audio. Elicit answers.

> 1 No.   2 Head of the design team in an advertising agency.

12 Go through the instructions and remind students to note key words and the first part of words, e.g. *uni* for *university, lang* for *language*. Play the audio and ask students to compare answers. Play the audio a second time if necessary before checking answers as a class.

> **first job:** in an old people's home   **further education:** night school, marketing and publicity   **current job:** head of design, international advertising agency

13 Go through the instructions. Direct students to *Leaving School* on >> p.32 and read question A and options 1 and 2. Elicit the option Karim chose (Q). Do the first stage as an example to demonstrate the activity. Students continue the activity in pairs, using their notes from exercise 12. Monitor and help as necessary. To go over answers, elicit each stage and check students understand the answer. Check any new vocabulary as you read each stage and the options. Refer students to audio script 3D.2 on >> p.152 to help if necessary.

> Q, S, R, M

Extra activity
Ask students to look at audio script **3D.2** on >> p.152 and point out the places where Karim hesitates, uses words like *you know, anyway*, and repeats what he's already said. Elicit or explain that speakers do these things to get time to think, and to signal to their listener that they haven't finished speaking (they want to keep their turn). Put students into pairs to practise using the audio script.

14 Read the instructions and direct students to their route in exercise 5. In pairs, students describe their careers. Ask students to make a note of each other's route and to show their partner at the end. Check students swap roles. Monitor and give positive feedback where students have used conversation fillers to hold the floor. Ask for volunteers to tell the class about their partner's career.

ABCD Put it all together

15 Go through the instructions and check students understand that this time they talk about their real education and career in their own country. Point out that they can extend their own experiences to include what they hope to do in order to get their ideal job. Encourage students to use their dictionaries and monitor and help as necessary.

16 Put students into pairs to talk about their education and career using their notes. Check students swap roles. They make a note of similarities and differences and report back to the class or another pair of students at the end of the activity.

Student performance
Students should be able give a short, factually-based description.

You can use this checklist to monitor and give feedback or to assess students' performance.

Coherence	Do students talk about their education and career in logical order? exercise 14
Fluency	Do students keep talking and use conversation fillers to keep the floor? exercise 13
Vocabulary	Do students use vocabulary to describe their education accurately? exercise 3

I can talk about my education and career.

Students tick *on my own* if they have done the activity using their notes. They tick *with some help* if they have looked at the vocabulary in exercise 7 once or twice for help.

Early finishers
Students repeat the activity without using their notes.

Additional material

www.oup.com/elt/result for extra practice activities
www.oup.com/elt/teacher/result for extra teacher resources

How to talk about your education and career

v education   P word endings which can affect stress

A Vocabulary education

1 What is the system of education in your country? Discuss with a partner.
Example We start primary school at the age of five.

2 Work with a partner. Guess the order of these British qualifications. What are the equivalents in your country?
- [ ] 'A' level [ ] Masters [1] GCSE
- [ ] doctorate [ ] degree (BA or BSc)

3 Complete the sentences with these words.

classes   college   ~~department~~   faculty
professor   school (x2)   teacher

1 She's a lecturer in the history _department_.
2 Is the economics department in the science or arts _____?
3 I left school at 16 and went to a further education _____.
4 He studied economics in evening _____.
5 At what age do children start secondary _____ in your country?
6 Her father was a university _____.
7 She used to be a school _____.
8 People study foreign languages at night _____.

B Read and make decisions

4 Read text A in **Leaving School** opposite. Work with a partner and discuss all the advantages and disadvantages of the two options.

5 Work alone. Choose option 1 or 2 in text A and follow the instructions. Make a note of your route. Don't worry if there are a few words you don't understand.

6 What happens in the end? Compare with a partner.

C Pronunciation word endings which can affect stress

7 Complete the boxes.

-tion		-ogy, -aphy, -ity	
verb	noun	noun or adjective	subject of study
●●●	●●●●	●●●	●●●●
ed**u**cate	edu**ca**tion	**tech**nical	tech**no**logy
●●●	●●●●●	●●●	●●●●
qualify	qualifi**ca**tion	**pho**tograph	_____
●●●	●●●●	●●	●●●●
graduate	_____	**pub**lic	_____
●●	●●●●		
ap**ply**	_____		

8 **3D.1▶** Listen and repeat. Copy the stress pattern.

9 Notice that the word endings in the box can affect the stress. Complete the rules.
1 In words ending with -_____, the stress is always one syllable from the end.
2 In words ending with -_____, -_____, or -_____, the stress is always two syllables from the end.

10 Work with a partner. Can you think of any more words with these endings?

D Listen and make notes

11 **3D.2▶** Listen to Karim talking about his education and career and answer the questions.
1 Did he go straight to university after leaving school?
2 What's his job now?

12 Listen again. Make notes about these topics for Karim.
leaving school   *left at 16*
first job
further education
current job

13 Follow Karim's route in **Leaving School** opposite. Work with a partner and use your notes from exercise 12.

14 Tell your partner about your own route through the reading maze in exercise 5. Listen to your partner's description and follow their route through the reading maze.

ABCD Put it all together

15 Write notes about your real education and career using the topics in exercise 12. If your career is still very short, imagine what might happen in the future.

16 Talk to other students. Use your notes to describe your education and career. Whose education and career is most similar to yours?

I can talk about my education and career.

Tick ✓ the line.   with a lot of help   with some help   on my own   very easily

Writing A CV

A Vocabulary review

1 Put these words in the correct column. Add two or more words about you in each column. You can use your dictionary. Be honest!

bad at maths   cycling   drawing   faculty   geography   ~~hard-working~~   lazy   manager   self-employed

education	work	personality	interests
		hard-working	

2 Underline any negative ideas in exercise 1. Would you include these in a job application? Discuss with a partner.

B Read a CV

3 Look at Patricia's CV. Find four pieces of information which you think she should cut from it.

4 Which of these careers would fit with Patricia's CV? Discuss with a partner.

accountant   computer technician   English teacher   French teacher   reporter   tour guide   web designer

5 Underline the best description of the CV from each pair. Why do you think it is like this?
  1 brief/conversational   *the reader wants a quick idea if the applicant is suitable*
  2 full sentences/phrases
  3 opinions/facts
  4 informative/entertaining
  5 quick notes/carefully written and checked

C Text building

6 Find the section in the CV where Patricia puts all this information in one brief bullet point. With a partner, write the information in 1–3 in brief bullet points.

I'm ambitious. I'm hard-working. I'm a school leaver. I've got good computer skills. I've got good language skills.

  1 I'm reliable. I'm punctual. I'm a graduate. I've got a driving licence. I've got a car.
  2 I'm qualified. I'm experienced. I'm a flight attendant. I've got good first-aid skills.
  3 I'm trained. I'm highly skilled. I'm a computer technician. I've got good qualifications. I've got good references.

7 Write two Personal Profile bullet points for you. Use your information in exercise 1.

Curriculum Vitae

Personal Details
Name   Patricia Leahy
Address   28 Coldhall Lane,
             Accrington, Lancs

Telephone   829 882 8887
Email   pleahy@telcom.net
Date of Birth 14/09/89

Personal Profile
- An ambitious, hard-working school leaver with good computer and language skills
- Good attitude and creative ideas
- Not very communicative in the mornings

Education
2006 to 2008	Nelson 6th Form College 16 Ribblesdale Road, Nelson, Lancs	
A-levels	• IT A • French B • Economics C	
2001 to 2006	Accrington Comprehensive 190 Kelvin Street, Accrington, Lancs	
GCSEs	• Maths A • Science A • French B • IT B	• History C • English Literature C • English Language C • Geography *Fail*

Work Experience
2008 to present   Unemployed
Summer 2007   Technical assistant *Computers R Us*
Summer 2006   Shop assistant *Carlin's Books*

Interests
- Website design   • Singing   • Basketball
- Graffiti painting • Clarinet

Referees

ABC Put it all together

8 Think of a job you would like to have. Write a list of qualifications, skills, and experience you would need. Compare your ideas with a partner.

9 Write a CV to go with your application for the job.

10 Check your spelling and punctuation.

11 Read your partner's CV. Do you think he/she will get the job?

I can write my CV.
Tick ✓ the line.   with a lot of help   with some help   on my own   very easily

Orientation

Context and Language

In this lesson, students practise writing a CV. Here the CV begins with a personal profile, followed by education (in reverse order) and work experience, and ends with the applicant's interests and referees. A CV is often referred to as a résumé in American English.

New language	words: *accountant, applicant, computer technician, hard-working, web-designer* phrases: *work experience*
Recycled language	words: *'A' level, career, cycling, faculty, fail, GCSE, lazy, manager, profile, skills, technical assistant* phrases: *bad at (Maths), self-employed*
Recognition language	*brief, bullet point, conversational, first-aid, highly skilled, referees, references*
Discourse	text building with *with* and *and*

End product

In *Put it all together*, students decide on a job they would like and write a CV. This is based on the model in exercise 3.

Warmer

Write *CV* on the board. Ask *What is it?* and *What do you put in it?* Ask volunteers for ideas.

Write *How to write a CV* on the board.

A Vocabulary review

1 Go through the instructions and check vocabulary. Ask students to write two or more words about themselves, using their dictionaries. Monitor and help. Ask volunteers to tell the class about the words they have added.

> **education:** geography, bad at Maths, faculty   **work:** manager, self-employed   **personality:** lazy   **interests:** drawing, cycling

2 Read the instructions and put students into pairs to discuss the question. Monitor and join in discussions before nominating individuals to report to the class.

B Read a CV

In this section, students analyse why a CV is organized this way.

3 Ask students to look at the information in the CV. They decide which four pieces of information should be cut. Set a short time limit to encourage them to scan the text. Students compare in pairs, before discussing as a class.

> not very communicative in the mornings, Geography Fail, 2008 to present: unemployed, interests: graffiti painting

4 Ask students to read the careers and check vocabulary. In pairs, they discuss which careers are appropriate for Patricia and explain why they think a certain career would be good.

> **Suggested answers**
> computer technician (she has the qualifications and the work experience); web-designer (she has technical qualifications and it's one of her interests)

5 Read the instructions and ask students to read items 1–5 and check vocabulary. Go through the example to demonstrate the activity. Students continue individually. Check answers as a class before putting students into pairs to discuss why they think a CV is organized in this way. Ask for volunteers to make suggestions.

> 2 phrases   3 facts   4 informative   5 carefully written and checked   The reader wants to be able to find relevant information quickly so he/she can decide whether or not to call the applicant for interview.

C Text building

6 Go through the instructions and ask students where they will find the information in the sentences *(Personal Profile)*. Copy the sentence onto the board and point out the use of the comma and *with* and *and* to highlight how information has been added.

Ask students to read the sentences in items 1–3 and check vocabulary. Students continue individually. They compare in pairs before checking answers as a class.

> 1 A reliable, punctual graduate with a driving licence and a car.
> 2 A qualified, experienced flight attendant with good first-aid skills.   3 A trained, highly-skilled computer technician with good qualifications and references.

7 Read the instructions and give students time to add more words to the table in exercise 1 if necessary. Students complete the activity individually. They show their bullet points to a partner, and give each other advice. Students choose one point to tell the class. The class says if it is correct and suggests any changes.

ABC Put it all together

8 Read the instructions and put students into pairs to exchange ideas. Monitor and help as necessary with vocabulary and encourage students to check vocabulary in their dictionaries.

9 Tell students to write a CV to go with an application for a job in their country. They use their own names for qualifications.

10 Ask students to check spelling and punctuation.

11 Put students into pairs to swap CVs. They should tell each other the job they have decided to apply for and if they will get the job. They explain why/why not.

Student performance

Students should be able to write a short CV.

You can use this checklist to monitor and give feedback or to assess students' performance.

Content	Have students included all the sections?
Coherence	Have students written coherent bullet points to describe their profile?
Vocabulary	Have students used a variety of adjectives to describe their qualities?

I can write my CV.

Students tick *on my own* if they have included all their notes in exercise 8 in the CV. They can tick *with some help* if they have missed one or two pieces of information.

Early finishers

Books closed. Students write a CV for another job.

Additional material

www.oup.com/elt/result for extra practice activities
www.oup.com/elt/teacher/result for extra teacher resources

Warmer

Remember the places

Books closed. Copy the clues below onto the board. In pairs or groups, students find the names of the places in the unit. Set a time limit of about three minutes. Groups swap answers and read the texts in lessons A–D again to check each other's answers.

1 school dining room 2 play area outside a school building 3 the first school young children go to 4 a place with lots of faculties 5 where English children take GCSEs 6 you can study there at night 7 doctors work there 8 where you look for a job 9 where you can take technical qualifications 10 where the teacher's pet sits

> 1 canteen   2 playground   3 primary school   4 university
> 5 secondary school   6 night school   7 hospital   8 a job centre
> 9 further education college   10 the front of the class

A Grammar

1   used to 3A exercise 9

Warm-up: Direct students to the pictures of the classrooms on **>> p. 26**. Set a time limit of two minutes for them to find the differences. Monitor for accuracy as students give answers and direct them to exercise 8 on **>> p. 27** if necessary.

Set-up: Read the instructions to the class and go through the first two examples to demonstrate the activity.

> 3 –   4 –   5 used to get   6 didn't use to be   7 used to have
> 8 –   9 didn't use to want

Follow-up: Students write five true/false sentences about themselves. They read their sentences to a partner who guesses which ones are false.

2   Present perfect and past simple 3B exercise 12

Warm-up: Write these time words and phrases on the board: *this year, in 2005, 10 minutes ago, in the last 10 minutes, when you were on holiday, last month*. Ask students to decide if they are used with the past simple or present perfect.

Set-up: Remind students to look at *Irregular verbs* on **>> p.148** for help if necessary.

> 2 went   3 haven't been   4 bought   5 phoned   6 Has/phoned
> 7 Have/bought   8 Did/go   9 didn't have   10 hasn't given

Follow-up: Students choose four sentences from 1–10 and change them into questions to ask a partner.

3   Phrasal verbs 3C exercise 7

Warm-up: Write the following phrasal verbs on the board and ask students to give the names of things (nouns) we can use them with: *put away, put on, take off, turn on, turn up*. Direct students to **>> p.31**, exercise 5, if necessary.

Set-up: Do the first example on the board with the class.

> b I'll turn the heating up.
> c Why don't you take them off?
> d I've put them away.
> e You should put your coat on.
> f I'll turn them off.
> 2 d   3 b   4 f   5 e   6 c

Follow-up: In pairs, students use different phrasal verbs from lesson 3C and write five similar questions for another pair.

B Vocabulary

4   Achievement words 3B exercise 2

Warm-up: Review vocabulary. Ask students the questions in exercise 2 on **>> p.29**.

Set-up: Direct students to read the text and say who wrote it. *(A teacher.)* Point out that students will need to use the past tense of most of the verbs in the list.

> 2 passed   3 managed   4 succeeded   5 kept   6 achievement
> 7 successful   8 failed   9 give up

Follow-up: Students write a similar text a teacher might write about them, using positive words only.

5   Hospitality phrases 3C exercise 11

Warm-up: Write the following words on the board: *don't, you, would, worry, like, why, help, I, shall, yourself, I.* Put students in pairs and give them two minutes to write hospitality phrases. Direct them to *Hospitality phrases* on **>> p.30** to check their answers.

> 2 me   3 Why   4 Help   5 if   6 alright   7 Shall   8 Don't

Follow-up: Students imagine Bernadette invited her school friend to her home. They write their own seven-line conversation with five gaps for another pair.

6   Education 3D exercise 3

Warm-up: Write the numbers on the board: *3, 6, 10, 15, 18, 20, 28*. Ask students for the names of education places people go to at these ages, and what they can study there.

Set-up: Ask students to read the clues and check vocabulary.

> 2 department   3 playground   4 evening   5 secondary
> 6 lecturer   7 maths   8 faculty   9 break   10 arts   11 degree
> 12 professor

Follow-up: In pairs, students choose five words from *Leaving School* on **>> p.32** and write clues. Students swap clues with another pair.

Early finishers

Students review the unit and write a list of education words they want to remember (or forget!). They use a dictionary and mark the stressed syllable(s).

Unit 3 Review

A Grammar

1 used to Change the verbs in blue to the *used to* form if possible. If not, put — in the gap.

As a child, I lived [1] *used to live* in a small village and the nearest school was ten miles away. On my first day of school, when my mum put [2]_____ — me on the bus, I cried [3]_____ for the whole journey. However, after a couple of weeks I started [4]_____ to enjoy it. Every Monday morning, I got [5]_____ on the bus happy to return to school after the weekend. There weren't [6]_____ many kids of my age in the village, so I was lonely, but at school I had [7]_____ lots of friends. Nowadays, I always look [8]_____ forward to the holidays, but at that time, I didn't want [9]_____ the school terms to end.

2 Present perfect and past simple Put the verbs in the present perfect or past simple.

1 I *'ve seen* some good films this week. see
2 I _____ to North Africa in 2004. go
3 I _____ to hospital since I was a child. not go
4 My parents _____ a new car last year. buy
5 Your sister _____ a few minutes ago. phone
6 _____ anyone _____ in the last few minutes? phone
7 _____ you _____ any new clothes this month? buy
8 _____ you _____ to a good school when you were a child? go
9 I _____ a summer holiday last year. not have
10 The teacher _____ us any homework this week. not give

3 Phrasal verbs Put the words in order to make sentences. Then put the sentences into the conversations below.

a up I it made *I made it up.*
b heating up I'll turn the
c don't take you off Why them ?
d put away them I've
e coat on You put should your
f them I'll off turn

1 **A** Is that story true?
  B No, *I made it up* .
2 **A** Hey Mum, where are my toys?
  B _____ .
3 **A** It's cold in here, isn't it?
  B Yes. _____ .
4 **A** We don't need the lights on any more.
  B No. _____ .
5 **A** Is it cold outside?
  B Yes. _____ .
6 **A** My shoes are wet.
  B Oh. _____ ?

B Vocabulary

4 Achievement words Complete the text with the correct form of these words.

~~achieve~~ achievement fail give up keep
manage pass succeed successful

Your daughter has [1] *achieved* a lot this year. She has [2]_____ nearly all her exams and she has [3]_____ to get an A in three of them. She has [4]_____ in improving her spelling and she has [5]_____ working hard on her maths. She has published an article in the school magazine – a great [6]_____! She has been a little less [7]_____ in music, and unfortunately she [8]_____ her violin exam. We think that perhaps she should [9]_____ playing the violin.

5 Hospitality phrases Write the best word in each gap.

A Hello Melinda, come in! [1] *Would* you like [2]_____ to take your coat?
B Oh yes, thanks.
A Just leave your umbrella here. [3]_____ don't you come into the kitchen?
B Thanks.
A [4]_____ yourself to some tea – I've just made a pot. Or I'll make you some coffee [5]_____ you like?
B Thanks. Tea is fine.
A Is everything [6]_____? Are you warm enough? [7]_____ I turn the heating on?
B No, I'm fine, thanks.
A OK, I'm going out now. [8]_____ worry about washing up. Just leave your cup in the sink.

6 Education Write the words for these definitions.

1 Studies after leaving school. *f u r t h e r* education
2 A history lecturer works in the history d_____ m_____ of the university.
3 Where school children play in the break. p_____ g_____
4 Night school. e_____ classes
5 After primary school. s_____ d_____ school
6 A teacher at a university. l___ t_____
7 A school subject with a lot of numbers. m_____
8 Is the economics department in the arts or science f_____?
9 Time between lessons in the school day. b_____
10 Not the science faculty. The a_____ faculty.
11 A university qualification. d_____
12 The head of a university department. p___ f_____

What's your idea of fun?

BASE Jumping

As soon as I saw someone BASE jumping off a Swiss mountain, I knew I wanted to do it. This guy just jumped off a cliff and fell for a few seconds before opening his parachute and floating down to land in the valley. It looked amazing.

BASE jumping's great because you don't have to go up in a plane. The word BASE comes from Building, Antenna, Span (the middle part of a bridge), Earth (mountain or cliff) – the four kinds of places that BASE jumpers jump from. I've jumped from all of these except an antenna, so that's my next objective.

The most important thing in BASE jumping is to stay calm when you're falling. You have to make very fast and accurate moves and the smallest mistake will kill you. Most people think my hobby is terrifying, but I actually enjoy being terrified!

Chuck Calderon Tennessee, USA

Karaoke

A lot of my friends say they feel embarrassed when they sing in front of people, but I don't think it's embarrassing at all. People are so worried about what other people think that they can't have fun any more. I think it's crazy. When I get up on stage, I just forget what people think of me.

Last year I entered a karaoke competition in my home town, Wicklow, and I won a place in the national championship. I was so excited! I went up to Dublin with all my friends and family, it was fantastic. There were some brilliant singers there from all over the country and I didn't think I had a chance, but in the end I won second place. Was I embarrassed? No, I wasn't!!!!

Shania Brady Wicklow, Ireland

Bodybuilding

I started bodybuilding when I was a teenager. I was in a hockey team and I went to the gym a lot to train. I discovered that I really enjoyed lifting weights and feeling my muscles work. I was fascinated by the photos of bodybuilders I saw in magazines and I wanted amazing muscles like that too. After a while I stopped playing hockey and spent all my time in the gym instead.

As a bodybuilder, I have to eat a lot of protein-rich food like meat and eggs, and I don't go out much at night because you need lots of sleep when you're working out a lot. That's probably the only bad thing about the sport. Some people say that bodybuilding is disgusting, especially for women, because they think enormous muscles aren't natural. I think they're just embarrassed about their own weak little bodies and too lazy to work out. I've got a great body now, and I've had my photo printed in several magazines.

Petra Bruneau Winnepeg, Canada

Sudoku

For me, there's nothing more satisfying than doing a sudoku. I love the way the numbers all fall into place. People think a sudoku is a boring mathematical puzzle, but it hasn't got anything to do with maths. The pieces of the puzzle are numbers, but you don't do any calculations with them. I suppose most people try to solve the puzzle by logic, but I don't. I put a number in place by intuition – because it looks right. Then one thing leads to another, and suddenly it's finished. I can usually do a difficult sudoku in under ten minutes. I sometimes do 15 or 20 puzzles one after the other, and I never get bored.

I was in the National Championship last year, and that was really exciting. There were 160 competitors and I finished in the top ten. My friends used to get annoyed about my sudoku habit. You can't have an interesting conversation with someone who is doing a sudoku! But now I think they accept it.

Jake Daniels Portsmouth, UK

How to say how you feel about things

Orientation

Context

In this lesson, students will practise using adjectives to describe what they do when they experience certain feelings.

The illustrated article, *What's your idea of fun?* contains four descriptions of hobbies which may not appeal to everyone. Each person explains why they enjoy the hobby, but admits that others might find them terrifying (BASE jumping, jumping off cliffs), embarrassing (Karaoke, singing in front of people), disgusting (Bodybuilding), boring (Sudoku).

Language

Focus grammar	*-ed* and *-ing* adjectives: *disgusted – disgusting, terrified – terrifying*
Focus words	*-ed* and *-ing* adjectives: *annoyed, boring, embarrassed, excited, fascinated, satisfying, worried*
Recognition vocabulary	words: *ashamed, bodybuilding, cliffs, concerned, enthusiastic, karaoke, unpleasant* phrases: *BASE jumping*
Recycled language	words: *achievements, afraid, angry, appeal, bridges, collections, fantastic, happy, hobby, horrible, interested, spare time, sports, stupid, sudoku, uninteresting* phrases: *art and music, outdoor activities*
Pronunciation	*-ed* endings: /d/, /t/, /ɪd/ **4A.1**

Language note

The pronunciation of *-ed* endings in passive adjectives follows the same pronunciation rules as regular past tense verbs. Students are unlikely to be misunderstood when they use passive (*-ed*) adjectives in context if they fail to make the final distinction between the final /t/ or /d/ consonant sound.

End product

In *Put it all together*, students write things they do at certain times. In pairs, they ask and answer about how they feel when they are doing the activities.

Preparation

Look at *Pairwork 4A* on **>> p.127** to help students with exercise 11, if necessary. Take dictionaries to class.

Warmer

Write these words and phrases on the board: *sports, outdoor activities, games and puzzles*. Ask students to use their dictionaries and to write two examples for each category, two they enjoy and two they don't. Elicit examples for each category around the class, and ask students why they like or don't like the activity.

Write *How to say how you feel about things* on the board.

A Read for detail

In this section, students use illustrations to predict the general content of texts before reading for detail to do a jigsaw reading.

1   Go through the instructions and check vocabulary in the hobby categories. Put students into pairs to talk about what they do in their free time. Monitor and help students get their ideas across and respond to what they say. Use some of the lesson adjectives to tell them how you feel about their sport. Ask for volunteers or nominate students to tell the class.

2   Direct students to *What's your idea of fun?* on **>> p.36** and photos a–d. Ask students about the activities, e.g. *Is this your idea of fun? Have you ever done this? Would you like to? Why? Why not?* Tell students not to read the texts but ask them to match the photos with the heading. Check answers.

> a Karaoke b Sudoku c Bodybuilding d BASE jumping

3   Put students into pairs. Ask student A to read about Chuck and Shania's hobbies and student B to read about Petra and Jake's.

Ask students to look at the topics in the exercise and check vocabulary as necessary. Explain that they should make notes about the people and their hobbies. Tell students they can use their dictionaries if necessary, but encourage them to try and guess the meaning of words they don't need to understand. Monitor and help as necessary.

Extra help

Put students who have read the same texts together to compare notes to check they have similar information before they do exercise 4.

4   Put students into pairs to tell their partner about the hobbies they read about. Monitor and help as necessary. Ask students to explain to the class which of the hobbies they would like to do and why. Listen out for the use of *-ed* and *-ing* adjectives, but do not correct at this stage as this is the focus of the next section.

Ask for information about the four activities using the topics in exercise 3.

> **Suggested answers**
> **Chuck Calderon:** BASE jumping, jumps off buildings, cliffs, bridges, likes being terrified, terrifying, dangerous, jumped from three different places
> **Shania Brady:** Karaoke, sings in front of people, fantastic, embarrassed, people worry about what other people think, won a place in a national competition
> **Petra Bruneau:** bodybuildng, lifts weights, enjoys the gym, disgusting, don't go out at night, had photo printed in several magazines
> **Jake Daniels:** sudoku, doing number puzzles, satisfying, boring, it's a mathematical puzzle, finished in the top ten of a national competition

B Grammar and vocabulary *-ed* and *-ing* adjectives

5 Read the title of the section and point to examples of *-ed* and *-ing* adjectives on the board. Elicit or explain that adjectives are used with the verb *to be*. Go through the instructions.

Do item 1 together and show students how, in *BASE Jumping* on >> p.36, there are words and phrases which help students find the adjective. Read through items 2–10 and tell students that they will look for words with similar meanings. Encourage them to try and guess the meaning of the vocabulary for parts of the words they already know, and to look in the texts for a word with the same general meaning. They should only use a dictionary if necessary.

Students continue the activity in pairs. Monitor and help as necessary to guide students to the general meaning of the words and the corresponding adjectives in the texts.

> **BASE jumping:** 2 terrified   **Karaoke:** 3 embarrassed   4 worried   5 excited   **Bodybuilding:** 6 fascinated   7 disgusting   **Sudoku:** 8 satisfying   9 boring   10 annoyed

6 Ask students to find the first word, *amazing*, in their dictionaries. Elicit or explain that the information in a dictionary often tells them which part of speech the word is, how to pronounce it, what it means and how it is used by giving an example sentence. Monitor and help as necessary as students check dictionaries for the words in exercise 5.

Teaching tip
While they are doing this exercise, students will naturally encounter *-ed* and *-ing* forms near each other in their dictionaries.

7 Direct students to the two sets of cartoons and elicit what they can see in each one. Point out that in each set, one cartoon focuses on the person showing how they feel. The caption begins *He's/She's*. In the other cartoons, the caption begins *It's* and this relates to the cause of the feeling.

Elicit which word matches with which cartoon, and ask students to spell the word before you accept the answer. Complete the rules together as a class.

> 2 disgusted   3 terrifying   1 terrified   4 disgusting
> **Rules:** *-ed, -ing*

Direct students to the definitions in exercise 5 and point out how *something* and *feeling* relate to the *-ed* and *-ing* endings.

8 Tell students that the sentences in the exercise are about the four people in *What's your idea of fun?* Ask students to read sentences 1–4 and to ignore the blanks. Check vocabulary. Do the first item together as a class, ask students to say if the word in the blank is about the person's feeling, or the cause of the feeling. Monitor and help as necessary as students continue individually. Check answers.

> 1 terrified   2 exciting, embarrassed   3 disgusted, fascinating   4 satisfied, bored

Extra help
Ask students to rewrite the sentences, using *-ed* and *-ing* adjectives to describe their own feelings.

C Pronunciation *-ed* endings

9 Direct students to the phonetic transcriptions of the adjectives. Ask them to say each one and to check in their dictionaries. Direct students to the pronunciation box and the phonetic symbols in each column. Explain that *amazed* is in the first column because the *-ed* ending is /d/.

Ask students to put the other words into the correct columns according to the pronunciation of the final *-ed*. Monitor and help as necessary and elicit answers to write in three columns on the board. Ask students to check their spelling.

Ask *When is* -ed *pronounced* /ɪd/? *(When the infinitive of the verb ends in the letter* t *or* d.)

> /d/ bored   /t/ embarrassed   /ɪd/ excited, fascinated, disgusted, interested

10 4A.1 Play the audio for students to listen and repeat. Give extra practice as necessary.

Extra help
Remove the words from the board and number the columns 1–3. Say the words for students to say the number of the column according to the pronunciation of the ending. Students continue testing a partner.

Extra plus
Write the following pairs of words on the board: *bored, bought; played, plate; stayed, state; weighed, weight; lived, lift*. Ask students to test a partner to see if they can pronounce and hear the difference between the final /d/ and /t/ sound.

ABC Put it all together

11 Tell students they will follow the instructions and write the names of different things on a piece of paper. Put students into A/B pairs and direct them to the appropriate *Pairwork* section.

Ask for volunteers to read the example conversation. Encourage them to keep the conversation going by asking and answering more questions. Students continue in pairs.

Student performance
Students should be able to give short explanations.

You can use this checklist to monitor and give feedback or to assess students' performance.

Content	Do students give detail in their answers? exercise 4
Vocabulary	Do students have enough adjectives to describe their feelings? exercise 5
Pronunciation	Do students pronounce adjective endings clearly? exercise 9

I can say how I feel about things.

Students tick *on my own* if they have answered most of their partner's questions without looking at the lesson. They tick *with some help* if they have looked at the vocabulary in exercises 5 and 9 a couple of times for help with vocabulary.

Early finishers
Students swap instructions and write their notes in a different order. They ask and answer about the activities.

Additional material

www.oup.com/elt/result for extra practice activities
www.oup.com/elt/teacher/result for extra teacher resources

How to say how you feel about things

G -ed and -ing adjectives   V -ed and -ing adjectives   P -ed endings

A Read for detail

1 Think of hobbies. Use these categories to help you. Tell your partner what you and people you know do in their spare time.

art and music   collections   games and puzzles
outdoor activities   sports

2 Look at the headings of **What's your idea of fun?** opposite and match them with photos a–d.

3 Work in pairs. Look at **What's your idea of fun?**
Student A read about Chuck and Shania's hobbies.
Student B read about Petra and Jake's hobbies.

Make notes about these topics for each person.
1 Person's name   *Chuck Calderon*
2 Name of hobby   *BASE jumping*
3 What this person does in their hobby   *jumps off* ...
4 Why he/she likes the hobby
5 What other people think of the hobby
6 One problem connected with the hobby
7 Something he/she has achieved

4 Describe the two hobbies you read about to your partner. Use your notes from exercise 3. Which of the hobbies would you like to try?

B Grammar and vocabulary -ed and -ing adjectives

5 Work with a partner. Find -ed or -ing adjectives in **What's your idea of fun?** to describe the following.

BASE Jumping
1 something fantastic   *amazing*
2 feeling very afraid

Karaoke
3 feeling stupid and ashamed
4 feeling concerned and afraid
5 feeling happy and enthusiastic

Bodybuilding
6 feeling very interested
7 something horrible and unpleasant

Sudoku
8 something pleasing that makes you feel good
9 something uninteresting
10 feeling a little angry

6 Check your answers in a dictionary.

7 Match these words with pictures 1–4. Then complete the rules.

☐ disgusted   ☐ terrifying   ☐ terrified   ☐ disgusting

1 He's ...   2 She's ...

3 It's ...   4 It's ...

Rules
Use adjectives ending with -_____ to talk about how a person feels.
Use adjectives ending with -_____ to talk about the cause of that feeling.

8 Finish the words in these sentences.
1 Chuck's hobby is terrif*ying*____, but he enjoys being terrif_____.
2 Shania thinks Karaoke is excit_____, and she never feels embarrass_____.
3 Some people feel disgust_____ by bodybuilding, but Petra thinks it's fascinat_____.
4 Jake feels satisf_____ when he finishes a puzzle – he never feels bor_____.

More practice? **Grammar Bank** >> p.139.

C Pronunciation -ed endings

9 Write these adjectives in the box in normal spelling according to how -ed is pronounced.
/əˈmeɪzd/   /ɪkˈsaɪtɪd/   /ˈfæsɪneɪtɪd/   /bɔːd/
/ɪmˈbærəst/   /dɪsˈɡʌstɪd/   /ˈɪntrəstɪd/

/d/	/t/	/ɪd/
amazed		

10 **4A.1▶** Listen and repeat.

ABC Put it all together

11 Work in pairs. Follow the instructions and write the answers in the shapes. Then ask about the words in your partner's shapes.
Student A Look at **Feelings** on >> p.127.
Student B Look at **Feelings** on >> p.134.

I can say how I feel about things. ▬▬▬▬▬▬▬▬▬
Tick ✓ the line.   with a lot of help   with some help   on my own   very easily

Are **you** into music?

Some people live for music while for others, it is just noise. But most of us lie somewhere between these two extremes. **What about you – how into music are you? Do this test and find out!**

1 Every few years, a new way of listening to music is invented. Put these in order from the oldest to the newest and tick the ones you've got at home.

a ☐ MP3 player
b ☐ 1 Radio
c ☐ Tapes
d ☐ CDs
e ☐ Records

2 People listen in different ways. Can you guess what the people below are listening to? Match the photos and descriptions. Which photo is missing?

a A Carlos Santana guitar solo.
b A news podcast.
c A Mozart symphony.
d A Spice Girls track.

3 Does music make you move? Tick the things you do when you're listening.

a Tap your feet.
b Sing along.
c Dance.
d 'Conduct' the orchestra like the old man in the photo in 2.
e Play the 'air guitar' like the young man in the photo in 2.

4 Some of these are more difficult to name than others. Which can you name? Write a name on the line – if you can!

a A singer   _____
b A composer   _____
c A guitarist   _____
d A drummer   _____
e A female drummer _____

5 What are the differences between these instruments?

a Which is bigger – a keyboard or a grand piano?
b Which is usually louder – a Spanish guitar or an electric guitar?
c Which is heavier – a saxophone or a recorder?
d Which are the biggest and smallest of these – a violin, a double bass, and a cello?

6 A lot of music fans are great collectors. How many of these have you got? Tick them.

a Books or magazines about music.
b A collection of CDs by one artist.
c A T-shirt with the name of a singer or group.
d An autograph of a famous musician.

7 Look at the six singers above. What styles of music are they singing? Which style is the oldest?

country jazz opera
rap reggae rock

8 Some fans prefer bigger venues, others prefer smaller, more intimate venues, and some people aren't interested in live music at all. How many of these have you been to? Tick them.

a A massive concert in a stadium or other outdoor venue.
b A big concert in a concert hall or other indoor venue.
c A small concert in a club or other small venue.

9 You're going on a long, boring car journey. What do you do? Tick your answer.

a Have a conversation.
b Listen to the radio.
c Take the first few CDs you find.
d Carefully choose some good 'driving music'.

How to talk about music

Orientation

Context

In this lesson, students will practise using comparatives and superlatives to exchange opinions.

The illustrated music quiz *Are you into music?* invites readers to answer various questions to examine how much they enjoy music. The *Answer Key* on >> **p.127** provides scores for each of the questions individually.

Language

Focus grammar	comparative and superlative sentences: *The guitar is cheaper than the piano., The best instrument., The most popular composer.*
Focus words	comparative and superlative adjectives and adverbs: *good, better, best; easy, more easily, most easily* quantifiers: *a bit, a lot, far, slightly, much* events and venues: *club, concert hall, stadium* instruments and musicians: *cello, composer, bass, drummer, guitarist, keyboard, recorder, saxophone, violin* music products: *CD, iPod, headphones, MP3 player, records, speakers, stereo system, tapes* styles of music: *classical, country, jazz, opera, pop, rap, reggae, rock*
Recognition vocabulary	words: *autograph, conduct, entertainment, fan, massive, noise, obsessed, podcast, symphony, track, venue* phrases: *air guitar, tap your feet*
Recycled language	words: *boring, convenient, interested, internet, invented, souvenir*
Pronunciation	comparative *-er* 4B.1

Language note

Sometimes Italian and Spanish speakers may sound as if they are using the comparative when they don't intend to. They might add an extra syllable at the beginning of words beginning with /s/, e.g. in the phrases *an old song* or *a big stage*. This makes the phrases sound like *an older song* or *a bigger stage*.

End product

In *Put it all together,* students exchange opinions about arts and entertainment. Students have listened to two people doing a similar activity in audio script **4B.2**.

Preparation

Think about one or two well-known or local singers or pieces of music for the different types of music if you want to do the *Warmer*. Look at *Pairwork 4B, Music* >> **p.128** so you can help students with exercise 14, if necessary. Take dictionaries to class if necessary.

Warmer

Team game. Write the following types of music on the board: *classical, country, pop, jazz, opera, rap, rock.* Put students into small teams and set a time limit of about three minutes for them to think of as many examples as they can. Elicit examples for the different types and ask the class if they agree. Award one point for each acceptable answer.

Write *How to talk about music* on the board.

A Read and respond

In this section, students read for detail to do a magazine quiz.

1 Students answer the question in pairs. Monitor and encourage students to give details about the type of music, their favourite singers and composers, where and when they listen to it. Ask for volunteers to tell the class about their partner.

2 Direct students to *Are you into music?* on >> **p.38** and ask them to look at the title, pictures and the introduction to decide what the quiz is about *(how much people enjoy music)*. Elicit or explain that *to be into* means *interested in* or *enthusiastic about.*

   Ask students to do the quiz. Tell them to guess the general meaning of new words in the quiz, and remind them that they will look at the vocabulary in more detail in the next section.

   Teaching tip

   Comprehension of the text does not depend on pre-teaching vocabulary. Reading the music-related words in context will remind students of words they may already know passively.

3 Put students into pairs and direct them to the *Answer Key* on >> **p.127**. Ask students to read through the instructions and check they understand that there are different instructions for different questions.

   Ask questions to help them guess new vocabulary in context, e.g. write the word *obsessed* on the board and ask *What type of word is it: noun, verb, or adjective? Does it describe a feeling or the cause of the feeling? Is it positive or negative? Can you think of another word to replace it?*

   Ask students to swap books and calculate each other's score and read the result to their partner. Monitor and help as necessary, asking students if they agreed with the results and encouraging them to comment. Ask volunteers to tell the class about their results and if they agree with them.

B Vocabulary music

4 Ask students to read items 1–6 and check vocabulary. Do the first item as a class to demonstrate the activity. Read the first item and ask students to identify key words to help them find the answer *(song, instrument)*. Tell students to look over the quiz again to identify the general topic of the question. Point out that sometimes, as in this case, it might be easier to decide in which questions they won't find the answer, e.g. questions 1, 3, 6, 8. Now ask students to read the other questions and answers more carefully to find the answer.

   Monitor as students continue individually, helping them locate the parts of the text where they might find the answer. Ask for volunteers to give answers and say the question number in the quiz where they found it. Model pronunciation as necessary.

   2 symphony   3 track   4 conduct   5 autograph   6 venue

   Extra help

   Before students do the quiz, ask them to match the following topics and questions. This will help them locate the places where they might find the answers more quickly. *People and what they do (4), places to listen to music (8), types of listening materials (2), styles of music (7), ways of listening to music (1), travelling and listening (9), moving to music (3), instruments (5), what people collect (6).*

5 Go through the instructions and items 1–4, checking vocabulary. Elicit one more example for each category before students continue individually. Monitor and help as necessary. Nominate students to give examples. Ask students to add more words to the lists or set this task for homework.

> **instruments and musicians:** composer, guitarist
> **styles of music:** classical, country, jazz, opera, pop, rap
> **music products:** MP3 player, records, tapes
> **events and venues:** club, concert hall

C Grammar comparatives and superlatives

6 Direct students to question 5 in *Are you into music?* to remind students of the concept and form. Ask *Which sentence is comparing one thing with another? Comparing one thing with all others of the same type? How do you make the comparative? How do you make the superlative?*

Read the instructions and ask students which instrument they prefer. *The guitar or piano?* Students read the text to check vocabulary. Remind them to ignore the blanks. Monitor and help as necessary as students complete the activity, making a note of common problems. Go over answers as a class, clarifying any areas of difficulty and checking that students remember the difference between adjectives and adverbs.

> 2 smaller   3 more convenient   4 more easily   5 better
> 6 smaller   7 best   8 more clearly   9 cheaper
> 10 more convenient   11 most popular

7 Say the adjectives in the text for students to call out *comparative* or *superlative* as a class.

8 Ask students to underline the words in the text in exercise 6 and elicit the rules.

> **Rules:** 1 much, far, a lot   2 slightly, a bit

9 4B.1 Direct students to the pronunciation box. Ask them to read the phrases in both columns and say what the difference is between them. *(The phrases in column A describe one thing, whereas the phrases in column B compare two things.)* Read the instruction and play the audio for students to say A or B as a class. Put students in pairs to test a partner. Monitor and give positive feedback for clear pronunciation.

> A, B   A, B   B, A   B, A   A, B

Extra help
Play the audio a second time and ask students to write A or B. They check their answers using audio script **4B.1** on **>> p.152** to identify any phrases where they didn't hear the difference. Say three phrases from column A and one from column B slightly more slowly to help students hear the contrast. Repeat with three phrases from column B and one from column A. Repeat the activity with the audio and pause after each pair to give students time to reflect.

10 Read the question and give students one or two minute's thinking time before they do the activity. Remind them to use the words and phrases in exercise 8. Put students into pairs to talk about which instrument they prefer. Monitor and go over any repeated errors at the end of the activity.

D Predict and listen for key words

In this section, students predict the main ideas in a conversation before listening to check.

11 Tell students that they will listen to a conversation in which two people compare CDs and MP3 players. Check students understand what each thing is and put them in pairs to list some good and bad points. Ask for suggestions around the class and write some notes on the board.

12 4B.2 Read the instructions and play the audio. Remind students to think about a topic before they listen, as this will help them be more effective listeners.

13 Read the instructions and direct students to the table. Check any new vocabulary in the first column, e.g. *iPod, speakers, headphones*. Play the audio and give students time to make notes. Students can compare in pairs and listen a second time if necessary before you go over answers as a class.

> **Andrea:** prefers CDs, prefers stereo system – more comfortable listening; prefers speakers – better sound
> **Jan:** prefers MP3s; iPod – smaller, much better; headphones – you can play music more loudly

Extra plus
Students write the reasons the speakers give for not liking something and listen again to check.

ABCD Put it all together

14 Direct students to *Music* on **>> p.128** and read the instructions. Monitor and help as necessary with ideas as students make notes. Students discuss the topic in pairs or small groups.

Student performance
Students should be able to use short statements to give and justify their opinions.

You can use this checklist to monitor and give feedback or to assess students' performance.

Grammar	Do students mostly use comparative phrases accurately? exercise 8
Vocabulary	Do students use a variety of music words? exercise 5
Pronunciation	Do students pronounce the final syllable on a comparative adjective audibly? exercise 10

I can **talk about music.**
Students tick *on my own* if they have explained their opinion using their notes. They tick *with some help* if they have looked at one or two quiz questions to help with vocabulary.

Early finishers
Students choose another topic to discuss. They make notes and repeat the activity.

Additional material

www.oup.com/elt/result for extra practice activities
www.oup.com/elt/teacher/result for extra teacher resources

How to talk about music

G comparatives and superlatives **V** music **P** comparative -*er*

A Read and respond

1 What music do you listen to? Tell a partner.

2 Read **Are you into music?** opposite and choose or write your own answers.

3 Exchange books with your partner. Look at the **Answer Key** on >> p.127 and calculate your partner's score. Read out the result to your partner. Do you agree with the result?

B Vocabulary music

4 Find words in the quiz with these meanings.

1 a part of a song where a single instrument is most important *solo*
2 a piece of classical music for an orchestra
3 a single song or piece of music
4 lead an orchestra with your hands
5 the signature of a famous person as a souvenir
6 any place where you see a concert or other live entertainment

5 Find words in **Are you into music?** to add to these lists. With a partner, add more words of your own.

1 instruments and musicians *saxophone, drummer* ...
2 styles of music *rock* ...
3 music products *CD* ...
4 events and venues *stadium* ...

C Grammar comparatives and superlatives

6 Complete the text with the comparative or superlative forms of the adjectives and adverbs in brackets.

Guitar or piano?

A guitar is ¹*cheaper*_____ (cheap) than a piano to buy and it's a lot ²_____ (small), so it's ³_____ (convenient) if you live in a small flat. Also, you can carry it much ⁴_____ (easily) so it's ⁵_____ (good) if you move around a lot. You can also buy special guitars for kids – these are slightly ⁶_____ (small) than normal guitars.

On the other hand, a piano is probably the ⁷_____ (good) instrument of all for learning about music. You can see all of the notes a bit ⁸_____ (clearly) than on a guitar. If a piano is too big and expensive, you could buy a keyboard. These are far ⁹_____ (cheap) and ¹⁰_____ (convenient). A toy keyboard is probably the ¹¹_____ (popular) instrument of all for small children.

7 Which adjectives in exercise 6 are comparatives? Which are superlatives?

8 Underline these words in the text in exercise 6 and complete the rules.

slightly   much   far   a bit   a lot

Rules

Use _____, _____, and _____ to compare two things that are very different.
Use _____ and _____ to compare two things that are NOT very different.

9 **4B.1▶ Pronunciation** Can you hear the difference? Listen and say *A* or *B*. Test a partner.

A	B
a nice venue	a nicer venue
an old song	an older song
a deep sound	a deeper sound
a big stage	a bigger stage
a small studio	a smaller studio

10 Which would you choose, a guitar or a piano? Tell a partner and say why.

More practice? **Grammar Bank** >> p.139.

D Predict and listen for key words

11 Which is better, listening to music on CD or MP3? List some good and bad points of both with a partner.

12 **4B.2▶** You will hear Andrea and Jan talking about how they listen to music. Do you hear any of your good and bad points from exercise 11?

13 Listen again. Underline what they prefer and write notes about the reasons.

	prefers ...	because ...
Andrea	CDs / MP3	*better quality, clearer sound*
	iPod / stereo system	
	speakers / headphones	
Jan	CDs / MP3	
	iPod / stereo system	
	speakers / headphones	

ABCD Put it all together

14 Work in pairs or small groups. Look at **Music** on >> p.128 and make notes about the music, venues, and entertainment you prefer. Discuss your ideas.

I can talk about music.

Tick ✓ the line.   with a lot of help   with some help   on my own   very easily

Restaurant Reviews

Thinking of going out for a meal? Why not try somewhere different?
Here are our top eight recommendations for the weekend …

Café Paradiso

You won't find pizzas as good as these anywhere in town. The pasta dishes are excellent too, and there's a salad bar where you can take all you can eat. This bright, cheerful restaurant is popular with families and it offers good value for money. If you prefer a quieter atmosphere, try it later in the evening when it isn't as busy as early evening.

$**$$$ **SEATS 96
OPEN 5.00 till midnight

The Chestnut

I've never had vegetarian food as tasty as this. Save space for something from the excellent dessert trolley, too. This tiny restaurant is often fully booked, so book as early as you can. Highly recommended, even for non-vegetarians!

$$**$$ **SEATS 16
OPEN 7.00 till 10.30

The Red Lion

This pub restaurant offers traditional home cooking in a warm, cosy atmosphere. The servings are very generous and the prices are reasonable. The staff are very friendly and the waitress likes to stop and chat – which means that the service isn't as quick as some people would like.

$**$$$ **SEATS 24
OPEN 5.30 till 10.00
FREE PARKING

El Paso

Nowhere serves steaks as big as the ones at the El Paso. And it doesn't stop – when you empty your plate, a waiter arrives with a skewer of meat and serves you more. But save your appetite – they bring the best meat last. This restaurant seats over 100 people, making it ideal for large groups. There's live music on Friday and Saturday evenings.

$$$**$$ **SEATS 110
OPEN 6.30 till 1.00
FREE PARKING

Chez Dominique

The modern art on the walls gives this place an elegant, stylish atmosphere. Everything on the menu is cooked to perfection, and the wine list is impressive. Yes, it's expensive, but you get what you pay for. But be warned – the main course servings aren't as big as you'd expect, so don't skip the starters!

$$$$**$ **SEATS 30
OPEN 7.00 till 11.30

Old Peking

The Old Peking is under new ownership, but it's just as good as ever. There are all the usual Chinese dishes and plenty of options I haven't seen elsewhere. The staff are friendly and do everything to make your meal as pleasant as possible. It's great value for money and you won't get a good meal as cheap as this anywhere else in town.

$**$$$ **SEATS 50
OPEN 6.00 till midnight

Bombay Palace

I've never had a curry as hot as the vindaloo at the Bombay Palace! But if you'd rather have something milder, there are plenty of other options on the menu. They don't serve wine, but you may take your own. There's a small charge for opening the bottle, but it isn't as expensive as a restaurant wine price.

$$**$$ **SEATS 50
OPEN eight till late

Home Sweet Home

This is home cooking at its best – your favourite recipes prepared just how you like them. There's no charge for opening the wine. You can stay as long as you want – nobody will ask you to leave. You can even watch the TV channel of your choice while you eat. There's friendly self-service, of course – and if there isn't, well, you can't complain. But don't forget to do the shopping!

How to compare and discuss preferences

Orientation

Context

In this lesson, students will practise using phrases to make and respond to suggestions.

The illustrated magazine feature, *Restaurant Reviews*, gives information about seven restaurants (the food, place, service, size, prices and opening hours). The review *Home Sweet Home* is a joke.

Culture note

Pronunciation in English plays an important part in politeness. For example, when a person refuses an offer or rejects a suggestion (which might be considered impolite), disagreement is usually signalled by a hesitant-sounding voice. Often, the intonation pattern in *Erm, well, I don't know* is enough to reject a suggestion without causing offence. (See *Pronunciation* below.)

Language

Focus grammar	comparing with *as*: *as tasty as, isn't as quick as, aren't as big as*
Focus words	adjectives: *bright, busy, cheerful, generous, elegant, impressive, popular, stylish, sweet, tasty* food and places: *cafeteria, Indian, restaurant, snack, take-away, three-course meal,* etc.
Focus phrases	expressing likes and dislikes: *absolutely adore, can't stand, don't mind, hate, love, like, not too keen on*
Recognition vocabulary	words: *atmosphere, chat, complain, dessert trolley, mild, reasonable, salad bar, skip, servings, starters* phrases: *be warned, cooked to perfection, fully booked, highly recommended, save your appetite, self-service, small charge, under new ownership, value for money*
Recycled language	words: *big, cheap, expensive, friendly, pleasant, plenty, small, traditional* phrases for making suggestions: *Let's, Shall we ...?, What about ...?, How about ...?, Why don't we ...?*
Pronunciation	intonation: *disagreeing politely* 4C.2

End product

In *Put it all together,* students work in small groups to agree a place to go to for dinner. Students' conversations are based on audio script 4C.3.

Warmer

Write the following foods on the board and ask students to put them in order according to whether they love or hate them: *pizza, vegetarian food, traditional home cooking, giant-size steaks.* Ask students to find two people who share their opinions, one who really loves the same food, and another who really hates it. Write numbers 1–6 on the board and ask for a show of hands for foods and how students feel about them. Write *absolutely adore* for position 1 and *can't stand* for position 6.

Write *How to compare and discuss preferences* on the board.

A Vocabulary expressing likes and dislikes

1   Ask students to read statements 1–4 and check vocabulary. Put students into pairs to discuss the statements and monitor and make a note of any problems with the following phrases: *can't stand + noun/gerund, don't mind what/gerund, absolutely adore + noun/gerund, not too keen on + noun/gerund.* Contribute to students' discussions as you monitor.

Extra help

Write the following phrases in a jumbled order on the board: *absolutely adore, love, like, don't mind, don't like, hate, can't stand.* Students place them in order on a vertical line. Review verb patterns as necessary.

2   Ask students to underline the phrases for expressing likes and dislikes in exercise 1. Read the instructions and example. Ask students to use the expressions to tell a partner what they like and don't like about restaurants and food. Monitor and help with vocabulary and pronunciation as necessary.

Ask for volunteers to share their opinions with the class for each of the statements in exercise 1. Encourage students either to explain why or to give an example of when they experienced food they liked and disliked.

Extra plus

Students do exercise 2 in small groups.

B Read for detail

In this section, students read short reviews for gist to identify a joke entry before scanning for detail.

3   Direct students to *Restaurant Reviews* on **» p.40** and ask them where they would find these texts. *(A local newspaper supplement or a regular entertainment guide.)* Put students into pairs and ask them to say how they would read this type of text if they were looking for somewhere to go for a meal at the weekend. Ask for suggestions. *(They would probably look quickly at the information in each text to decide which places sounded good before reading in detail.)*

Check students understand the instructions and tell them to look at each text quickly to find the joke review. Go over the answer as a class and ask students to say what information in the text helped them decide.

Home Sweet Home. The text describes various aspects of eating at home, for example, advantages such as favourite recipes, no charge for opening wine, no time limit on how long you stay, and the disadvantage of having to do the shopping.

Teaching tip

Students often fail to use the same reading techniques they use in their own language with different text types. Pointing out that they should choose appropriate ways to read texts according to different types will help improve students' success and confidence in reading.

4   Go through the instructions and check students understand that they should find two examples for each person (what they would and wouldn't like). Go through the example with the class to demonstrate the activity and explain that students will scan the reviews for the key words from exercise 1. Ask students to find the restaurant which John would like, ones which aren't busy or noisy. *(Café Paradiso in the evening.)*

Point out that there might be more than one possible place, and that students can use the symbols under each review to find out more information about the places. In pairs, students continue the activity. Monitor and help as necessary. Nominate different students to give answers and see if the class agrees.

> John would like *Café Paradiso* in the evening, *The Red Lion*; wouldn't like *The Chestnut* or *El Paso*.
> Ali would like *The Red Lion*, *El Paso*; she wouldn't like *Chez Dominique*.
> Sue would like *Café Paradiso*, she wouldn't like the others.
> Dick wouldn't like *Bombay Palace*.

5 Ask students to read sentences 1–7 and check vocabulary. Point out that students should only use *Doesn't say* if there is no information given in the review. Monitor and help as necessary. Ask for volunteers to give answers and elicit reasons why a statement is true or false. Check students understand vocabulary as you go over the reasons.

> 2 True. They are often fully booked.   3 False. The waitresses like to stop and chat.   4 Doesn't say.   5 False. You shouldn't skip the starters.   6 True. The staff are friendly.   7 Doesn't say.

C Grammar comparing with *as*

6 Read the instructions and ask students to find the first example in the reviews (*Café Paradiso*). Ask students to read items 2–9 and check vocabulary. Monitor and help as students continue the activity individually. Ask for volunteers to say in which review they found the information when they give the answers. Monitor answers for accuracy.

> 2 as tasty as   3 isn't as quick as   4 as big as   5 aren't as big as
> 6 as pleasant as   7 as hot as   8 isn't as expensive as
> 9 as long as

7 Read the instructions. Ask students to read sentences 1 and 2 and the options. Check vocabulary as necessary. Write the sentences on the board while students answer the questions individually. Go through the answers with the class.

> 1 b   2 b

Extra help
Ask students to make positive and negative sentences similar to those on the board to compare two restaurants using these adjectives: *small, expensive, busy, noisy*. Give the following example: *The Old Peking is as small as The Bombay Palace*.

8 Go through the instructions and items 1–4 and check vocabulary. Students continue the activity in pairs. Give positive feedback for accurate or creative comparisons.

D Listen for specific information

In this section, students listen to a conversation between friends for key words and specific information.

9 4C.1 Read through the instructions and ask students how they are going to listen. *To every word or for the names of the restaurants? (Names of restaurants.)* Tell students to tick the places they hear. Play the audio.

> Café Paradiso   The Old Peking   The Bombay Palace
> Chez Dominique   The Chestnut

10 Go through the instructions and check students understand the activity. Play the audio again. Students can compare answers in pairs and listen again if necessary. Check answers.

> Café Paradiso: full of children   The Old Peking: Sarah isn't too keen on Chinese food   The Bombay Palace: Tom isn't sure (but doesn't say why)   Chez Dominique: too expensive

11 Read the instructions and the phrases for making suggestions. Direct students to audio script 4C.1 on >> p.152 to underline the phrases. Check answers as a class.

12 4C.2 Read the instructions. Explain that, in English, speakers use intonation to sound polite, especially when they reject a suggestion made by another person. Direct students to the face icons and the intonation contours for each one. Play the audio and pause after each phrase for students to hear the intonation pattern. Play the audio a second time for students to repeat each phrase, encouraging them to copy the pattern. Give extra practice as necessary.

13 4C.3 Go through the instructions and check students understand the activity. Ask students to listen and identify the tone of voice. Play the audio, pausing after each conversation for students to call out the answer as a class. Play the audio a second time if necessary.

> 1 disagree   2 agree   3 agree   4 disagree

Extra help
Play the audio again for students to repeat the melody at the end of each conversation.

Extra activity
Students take turn to test a partner by humming the tone. The partner says if they are agreeing or disagreeing.

ABCD Put it all together

14 Read the instructions and check students understand the activity. Suggest students look again at *Restaurant Reviews* on >> p.40 for ideas, if necessary.

15 Put students into small groups and read the instructions. Ask two students to read the example and invite a third student to agree or disagree with B's opinion. Students continue. At the end of the activity, see which restaurants students have decided to go to.

Student performance
Students should be able to give short explanations.

You can use this checklist to monitor and give feedback or to assess students' performance.

Interaction	Do students use suggestion phrases appropriately? exercise 11
Vocabulary	Do students use a variety of adjectives? exercise 8
Pronunciation	Do students try to use intonation when disagreeing? exercise 12

I can **compare and discuss preferences.**

Students tick *on my own* if they have explained their point of views using their notes. They tick *with some help* if they have looked at the phrases in exercise 12 once or twice.

Early finishers
Tell students that the restaurant they have chosen is fully booked. They repeat the activity to agree another place to go.

Additional material

www.oup.com/elt/result for extra practice activities
www.oup.com/elt/teacher/result for extra teacher resources

How to compare and discuss preferences

G comparing with *as*   V expressing likes and dislikes   P disagreeing politely

A Vocabulary expressing likes and dislikes

1 Do you agree with these statements? Tell a partner.

John   I can't stand busy, noisy restaurants.
Ali   I don't mind what I eat, I just want a lot of it.
Sue   I absolutely adore Italian food.
Dick   I'm not too keen on curry or hot food in general.

2 Make true sentences for you about restaurants and food using the phrases in red in exercise 1. Tell a partner.
Example   I can't stand restaurants with lots of smoke.

B Read for detail

3 Read **Restaurant Reviews** opposite. Which one is a joke?

4 Work with a partner. Which restaurants would the people in exercise 1 like and not like?
Example   John would hate the Café Paradiso when it's busy.

5 Read the sentences. Write *true*, *false*, or *doesn't say*.
1 Café Paradiso has the best pizzas in town.   *True*
2 The Chestnut is often full.
3 The service at the Red Lion is fast.
4 The vegetables at the El Paso are very fresh.
5 They don't serve starters at Chez Dominique.
6 The people are nice at the Old Peking.
7 They only serve Indian food at the Bombay Palace.

C Grammar comparing with *as*

6 Underline phrases in **Restaurant Reviews** with these meanings. All the phrases include the word *as*.
1 when it's quieter than early evening
   when it isn't as busy as early evening
2 such tasty vegetarian food
3 slower than some people would like
4 nowhere serves bigger steaks than
5 servings are smaller than you'd expect
6 your meal couldn't be more pleasant
7 I've never had such a hot curry
8 it's cheaper than a restaurant wine price
9 you can stay for any length of time

7 Read the sentences and say if the meanings are *a* or *b*.
1 The Red Lion is as cheap as the Old Peking.
   a The Red Lion is cheaper.
   b You pay about the same at both.
2 The Café Paradiso isn't as big as the El Paso.
   a Both of them are the same size.
   b The El Paso is bigger.

8 Work with a partner and compare your opinions. Use *as … as* to compare things in these lists. You can use these adjectives or others.
big small cheap expensive sweet tasty
1 Cuisine: Italian French Indian Chinese other
2 Places to eat: take-away cafeteria restaurant
3 Meals: a quick snack a three-course meal dinner
4 Fruit: melons bananas strawberries apples

More practice? **Grammar Bank** >> p.139.

D Listen for specific information

9 4C.1▶ Listen to Sarah and Tom deciding which restaurant to go to. Which places do they mention?

10 Listen again. Why do they decide *not* to go to the first four places they mention?

11 Look at the audio script on >> p.152. Underline phrases for making suggestions, starting with these words.
Let's …   Shall we …?   What about …?
How about …?   Why don't we …?

12 4C.2▶ **Pronunciation** Listen and repeat these phrases from the conversation. Copy the tone of voice.

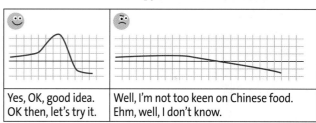

🙂	🙁
Yes, OK, good idea. OK then, let's try it.	Well, I'm not too keen on Chinese food. Ehm, well, I don't know.

13 4C.3▶ You will hear Sarah making suggestions. You don't hear the words in Tom's replies, only his tone of voice. Is he agreeing or disagreeing?

ABCD Put it all together

14 Look at **Restaurant Reviews** again and choose two you would love to visit, two you wouldn't mind visiting, and two you wouldn't like. Make notes of your reasons.

15 Work in small groups. You want to go for a meal together on Friday evening. Try to agree which restaurant to go to. Remember to use the phrases from exercises 1 and 11.
Example   A Shall we go to Chez Dominique?
              B I'm not too keen on French food. How about …

I can compare and discuss preferences. ▮▮▮▮▮

His film or her film?

1 THE QUEEN

63ᵐᵉ Mostra de Venise
Compétition

HELEN MIRREN

UN FILM DE STEPHEN FREARS

2 MATRIX

3 THE LORD OF THE RINGS
THE FELLOWSHIP OF THE RING

4 Disaster is just a small step away

ROWAN ATKINSON
MR. BEAN'S HOLIDAY

5 TOM CRUISE
M:i:III
THE MISSION BEGINS MAY 5

6 MAMMA MIA!

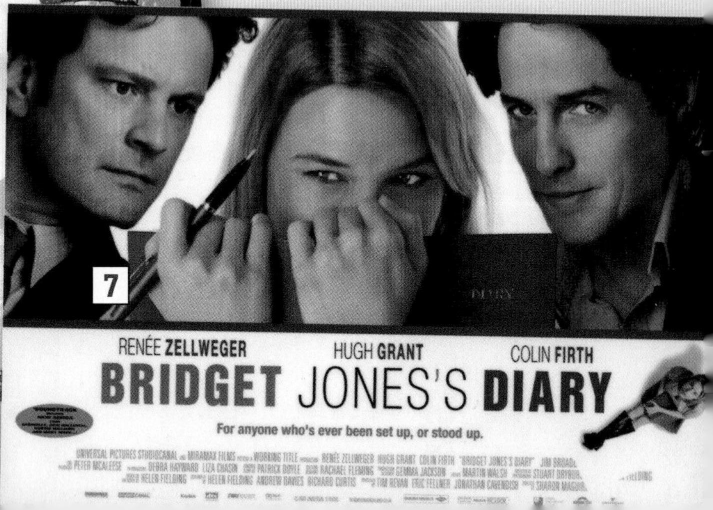

7 RENÉE ZELLWEGER   HUGH GRANT   COLIN FIRTH
BRIDGET JONES'S DIARY
For anyone who's ever been set up, or stood up.

READERS' REVIEWS

Great fun and so true!
★★★★★

It's a film about a single woman who is looking for the right man to start a relationship with. It's one of my favourites because it's really funny and it shows things that really happen to women. I can really identify with the situations which the woman finds herself in. I LOVE this film!

A load of rubbish!
★☆☆☆☆

I can't stand films like this. It's about a woman who is unhappy because she hasn't got a man. She goes out with one guy who is selfish and another guy who is boring, and that's all. End of story. I prefer films which have a plot and a bit of action.

Quite funny
★★★☆☆

I don't usually like chick flicks, but this one was entertaining. It's about an English woman who wants a relationship but she can't find a man who she likes. She gets into some situations which are really embarrassing. The actress that plays the woman is really good. It's not brilliant, but it's one of those films that leaves you feeling good.

How to explain what a film is about

Orientation

Context

In this lesson, students will practise using defining relative clauses to give information about a film (without mentioning the name). The film posters in *His film or her film?* on **>> p.42** are: *1 The Queen 2 Matrix 3 The Lord of the Rings 4 Mr Bean 5 Mission Impossible III 6 Mamma Mia! 7 Bridget Jones' Diary*. They illustrate the vocabulary in *Types of film*.

Readers' Reviews has three different reviews and star ratings of the same film, *Bridget Jones*.

Language

Focus grammar	subject and object defining relative clauses: *a woman who is unhappy, things that happen to women, a man (who) she goes out with, a situation (that) she is in*
Focus words	films: *action, comedy, drama, fantasy, musical, romance, science fiction* others: *action, attractive, brilliant, character, classic, dialogue, emotion, excitement, fighting, literature, relationships, plot, situations, speed*
Recognition vocabulary	words: *selfish* phrases: *chick flicks, feeling good, identify with, goes out with*
Recycled language	words: *boring, embarrassing, entertaining, funny, love* phrases: *can't stand, don't like*

End product

In *Put it all together*, students work in pairs and give a description of a film: the characters and action. The description is based on the texts in *Readers' Reviews* on **>> p.42**.

Preparation

Think of the names of recent films your students will be familiar with for the *Warmer* and exercise 1. If you have newspaper or magazine adverts of some latest releases, you could use these for the *Warmer*. Read *Research results* on **>> p.128** so you are familiar with them for exercise 4.

Warmer

Write the names of some different types of recent national and international films on the board and ask for a show of hands to see who has seen them, plans to see them, or definitely doesn't want to see them. Encourage students to say why or why not.

Encourage students to give their reasons, and help them get their ideas across, supplying vocabulary as necessary. Do not overcorrect for accuracy at this stage.

Write *How to explain what a film is about* on the board.

A Vocabulary films

1   Read the instructions and put students into pairs to do the activity. Tell students that they can use the names of the film in their own language or explain what it's about. Ask for volunteers to tell the class.

2   Direct students to *Types of film* and the posters in *His film or her film?* on **>> p.42**. See if students know the names of the films in the posters (see *Context* opposite).

Students continue the activity in pairs. Encourage them to use their dictionaries if necessary. Monitor and make a note of any problem pronunciation of the words in *Types of film*. Go through each poster, eliciting the answer. Model and help with pronunciation as necessary.

> 1 drama   2 science fiction   3 fantasy   4 comedy   5 action
> 6 music   7 romance

Extra help

Say the number of a poster for students as a class to call out the film type.

Extra plus

In pairs, students say the poster number and genre. Their partner repeats if the information is correct and stays silent if it isn't.

3   Draw two columns on the board, labelled *men* and *women*. Read the instructions and ask for the most popular type of film for men and women. Do not comment at this stage. Ask students to write their own lists in order of popularity. Put students into pairs or small groups to compare their lists.

4   Direct students to *Research results* on **>> p.128**. Give them time to compare their lists with the research findings and ask for comments about similarities and differences around the class.

B Listen to a radio programme

In this section, students discuss the topic and anticipate what they expect to hear, before listening to a radio interview.

5   Read the instructions and ask students to check vocabulary in their dictionaries if they need to. Monitor and help as necessary. Go through each item as a class, asking for a show of hands. If students are not sure or do not agree, encourage them to explain why.

6   4D.1 Explain that a team of university professors researched this topic in the 1990s. Point out that the radio interview is mainly about women's films, but they do talk a little bit about what men prefer. Play the audio for students to tick the words they hear.

> ✓ relationships   dialogue   action   attractive   men

Extra help

If necessary, pause the audio after each question to give students time to make notes.

Teaching tip

Point out that when we listen to the radio in our own language, we usually have an idea of the type of information we will hear. Tell students that thinking about a topic before they listen will help them understand people speaking English.

7 Go through the instructions and ask students to read questions 1–4. Check vocabulary as necessary. Play the audio for students to listen and make notes. Ask students to compare answers and play the audio a second time if necessary. Nominate students to give answers and see if the class agrees.

> 1 They focus on people and dialogues.
> 2 a They are films which have women as the main characters and women can identify with.
>   b The men women find attractive.
>   c An example of a film from classic literature.
> 3 No, there are too few women's films.
> 4 She prefers reading books.

Extra activity

Students could listen to or read the text again. They tell a partner if they agree with Janet Shaw's opinion and say why or why not.

8 Direct students to the film posters on **>> p.42**. In pairs or small groups, students discuss which of the film posters are women's films. Monitor and help with ideas, encouraging students to give examples and extra details. Monitor for use of defining relative clauses but do not correct for accuracy at this stage.

Ask for a spokesperson from each group to report their ideas to the class and encourage other to express agreement or disagreement.

C Grammar defining relative clauses

9 Direct students to *Readers' Reviews* on **>> p.42**. Ask students to say what they think the writer's opinion is from the titles and symbols. Students read the reviews. Answer item 1 together as a class. *(Bridget Jones.)* Put students into pairs to answer the questions. Monitor and help with vocabulary in the texts as necessary. Go through each of the questions in turn, asking for volunteers to share their answers with the class.

> 1 Bridget Jones' Diary   2 Student's own answers.
> 3 Suggested answers: text 1 female; text 2 male; text 3 either

10 Ask students to underline the relative pronouns in the text and go through the rules together as a class.

> **Rules:** that   which   who

11 Direct students to the pictures and read the sentences. Ask students what the verb is in the words in red. Write *like* on the board. Do items 1–2 and complete the rule together as a class.

> 1 d   2 **Rule:** object

Extra help

Drill sentences a–d, encouraging students to run phrases which include the relative pronoun together to sound fluent.

Extra activity

Draw three columns on the board, labelled *who, that,* and *which*. Ask students to look again at *Readers' Reviews* and make a note of general subjects and objects in each column. *(Who = a single woman, a woman, one guy, another guy, an English woman; a man; That = things, the actress, a film; Which = situation, films.)* Point out that all the words are general. They do not tell us exactly which woman, man, film, etc. the writer is talking about. Ask students which relative pronouns can be omitted. *(Text 1: situations (which) the woman Text 3: man (who) she.)*

12 Read the instructions. Ask students to read sentences 1–7 and to tell you the name of the film *(Bridget Jones)*. Check vocabulary. Do item 1 as a class to demonstrate the activity. Monitor and help as necessary. Put students into pairs to compare answers before checking as a class.

As you go over answers, point out how the subjects and objects referred to by the relative pronouns are very general, e.g. the guy, a situation, the actress, everything, the guy, the actor, and these are typical topics we use to talk about films.

> Pronouns can be cut from sentences 3, 5, 6.

Extra help

Ask students to think of their favourite films and to write sentences similar to those in exercise 12 about a woman, an actor, and a situation using relative pronouns. Monitor and help as necessary. Ask students to read their sentences to a partner. The partner guesses the film.

Extra plus

Students write a short paragraph similar to one of the *Readers' Reviews* on **>> p.42**. They read their paragraph to the group or class. The others guess the film.

ABC Put it all together

13 Go through the instructions and monitor and help with ideas as necessary. Tell students not to use the names of people or places, and to use vocabulary from *Types of film*. Direct them to *Readers' Reviews* and the sentences in exercise 12 for ideas.

14 Put students into pairs and check they understand the activity. Read the beginning of the opening sentence and remind students to use relative pronouns so their partner doesn't find out the name of the film too easily. Give students a little more thinking or rehearsal time if necessary.

Students complete the activity in pairs. Check they swap roles. Tell students that if they can't guess the film, they can ask their partner questions, e.g. *What's the name of the actor who lives in ...?*

Student performance

Students should be able to give a short description.

You can use this checklist to monitor and give feedback or to assess students' performance.

Content	Do students give enough information about the film? exercise 9
Grammar	Do students mostly use defining relative pronouns *who* and *which* accurately? exercise 12
Vocabulary	Do students have enough vocabulary to talk about a film? exercises 1, 5

I can **explain what a film is about.**

Students tick *on my own* if they have described their film using their notes. They tick *with some help* if they have looked at *Types of film* and sentences a–d in exercise 11 once or twice for help.

Early finishers

Students repeat the activity with a different film. They have to use five relative pronouns in their descriptions.

Additional material

www.oup.com/elt/result for extra practice activities
www.oup.com/elt/teacher/result for extra teacher resources

How to explain what a film is about

G defining relative clauses   v films

A Vocabulary films

1 List five or more of your favourite films. Tell your partner why you like them.

2 Match the **Types of film** opposite with film posters 1–7 in **His film or her film?** You can use your dictionary.

3 What types of film do men and women usually prefer? Put them in order from 1–7 for men and women.

4 Look at **Research results** on ≫ p.128. Does anything surprise you? Tell a partner.

B Listen to a radio programme

5 Work with a partner and decide which of these things men usually want and which ones women usually want.

action   a good story   attractive men
attractive women   dialogue   emotion   excitement
fighting   love   relationships   speed

6 **4D.1▶** Listen to Janet Shaw, a professor of Media Studies, talking about women's films on a radio programme. Which of the things in exercise 5 does she mention?

7 Listen again and answer the questions.
1 What do women's films focus on?
2 What does Dr Shaw use the examples below to show?
   a the films *Thelma and Louise* and *Alien*
   b the actors Nicolas Cage, Hugh Grant, and Mel Gibson
   c the book *Pride and Prejudice*
3 Do women watch only women's films?
4 Which kind of film does Dr Shaw prefer?

8 Which of the films in **His film or her film?** do you think are women's films? Tell a partner.

C Grammar defining relative clauses

9 Work with a partner. Read **Readers' Reviews** opposite and answer the questions.
1 Which film are the reviews about?
2 Do you agree with any of the reviews?
3 Do you think the writers are male or female?

10 Underline all the examples of the relative pronouns *who*, *which*, and *that* in **Readers' Reviews** and complete the rules.
Rules _____ refers to people or things.
_____ refers only to things.
_____ refers only to people.

11 Read the sentences and answer the questions. The red part of these sentences is called a relative clause.

a She's found a man who she likes.
b She's found a man she likes.

c She's found a man who likes her.
d She's found a man likes her.

1 One of sentences a–d above is incorrect. Which one? ~~Cross~~ it out.
2 In sentence a, who is the *object* of the verb likes. In sentence c, who is the *subject* of the verb likes. Underline the correct word in this rule.

Rule You can leave out the pronouns *who*, *that*, or *which* if they are the **subject/object** of the verb in the relative clause.

12 Is it possible to leave out the pronouns *who*, *which*, and *that*? If it *is* possible to cut it, ~~cross~~ it out.
1 It's about the guys ~~who~~ she goes out with.
2 It's about a situation which is embarrassing.
3 It's about the situation that she is in.
4 The actress who plays Bridget is called Renée Zellweger.
5 The film is about everything that she writes in her diary.
6 The first guy who she goes out with is her boss.
7 The actor who plays her boss is Hugh Grant.

More practice? **Grammar Bank** ≫ p.139.

ABC Put it all together

13 Choose a film you remember and think of the answers to these questions.

What type of film is it?   Who's in it?
What's the story?   Why do you like it?

14 Describe your film to a partner but don't say the title. Listen to your partner's description. Can you guess which film it is? Would you like to see it?

Example This is an action film about a woman who …

I can explain what a film is about.

Tick ✓ the line.   with a lot of help   with some help   on my own   very easily

Writing A description of a film or book

A Read and order

1 Have you seen this film, or would you like to? Tell a partner.

2 Put the film description in order. Use this structure to help you.

Structure

paragraph 1   title; type of film; setting

paragraph 2   the main star(s); the key characters; how the story begins

paragraph 3   a good moment in the film; a final opinion about the film and actors

THE SUSPENSE *of ALIEN!*
THE EXCITEMENT *of JAWS!*
THE FUN *of BACK TO THE FUTURE!*

HOLLYWOOD PICTURES *and* AMBLIN ENTERTAINMENT *present*

ARACHNOPHOBIA

- [ ] However, his patients start to die and people in the town think he's a bad doctor.
- [ ] He plays Doctor Jennings, who moves to the town but can't find work because an old man called Doctor Metcalf already works there.
- [ ] But the film is also very amusing, and Jeff Daniels is really funny.
- [ ] When the old doctor is killed by the spiders, Doctor Jennings takes over.
- [ ] I nearly jumped out of my seat!
- [1] I saw a great film recently called 'Arachnophobia'.
- [ ] It's a comedy horror film about deadly spiders who invade a small Californian town.
- [ ] Jeff Daniels is the star of the film.
- [ ] The most frightening moment is when Doctor Jennings finds the queen spider in his own house.

3 Work with a partner. Explain who or what the highlighted words in the text (a pronoun or *the* + noun) refer to.

Example   the town = the town where Doctor Jennings lives

4 The writer of the text decided to cut these sentences. Why is the text better *without* them? Match the sentence and the reason. There may be more than one reason.

1 There are two restaurants in the town.

2 Doctor Metcalf's secretary is woman called Mercedes with a dog called Mary Kate.

3 I went to California once.

4 At the end of the film, the doctor kills the queen spider and everyone in the town is saved.

a [ ] It reveals the end and spoils it for the reader.

b [ ] It is a boring detail.

c [ ] It's long and unnecessary in a brief description.

d [ ] It isn't relevant.

B Content and organization

5 Work with a partner. Read this film description and underline examples of these problems. Write 1, 2, or 3 next to the examples you find.

1 this information is in the wrong order

2 this is an irrelevant or unnecessary detail

3 this should use a pronoun or *the* + noun to refer back

The terrifying motion picture from the terrifying No.1 best seller.

JAWS

ROY SCHEIDER   ROBERT SHAW   RICHARD DREYFUSS

JAWS

I saw a film from the DVD shop near my house. The DVD was very cheap. The film from the DVD shop was called 'Jaws'. 'Jaws' is a thriller about a killer shark.

A girl goes for a swim in the sea and a shark kills the girl. It's a very frightening film. The most frightening moment is when a shark jumps on the boat.

The chief of police and two other men go out in a boat to hunt for a shark, but a shark hunts them. A shark eats one of the men. In the end, they kill a shark and swim back to the beach.

6 Look at the structure in exercise 2. Is any information missing in the Jaws text? Compare with a partner.

7 Rewrite a better version of the Jaws text.

C Getting ideas to write about

8 Think of a film you have seen recently or a book you have read. Write a description of the story very quickly (five minutes maximum). Don't worry about mistakes or organization for now.

9 Work with a partner. Read your descriptions aloud and discuss any changes which would make it better.

ABC Put it all together

10 Rewrite your description, making changes from your discussion in exercise 9.

11 Now check your grammar and spelling and make corrections.

12 Give your description to another partner. Have you seen the film? Would you like to? Tell your new partner.

I can write a description of a film or book.

Tick ✓ the line.   with a lot of help   with some help   on my own   very easily

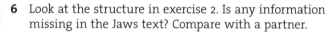

Orientation

Context and Language

In this lesson, students analyse, write, and review a description of a film or book.

Preview grammar	the definite article
Recycled language	words: amusing, cheap, comedy, frightening, funny, horror, setting, spiders, terrifying grammar: -ed and -ing adjectives
Recognition language	words: deadly, key characters, relevant, spoils phrases: takes over
Discourse	substitution to avoid repetition: Arachnophobia – the film

End product

In *Put it all together*, students write a description of a film or book they know. After reviewing a first draft for organization and a second for grammar and spelling, partners comment on the description.

Warmer

Write film types from 4D on the board. In pairs, students choose two and write associated vocabulary. Go through each one eliciting examples. Students read the vocabulary, the class guesses the film type.

Write *How to write a description of a film or book* on the board.

A Read and order

In this section, students analyse content and coherence in a film description.

1 Direct students to the picture. They discuss the question in pairs. Ask for a spokesperson from each pair to report their opinions.

2 Go through the instructions and the paragraph structure. Check vocabulary. Ask students to read the sentences from the description. Students do the activity in pairs, remind them to ignore the highlighted words. Check answers.

> 2 It's a comedy …   3 Jeff Daniels …   4 He plays …
> 5 When the old doctor …   6 However, his patients …
> 7 The most frightening …   8 I nearly …   9 But the film is …

3 Read the instructions and go through the example as a class. Students compare in pairs before you check answers as a class. Ask why the writer has not repeated the same words. *(The writer and reader both know what is being talked about so the topics don't need to be written in full again.)*

> He = Jeff Daniels   the film = Arachnophobia
> the old doctor = Doctor Metcalf   It's = Arachnophobia

4 Read the instructions and ask students to read sentences 1–4. Check vocabulary. Direct students to reasons a–d. Go through each one in turn to check understanding. Do the first sentence together as a class to demonstrate the activity. Students continue individually. Check answers.

> 1 b, d   2 b, c   3 d   4 a, c

B Content and organization

In this section, students sequence a description according to a three-paragraph structure.

5 Read through the instructions and items 1–3. In pairs, students continue the activity. Check answers. Read the modified text aloud, so students can hear how coherent and logically ordered it is.

> 1 information out of order: *It's a very frightening film …* (should be in paragraph 3)   2 irrelevant / unnecessary detail: *the DVD was very cheap; the DVD shop*   3 pronoun, or *the + noun*: paragraph 1: 'Jaws' – the film   paragraph 2: the girl – her   paragraph 3: the shark – it

6 Direct students to the paragraph structure in exercise 2 and put them into pairs to check to see if there is any information missing. Go through each of the points in turn, and ask for examples from the text *(the main actors, final opinion)*.

7 Tell students to write a better version of the text, using the structure in exercise 2 and their notes from exercise 6. Put students into pairs to compare their version and to say why they think it's better than the text in exercise 6.

C Getting ideas to write about

In this section, students focus on text organization and grammar.

8 Go through the instructions and tell students to look back at lesson 4D for ideas. Point out that the first thing to do is to get their ideas on paper. Explain that it's more difficult to make changes to organization than grammar and vocabulary once a text has been written. Monitor and help with ideas as necessary.

9 Put students into pairs to read their texts aloud. Ask the student listening to say if the text is easy to follow and understand. Monitor and contribute to students' discussions.

ABC Put it all together

10 Read the instructions to the class. Suggest students write numbers next to the sentences to show the order they want to use when they rewrite their text.

11 Ask students to check their grammar and spelling, and to check they have used pronouns and *the + noun* to refer back. Encourage students to use symbols for any mistakes.

12 Students swap descriptions and say if they would like to see the film or read the book.

Student performance

Students should be able to produce a short description of 90 words.

You can use this checklist to monitor and give feedback or to assess students' performance.

Content	Have students included the main points?
Organization	Have students organized their writing logically?
Coherence	Have students referred back to nouns correctly?

I can **write a description of a film or book.**

Students tick *on my own* if they are happy with their description after they have reviewed it for organization and accuracy. They can tick *with some help* if they would like to make one or two more changes after doing exercise 12.

Early finishers

Students write a final draft of their text for display.

Additional material

www.oup.com/elt/result for extra practice activities
www.oup.com/elt/teacher/result for extra teacher resources

Warmer

Remember the questions

Put students into small teams to write as many questions as they can using the words below. Set a three-minute time limit.

what, is, are, your, meal, why, does, idea, not, her, out, watching, shall, don't, you, of, make, his, try, into, we, about, music, or, something, film, move, a, different, go, for, where, fun.

Students can use the words as many times as they want. Give a student from each team a turn to say a question. Ask the class to decide if the question is correct. If it is, award two points. If it isn't, award a point to the first team to correct the question.

> **Suggested answers**
> What is your idea of fun?   Are you into music?   Does music make you move?   Why not try something different?   His film or her film?   What about watching a film?   Why don't we try something different?   Shall we go out for a meal?   Where shall we go?

A Grammar

1   -ed and -ing adjectives 4A exercise 5

Warm-up: Read a few of the definitions from exercise 5 on >> p.37 and elicit -ed and -ing adjectives.

Set-up: Go through the example and check students understand the activity.

> 2 boring; bored   3 excited; exciting   4 disgusting; disgusted

Follow-up: Ask students, in pairs or small groups, to write five questions for a survey called *What's your idea of fun?* The questions are based on the activities in lessons A–D. Students interview four or five others and see who likes and dislikes the same things.

2   Comparatives and superlatives 4B exercise 6

Warm-up: Ask *Cinema, theatre, or concert?* Ask students which they prefer and why.

Set-up: Go through the instructions and the example. Explain that students choose one of the topics after the list of things.

> **Suggested answers**
> 2 Instant coffee is a bit easier to make. / Real coffee tastes much better than instant coffee.
> 3 Reggae is much better to dance to. / Rock is far more exciting.
> 4 Seeing films on DVD is a lot cheaper and more convenient.
> 5 A weekend break in the city is much more relaxing.
> 6 An email is much cheaper to send. / A text message is a bit quicker to write.
> 7 Cards are slightly easier to learn. / A game of cards is played more quickly than a game of chess.

Follow-up: Students choose topics from Unit 4 and ask for a partner's opinion. They must use *slightly, much, far, a bit,* or *a lot* in their answers.

3   Comparing with *as* 4C exercise 6

Warm-up: Write *Saxophone or recorder?* on the board and ask students to make sentences about the two instruments with *as.*

Set-up: Ask students to read items 2–4 and underline the nouns that are being compared.

> 2 A hamburger isn't as expensive as a steak.
> 3 Driving isn't as good for you as cycling.
> 4 Folk music isn't as complicated as classical music.

Follow-up: In pairs, students choose two items and write comparative sentences. They swap items with another pair, and write sentences. At the end of the activity, they compare sentences.

4   Defining relative clauses 4D exercise 12

Warm-up: Read the first part of the sentences in exercise 12, >> p.43, pausing before the relative pronoun for the class to say which word comes next. Direct students to exercise 10, >> p.43 to revise if necessary.

Set-up: Ask students to read sentences 1–4. Ask for the name of the film. *(Titanic.)*

> 2 They're on a ship that's crossing the Atlantic.
> 3 He meets a woman who can see the future.
> 4 They say he'll never marry the girl he loves.

Follow-up: In pairs, students write four sets of sentences about a film. Pairs swap sentences and join them together. They guess the name of the film.

B Vocabulary

5   Music 4B exercises 4, 5

Warm-up: Set a two-minute time limit for students to write as many words as they can connected with the theme *music.* They look back at lesson 4B and check spellings.

Set-up: Read the instructions and ask students to read the clues. Check vocabulary as necessary.

> 2 drummer   3 musician   4 saxophone   5 keyboard
> 6 composer   7 guitarist   8 track   9 stadium
> Hidden word: orchestra

Follow-up: In pairs, students use their dictionaries to write clues for five more words connected with *music.* They swap clues with a partner and see which pair can find the answers first.

6   Expressing likes and dislikes 4C exercises 1, 8

Warm-up: Write the following words on the board for students to make phrases they could use to talk about likes and dislikes: *not, absolutely, can't, too, don't, keen, stand, mind, adore, on.* Students look back at lesson 4C, exercise 1 to check their answers.

Set up: Go through the example with the class.

> 2 not too keen on   3 absolutely adore   4 can't stand
> 5 don't mind

Follow-up: Students choose a restaurant from *Restaurant Reviews* on >> p.40 and have conversations with others in the class to see how many people they can get to go to dinner with them.

7   Films 4D exercise 2

Warm-up: Say the names of different films for students to call out the type. Use the films on >> p. 42 or local films your students are likely to know.

Set-up: Go through the example with the class.

> 2 science fiction   3 fantasy   4 musical   5 action   6 drama
> 7 comedy

Follow-up: Students write some true sentences about their own opinions of the films, without mentioning the type. They swap sentences with a partner and guess the film types.

Early finishers

Students review the unit and make a list of adjectives they want to remember. They write a sentence for each one.

Unit 4 Review

A Grammar

1 *-ed* and *-ing* adjectives Finish the words in these sentences.

1 I'm not usually interest*ed__* in history, but this book was quite interest*ing__*.

2 I thought the show was bor____. Everybody else was bor____, too.

3 I used to be really excit____ on New Year's Eve, but now I don't find it excit____ at all.

4 I thought the food was disgust____ but Dad didn't seem disgust____ by it.

2 **Comparatives and superlatives** Give your opinion using comparatives or superlatives. Use the adjectives given and one of the words below.

a bit   a lot   far   much   slightly

1 Brown or white bread?   good for you/tasty
I think brown bread is better for you and it's much tastier.

2 Real or instant coffee?   easy to make/taste good

3 Reggae, rock, or jazz?   good to dance to/exciting

4 Films at the cinema or on DVD?   convenient/cheap

5 A weekend break in the country or the city? exciting/relaxing

6 Text message, email, or letter? quick to write/cheap to send

7 Chess or cards?   learn easily/play quickly

3 **Comparing with** *as* Put the words in order to make sentences.

1 as as bus isn't quick The the Underground
The bus isn't as quick as the Underground.

2 as a expensive as hamburger isn't A steak
_____

3 as cycling Driving for as good isn't you
_____

4 classical as complicated Folk isn't music as music
_____

4 **Defining relative clauses** Join the two sentences using relative pronouns to make one longer sentence.

1 It's a story about a poor boy. He falls in love with a rich girl.
It's a story about a poor boy who falls in love with a rich girl.

2 They're on a ship. It's crossing the Atlantic.
_____
_____

3 He meets a woman. She can see the future.
_____
_____

4 They say he will never marry the girl. He loves her.
_____
_____

B Vocabulary

5 **Music** Complete the puzzle and find the hidden word.

	1	C	O	N	D	U	C	T

Clues
1 To direct an orchestra.
2 A person who plays the drums.
3 A person who plays music.
4 An instrument made of a long, curved metal tube.
5 An instrument like a piano.
6 A person who writes pieces of music.
7 A person who plays the guitar.
8 One song or piece of music on a record or CD.
9 A massive music venue which is normally used for sport.

6 **Expressing likes and dislikes** Complete the words in this conversation.

A Let's go out to eat.

B OK. [1]*How__* a*bout* *going* *to*____ a Chinese restaurant?

A I'm [2]n____ t____ k____ o____ Chinese food, actually. How about an Indian restaurant? I [3]a____ a____ Indian food.

B Oh no, I [4]c____ s____ it! Do you like Italian food?

A Well, I [5]d____ m____ pizzas.

B OK, let's go to an Italian then.

7 **Films** Match the film types and the people.

action   comedy   drama   fantasy
musical   ~~romance~~   science fiction

Kate I like love films.   *romance*
Jim   I like films set in the future.
Mick I like films about imaginary, magical worlds.
Sara I like films with lots of singing and dancing.
Ed   I like films with lots of excitement and adventure.
Liz   I like serious films with good dialogue.
Jo   I like films which make me laugh.

Politics

capital /ˈkæpɪtl/   con**serv**ative /kənˈsɜːvətɪv/   de**moc**racy /dɪˈmɒkrəsi/   e**lect**ions /ɪˈlekʃnz/
head of state /hed əv ˈsteɪt/   **nat**ional /ˈnæʃnəl/   po**lit**ical /pəˈlɪtɪkl/   **pres**ident /ˈprezɪdənt/
repre**sent** /reprɪˈzent/   re**pub**lic /rɪˈpʌblɪk/   **soc**ialist /ˈsəʊʃəlɪst/   U**nit**ed **Nat**ions /juˈnaɪtɪd ˈneɪʃnz/

Symbols *of* Power

An Object

The ballot box has perhaps become one of the great symbols of democracy. It represents the power of the voters to elect their own leaders. The name 'ballot' comes from 'ball'. At one time voters used  a small black ball to vote in elections, instead of paper, or nowadays, an electronic vote. Many ballot boxes are transparent so that people can see that they were empty at the beginning of voting. The idea of transparency, that people can see everything, has become a symbol, too – of honesty.

Directions

The directions left and right are used as symbols for political views. Political parties with more socialist views are called left wing, while parties with more conservative views are 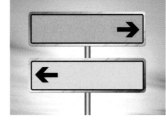 called right wing. This symbolism comes from the French Revolution, where liberal members of parliament sat to the left of the president and conservatives sat to the right.

Colours

Light blue is the colour of the United Nations. It was chosen because it is the colour of the sky above every nation on Earth. The colour is used as a protective sign on the hats of peacekeeping forces so that they are not mistaken for the enemy. Other colours with political meaning are red and green. Red is the traditional colour for socialism and communism, while green is a symbol for parties mainly concerned with the environment.

Buildings

Government buildings are symbols of power and they are often designed to be large and impressive. In the USA, many public buildings were built to look like buildings from ancient Greece and Rome. There was a political message here – like the USA, ancient Greece and Rome were republics, too. Meanwhile, during the time of the Soviet Union, government buildings were massive to remind the public of the great power of the state.

A Shape

The five-pointed star is a very common symbol of military power, and is used on military vehicles and uniforms in many countries. It is also a very common national symbol and is used on the flags of 35 countries. For example, there are 50 stars on the flag of the USA, and they represent the states in that country. The symbol for the European Union also includes stars to represent the member nations.

Animals

Countries often have an animal as a national symbol. Lions and eagles are very popular symbols because they represent strength. For example, Bulgaria, England, and the Netherlands have the lion as the national animal, and the USA, Mexico, and Austria have various kinds of eagle. Other countries use animals which are very characteristic of the region, for example the kiwi in New Zealand or the springbok antelope in South Africa.

How to talk about countries and governments

Orientation

Context

In this lesson, students will practise using *politics* vocabulary to talk about their own country.

The illustrated article, *Symbols of Power*, describes symbols that are common to many countries. The photos show: *1 casting a vote in a transparent ballot box 2 directions left and right (symbols for political opinions) 3 a United Nations soldier with a light blue beret 4 a poster asking people to vote 'green' (for the environment) 5 the Parthenon, Greece 6 soviet-style building in Warsaw 7 star symbols (on flags and a jeep) 8 a lion statue 9 an eagle on a flag.*

In *Politics*, phonetic transcriptions of key vocabulary is given.

Language

Focus grammar	*the* or no article in names of institutions
Preview grammar	the passive: *are used as, was chosen*
Focus words	politics: *capital, conservative, democracy, elections, head of state, national, political, president, represent, republic, socialist, United Nations*
Recognition vocabulary	words: *ancient, ballot box, elect, electronic, enemy, environment, headquarters, honesty, impressive, massive, military, protective, represent, strength, transparent, vehicles, vote* phrases: *left/right wing, peacekeeping forces*
Recycled language	capital letters for proper nouns (names, countries) *the* before geographical names
Pronunciation	*the: the president* /ðə/, *the English* /ði/ **5A.4**

End product

In *Put it all together*, students give a short presentation to a partner about politics in their own country or one they know about. They have previously rehearsed the presentation and use their notes.

Preparation

Copy the place names from exercise 8, lesson 2A onto the board before students arrive if you want to do the *Warmer*. Think about classroom organization for the group work activity in exercise 7. Collect answers for different countries to the questions on **>> p.128** for exercise 16 if you feel your students will need extra help.

Warmer

Team game. Direct students to the names of places on the board (see *Preparation*). Put students into small teams to decide if the geographical names need the definite article. Give one point for correct answers and award another point if teams can give you an extra fact about the places.

Write *How to talk about countries and governments* on the board.

A Read for specific information

In this section, students read an article for specific information before focussing on vocabulary.

1   Direct students to the photos on **>> p.46**, the title, and sub-titles in *Symbols of Power*. In pairs, students talk about what they can see in the photos. Monitor and help as necessary. Elicit information around the class about each photo.

> See *Context* for answers.

2   Read the instructions and set a short time limit to encourage students to scan the article. Tell them to continue individually and to ignore any unknown vocabulary. Put students into pairs to exchange information and monitor for pronunciation.

Ask students to choose one fact they know, and one they don't. Nominate students to tell the class and help them get their ideas across. Do not overcorrect for accuracy. Monitor and make a note of vocabulary in *Politics* on **>> p.46** which might need extra pronunciation work in section B.

3   Ask students to read sentences 1–6 carefully and check new vocabulary. Do item one together, eliciting the reason why the answer is false. *(The text says many ballot boxes are transparent, implying some aren't.)* Monitor and help as necessary as students continue individually. Check answers as a class.

> 2 False. (They were used after the French Revolution in 1789.)
> 3 True.   4 True.   5 False. (The stars represent member nations.)
> 6 True.

4   Read the instructions and meanings 1–4 with the class. Elicit or explain that the questions ask about word class, e.g. *educate (v), education (n)*. Write the words on the board to show students that thinking about the type of word and its relationship to another is a useful strategy for guessing meaning.

Do the first item together to demonstrate the activity. Monitor and help as students continue individually. Ask for volunteers to give answers and to spell the new word. Write the answers on the board before students find them in the text.

> 2 symbolism   3 protective   4 ancient   5 strength

Extra activity

In pairs, students find and underline other related words, e.g. *transparent – transparency*. Encourage them to guess meanings, using their existing knowledge and the context. Students can check in a dictionary for homework.

Teaching tip

Students often believe a text is too difficult for them to read when they come across a word they don't know, even in their own language. Raising awareness to strategies for guessing meaning might stop students giving up too easily, and so develop their reading skills.

B Vocabulary politics

5   Direct students to *Politics* on **>> p.46** and read the instructions. Say each word and ask students if a similar word exists in their language. Use the transcriptions to draw attention to word stress. Model and give pronunciation practice as necessary.

6 Ask students to read the text, ignoring the blanks. Check vocabulary. Students continue individually and compare in pairs. To check answers, read the text aloud and pause before a blank. Elicit the answer and monitor for pronunciation.

> 1 president 2 republic 3 democracy 4 elections 5 political
> 6 socialist 7 conservative 8 capital 9 United Nations
> 10 represent 11 national

Extra activity

In pairs, students find one true and one false fact about their own country. They tell a partner.

C Listen for key information

In this section, students use key information to understand short quiz questions.

7 5A.1 Read the instructions and check students understand. In small groups, students read and listen, ignoring any new vocabulary. Play the audio and ask students to compare their answer with other members in the group *(c)*.

8 Read the instructions and direct students to the question in exercise 7. In pairs, students underline the key words. Check answers. To help build students' listening confidence, remind them that it is not always necessary to understand every word.

> **key words:** country, 1893, first, women, vote

Teaching tip

Students might want to underline more words. Elicit or explain that although it might help to understand *first nation*, or *vote in an election*, understanding the words *first* and *vote* are more important. We can guess and remember the rest from context.

9 5A.2 Ask students to write their answers after each question. Play the audio, pausing for students to reflect on the question and giving them time to write their answer. Students compare answers in pairs. Play the audio a second time if necessary. Do not check answers at this stage as students will listen and check in exercise 10.

10 5A.3 Play the audio for students to check their answers. See who has the highest score.

> 2 b   3 a   4 a   5 c   6 a   7 b   8 c

11 Read the instructions and direct students to audio script 5A.3 on >> p.153. Monitor and help as necessary.

D Grammar *the* or no article in names of institutions

12 Do the activity as a class. Direct students to the grammar box and say a category word, e.g. *individual people*. Elicit an example and ask *The or no the?* Continue for each of the categories and ask students to copy the table and add the information at the end. Guide students to the use of the definite article as necessary as they write the name in the appropriate column. Ask students to complete the rule in pairs and check as a class.

> **individual people:** King Richard III, Queen Elizabeth
> **positions:** the Australian prime minister, the head of state
> **organizations:** the Irish government, the Liberal Party
> **Rule:** Use *the* with **positions** and **organizations** but not with **individual** people.

Extra help

Show students how the rules are generative. Ask students to give more examples for each column from non-political contexts, e.g. The Beatles, The Simpsons.

13 Go through the instructions and the example. Point out the use of *the* before *name* in the example. Remind students or elicit that we use *the* in this case because we are talking about something unique. Students continue individually.

Nominate students to give answers and ask the class to listen and say if they agree or not. Focus on question 6 and check students understand why *president of Tanzania* is preceded by *the* (the word *president* is used as a general noun here).

> 2 the leader/the Conservative   3 the headquarters/the United Nations   4 – Prince/the United Kingdom   5 the Czech Republic/the European Union   6 – President/the president

Extra help

Students find and underline examples of titles, positions, and organizations in *Symbols of Power* on >> p.46. They can revise the grammar in lesson 2A.

14 Read the question and direct students to the information in the box. Point out or elicit that *European* starts with a consonant sound, despite its spelling.

> *The* is pronounced *thee* /ði/ before a vowel sound.

15 5A.4 Direct students to exercise 12. In pairs, students discuss the pronunciation of *the*. Play the audio, pausing after each item for students to check and repeat. Give extra practice as necessary.

Extra plus

In pairs, students decide how *the* is pronounced in the questions in exercise 13.

ABCD Put it all together

16 Read the instructions and direct students to the questions on >> p.128. Students can look back at *Symbols of Power* on >> p.46 and the information in audio script 5A.2 for extra ideas. Students complete the activity in pairs. Monitor and help as necessary. Check they are writing notes not sentences and give students time to rehearse their presentations together.

17 Put students into different pairs to tell a new partner about their country. At the end of the activity, ask for volunteers to say if they learned anything surprising or interesting.

Student performance

Students should be able to give a short factual presentation.

You can use this checklist to monitor and give feedback or to assess students' performance.

Grammar	Do students mostly use the definite article correctly? exercise 13
Vocabulary	Do students have sufficient vocabulary to do the task? exercise 6
Pronunciation	Do students mostly pronounce *the* correctly? exercise 15

I can talk about countries and governments.

Students tick *on my own* if they have given their presentation using their notes. They tick *with some help* if they have looked at *Politics* on >> p.46 occasionally.

Early finishers

Students try to do the activity from memory, using the photos on >> p.46 to help.

Additional material

www.oup.com/elt/result for extra practice activities
www.oup.com/elt/teacher/result for extra teacher resources

How to talk about countries and governments

A Read for specific information

1 Look at the photos in **Symbols of Power** opposite. Tell a partner what they show.

2 Read **Symbols of Power**. Find two facts you already knew and two facts you didn't. Tell a partner.

3 Read the sentences. Write *true* or *false*.
1 Ballot boxes are all transparent.   *False*
2 Left and right have always been symbols for political views.
3 UN peacekeepers wear blue hats so they are not mistaken for the enemy.
4 US public buildings follow Greek and Roman style because it is impressive.
5 The European Union flag has stars to represent the years since it started.
6 Strong animals are popular as national symbols.

4 Find words with these meanings.
1 a noun from the word *symbol* (para 2)
2 an adjective from *protect* (para 3)
3 an adjective meaning *very old* (para 4)
4 a noun from the word *strong* (para 6)

B Vocabulary politics

5 Look at the words in **Politics** opposite. Are any of them similar in your language? Compare with a partner.

6 Complete the text with the words from **Politics**.
In my country, the ¹ *head of state* is the ²_____.
We don't have a king or queen – our country's a
³_____. The people vote to elect the members
of parliament – it's a ⁴_____. We have ⁵_____
every five years. There are two main ⁶_____
parties. The ⁷_____ Party is more left wing and
the ⁸_____ Party is more right wing. The main
government buildings are in the ⁹_____. My
country is a member of the ¹⁰_____ _____.
Our flag has three colours to ¹¹_____ the sea, the
land, and the sky. Our ¹²_____ animal is the eagle.

C Listen for key information

7 **5A.1▶** Work in a group. Read and listen to question 1 from a quiz. Choose the correct answer.
1 An election is a system in which the people choose their political leaders. In the past, only men were allowed to vote. Which country, in 1893, became the first nation to allow women to vote in elections?
   a The United Kingdom   b Indonesia   c New Zealand

8 Which words in the question <u>must</u> you hear correctly in order to be able to choose the answer? <u>Underline</u> them.

9 **5A.2▶** Listen to questions 2–8 and choose *a*, *b*, or *c*.

10 **5A.3▶** Listen to the correct answers and count your score. Who has the highest score?

11 Choose two of your correct answers. Look at the questions and answers in the audio script on **»** p.153 and <u>underline</u> the words which helped you.

D Grammar *the* or no article in names of institutions

12 Write these names in the grammar box. Add *the* if necessary. Then complete the rule.
Australian prime minister   head of state   Irish government
King Richard III   Liberal Party   Queen Elizabeth

individual people	positions	organizations
Princess Diana	the emperor of Japan	the European Union
President Kennedy	the US president	the United Nations

Rule Use *the* with _____ and _____, but not with _____ people.

13 Add the missing *the* to these questions.
1 What's *the* name of *the* president of *the* USA?
2 Who's leader of Conservative Party?
3 Where's headquarters of United Nations?
4 Is Prince William from United Kingdom?
5 Is Czech Republic in European Union?
6 Did President Mandela meet president of Tanzania?

14 Pronunciation *the* is pronounced differently in A and B. Can you see why?

A	B
the president /ðə ˈprezɪdənt/ the European Union /ðə jʊərəˈpiːən ˈjuːniən/	the EU /ði iː ˈjuː/ the English /ði ˈɪŋglɪʃ/

15 **5A.4▶** Look at the phrases in exercise 12. Is *the* pronounced A or B? Listen, check, and repeat.
More practice? **Grammar Bank »** p.140.

ABCD Put it all together

16 Work with a partner. Write notes about politics in your country, or in another country you know. Try to answer the **Politics** questions on **»** p.128.

17 Change partners. Tell your new partner about the country from exercise 16. Listen to your partner's description. Is any information surprising?

I can talk about countries and governments. ▬▬▬▬▬▬

Signs

Proceed with caution.

allow /əˈlaʊ/ *verb* [T] to give permission for sb to do sth

forbid /fəˈbɪd/ *verb* [T] [usually passive] to not allow sth

permit /pəˈmɪt/ *verb* [T] *(formal)* to allow sb to do sth

prohibit /prəˈhɪbɪt/ *verb* [T] *(formal)* to say that sth is not allowed by law

Laws for Paws

A tour of weird and wonderful animal laws in the USA ...

You mustn't take your dog into a barber's!

If you're travelling around the United States with a pet, there are local laws you need to know. For example, if you go for a haircut in Juneau, Alaska, you'll have to leave your dog outside. It's illegal to take a pet into a barber's.

You mustn't travel with an animal on the roof!

Meanwhile, in Sun Prairie, Wisconsin, dogs and cats aren't allowed in cemeteries. In the Californian town of Glendale, you mustn't take a dog in a lift, and in Cathedral City, you can't take one into a school. You can walk your dog in Waterboro, Maine, but the lead must be shorter than 8 feet (about 2.4 metres). And remember, you mustn't travel with an animal on the roof of your car in Anchorage, Alaska.

You mustn't take a skunk into Tennessee!

If you have a pet skunk, you mustn't take it into Tennessee – it's forbidden to enter the state with one of these smelly animals. And remember, pet rats aren't allowed in Billings, Montana.

If your pet suddenly dies, don't forget – you can't leave a dead animal on anybody else's property in Conyers, Georgia.

There are laws about hunting animals, too. While you're in Virginia, don't forget that hunting isn't allowed on Sundays – except for racoons. You can kill a racoon any time before 2 a.m. In Arizona, hunting camels is forbidden. And you must never shoot a fish in Wyoming!

You can kill a racoon any time before two o'clock in the morning.

What about selling animals? Well, if you're planning to sell chicks or ducklings in Kentucky, you mustn't dye them a different colour first. And of course, you mustn't steal animals. In fact, in Louisiana there is a specific law which says it's illegal to steal alligators.

You mustn't dye a chick blue!

You've been warned!

GLOSSARY	
duckling *n* baby duck	
dye *vb* to change the colour of something	
hunt *vb* to search for and kill animals, for food or sport	
smelly *adj* has a bad smell	

How to talk about rules and laws

Orientation

Context

In this lesson, students will practise using modals of obligation to talk about what can and can't be done.

Signs on >> **p.48** illustrates the meaning of some of the dictionary entries.

The illustrated magazine article *Laws for Paws* describes weird and wonderful laws in different US states.

Glossary explains some key vocabulary.

Culture note

We often assume that rules and laws in different countries, e.g. about animals, driving or throwing away rubbish, are the same. Politeness. In English, we often use the phrase *I don't know* to signal that we are unsure of something rather than not actually knowing about it. This phrase and others are used to invite confirmation from the listener (see *Focus phrases* below).

Language

Focus grammar	modals of obligation: *must, mustn't, have to, don't have to, can, can't*
Preview grammar	the passive: *it's forbidden* gerunds: *parking, smoking, taking photographs,* etc. question tags: *It isn't allowed, is it?*
Focus words	*allow, forbid, illegal, permit, prohibit*
Focus phrases	expressing uncertainty: *I don't know., It isn't …, … is it?, I'm not sure.*
Recognition vocabulary	words: *alligator, barber's, camel, caution, cemeteries, chase, chick, duckling, dye, guard/guide dog, hunting, lead (n), licence, local, obligation, permission, pet, proceed, racoon, rat, rubbish, shoot, skunk, smelly, warning, weird* phrases: *get rid of, give away, keep under control, take away, throw away*
Recycled language	words: *dangerous, law, lift, prefer, roof, steal* phrases: *clean up* grammar: *superlatives*
Discourse	giving explanations with *because*

End product

In *Put it all together*, students talk about laws they know about in their own country. They give short explanations and invite confirmation. Their conversations are based on audio script **5B.1**.

Preparation

Think about classroom organization so students can work in groups for exercise 6 and 17. Take dictionaries to class if necessary.

Warmer

Show or draw a simple sketch of a mobile phone on the board. Draw two columns, one with a tick and the other with a cross. Ask students to write a list of laws they would like to see for the use of mobile phones. Put students into small groups and set a short time limit. Ask for a spokesperson to read out the group list. Monitor and make notes of students' use of modal verbs. Ask the class to vote on the best law, and nominate individuals to say why.

Write *How to talk about rules and laws* on the board.

A Vocabulary permission words

1 Read the instructions and put students into pairs to talk about the topic. Monitor and join in with conversations. Help students express their ideas but do not overcorrect for accuracy. Ask for volunteers to tell the class anything interesting they found out about their partner.

2 Direct students to *Signs* on >> **p.48**. Ask what they can see in each picture and where they might see the sign (ignore the captions for the moment). Ask students to look at the dictionary entries and check they understand the abbreviations *sb* (somebody) and *sth* (something).

Go through each picture and ask the class for suggestions.

> **Suggested answers**
> 1 Feeding the birds is forbidden.   2 You are permitted / allowed to continue, but you should be careful.   3 Dogs are forbidden/prohibited.

3 Direct students to the dictionary entries on >> **p.48** and read through the definitions. Direct students to the table and check they understand the concept of formality. Ask about how people speak or write to others: friends, family, colleagues, a boss, an important person. Point out the headings of the two columns. Do the activity as a class.

> **you can do it:** permit   **you can't do it:** forbid, prohibit

Extra help

Ask students to say which of these pairs of contexts would contain formal language: *a parent talking to a child or an official document; a sign or a postcard; a Sunday magazine or a law; government website or a friendly email.*

4 Read the instructions and ask students to read sentences 1–4. Check vocabulary as necessary and ask students to suggest where the signs might be found (*government buildings, schools, clubs, restaurants*). Go through the example as a class, pointing out the use of *isn't*. Monitor and help as necessary as students write the sentences. Go over answers as a class.

> 2 Parking isn't permitted.   3 Mobile phones are forbidden.
> 4 Taking photographs is prohibited.

B Read and interpret

In this section, students think about the reasons behind various facts in a magazine article.

5 Direct students to *Laws for Paws* on >> **p.48**. Ask them to look at the title, headline and pictures and suggest what the text is about. Check they understand that, in this context, a law is nationally binding (rather than a rule for a particular place). Go through the instructions and descriptions a–c and set a short time limit to encourage students to read the text quickly. Read each description and ask for a show of hands. Nominate a few students to explain their reasons.

> b Option a isn't the best as the text isn't about **all** animals in the USA. Option c isn't the best as the text only mentions **some** laws, those which are funny.

6 Give students time to read the text in more detail before putting them into pairs to compare ideas. Direct students to the glossary on >> p.48 and remind them to use their dictionaries to help with key words only. Students exchange opinions in groups of four. Monitor and encourage quieter students to join in.

7 Go through the instructions and the example conversation. Elicit other possible explanations. Put students into pairs to continue and check students' explanations are logically connected to the topic. After a few minutes, nominate students to share ideas with the class.

Extra plus
Students can discuss which rules they agree with (why and why not) in groups or as a class.

C Grammar modals of obligation

8 Elicit the law about dogs and hairdressers and write *You mustn't take your dog into a barber's.* on the board. Ask *Have you got a choice? What will happen if you do?* Read the instructions. Monitor and help as students continue the activity individually. Do not focus on the meaning of these modals as students will talk about this in the next activity.

9 Ask students to look at statements 1–6 and check vocabulary. Go through the example to demonstrate the activity. Point out that students can find the information in the text by using key words in the question and they can use the pictures to help locate the answer. They should then read more carefully. Monitor and check they are using appropriate reading strategies, and offer guidance as necessary. Nominate students to give answers and see if the class agrees.

2 False. (You have no choice. You *mustn't* take your dog in a lift.)
3 False. (You *can* walk your dog as long as the lead is short.)
4 True.   5 True.   6 False. (You can (if you want) kill one before 2 a.m. but you must kill it after 2 a.m.)

10 Direct students to the grammar box and read the instructions. Refer students back to their answers in exercise 9 and *Laws for Paws* on >> p.48. Do the exercise as a whole class.

forbidden: mustn't; can't   **an obligation:** must; have to
not an obligation: don't have to

11 Go through the instructions and ask students to read rules 1–7. Do the first item as a class. Students continue individually. Monitor and direct students back to the grammar box as necessary. Elicit answers and encourage students to say full sentences when they answer.

2 don't have to   3 have to   4 must   5 can   6 have to   7 can

Extra help
Students write out the correct version of the rules.

Extra plus
Students use their dictionaries and write sentences about rules in their country. Some should be true, others false. They read them in small groups for the others to guess *true* or *false.*

D Listen for the general idea

In this section, students identify the main idea of a conversation, before listening for detail.

12 5B.1 Read the section title and instructions for the activity. Ask students how they need to listen to understand the general idea. *(Listen for key words and phrases in the questions.)*

Check students understand vocabulary in questions 1–4 and ask them to underline key words and phrases to listen for. Play the audio. Ask students to compare answers and play the audio

a second time if necessary. Give the answer and ask students how they guessed.

2 (key words in question: throw away; key words in audio: rubbish bins, take it away)

13 Check students understand the questions before you play the audio again. Put students into pairs to compare answers before going over them as a class.

1 You can't do that, it isn't allowed.   2 No.   3 The shop where he bought a new fridge took the old one away.

14 Read the instructions and direct students to audio script 5B.1 on >> p.153.

Extra activity
Students use audio script 5B.1 on >> p.153 to practise using the phrases. They swap roles.

15 Go through the instructions and check students understand. Ask for volunteers to ask you the questions in exercise 12. Respond using some of the phrases from the listening to show you're not sure. Students continue in pairs. Give positive feedback when students use appropriate phrases.

Extra activity
Write these questions on the board: *Are there laws about: taking children in cars and wearing seat-belts? Can cyclists ride side by side?* Students discuss in pairs.

ABCD Put it all together

16 Put students into pairs to discuss the topic. Encourage them to use the ideas in *Laws for Paws* and exercises 11 and 12. They can make notes, and should add explanations for the laws. Refer them back to exercise 7 for further help with explanations, if necessary. Monitor and help with ideas.

17 Reorganize students into small groups and so they are not working with the same partner from exercise 16. Tell students to explain the laws to others, saying when they are uncertain of their reasons. Ask a spokesperson from each group to give an example of a useful law to tell a visitor and why.

Student performance
Students should be able to make short factual statements and give explanations.

You can use this checklist to monitor and give feedback or to assess students' performance.

Coherence	Do students give logical explanations for the laws? exercise 7
Grammar	Do students use a variety of modals to talk about obligation? exercise 11
Vocabulary	Do students use phrases to indicate they are unsure? exercise 15

I can talk about rules and laws.
Students tick *on my own* if they have given rules and explanations looking up from their notes a couple of times. They tick *with some help* if they have mostly looked at their notes.

Early finishers
Students rank *Laws for Paws* from the point of view of a visitor, starting with the most useful ones. They compare with a partner.

Additional material

www.oup.com/elt/result for extra practice activities
www.oup.com/elt/teacher/result for extra teacher resources

How to talk about rules and laws

G modals of obligation   v permission words

A Vocabulary permission words

1   Do you have a pet, or have you had one in the past? Tell your partner about it.

2   Read **Signs** opposite. What do they mean? Use the dictionary definitions.

3   Write the verbs from the dictionary definitions in **Signs** in the box.

	you can do it	you can't do it
less formal	allow	
more formal		

4   Write a sentence with the same meaning using the word in green.
   1   Smoking is forbidden. allowed   *Smoking isn't allowed.*
   2   Parking is prohibited. permitted
   3   Mobile phones aren't allowed. forbidden
   4   Taking photographs is not permitted. prohibited

B Read and interpret

5   Read **Laws for Paws** opposite quickly. What is the best description of the topic of the text?
   a   animals in the USA
   b   funny animal laws
   c   laws connected with pets

6   Read the text again and decide with a partner which law is the strangest and the funniest. Compare your ideas with other pairs.

7   Can you think of explanations for the laws? Discuss with a partner.
   Example   A   Why do you think dogs are forbidden in hairdressers'?
                 B   Maybe it's because they aren't clean ...

C Grammar modals of obligation

8   Underline examples in **Laws for Paws** of *must, mustn't, have to, don't have to, can,* and *can't.*

9   Write *true* or *false*. If the sentence is false, say why.
   1   You can leave your dog outside the barber's if you prefer. *False. You haven't got a choice – you have to leave your dog outside.*
   2   You don't have to take your dog in a lift in Glendale.
   3   You mustn't walk your dog in Waterboro.
   4   The lead has to be shorter than 8 feet.
   5   You can't take a skunk into Tennessee.
   6   You must kill a racoon if you see it before 2 a.m.

10   What can you use the modal verbs for? Write them in the grammar box.

to say it's allowed	to say it's forbidden	to say it's an obligation	to say it's not an obligation
can			

11   Work with a partner and guess what the rules are. Underline the best modal verb.
   Dog Ownership in Britain ...
   1   Your dog's collar must/can't have your name and address on it.
   2   You mustn't/don't have to have a dog licence.
   3   You have to/can clean up after your dog.
   4   Dogs can/must be kept under control on main roads.
   5   Farmers can/must shoot a dog if it chases their cows.
   6   If you have a guard dog, you have to/don't have to put up a warning sign.
   7   Blind people must/can take guide dogs on buses.

   More practice? **Grammar Bank** >> p.140.

D Listen for the general idea

12   5B.1▶ Listen to two friends, Jeff and Sally, talking about one of the questions below. Which question are they talking about?
   1   Can you light a fire in your garden?
   2   Can you throw an old fridge away?
   3   Do you have to buy a licence for a TV?
   4   Do you have to wear a seat belt on a bus?

13   Listen again and answer the questions.
   1   What is Jeff's answer to the question in exercise 12?
   2   Is he sure about it?
   3   What happened when he had the same problem?

14   Look at the audio script on >> p.153. Underline the phrases Jeff uses to show that he isn't sure.
   Example   it isn't allowed, is it?

15   What do you think the correct answers are for the questions in exercise 12 in Britain or your country? Discuss with a partner. If you aren't sure, use some of the phrases you underlined in exercise 14.

ABCD Put it all together

16   Do you know any laws that people coming to live in your country should know? Discuss with a partner.

17   Work in small groups. Explain the laws to the others. Who talked about the most useful laws for a visitor?

I can talk about rules and laws.

Tick ✓ the line.   with a lot of help   with some help   on my own   very easily

Captions

SOME STOLEN EARRINGS HAVE BEEN FOUND BY A TREE

A MAN HAS BEEN ATTACKED BY A CASH MACHINE

A WOMAN HAS SHOT A ROBBER WITH A BASEBALL BAT

COW CABS AGAINST CRIME

CHILE – Juan Geraldo has not been robbed since he disguised his car as a cow.

Juan, a 46-year-old taxi driver from Santiago, is tired of being robbed. He has been attacked four times already. The first time, his car was stolen and he was thrown naked into a blackberry bush. The last time, he was attacked with a knife and just managed to drive himself to hospital.

Mr Geraldo got the idea to customize his vehicle from a TV advert showing a sports car lined with cowhide. He went out, bought a roll of cowhide material and covered the inside of his taxi from floor to ceiling. He even covered the steering wheel and changed the sound of his car horn to a cow moo.

The taxi looks very strange, but it is even more impressive at night. Mr

A taxi like this is going to be noticed

Mr Geraldo was thrown naked into a blackberry bush

Geraldo put neon lights on the ceiling, so you can clearly see the black and white cowhide in the bright light as it goes along the street. To complete the picture, Mr Geraldo wears a cowhide jacket and hat.

A taxi like this will be noticed and remembered, and that's exactly the idea. Now, when robbers get in, they get straight out again. 'They don't want to rob me because they'll be seen by everybody,' says Mr Geraldo. Customers like it too, and 80% of Juan's clients are women who

feel safer in the brightly lit cow cabs.

Many customers who call for a cab specifically ask for a cow cab. These clients include government ministers, TV celebrities, and parents organizing birthday parties for their children. They are so popular that Mr Geraldo's business has grown, and now he has seven cow cabs. What's next? Mr Geraldo is keen to develop his idea and is already thinking of making a zebra cab or a lion cab. 'It's a question of using your imagination,' he says.

How to talk about stories in the news

Orientation

Context

In this lesson, students use the passive to talk about events in which the object of an action is more important than the subject.

The style of British newspaper headlines sometimes results in a text with two meanings. The illustrations in *Captions* show the wrong meaning of typical ambiguities caused by prepositional phrases.

The newspaper article, *Cow Cabs Against Crime*, reports the story of how a Chilean taxi driver decorated his taxi so everyone would notice it. His purpose was to deter potential robbers.

Culture note

Newspapers have different journalistic styles for headlines in different countries. In British newspapers, journalists aim to make their headlines as short as possible. They achieve this by deleting non-essential grammatical words like articles and auxiliary verbs, which sometimes create amusing ambiguities.

Language

Focus grammar	active or passive: *A woman has shot a robber.*, *A robber has been shot by a woman.*
Focus words	crime verbs: *arrest, attack, criminal, escape, hijack, kidnap, kill, murder, rob, shoot, steal, thief, victim*
Focus phrases	prepositional phrases: *by a cash machine, by a tree, with a baseball bat*
Recognition vocabulary	words: *alarms, cab, cow (moo), cowhide, customize, earrings, imagination, impressive, lined, naked, neon lights, specifically, steering wheel, valuable, youths, zebra* phrases: *switch off*
Recycled language	words: *already, celebrities, ceiling, cover, customers, delete, gallery, guards, managed, worth* grammar: *past simple and present perfect*
Pronunciation	compound nouns: *sports car* ● ●, *baseball bat* ● ● ●, *birthday party* ● ● ● ● 5C.1

End product

In *Put it all together*, students role play being a radio news reporter and give the latest news report for one story. This is based on audio script 5C.2.

Preparation

Think about classroom organization for exercise 14. Take dictionaries to class.

Warmer

Write the following words on the board: *attack, baseball bat, cash machine, earrings, found, robber, police officer, shot, thief, tree.* Put students into small groups and set a time limit of about four minutes for them to write a story using as many of the words as they can. A spokesperson from each group tells their story to the class. Ask students where they might find stories like these. *(In newspapers or on the radio.)*

Write *How to talk about stories in the news* on the board.

A Vocabulary crime verbs

1 Read the questions and put students into pairs or small groups to exchange information. Write the following cues on the board: *Read – every page, some articles, some sections?* Monitor and join in the discussions before bringing the class together to exchange information.

2 Go through the instructions and direct students to sentences 1–4 and the three verbs. Explain that these verbs have similar meanings and ask students to look them up in their dictionaries. Go over the example with the class and put students into pairs to continue the activity. Check answers and elicit or explain that we use *rob* when people steal something in a violent way.

Continue section by section. In sentences 5–7, elicit or explain that *murder* is used to describe a planned action. Model and give pronunciation practice as necessary.

> 2 attacked   3 stole   4 robbed   5 murdered/killed
> 6 killed/shot   7 shot   8 kidnapped   9 hijack   10 arrested

3 Read the instructions for the activity. Direct students to *Captions* on >> **p.50** and the caption below the first picture. Go through the example as a class. Elicit or tell students that the phrase *by a tree* could either mean that the tree is the subject of the verb *find*, or *by* could mean *near*.

Check vocabulary in the captions. Students continue the activity in pairs. Monitor and help as necessary. Check answers.

> 2 The cash machine didn't attack the man. The man was near the cash machine when he was attacked.
> 3 The woman didn't use the baseball bat to shoot the robber. The robber was carrying the baseball bat.

B Read for detail

In this section, students anticipate the content of a newspaper article, using the photo and headline, before reading and inferring information.

4 Read the instructions and direct students to the photos and headline on >> **p.50**. Put students into pairs to answer the question. Ask for volunteers to report their suggestions and to give a reason. Take a vote on the most popular or entertaining suggestions but do not comment at this stage.

5 Read the question and check understanding. Tell students to read the article carefully, ignoring any new vocabulary.

> Geraldo's life has improved because he hasn't been attacked again, his business has grown and he now has seven cabs.

6 Ask students to read sentences 1–6 and check vocabulary as necessary. Do the first item together to demonstrate that sometimes students need to think carefully about what *isn't* said in the text, e.g. the text doesn't say anything about his car being stolen, but it does say *he drove himself ...*

Monitor and help as students continue individually. Go through the answers as a class, asking for reasons why if a statement is false. Take a vote on how many students think Geraldo's idea is a good one, and if they would use his taxi service.

> 2 True.   3 True.   4 False. (He put them on the ceiling.)   5 True.
> 6 False. (He's thinking of making one in the future.)

Extra activity

Students find words in the text with the following meanings: *with no clothes on (naked, para 1); change or decorate your own car (customize, para 2); covered on the inside (lined, para 2); amazing (impressive, para 3).* They choose five more unknown words to guess the meaning of, checking in a dictionary.

Extra plus

Discussion topic. *Robbers won't rob you if everybody's looking.* Work with a partner and think of some other ways a taxi driver could make everybody look.

C Pronunciation compound nouns

7 5C.1 Direct students to the words above the box and elicit or explain that they are all compound nouns (two nouns which, when used together, refer to one particular thing). Check students understand the meaning of the compound nouns.

Copy the stress patterns onto the board and number the columns 1, 2, and 3. Read the instructions and play and pause the audio after each one for students to say which stress pattern it is.

Play the audio a second time, pausing for students to repeat. Encourage students to run the two words together and give extra pronunciation practice as necessary.

1 earrings, headline, sports car   2 cash machine, steering wheel
3 birthday party, taxi driver

8 Read the information and ask students where the main stress falls. *(On the first syllable.)* Explain that, in compound nouns, the stress is normally on the first word. However, if the first word in a compound noun is the material, e.g. *straw hat, neon light* then both words are stressed.

Extra activity

In pairs, students say the number of a column for a partner to say a compound noun with the corresponding stress pattern. Students swap roles.

D Grammar active or passive?

9 Read the section title and the instructions. Ask students to underline the verbs *attack, steal,* and *throw* in the first paragraph of *Cow Cabs Against Crime* on >> p.50. Write the following sentences from the text on the board: *He has been attacked four times already. His car was stolen. He was thrown into a blackberry bush.* Go through questions 1 and 2 as a class.

1 attack – robbers; steal – robbers; throw – robbers
2 a (*He* is in subject position, even though he's the object of each of the verbs.)

10 Read the instructions and do the example as a class. Elicit or explain that the bike is in subject position in the sentence. It didn't do the action (steal) so we use the passive.

Ask students to read sentences 2–6 and check vocabulary. Monitor and help as necessary as students continue individually. Nominate students to read the whole sentence as you go over the answers. Check students understand why the tense is used in each sentence.

2 robbed   3 have arrested   4 was taken   5 has been hijacked
6 was killed

Extra help

Transformation drill. Use the information in exercise 2. Make cues for students to say or write sentences using the active and passive. *T man/rob/lady* **SS** *A man robbed a lady.* *T A lady* **SS** *A lady was robbed by a man.* etc.

11 Go through the instructions. Read the first part of the text aloud and then ask students to read the nouns and verbs. Check vocabulary as necessary. Direct students to the example and elicit one or two example sentences to check students understand the activity. Put students into pairs to continue and monitor and help as necessary.

Read the second sentence, beginning *Some news ...* and elicit the final sentence of the news report.

12 5C.2 Read the instructions and play the audio. Play the audio a second time if necessary. Ask for volunteers to tell the class about any differences in their story and the audio. Point out that the story should include the following information: when and where the event happened, who was involved, how it happened and include details.

Extra help

In pairs, students take turns to role play being a radio presenter and read the news report.

Extra plus

Books closed. Students role play being a radio presenter and tell the story to another partner.

ABCD Put it all together

13 Go through the instructions and put students into pairs. Direct them to the headlines on >> p.128 and check any vocabulary. Read the questions and check students understand the activity. Monitor and help with ideas as necessary. Encourage students to practise telling their stories to each other.

14 Put students with a new partner or into groups to tell their stories. Ask students to tell the class about interesting news stories they were told.

Student performance

Students should be able to tell a short narrative.

You can use this checklist to monitor and give feedback or to assess students' performance.

Content	Do students give all the main points of the story? exercise 12
Grammar	Do students mostly use the passive appropriately? exercise 11
Vocabulary	Do students have enough vocabulary to do the activity? exercise 2

I can talk about stories in the news.

Students tick *on my own* if they have told their story using their notes. They tick *with some help* if they have paused on several occasions to think about vocabulary.

Early finishers

Students choose a different story from *Headlines* on >> p.128. They make notes and then take turns to tell a partner. Partners count how many times they hear the passive.

Additional material

www.oup.com/elt/result for extra practice activities
www.oup.com/elt/teacher/result for extra teacher resources

How to talk about stories in the news

G active or passive?   v crime verbs   P compound nouns

A   Vocabulary   crime verbs

1   When and how often do you read newspapers? What type of stories do you read? Tell a partner.

2   Choose the best verbs to complete the sentences.

steal   rob   attack

1   A young man *robbed* an old lady.
2   A dog _____ the postman.
3   A thief _____ my bicycle.
4   Three men _____ the bank.

shoot   murder   kill

5   The man _____ the victim with a knife.
6   Police _____ the escaping criminal.
7   He _____ himself in the foot.

kidnap   hijack   arrest

8   Some criminals have _____ a politician.
9   Three men tried to _____ a plane.
10 Police _____ the three men.

3   The **Captions** opposite have two meanings. The pictures show the wrong meaning. What do you think the correct meaning is? Compare with a partner.

Example   The tree didn't find the earrings. The stolen earrings were found *next to* the tree.

B   Read for detail

4   Look at the headline and photos in **Cow Cabs Against Crime** opposite, but don't read the text. What do you think it will be about? Tell a partner.

5   Read the article. How has Juan Geraldo's life improved since he made his first cow cab?

6   Write *true* or *false*. If the sentence is false, say why.

1   The last time Juan was attacked, his car was stolen.
    False. He drove himself to hospital.
2   He first saw a cow taxi on a TV advert.
3   His taxi horn makes the same noise as a cow.
4   He put neon lights on the outside of the car.
5   Robbers don't attack because everybody notices the taxi.
6   Juan has also made a zebra cab.

C   Pronunciation   compound nouns

7   **5C.1▶** Listen and write these words in the box according to the stress pattern. Then practise saying the words.

~~baseball bat~~   birthday party   cash machine   earrings
headline   sports car   steering wheel   taxi driver

● ●	
● ● ●	baseball bat
● ● ● ●	

8   Nouns made from two shorter nouns are compound nouns. What is the stress rule for these words?

D   Grammar   active or passive?

9   Look at the first paragraph of **Cow Cabs Against Crime** and underline these verbs. Then answer the questions.

attack   steal   throw

1   Who did these actions – Juan or the robbers?
2   Why did the writer put these verbs in the passive?
    a   To put the focus on Juan, not the robbers.
    b   To put the focus on the robbers, not Juan.

10 Active or passive? Underline the correct form of the verb.

1   Oh no! My bike has stolen/has been stolen.
2   While Jade was walking home, a young man robbed/was robbed her.
3   After a fight, the police have arrested/have been arrested three youths.
4   Someone broke into Harry's flat, but nothing took/was taken.
5   A flight to Paris has hijacked/has been hijacked.
6   There was a train crash yesterday, but fortunately nobody killed/was killed.

11 Work with a partner. What happened in this story? Make sentences from the nouns and verbs.

Example   The door was left open.

A Renoir painting worth three million euros has been stolen from the National Gallery. Police believe it was done with the help of someone who works in the gallery …
door / leave open   alarms / switch off
security guards / drug
film from security cameras / delete
less valuable paintings / not take

Some news is just coming in. We've just been informed that …
painting / find in Hong Kong   three men / arrest

12 **5C.2▶** Listen to the radio report of the story. Are there any differences from your version of the story in exercise 11? More practice? **Grammar Bank** >> p.140.

ABCD   Put it all together

13 Work with a partner. Choose a true story from the news or one of the **Headlines** on >> p.128 and invent the story. Write notes to answer the questions.

14 Work with a new partner or group. Tell your news story. Which story is the most interesting?

I can talk about stories in the news.

Tick ✓ the line.   with a lot of help   with some help   on my own   very easily

Mystery in the Tower

The princes disappear

On 9th April, 1483, King Edward IV of England died. He had two sons – Edward, aged 12 and Richard, aged 9. The boys' uncle, also called Richard, was asked to look after them and govern the country until Edward was old enough to be king. This never happened. Uncle Richard put the princes in the Tower of London to 'protect' them, and they were never seen again. They simply disappeared. Meanwhile, their uncle took power and became King Richard III of England.

Richard III is killed

So what happened to the princes? Nobody knows. But later that year, the stories began. People said that Richard had murdered the boys. A lot of people were against Richard and rebelled. Richard's enemy, Henry Tudor, had spent some time in France, but now he returned to England and the rebels joined him. On August 22nd, 1485, their two armies fought at the battle of Bosworth Field. King Richard was killed and Henry became King Henry VII of England.

A forced confession?

Were the boys really dead? Many people thought they were still alive, and perhaps Edward could become king. But King Henry was quite clear: Richard had killed them. In 1502, Richard's friend, Sir James Tyrell, confessed. He had murdered the boys on Richard's orders – although he didn't say what had happened to their bodies.

History is written

In 1674, the bones of two children were found under the stairs of the church in the Tower of London. Now it seemed clear: Richard III had ordered Sir James to kill the princes in the Tower and put their bodies under the stairs. In Shakespeare's play, *Richard III*, Richard was an evil monster, a murderer with a deformed body. The most famous painting from that time shows that Richard had one shoulder bigger than the other. At that time, people thought that a deformed body was a sign of an evil mind. And so history was written. The story was complete. Or was it?

King Edward —— *brother* — Richard — *enemy* — Henry
IV   Tudor

Prince   Prince
Edward   Richard
(12)   (9)

GLOSSARY

army *n* /'ɑːmi/ very large organized group of soldiers
battle *n* /'bætl/ fight between two armies
confess *vb* /kən'fes/ to say 'I did the crime'
deformed *adj* /dɪ'fɔːmd/ not the normal shape
enemy *n* /'enəmi/ opposite of friend
evil *adj* /'iːvl/ very bad
protect *vb* /prə'tekt/ keep safe
rebel *vb* /rɪ'bel/ fight against the government
rebel *n* /'rebl/ a person who fights against the government

How to talk about past events

Orientation

Context

In this lesson, students practise using the past perfect and past simple to connect past events in a narrative.

The illustrated text, *Mystery in the Tower*, recounts the main events surrounding the murder of two young English princes around the late 15th century. The murderers still haven't been identified.

Glossary gives the meanings of some key words.

Language

Focus grammar	past perfect: *Richard had killed them., He hadn't killed them., Had he killed them?*
Focus words	war and power: *army, battle, confess, enemy, govern, protect, rebel (n, v), take power*
Recognition vocabulary	*belonged, bones, deformed, evil, forced, historian, monster, orders, rebellion, solved, torture, ugly*
Recycled language	words: *answer, happen, kill, king, murder, power, prince, shoulder, stairs, uncle* grammar: *past passive*
Pronunciation	stress in two-syllable nouns and verbs: *battle* ● •, *become* • ●

Language note

In two-syllable nouns, the stress is usually on the first syllable. In two-syllable verbs, it falls on the second syllable. This is demonstrated with *rebel*, which can be both noun and verb. This is a useful pattern to use to predict the pronunciation of new words. However, there are exceptions, e.g. *murder, happen, answer* which occur in *Mystery in the Tower*.

End product

In *Put it all together*, students work with a partner to tell a story from picture prompts and notes. They have discussed the contents of the story during the lesson.

Preparation

Think about significant dates of past events which could include local events, e.g. the end of term or an exam to include in the *Warmer*. Read *Mystery in the Tower* and audio script **5D.1** so you are familiar with the story.

Warmer

Write some significant dates on the board (or you could use the following significant English historical dates: *1066 – the French invade England, 1564 – William Shakespeare born, 1605 – the Gun Powder Plot, 1912 – the Titanic sinks, 1919 – first flight across the Atlantic*). Put students into pairs or small groups to see if they can name the event.

Write *How to talk about past events* on the board.

A Read and understand reasons

In this section, students think about the content of a history text using visuals, before interpreting detail.

1 Read the instructions. Students discuss important historical dates in pairs. Ask for volunteers to say dates people talk about in their country for the class to guess the event.

2 Direct students to the pictures in *Mystery in the Tower* on **>> p.52**. Elicit ideas about the content of the text and write key words on the board.

3 Go through the instructions. Elicit or explain that the section headings in the exercise are the same as those in the text on **>> p.52**. Tell students to read questions 1–8 and check vocabulary.

Ask students to read questions 1 and 2 again, before reading the corresponding part of the text to find the answers. Do the first question together as a class, and direct students to the family tree at the bottom of **>> p.52**.

Go over answers at the end of each part. Monitor for the use of the past perfect, but do not correct for accuracy at this stage.

> **Possible answers**
> 1 They were brothers. Their father was King Edward and their uncle (father's brother) was Richard.
> 2 He was too young; he disappeared; Richard took power.
> 3 They thought he was a murderer.
> 4 He killed King Richard.
> 5 No, some thought they were alive.
> 6 Sir James Tyrell confessed. He murdered the boys on Richard's orders.
> 7 Students' own answers.
> 8 People thought a deformed body was a sign of an evil mind. More evidence that Richard was the murderer!

Extra activity

Write the following key dates on the board: 1483, 1485, and 1502. Ask students what happened and write notes on the board. (*King Edward IV died and Richard governs the country. Richard was killed and Henry VII became King of England. Sir James Tyrell confessed to murder.*)

B Pronunciation stress in two-syllable nouns and verbs

4 Read the section heading and instructions. Direct students to the words above the box and the glossary on **>> p. 52**. Point out that the word *rebel* is a noun and a verb. Draw two columns and the stress patterns and examples on the board.

Monitor and help by modelling the words as students continue individually. Check answers.

> ● • body, happen, power, rebel (n), shoulder
> • ● complete, confess, protect, rebel (v), return

5 Read the instructions and do the activity together as a class. Go over the answers and point out that the rule is a general one. There are some exceptions.

> The words with ● • pattern are nouns. The others are verbs. The first syllable is usually stressed in nouns. The second syllable is usually stressed in verbs. *Happen* breaks the rule.

Extra help

Do a minimal pair drill with *rebel* (n and v). Face the class and say *'rebel* (n) several times and then *re'bel* (v) as a verb. Say each word alternately to help students hear the difference. Turn your back to the class and change the pronunciation at random. Students say *noun* or *verb*. They continue in pairs.

Extra plus

Students take turns to say a word from exercise 4. Their partner says if they heard the correct pronunciation.

C Predict before you listen

In this section, students anticipate the content of a radio interview before listening to check.

6   Go through the instructions and ask students to read questions 1–5. Check vocabulary as necessary. Do the first item together as class. Monitor and join in, as students continue in pairs. Encourage students to give reasons for their answers.

> **Suggested answers**
> 1 They supported Richard's enemy, Henry.
> 2 To protect Richard.
> 3 No, only the bones were found.
> 4 According to the text, yes.
> 5 Students' own answers.

7   5D.1 Read the instructions and play Part 1 of the audio. Ask students about their predictions for question 1 in exercise 6. Play Part 2 of the audio and ask about students' predictions for questions 2 and 3. Play part 3 of the audio and check predictions for questions 4 and 5. Ask students who they think killed the princes. *Richard, Henry, or Sir James Tyrell?*

Teaching tip

Give students positive feedback and explain that by thinking about what they will hear before they listen, they have managed to understand the main detail in a difficult text. Point out that doing this will help them become more successful listeners.

Extra activity

Direct students to read audio script 5D.1 on >> p.153–54 and play the audio again. Ask students to underline the parts of the interview they guessed before they listened to it for exercise 7.

D Grammar past perfect

8   Copy the time line onto the board and go through the exercise with the class. Read sentences 1 and 2, and elicit or explain that both sentences could be true, depending on who killed the princes. Ask *Who killed the princes in sentence 1? (Henry.) And sentence 2? (Richard.)* Guide students to match sentences 1 and 2 with times A and B and check they understand the answers.

> 1 B   2 A

9   Go through the exercise with the class, to check they understand the sequence of events. Elicit or explain that we use *had + past participle* to show that one event happened before another in the past.

> 1 a then b   2 b then a

10 Direct students to the grammar box and write *He had killed them.* on the board. Underline *had* and *killed*. Tell students that this tense is called the past perfect. Elicit the negative and question forms and write these on the board for students to copy into the grammar box.

> – He **didn't kill** them.   ? **Had** he **killed** them?

11 Ask students to find six examples of the past perfect in *Mystery in the Tower.* Students can compare in pairs before you go over answers. Nominate students to read the sentences and monitor for accuracy of form.

Extra help

Ask *yes/no* questions to check students are clear about the form, e.g. *Do we use the past of the auxiliary* have *to make the past perfect? Do we make the question for the past perfect with the past of do? Do we use the negative after the auxiliary* had? *Do we use the past tense of the main verb?*

12 Read the instructions and ask students to read sentences 1–6. Check vocabulary as necessary. Do item one together as a class, reminding students to look at *Irregular verbs* on >> **p.148** to check past participles. Monitor and help as necessary as students continue individually.

Put students into pairs to compare their answers. Nominate individuals to give answers and to read the complete sentence. See if the class agrees before giving feedback.

> 1 had killed   2 killed, took   3 put, had died   4 died, put
> 5 began, had spent   6 examined, had changed

Extra help

Students choose three items and copy the sentences. They draw a time line (see exercise 8) for each item and mark the events.

Extra plus

Students use the facts in *Mystery in the Tower*, to make three similar items for a partner.

ABCD Put it all together

13 Go through the instructions and check students understand. Go through the example with the class and elicit the end of the sentence. Give students time to make some notes about each of the pictures and monitor and help as necessary.

Put students into pairs to continue the activity. Monitor and check students swap roles.

Student performance

Students should be able to present a short part of a narrative.

You can use this checklist to monitor and give feedback or to assess students' performance.

Content	Do students give two or three facts about each picture? exercise 3
Grammar	Do students use the past perfect occasionally? exercise 12
Vocabulary	Do students have enough vocabulary to do the task? exercise 3

I can talk about past events.

Students tick *on my own* if they have talked about the pictures using their notes. They tick *with some help* if they have looked at the sentences in exercise 12 for help.

Early finishers

Students take turns to tell the whole story of *Mystery in the Tower* using their notes.

Additional material

www.oup.com/elt/result for extra practice activities
www.oup.com/elt/teacher/result for extra teacher resources

How to talk about past events

A Read and understand reasons

1 What dates or events in history do people in your country usually remember from school? Tell a partner.
Example Columbus crossed the Atlantic in 1492.

2 Look at the pictures in **Mystery in the Tower** opposite. What do you think the mystery was?

3 Read **Mystery in the Tower** and discuss the questions after each part.

The princes disappear
1 There are two Edwards and two Richards. How are they all related to each other?
2 Why didn't Prince Edward become king?

Richard III is killed
3 Why were people against Richard?
4 How did Henry become king?

A forced confession?
5 Was everybody sure that the princes were dead?
6 In 1502, people thought the mystery was solved. Why?

History is written
7 Who do you think the bones belonged to?
8 The picture showed Richard was deformed. Why was that important?

B Pronunciation stress in two-syllable nouns and verbs

4 All of these words have two syllables. Put them in the correct box. Use the glossary to help with new words.

~~battle~~ ~~become~~ body complete confess happen
power protect rebel *n* rebel *vb* return shoulder

| ● ● | *battle* |
| ● ● | *become* |

5 Are the words in exercise 4 nouns or verbs? What is the general rule? Which word breaks the rule?

C Predict before you listen

6 You will hear a historian talking about the murder of the princes. Predict his answers to these questions.
1 The people who first wrote about the princes in the tower were against Richard. Why?
2 Why did Sir James confess?
3 Do we *really* know what happened to the bodies?
4 The painting shows Richard was deformed. But was he really?
5 Who really killed the princes in the Tower?

7 **5D.1▶** Listen to the programme in three parts. After each part, discuss if your predictions were correct.

D Grammar past perfect

8 Look at the diagram. Match the sentences below with A and B on the time line.

1483 Richard took power.   1485 Henry took power.

1 ☐ When Henry took power, he killed the princes.
2 ☐ When Henry took power, Richard had killed the princes.

9 Answer the questions about the sentences in exercise 8.
In sentence 1, which happened first?
a Henry took power.
b The princes died.

In sentence 2, which happened first?

10 Complete the grammar box.

+	–	?
He had killed them.	He _____ _____ them.	_____ he _____ them?

11 Underline six examples of the past perfect in **Mystery in the Tower**.

12 Put the verbs in brackets in the past simple or past perfect. Compare with a partner.
1 Henry _took_ (take) power in 1485. His army _____ (kill) Richard in battle.
2 Henry's army _____ (kill) Richard in battle and _____ (take) power.
3 Richard _____ (put) the boys in the Tower in June. Their father _____ (die) in April.
4 Edward IV _____ (die) in 1483 and Richard _____ (put) his two sons in the Tower.
5 Before the rebellion _____ (begin), Henry _____ (spend) some time in France.
6 Experts _____ (examine) the painting with X-rays. They discovered that somebody _____ (change) it.

More practice? **Grammar Bank ≫** p.140.

ABCD Put it all together

13 Work with a partner. Tell the **Mystery in the Tower** story together. Use the pictures to help you.
Example This painting shows the two princes, Edward and Richard, in the Tower. They were put there by …

I can talk about past events. ▬▬▬▬▬▬

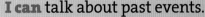

Tick ✓ the line.   with a lot of help   with some help   on my own   very easily   53

Writing Narrating a story

A Read and identify narrative strategies

1 Why do people read books? Compare with a partner.
Example To find information ...

2 Read this story. What is the purpose of the text? Choose the best answer.
   a To give information to the reader.
   b To explain something to the reader.
   c To entertain the reader.

It was the worst possible moment for my mobile to start ringing.

There was a burglar in the building and I was hiding behind the photocopier. I'd been working late and I was the last person in the office. When I heard the breaking glass, I knew immediately what was happening. I quickly found a dark corner and hid.

Then my phone rang and I heard the burglar stop. He was listening. Then he started walking towards the photocopier! I looked around me for a weapon, but I could only find a ball-point pen. It was blue, I think.

Then he called my name. 'Is that you, Jo?' he asked. It was Tom, my boss. He'd left his keys on his desk and he couldn't get into his house.

3 Put the events in the order they actually happened.
   ☐ Jo heard breaking glass.
   ☐ Jo hid.
   1 Tom left his keys on his desk.
   ☐ Jo thought it was a burglar.
   ☐ Jo worked late.
   ☐ Tom asked, 'Is that you, Jo?'
   ☐ Jo's mobile rang.

4 Here is another version of the story in exercise 2. Think of three reasons why it is less interesting.

Tom left his keys in the office and went back to get them. Jo was working late and thought Tom was a burglar.

5 Work with a partner. Find examples of the strategies below in the text in exercise 2.
Narrative strategies
   1 Start in the middle of the story to catch the reader's attention quickly.
   2 Go back to earlier events to explain the background to the situation.
   3 Give details about the most exciting moments to get the reader interested in what's going to happen next.
   4 Keep a surprise for the end of the story which explains everything that happened.

B Use narrative tenses to order the story

6 What is the order of the actions? Match a–c with 1–3.

   My phone rang ... a ... and then I left the office.
                      b ... after I'd left the office.
                      c ... while I was leaving the office.

   1 [b] first green, then blue
   2 ☐ first blue, then green
   3 ☐ green and blue at the same time

7 What tense are the verbs in green in exercise 6?

8 Order these actions using the three narrative tenses.
   1 watch TV   have dinner
      Example I watched TV and then I had dinner.
                 I watched TV after I'd had dinner.
                 I watched TV while I was having dinner.

   2 listen to the radio   make lunch
   3 read the newspaper   travel to work

C Think about your reader

9 Work with a partner. Rewrite this story using the strategies in exercise 5 to make it more exciting.

I was staying in a hotel in Barcelona. I went to a concert one night and I took a taxi back to the hotel. It couldn't take me to the door because the hotel was in a pedestrian area, so I had to walk the last 500 metres. I left my bag in the taxi by mistake, got out, and started walking. It was late and I was alone. Then I heard footsteps behind me. I was frightened. I thought it was a robber. I ran to the hotel. The person followed me in. He was the taxi driver and he was returning my bag.

10 Read **Narrating a story** on >> p.128. Which story is more exciting, yours or the one on >> p.128? Why?

ABC Put it all together

11 Work with a partner. Choose one of the sentences below to start a story. Make notes on the main events.
   The moment I walked into the house, I knew something was wrong.
   I'm not usually afraid of dogs, but this one was different.
   I'd never ridden a motorbike before and I had no idea where the brakes were.

12 Write a story of about 100 words starting with one of the sentences. Try to make the story entertaining.

13 Work in small groups. Read your classmates' stories. Try to guess the ending before you finish. Which story is the most entertaining?

I can narrate a story.
Tick ✓ the line.   with a lot of help   with some help   on my own   very easily

Orientation

Context and Language
In this lesson, students practise using different past tenses to connect events in a narrative.

New language	burglar, to return (give back), weapon
Recycled language	words: attack, breaks, concert, robber, safe phrases: pedestrian area grammar: past simple, past continuous and past perfect discourse: after, because, but, so, then, until, while
Recognition language	words: attacker, footsteps, night porter, scared phrases: dark corner grammar: past perfect continuous

End product
In *Put it all together*, students write a story in about 100 words, using narrative strategies in exercise 5 and the model in exercise 2.

Preparation
Read *Narrating a story* on >> p.128 so you can help students with exercise 10. Think about classroom organization if you want students to work in groups for exercise 13.

Warmer
Ask *What do you look for in a good book?* Put students into groups to exchange ideas and ask for a spokesperson from each group to tell the class. Help students get their ideas across.

Write *How to narrate a story* on the board.

A Read and identify narrative strategies

In this section, students analyse a story for strategies a writer uses to entertain a reader.

1 Put students into pairs to discuss the question. Encourage them to give examples. Ask for volunteers to suggest reasons.

2 Ask students to read answers a–c. Direct them to the text. Take a vote on the best answer *(c)*, and nominate students to explain why. Check vocabulary.

3 Read the instructions. Ask students to read the sentences and check vocabulary before they continue individually. Students compare ideas in pairs. Check answers.

> 2 Jo worked late.   3 Jo heard breaking glass.
> 4 Jo thought it was a burglar.   5 Jo hid.
> 6 Jo's mobile rang.   7 Tom asked, 'Is that you, Jo?'

4 Read the second version of the story. In pairs or small groups, students discuss why it is less interesting. Elicit ideas.

> **Suggested answers**
> The events are written chronologically; there is no detail; it isn't written from the point of view of a person involved; there are no adjectives and adverbs; there is no direct speech.

5 Read the instructions. Ask students to look at strategies 1–4 and say what *narrative strategies* means *(ways of telling a story)*. Go through each one, eliciting an example from exercise 2.

B Use narrative tenses to order the story

6 Go through the instructions. Do the example with the class to demonstrate the activity. Students continue in pairs. Monitor and help as necessary. Check answers.

> 2 a   3 c

7 Ask students to identify the tenses of the verbs in green in exercise 6. Explain that using different tenses helps make the story more interesting.

> a past simple   b past perfect   c past continuous

8 Go through the example to demonstrate the activity. Nominate students to say different ways of narrating the two events. Monitor for accurate use of tenses and linkers.

> 2 I listened to the radio and then I made lunch.
>   I listened to the radio after I'd made lunch.
>   I listened to the radio while I was having lunch.
> 3 I read the newspaper and then I travelled to work.
>   I read the newspaper after I'd travelled to work.
>   I read the newspaper while I was travelling to work.

C Think about your reader

9 Go through the instructions and read the text aloud to the class. Ask students to read the strategies in exercise 5, before they rewrite the story. Give positive feedback for accurate use of the grammar, linkers, and strategies.

10 Read the instructions and direct students to *Narrating a story* on >> p.128. Monitor and encourage students to be positive about their own writing.

ABC Put it all together

11 Read the instructions and the three sentences. In pairs, students choose a topic and make notes on the main events.

12 Ask students to write their stories, making them as entertaining as possible for their reader.

13 Put students into small groups to exchange and read each other's stories. Ask them to stop about two or three sentences before the end and to guess the ending.

Student performance
Students should be able to narrate a story of about 100 words.

You can use this checklist to monitor and give feedback or to assess students' performance.

Content	Have students given details about the most exciting moments?
Organization	Have students told the events in an interesting way?
Grammar	Have students used a variety of past tenses appropriately?

I can **narrate a story.**

Students tick *on my own* if they followed the narrative strategies in exercise 5. They can tick *with some help* if they would make one or two changes when they write a second draft.

Early finishers
Students review their writing and make notes about what they would change (if anything) if they were to write a second draft.

Additional material
www.oup.com/elt/result for extra practice activities
www.oup.com/elt/teacher/result for extra teacher resources

Warmer

Remember the topic

Write the unit letters and the following topics on the board:
*A Countries and governments, B Rules and laws, C Stories in the news,
D Past events.*

Read the following sentences for students to call out or write the
letter of the topic.

*1 You can't hunt on Sundays in Virginia. 2 The Netherlands has the
symbol of a lion on its flag. 3 Green is the colour mainly concerned
with the environment. 4 Juan Geraldo has been attacked four times.
5 Richard's enemy, Henry Tudor, had spent some time in France. 6 A
man has been attacked by a cash machine. 7 You must leave your
dog outside the barber's in Alaska. 8 Richard III became King of
England. 9 In the USA, many public buildings look like buildings from
ancient Greece and Rome. 10 Experts discovered that somebody had
changed the painting.*

| 1 B | 2 A | 3 A | 4 C | 5 D | 6 C | 7 B | 8 D | 9 A | 10 D |

A Grammar

1   the or no article in names of institutions 5A exercise 13

Warm-up: Draw three columns on the board: *individual people, titles
and positions*, and *organizations*. Elicit an example for each column.
Direct students to >> **p.47**, exercise 12, to revise the grammar if
necessary.

Set-up: Go through the instructions and example.

2 the   3 the   4 –   5 –   6 the   7 the   8 the   9 –

Follow-up: In pairs, students prepare five similar sentences. They
swap with another pair and then correct each other's answers.

2   Modals of obligation 5B exercise 11

Warm-up: Write the following animal words on the board: *dog, cat,
skunk, pet rat, racoon, camel, ducklings, alligators.* In pairs, students
try to remember the laws about them. Direct students to *Laws for
Paws* on >> **p.48** to check how many they remembered correctly.

Set-up: Do the example with the class. Elicit another possible
answer. *(You can wear your seat belt.)* Tell students to write as many
possible answers as they can.

2 You must switch off .../You can't use ...   3 You can put .../
You don't have to put ...   4 You can't leave ...   5 You don't have
to have ...   6 You must show ...   7 You can't use ...   8 You can
use .../You don't have to use   ...

Follow-up: Students write four questions similar to those in
exercise 12 on >> **p.49** to ask a partner about rules in their country.

3   Active or passive? 5C exercise 10

Warm-up: Write the following words on the board for students to
make a sentence: *dog, by, boy, bitten, the, was, the.*

Set-up: Go through the example as a class to demonstrate the
activity.

2 The film was watched by the girl.   3 The man was hurt by
the falling rocks.   4 The thief was caught by the police.
5 You were burned by the midday sun.

Follow-up: In pairs, students write five jumbled sentences for
another pair.

4   Past perfect 5D exercise 12

Warm-up: Copy the time line from >> **p.53**, exercise 8. Write the
first part of sentences 1 and 2 and elicit the second part.

Set-up: Ask students to read the text and say what happened.

2 had been   3 (had) walked   4 went   5 was
6 had broken   7 had stolen   8 phoned

Follow-up: In pairs, students draw a time line to show four
different dates and events, similar to the one on >> **p.53**, exercise 8.
They swap with another pair and write three sentences to describe
the story.

B Vocabulary

5   Politics 5A exercise 6

Warm-up: Books closed. Write *Politics* on the board and set a two-
minute time limit for students to write words connected with the
topic. Students check with the vocabulary panel on >> **p.46**.

Set-up: Ask students to read the clues and check vocabulary.

2 capital   3 national   4 left   5 represent   6 president
7 democracy   8 state   9 election   10 conservative   11 political
12 republic

Follow-up: Students make anagrams of five *Politics* words and
swap with a partner.

6   Permission words 5B exercise 4

Warm-up: Put students into pairs to choose four sentences from
exercise 2. Students rewrite them using the words *permit, allow,
forbid,* and *prohibit.* They can refer to >> **p.49**, exercise 10, if
necessary.

Set-up: Ask students about the topics of the illustrations. Go
through the example with the class.

2 Feeding the birds is prohibited.   3 Taking photos is not
permitted.   4 Bicycles are forbidden.   5 Food isn't allowed.

Follow-up: Students write three laws for people coming to live
in their country. They tell a partner the topics, for the partner to
guess the laws.

7   Crime verbs 5C exercise 2

Warm-up: Ask students to look at the words in the word pool and
write the past tense and past participle. They check in *Irregular
verbs* on >> **p.148**.

Set-up: Go through the first item. Remind students to think about
which verb is used with the noun.

2 attacked   3 robbed   4 killed   5 hijacked   6 shot   7 arrested
8 kidnapped

Follow-up: In pairs, students write three gapped sentences for
another pair. They write the verbs on the paper and swap with
another pair.

Early finishers

Students choose a grammar point they want to remember from
Unit 5. They write an example of a positive and negative sentence
and translate each one into their own language.

Unit 5 Review

A Grammar

1 *the* or no article in names of institutions Write *the* or nothing in each gap.

Everybody was there – leaders from ¹ *the* European Union, ² _____ Secretary-General of ³ _____ United Nations, ⁴ _____ King Leopold, ⁵ _____ Princess Leida, the leaders of ⁶ _____ Conservative and Socialist Parties, ⁷ _____ president of ⁸ _____ United States and ⁹ _____ Prince Edward.

2 Modals of obligation Write sentences with *must, can't, can,* or *don't have to*.

Instructions when flying

1 The seat belt sign is not switched on.
   You don't have to wear your seat belt.

2 Switch off your mobile phones now.
   _____

3 Put your bags under the seat in front if you want.
   _____

4 Don't leave your seat during landing.
   _____

5 A passport isn't necessary on an internal flight.
   _____

6 Show your ID when you get on the plane.
   _____

7 Don't use electronic equipment during take-off.
   _____

8 Use the overhead light if you want to read.
   _____

3 Active or passive? Which sentence is unlikely in the active? ~~Cross~~ it out and write it in the passive.

1 The boy walked the dog.
   ~~The boy bit the dog.~~   *The boy was bitten by the dog.*

2 The film watched the girl.
   The film amazed the girl.

3 The man has seen the falling rocks.
   The man has hurt the falling rocks.

4 The thief caught the police.
   The thief heard the police.

5 You saw the midday sun.
   You burned the midday sun.

4 Past perfect Put the verbs in the past simple or past perfect.

Dennis ¹ *arrived* (arrive) home very late, tired, and wet. He ² _____ (go) to a party and he ³ _____ (walk) home in the rain. When he ⁴ _____ (go) into the house, he ⁵ _____ (be) shocked to find everything in a complete mess. Somebody ⁶ _____ (broken) in through the window and they ⁷ _____ (steal) his computer and TV. He ⁸ _____ (phone) the police immediately.

B Vocabulary

5 Politics Write the words for these definitions.

1 e *l e c t* To choose your leaders.
2 c _____ City of government.
3 n _____ n ___ Of the nation. *adj*
4 l _____ wing Socialist or similar.
5 Leaders r __ p _____ the people.
6 p _____ Leader of a republic.
7 d _____ c _____ Political system in which people vote.
8 Head of s _____.
9 e _____ Method of choosing governments.
10 c ___ s _____ Opposite of socialist.
11 p _____ c ___ Of politics. *adj*
12 r _____ b _____ Country without kings or queens.

6 Permission words Complete the sentence for each sign in the passive. Use the verb given.

1 allow   Dogs *aren't allowed* _____.

2 prohibit   Feeding the birds _____.

3 permit   Taking photographs _____.

4 forbid   Bicycles _____.

5 allow   Food _____.

7 Crime verbs Complete the sentences with the correct form of these verbs.

arrest attack hijack kidnap kill rob shoot ~~steal~~

1 Someone has *stolen* my wallet!
2 I was _____ by a young man with a knife.
3 A gang of criminals _____ the bank and escaped with €20,000.
4 There was a road accident, but nobody was _____.
5 The plane was _____ by a group of terrorists.
6 The boy _____ himself in the foot by accident with his father's gun.
7 The police have _____ two men in connection with the robbery.
8 The criminals _____ Dr Jennings and demanded €150,000 to set him free.

Extreme adjectives

amazing awful brilliant dreadful enormous exhausted
fantastic furious terrible terrified wonderful

How to express strong feelings

Orientation

Context

In this lesson, students will practise using extreme adjectives to talk about experiences.

In the photo story *Crash!*, Suzi crashes into Paul's car. They used to be a couple, but Paul left her for a model called Mercedes (a Spanish Christian name and the make of a car – Mercedes Benz). Suzi feigns delight at meeting up, and suggests they celebrate. This is her way of exacting revenge as, when the police arrive, Paul will be suspected of drink-driving.

Extreme adjectives shows syllable stress in key vocabulary.

Language

Focus grammar	*so* and *such: I'm so exhausted., It's such an amazing story.*
Focus words	extreme adjectives: *amazing, awful, brilliant, dreadful, enormous, exhausted, fantastic, furious, terrible, terrified, wonderful*
Focus phrases	*Really?, Yeah, I know., Wow! Sounds good., Oh no!, Poor you!*
Recognition vocabulary	words: *coincidence, fault, a fool, unbelievable* phrases: *absolutely amazing, split up*
Recycled language	superlatives: *the best/worst film*
Pronunciation	high intonation **6A.2**

Language notes

Words like *amazing, brilliant, fantastic,* and *wonderful* are close synonyms. They have similar meanings but are often used in different situations (collocation). Dictionaries usually provide example sentences which illustrate the kinds of contexts in which these intensifying adjectives (and adverbs) can be used.

So is often used with a *that* clause to suggest the cause of an action, e.g. *He was so tired that he fell asleep immediately. So* suggests his tiredness was the cause of his falling asleep.

End product

In *Put it all together*, students have a conversation about a good or bad experience. They ask questions and express sympathy to encourage their partner to continue. The conversation is based on audio script **6A.3**.

Preparation

Listen to audio script **6A.2** so you can point out intonation patterns as students listen in exercise 11. Look at *Tell a story* on >> **p.128** to help students with exercise 16. Take dictionaries to class.

Warmer

Write the following nouns on the board: *car, film, meal, driver, holiday.* Set a short time limit and put students into small groups to think of as many adjectives as they can to describe each item. Elicit ideas around the class and monitor for pronunciation of extreme adjectives. Do not overcorrect for accuracy at this point.

Write *How to express strong feelings* on the board.

A Read and follow meaning

In this section, students read a conversation for gist before inferring meaning from context.

1   Read the question and go through the example as a class. Put students into pairs to discuss tips for driving safely and monitor and contribute to discussions.

2   **6A.1** Direct students to the title and pictures in *Crash!* on >> **p.56** and ask them to say what's happened. Do not confirm students' suggestions at this point.

Go through questions 1 and 2. Play the audio while students read the conversation. Elicit answers around the class and see if others agree or disagree. Encourage students to give reasons.

> 1 He left her for a super model named Mercedes.
> 2 She encourages Paul to drink some champagne so that when the police arrive, he'll be in more trouble.

3   Go through the instructions and questions 1–5. Check vocabulary as necessary and do the first item as a class. Encourage students to give reasons and guide them to see that they will have to find meanings that are not directly explained in the text. Monitor and help, making sure students explain their answers. Nominate students to give answers.

> 1 Yes. Paul is angry with her.   2 No. She's still angry with him and wants to take revenge.   3 Yes. Paul refers to leaving her. 4 No. She says this to make him feel comfortable with her so he won't suspect what she's about to do.   5 No. He drinks the champagne and offers Suzi more.

4   Put students into pairs to discuss what they think will happen next. Monitor and respond to students' reasons, saying if you agree or not and why. Put students with a different partner or into small groups to compare their answers. Ask for volunteers to tell the class.

Extra activity

Students read the conversation between Suzi and Paul, and continue for two or three turns.

B Vocabulary extreme adjectives

5   Ask students to look at the title of the section and say what they think *extreme adjectives* are. Elicit or give one or two examples. Direct students to *Extreme adjectives* on >> **p.56** and point out or elicit that the stressed syllable is in bold.

Go through the instructions and the example as a class. Check vocabulary as you do each item. Monitor and give extra pronunciation practice as necessary.

> very tired – exhausted   very frightened – terrified
> very angry – furious   very surprising – amazing

6   Do the activity as a class. Direct students to the diagram and make phrases using the words at either end of the line to help students understand, e.g. say *a wonderful day*, and ask if it was good, say *a terrible day*, and ask if it was bad. Explain or elicit that the words in between are used to describe things which are not so extreme.

Direct students to *Extreme adjectives* again on >> **p.56** to find the synonyms. Monitor and give positive feedback for accurate syllable stress. As you go over answers, ask students to read any example sentences in their dictionaries. Use these to point out what type of things the adjectives are used to describe.

> **terrible:** awful, dreadful
> **wonderful:** amazing, brilliant, fantastic

7 Go through the instructions and do the first item as a class to demonstrate the activity. Ask about people's feelings about *high buildings*, e.g. *Do they make people feel exhausted or furious?* Monitor and help students make effective use of the information in their dictionaries. To check answers, ask for volunteers to read the whole sentence and see if the class agrees with the suggested answer. If there is a difference of opinion, guide students to the answer by eliciting information about what the adjectives can be used to describe.

> 1 terrified   2 exhausted   3 brilliant   4 an amazing   5 furious

Extra activity

Draw students' attention to the word *absolutely* in *Crash!* Ask *What word do we use instead of* very *before an extreme adjective?* Students find it in the story.

C Grammar *so and such*

8 Do the exercise together. Read the rules aloud (ignoring the blanks for the moment) before directing students to read the three sentences. Ask students to underline a noun *(driver)*, two adjectives *(happy, awful)*, and an adverb *(badly)*. Elicit the rules and point out the indefinite article after *such*.

> **Rules:** Use *such* to make a noun more extreme. Use *so* to make an adjective and adverb more extreme.

9 Ask students to look at *Crash!* again to find and underline examples in the conversation.

10 Read the instructions and the example to check students understand the activity. Ask for volunteers to make the sentences more extreme.

> 2 It's such an amazing story.   3 I'm so exhausted!   4 Why do you drive such an enormous car?   5 Why do you drive so fast?

11 6A.2 Play the first two sentences, pausing after each one. To help students hear the intonation pattern, trace it in the air as they listen. Continue with the audio, pausing after each sentence for students to repeat. Give extra practice as necessary.

Extra activity

Ask students to look back at the photo story and make sentences, e.g. *Suzi's so beautiful. Paul's such a typical man. Suzi's plan is so clever. Paul is so stupid to drink the champagne.* etc.

D Listen and identify the topic

In the main listening activity, students listen to short conversations to identify the topic before identifying specific words and phrases.

12 6A.3 Tell students they will listen to three different conversations. Read the instructions and ask students to brainstorm some words associated with each of the topics. Play the audio. Ask for volunteers to say the topics of each of the conversations and see if the class agrees. Play the audio a second time if necessary.

> 1 a film   2 a holiday   3 exam results

13 Read the instructions and go through the example to check students understand the activity. Play the audio, pausing after each conversation for students to make notes. Ask around the class for words and phrases associated with the topic. Play the audio again if necessary.

> **Conversation 1:** see it again   **Conversation 2:** it, a brilliant time, the place, go again next year, maybe I'll go
> **Conversation 3:** them, awful, parents won't let me, have to do them again, spend all summer preparing

Teaching tip

Sometimes, a good listening strategy is to have a topic in mind beforehand and then to listen for clues to confirm or change your idea. Pointing out this strategy helps students see that listening is not a passive activity, and that they shouldn't give up easily.

14 Read the instructions and check students understand the activity. Direct students to audio script 6A.3 on >> p.154 and go through the first conversation to demonstrate the activity. Monitor and help as students continue individually. Check answers as a class and play the audio again for students to listen and read.

> **Conversation 2:** Oh really?   So you liked the place, then?
> **Conversation 3:** So how are they?   Oh no!   What – were they so terrible then?

15 Read the instructions. Ask for two volunteers to read the first conversation to the class and remind them to use high intonation to show interest. Monitor and give praise for the use of high intonation as students continue in pairs. Check students swap roles.

ABCD Put it all together

16 Direct students to *Tell a story* on >> p.128. Go through the information and check any vocabulary as necessary. Tell students to make notes to prepare for the activity and monitor and help as necessary. Give students time to rehearse by mumbling the story to themselves.

17 Go through the instructions and put students into pairs to tell their stories. Check students swap roles.

Student performance

Students should be able to show they are interested listeners.

You can use this checklist to monitor and give feedback or to assess students' performance.

Interaction	Do students use phrases to encourage their partner to continue? exercise 15
Vocabulary	Do students use extreme adjectives appropriately? exercise 7
Pronunciation	Do students attempt to use high intonation? exercise 11

I can express strong feelings.

Students tick *on my own* if they have used phrases to encourage their partner to continue a conversation from memory. They tick *with some help* if they have looked at their answers to exercise 14 or the board once or twice for help.

Early finishers

Students tell their stories from memory or choose and prepare a different topic from *Tell a story*.

Additional material

www.oup.com/elt/result for extra practice activities
www.oup.com/elt/teacher/result for extra teacher resources

How to express strong feelings

G *so* and *such*   V extreme adjectives   P high intonation

A Read and follow meaning

1 What are the best tips for driving safely? Discuss with a partner.
Example Watch the other cars carefully.

2 **6A.1▶** Read and listen to **Crash!** opposite and answer these questions.
1 What reasons has Suzi got to be angry at Paul?
2 What does she do about it?

3 Read the story again. Work with a partner and answer the questions. Give reasons.
Do you think ...
1 Suzi was responsible for the crash?
2 Suzi is happy to see Paul again?
3 Suzi and Paul used to have a relationship?
4 Suzi really means it when she says 'you're so kind'?
5 Paul understands what Suzi is doing?

4 Work with a partner. What do you think is going to happen next? Compare your answer with other students.

B Vocabulary extreme adjectives

5 Look at **Extreme adjectives** opposite and match one adjective with each of these meanings. You can use a dictionary.

very big *enormous*   very angry
very tired   very surprising*
very frightened
* also often used to mean *very good*

6 Find synonyms for *terrible* and *wonderful* in **Extreme adjectives**. Write them in this diagram.

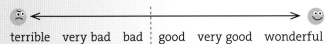

terrible   very bad   bad ┊ good   very good   wonderful

_____   _____

7 Work with a partner. Underline the best word to complete the sentences.
1 He was exhausted/terrified/furious of very high buildings.
2 She was terrified/furious/exhausted after the walk, and needed to rest for a while.
3 I went to see a/an enormous/brilliant/furious film last night.
4 We had such a/an amazing/furious/terrified lunch!
5 She was terrified/furious/exhausted after he damaged her expensive new car.

C Grammar *so* and *such*

8 Look at the examples and complete the rules.
You were driving so badly.
I'm just so happy.
You always were such an awful driver.

Rules
Use _____ to make a noun* more extreme.
Use _____ to make an adjective or adverb more extreme.
*There may be other words between *such* and the noun.

9 Underline examples of *so* and *such* in **Crash!**

10 Make these sentences more extreme with *so* or *such*.
1 Why was Paul furious?   *Why was Paul so furious?*
2 It's an amazing story.
3 I'm exhausted!
4 Why do you drive an enormous car?
5 Why do you drive fast?

11 **6A.2▶** Pronunciation Listen and repeat the sentences on the audio.

I'm **so** ex**haust**ed!   It's **such** a **brill**iant **film**!

Notice that to express strong feelings, the voice goes high on the main syllables.

More practice? **Grammar Bank** ≫ p.141.

D Listen and identify the topic

12 **6A.3▶** Listen to three conversations. Guess what the people are talking about from the list below.
a restaurant   a shop   a holiday   a film
exam results   a job interview

13 Listen again. Make a note of the words and phrases that helped you identify the topic. Compare with a partner.
Example Conversation 1 – ending, story, music, see

14 Look at the audio script on ≫ p.154. Underline questions and expressions of sympathy which encourage the other person to continue.
Example Really?

15 Choose two of the conversations and practise them with a partner. Use a high voice to express strong feelings.

ABCD Put it all together

16 Prepare to tell your partner a story. Look at **Tell a story** on ≫ p.128.

17 Tell your story to your partner. Listen to your partner's story. Encourage him/her to continue by asking questions and expressing sympathy.

I can express strong feelings.

Tick ✓ the line.   with a lot of help   with some help   on my own   very easily

Lost *and* **found**

When Doug Schmitt left his wallet at a petrol station in 1967, he didn't expect to see it again.

Mr Schmitt had stopped to buy petrol in Logan, Utah. In those days, he was a student at Utah State University. He forgot to pick up his wallet after paying and drove away. When he noticed, it was too late to go back.

39 YEARS IN A DRAWER

The owner of the petrol station put the wallet in a drawer and hoped that Mr Schmitt would return to collect it. 39 years later, the petrol station owner died and his wife decided to clear out his office. She found the wallet, which contained $5 in cash, some old stamps, a dry-cleaning ticket, Mr Schmitt's university ID card, and some photos of his high school girlfriends. She asked her son-in-law, Ted Nyman, to find the owner of the wallet. Mr Nyman looked on the Internet and discovered that Mr Schmitt runs an antiques business in Lake Ariel, Pennsylvania. He contacted Mr Schmitt and sent him the wallet.

A FULL HEAD OF HAIR

Mr Schmitt was very surprised to get the wallet back and praised the 'good, honest' people of Utah. He said it was strange to receive a little piece of his own history and nice to see the photo on his ID card. 'I had a full head of hair back then,' he said.

DRY CLEANING

Mr Schmitt's wife Vickie decided to contact the local TV station with the story. She said, 'It's wonderful that people are kind enough to do this for a complete stranger.' She added, 'It's great to see how Doug looked when he was at college.'

Mr Schmitt says he must remember to collect his dry-cleaning next time he's in Utah.

When Ray Heilwagen lost his wallet in France during World War II, he didn't expect to see it again.

Mr Heilwagen, from Hannibal, Missouri, had fallen into a river after being hurt in the leg by a bomb. While he was waiting for the medics to come, he remembers taking out his wallet to look at the photos. But the next morning, before being moved to hospital, he couldn't find it.

A SURPRISE PHONE CALL

62 years later, he received a phone call from a man who said he had found it. The man, called Stephen Breitenstein, from Illinois, said his father had died recently and he had found the wallet among his things. Mr Breitenstein's dad had been in France during the war and had found the wallet and brought it home hoping to find the owner. However, he didn't know how to do it and finally stopped looking. He left the wallet in a drawer.

'SORRY IT TOOK OVER 60 YEARS'

Mr Breitenstein found the wallet, which contained a few francs, some receipts, some photos, and Mr Heilwagen's social security card. He decided to look for Mr Heilwagen on the Internet, found him, and sent him the wallet. Mr Breitenstein also sent a note saying he was very happy to find Mr Heilwagen, and he apologized for taking over 60 years to return the wallet.

THE KINDNESS OF STRANGERS

Mr Heilwagen was very surprised to get the wallet back. 'I could hardly believe it,' he said. He was amazed that a complete stranger would be kind enough to look for him and return the wallet after so many years, and he really enjoyed seeing his old things again.

Dictionary extracts

GRAMMAR If you **stop to do sth**, you stop in order to do it: *On the way home I stopped to buy a newspaper.* If you **stop doing sth**, you do not do it any more: *I stopped smoking 3 months ago.*

GRAMMAR If you **remember to do sth**, you don't forget to do it: *It's my mother's birthday. I must remember to phone her.* If you **remember doing sth**, you have a picture or memory in your mind of doing it: *Do you remember going to the cinema for the first time?*

Notes from *Oxford Wordpower Dictionary* © Oxford University Press 2006

How to tell and show interest in an anecdote

Orientation

Context

In this lesson, students will practise telling an anecdote and being an interested listener.

The two texts on >> p.58 are true stories which have several things in common. Two people lost their wallets and never expected to see them again and both wallets were returned after a long period of time. There are photos of the people who lost the wallets.

Dictionary extracts gives grammatical information about the use of *to* + infinitive and gerunds after the verbs *stop* and *remember*.

Language

Focus grammar	infinitives and gerunds: *after paying, before being moved, expect to see, kind enough to look, remembers taking out, stopped to buy, too late to go back*
Preview grammar	reported speech
Focus words	verbs: *decide, don't mind, enjoy, expect, fancy, finish, forget, hope*
Focus phrases	*after/before ...ing, it's great to ..., kind enough to ..., thanks for ... ing, too late to ...*
Recognition vocabulary	words: *antiques, bomb, medics, notice, paperwork, praised, stamps, son-in-law* phrases: *a complete stranger, dry-cleaning, social security card*
Recycled language	words: *amazed, bank cards, cash, documents, drawer, handbag, ID card, mobile phone, ticket, wonderful* phrases: *pick it up* grammar: *past perfect; too ... to, enough; gerund/infinitive*
Discourse	conversation building

Language note

Information and example sentences usually given in dictionaries will help students to decide if a verb is followed by an infinitive or a gerund.

The verbs *stop* and *remember* can be followed by *to* + infinitive or a gerund, but with a difference in meaning.

End product

In *Put it all together*, students use their notes to tell different stories based on pictures in *Pairwork*. The conversation is based on audio script 6B.1.

Preparation

Read the phrases in exercise 14 so you can use them in the *Warmer*. Look at the picture story on >> p.129 so you can help students in exercise 16, if necessary. Take dictionaries to class.

Warmer

Ask students when they last lost an everyday object, e.g. an umbrella. Encourage students to tell the class about their experiences and ask *wh-* questions to elicit extra details. Use phrases from exercise 14 to show you are interested in their stories.

Write *How to tell and show interest in an anecdote* on the board.

A Read and follow the main events in a story

In this section, students read true stories for specific information.

1   Read the question and put students into pairs to tell their stories. Monitor and join in conversations. Nominate students to tell the class.

2   Put students into A/B pairs and direct them to the stories on >> p.58. Make sure half the class reads one story and half reads the other. Set a time limit of about three minutes to encourage students to read for the main ideas only. Ask for suggested titles and write them in two columns on the board. Do not comment at this stage if the titles are similar.

3   Read questions 1–8 and check vocabulary as necessary. Ask students to read their text again, and encourage them to use a dictionary to find the meaning of essential words only. Monitor and help if necessary as students continue individually. Ask both A and B students to give answers to the questions and write notes in the columns on the board.

> **text A:** 1 He forgot to pick it up in a petrol station in Utah. 2 The owner of the petrol station.   3 In a drawer.   4 His wife. 5 $5 cash, old stamps, a dry-cleaning ticket, university ID card, some photos of friends.   6 On the Internet.   7 He was very surprised.   8 39 years.
> **text B:** 1 He lost it in France in the Second World War. 2 Mr Breitenstein's father.   3 In a drawer.   4 Mr Breitenstein. 5 A few francs, some receipts, some photos, a social security card.   6 On the Internet.   7 He was very surprised.   8 62 years.

4   Go through the instructions. In pairs, students tell each other about the stories they read. Ask for volunteers to tell the class about any similarities and differences they found.

Extra help

Draw a vertical time line on the board and choose one of the stories. Write *man lost wallet*, at the top, and *man got wallet back* at the bottom. Elicit events to add to the time line and monitor for correct use of the past perfect. Review the use and form of past tenses if necessary.

Extra activity

Students draw a vertical time line and mark the main events for the other story.

5   Read the instructions, phrases and example with the class. Monitor and help as necessary as students continue in pairs.

Extra activity

Return to students' suggested titles for exercise 2. The class votes on the best title for the stories.

B Grammar infinitives and gerunds

6   Write this sentence on the board: *He didn't expect to see his wallet again.* Underline *didn't expect* and *to see* and ask if these are *nouns* or *verbs*. (Verbs.) Ask *Which verb is the to + infinitive form?* (To see.)

Direct students to the two columns in the grammar box. Tell students that when two verbs are used together, the first verb might be followed by either an infinitive or gerund. Ask students to find an example of a *verb + gerund* in the phrases in exercise 5 *(remembers taking out)*.

Read the instructions and check vocabulary. Ask students to find the verbs in the texts and to look at the form of the next verb. Go over answers as a class, before students write the verbs in the appropriate column.

> **use a gerund after:** enjoy, forget   **use *to* + infinitive after:** decide, expect, hope

7 Read the instructions and sentences 1–8. Check vocabulary as necessary and go through the first item as a class. Remind students that their dictionaries usually give information and examples which will help them decide if a verb is followed by an infinitive or a gerund. Monitor and help students as they continue individually.

Ask for volunteers to give answers and see if the class agrees. Ask students to find another example of a verb in items 1–8 to add to the grammar box in exercise 6. (They add *don't mind* to the first column of the box.)

> 2 eating   3 to meet   4 driving   5 to look   6 going   7 doing   8 to take

8 Go through the examples in the box together as a class, focussing attention on the words in blue. Put students into pairs to underline or highlight examples in the texts.

Extra help

Write *infinitive + to (A)* and *gerund (B)* on the board. Say some of the verbs and phrases from the boxes in exercises 6 and 8 for students to say A or B. Students continue in pairs.

Extra plus

In pairs, students take turns to say a sentence stem for a partner to continue, e.g. *A He didn't expect … B to pass his exam.*

9 Tell students to read the text, ignoring the blanks. Ask *Did the person feel happy at the end? (Yes.)* and elicit why. Check vocabulary as necessary and do the example together, pointing out the preposition *after* and directing students to the information in the box in exercise 8. Monitor and help as necessary as students continue individually. To check answers, read the text aloud. Pause at each blank for students to say the answer as a class.

> 2 to return   3 going   4 bringing   5 helping   6 to know   7 to do

10 Read the information to the class and direct students to *Dictionary extracts* on **>> p.58**. Ask students to find examples in each of the texts. Check students understand the difference in meaning by asking, in each case *Which action happened first?*

> **text A:** stopped to buy, remember to collect
> **text B:** remembers taking out, stopped looking

Extra activity

Read the following situations and ask students to answer the question *What do you do?*
1 You pass your friend in the street. Do you *Stop talking* or *Stop to talk?*
2 The exam's starting. Do you *Stop talking* or *Stop to talk?*
3 What do you do before leaving a café? Do you *remember to pay* or *remember paying?*
4 After you've left the café, you think about the bill. Do you *remember paying* or *remember to pay?*

C Listen and show interest

In this section, students listen for detail and to identify how a person shows they are interested in a story.

11 Read the instructions and ask students to make a list of items people normally have in a handbag. Remind students that it's usually easier to understand if they think about things they expect to hear. Elicit ideas around the class.

12 6B.1 Play the audio for students to tick the words on their list. Play the audio a second time if necessary.

13 Ask students to read questions 1–4 before listening a second time. Play the audio and check answers as a class at the end.

> 1 To tell Ben about a similar experience she'd had.
> 2 She left it on a train.   3 No, she didn't.
> 4 She cancelled her credit cards.

14 Read phrases 1–4 and meanings a–d and check vocabulary as necessary. Do the first item together as a class to demonstrate the activity. Check answers as a class.

> 1 b   2 d   3 a   4 c

15 Read the instructions and direct students to audio script 6B.1 on **>> p.154** to find more examples of Ben showing he's interested in Julia's story. Monitor and help as students continue individually. Play the audio again for students to listen to Ben. Ask students to take turns saying the conversation and check they swap roles.

ABC Put it all together

16 Put students into A/B pairs and direct them to the appropriate *Pairwork* activity. Ask students to make notes about what happened. Monitor and encourage them to add extra details, e.g. when and where the event took place, how they felt, etc. Direct them to the questions in exercise 3 for ideas.

17 Read the instructions and remind the listeners to sound interested. Ask the story teller to tell their partner if they felt they sounded interested. Check students swap roles.

Student performance

Students should be able to tell a short narrative and respond as an interested listener.

You can use this checklist to monitor and give feedback or to assess students' performance.

Content	Do students give sufficient detail? exercise 3
Interaction	Do students show they are interested listeners? exercise 15
Vocabulary	Do students have enough vocabulary to do the task? exercise 11

I can tell and show interest in an anecdote.

Students tick *on my own* if they have had the conversation using their notes. They tick *with some help* if they looked at the grammar boxes in exercises 6 or 8 on **>> p.59** occasionally.

Early finishers

Students retell the story without using their notes. Their partner asks four questions to find out more and to show interest.

Additional material

www.oup.com/elt/result for extra practice activities
www.oup.com/elt/teacher/result for extra teacher resources

How to **tell and show interest in an anecdote**

G infinitives and gerunds

A Read and follow the main events in a story

1 Have you ever lost something valuable? Tell a partner.

2 Work with a partner. Look at **Lost and found** opposite. **Student A** read text A and **Student B** read text B. Write a title for your text.

3 Answer these questions about the article you read.

1 How and where did the man lose his wallet?
2 Who found the wallet first?
3 Where did he keep the wallet all these years?
4 Who found the wallet again?
5 What was in the wallet?
6 How did they find the owner of the wallet?
7 How did the owner feel about getting it back?
8 How long did it take to get his wallet back?

4 Tell your partner about the story you read and make a list of similarities and differences between the stories.

5 Can you remember how these phrases came into the stories? Tell a partner.

after paying   before being moved   expect to see
kind enough to look   remembers taking out
stopped to buy   too late to go back

Example expect to see – The man lost his wallet in the war. He didn't expect to see it again.

B Grammar infinitives and gerunds

6 Find these words in **Lost and found** and write them in the box.

decide   enjoy   expect   forget   hope

use a gerund after ...	use *to* + infinitive after ...
mind fancy finish	want

7 Complete the sentences with the infinitive or gerund of the verbs. You can use your dictionary.

1 I didn't expect _to see_ my wallet again. see
2 We really enjoy _____ out. eat
3 I hoped _____ the man who found my wallet. meet
4 I don't mind _____ you to the station. drive
5 She decided _____ for the owner of the wallet. look
6 Do you fancy _____ to the cinema tonight? go
7 I haven't finished _____ my homework yet. do
8 Don't forget _____ your passport with you. take

8 Read the rules below. Underline examples in the texts.

use a gerund after prepositions	use *to* + infinitive after adjectives (often with *too / enough*)
after being hurt	it's great to see
before being moved	too late to go back
thanks for helping me	kind enough to do this

9 Work with a partner. Complete the text with infinitives or gerunds.

bring   do   go   help   know   ~~leave~~   return

I dropped my wallet on the pavement after [1] _leaving_ a café. When I noticed, it was too late [2] _____ to the place and look for it. I phoned the bank to cancel my credit cards before [3] _____ to bed. The next day, a man came to my house and returned my wallet to me. I thanked him for [4] _____ it back and offered him €20 for [5] _____ me. He refused the money and left. It's nice [6] _____ that there are people honest and friendly enough [7] _____ something like this!

10 *Stop* and *remember* can be followed by an infinitive or gerund, but the meaning is different. Read **Dictionary extracts** opposite and find examples of each meaning in **Lost and found**.

More practice? **Grammar Bank** >> p.141.

C Listen and show interest

11 You will hear Julia telling Ben about losing her handbag. What do you think was in the handbag? Make a list.

12 **6B.1▶** Listen. Which things on your list do you hear?

13 Listen again and answer the questions.

1 Why did Julia start telling her story?
2 Where did Julia leave the handbag?
3 Did she get it back?
4 What did Julia do after losing the handbag?

14 Ben is an interested listener. Match phrases 1–4 from the audio script with meanings a–d.

1 ☐ What a pain!
2 ☐ Mmm ...
3 ☐ And did you get it back?
4 ☐ Yeah, all the paperwork and everything.

a Ben asks questions to show he's interested.
b He expresses sympathy.
c He adds details to show he can understand what she's saying.
d He makes sounds to show he's still listening.

15 Underline these and more examples in the audio script on >> p.154. Then practise saying them with a partner.

ABC Put it all together

16 Work with a partner. Prepare to tell a story.

Student A Look at **Picture story** on >> p.129.
Student B Look at **Picture story** on >> p.134.

17 Tell your story to your partner. Listen with interest to your partner's story. Use some of the responses that Ben uses in exercise 14.

I can tell and show interest in an anecdote.

Tick ✓ the line.   with a lot of help   with some help   on my own   very easily

Behaviour

a bully /'bʊli/   to fight   friendly   helpful
kind   naughty   noisy /'nɔɪzi/   nosy /'nəʊzi/
polite   rough /rʌf/   rude   to swear
well-behaved /wel bɪ'heɪvd/

TODAY'S TV CHOICE

Nightmare Neighbours

TBC1 21.30 – 22.00

This is the first of a new documentary series about problem neighbours. In this programme, we follow the lives of the Dicksons – a retired couple in Plymouth, and their next
05 door neighbours, the Lanes – a single mother and her two children.

The Dicksons say that the Lanes are noisy and rough. They say they can't sleep because of the fighting and shouting from next door. Mrs Dickson
10 says she caught Mrs Lane's daughter painting graffiti on their garage wall, and according to Mr Dickson, the Lanes leave rubbish by the front door. He says the smell is terrible and it's a health hazard.

15 But of course, there are two sides to every dispute. According to Mrs Lane, the Dicksons just want to make trouble because she is separated from her husband. She says they enjoy complaining because they're bored and haven't
20 got anything else to do.

There's something fascinating about looking at other people's everyday lives, and this is the secret of reality TV's success. In the series Nightmare Neighbours, we see how tiny disputes
25 can become wars which last for many years. We'll see a woman who set fire to her neighbour's door because he parked his car in the wrong place, and a man who shot his neighbour's dog because it was barking too loudly. We'll see a couple who
30 installed a security camera in their home and pointed it towards their neighbour's front door. At the end of these shows, you come away thinking, 'Why don't these people just talk to each other?!'

Love Your Neighbours

Mrs Dickson thinks the Lanes
Are noisy and rough
She says the kids are naughty
She says ¹_____'s had enough
Mr Dickson says ²_____ leave
Their rubbish by the door
'You can't complain,' says Mrs Lane
'It's not against the law'

Love Your Neighbours ...

Mrs Dickson says their children
Play their music loud
She says ³_____ hears them swearing
It shouldn't be allowed
Mr Dickson says ⁴_____ hears them
Fighting all night long
'You can't complain,' says Mrs Lane
'We're doing nothing wrong'

Love Your Neighbours ...

Mrs Dickson says ⁵_____ kick
Their ball along the hall
She says ⁶_____ saw their daughter
Writing on the wall
Mr Dickson says ⁷_____ hears them
Talking on the phone
'Don't complain,' says Mrs Lane
'Leave us all alone'

Love Your Neighbours ...

60   **6C**

How to talk about people in your neighbourhood

Orientation

Context

In this lesson, students use reported speech to explain what others have said.

The photos illustrate the concept of problem neighbours in general.

Today's TV Choice is an illustrated TV review of a new reality TV documentary, *Nightmare Neighbours*. The programme explores the conflict between two families, the Dicksons and the Lanes. The verse, *Love Your Neighbours*, is also about the two families. There is a song version on the audio (6C.2).

Behaviour gives phonetic transcriptions of some key vocabulary which is not obvious from spelling.

Language

Focus grammar	pronouns in reported speech: *He says he ..., He says, 'I ...'*
Focus words	behaviour: *bully, fight, friendly, helpful, kind, naughty, noisy, nosy, polite, rough, rude, swear, well-behaved*
Recognition vocabulary	words: *bark, dispute, documentary, graffiti, health hazard, mentioned, recommended, security camera* phrases: *according to, doing nothing wrong, feel sorry for, had enough, separated from, set fire to*
Recycled language	words: *allowed, bored, complain, divorced, fascinating, garage, loud, Mr, Mrs, Ms, retired, single* phrases: *against the law* grammar: *personal and possessive pronouns*
Pronunciation	spelling and pronunciation *gh*
Discourse	coherence in pronouns

Language notes

In reported speech, when the reporting verb is in the present tense, the tense of the reported speech is the same as it was when spoken. We deal with this area in the next lesson.

The letters *gh* aren't usually pronounced. Occasionally, the letters form the consonant /f/, as in *rough* and *enough* /f/.

End product

In *Put it all together*, students work in pairs or small groups. Using their notes, they report what another person has told them.

Preparation

Read *Are you a good neighbour?* on **>> p.129**, so you are familiar with the activity for exercise 17. Think about classroom organization for pair and group work in exercise 18. Take dictionaries to class if necessary.

Warmer

Write the word *neighbours* on the board. Set a short time limit for students, in groups, to list good and bad points about living near other people. Elicit suggestions and write five ideas for each on the board. Ask students to put the good points in order (starting with the best first) and to compare ideas.

Write *How to talk about people in your neighbourhood* on the board.

A Vocabulary behaviour

1 Draw two columns on the board: *positive* and *negative*. Direct students to *Behaviour* on **>> p.60** and elicit a word for each column. Ask students to use their dictionaries and monitor and help as necessary as students continue individually.

Check answers as a class and give extra pronunciation practice as necessary. Ask students to make sentences with the words to check they understand. Listen and check they use the word correctly, e.g. *to fight* as a verb, *rough* as an adjective.

> **positive:** friendly, helpful, kind, polite, well-behaved
> **negative:** a bully, naughty, noisy, nosy, rough, rude, to fight, to swear

2 Go through the instructions and check students understand the complaints. Monitor and encourage them to talk about their reasons as they continue in pairs. Nominate students to explain their order and encourage others to comment.

3 6C.1 Read the instructions and ask students how they are going to listen. *To every word or for key words? (For key words in the complaints.)* Play the audio and ask students to compare answers in pairs. Play the audio a second time if necessary. Elicit answers and give extra pronunciation practice of key vocabulary.

> 1 noise   2 rough behaviour   3 naughty children   4 walls and fences   5 car parking   6 animal problems   7 rubbish

Extra activity

Ask students how the list compares to where they live.

B Read a TV review

In this section, students scan a TV review for specific information before reading intensively for detail.

4 Direct students to *Nightmare Neighbours* on **>> p.60** and ask *Is it a dictionary entry, a verse, or a TV review? (A TV review.)* Direct students to the pictures and ask if they think it is going to be about good or bad neighbours. *(Bad.)* Set a short time limit for students to read the text and identify the people in the photos.

> The Dicksons, Mrs Lane's son, Mrs Lane's daughter

5 Go through the instructions and the example with the class. Ask students how they are going to read the text. *(Scan to find the words from exercise 2 and then read that part of the text more carefully to check.)* Ask students to continue, ignoring new vocabulary for the moment. Monitor and help if necessary. Ask for volunteers to give answers and see if the class agrees before giving feedback.

> animal problems (line 28)   car parking (line 27)
> walls and fence problems (line 11)
> noise (line 9)   rubbish (line 12)

6 Ask students to read meanings 1–5 and check vocabulary as necessary. For each item, ask students what type of word they are looking for. *(A noun, verb, or adjective.)* Do item 1 together and ask students how they found the answer. Check answers.

> 1 a health hazard   2 dispute   3 separated   4 bark   5 install

7 Read sentences 1–6 and ask students to say *true* or *false* from memory. Write students' answers on the board. Ask students to read *Nightmare Neighbours* again to check their answers. Go over answers together and ask students to give reasons if a statement is false. Monitor for pronunciation of *Mr*, *Mrs*, and *Ms*.

> 2 True.   3 True.   4 False. (Both Mr and Mrs Dickson say they can't sleep.)   5 False. (She's separated.)   6 True (according to Mrs Lane).

8 Read questions 1–3 to check understanding. Students continue the activity in pairs. Monitor and join in with discussions. Give positive feedback when students support their opinion with reasons or examples from the text. Bring the class together and go through the questions. Nominate a student to share their opinion and invite others to add their comments.

Extra activity
Ask students to choose three new words or phrases from the text. They guess the meaning before checking in a dictionary.

C Grammar pronouns in reported speech

9 Direct students to *Love Your Neighbours* on >> **p.60**. Ask them about the text. *Is it a dictionary entry, a verse, or a TV review? (Verse.)* Check vocabulary as necessary. Tell students to underline the verb *to say* and ask *Do the people say these things once or often? (Often. The verb* say *is in the present tense.)*

Do the first item together to show students that they might need to look at the information before and after the blank. Students continue individually and write the missing pronouns. Do not go over the answers at this stage.

10 6C.2 Play the audio for students to listen and check answers.

> 1 she   2 they   3 she   4 he   5 they   6 she   7 he

11 Draw two columns on the board: A and B. Copy the first sentence from each column in the grammar box and ask *Which sentence reports the actual words Mrs Dickson says? (A.) Which sentence simply reports what she said? (B.)* Elicit or explain the punctuation differences between the two sentences.

Direct students to the grammar box and read the sentences row by row. Do the activity together and check students understand why the missing pronouns are different. *(Reported speech, in column A, gives the actual words the speaker used, whereas in column B the person reporting what was said isn't the person who spoke.)* Complete the rule as a class.

> He says, 'I hear them.'   She says **she** saw …
> **Rule:** sometimes have to

Extra help
Say *I'm tired.* and nominate a student to report what you said. Ask the student to repeat the statement *I'm tired.* and to nominate another to report what was said. Monitor for accuracy of changes in the pronoun for reported speech.

12 Go through the instructions and the example. Check students understand. Point out the pronoun change. Elicit one or two more examples. Students continue in pairs.

> She says their kids …/She says, 'Your kids …'
> Mr Dickson says they leave their rubbish   …/He says, 'You leave your rubbish …'
> She says she hears them …/She says, 'I hear them …'
> He says he hears them …/He says, 'I hear them …'
> She says they kick their …/She says, 'They kick their ball …'
> She says she saw their …/She says, 'I saw your daughter …'
> He says he hears them …/He says, 'I hear them …'

Extra help
Students work in pairs. One reports what was said, the other says the words in a complaining tone of voice. They swap roles.

Extra plus
Students role play the Dicksons and Lanes having an argument.

13 Read the instructions and example and check students understand the activity. Students continue the activity in pairs. Monitor and help as necessary. Ask for volunteers to tell the class about what people they know often say.

D Spelling and pronunciation *gh*

14 Read the instructions. Ask students to look at the phonetic transcriptions and to listen to the words to hear the difference. Say *fit* and *fight* several times for students to tune in to the difference in pronunciation. Read a and b and ask which one is correct. (a.) Explain that, in *fight*, the letters *gh* aren't pronounced.

15 Direct students to *Love Your Neighbours* on >> **p.60** and ask them to find the first example of a word containing the letters *gh*. (*In the title* Neighbour.) Students continue individually.

As you go over answers, ask which two words end in the /f/ sound (*rough, enough*). Students confirm this by using their dictionaries and checking the phonetic transcriptions.

> neighbour (three times)   rough   naughty   enough   fighting   night   daughter

16 Direct students to the verse on >> **p.60** to practise saying the lyric. Play the audio again if students enjoy singing along.

ABCD Put it all together

17 Read the instructions and direct students to *Are you a good neighbour?* on >> **p.129**. Use the example and nominate a student to ask you the question. Read the reply. Ask students to make notes of their partner's answers for the next activity. Put students into pairs to do the interview. Check they swap roles.

18 Reorganize students so they are working with a different partner or in a small group. Read the instructions and example to demonstrate the activity. Students continue.

Student performance
Students should be able to report short statements.

You can use this checklist to monitor and give feedback or to assess students' performance.

Coherence	Do students use pronouns accurately? exercise 13
Vocabulary	Do students have enough vocabulary to do the activity? exercise 1
Pronunciation	Do students usually pronounce words with *gh* accurately? exercise 16

I can **talk about people in my neighbourhood.**
Students tick *on my own* if they did the activity without looking at the grammar box in exercise 11. They tick *with some help* if they have looked at the grammar box occasionally.

Early finishers
Put students into groups of three. Two are in an argument and will not talk to each other. The third acts as a go-between, taking messages from one to the other.

Additional material
www.oup.com/elt/result for extra practice activities
www.oup.com/elt/teacher/result for extra teacher resources

G pronouns in reported speech V behaviour P spelling and pronunciation *gh*

A Vocabulary behaviour

1 Look at **Behaviour** opposite. Which words do you think are positive and which are negative? Use a dictionary to help you.

2 Which of these complaints about neighbours are most common? Work with a partner and number them 1–7.

☐ animal problems   ☐ noise
☐ car parking   ☐ rough behaviour
☐ naughty children   ☐ rubbish
☐ walls and fence problems

3 **6C.1▶** Listen to the results of a survey in Britain. What is the order of the complaints in exercise 2?

B Read a TV review

4 Read **Nightmare Neighbours** opposite. Who do you think the people are in the photos?

5 Which of the problems in exercise 2 are mentioned? Say where they are in the text.

Example noise – lines 7–9 and 28–29

6 Find words with these meanings.
1 a thing which may be dangerous
2 an argument or disagreement between people
3 no longer living with your wife, husband or partner
4 the noise made by a dog
5 to fix equipment into position so that it can be used

7 Write *true* or *false*. If the sentence is false, say why.
1 Mr Dickson works in a bank. *False – he's retired.*
2 The Lanes live next door to the Dicksons.
3 There are three people living in the Lane's house.
4 Mrs Dickson says she can't sleep.
5 Mrs Lane isn't married.
6 The Dicksons definitely enjoy complaining.

8 Answer the questions with a partner.
1 Who do you feel more sorry for – the Dicksons or the Lanes?
2 Which do you think is the worst behaviour mentioned?
3 Why do you think the writer recommends this programme?

C Grammar pronouns in reported speech

9 Read **Love Your Neighbours** opposite. Write the missing pronouns in the gaps.

10 **6C.2▶** Listen and check.

11 Write the missing pronouns in the grammar box. Then underline the correct word in the rule.

direct speech (present tense)	reported speech (present tense)
She says, 'They swear.'	She says they swear.
He says, '_____ hear them.'	He says he hears them.
She says, 'I saw their daughter.'	She says _____ saw their daughter.
She says, 'You can't complain.'	She says we can't complain.

Rule
When you change direct speech into reported speech, you always have to / sometimes have to change the pronouns.

12 Work with a partner. Imagine the Dicksons are speaking directly to Mrs Lane. Find more examples of reported speech in the song and say them in direct speech.

Example She says she's had enough. She says, 'I've had enough.'

13 Think of people you know well. What do they often say? Tell a partner.

Example My mother often says she hates the traffic …

More practice? **Grammar Bank** >> p.141.

D Spelling and pronunciation *gh*

14 Look at this pair of words. What difference do the letters *gh* make to the pronunciation? Choose the best answer.

fit /fɪt/   fight /faɪt/
a They change the sound of the vowel.
b They change the sound of the last consonant.

15 Underline nine words with *gh* in **Love Your Neighbours**. Answer the question.

gh is usually part of a vowel sound. In which two words is it the consonant sound /f/?

16 Practise saying the song lyric.

ABCD Put it all together

17 Look at **Are you a good neighbour?** on >> p.129. Interview your partner and tick ✓ the answers which are true for him / her.

Example **A** Who do you know in your neighbourhood?
B Well, I don't know one of my next door neighbours very well, because they just moved in last month, but I know the other one …

18 Work with a different partner or group. Tell your new partner(s) what your first partner says about his / her neighbours. Who gets on best with their neighbours?

Example Sonia says she doesn't know her next door neighbours very well because …

I can talk about people in my neighbourhood.

THE MAN WHO SOLD THE EIFFEL TOWER

1 **Paris, 1925.** World War I had finished and the city was full of people with cash looking for business opportunities. Victor Lustig was reading the newspaper one day and found an article about the Eiffel Tower. It said the tower was being neglected because it was too expensive to maintain. Lustig saw a great 'business opportunity' – he would sell the Eiffel Tower!

2 Lustig wrote to six important businessmen in the city and invited them to a secret meeting in a well-known Paris hotel. He said he was a government official and he told them that he wanted to talk about a business deal. All six of the businessmen came to the meeting.

3 At the meeting, Lustig told them that the city wanted to sell the Eiffel Tower for scrap metal and that he had been asked to find a buyer. He said that the deal was secret because it would not be popular with the public. The businessmen believed him, perhaps because the Eiffel Tower was never planned to be permanent. It had been built as part of the 1889 Paris Expo, and the original plan had been to remove it in 1909.

4 Lustig rented a limousine and took the men to visit the tower. He showed them around. After the tour, he said that if they were interested, they should contact him the next day. Lustig told them he would give the tower contract to the person with the highest offer. One of the dealers, Andre Poisson, was very interested, but he was also worried.

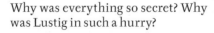
Why was everything so secret? Why was Lustig in such a hurry?

5 The two men had a meeting, and Lustig confessed that he wasn't looking for the highest offer. He said he would give the contract to anybody – for a price. Poisson understood: Lustig wanted a little extra money 'under the table' for himself. That explained why the deal was secret. This was Lustig's cleverest lie, because now Poisson believed him completely.

6 Lustig sold Poisson a false contract for the Eiffel Tower – and on top of that, Poisson paid him a little extra money 'under the table'. Lustig put

Scrap metal

Victor Lustig

Lustig being arrested

Alcatraz

all the money in a suitcase and took the first train to Vienna. Poisson never told the police what had happened – he was too embarrassed. After a month, Lustig returned to Paris and tried to sell the Eiffel Tower again, but this time somebody told the police and he had to escape to America. There, he continued his criminal career and finished his days in the famous Alcatraz prison.

How to report what people said

Orientation

Context

In this lesson, students will practise retelling a story using reported speech.

The illustrated text, *The Man Who Sold the Eiffel Tower,* tells the true story of Victor Lustig, an enterprising businessman who convinced another man, Andre Poisson, to buy the Eiffel Tower. Poisson was too embarrassed to go to the police and Lustig disappeared to Vienna with his money. The temptation for Lustig to try the trick again was great and so he returned to Paris a month later. He didn't manage to sell the tower this time, and had to escape to America. He was eventually arrested for other crimes and ended his days in the famous Alcatraz prison.

Language

Focus grammar	tenses in reported speech: *He said he tried to help., He said he'd tried to help., He said he'd try to help.*
Focus words	*say* and *tell*
Focus phrases	*I said (that)..., I told him to ..., I said, 'We will ...'*
Recognition vocabulary	words: *confessed, contract, dealer, estate agent, maintain, neglected, permanent* phrases: *business opportunity, in a hurry, scrap metal, under the table*
Recycled language	words: *embarrassed, interested, secret, worried* grammar: *past simple and past perfect tenses; subject and object pronouns*
Pronunciation	*'d 6D.2*
Discourse	pronouns in reported speech

Language note

This is the first presentation of tense shift in reported speech and the examples in the lesson are restricted to the simple forms of the past, present, and future. Other structures will be focused on later in the course.

End product

In *Put it all together,* students retell two parts of a connected story in *Pairwork* from memory. They discuss their answers to some questions to find out how their stories are connected and are directed to >> **p.133** to read the solution.

Preparation

Read the *Extra activity* notes for exercise 3. Take dictionaries to class, if necessary.

Warmer

Ask students to think about the last thing that somebody said to them just before they came to class, just before they left home this morning, last thing last night. Ask volunteers to tell the class. Monitor for the use of *say* and *tell* and use of tenses. Do not correct for accuracy at this stage.

Write *How to report what people said* on the board.

A Read and understand the main ideas

In this section, students skim and scan an article for the main ideas, ignoring or guessing the meaning of unknown vocabulary.

1 Direct students to the pictures and title of the article on >> **p.62**. In pairs, students predict the content of the story. Ask for suggestions but do not comment at this stage.

2 Ask students to read the article and answer the two questions. Set a short time limit to encourage students to skim the text.

> Victor Lustig sold it.   Andre Poisson bought it (or thought he had, but he had a false contract).

3 Read the instructions and summaries a–f. Check vocabulary. Go through the example as a class to demonstrate that students might have to think about the language in the summaries and look for connected ideas in the text. Do the next paragraph together if necessary, asking students to say which key words in the questions and summaries helped them find the answer.

Monitor and help as necessary as students continue individually. Elicit key words in the summaries and corresponding detail in the text as you check answers. At the end of the activity, ask students if they would have bought the Eiffel Tower and encourage them to give reasons.

> 2 e   3 f   4 c   5 a   6 d

Extra activity

Ask students to find the following words and phrases in the text and to guess their meanings: *neglected (para 1), business deal (para 2), permanent (para 3), in a hurry (para 5), under the table (para 5).* Students check in their dictionaries. Put students into pairs to compare guesses and to check in their dictionaries. Ask students to tell each other how they guessed the meaning and to decide which approach worked best and why.

B Vocabulary *say* and *tell*

4 Ask students to underline or highlight examples of *said* and *told* in the text. Direct students to sentences 1–3 and check vocabulary. Ask students to underline the correct word in each sentence, using the examples in the text to help. Point out the form as you go over answers. Elicit or explain that *tell* always has a personal object.

> 1 said   2 told   3 said

5 Ask students to read the text and ignore the blanks. Explain any new vocabulary. Read the first two sentences and elicit or explain why *told* is the correct word. *(We use* tell *with a personal pronoun.)* Students continue individually. Monitor and help as necessary. To check answers, read the text, pausing at the blank and ask students as a class to call out the answer.

> 2 said   3 said   4 told   5 said   6 told

C Grammar tenses in reported speech

6 Read the instructions and direct students to the grammar box and column headings. Copy the sentences in the two columns in the first row onto the board. Underline the verbs in both sentences, *'m, told,* and *was*. Ask *Which was said first, the sentence in direct or reported speech? (Direct speech.)* Elicit or explain that we usually show this by changing the tense in the reporting verb (*told*), and the verb *'m* in the example changes to *was*. Read the information in the third column.

Ask students to find the sentences in the first column in reported speech in the text. Remind students to think about pronouns. Go over answers as a class and elicit the rule.

reported speech: He said that they had ('d) asked him to sell it.   change past simple to **past perfect**.
He said that he would ('d) buy it. change *will* to **would ('d)**.
Rule: change

7 Direct students to the grammar box and the column headings. Ask students about the tense of the three examples in row 1 for the verb *try* in the direct speech column (present, past, and future). Say each sentence for the class to report what you said, reading from the second column. Elicit or explain *'d* in the reported speech form 1b and 1c (in 1b *'d* is *had*, in 1c *'d* is *would*).

Ask students to continue the activity, looking again at the sentences for *try* if necessary. Monitor and help, making a note of any problems to review at the end of the section.

2 a needed   b had ('d) needed   c would need ('d)

8 6D.1 Explain to students that they might find it difficult to hear *'d*. Read the phrases in items 1 and 2. Play the audio for students to listen and tune in to the speaker's voice. Play the audio a second time, pausing after each item for students to repeat. Give extra practice as necessary.

9 6D.2 Read the instructions and the example to demonstrate the activity. Play the audio, pausing after each one for students to say the letter. Give positive feedback for correct answers. In pairs, students test a partner. Monitor and help with pronunciation.

1 b, a, c   2 c, a, b

10 Go through the instructions and check students understand *small lies*. Read the actual words people said aloud and do the first item with the class to demonstrate the activity.

Ask students to read items 2–6 and check vocabulary. Monitor and help as students continue individually. To check answers, ask for volunteers to read the full sentence. Tell the class to listen and say if they agree or not. If there is disagreement, explain the answer referring back to the grammar box in exercise 7.

2 ... he would ('d) be fine.   3 ... he had ('d) bought it.
4 ... Santa Claus had ('d) brought it.   5 ... she looked lovely.
6 ... he didn't feel very well.

11 Read the instructions and check students understand the activity. Put students into pairs to decide the order of the lies, starting with the worst first. Monitor for accuracy and encourage students to give reasons. Nominate a few students to tell the class the order of their lies and encourage them to explain their order. Help students to express their ideas.

ABC Put it all together

12 Read the instructions and check students understand the activity. Put students into A/B pairs and direct them to the appropriate *Pairwork* story on >> **p.129** and >> **p.134**. Give students time to make notes of key parts of the story and to remember it. Monitor and help as necessary.

Read through the second part of the instructions in *Pairwork*. Ask students to discuss the answers to the questions using the information from their stories. Bring the class together and go over the answers. Finally, direct students to >> **p.133** to read the solution. Ask students if they guessed the solution before they read it and encourage them to explain how they worked it out.

Student performance

Students should be able to report short statements.

You can use this checklist to monitor and give feedback or to assess students' performance.

Coherence	Do students use pronouns appropriately? exercise 10
Vocabulary	Do students mostly use *say* and *tell* appropriately? exercise 5
Pronunciation	Do students pronounce *'d* audibly? exercise 9

I can **report what people said.**

Students tick *on my own* if they have mainly told their story to a partner from memory. They tick *with some help* if they have looked at the sentences in the grammar box in exercise 7 occasionally.

Early finishers

Students swap roles and repeat the activity in exercise 12.

Additional material

How to report what people said

G tenses in reported speech   V *say* and *tell*   P *'d*

A Read and understand the main ideas

1 Look at the title and photos opposite. What do you think the story will be about? Tell a partner.

2 Read **The Man Who Sold the Eiffel Tower**. Who sold the tower? Who bought it?

3 Read the text again. Match summaries a–f with paragraphs 1–6. Compare with a partner.
   a ☐ explaining the sale
   b ☐1 a great idea
   c ☐ how to buy the Eiffel Tower
   d ☐ Lustig gets rich
   e ☐ organizing a meeting
   f ☐ reasons why it's a secret

B Vocabulary *say* and *tell*

4 Underline examples of *said* and *told* in the text. Then underline the correct words in these sentences.
   1 I said/told that I had a deal to offer him.
   2 I said/told him to give me the money.
   3 I said/told, 'We will both be rich!'

5 Work with a partner. Complete the text with *said* or *told*.
   In 1924, Arthur Ferguson met an American tourist in Trafalgar Square. He ¹ _told_____ the man that he was an estate agent. He ² _____ that the British Government was short of money and wanted to sell Nelson's Column. He ³ _____ they had asked him to sell it. He ⁴ _____ the tourist that the deal was secret. The tourist ⁵ _____ he would buy it. Ferguson ⁶ _____ him he needed a deposit of £6,000. The tourist paid.

C Grammar tenses in reported speech

6 Find these sentences reported in the text in exercise 5 and write them below. What are the differences in tense? Underline the correct word in the rule.

direct speech	reported speech	
'I'm an estate agent.'	*He told the man that he was an estate agent.*	change present simple to _past simple_
'They asked me to sell it.'		change past simple to _____
'I'll buy it.'		change *will* to _____

Rule
If the reporting verb (e.g. *say* or *tell*) is in the past, you change/don't change the tense in the reported speech.

7 Complete the sentences in the box. Note that *had* and *would* can both be reduced to *'d*.

		direct speech	reported speech	
1	a	I try to help.	He _said he tried____	to help.
	b	I tried to help.	He _said he'd tried__	to help.
	c	I'll try to help.	He _said he'd try___	to help.
2	a	I need money.	She said she _____	money.
	b	I needed money.	She said _____	money.
	c	I'll need money.	She said _____	money.

8 **6D.1▶ Pronunciation** Can you hear the *'d*? Listen to the difference and repeat.
   he tried to   he'd tried to
   she needed   she'd needed

9 **6D.2▶** Listen to the reported speech sentences from exercise 7 and say if they are *a*, *b*, or *c*. Test a partner.
   Example He said he'd tried to help. = b!

10 The people below tell small lies. These are their actual words. Complete the reported sentences.
   'You'll be fine.'   'Santa Claus brought it.'   'You look lovely.'
   'I bought it.'   'I don't feel very well.'   ~~'I'll have a little more.'~~
   1 Beth finished her meal and was full. To be polite, she said _she'd have a little more_.
   2 Edgar's doctor said _____. Edgar was ill for six more months.
   3 Frank found a winning lottery ticket on a train seat. He said _____.
   4 Linda got a new doll for Christmas. Linda's mum told her _____.
   5 Tina looked awful in her new dress. Her friend told her _____.
   6 Tom was fine, but he didn't want to go to school. He said _____.

11 Work with a partner. Do you think the lies in exercise 10 are bad? Put them in order.
   More practice? **Grammar Bank** >> p.141.

ABC Put it all together

12 Work with a partner. Read a story carefully and try to remember it. Tell your part of the story to your partner. Use reported speech instead of direct speech.
   Student A Look at **The Violin Story Part A** on >> p.129.
   Student B Look at **The Violin Story Part B** on >> p.134.

13 Now read **The Violin Story solution** on >> p.133.

I can report what people said. ▬▬▬▬▬▬▬▬

Writing Exchanging news in a personal letter

A Vocabulary responding to news

1 Work with a partner. Match the news and responses. Sometimes more than one answer is possible.

1 [d] My birthday is the same day as yours.	a How terrible! Poor you!
2 ☐ My aunt has died.	b Oh no, I'm so sorry.
3 ☐ I can't go on holiday – I've broken my arm.	c That's absolutely fantastic! Well done!
4 ☐ I've been chosen for the national team!	d Wow, what a coincidence!
5 ☐ I've resigned from my job!	e That's wonderful news. I'm so pleased for you!
6 ☐ We're going to have a baby!	f What a surprise!

2 Think of one piece of good news and one piece of bad news. Tell your partner and practise responding.

Example **A** I've passed my driving test!
            B That's absolutely fantastic! Well done!

B Read a personal letter

3 Look at the photo of Ashley's flat. Guess what's happening and how Ashley feels about it. Tell a partner.

4 Read Ashley's letter to Fran and check your guesses.

Dear Fran,

How are you? I'm fine. I've just moved into my new flat and it's brilliant. It's such a great feeling having a place of my own, although I'm absolutely exhausted after moving all my boxes!

My neighbours Angela and Bruce are nice, although their kids are quite noisy. However, school term starts next week, and Angela says they'll be quieter then. Anyway, I can't complain – I'm quite noisy myself, as you know!

By the way, bad news about me and Gabi. We've split up. It was really hard but I think it was the right thing to do. I'll tell you all about it next time we meet.

Last time we met, you said you were going to move flat as well. Have you moved yet? What's the new place like? Is it a nice area? Do you get on with the neighbours? Write soon and tell me all about it!

Love from Ashley

5 Find the words or phrases below in Ashley's letter. Match them with the meanings in 1–4.

☐ by the way   ☐ however   ☐ anyway   ☐ although

1 A word meaning *but* which isn't followed by a comma.
2 A word meaning *but* which is followed by a comma.
3 A word meaning *also* or *and*.
4 A phrase used to introduce an unconnected topic.

C Connect ideas

6 Write sentences with the same meaning using the blue words. Look at Ashley's letter for help with punctuation. Compare with a partner.

1 They're nice, although their kids are noisy. however
   They're nice. However, their kids are noisy.
2 I'm happy. However, I'm very tired. although
3 I don't want it. It's too expensive and I don't even like it. anyway
4 We did it. However, it wasn't easy. although
5 It's boring, although it's very well paid. however
6 I don't take sugar. I don't like it. Also, it's bad for you. anyway

D Think about your reader

7 Look at Ashley's letter again. What is Ashley's relationship to Fran? Choose the best answer.

a Complete strangers.
b Good friends.
c Acquaintances.

8 How does Ashley make the letter like a conversation with a friend? Work with your partner and find examples of 1–4 in the letter.

1 asking the reader questions
2 writing about people and facts the reader knows
3 expressing personal feelings about the news in the letter
4 using written expressions similar to *hello* and *goodbye* in spoken dialogue

9 Imagine Fran and Ashley meet and have the conversation face to face. Role play the conversation. Add more news and use expressions from exercise 1.

ABCD Put it all together

10 You are Fran. Write a reply. Respond to all the news in Ashley's letter and answer his questions. Connect your ideas and add some news about you and people you know.

11 You are Ashley. Read your partner's letter. Does it give you all the news you wanted to hear?

I can exchange news in a personal letter.

Tick ✓ the line.   with a lot of help   with some help   on my own   very easily

Orientation

Context and Language

In this lesson, students practise using connectors to write a 'newsy' letter to a friend. This is based on a model in exercise 4.

Recycled language	words: *absolutely, acquaintances, dialogue, exhausted, neighbours, noisy, strangers* phrases: *split up* grammar: *so, such* discourse: *also, and, but*
Recognition language	words: *coincidence, expressing, resigned*
Discourse	connectors: *anyway, although, by the way, however*

End product

In *Put it all together*, students reply to the letter in exercise 4. They swap letters and decide if it contains the news they expect to hear.

Warmer

Tell students to imagine they are writing a letter to a friend who lives in a different town. Ask them to think about what they've been doing recently and what they could tell their friend about. Put students into pairs or small groups to exchange ideas. Elicit suggestions around the class.

Write *How to exchange news in a personal letter* on the board.

A Vocabulary responding to news

1 Go through the instructions and ask students to read the information in both columns and check vocabulary as necessary. Put students into pairs to continue. Check answers.

> 2 b   3 a   4 c, e   5 a, f   6 e

Extra activity

Say a sentence from news items 1–6 and nominate a student to respond. That student then says a different news sentence and nominates another to respond.

2 Read the instructions and go through the example with the class before students continue in pairs. Monitor and give positive feedback for appropriate responses.

B Read a personal letter

In this section, students use a photo to guess what news a person gives in a letter before analysing it for informal discourse features.

3 Read the instructions and direct students to the photo of Ashley's flat. Put students into pairs to compare ideas and monitor and contribute to students' suggestions.

4 Ask students to read the letter and check their guesses, ignoring any new vocabulary for the moment. Ask for volunteers to tell the class about what they guessed correctly.

5 Read items 1–4 and do the first item as a class to demonstrate the activity. Monitor and help as students continue in pairs. Go over answers as a class.

> 1 although   2 however   3 by the way   4 anyway

C Connect ideas

6 Go through the instructions and example. Monitor and help as students continue individually. Students compare answers in pairs. Elicit answers and write them on the board.

> 2 I'm happy, although I'm very tired.   3 I don't want it. It's too expensive. Anyway, I don't even like it.   4 We did it, although it wasn't easy.   5 It's boring. However, it's very well paid. 6 I don't take sugar. I don't like it. Anyway, it's bad for you.

D Think about your reader

In this section, students think about the similarities between face-to-face conversation and an informal letter between friends.

7 Read the instructions and do the activity as a class. Elicit the best answer from students *(b)* and ask them to explain how they can tell that Ashley and Fran are good friends.

8 Go through the instructions and read items 1–4 with the class. Do the first item together to demonstrate the activity. Monitor and help as necessary, guiding students to the relevant parts of Ashley's letter. Check answers.

> 2 Ashley gives information about Gabi.   3 Ashley expresses personal feelings about his new flat, his neighbours and the end of his relationship.   4 He uses *Dear* for *Hello* and *Love from* for *goodbye*.

9 Read the instructions. Give students time to plan their conversations and to think of answers to the questions at the end of Ashley's letter. Remind them to use some expressions from exercise 1. Monitor and give positive feedback for 'newsy' conversations and check students swap roles. Volunteers have their conversations for the class.

ABCD Put it all together

10 Go through the instructions and remind students to use the expressions in exercise 5.

11 Tell students to swap letters and imagine that they are Ashley. Ask them to make a note of any more information to ask their partner at the end.

Student performance

Students should be able to write a reply to a personal letter.

You can use this checklist to monitor and give feedback or to assess students' performance.

Content	Have students included all the information? Have students written in a conversational style?
Coherence	Have students connected ideas appropriately?

I can **exchange news in a personal letter.**

Students tick *on my own* if they think they have given the news their friend would expect. They can tick *with some help* if they feel they need to add one or two more pieces of information.

Early finishers

Students imagine that a friend has just moved to another town. They write a personal letter, giving and asking for news.

Additional material

www.oup.com/elt/result for extra practice activities
www.oup.com/elt/teacher/result for extra teacher resources

Warmer

Remember who

Read (or write on the board) the sentences below from Unit 6. In small groups, students write down who said or wrote them. Students look through the unit to check their answers at the end.

1 Your kids are naughty. 2 I had a full head of hair back then. 3 I'm a government official. 4 Look what you've done to my car! 5 I've moved into my new flat and it's brilliant. 6 I'm sorry it took over 60 years. 7 I'd like to buy the Eiffel Tower. 8 Bad news about me and Gabi! 9 Let's have a drink to celebrate. 10 I could hardly believe it.

> 1 Mrs Dickson 2 Doug Schmitt 3 Victor Lustig 4 Paul
> 5 Ashley 6 Mr Breitenstein 7 Andre Poisson 8 Ashley
> 9 Suzi 10 Mr Heilwagen

A Grammar

1 so and such 6A exercise 8

Warm-up: Say the following words for students to call out *so* or *such* to make a phrase: *restaurant, big meal, tired, short holiday, frightened, wonderful film, bad interview, exhausted*. Direct students back to exercise 8 on >> **p.57** to revise, if necessary.

Set-up: Students underline the stressed word in the example.

> 2 We ate outside because it was such a beautiful day.
> 3 Why are fresh vegetables so expensive these days?
> 4 I didn't know it was such a long journey.
> 5 I didn't know it was so far away.

Follow-up: Students write some factually true or false sentences about Paul and Suzi in *Crash!* on >> **p.56**. They say their sentences for a partner. They repeat the factually correct ones.

2 Infinitives and gerunds 6B exercise 7

Warm-up: Books closed. Draw two columns on the board: *A use a gerund after …* and *B use to + infinitive after …* Call out the following verbs for the class to say A or B: *don't mind, fancy, want, finish, expect, enjoy, decided.*

Set-up: Go through the instructions and point out the pairs of similar sentence endings in a–h.

> 2 e 3 f 4 c 5 g 6 h 7 a 8 d

Follow-up: Write these pairs of sentence beginnings on the board: *Do you fancy …?/Do you want …?; I don't mind …/I hope …; Don't forget …/Have you finished …?* In pairs, students write similar sentence endings for each pair. Students change the order of their sentence endings and swap with a partner to do the exercise.

3 Pronouns in reported speech 6C exercise 11

Warm-up: Ask students what Mr and Mrs Dickson said about the Lanes. Direct students to *Love Your Neighbours* on >> **p.60** to check.

Set-up: Ask students to read the paragraph and say what Holly thinks of Justin.

> Holly says she shares the office with a man called Justin. She says they sometimes have lunch together. She says she'll introduce me to him one day. She says she thinks he's really funny.

Follow-up: Ask students to tell their partner why they think they are good neighbours. They change partners and tell a new partner.

4 Tenses in reported speech 6D exercise 6

Warm-up: Write the following sentences on the board: *I try to help.* and *I need money.* Ask students to write the sentences in the past and future, and then to write all of them in reported speech. Direct students to the grammar box on >> **p.63** to check their answers.

Set-up: Go through the example with the class.

> 2 He said she'd be fine. 3 She said she hadn't studied enough. 4 He said she always passed her exams. 5 She said she had got a C in December. 6 He said there was still time to study. 7 She said she didn't understand maths. 8 He said he'd help her.

Follow-up: In pairs, students write a similar short conversation for another pair to change into reported speech.

B Vocabulary

5 Extreme adjectives 6A exercise 7

Warm-up: Read the extreme adjectives and elicit nouns that the adjectives could describe.

Set-up: Ask students to underline the noun in the example sentence.

> 2 terrified 3 furious 4 enormous 5 amazing 6 exhausted

Follow-up: Students write gap-fill sentences for a partner using *Extreme adjectives* on >> **p.56**.

6 Behaviour 6C exercise 1

Warm-up: Set a short time limit for students to study the vocabulary in *Behaviour* on >> **p.60**. Books closed. Students write as many words as they can remember and compare with a partner.

Set-up: Ask students to read the clues and check vocabulary as necessary.

> 2 behaved 3 friendly 4 rude 5 noisy 6 rough 7 swear
> 8 fight 9 helpful 10 nosy

Follow-up: In pairs, students prepare a word search for another pair, using the vocabulary on >> **p. 60**. Tell students to draw a grid with 11 columns and 6 rows. They write the words horizontally and vertically.

7 say and tell 6D exercise 5

Warm-up: Say sentences to different students and nominate others to report what you said using *say* and *tell*. Suggested sentences: *Your bag's nice. You look tired. I worked hard yesterday. I'll help you.*

Set-up: Ask students to read the text and find the name of the dog.

> 2 told 3 said 4 said 5 told 6 said 7 said

Follow-up: Direct students to >> **p.63**, exercise 10. In pairs, students write three 'small lies' sentences for another pair to change into reported speech.

Early finishers

Students look through the grammar in Unit 6 and write the topics in order of difficulty. They write five personal information sentences to help them remember the most difficult area.

Unit 6 Review

A Grammar

1 *so and such* Make these sentences more extreme using *so* or *such*.

1 You don't need to speak loudly.
   You don't need to speak so loudly.

2 We ate outside because it was a beautiful day.
   _____

3 Why are fresh vegetables expensive these days?
   _____

4 I didn't know it was a long journey.
   _____

5 I didn't know it was far away.
   _____

2 Infinitives and gerunds Match 1–8 with a–h.

1 [b] It's warm and sunny. Do you fancy ...
2 [ ] It's a nice day. Do you want ...
3 [ ] After leaving school, I hope ...
4 [ ] I'm going to take a year out before ...
5 [ ] There were dark clouds, so I decided ...
6 [ ] It was raining, but I don't mind ...
7 [ ] You can watch TV when you finish ...
8 [ ] Please don't forget ...

a doing your homework.
b going to the beach?
c going to university.
d to do your homework.
e to go for a picnic?
f to go to university to study economics.
g to take my umbrella.
h walking in the rain.

3 Pronouns in reported speech Report what Holly says about her work using *says*.

'I work in an office. I share the office with a man called Justin. We sometimes have lunch together. I'll introduce you to him one day. I think he's really funny.'

She says she works in an office. She says she shares ...

4 Tenses in reported speech Write this conversation in reported speech using *said*.

Anna ¹ I'm worried about the maths exam.
   Anna said she was worried about the maths exam.
Ben ² You'll be fine.
A ³ I didn't study enough.
B ⁴ You always pass exams.
A ⁵ I got a C in December.
B ⁶ There's still time to study.
A ⁷ I don't understand maths.
B ⁸ I'll help you.

B Vocabulary

5 Extreme adjectives Complete the sentences with these adjectives.

amazing ~~brilliant~~ enormous
exhausted furious terrified

1 Her first book was good, but her second was *brilliant*.
2 She's _____ of spiders and snakes.
3 He's _____ because I broke his computer.
4 The Atlantic's big, but the Pacific's _____.
5 Greg's a magician and he can do some _____ tricks.
6 He was _____ after walking for ten hours.

6 Behaviour Find the answers to clues 1–10. Some letters are used twice.

```
A  C (N  A  U  G  H  T  Y)
E  B  E  H  A  V  E  D  N
F  R  I  E  N  D  L  Y  O
I  R  R  U  D  E  P  U  S
G  N  O  I  S  Y  F  H  Y
H  A  E  S  R  O  U  G  H
T  S  W  E  A  R  L  O  P
```

Clues
1 Bad behaviour. (adj) *naughty*
2 Opposite of 1. Well-_____.
3 Behaves like a friend. (adj)
4 Opposite of polite.
5 Opposite of quiet.
6 Not polite, may be violent.
7 To use bad words.
8 To attack each other.
9 Likes to help. (adj)
10 Curious about other people's personal life.

7 *say* and *tell* Complete the story with *said* or *told*.

There was a boy with a dog on the train. I ¹ *said*, 'Your dog's nice. What's his name?' The boy ² _____ me his dog was called Boris. 'He looks like a good dog,' I ³ _____. 'Does he bite?' The boy ⁴ _____ he didn't. Then I reached over to touch the dog and it bit me. 'Ouch! You ⁵ _____ me Boris didn't bite!', I ⁶ _____. 'He doesn't,' ⁷ _____ the boy, 'That's not Boris.'

DOES YOUR DOG LOOK LIKE YOU?

You often hear people say that dogs look like their owners. It sounds like a crazy idea, but a new study from California suggests that it's true – but only in certain circumstances.

Researchers wanted to find out if people really do look like their dogs, and just how this happens. First of all, they took photos of 45 dogs and their owners. They mixed the photos up and asked a group of people to match them.

The people who took part in the research were able to match most of the owners with their dogs if they were pure-bred – dogs whose parents are both the same type of dog. However, they weren't able to do the matching for mongrels

– dogs with parents of two different types. The researchers have suggested that this may be because people choose dogs which look like themselves, and people who want pure-bred dogs choose their pets more carefully.

The researchers say it isn't clear how the people in their study were able to do the matching. They didn't simply match hairy dogs with hairy people or big dogs with big people. It seems that they used a more complicated method, such as matching friendly-looking dogs with friendly-looking people.

What do you think? Try it for yourself. Can you match these dogs with their owners?

Character	Looks	Age
active ag**gres**sive am**bit**ious	**bush**y **eye**brows mou**stache** fringe	in her late teens
ar**tist**ic con**fid**ent **gen**erous	clean-**shav**en round face high **fore**head	in his early twenties
im**ag**inative kind **live**ly **ner**vous	**curl**y hair **ging**er hair straight hair	in his mid thirties around fifty
out**go**ing **ser**ious shy un**friend**ly	**wav**y hair **shoul**der-length hair	in his seventies

How to say how people look

Orientation

Context

In this lesson, students practise using adjectives to describe the character, looks, and age of a person.

The photos show six people and dogs who closely resemble them. The text *Does your dog look like you?* discusses recent research on the topic.

Word stress is shown in the adjectives and noun phrases in the vocabulary panels *Character* and *Looks*. The phrases in *Age* give examples of how to refer to approximate age.

Culture note

English speakers often use contrastive stress to clarify misunderstandings. It is more polite as it avoids telling a person directly that they are wrong. It can also be used to ask for clarification (see *Pronunciation* below).

Language

Preview language	*maybe, probably*
Focus words	looks: *bushy eyebrows, clean-shaven, curly, fringe, ginger, high forehead, moustache, round face, shoulder-length, straight, wavy* character: *active, aggressive, ambitious, artistic, confident, generous, imaginative, kind, lively, nervous, outgoing, serious, shy, unfriendly*
Focus phrases	*look* and *look like*: She looks very happy., She looks like my grandmother. age: *in her late teens, in his early twenties, in his mid thirties, around fifty, in his seventies*
Recognition vocabulary	*circumstances, hairy, mongrel, pure-bred, researchers, smile*
Recycled language	words: *beard, black, brown, face, friendly, grey, hair, intelligent, long, nose, owners, parents, short, white* grammar: *closed questions; adjective order in noun phrases*
Pronunciation	contrastive stress: Has she got **short** fair hair? No, she's got **long** fair hair. 7A.4

End product

In *Put it all together*, students work in small groups and ask closed questions to identify a picture.

Preparation

Take photos of famous people to class if you want to use them for the *Warmer*. Look at *Portraits of Men* on >> **p.129** to familiarize yourself with exercise 15. Think about classroom organization for group work in exercise 15. Take dictionaries to class.

Warmer

Put students into small groups. Ask each one to choose a famous person or a student in the class. The others have to ask yes/no questions about appearance to identify the person. Monitor for use of adjectives, but do not overcorrect for accuracy at this stage. Write an example question on the board, e.g. *Has she got long brown hair?*

Write *How to say how people look* on the board.

A Read for detail

In this section, students read an article for gist and detail.

1   Read the questions and direct students to the photos on >> **p.66**. Put students into pairs to discuss the questions. Monitor and join in. Listen to students' use and pronunciation of adjectives. Ask volunteers to share their ideas with the class.

2   Direct students to the text *Does your dog look like you?* on >> **p.66**. Read the question and answers a–d and check vocabulary as necessary. Set a short time limit to encourage students to read for gist. Take a class vote on the best option and nominate students to say why or why not (c).

3   Read the instructions and ask students to read sentences 1–6. Check vocabulary as necessary. Ask students how they will read the text. (*Use key words in the question to help them locate the information in the text.*) Monitor and help as necessary. Ask for volunteers to say *true* or *false* and to explain reasons for any *false* answers.

> 1 True.   2 False. (They asked other people to match the photos, not the owners.)   3 False. (Mongrels don't.)   4 True. 5 False. (They used a more complicated method.)   6 True.

Teaching tip

Exercises 2 and 3 require different reading strategies. Students often read texts the same way, irrespective of why they are reading. Explain that they will become much better readers if they choose a strategy which suits their purpose.

4   Go through the instructions and example and check understanding. Put students into pairs to continue the activity. Monitor and give positive feedback for interesting explanations. Go over answers as a class, nominating a different student to say how they matched the dog with its owner. Listen to pronunciation but do not overcorrect for accuracy.

> 4 and 6   5 and 3   7 and 9   10 and 8   12 and 1

B Vocabulary looks and character; *look* and *look like*

5   Direct students to the example sentences. Ask students to find a noun *(dog)* and an adjective *(friendly)*. Read sentences 1 and 2 and complete the rules as a class.

> 1 look like   2 look

Language note

In rules 1 and 2 in exercise 5 it would be more accurate to say noun phrase and adjective phrase, since there may be other words along with the noun or adjective, such as *her* before a noun, or an adjective, e.g. *He looks like a nice man*; or *very* before an adjective, e.g. *He looks very nice*. Point out the extra words to your students as you check answers.

6   Read the instructions and go through the example as a class. Check students understand why *looks like* is the correct answer and point out the *s* on the third person. Monitor and help as students continue individually. To check answers, nominate students to read the full sentence.

> 2 looks   3 looks like   4 look   5 looks like   6 look like

7 Direct students to *Character, Looks,* and *Age* on >> p.66. Put students into pairs and ask them to use their dictionaries to match the words and phrases with the people in the photos. Monitor and help, eliciting suggestions around the class. Give extra pronunciation practice as necessary. Point out the syllable stress in bold.

> photo 2: (woman) late sixties, curly hair, kind, generous, active, lively
> photo 4: (man) mid thirties, clean shaven, round face, high forehead, unfriendly, aggressive
> photo 5: (man) seventies, shoulder-length hair, moustache, beard, bushy eyebrows, lively
> photo 7: (woman), early fifties, wavy hair, ambitious, confident
> photo 10: (girl) late teens, early twenties, ginger hair, no fringe, outgoing, imaginative, artistic
> photo 12: (man) early twenties, straight hair, nervous, shy

8 Read the instructions and the example. Ask students which photo the text describes (photo 2). Students continue the activity in pairs. Monitor and give positive feedback where students have given two or more pieces of information. Make a note of repeated pronunciation problems to go over at the end.

Teaching tip

Listen out for L1 interference. Students might say *He's got 21.* or *He's 21 years.*

Extra activity

In pairs, small groups or as a class, students describe a picture and the other(s) guess which one is being described. If the other(s) can't guess, encourage the student describing the picture to give more detail. Point out that students can also make negative sentences, e.g. *He hasn't got a beard.*

C Listen for key words

In this section, students listen to a short monologue and identify the key words they need to identify the subject of a description.

9 7A.1 Go through the instructions and check students understand the activity. Play the audio and give students time to use their underlined words to identify the photo before checking answers *(photo 12)*. To check answers, read the text aloud for students to indicate key words. Check the class agrees before giving feedback. Ask students which words aren't key words *(articles, some pronouns, prepositions, conjunctions).*

> **Suggested answers**
> man, early twenties, he, straight, dark, long face, nose long, thin, eyes, wide open, surprised, shy
> (Note: students might underline fewer than these suggestions.)

Teaching tip

This activity helps to build students' confidence. Most students find listening very difficult and often feel discouraged by what they can't understand. The underlined words and phrases demonstrate just how much (or little) they need to understand to do the activity.

10 7A.2 Go through the instructions and play the audio, pausing after each description for students to identify the photo. In pairs, students compare their answers.

> a photo 7   b photo 10   c photo 4   d photo 2   e photo 5

11 Read the instructions and check students understand the activity. Play the audio. Check answers.

D Pronunciation contrastive stress

12 7A.3 Read the instructions and check students understand the activity. Ask students how they will listen. *(For key words, pronouns, adjectives.)* Play the audio. Ask for answers and the words which helped students guess.

> photo 5 (the older man) (key words = man, long white hair)

13 7A.4 Read the instructions and direct students to columns A and B. Explain that the sentences are exactly the same except for the words in bold and these are the words the speaker chooses to give prominence or main stress to.

Ask students to listen and say A or B when you stop the recording. Play the audio, pausing at the end of each item.

> 1 B, A   2 A, B   3 A, B   4 B, A

Extra activity

In pairs, students test a partner. Student take turns to say a sentence from the box, the other says A or B.

14 Read the instructions and do the example as a class to demonstrate the activity. Ask students to identify which sentences from exercise 13 (1A or B) answers each question. Underline the stressed word to show the relationship between the question and answer. Put students into pairs to continue the activity.

Check answers as a class before students ask and answer in pairs. Explain that using contrastive stress in answers is a polite way of correcting information.

> 2 A, B   3 A, B   4 B, A

Extra activity

Students take turns to ask and answer about the people in the photos 1–12. They imagine they haven't heard the information correctly, and ask a question for confirmation.

ABCD Put it all together

15 Put students into small groups. Direct them to *Portraits of Men* on >> p.129 and go through the instructions and the example. Tell students to take turns to choose a photo.

Student performance

Students should be able to give short descriptions in answers to questions.

You can use this checklist to monitor and give feedback or to assess students' performance.

Interaction	Do students use contrastive stress to check information? exercise 14
Vocabulary	Do students a variety of adjectives? exercise 8
Pronunciation	Do students use contrastive stress accurately? exercise 14

I can **say how people look.**

Students tick *on my own* if they have done the activity without looking at *Character, Looks,* and *Age* on >> p.66. They tick *with some help* if they looked at the vocabulary panels occasionally.

Early finishers

Students decide which dog they think the people in *Portraits of Men* would choose. They compare with a partner and explain why.

Additional material

www.oup.com/elt/result for extra practice activities
www.oup.com/elt/teacher/result for extra teacher resources

How to say how people look

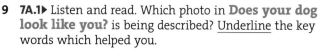
v looks and character; *look* and *look like* **p** contrastive stress

A Read for detail

1 Which dogs in the photos opposite do you prefer? Why? Tell a partner.

2 Read **Does your dog look like you?** opposite quickly. What is the text about? Choose the best answer.
   a Different types of dog.
   b People who try to look like dogs.
   c Research on the appearance of dogs and their owners.
   d People and their dogs in California.

3 Read the text again. Write *true* or *false*.
   1 Researchers mixed the photos of the dogs and owners.
   2 They asked the dog owners to find their dogs.
   3 All dogs look like their owners.
   4 People are careful when they choose pure-bred dogs.
   5 People simply matched hairy dogs with hairy people.
   6 People matched friendly-looking people and dogs.

4 Work with a partner and match the people in the photos with their dogs. Explain how you did it.
   Example photo 2 and 11 – the woman and her dog both have the same curly hair and it's the same colour ...

B Vocabulary looks and character; *look* and *look like*

5 Look at the example sentences and underline the correct word in the rules.
   He looks friendly. He looks like his dog.
   1 Use look/look like before a noun, to compare appearances.
   2 Use look/look like before an adjective, to guess a person's character from their appearance.

6 Complete the sentences with the correct form of *look* or *look like*.
   1 He _looks like_ a student.
   2 She _____ very happy.
   3 She _____ her sister.
   4 He doesn't _____ very kind.
   5 She _____ my grandmother.
   6 He doesn't _____ anyone I know.

7 Work with a partner. Look at **Character**, **Looks**, and **Age** opposite. Match the words and phrases with people in the photos. Use a dictionary to help.

8 Make sentences to describe the people in the photos. Compare with a partner.
   Example She looks generous. She doesn't look aggressive. She's got curly hair. She's probably in her late sixties. She looks like my grandmother ...

C Listen for key words

9 7A.1▶ Listen and read. Which photo in **Does your dog look like you?** is being described? Underline the key words which helped you.
   This man's in his early twenties, and he's got straight dark hair ... ehm ... it's quite long. He's got quite a long face, and his nose is long and thin too. His eyes are wide open – he looks a bit suprised. He looks a bit shy, nervous perhaps, I don't know.

10 7A.2▶ Listen to these descriptions and match them with people in the photos. Compare with a partner.

11 Work with a partner. Before you listen again, write down any key words you can remember about each photo. When you listen, tick ✓ your words if you hear them.

D Pronunciation contrastive stress

12 7A.3▶ Listen to two people playing a guessing game. Say which person in **Does your dog look like you?** they're talking about.

13 7A.4▶ Which word is stressed? Listen and say *A* or *B*.

	A	B
1	No, **long** fair hair.	No, long **fair** hair.
2	No, curly **ging**er hair.	No, **curly** ginger hair.
3	No, **late** twenties.	No, late **twen**ties.
4	No, big **brown** eyes.	No, **big** brown eyes.

14 Work with a partner. Match the answers in exercise 13 with these questions. Then ask and answer.
   1 [B] Has he got long dark hair?
     [A] Has he got short fair hair?
   2 [ ] Has she got curly grey hair?
     [ ] Has she got straight ginger hair?
   3 [ ] Is he in his early twenties?
     [ ] Is he in his late thirties?
   4 [ ] Has she got small brown eyes?
     [ ] Has she got big blue eyes?

   Example A Has he got long dark hair?
           B No, long **fair** hair.

ABCD Put it all together

15 Work in groups. Look at **Portraits of men** on ≫ p.129. Take turns to choose a photo. The other students ask closed questions to guess the photo.

Compound adjectives

clean-shaven	loose-fitting	well-known
fashion-conscious /ˈfæʃn kɒnʃəs/	old-fashioned	well-mannered
good-looking	well-dressed	well-off

The Kings of Cool

Brazzaville, Congo – Bienvenu Mouzieto knows what he likes. Clothes. He's standing in front of his house in the poor and dusty Bacongo neighbourhood, wearing a loose-fitting grey suit, leather shoes, a hat, and a tie. He's even wearing a white scarf. His outfit is possibly worth more than his house. He is elegant in an old-fashioned 1930's style. It's not what you expect to see in one of the world's poorest countries.

But Mouzieto is not the only well-dressed person around here. He is one of a large group of fashion-conscious men called the *sapeurs*. They are mostly poor and unemployed, but they would rather spend their money on clothes than food. For them, looking cool is everything. Style is their identity – they believe in the motto, 'You are what you wear'. The *sapeurs* know what they like, and what they like is expensive. It's Armani. It's Gucci. It's Prada. When they get dressed up and go out, it's a battle of designer labels. The winner is the person with the most elegant and expensive outfit.

The *sapeurs* know how to show off their clothes. They spend hours in front of the mirror practising their own favourite ways of standing. They learn how to walk with style. They know which colours look good together and they only use three colours in any outfit, including the accessories. The socks will match the hat, perhaps, or the belt will match the watch strap. The *sapeurs* are clean-shaven and well-mannered, and they are all well-known in their local neighbourhoods.

Most *sapeurs* can't really afford their lifestyle. They are not well-off, and it's difficult to find the money for such expensive tastes. Sometimes they borrow clothes – after all, only the person who lent the clothes knows where they came from. Sometimes they turn to crime, and many have spent time in prison.

What makes a *sapeur* go to such extremes to look good? Photographer Héctor Mediavilla has been studying the *sapeurs* since 2003. He understands why they like dressing up. 'When they go out dressed up, they walk differently,' he says. They behave as if they are important people – 'They show off. Sometimes they refuse to talk to other people – even their friends. They act as if they really were famous and important. They're stars for that night. It's worth it, isn't it?'

How to talk about fashion

Orientation

Context

In this lesson, students use *wh-* clauses and compound nouns to discuss fashion.

The magazine article, *The Kings of Cool,* is written by a journalist who has been studying a group of people, *sapeurs.* They come from very poor backgrounds and yet go to enormous lengths to look good.

In the article, the journalist points out that wearing designer clothes can temporarily change the way people feel about themselves. In this case, they feel like 'stars'.

Compound adjectives gives focus vocabulary from the article.

Language

Focus grammar	*wh-* clauses: *I don't care what people think., I don't know how much an Armani suit costs., I don't mind what I wear., I know which colours look good together.,* etc.
Focus words	compound adjectives: *clean-shaven, fashion-conscious, good-looking, loose-fitting, old-fashioned, well-dressed, well-known, well-mannered, well-off*
Recognition vocabulary	*accessories, designer label, dusty, show off, unemployed, watch strap*
Recycled language	words: *outfit, rich, smart, tight* phrases: *looks + adjective, looks like, suit me, to be worth it*
Pronunciation	*t* at the end of a word 7B.2

Language notes

Wh- clauses often relate to mental or verbal process, e.g. don't mind, don't care, decide, explain, forget, guess, imagine, know, remember, say, tell, think, understand, wonder.

Compound nouns. Whether or not two nouns are joined with a hyphen is often difficult to decide. Different dictionaries often give different information.

End product

In *Put it all together*, students make a statement and justify it giving reasons. This is based on audio script 7B.1.

Preparation

Think of a famous person to introduce exercise 3. Take dictionaries to class, if necessary.

Warmer

Review clothes vocabulary. Set a time limit of about two minutes and ask students to write as many words for clothes as they can remember. Do a quick class brainstorm and write vocabulary on the board, checking students' understanding as necessary.

Ask students to talk about the clothes they're wearing at the moment, e.g. where they got them, if they prefer smart or casual, cheap or expensive clothes. Respond to students' comments by expressing your opinion and giving reasons.

Write *How to talk about fashion* on the board.

A Vocabulary compound adjectives

1 Go through the instructions and remind students to use the adjectives from lesson 7A. Monitor and join in as students continue in pairs. Ask for volunteers to describe what another student is wearing. The class guesses who it is.

2 Direct students to *Compound adjectives* on >> **p.68** and ask students to use the words to describe the people in the photos accompanying the article. Point out that they can use *is/isn't*. Encourage students to think about meaning by using what they already know about parts of the compound adjectives, e.g. *clean + shave* = somebody without a beard or moustache. Monitor for pronunciation and give extra practice as necessary.

Extra activity

Give students brief definitions for students to say a word in *Compound adjectives*, e.g. interested in modern clothes = *fashion-conscious*.

3 Read the instructions and demonstrate the activity by describing a famous person. Monitor and help as necessary as students continue in pairs. Nominate students to describe people for the class to guess who they are.

Extra help

In pairs, students look back at the pictures for lesson 7A and see who they can describe using the adjectives.

B Read for detail

In this section, students read a magazine article for specific information and infer for detail.

4 Direct students to the photos and title in *The Kings of Cool* on >> **p.68**. In pairs, students answer the question. Elicit suggestions and ask what they think the title of the text means.

> **Suggested answers**
> **the place:** It's probably Brazzaville, Congo, it's poor.
> **the people:** They're well-dressed, wearing smart (not casual) loose-fitting clothes, etc.

5 Go through the instructions and ask students to read sentences 1–6. Check vocabulary. Ask students how they are going to read the text. *Word by word or use key words in the question to locate the information in the text? (Use key words.)* Encourage students to guess the meaning of any new vocabulary as they read or to ignore them.

Do the first item as a class to demonstrate the activity. Students continue individually. Ask for volunteers to give answers. Check the class agrees before giving feedback.

> 2 True.   3 False. (They are mostly poor and unemployed.)
> 4 True.   5 False. (Many have spent time in prison.)   6 True.

6 Direct students to read questions 1–4 and check vocabulary. Explain that students might not find the answer in the text. Do item 1 to demonstrate the activity. Monitor and help as students continue individually.

Put students into pairs to compare ideas. Monitor for interesting contributions and give positive feedback whenever possible. Check answers.

7 Go through the instructions and ask students to guess the meaning of the words. Students compare their guesses in pairs. Ask for volunteers to share their guesses with the class, and say how they guessed. If there is more than one suggestion for a particular word, ask the class which one they think is best.

Ask students to find the words in their dictionaries. Monitor and help students find and notice how compound nouns and phrasal verbs are listed in their dictionaries, e.g. *designer label* may not be an individual entry but students could look up *design* or *designer*. Go over answers as a class.

Teaching tip
Remind students that, to guess the meanings of words in a text, they can think about the word class or part of speech; look at the unknown word in context and see if it is part of a larger phrase, e.g. *show off* and see if they already know a part of the word. Point out that using more than one strategy will help them become more successful readers.

C Grammar *wh-* clauses

8 Read the instructions and direct students to *The Kings of Cool* on >> **p.68**. Ask students to read sentences 1–7 and check vocabulary. Direct students to the section heading and elicit or explain that a *wh-* word is a collective name for interrogative pronouns, most of which begin with *wh*. *How* is also called a *wh* word.

Do the first item together to demonstrate the activity. Elicit or explain that the word in the blank relates to the phrase which follows it. Monitor and help, noting any common mistakes to review at the end. Nominate individuals to say the complete sentence as they give their answer.

2 what   3 how   4 how   5 which   6 where   7 why

9 Read the instructions and go through the example. Ask students to read items 2–7 and check vocabulary. Monitor and help as students continue individually. Ask for volunteers to give answers and see if everyone agrees.

I know/don't know:
2 why people buy designer clothes.
3 what my UK shoe size is.   4 where my shoes were made.
5 how tall I am.   6 who invented jeans.
7 what colours suit me.

10 Read the instructions and ask the example question to several students. Elicit or explain that only the first part *I don't know* changes to make the question form. Do one or two more examples, encouraging students to add information, e.g. speaker B could say, *No, I don't. I've never bought shoes in the UK.* Monitor and give positive feedback for accurate word order in questions as students continue in pairs.

Extra activity
Open pairs questions. Ask a question and nominate a student to answer. The same student asks another question and then nominates another to answer. Continue, encouraging students to increase fluency when they ask the questions. You could click your fingers to suggest they speak more quickly.

D Listen for specific information

In this section, students anticipate what a person will say and listen to check.

11 Direct students to the photos of the three women and ask students to describe them, using *She looks like …* and *She looks … .*

Ask students to read sentences 1–6. Check they understand the difference between *I don't mind.* and *I don't care.* Check vocabulary. Read the instructions and do the first item as a class to demonstrate. Go through each sentence asking for volunteers to make suggestions and give reasons. Do not comment at this stage as students will listen to check predictions in the next exercise.

12 7B.1 Play the audio for students to check their predictions. Students compare in pairs and listen a second time or check answers using the audio script on >> **p.155**.

1 WL   2 H   3 WL   4 M   5 WL   6 M

Extra plus
Students decide who they agree with most. They compare and explain why in small groups.

13 7B.2 Read the instructions and direct students to the sentences in exercise 11. Play the audio, pausing for students to repeat. Ask about the pronunciation of *t* and elicit or explain that it isn't pronounced, unless the following word begins with a vowel. Play the audio a second time if necessary, encouraging students to sound more fluent.

ABCD Put it all together

14 Ask students to read questions 1–6 and go through the instructions with the class. Monitor and check students are making notes rather than writing full sentences.

15 In pairs, students make their 'fashion statement' to a partner. They swap partners or work in groups to make their fashion statement again. Students say whose opinion is similar.

Student performance
Students should be able to state their opinion and give short explanations.

You can use this checklist to monitor and give feedback or to assess students' performance.

Fluency	Do students give their opinions without a lot of hesitation? exercise 13
Grammar	Do students use a variety of *wh-* clauses? exercise 10
Vocabulary	Do students use a few compound adjectives? exercise 3

I can **talk about fashion.**
Students tick *on my own* if they have made their statement using their notes. They tick *with some help* if they have also looked at the vocabulary panel or exercise 11 occasionally.

Early finishers
Students make a fashion statement for a *sapeur,* and compare with a partner.

Additional material

www.oup.com/elt/result for extra practice activities
www.oup.com/elt/teacher/result for extra teacher resources

How to talk about fashion

G *wh-* clauses   V compound adjectives   P *t* at the end of a word

A Vocabulary compound adjectives

1 Describe what another person in the class is wearing, but don't say their name. Your partner must guess who you are talking about.

2 Look at **Compound adjectives** opposite. Which ones can you use to describe the people in the photos?

3 Can you describe anybody you know with the **Compound adjectives**? Tell a partner.

B Read for detail

4 Look at the photos in **The Kings of Cool** opposite. What can you say about the place and the people? Tell your partner.

5 Read **The Kings of Cool**. What do you find out about Bienvenu Mouzieto? Write *true* or *false*.
   1 He lives in Brazzaville, Congo.   *True*
   2 He's part of a group called the *sapeurs*.
   3 *Sapeurs* are rich.
   4 They like expensive clothes.
   5 They've all spent time in prison.
   6 *Sapeurs* behave differently when they're dressed up.

6 Answer the questions and compare with a partner.
   1 Why is Mouzieto's appearance surprising?
   2 What do *sapeurs* do when they go out?
   3 Why do you think they're well-known in their neighbourhoods?
   4 Mediavilla says, 'It's worth it.' What does he mean?

7 Find these words in **The Kings of Cool** and guess their meanings. Compare with a partner and say how you guessed. Check the words in a dictionary.

   dusty outfit designer labels show off
   accessories watch strap

C Grammar *wh-* clauses

8 Write the *wh-* words below in the sentences and then check in **The Kings of Cool**.

   which why ~~what~~ what where how how

   1 Bienvenu Mouzieto knows __*what*__ he likes.
   2 'You are _____ you wear.'
   3 The *sapeurs* know _____ to show off their clothes.
   4 They learn _____ to walk with style.
   5 They know _____ colours look good together.
   6 Only the person who lent the clothes knows _____ they came from.
   7 He understands _____ they like dressing up.

9 We often use a *wh-* clause after *know*. Make sentences from the words below beginning with *I know* or *I don't know*.
   1 how much/costs/an Armani suit
      I don't know how much an Armani suit costs.
   2 people/why/designer clothes/buy
   3 is/my UK shoe size/what
   4 my shoes/where/were made
   5 how tall/am/I
   6 jeans/invented/who
   7 what/suit me/colours

10 Make questions beginning *Do you know* from the sentences in exercise 9 and ask a partner.
    Example   **A** Do you know what your UK shoe size is?
                B No, I don't.

    More practice? **Grammar Bank** >> p.142.

D Listen for specific information

11 Look at the photos of Wang Li, Heather, and Marcela. Predict who will say these sentences.
    1 I don't mind what I wear.
    2 I don't care what people think!
    3 I never look at labels.
    4 If you're well-dressed, they treat you differently.
    5 I wear what I'm expected to wear.
    6 My outfit changes how I feel.

Wang Li

12 **7B.1▶** Listen and check your predictions.

13 **7B.2▶** Pronunciation Listen and repeat sentences 1–6 in exercise 11. When is the letter t pronounced?

Heather

ABCD Put it all together

14 Make notes to answer four or more of these questions.
    1 What do you wear ... at work? at home? to go out in the evenings? on holiday?
    2 Where/How often do you shop for clothes?
    3 How much do you spend on clothes?
    4 Do you have any favourite ... designer labels? outfits?
    5 Do you think clothes are important? Why?
    6 Are you fashionable? What is fashion to you?

Marcela

15 Use your notes to make a personal 'fashion statement' to a partner. Then make your fashion statement again to another partner or group. Whose opinions are most similar to yours?

I can talk about fashion.

Tick ✓ the line.   with a lot of help   with some help   on my own   very easily

My week of living *differently*

In this new series of articles, we ask different people to change their lifestyle completely for one week and keep a diary of their experiences. This week we follow web-designer **Dwight Miller**'s week of living differently.

Dwight doesn't think much about his body and appearance. He's a scruffy couch potato. So we challenged him to spend a week paying more attention to his image.

Here's Dwight's diary …

Sunday Evening

My week of living differently starts tomorrow. I'm going to do lots of things I've never done before in my life. First of all, I'm having a complete style makeover.

Monday *Makeover day*

I don't normally waste time on my hair. I don't even comb it. For me, a good haircut is a fast haircut – fifteen minutes maximum. But today, I spent two and a half hours in the chair, bored out of my mind. They put red highlights in my hair and then they gave me a funny red jacket to match. When I came out, my girlfriend said I looked like Ronald McDonald.

Tomorrow, I'm going to have a Pilates class. I'm not sure what Pilates is, but I'll check on Wikipedia when I get home …

Tuesday *Pilates day*

OK, so now I know. Pilates is an exercise method where you have to think a lot about breathing. We spent a lot of time breathing deeply. It was quite relaxing, really. I'll go to bed early tonight. Tomorrow's tango day: I'm going to have a dance class.

Wednesday *Tango day*

It was great fun until I stepped on my partner's toe! But I think I'll continue. Tango looks really cool when you can do it well. I'll probably buy some good shoes, though. Trainers don't look right.

Tomorrow, I'm doing something which sounds very exciting and dangerous – Thai boxing!

Thursday *Thai Boxing day*

Thai boxing is called 'The Science of the Eight Limbs' because you use your knees and elbows as well as hands and feet. But for me, it was the science of one limb. I lifted my leg to kick, the instructor kicked my other leg and knocked me over. I fell on my thumb and now it's really painful. I don't think I'll do that again.

Tomorrow's the last day of my lifestyle makeover, and I'm going to do something calm and relaxing – a Turkish bath.

Friday *Turkish Bath day*

Normally, I can't spend more than five minutes doing nothing. I have to be at my computer, or watching the TV, or reading a magazine. But today I sat in a steam bath for two hours doing absolutely nothing and it was fantastic. I got a massage, too, and I came out feeling brilliant – totally refreshed – a new man! I'll definitely do that again. What a great way to end my lifestyle makeover week!

Next week, read about librarian Linda Smith's week living and working as a fashion model in Tokyo …

How to talk about plans and intentions

Orientation

Context

In this lesson, students will practise using future forms to talk about their coming week.

The illustrated article *My week of living differently*, introduces a new TV series about people who have makeovers; temporary life style changes. The article includes Dwight's diary, in which he explains and comments on his different activities.

Language

Preview language	maybe, probably
Focus grammar	future intentions: *I'm ...ing, Are you doing ...?, I'm going to ..., Are you going to ...?, I'll do ..., Will you do ...?*
Focus words	body and exercise: *climbing, comb, elbow, gym, haircut, jogging, knee, limb, massage, shave, steam bath, thumb, toe, walking, yoga*
Recognition vocabulary	words: *makeover, scruffy, refreshed* phrases: *body care, bored out of my mind, couch potato, waste time*
Recycled language	words: *active, appointment, arrangement, attractive, celebrate, bored, elegant, fashionable, fantastic, ill, interested, plan, style, tired, untidy* phrases: *fashion conscious* grammar: *present perfect and past simple; adverbs of frequency; reported speech*
Pronunciation	silent letters: *b, k, l*

Language note

English has no future tense like many other languages. Instead, we generally choose between the present continuous, *going to,* and *will*. The distinction between the three forms is often very subtle as it depends on context and what the speaker wants to convey. Arrangements are likely to be plans a person has had for a while, so both *going to* and present continuous are possible. However, arrangements usually involve other people, e.g. meeting at a certain time, going somewhere with somebody so the present continuous can also be used in these contexts. *Going to* is used for plans which are private and personal such as *read a book* because these activities haven't been arranged with others.

End product

In *Put it all together*, students plan a 'makeover' week for a partner. The partner explains this to another student.

Preparation

Think about classroom organization for the stages in *Put it all together*. Take dictionaries to class. For the next lesson, ask students to bring a photo of a room in their house.

Warmer

Write *Next week?* on the board. Give students time to think about what they will be doing and ask for volunteers to tell the class. Monitor for the use of future forms but do not overcorrect for accuracy at this stage. See who has the most exciting week ahead.

Write *How to talk about plans and intentions* on the board.

A Vocabulary body and exercise

1 Read the instructions and ask students to look at the vocabulary box. Check students understand the title of each column by asking them to give another word for each one. Monitor and help as students continue individually.

To check answers, go through each column in turn and elicit answers around the class. Check and help with pronunciation if necessary but do not comment on silent letters as this will be focused on in exercise 3.

Ask for additional words and write them on the board. Encourage students to check for meaning in their dictionaries as necessary.

> **parts of the body:** knee, limb, thumb, toe
> **exercise activities:** gym, jogging, steam bath, walking, yoga
> **body care:** haircut, massage, shave

2 Read the instructions and direct students to the example. Ask other questions, e.g. *Do you ever go climbing?* Monitor and help as necessary as students complete the exercise individually. Go over answers as a class.

> **Do you ever go:** climbing, to the gym, to yoga, walking?
> **Have you ever had a:** massage, steam bath?
> **How often do you have a:** haircut, shave?
> **Have you ever hurt your:** elbow, knee, limb, toe?

Ask question 1 and nominate different students to answer. Remind students of frequency adverbs, e.g. *sometimes, often* they could use to answer the questions if necessary. Repeat with question 2, drawing attention to the type of answers for *Have you ever ...?* questions (*never, once,* etc.). Put students into pairs to ask and answer the questions. Monitor and note common pronunciation problems to go over at the end of the section. Check students swap roles.

Extra help

Review *go, have, do* + sports and activities, if necessary.

Extra activity

Ask a question and nominate a student to answer. The student asks a different question and then nominates another student to answer.

3 Go through the instructions and examples for each letter. Ask students how they can find out if letters are pronounced or not. *(In their dictionaries.)* Monitor and help as students continue individually. Ask students to compare with a partner before nominating individuals to give answers. Give extra pronunciation practice as necessary.

> **silent b:** comb, limb, thumb
> **silent k:** knee
> **silent l:** walking

B Read and infer

In this section, students read a magazine article for gist before inferring information not directly stated in the text.

4 Read the question and direct students to *My week of living differently* on **>> p.70**. Set a time limit of about two minutes to encourage students to skim the text to answer the question. Put students in pairs to share their information with a partner.

5 Read the instructions and questions 1–4 with the class. Direct students to the title of the section and ask them what *infer* means. Elicit or remind students that it refers to a reading activity we do when we think about information that isn't directly stated in the text. Ask students if they do this when they read texts in their own language.

Do question 1 together as a class to demonstrate. Ask *How do we know that Dwight enjoyed dancing tango? (He says it was great fun.)* Ask students to find two more activities that Dwight enjoyed and ask students to explain why. *(Pilates. He says it was quite relaxing. Turkish bath. He says it was fantastic.)*

Tell students to ignore new vocabulary for the moment and to read the text again to find the answers to questions 2–4. Ask for volunteers to explain their choices.

> 2 Tango. He says it looks cool when you can do it well.
> 3 None of them. The experience was a week of living differently.
> 4 The Makeover Day. He says he was bored. Thai Boxing Day. He says he doesn't think he'll do it again.

6 Go through the instructions and do item 1 as a class to demonstrate the activity. Direct students to the word *scruffy* (in the first paragraph). Encourage students to read before and after the word to find information which will help them guess the meaning of the word. *(He doesn't think much about his image.)* Ask students to use their dictionaries as necessary to help them choose the best answer *(untidy)*.

Monitor and help as necessary as students continue individually. Ask for volunteers to give answers and to explain which words and phrases helped them guess the meaning.

> 2 a person who isn't very active (from the accompanying picture)
> 3 a complete change of style (haircut)
> 4 very bored (spent two and a half hours in the chair)
> 5 the opposite of bored (brilliant, a new man)

Teaching tip
Successful readers look at text surrounding an unknown word or phrase. Students often only focus on the preceding text. If they can't guess meaning they might give up, thinking that the text is too difficult for them. Encouraging students to look more widely will help build their confidence in dealing with texts they perceive as being difficult.

7 Ask students to read questions 1–3 and put them into pairs to discuss answers. Monitor and join in discussions. Bring the class together and ask for volunteers to tell the class about their activities. Monitor for the use of future forms, but do not overcorrect for accuracy at this stage.

C Grammar future intentions

8 Ask students to read sentences 1–3 and a–c. Check they understand the difference between an appointment *(fixed day and time)* and a plan *(or intention which hasn't been organized yet)*. Monitor and help as necessary as students continue. Read each sentence in turn and ask the class to say a, b, or c.

> 1 b   2 a   3 c

9 Go through the rules with the whole class. For each one, read the corresponding sentence in exercise 8 and elicit the tense.

> **Rules:** 1 present continuous   2 will   3 going to

Extra activity
Ask students to ask and answer the questions in exercise 7 with a new partner. Monitor for accuracy.

10 Direct students to *My week of living differently* on >> **p.70** and ask them to underline examples of the future forms. Check answers and ask if the sentence is use a, b, or c.

11 Tell students to read the conversation, ignoring the blanks to answer *Who has the most exciting week ahead? A or B? (B.)* Do item 1 as a class and direct students to the rules in exercise 9. Check vocabulary in the rest of the conversation. Monitor and help as students complete the activity individually.

12 7C.1 Ask students to compare answers with a partner. Play the audio and pause after each item for students to check. Ask about the context. *Is it a, b, or c?* (in exercise 8).

> 1 Are you doing   2 I'm doing   3 I'm going to   4 you're not going   5 I'll   6 Are you doing   7 I'm starting   8 We're going to

Extra help
Draw three columns on the board: *arrangement, plan,* and *decide now.* Ask students to copy an example sentence from *My week of living differently* for each use and to write their answers from exercise 7 in the appropriate column.

Extra activity
Students take turns to be A and B and practise the conversation.

Extra plus
In pairs, students ask and answer about their plans and arrangements for the coming week.

ABC Put it all together

13 Read the instructions and the example activities. Check vocabulary by eliciting some examples for each topic. Set a time limit of about two to three minutes for students to make notes. Tell students to look back at section A for ideas if necessary. Put them into pairs and ask them to swap diaries.

14 Go through the instructions and check students understand. Remind them of Dwight's normal week and the different things he did. Students write notes to prepare a plan for a partner.

15 Organize students into different pairs. Go through the instructions and example and check students understand the activity. At the end, ask for volunteers to tell the class about the new plan and if they would like to do it.

Student performance
Students should be able to make simple statements.

You can use this checklist to monitor and give feedback or to assess students' performance.

Grammar	Do students use a range of future forms to talk about their intentions? exercise 11 Do students use future forms appropriately? exercise 11
Vocabulary	Do students use a variety of body and exercise words? exercise 2

I can **talk about my plans and intentions.**
Students tick *on my own* if they have done the activity using the notes. They tick *with some help* if they have looked occasionally at exercise 6 or the notes on the board for help.

Early finishers
Students repeat exercises 14 and 15 with a different partner.

Additional material
www.oup.com/elt/result for extra practice activities
www.oup.com/elt/teacher/result for extra teacher resources

How to talk about plans and intentions

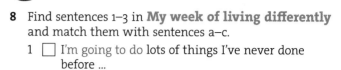

G future intentions   V body and exercise   P silent letters

A Vocabulary body and exercise

1 Write these words in the correct box. Add five more words of your own. You can use a dictionary.

~~climbing~~ ~~comb~~ ~~elbow~~ gym haircut jogging
knee limb massage shave steam bath
thumb toe walking yoga

parts of the body	exercise activities	body care
elbow	climbing	comb

2 Which words from exercise 1 could go in the gaps? Complete the questions and ask your partner.

1 Do you ever go _____?
   Example Do you ever go jogging?
2 Have you ever had a _____?
3 How often do you have a _____?
4 Have you ever hurt your _____?

3 **Pronunciation** Some letters in words are not pronounced. Find words in exercise 1 to add to these lists. Compare with a partner.

Silent b   *climb ...*
Silent k   *know, knife ...*
Silent l   *calm, half ...*

B Read and infer

4 Read **My week of living differently** opposite. Is Dwight Miller similar to you? Tell a partner.

5 Answer the questions.
Which activity or activities do you think Dwight ...
1 enjoyed doing? *Tango dancing*
2 would like to do better?
3 had done before?
4 probably won't repeat?

6 Find these words and phrases in the text and guess the meaning. Underline the best description.

1 scruffy = elegant/untidy/fashionable
2 couch potato = a person who isn't very active/attractive/fashion conscious
3 makeover = a complete change of ideas/activity/style
4 bored out of my mind = very interested/quite bored/very bored
5 refreshed = the opposite of tired/ill/bored

7 Answer the questions with a partner.
1 Which activities in the diary have you done?
2 Which do you or would you enjoy doing?
3 What activities would your own week of living differently include?

C Grammar future intentions

8 Find sentences 1–3 in **My week of living differently** and match them with sentences a–c.

1 ☐ I'm going to do lots of things I've never done before ...
2 ☐ I'm having a complete style makeover.
3 ☐ I'll definitely do that again.

a He probably has an appointment.
b He's probably had this plan for some time.
c He's probably decided this just now.

9 Complete the rules with *will*, *going to*, or *present continuous*.

Rules
1 Use _____ for arrangements and appointments.
2 Use _____ for plans you've just decided.
3 Use _____ for plans you've had for a while.

10 Underline examples of future forms in **My week of living differently**. Compare with a partner.

11 Underline the best future forms in this conversation.

A ¹Are you doing/Will you do anything interesting this week?
B No, not much. ²I'll do/I'm doing my French exam on Monday, so ³I'm going to/I'll stay home and study.
A So ⁴you won't go/you're not going out at the weekend?
B No. Maybe ⁵I'll/I'm going to go out to celebrate after the exam! What about you? ⁶Will you do/Are you doing anything special?
A Well, ⁷I'm starting/I'll start dance classes on Thursday.
B Really? What sort of dancing?
A ⁸We'll/We're going to study salsa, tango, rumba ... that sort of thing.
B Wow, sounds great.

12 7C.1▶ Listen and check.
More practice? **Grammar Bank** >> p.142.

ABC Put it all together

13 What do you normally do in a typical week? Write a Monday–Friday diary and write ideas for each day about some of the topics below. Give it to a partner.

times (getting up, meals, going to bed)   work routines
leisure activities   exercise   journeys   house work

14 Look at your partner's normal week. Prepare a plan for a 'week of living differently' and give it to him or her.

15 Look at your plan and tell a different partner about it. Do you think you will enjoy the week? Why?

Example I'm going to drive a Formula 1 car. I've always wanted to do that!

I can talk about my plans and intentions. ▮▮▮▮▮▮

Room Detectives

You can learn a lot about a person by looking at their room. If you look carefully, you will find clues to the person's age and occupation, their interests, habits, and personality. Look at this picture, for example …

It shows a man's bedroom. It must be a man's room because there are men's clothes hanging behind the bed. It doesn't look very comfortable, the furniture is cheap and simple, so he can't have a lot of money. There's a wooden bed, two chairs and a table. I think the man must clean and tidy a lot, because the room is neat and there's nothing on the floor. Or perhaps he tidied the mess for the picture!

The room is quite small, and there are two doors and a window. I guess the shutters of the window must be closed because there isn't much light coming in. There are paintings on the wall – I suppose the man might be an artist, or maybe he just likes pictures. Two of them are portraits of people – they might be members of the man's family or people he knows. There aren't any books in the room, so the man can't enjoy reading much.

The room is old-fashioned. There's no electrical equipment, not even a light. In one corner of the

Room 1

room, there's a jug of water, a bowl, a piece of soap, a mirror, and a towel. I guess this must be a washing area – perhaps there's no bathroom. Maybe this is in a place without electricity or running water, or perhaps it's a long time in the past, before these things were common.

Room 2

How to express guesses

Orientation

Context

In this lesson, students will practise using modal verbs and adverbs to talk about deductions and to speculate.

Room Detectives invites a reader to make guesses about people from what they have in their room. In *Room 1* the writer is speculating about the owner of bedroom in the first picture, a room Van Gogh shared with others when he lived in Arles (towards the end of his life). *Room 2* shows a different bedroom.

Language

Focus grammar	modals of deduction; *must, might, can't*
Focus words	adverbs for guessing: *perhaps, maybe, probably*
Recognition vocabulary	words: *bowl, common, detectives, hanging, jug, mess, neat, old-fashioned, portrait, shutters, simple* phrases: *electrical equipment, graduation photo, running water*
Recycled language	*bathroom, bedroom, behind, chair, cheap, clean and tidy, clothes, comfortable, doors, expensive, floor, mirror, neat, poor, rich, soap, table, window, wooden*

Language note

Adverbs of speculation, e.g. *probably* are used to indicate how *certain* a person is about a deduction. *Probably* is used to say that something is likely to be true or likely to happen. *Perhaps* is used to say that something is possible or that the speaker is not certain about something. *Maybe* is used to say that something is possible or might be true.

End product

In *Put it all together*, students make deductions and speculate about the owners of rooms in *Pairwork*. They check their guesses at the end of the activity, using information on **>> p.134**.

Preparation

Look at *Two rooms – the photos* on **>> p.130** so you are familiar with the activities in exercise 15. Take dictionaries to class.

Warmer

Write the title *Room Detectives* on the board, and put students into small groups to discuss what it means. Do not respond to suggestions at this point.

If students have brought photos of a room in their house, collect and redistribute the photos. If students haven't brought photos in, ask them to choose a room in their house and to make some notes about what it looks like. Collect and redistribute the notes.

Students deduce information about the owner and guess who lives there and report back to the class.

Write *How to express guesses* on the board.

A Read and find reasons

In this section, students read a description for gist and detail.

1 Put students into pairs to describe their bedroom. Monitor and encourage students to give detail. Ask for volunteers to tell the class about their partner's bedrooms.

2 Direct students to *Room Detectives* on **>> p.72**. Ask them to look at the picture and read *Room 1* to decide if they agree with the writer's guesses or not. Set a short time limit to encourage students to read for gist. Put students into pairs to exchange ideas and elicit suggestions around the class.

3 Ask students to read questions 1–7 and check vocabulary. Students read the text again, ignoring new vocabulary for the moment. Put students into pairs to answer the questions. Nominate students to give answers and invite other students to say if they agree or disagree and say why/why not.

> 2 Because the furniture is cheap and simple.
> 3 Because the room is tidy and there's nothing on the floor.
> 4 Because there isn't much light in the room.
> 5 Because there are paintings on the wall.
> 6 Because there aren't many books.
> 7 Because there's no electricity or running water.

4 Direct students to *The Bedroom in Arles* on **>> p.130**. They read the information and decide which of the writer's guesses it confirms.

> 1 It was a man's room.
> 2 The man isn't rich (Vincent Van Gogh was poor).
> 5 The man might be an artist (Vincent Van Gogh).
> 7 This might be a long time in the past (1888).

Extra activity

Students choose five new words in the texts and look for clues to guess meanings. They check in a dictionary.

B Grammar modals of deduction *must, might, can't*

5 Go through the instructions, sentences 1–3 and options a and b. Read sentence 1 and options a and b to the class. Direct students to the first paragraph to decide how sure the writer is. Elicit the answer *(a)* and a reason. *(The writer says there are men's clothes hanging behind the bed.)* Students continue individually, ignoring any unknown vocabulary for the moment.

> 2 b The furniture is cheap and simple. 3 b It's possible that the man likes paintings rather than paints himself.

6 Copy the time line onto the board and do the activity as a whole class. Tell students that the line represents how certain we are of something and elicit or give two examples, one for each end of the line, e.g. *This is Juan's book. This isn't Juan's book.*

Read the instructions and direct students back to exercise 5 to help them decide where the modals should be placed. Elicit answers and write them on the board.

> can't be   might be   must be

Extra activity

Put students into pairs or small groups. Set a short time limit for them to make more deductions about the room's owner. Ask for suggestions around the class and see if the others agree or disagree.

7 Go through the instructions and ask students to read sentences 1–6. Check vocabulary as necessary. Do item 1 together to demonstrate the activity, and elicit a couple more suggestions, e.g. *She might be American. She might be Australian.*

Students continue in pairs. Elicit a few suggestions for each item, encouraging students to use a range of modals (*must, might, can't* along with *is* and *isn't*). Ask for suggestions about who the person is. Direct students to the answer on **>> p.134**.

> **Suggested answers**
> 2 She must be married. She can't be single. She might have children.
> 3 She might be a foreign journalist. She can't be a waitress.
> 4 She must be Australian. She might have lived in Australia for a long time. She might have learned English in Australia.
> 5 She must be famous. She might be married to a member of a royal family.
> 6 She must be an actress. She isn't a housewife.

8 Direct students to the picture of *Room 2* on **>> p.72**. Read the instructions and check vocabulary. Read the example and point out that it contains a guess and a reason. Put students into pairs to continue the activity. Make a note of any common mistakes to go over at the end of the exercise.

To check answers, ask for volunteers to give information about the person and the reason why they've reached this conclusion. See if the class agrees. Encourage students to talk about their different deductions. Do not confirm answers at this stage.

Extra activity

Put students into pairs to choose another famous person and to write similar statements to those in exercise 7. Point out how the sentences begin with general statements and become more informative at the end. Students change partners. They read their sentences to a new partner, who guesses the identity using modals of deduction.

C Listen for detail

In this section, students listen to a description to identify main points and detail.

9 7D.1 Read the instructions and check students understand the activity. Play the audio. Ask pairs to say if the speaker agreed with any of their ideas in exercise 8.

10 Read the instructions and check vocabulary. Play the audio a second time for students to make notes about what the speaker says about each of the topics. Pause the audio occasionally to give students time to make notes. Students compare answers in pairs.

Bring the class together and elicit what the man said about each point. Ask for volunteers to say if they agree with the deductions or not. Encourage them to give reasons.

> **birthday:** perhaps her 18th or 21st (an important birthday because the dresses are expensive)
> **party dresses:** she must be having a party; must be deciding which one to wear
> **graduation photo:** might be a student
> **babies:** she must like them
> **portrait:** might be her sister or a friend

11 Read the instructions and ask students to complete the blanks from memory. Monitor and help as necessary. Direct students to audio script 7D.1 on **>> p.155** to check.

D Vocabulary adverbs for guessing

12 7D.2 Read the information to the class. Play the audio, pausing for students to repeat the sentences. Encourage them to sound more fluent by running words together.

13 Read the instructions and direct students to the sentences in the box. Elicit or explain that *maybe* and *perhaps* are adverbs which are also used when a person isn't certain of something. *Probably* is an adverb used when a person thinks that something is likely to happen. Read through rules a–c as a class and elicit answers.

> a after   b before   c more

14 Ask students to read sentences 1–5 and check vocabulary. Do the first item as a class. Monitor and help as students continue individually. To check answers, nominate students to read the full sentence and see if the class agrees. Direct students back to the example sentences in exercise 13 if necessary.

> 1 probably   2 Maybe   3 Perhaps   4 probably   5 probably

Extra activity

Students use *perhaps, maybe,* and *probably* to make three more sentences about the person who owns *Room 1* in *Room Detectives*. They base their sentences on what they can see in the picture. Elicit suggestions around the class and ask other students to say if they agree or not and why.

ABCD Put it all together

15 Direct students to the photos of two rooms on **>> p.130**. Read through the instructions and the example conversation to demonstrate the activity. Remind students to talk about the topics in exercise 8. Students continue the activity in pairs.

At the end of the activity, direct students to *Two rooms – the people* on **>> p.134** to find out about the people.

Student performance

Students should be able to make short hypothetical statements and support them with reasons.

You can use this checklist to monitor and give feedback or to assess students' performance.

Content	Do students talk about four or five different topics? exercise 8
Grammar	Do students use a variety of modals to talk about deductions? exercise 7
Vocabulary	Do students have enough vocabulary to do the task? exercises 3, 14

I can express guesses.

Students tick *on my own* if they have explained their reasons for guesses without a lot of hesitation. They tick *with some help* if they have looked at the diagram in exercise 6 or the box in exercise 13 occasionally for help.

Early finishers

Students imagine another room in the house of one of the people from the *Pairwork* photos. They make some notes and compare their ideas to see if they agree.

Additional material

www.oup.com/elt/result for extra practice activities
www.oup.com/elt/teacher/result for extra teacher resources

How to express guesses

G modals of deduction *must, might, can't* V adverbs for guessing

A Read and find reasons

1 What's your bedroom like? Describe it to a partner.

2 Read **Room Detectives** opposite. Do you agree with the writer's guesses? Tell a partner.

3 Read the text again and answer the questions with a partner.
   Why does the writer think …
   1 it's a man's room?
      There are men's clothes hanging behind the bed.
   2 the man isn't rich?
   3 the man's clean and tidy?
   4 the shutters are closed?
   5 the man might be an artist?
   6 the man doesn't read much?
   7 this might be a long time in the past?

4 Read the true information about **The Bedroom in Arles** on >> p.130. Which guesses in exercise 3 does it confirm?

B Grammar modals of deduction *must, might, can't*

5 Read these sentences from **Room Detectives**. For each sentence, decide how sure the writer is – a or b.
   1 It must be a man's room.
   2 He can't have a lot of money.
   3 The man might be an artist.

   a The writer feels sure about these guesses.
   b The writer thinks this is possible, but isn't sure.

6 Write *must, might*, and *can't* in the diagram.

   ━━━━━━━━━━━━━━━━━━━━━━▶ +
   isn't _____ be _____ be _____ be is

7 Write sentences with *must, might*, or *can't* about this mystery person. Who do you think it is? Check the answer on >> p.134.
   1 She's got big houses in the USA and Australia.
      She must be rich. or *She can't be poor.*
   2 She wears a wedding ring.
   3 She travels a lot for work.
   4 She speaks with an Australian accent.
   5 Photographers follow her everywhere.
   6 She's won an Oscar.

8 Look at **Room 2** opposite. Work with a partner and make guesses about the person whose room this is.
   name age nationality occupation marital status
   hobbies and interests future plans
   Example Her name must be Liz, because there's a birthday card to Liz on the wall.

   More practice? **Grammar Bank** >> p.142.

C Listen for detail

9 7D.1▶ Listen to a man guessing the information about Liz in exercise 8. Does he talk about the same things as you?

10 Listen again. What does he say about these things? Do you agree? Compare your ideas with a partner.
   birthday party dresses graduation photo
   babies portrait

11 Can you remember the missing words in these phrases? Check the audio script on >> p.155.
   1 perhaps it's her _____ or _____ birthday
   2 maybe it's a room in her _____ _____
   3 she probably isn't _____
   4 she probably plans to get _____ and have _____
   5 perhaps the girl likes _____

D Vocabulary adverbs for guessing

12 7D.2▶ The red words in exercise 11 are also used to make guesses. Listen and repeat the sentences.

13 In the sentences below, *he* is the subject of the verb. Underline the correct word in the rules.

Perhaps	he	lives alone.
Maybe		doesn't live alone.
He	probably	lives alone.
		doesn't live alone.

   a We usually put *probably* before / after the subject.
   b We usually put *perhaps* and *maybe* before / after the subject.
   c *Probably* is more / less certain than *perhaps* and *maybe*.

14 Underline the best adverb.
   1 The man perhaps / probably likes the colour blue.
   2 Maybe / Probably he likes living alone.
   3 Probably / Perhaps he's expecting guests.
   4 He probably / maybe wants some peace and quiet.
   5 He probably / perhaps doesn't read much.

ABCD Put it all together

15 Look at the photos of two rooms on >> p.130 and make guesses about the owners of the rooms. Discuss with a partner. Then check if your guesses were correct.

Writing A letter of application

A Read and think about context

1 Read the job ad and answer the questions.
  1 What are they looking for and what are they offering?
  2 How is it different from a more typical job ad?
  3 What should you do if you want to apply?

B Think about the content

2 Read Edith's letter of application (Don't worry about the spelling mistakes). Do you think it will make a good impression? Discuss with a partner.

3 Does Edith's letter follow <u>all</u> the instructions in the ad?

C Check spelling and structure

4 Find six typing errors in Edith's letter. Why do you think the spellchecker on her computer didn't show them? Compare with a partner.

5 Look again at Edith's letter of application. What are the rules of a formal letter? Discuss with a partner.

D Get ideas to write about

6 Complete the information about Edith in this table.

	Edith	me
age and background	20 immigrant from Hong Kong	
appearance		
clothes		
personality		
attitude	like being different don't mind what people think	
availability		

7 Complete the same information about you.

ABCD Put it all together

8 Write a letter of application for the reality show in the advert. Work with a partner and plan what you will include in the paragraphs. Use Edith's letter as a model.
  Example para 1: reason for writing ...

9 Read your partner's letter and comment on the content and accuracy. Do you think your partner will be chosen?

YOUR CHANCE TO APPEAR ON TV!

We are looking for 15 people to take part in a reality show. Participants will spend four months living together on a Pacific island and some will be voted off the island by the viewers every two weeks. There will be BIG CASH PRIZES for the last three people on the island.

We are looking for the widest possible variety of background, appearance, and personality.

Please send a brief handwritten letter (120–150 words) with a photo. Your letter should describe your appearance and personality. We will choose 300 candidates to attend an audition in June.

Please send applications to:
Change Your Life TV, PO Box 2998, Bexhill, Surrey

---

12 Rose Lane
London SE20 9ST

Change Your Life TV   12 February 2009
PO Box 2998
Bexhill, Surrey

Dear Sir or Madam

I'm writing in response to your advert in the Evening Times for participants in a TV reality show. You said you wanted a variety of people of different appearance, personality an background. I think I wood be a good candidate for your programme.

I'm 20 years old and my family moved to this country from Hong Kong when I was too. I'm medium height and slim. I've got a round face and my hair is dyed bright red. I enjoy wearing unusual, imaginative cloths. I'm lively, confident and outgoing. I like being different and I don't mind what people think of me.

I'm working freelance at he moment, so I will be easily available to participate in you're programme. Please find my photograph enclosed.

I look forward to hearing from you.

Yours faithfully

Edith Chan

Edith Chan

I can write a letter of application.

Tick ✓ the line. with a lot of help with some help on my own very easily

Orientation

Context and Language

In this lesson, students write a letter of application to appear on a TV reality show, responding to a newspaper advertisement.

New language	words: *candidate, dyed, enclosed, participate* phrases: *yours faithfully*
Recycled language	words: *appearance, apply, application, background, confident, imaginative, immigrant, lively, outgoing, personality, slim, variety* grammar: *wh- clauses*
Recognition language	words: *attitude, availability, brief, freelance, handwritten, unusual, viewers* phrases: *bright red, make a good impression, medium height, spellchecker, voted off*

End product

In *Put it all together*, students write a formal letter of application based on a model letter. Students exchange letters and decide if their partner would be chosen for interview.

Warmer

Put students into small groups to discuss reality TV shows. Choose two or three questions and write them on the board. Bring the class together and ask for volunteers to report the group's opinions.

Write *How to write a letter of application* on the board.

A Read and think about context

In this section, students skim and scan a job ad to find key information.

1 Read questions 1–3 and direct students to the advertisement. Set a short time limit to encourage students to scan the ad to find the answers. Ask students to compare in pairs before asking for volunteers to give answers.

> 1 They are looking for 15 people to take part in a reality TV show. They offer big cash prizes.   2 It is an advert for people to take part in a competition, rather than work for a salary. 3 To apply, you write a brief handwritten letter describing your appearance and personality.

B Think about the content

In this section, students review a letter of application for detail.

2 Read the instructions and check students understand the activity. Students complete the activity in pairs. Elicit answers, encouraging students to give examples from the letter.

3 Read the instructions and ask students to underline the instructions in the ad before they look at Edith's letter in more detail. Tell students to use their dictionaries to help with vocabulary in Edith's letter. Monitor and help as students continue individually.

Nominate students to give an instruction from the ad and to explain in which paragraph Edith gives the information.

C Check spelling and structure

4 Go through the instructions and check students understand the activity. Students continue individually. They compare answers in pairs and discuss the question. Elicit the spelling mistakes and write the corrected words on the board.

> **paragraph 1:** an – and; wood – would
> **paragraph 2:** too – two; cloths – clothes
> **paragraph 3:** he – the; you're – your
> A computer spellchecker doesn't show words which are correct, but which may be wrong in a particular context.

5 Read the instructions and put students into pairs to discuss the rules of a formal letter. Monitor and guide students to parts of the text, e.g. the position of the address, the greeting and closing. Elicit suggestions around the class.

> Put your own address top right; put the date below your address, put the reader's address top left; use *Dear Sir or Madam* if you don't know who you are writing to; give your reason for writing in the first paragraph; if you don't know who you are writing to, close with *Yours faithfully*.

D Get ideas to write about

6 Direct students to the table and the information in the first column. Tell students to look at the information about Edith and to complete the missing information. Students compare ideas in pairs. Check answers.

> **appearance:** medium height, slim, round face, dyed hair
> **clothes:** unusual, imaginative
> **personality:** lively, confident, outgoing
> **availability:** easily available

7 Ask students to complete the second column with information about themselves. Remind them to look at *Character* and *Looks* on >> p.66 and to use their dictionaries.

ABCD Put it all together

8 Read the instructions with the class. Monitor and encourage a collaborative working atmosphere. Remind students to use *Why don't you ...?* and *You could ...* to make suggestions.

Ask them to follow the rules in exercise 5 and review their letters for content and accuracy.

9 Tell students to imagine that they work for *Change Your Life TV*. Ask them to read their partner's letter and tell their partner if they would be chosen for interview.

Student performance

Students should be able to write a formal letter of application of about 120 words.

You can use this checklist to monitor and give feedback or to assess students' performance.

Content	Have students included all the information? Have students written in a conversational style?
Vocabulary	Have students spelt words correctly?

I can **write a letter of application.**

Students tick *on my own* if they have included all the points. They can tick *with some help* if they have forgotten to include a piece of information.

Early finishers

Students rewrite their letters to include any missing information and correct spelling. They add two more pieces of information about their appearance, personality, or attitude.

Additional material

www.oup.com/elt/result for extra practice activities
www.oup.com/elt/teacher/result for extra teacher resources

Warmer

Remember the situations

Write lessons A–D *How to* titles on the board: *A … say how people look, B … talk about fashion, C … talk about plans and intentions, D … express guesses.* Say sentences 1–10 below for students to call out the lesson letter.

1 I don't think I'll do that again! 2 He looks a bit shy and nervous. 3 I don't mind what I wear. 4 I'm starting dance classes on Thursday. 5 She's in her early fifties. 6 He can't have a lot of money. 7 He knows which colours look good together. 8 It must be a man's room. 9 I don't know how much an Armani suit costs. 10 He doesn't look like his dog!

> 1 C 2 A 3 B 4 C 5 A 6 D 7 B 8 D 9 B 10 A

A Grammar

1 wh- clauses 7B exercises 8, 9

Warm-up: Write *wh-* words *(what, why, where, which, how)* on the board. Students make sentences about *sapeurs* with each one once.

Set-up: Go through the example and remind students that they find the sentences by looking horizontally and vertically.

> 2 Does he know why you left him?
> 3 Do you know where Panama is?
> 4 I don't know who you are.
> 5 I know what happened.
> 6 She knows how to look after herself.
> 7 I don't know where he went.

Follow-up: Students use the questions in exercise 14, >> p.69 to help them write a fashion statement for a famous person. In groups, they read their statement for the others to guess who.

2 Future intentions 7C exercise 11

Warm-up: Ask students to write three sentences about an appointment, a plan, and something they've just decided. Direct them to >> p.71, exercise 8 to check their use of future tenses.

Set-up: Go through the instruction and check students understand the activity.

> 2 I'm going to 3 I'm going 4 I'm going to buy 5 I'll help
> 6 They're coming

Follow-up: Students write their plans for next month. In groups, they compare their plans to see if anyone shares the same hobbies and interested.

3 Modals of deduction 7D exercises 7, 8

Warm-up: Copy the diagram from >> p.73, exercise 6 onto the board. Write *is* and *isn't* at either end and ask students where you should place *must, might,* and *can't*.

Set-up: Ask students to read the text and sentences 1–6 to check they understand the activity.

> 2 can't 3 must 4 can't 5 might 6 must

Follow-up: In pairs, students write a similar paragraph and exercise. They write the answer key on a different piece of paper. They swap with another pair and complete the sentences before checking their answers against the key.

B Vocabulary

4 Looks and character 7A exercise 7

Warm-up: Draw three columns on the board: *Character, Looks,* and *Age.* Set a short time limit for students to write words and phrases they can remember. Direct students to >> p.66 to check.

Set-up: Ask students to read the crossword clues and check vocabulary as necessary.

> 2 mid 3 active 4 outgoing 5 confident 6 generous
> 7 wavy 8 artistic 9 ginger 10 nervous 11 aggressive
> Hidden word: imaginative

Follow-up: Students choose somebody they know in the class and write adjectives to describe the person. They tell a partner the name of the person and their partner writes adjectives. Students compare their lists at the end.

5 Compound adjectives 7B exercise 2

Warm-up: Books closed. In pairs, students think of compound adjectives they could use to describe *The Kings of Cool.* They compare with the list on >> p.68.

Set-up: Ask students to read the words and check vocabulary.

> 2 f 3 d 4 e 5 g 6 a 7 c

Follow-up: Students describe one of the women on >> p. 69 for a partner to guess who it is.

6 Body and exercise 7C exercise 1

Warm-up: Books closed. Students write a list of activities Dwight did in his week of living differently. They compare with a partner before checking on >> p.70.

Set-up: Go through the instructions and tell students to think carefully about spelling.

> 2 massage 3 elbow 4 haircut 5 knee 6 jogging 7 toe
> 8 yoga 9 climbing

Follow-up: In pairs, students design a word search using the vocabulary on >> p.71, exercise 1. They write the number of words in the word search and swap with another pair.

Early finishers

Students look back at lesson 7C, exercises 8 and 9. They work with a partner and exchange ideas on different things they could do to remember the grammar.

Unit 7 Review

R7

A Grammar

1 *wh-* clauses Find seven sentences with *wh-* clauses.

1 I	2 Does	3 Do	you	know	where
don't	he	know	why	you	Panama
know	what	to	4 I	left	is?
5 I	6 She	wear.	don't	him?	are.
know	knows	how	know	who	you
what	7 I	to	look	after	herself.
happened.	don't	know	where	he	went.

2 Future intentions Underline the correct verb forms.

1 **A** Tea or coffee, sir?
   B I think I'll have/I'm having a tea, please.
2 **A** Have you got any plans for this evening?
   B Yes. I'm going to lie/I'll lie on the sofa and read a book!
3 **A** Have you made any arrangements for Friday night?
   B Yes, I'll go/I'm going out with Sophie – we're going to the cinema.
4 **A** Why are you saving your money?
   B I'm buying/I'm going to buy a saxophone and learn to play it.
5 **A** I can't do my homework!
   B Don't worry, I'm going to help/I'll help you if you like.
6 **A** Do you want to go out tonight?
   B I can't. I've invited Alec and Liz. They'll come/They're coming round at eight.

3 Modals of deduction Read about Louise and complete the sentences about her with *must*, *might*, or *can't*.

Louise Armstrong is from North America. She works as a flight attendant on international flights and she never has time to put away her suitcase. She often visits Ireland in her holidays, and she always stays in other people's homes there. She doesn't want to change her job – even if she could make more money doing something else.

1 She _might_ be Canadian.
2 She _____ be from France.
3 She _____ travel a lot for work.
4 She _____ spend much time at home.
5 She _____ have family in Ireland.
6 She _____ enjoy her work.

B Vocabulary

4 Looks and character Do the puzzle and find the hidden word.

Clues
1 Wants to be very successful, rich, etc.
2 He's in his _____ thirties.
3 Always busy doing things.
4 Opposite of *shy*.
5 Feeling sure about your abilities.
6 Gives people a lot of money, help, etc.
7 Hair: not curly, but not straight.
8 Character like an artist.
9 Hair colour: red or orange.
10 Afraid of things, not confident.
11 Behaving in an angry way.

| 1 | A | M | B | I | T | I | O | U | S |

5 Compound adjectives Match the two parts of the compound adjectives.

1 *b* well-   a conscious
2 ☐ well-   b dressed
3 ☐ old-   c shaven
4 ☐ loose-   d fashioned
5 ☐ good-   e fitting
6 ☐ fashion-   f mannered
7 ☐ clean-   g looking

6 Body and exercise Label the pictures.

1 thumb
2
3
4
5
6
7
8
9

75

On the Phone

1 Look, I'm with a client and I can't get away right now. Can I ring you back tomorrow?

2

3

a Hi, Lucy. It's me. I'm calling from the hospital. Gloria has had the baby. It's a beautiful boy! Hang on, I'll hand you over to Gloria ...

b Look, I've tried that number already, but I can't get through. I either get cut off or I just get the engaged signal. Is there another number I can call? Please don't hang up!! Hello?

c Hello, can you put me through to the emergency rescue service, please. My car's broken down ... Thanks.

d Extension 483? Who's calling please? ... Hold on. I'll put you through ... I'm sorry, the line's busy right now. Would you like to leave a message or call back in five minutes?

e Hello, it's Mike calling from Bike World. I'm calling to let you know the spray paint you ordered has arrived, so you can call by and pick it up some time ...

f Have you got her mobile number, please? ... Great. Hang on, I'll just get a pen to write it down ... OK, go ahead.

4

5

6

7

Phrasal verbs in the dictionary

- [ ] **break down**
- [ ] **call by** (*informal*)
- [ ] **cut sb off** [often passive]
- [ ] **get away (from …)**
- [ ] **get through (to sb)**
- [*a*] **hand (sb) over to sb**
- [ ] **hang on** (*informal*)
- [ ] **hang up**
- [ ] **put sb through**
- [ ] **ring (sb) back** (*Brit**)

*call back is an alternative for ring back

a (used at a meeting or on the phone) to let sb speak or listen to sb
b to end a telephone conversation and put the phone down
c (used about a vehicle or machine) to stop working
d to stop or interrupt sb's telephone conversation
e to telephone sb again or to telephone sb who has telephoned you
f to succeed in speaking to sb on the telephone
g to make a short visit to a place or person as you pass
h to succeed in leaving or escaping from sb or a place
i to wait for a short time
j to make a telephone connection that allows sb to speak to sb

How to talk on the phone

Orientation

Context

In this lesson, students practise using telephone words and phrases.

Photos 1–7 in *On the Phone* on **» p.76** show people in different situations making telephone calls. Speech bubbles a–f contain what the callers and answerers in photos 2–7 say.

Phrasal verbs in the dictionary lists key vocabulary and definitions which students will match and use during the lesson. The following information is also given: if a phrase is formal or informal; how it is usually used; other words it is used with; and whether a noun or pronoun can or must be used after the verb but before the particle (shown by the use of *sb*, with or without brackets).

Language

Focus grammar	phrasal verbs: *cut me off, get away, get through, hand over, hang on, hang up, ring me back, on the line, put through*
Focus words	telephone: *business deal, busy, called by public phone/called by this morning, connect, earn, engaged signal, extension, go ahead, message, mobile*
Focus phrases	*Can I help you?, Hello, can you ...?, Go ahead, I'm calling from ..., I'm calling to ...*
Recognition vocabulary	words: *client, engine, spray paint, urgently, vehicle* phrases: *call out service, emergency services*
Recycled language	words: *colleague, golf, interrupt, mechanic, pretend* phrases: *break down, call back later, escaping, get cut off, hold the line, I'm sorry, leave a message, put you through, the line's busy right now, wrong number*
Pronunciation	stress in phrasal verbs: *I **called by** this **morning**.* **8A.2**

Language note

The language presented in this lesson reviews and builds on what students studied in lesson 6A, *English Result Pre-intermediate*.

End product

In *Put it all together*, students role play being a caller and answerer using the information in *Phoning Frank* on **» p.130**. The conversation is based on audio script **8A.3**.

Preparation

Think about classroom organization if you'd like students to sit back-to-back in exercise 12. Read *Phoning Frank* on **» p.130** so you are familiar with the task in exercise 13. Take dictionaries to class.

Warmer

Write the following words on the board: *a, at, back, busy, call, cut, get, hang, hold, later, leave, line message, moment, number, off, out, put, the, through, up, wrong, you.* Ask students to guess a topic that connects all these words. *(Telephoning.)*

Put students into pairs or small groups to write telephone phrases they remember from *English Result Pre-intermediate*. Set a short time limit. Elicit suggestions around the class and write the phrases on the board.

Write *How to talk on the phone* on the board.

A Read and think about the situation

In this section, students read short parts of telephone conversations for detail.

1   Read the questions and put students into pairs to discuss their answers. Monitor and contribute to the conversations. Listen out for interesting comments and nominate students to tell the class. Encourage other students to add comments.

2   Direct students to photo 1 in *On the Phone* on **» p.76**. Read questions 1–3 and check vocabulary as necessary. Students continue the activity in pairs. Monitor and encourage students to use *maybe, perhaps, possibly, could be, might be,* and *can't be* in their discussions. To check answers, ask for suggestions and reasons. See if the class agrees before giving feedback.

> 1 They are friends or business associates. They are in a bar.
> 2 He is talking to a friend, partner, or colleague.
> 3 Maybe – it depends on what his relationship is with the woman and who he's talking to.

3   Read the instructions and direct students to photos 2–7 and speech bubbles a–f in *On the Phone* on **» p.76**. Go through the example to demonstrate the activity. Direct students back to questions 1–3 in exercise 2 and point out that they can also use clues in the photos, e.g. the man in photo 2 is writing something on a piece on paper as he's speaking. Students complete the activity.

Students compare answers in pairs. Do not go over answers at this stage as they will listen and check in exercise 4.

4   **8A.1** Play the audio and pause after each item. Elicit answers and ask for words, phrases, and any clues in the photos which helped students find the answers. Check vocabulary.

> 3 b can't get through, get cut off, another number
> 4 a hospital, had the baby, beautiful
> 5 d extension 483, I'll put you through, the line's busy
> 6 c emergency, rescue, car's broken down
> 7 e spray paint, ordered, call by

5   Ask students to read descriptions 1–6 and check vocabulary as necessary. Do the first item together to demonstrate the activity. Put students into pairs to continue. Monitor and help, encouraging students to give reasons for their answers. Nominate one student to give an answer and another to suggest a reason, if they agree.

> 2 photo 3   3 photo 7   4 photo 6   5 photo 2   6 photo 5

6   Read the instructions and ask students to read meanings 1–8, ignoring the blanks. Check vocabulary. Do the example as a class to demonstrate the activity. Explain that some answers are phrasal verbs and remind students that sometimes the verb and particle can be separated, e.g. *put you through*.

> 2 get through   3 engaged   4 calling   5 busy
> 6 leave a message   7 let you know   8 pick it up

Extra activity

In pairs, students take turns to give a partner the meaning of a phrase. The partner says the phrase.

7 Read the instructions and ask *What's a phrasal verb? (A verb and a particle which have a particular meaning.)* Direct students to *Phrasal verbs in the dictionary* and *On the Phone* on **>> p.76** to read the list of phrasal verbs. Elicit or explain that, in dictionaries, *sb* refers to *somebody*. It shows when a verb can or must be separated from a particle by a noun or pronoun. Ask students to find an example in speech bubble a *(hand you over)*.

Direct students to read definitions a–j and check vocabulary as necessary. Tell students to find the phrasal verbs in the speech bubbles to help them guess the meaning. Monitor and help as necessary as students continue individually.

To go over answers, say the phrasal verb for the class to call out the letter of the definition. Check students understand the extra information given with some of the phrasal verbs (see *Context*) as you go through the answers.

> break down c   call by g   cut sb off d   get away h
> get through f   hang on i   hang up b   put sb through j
> ring (sb) back e

Teaching tip
Students might fail to recognize phrasal verbs in a text if they don't look beyond the first word after the verb, e.g. in *hand you over*. Encouraging students to look for phrases across several words will help them understand texts more easily.

8 Ask students to read the text and say how many times Stephanie made a phone call. *(Four.)* Check vocabulary. Students continue individually. Monitor and check students are using the past tense form of the verbs. To check answers, read the text aloud and pause for students to call out answers.

> 2 call   3 Hang   4 put   5 cut   6 got   7 handed   8 call   9 hung

9 8A.2 Do the exercise as a class. Direct students to sentence a and ask *What does* by *mean? (To use.)* Play the audio for students to listen to the pronunciation of the sentences and read the rule to the class. Point out that *by* is a preposition here.

Read sentence b and ask students what the phrasal verb *called by* means. *(A short visit.)* Point out that *by* is a particle in this sentence. Play the audio for students to listen to stress in the phrasal verb in the second sentence.

Play the audio a second time for students to listen to both sentences. Tap the desk to help students hear the difference.

Extra help
Direct students to audio script 8A.1. In pairs, students find and underline the phrasal verbs and mark the stress on the particles. Monitor and help as necessary.

Extra activity
Students underline the particles in speech bubbles a–f. In pairs, they take turns to read the information and listen to see if their partner stresses the particle correctly.

C **Listen for detail**

In this section, students listen to the start of telephone conversations for specific information and detail.

10 8A.3 Read the instructions and check students understand the activity. Ask students to read items 1–5 and check vocabulary as necessary. Play the audio. Ask students to compare in pairs and play the audio a second time if necessary. To check answers, ask about each item in turn.

> 2 ✓   3 ✗   4 ✓   5 ✗

11 Go through the instructions and play the audio, pausing after the first telephone conversation. Elicit the name of the garage. Continue with the audio for students to make notes about the new information. Direct students to audio script 8A.3 on **>> p.155** to check answers. Nominate students to give answers.

> ✓ 1 Max Motors   2 side of main road near Stratford upon Avon   4 the engine won't start

12 Ask for two volunteers to read the conversation, encouraging the student playing the role of Stephanie to sound more desperate as she makes each new phone call. Remind students to ask for clarification or repetition when they are on the phone. Elicit a few phrases, e.g. *Sorry, can you say that again, please?* and write them on the board.

Put students into pairs to role play the conversation. Monitor and give positive feedback when students speak with attitude. Check students swap roles.

Extra activity
Students repeat the role play, looking up from their books as much as possible.

Extra plus
Students repeat the role play, sitting back-to-back and looking at their books as little as possible.

ABC **Put it all together**

13 Go through the instructions and check students understand. Direct students to *Phoning Frank* on **>> p.130** and check vocabulary if necessary. Give students time to plan what they will say before they do the activity. Check students swap roles.

Student performance
Students should be able to talk about services on the telephone.

You can use this checklist to monitor and give feedback or to assess students' performance.

Vocabulary	Do students a variety of telephone words and phrases? exercise 8 Do students use most phrasal verbs accurately? exercise 12
Pronunciation	Do students pronounce particles clearly? exercise 12

I can talk on the phone.
Students tick *on my own* if they have given the necessary information to their partner. They tick *with some help* if they have forgotten to give information and a partner has had to ask questions once or twice.

Early finishers
Students choose two situations from *On the Phone* on **>> p.76** and role play the telephone conversation.

Additional material
www.oup.com/elt/result for extra practice activities
www.oup.com/elt/teacher/result for extra teacher resources

How to talk on the phone

G phrasal verbs (2) **V** phrasal verbs; telephone words and phrases **P** stress in phrasal verbs

A Read and think about the situation

1 How much do you use the phone, and what do you use it for? Tell a partner.

2 Look at photo 1 in **On the Phone** opposite. Discuss the questions with a partner.
   1 Who are the people and where are they?
   2 Who do you think the man is talking to?
   3 Do you think he's lying? Why? Why not?

3 Match photos 2–7 in **On the Phone** with texts a–f. Say which words helped you decide.
   Example 2 = f pen; write it down

4 **8A.1▶** Listen and check.

5 Work with a partner. Match photos 2–7 with these descriptions.
   This person …
   1 is giving some good news to a friend or relative. *photo 4*
   2 has tried to phone already, but without success.
   3 is definitely speaking to a customer.
   4 has called a person who she doesn't know.
   5 is trying to get in touch with a woman.
   6 is responding to a caller – she definitely didn't phone the other person.

6 Find phrases in **On the Phone** with these meanings.
   1 I'm phoning from …   *I'm calling from …*
   2 I can't connect to that phone number
      I can't g_____ _____
   3 get the signal that means that someone is on the phone   *get the _____ signal*
   4 What's your name?   *Who's _____, please?*
   5 someone's talking on the line already
      the line's _____
   6 Would you like me to tell him/her?   *Would you like to _____ _____ _____?*
   7 I'm calling to tell you …   *I'm calling to _____*
      _____ _____ …
   8 collect it   *_____ it _____*

B Grammar and vocabulary
phrasal verbs (2)

7 Look at **Phrasal verbs in the dictionary** opposite. Find the phrasal verbs in **On the Phone**. Match the phrasal verbs and the definitions.
   Example hand over = a

8 Complete the text with verbs from exercise 7. Compare with a partner.
   Stephanie's car ¹ *broke* down on the way to work, so she had to ring a garage for help. A recorded message said, 'I'm sorry, all our lines are busy. Please ² _____ back in five minutes.' When Stephanie called a second time, a secretary answered and said, '³ _____ on, I'll ⁴ _____ you through.' Then she got ⁵ _____ off so she had to call back a third time. Finally, she ⁶ _____ through to a mechanic. He said he was busy and ⁷ _____ her over to a colleague. The colleague said, 'If you ⁸ _____ by, I'll check your car and see what the problem is.' She explained that she couldn't move her car. 'Then I can't help you,' replied the mechanic, and he ⁹ _____ up.

9 **8A.2▶ Pronunciation** Listen to the examples and read the rules.
   a I **called** by **pub**lic **phone**.
   Rule *by* isn't part of a phrasal verb. We don't usually stress prepositions.

   b I **called by** this **morn**ing.
   Rule *by* is part of a phrasal verb. We stress the particles in phrasal verbs.

   More practice? **Grammar Bank ➤➤** p.143.

C Listen for detail

10 **8A.3▶** Listen to Stephanie's phone calls to the garage from exercise 8. You will hear some extra information. Tick ✓ the information you hear.
   1 the name of the garage ✓
   2 where Stephanie is
   3 the time
   4 the problem with the car
   5 the names of the mechanics

11 Listen again and make notes about the new information in exercise 10. Read the audio script on ➤➤ p.155 and check.

12 Work with a partner. Role play the phone call.
   Student A Say Stephanie's lines.
   Student B Say the lines of the other characters.

ABC Put it all together

13 Work with a partner. Look at **Phoning Frank** on ➤➤ p.130. Choose the Caller or the Answerer role and read it. Plan what you are going to say before you start. Change partners and do the role play again.

Intelligent Animals

Smart Alex

An African grey parrot called Alex has amazed scientists with his language abilities. This clever bird can identify 50 different objects using English words, and he can also answer questions about their shape, colour, and number. But it's not just words – Alex can even make sentences in requests like 'I want X' or 'I wanna go Y'.

Alex is Irene Pepperberg's star pupil

African grey parrots have enjoyed popularity for thousands of years. They've been popular pets since ancient Egypt, perhaps because they're sociable and fun. They are able to repeat words and phrases they hear, and they can even copy the sound of laughter or a ringing phone. However, Alex's abilities show that parrots can actually use language, not just repeat it.

Training a parrot to speak

Animal psychologist Dr Irene Pepperberg has studied parrot intelligence since 1977. Alex is her star pupil and he's able to answer complicated questions like 'What object is green and has three corners?' Through her work, Pepperberg has made Alex famous. She's been able to show that parrots can actually think.

Birds get bored too

Because they are so intelligent, parrots can get bored easily. They're very active and they need things to stimulate their curiosity. Pepperberg created a computer program for Alex, so he could choose from four activities – watching a video, listening to music, seeing pictures, or playing a game. To begin with, Alex was curious and played with the system for an hour a day, but then he got bored with it. However, Pepperberg managed to get him interested again by changing the content of the program.

'You have to put this bird on the camera!'

A sense of humour?

Another African grey parrot who has been in the news is N'kisi, from New York. Apparently, N'kisi has a vocabulary of 950 words and can even make jokes. Once, when he saw another parrot hanging upside down, he said they should 'put this bird on the camera'.

Clever Rico

Rico, a border collie from Germany, is a surprisingly clever dog. Although Rico can't speak, he can understand more than 200 words, and he's able to learn the names of new toys easily. What's more, Rico can remember the new vocabulary weeks later.

Border collies can be trained as rescue dogs

Border collies are well-known to be intelligent animals. They are used as sheepdogs and can respond to many different whistles. They can also be trained as rescue dogs, for finding people lost under the snow, for example. However, Rico's abilities show that collies are even cleverer than we thought.

Famous on TV

Professor Julia Fischer of the Max-Planck Institute in Leipzig first saw Rico on television, on a popular German TV programme called 'Wetten Dass?' Millions of viewers were amazed to see how Rico could understand his owner's instructions and fetch things. He could go and get the correct toy from among many in his collection.

Rico's abilities have amazed TV viewers

A mathematical horse?

Fischer was suspicious because she remembered the case of the horse called Clever Hans. Hans was able to answer mathematical problems by tapping his foot the correct number of times. However, a psychologist discovered that in reality, the horse's owner was giving signals to Hans with his eyebrows. Fischer decided to test the possibility that Rico's owner was doing the same thing.

Rico passes his exams

Fischer put Rico and his owner in one room and placed Rico's toys in a different room. She asked the dog's owner to request different toys in a random order. It wasn't possible for Rico's owner to point to the toys, but Rico was able to fetch the correct toy 37 times out of 40. In one test, he also managed to learn the name of a new toy after hearing it once. A new toy was placed in his collection, and when Rico heard the name, he was able to correctly fetch the toy. 'This tells us he can do simple logic,' says Fischer, 'He's actually thinking.'

How to **talk about ability**

Orientation

Context

In this lesson, students use *can, could, be able to,* and *manage to* to talk about ability.

The two magazine articles are about animals with amazing language skills. Smart Alex, a parrot, can identify objects, answer questions, and make requests. Rico, a dog, is able to remember new vocabulary. He can also use simple logic and think.

Language

Focus grammar	ability: *can, could, be able to, manage to*
Focus words	adjectives and nouns: *able – ability, active – activity, curious – curiosity, popular – popularity, possible – possibility, real – reality*
Recognition vocabulary	words: *actual, ancient, collection, complicated, fetch, laughter, logic, occasion, random, sheepdogs, sociable, stimulate, surprisingly, suspicious, tapping, trained, toys, whistles* phrases: *hanging upside down, star pupil*
Recycled language	*amazed, clever, bored, enjoyed, eyebrows, famous, fun, intelligence, interested, scientists, shape*
Pronunciation	stress in words ending *–ity: ability* **8B.1**

End product

In *Put it all together*, students use their notes to tell a partner about a time when they were or weren't able to do something.

Preparation

Look at *Ideas* on **>> p.130** so you are familiar with the task in exercise 12. Take dictionaries to class if necessary.

Warmer

Write the following nouns on the board: *a bike, chess, clothes, a computer, crosswords puzzles, dinner, golf, guitar, jigsaws, a horse, table tennis.*

Draw four columns: *make, do, play, others.* Put students into pairs to classify the words according to the verbs they are used with. Ask students to add four more activities they can or can't do to the columns.

Students tick the things they can do and note when they first learnt to do them. Ask students to find out four other students' abilities. Monitor and join in, listening for students' use of modal verbs. Do not overcorrect for accuracy at this stage.

At the end of the activity, ask for volunteers to tell the class anything interesting they found out about others.

Write *How to talk about ability* on the board.

A **Read and summarize**

In this section, students read different articles and summarize information in note form.

1   Put students into pairs to discuss the question. Monitor and encourage students to think about *animals which can communicate with people* and *animals which are useful to people.*

Ask for volunteers to share their ideas with the class and encourage students to respond to each other's opinions.

2   Put students into pairs and direct them to the texts on **>> p.78**. Ask As to read *Smart Alex,* and Bs to read *Clever Rico* to find the most interesting fact. Tell students to guess the meaning of unknown but important words at this stage. Remind them to look at words and phrases around the words they are unsure of.

Ask for volunteers to tell the class which fact they found the most interesting and to say why. Monitor for the use of modal verbs to talk about ability but do not correct for accuracy at this point as students will focus on this in the next section.

3   Direct students to the box and ask them to read the first column. Check vocabulary. Check students understand the activity and monitor and help as necessary as students continue individually. Do not go over answers for exercise 3 at this point, as students will tell a partner about the text they read in the next exercise.

Smart Alex	**Clever Rico**
human use: pets	**human use:** rescue dog
language ability: can identify 50 different objects, can answer questions	**language ability:** can understand more than 200 words
why famous: he's a star pupil	**why famous:** finding the correct toy from many
who studied it: Irene Pepperberg	**who studied it:** Julia Fischer
other animal: N'kisi	**other animal:** Clever Hans (horse)

Extra help

Put students who read the same text into pairs to compare their answers. Monitor and help as necessary.

4   Read the instructions and the example. Put students into A/B pairs and monitor and encourage them to make eye contact with their partner as they exchange information (so they are listening to each other rather than copying each other's notes). Give positive feedback when students look up from their notes.

Extra activity

Ask students to cover the notes they made in exercise 4. Put students into pairs to tell a partner about their animal using the subtitles on **>> p.78**. Partners listen and tick the information in the box that their partner remembers.

5   In pairs, students decide which of the two animals is more amazing and why. Ask for a show of hands for each animal and nominate students to explain why. If there is a difference of opinion between students, nominate individuals with opposing views to discuss the topic further.

Extra activity

In pairs, students choose five new words and guess meaning. They check in their dictionaries.

B Grammar ability *can, could, be able to, manage to*

6 Direct students to the grammar box. Ask them to read the examples and check vocabulary as necessary. Students then underline the verbs in the section title.

Ask students to find the sentences in the texts on >> **p.78** and to match rules 1–4 with the verbs in a–d. Monitor and help as necessary. Check answers as a class but do not go into differences in meaning between *managed* and *be able to* at this point as this will be dealt with in the next level.

> 1 c 2 d 3 a 4 b

Extra help
Ask students to underline examples of *can, could, managed to,* and *be able to* in *Smart Alex* and *Clever Rico*. They identify the rule and write a number from 1–4 next to each sentence.

Extra activity
In pairs, students take turns to tell each other about the animal they read about, using the verb forms in a–d.

7 Ask students to read sentences 1–7 and check vocabulary. Go through the first item as a class and point out that there might be more than one answer. Students continue individually. Monitor and guide them to use the correct tense as necessary. Students compare answers in pairs. Nominate students to give answers and encourage them to read the full sentence.

> 2 could, was able to   3 can, is able to   4 be able to
> 5 managed to, was able to   6 could, were able to
> 7 been able to

Extra activity
Write these cues on the board: *now, last week, when you were a child*. Ask students to write a note of one example of an activity they could or couldn't do for each time period. Put them in pairs or small groups to tell each other about their abilities.

Extra plus
Books closed. Students mingle and tell each other about their abilities past and present. They see if they can find anybody who can and can't do the same things.

C Pronunciation stress in words ending -*ity*

8 Read the instructions and the table headings. Go through the first example and point out the spelling change. Ask students to continue with the activity and monitor and encourage them to check spellings in their dictionaries. Elicit answers from the class as a whole and nominate individuals to spell the word.

> **adjectives:** active, curious
> **nouns:** popularity, reality, possibility

9 8B.1 Play the audio, pausing after each set of words for students to repeat. Nominate different students to say the pairs of words and monitor for correct syllable stress. Play the audio a second time to give extra pronunciation practice if necessary.

10 Go through the exercise with the class. Say the words *able* and *ability,* and exaggerate the stressed syllable to help students hear the difference. Read rules a–c and elicit the answer *(c).*

Extra help
Put students into pairs and ask them to underline the stressed syllables in the words in the table in exercise 8. Monitor and encourage students to use their dictionaries to check their ideas. Elicit answers as a class and give extra pronunciation practice as necessary.

> popular – popularity   active – activity   curious – curiosity
> real – reality   possible – possibility

11 Demonstrate the activity by saying an adjective for the class to say the noun. Repeat with one or two more examples before putting students into pairs to continue. Monitor and give positive feedback for accurate pronunciation. Check students swap roles.

Extra help
Put students into different pairs to repeat the activity.

Extra plus
Ask for pairs of volunteers to repeat exercise 11 for the class. The class decides if the students say the words with correct syllable stress.

ABC Put it all together

12 Read the instructions and direct students to *Ideas* on >> **p.130**. Check vocabulary as necessary. Make sure students understand that they should write notes for each of the points and that these will help them tell a story about something that happened in the past. Tell students to use their dictionaries to help. Encourage them to practise saying their stories to themselves when they have finished making notes. Put students into pairs to tell their stories.

Student performance
Students should be able to relate a short narrative.

You can use this checklist to monitor and give feedback or to assess students' performance.

Grammar	Do students use modal verbs accurately? exercise 7
Vocabulary	Do students use a variety of ways of talking about ability? exercise 7
Pronunciation	Do students try to place stress on words ending in -*ity* correctly? exercise 11

I can talk about ability.
Students tick *on my own* if they have told their story using their notes. They tick *with some help* if they looked at the grammar box in exercise 6 once or twice for help.

Early finishers
Students choose a different topic from *Ideas* on >> **p.130** and repeat the activity.

Additional material

www.oup.com/elt/result for extra practice activities
www.oup.com/elt/teacher/result for extra teacher resources

How to talk about ability

G ability *can, could, be able to, manage to*   **P** stress in words ending *-ity*

A Read and summarize

1 Which animals do you think are the most intelligent? Discuss with a partner.

2 Work with a partner. Look at **Intelligent Animals** opposite. What is the most interesting fact in your text?
   Student A Read **Smart Alex**.
   Student B Read **Clever Rico**.

3 Complete the notes about your text in the box.

	Smart Alex	Clever Rico
animal	African grey parrot	border collie dog
human use of animal	_____ since Ancient Egypt	sheepdog and
language ability	can identify _____ can _____ complicated questions	can understand _____
Why famous?		
Who studied it?	Dr _____ _____	Prof. _____ _____
other animal in text		

4 Use your notes. Tell your partner about your text. Listen and complete the notes in the box.
   Example My text is about an African grey parrot …

5 Decide with a partner which animal is more amazing.

B Grammar ability *can, could, be able to, manage to*

6 Look at the examples in the box and then match rules 1–4 with a–d.

present simple	Rico can understand … Parrots are able to repeat …
past simple	Rico could understand … Rico also managed to learn … Hans was able to answer … Rico was able to fetch …
other tenses and modals	Irene's been able to show …

Rules

1 ☐ For ability in the present simple,
2 ☐ For general ability in the past simple,
3 ☐ For ability on one occasion in the past simple,
4 ☐ In other tenses or after modal verbs,

a use *was/were able to* or *managed to*.
b use *be/been able to*.
c use *can* or *is/are/am able to*.
d use *could* or *was/were able to*.

7 Complete the sentences with the forms in exercise 6. Compare with a partner.
   1 Yesterday, my dad _was able to_ (or _managed to_) finish the crossword for the first time ever!
   2 When I was a child, I _____ sing very well.
   3 My cat's very clever. I think she _____ understand me.
   4 In the future, we will _____ communicate with dolphins.
   5 I lost my key this morning, but I _____ open the door with a credit card.
   6 Some dinosaurs _____ fly.
   7 I've never _____ to do maths very well.

   More practice? **Grammar Bank >>** p.143.

C Pronunciation stress in words ending *-ity*

8 Complete the table. The words you need are in **Smart Alex** or **Clever Rico**.

adjective	noun
able	ability
popular	
	activity
	curiosity
real	
possible	

9 **8B.1▶** Listen and repeat the words in exercise 8. Be careful to put the stress on the correct syllable.

10 The stress is in a different place in the adjective and noun. Choose the correct ending to the rule.

    <u>a</u>ble   a<u>bil</u>ity

    In words ending with *-ity*, always put the stress on …
    a the last syllable.
    b the second-to-last syllable.
    c the syllable before *-ity*.

11 Test a partner. Choose an adjective for your partner to say the noun. Is the stress correct?

ABC Put it all together

12 Think of a time you were or weren't able to do something. Look at **Ideas** on **>>** p.130. Write notes about your story. Tell your story to your partner.

I can talk about ability.   ▬▬▬▬▬▬▬▬

Tick ✓ the line.   with a lot of help   with some help   on my own   very easily

Two Guys in BBC surprise

In the waiting room

When Guy Goma went for an interview for an IT job at the BBC, he didn't expect to become a TV celebrity. Mr Goma, a business studies graduate from Congo, was sitting in a waiting room with the other candidates for the job. At the same time, Guy Kewney, a British technology expert, was sitting in another room waiting to be called for a live TV interview on the subject of online music downloads.

Mistaken identity

Five minutes before the start of the programme, the producer went to the receptionist and asked where Guy Kewney was. She pointed to Guy Goma, so the producer approached him and asked him if he was Guy Kewney. Mr Goma thought that perhaps the man couldn't pronounce his surname and answered yes.

Mr Goma was taken to a TV studio where they put make up on his face and a microphone on his shirt, and sat him down in front of the cameras. This was a very strange job interview, he thought, but he decided to do his best. Finally, the live broadcast began.

The interview

The topic of the programme was a famous court case involving Apple Computers. The results of the court case had come out that day. The interviewer, Karen Bowerman, asked Mr Goma what he thought about the results of the case. She wanted to know if he was surprised at what had happened. Thinking that perhaps she was talking about the job interview, Guy replied that yes, he was very surprised.

The court case had been about downloading music from the Internet, and Ms Bowerman asked Guy if more people would download music online in the future. Guy thought this was another strange question, but he said yes, they would. However, by now it started to become clear that there had been a mistake and Ms Bowerman was surprised that Mr Goma had so little to say. He was obviously not an expert on the subject, and the interview ended shortly afterwards.

TV celebrity

The programme was seen all over the world and Guy Goma quickly became a celebrity.

Since his hilarious interview on the BBC, he has been invited to appear on Channel 4 News, CNN International, and other TV channels. So what about his interview for the IT post at the BBC? Unfortunately, he didn't get the job.

GLOSSARY
IT *n* information technology
BBC *n* British Broadcasting Corporation

How to **report an interview**

Orientation

Context

In this lesson, students practise using reported questions to talk about an interview.

The illustrated newspaper article, *Two Guys in BBC surprise* on **>> p.80**, reports on what happened when two men with the same christian names, Guy, were waiting for an interview at the BBC. One was there for a job interview, the other (a British technology expert) was waiting to be called for a live TV interview about online music downloads. The wrong 'guy' was taken to the studio for the TV interview, which was broadcast live as planned on BBC television. The headline of the article plays with the name *Guy* and the word *guy*, which is informal for *man*.

Language

Focus grammar	reported questions: *I asked him where he was from.*, *I asked him if he was Guy Kewney.*
Focus vocabulary	words: *candidates, company, CV, expert, post, salary, staff* phrases: *work for somebody*
Recognition vocabulary	words: *accountant, afterwards, approach, broadcast, celebrity, computer technician, court case, expert, graphic designer, guy, hilarious, identity, interpreter, lifeguard, microphone, nurse, reporter, sauna, star sign, taxi driver* phrases: *become clear, lined up, online download*
Recycled language	words: *appear, mistake, pointed, replied, said, surprised, thought, unfortunately* grammar: *pronouns in reported speech*

End product

In *Put it all together*, students report a job interview they role played in exercise 14. The activity is based on audio script **8C.1**.

Preparation

Read the *Teaching tip* after exercise 5. Think about different ways of guessing the meaning of vocabulary for the words in exercise 5 if you want to do the activity with the class. Think about how students will change partners for exercises 13–15. Take dictionaries to class if necessary.

Warmer

Put students into small groups. Ask them to make a note of what people do before they go for a job interview. Elicit suggestions around the class and encourage students to add details about how the person being interviewed might feel.

Ask students to tell the class about any experiences they (or anyone they know) have had at interviews. Monitor for the use of past tenses and reported speech. Do not overcorrect for accuracy but help students get their ideas across.

Write *How to report an interview* on the board.

A Read and predict

In this section, students read a news article paragraph by paragraph to predict content.

1 Set a short time limit. In pairs, students brainstorm a list of interview questions. Monitor for word order but do not correct at this stage. Elicit suggestions around the class and write the questions on the board.

2 Go through the instructions and ask students to read questions 1–3. Check vocabulary and direct students to the first paragraph of *Two Guys in BBC surprise* on **>> p.80**. Students answer the questions in pairs. Nominate students to give answers and check the class agrees before giving feedback.

> 1 Guy Goma, Guy Kewney
> 2 They are waiting for an interview. Guy Goma is waiting for a job interview and Guy Kewney is waiting for a live TV interview.
> 3 The wrong man will probably be called for the live TV interview. The clues in the text are: in the title *Two Guys*, referring to the coincidence of the two names; and in the first sentence, '*he didn't expect to become ...*' suggests that he will, in fact, become a TV celebrity.

3 Direct students to the second paragraph to read and answer the questions. Tell students to ignore any new vocabulary for the moment. Nominate students to suggest answers.

> **Two misunderstandings:** The receptionist confused the two men and Mr Goma thought the BBC man couldn't pronounce his name correctly. Mr Goma goes for the TV interview.

4 Direct students to the third paragraph and ask them to read questions 1–3. Check vocabulary as necessary before students continue reading to answer the questions. Go over answers before students read the final part of the story.

> 1 He probably felt nervous.
> 2 The interviewer began to understand the mistake as Guy Goma's answers to the questions were very short.
> 3 Students' own answers.

5 Go through the instructions. Put students into pairs and ask them to choose four words from the word pool. Ask students to find the words in the text and to guess their meaning. Monitor and help students explain what they did as necessary.

Teaching tip

Bring the class together. Ask students to choose a word and to tell the class how they guessed the meaning. Write notes of different ways of guessing on the board. Ask students to choose another word and to try to use a different way of guessing. Go through the list of ideas on the board and point out that it's a good idea to use more than one strategy to guess and check the meaning of a word.

Extra activity

Put students into pairs or small groups to discuss the event. Write the following questions on the board: *Do you think the story is funny? Why? Why not? How do you think Mr Goma felt: during the interview, when the interview ended, when he saw himself on TV? How do you think the BBC receptionist felt?*

Bring the class together. Ask students to report any interesting comments made by another student in the group. Monitor for reported speech but do not overcorrect for accuracy.

B Grammar reported questions

6 Direct students to the grammar box and the column headings. Ask students to read the sentences. Elicit or explain that open questions are questions which have many possible answers.

Copy the sentences in row A onto the board and go through questions 1–4 as a class. Highlight the word order in reported questions and point out that the position of the subject and verb does not change as it does in normal questions.

> 1 open question: after   reported question: before
> 2 open question
> 3 No. The verb and subject are in a different order.
> 4 No. The verbs in the open questions are in the present tense, whereas the verbs in the reported questions are in the past simple.

Extra activity

Ask students to find two examples of reported open questions in the text. (*... asked where Guy Kewney was. ... asked Mr Goma what he thought about the result of the case*).

7 Read the instructions and go through the example as a class. Point out the use of *ask* as the reporting verb for questions. Remind students that pronouns and tenses often change in reported speech, depending on the context.

Monitor and help as students continue individually. Ask volunteers to give answers and monitor for accuracy.

> 2 She asked me what I did.   3 She asked me where I worked.
> 4 She asked me what my nationality was.   5 She asked me who I wanted to see.

Extra activity

Students write the questions they talked about in exercise 1 in reported speech.

8 Check students understand the term *closed questions (questions begin with verbs such as* Are, Was, Do, Did, Can, Will *etc. and have only two possible answers, e.g.* yes/no, big/small, driving or walking). Put students into pairs to look at *Two Guys in BBC surprise* to complete the sentences. Go over answers as a class.

> He asked him if he was Guy Kewney.   She wanted to know if he was surprised at what happened.   She asked Guy if more people would download music online.
> For closed questions, we use *if* + ... after the reporting verb.

9 Explain that questions 1–8 are real questions that candidates have asked at an interview. Go through the questions and check vocabulary. Ask students why the questions are strange and help them express their ideas. Go through the example and put students into pairs to continue. Nominate students to give answers and ask the class if they agree before giving feedback.

> 2 He asked me why I wanted his CV.
> 3 She asked me what my star sign was.
> 4 He asked if he could bring his dog to work.
> 5 She asked me if she had to wear shoes.
> 6 He asked me if I was happily married.
> 7 She asked me if we had a sauna in the building.
> 8 He asked me where the company golf course was.

Extra help

Backchain drill. Help students remember reported questions. Use the answers to questions 1–8. Say the last word and add one word at a time for students to repeat. This will help increase students' fluency.

Extra activity

Put students in pairs to role play Mr Goma telling a friend about his interview. Check they swap roles.

C Listen for detail

In this section, students listen to an interview for gist and detail.

10 8C.1 Read the instructions, and play the audio. Take a yes/no vote and ask around the class and ask for reasons.

> No. She couldn't think of answers to the interviewer's questions. She didn't have the skills required. She expected too high a salary. The interviewer suggested she wouldn't.

11 Ask students to read sentences 1–4 and check vocabulary. Play the audio. Ask students to compare answers and play the audio a second time if necessary.

> 2 True.   3 True.   4 False. (Cath asked for £30,000 a year.)

12 Direct students to audio script 8C.1 on ≫ p.155. Ask students to read it through silently and check vocabulary. Point out the use of different reporting verbs (*asked, said, wanted to know, told, thanked*) in the audio script. Go through the instructions and check students understand that they role play the interview, not Cath and Richard's conversation. Ask for two volunteers to read the example.

ABC Put it all together

13 Read the instructions and encourage students to use dictionaries if necessary. Put students into pairs to choose and make notes about a job. Monitor and direct students to exercises 7 and 12 for ideas. Give students time to practise asking each their questions.

14 Put students into new pairs. Ask them to tell each other which job they are being interviewed for before they ask their questions. Monitor and check students swap roles.

15 Go through the instructions and ask for two volunteers to read the example. Encourage them to continue by eliciting a follow-up question, e.g. *What did you say?* Pair students with their original partners to talk about their interview.

Student performance

Students should be able to talk about an interview.

You can use this checklist to monitor and give feedback or to assess students' performance.

Content	Do students talk about four or more interview questions? exercise 12
Fluency	Do students report questions without a lot of hesitation? exercise 7
Vocabulary	Do students use appropriate reporting verbs? exercise 9

I can report an interview.

Students tick *on my own* if they have told their partner about the five questions. They tick *with some help* if they have looked at the grammar boxes occasionally.

Early finishers

Students choose another job and repeat exercises 13–15.

Additional material

www.oup.com/elt/result for extra practice activities
www.oup.com/elt/teacher/result for extra teacher resources

How to report an interview

A Read and predict

1 What questions do people usually ask at a job interview? Discuss with a partner.

2 Look at **Two Guys in BBC surprise** opposite. Read the first paragraph **In the waiting room** and answer the questions with a partner.
　1 What are the names of the two people?
　2 Why are they waiting?
　3 Can you guess what will happen later in the story? What are the clues?

3 Read **Mistaken identity**. What are the two misunderstandings? What do you think happens?

4 Read **The interview** and answer the questions with a partner. Then read the final part of the story.
　1 How do you think Mr Goma felt when the interview began?
　2 How did the interviewer begin to understand that there had been a mistake?
　3 What will happen to Mr Goma? Will he get the job he's applying for?

5 Work with a partner. Choose four of these words in the text and guess the meaning. Say how you guessed. Then check in a dictionary.

expert approach microphone broadcast case
download afterwards hilarious post

B Grammar reported questions

6 Look at the examples and answer the questions.

	open question	reported question
A	Where's he from?	I asked him where he was from.
B	Where does he live?	I asked him where he lived.

　1 In **A**, does the verb to be come before or after the subject?
　2 In **B**, which sentence has an auxiliary verb?
　3 Is the word order the same in the questions and the reported questions?
　4 Is the tense the same in the questions and the reported questions?

7 Imagine a female receptionist asked you these questions. Later, you tell a friend about it. Write the questions in reported speech.
　1 What's your name? *She asked me what my name was.*
　2 What do you do?
　3 Where do you work?
　4 What's your nationality?
　5 Who do you want to see?

8 Work with a partner. Complete the grammar box with sentences from **Two Guys in BBC surprise**. How are open and closed questions reported differently?

closed question	reported question
Are you Guy Kewney?	He asked him _____.
Are you surprised at what happened?	She wanted to know _____.
Will more people download ...?	She asked Guy _____.

9 Here are some unusual questions which *candidates* have asked at job interviews. Work with a partner and report the questions from the interviewer's point of view.
　1 **Woman** 'What does your company do?'
　　　　　She asked me what our company did.
　2 **Man** 'Why do you want my CV?'
　3 **Woman** 'What is your star sign?'
　4 **Man** 'Can I bring my dog to work?'
　5 **Woman** 'Will I have to wear shoes?'
　6 **Man** 'Are you happily married?'
　7 **Woman** 'Do you have a sauna in the building?'
　8 **Man** 'Where's the company golf course?'

More practice? **Grammar Bank** >> p.143.

C Listen for detail

10 **8C.1▶** Listen to Ricardo and Cath talking about a job interview. Do you think Cath will get the job?

11 Listen again and write *true* or *false*.
　1 Cath thinks the interview went well. *False*
　2 They asked why Cath wanted to work for them.
　3 They asked about Cath's language abilities.
　4 They said the salary was £30,000 a year.

12 Look at the audio script on >> p.155. What did Cath and the interviewers say? Role play the interview.
　Example A Why do you want to work for us?
　　　　　　 B I need the money.

ABC Put it all together

13 Work with a partner. Choose one of these jobs and think of five questions which an interviewer might ask.

accountant computer technician graphic designer
interpreter lifeguard nurse reporter taxi driver

14 Change partners. Interview your new partner using your questions from exercise 13.

15 Tell your first partner about your interview. Guess what job your partner was interviewed for.
　Example A What did the interviewer ask you?
　　　　　　 B She asked me what languages I spoke ...

I can report an interview.

Tick ✓ the line.　with a lot of help　with some help　on my own　very easily

Vikram's Story

I quite often travel to France for work. One time, I was in the Gare du Nord in Paris. I'd just arrived on the Eurostar train from London and while I was walking towards the exit, a man approached me. He looked very tired and hungry and I thought maybe he was homeless. He asked me whether I spoke English, and I told him I was English. He told me he was English too and he asked me to help him.

He said he'd been robbed and only had 80 euros cash to get home – but the ticket was 90 euros. He asked me to give him the 10 euros. He even promised to post it back to me when he got home. I agreed to give him the money, but when I looked in my pocket, I only had a couple of 50 euro notes.

I told him to wait while I went to get change. Then I gave him the money and invited him to join me for a coffee. While we were drinking the coffee, he advised me to be careful – he'd been robbed by a thief working in the station. Before he said goodbye, he asked me to give him my address so he could send me the money. I told him not to worry – he could keep it. I offered to give him five pounds for when he arrived in London, but he refused to take the money. He thanked me and walked away towards the ticket office. I left the station feeling I'd done something good.

The next day, I was in the station again. Another London train had just arrived and a crowd of passengers was leaving the station. Then I saw him – the same man from yesterday. He was asking a woman to give him money. I was so angry that I went over and warned the woman not to give him anything.

Vikram Shenoy
Leicestershire, UK

Reporting verbs

- [ ] **agree (not) to**
- [ ] **advise sb (not) to**
- [ ] **invite sb to**
- [a] **offer to**
- [ ] **refuse to**
- [ ] **promise (not) to**
- [ ] **warn sb (not) to**

a to ask if sb would like sth or to give sb the chance to have sth

b to ask sb to come somewhere or do sth

c to say yes to sth

d to say definitely that you will do or not do sth or that sth will happen

e to say or show that you do not want to do, give, or accept sth

f to tell sb about sth unpleasant or dangerous, so that they can avoid it

g to tell sb what you think they should do

How to report a conversation

Orientation

Context

In this lesson, students use different reporting verbs to talk about a conversation.

The travel magazine article *Vikram's Story* on >> **p.82**, recounts an experience he had when travelling to Paris, a trip he often did for work. On this occasion he was tricked out of ten euros by a man who pretended to have been robbed. The next day, Vikram realized he had been tricked when he saw the same man doing the same thing to another unsuspecting tourist. The photos show the main events in the story.

Reporting verbs lists key verbs and definitions which students will match and use during the lesson. The following information (often found in dictionaries) is also given: whether a noun or pronoun is used after the verb but before *to + infinitive* (shown by the use of *sb*) and the position of *not* when the reporting clause is negative, if the word is used to talk about somebody *sb* or something *sth*.

Language

Focus grammar	reported imperatives and requests: *He asked me to help him., I told him not to worry.*
Focus words	reporting verbs: *advise, agree, invite, offer, promise, refuse, warn*
Recognition vocabulary	words: *homeless, tricked* phrases: *leave me alone*
Recycled language	words: *approached, crowd, lie, robbed, say, tell, thanked, thieves, victim* grammar: *past tenses: past simple, past perfect, past continuous; pronouns in reported speech, say and tell*
Pronunciation	linking after *asked* and *told* **8D.1**
Discourse	pronouns in reported imperatives and orders

Language note

The reporting verbs studied in this lesson are more descriptive than *say, ask,* and *tell* as they give information about the function of what was said.

End product

In *Put it all together*, students recount a conversation they had with somebody they didn't know. They can use their notes.

Preparation

Look at *Questions* on >> **p.131** so you are familiar with the task in exercise 15.

Warmer

Write these words on the board: *agree, invite, offer, promise, suggest.* Put students into pairs or small groups to write the words a person might say when they want to do these things, e.g. *agree: Yes, I think you're right.*

Elicit examples from a spokesperson in each group. As you do so, nominate another student to report the previous student's answer. Encourage them to use the reporting verbs rather than *say, ask,* or *tell.* Monitor for accuracy but do not overcorrect at this stage.

Write *How to report a conversation* on the board.

A Read and follow a story

In this section, students predict content using photos before reading an article for gist and detail.

1 Direct students to the photos on >> **p.82**. Ask students who they can see. *(A young man, probably Indian.)* In pairs, students continue discussing the other photos. Monitor and help with vocabulary. Nominate students to talk about each photo in turn, inviting each other to add information.

> **clockwise:** railway station (Gare du Nord, Paris), a Eurostar train ticket, Vikram, one €10 note, a Eurostar train with passengers getting off, a cup of coffee on a bar, two €50 notes

2 Go through the instructions and answers a–c. Check students understand the meaning of *tricked* and *robbed*. *(A trick involves more than just taking something from somebody.)*

Direct students to *Vikram's Story* on >> **p.82** and ask how they are going to read the text. *Carefully or quickly? (Quickly.)* Set a short time limit to encourage students to read for gist. Take a vote on the best answer, encouraging students to add some facts from the story to explain their choice *(a)*.

3 Read questions 1–5 and check vocabulary. Tell students to read *Vikram's Story* again and to ignore unknown vocabulary for the moment. Do the first item as a class and elicit or remind students to use key words in the question to locate the parts of the text where they might find the answers. Point out that they will also need to read carefully as some information is not directly stated in the text.

Monitor and help as students continue in pairs. Ask for volunteers to give answers. Help students get their ideas across.

> 1 To check they could understand each other, maybe to see if Vikram might be sympathetic to his situation.
> 2 To give Vikram the impression that he was honest.
> 3 To make out that he was going to buy the train ticket that he'd needed the money for.
> 4 He saw the same man the following day.
> 5 Students' own answers.

Extra activity

Students work with a partner and find three new words in the text. They guess the meaning and check in a dictionary.

B Grammar reported imperatives and requests

4 Direct students to the grammar box. Ask students to look at the example sentences and elicit the difference between a request and an imperative. *(A request is asking somebody to do something, or for permission to do something. An imperative gives an order or advice.)*

Direct students back to *Vikram's Story* to find and underline the two sentences and to copy them into the reported speech columns.

Answer the questions below the box as a class. Point out that *ask* can be followed by the object + *to* + infinitive, and that *not* in a negative imperative is placed after the object pronoun and followed by *to* + infinitive.

> He asked me to help him.   I told him not to worry.
> a ask   b told

5 Go through the instructions and do the first item as a class. Monitor and help as students continue individually. Nominate students to give answers and see if the class agrees before you give feedback.

> 2 She told me not to wait.   3 I told him not to go.
> 4 He asked me to go.

6 8D.1 Read the information about pronunciation and play the audio, pausing after each sentence for students to repeat. Play the audio again and give extra practice as necessary.

7 Ask students to read conversations 1–4 and check vocabulary. Go through the example as a class to demonstrate the activity and remind students of changes in pronouns in reported speech. Monitor and help as students continue in pairs. Nominate students to give answers. Review any general problems with the class at the end, referring back to the grammar box. Revise the grammar of *ask* and *tell* as necessary.

> 2 I asked him to tell me the way to the station and he told me to follow him.
> 3 He told me to be careful and I told him not to worry.
> 4 She asked me to give her €10 and I told her to leave me alone.

Extra help

Transformation drill. Nominate different students and make a request or give an imperative for students as a class to report, e.g. *T Pablo, can you help me? SS She/He asked Pablo/him to help her/him.*
Reported requests: *Can you wait please?; Will you go please?; Can you help me, please?; Can you show me the way to the station?; Can you give me €10 please?*
Reported imperatives: *Don't worry!; Don't wait!; Don't go!; Follow me!; Be careful; Leave me alone.*

Extra activity

Say the imperatives and requests to different students. Encourage another student to ask *What did she/he say?* so the original student is cued to report what you said.

C Vocabulary reporting verbs

8 Direct students to *Reporting verbs* on >> **p.82**. Go through each one and draw attention to the grammatical information given in the list, e.g. *advise sb (not) to* tells us that *advise* must be used with a pronoun, and that the negative is placed between the pronoun and *to*. Direct students to *Vikram's Story* to find and underline examples of the reporting verbs.

9 Ask students to read definitions a–g and check vocabulary. Put students into pairs to match the reporting verbs and definitions. Monitor and help as necessary. To check answers, read the definitions and ask the class to say the letter of the definition. Check students understand the information about how the verbs are used (see *Context*).

> agree c   advise g   invite b   refuse e   promise d   warn f

10 Ask students to read sentences 1–3 and check vocabulary as necessary. Do the first item as a class to demonstrate the activity, encouraging students to think about was actually said and to decide if it is advice, a warning, or an offer. *(Advice.)* Students continue individually and compare in pairs.

> 1 advised   2 invited   3 offered, refused

11 Direct students to *Reporting verbs*. Do the first two items together to demonstrate the activity. Monitor and help as necessary. Students continue individually. Give extra pronunciation practice of the past tenses verbs if necessary.

> 3 offered to come   4 refused to come   5 invited her to come
> 6 agreed to go   7 advised him to go/come

D Listen and show interest

In this section, students listen for gist and detail in a conversation about *Vikram's Story*.

12 8D.2 Read questions 1 and 2 and check vocabulary. Play the audio. Ask students to compare answers and play the audio a second time if necessary. Check answers.

> 1 He was very kind.   2 He was right to do it.

13 Read the instructions and direct students to audio script 8D.2 on >> **p.155**. Elicit one or two more examples as a class. Monitor and help as necessary as students continue individually. Check answers and explain that these are ways of showing interest and developing a conversation.

> **questions:** So, did you give it to him?   Did you say anything?
> **comments:** That was very nice of you.   Uh huh.   Mmm.
> So that story about ... was a lie.   Quite right too!

14 Put students into pairs to practise the conversation. Check students swap roles and give positive feedback.

ABCD Put it all together

15 Read the instructions and direct students to *Questions* on >> **p.131**. Check students understand the activity and monitor and help with ideas if necessary.

16 Put students into pairs to exchange stories. Remind them to be interested listeners. Check students swap roles.

Student performance

Students should be able to recount a conversation.

You can use this checklist to monitor and give feedback or to assess students' performance.

Coherence	Do students use pronouns appropriately? exercise 7
Fluency	Do students use reporting phrases without a lot of hesitation? exercise 6
Vocabulary	Do students use different reporting verbs appropriately? exercise 11

I can report a conversation.

Students tick *on my own* if they have told their story without looking at *Reporting verbs*. They tick *with some help* if they have looked at the vocabulary panel once or twice for help.

Early finishers

Students imagine they are Vikram. They tell their story to their partner. The partner listens carefully to pronouns and says if the story was easy to follow or not.

Additional material

www.oup.com/elt/result for extra practice activities
www.oup.com/elt/teacher/result for extra teacher resources

How to report a conversation

G reported imperatives and requests   V reporting verbs   P linking after *asked* and *told*

A Read and follow a story

1 Look at the photos opposite. What do you think the story is about? Discuss with a partner.

2 Read **Vikram's Story** opposite. What happened? Choose the best answer.
   a He was robbed.   b He was tricked.   c He got lost.

3 Answer the questions with a partner.
   1 Why did the man ask Vikram if he spoke English?
   2 Why did the man refuse the five pounds?
   3 Why did the man walk towards the ticket office after saying goodbye?
   4 How did Vikram know the man had tricked him?
   5 Would you do the same as Vikram in this situation? Why? Why not?

B Grammar reported imperatives and requests

4 Find the reported form of these sentences in **Vikram's Story**. Then answer the questions below.

	direct speech	reported speech
request	'Can you help me?'	
imperative	'Don't worry!'	

Which verb do we use ...
a for reported requests?   b for reported imperatives?

5 Put these sentences in reported speech.
   1 I/her   'Can you wait, please?'   *I asked her to wait.*
   2 She/me   'Don't wait!'
   3 I/him   'Don't go!'
   4 He/me   'Will you go, please?'

6 **8D.1▶ Pronunciation** Listen and repeat the answers to exercise 5. Notice that you don't hear the past tense endings in ask<u>ed</u> and tol<u>d</u> before *me*.

7 Work with a partner. Report these mini-conversations.
   1 **Me**   Can you help me?
     Woman Could you wait a moment, please?
               I asked her to help me and she asked me to wait a moment.

   2 **Me**   Can you show me the way to the station, please?
     Man Follow me.

   3 **Man** Be careful!
     Me   Don't worry!

   4 **Woman** Can you give me €10, please?
     Me   Leave me alone.

More practice? **Grammar Bank** >> p.143.

C Vocabulary reporting verbs

8 Look at **Reporting verbs** opposite and <u>underline</u> examples of the verbs in **Vikram's Story**.

9 Match the reporting verbs with the definitions. Compare with a partner.

10 <u>Underline</u> the best option in these sentences.
   1 They advised/warned/offered me to take the bus because it was cheaper.
   2 Tom offered/promised/invited me to stay in his flat during the holidays.
   3 I invited/offered to lend her €20, but she offered/refused to take it.

11 Report these sentences using all of the reporting verbs.
   1 I'll come, I promise.   *He promised to come.*
   2 If you go, there will   *She warned me not to go.*
     be trouble!
   3 I'll come, if you want.   *He ...*
   4 No, I'm not coming!   *She ...*
   5 Would you like to come?   *He ...*
   6 Yes, OK, I'll come.   *I ...*
   7 You should come.   *She ...*

D Listen and show interest

12 **8D.2▶** Listen to Vikram telling his story to his friend Anita and answer the questions.
   What does Anita think about ...
   1 Vikram telling the man to keep the money?
   2 Vikram warning the woman about the man at the end of the story?

13 Anita is an interested listener. She asks a lot of questions and makes comments. Look at the audio script on >> p.155 and <u>underline</u> them.
   Example   Why? What happened?

14 Work with a partner and practise the conversation.

ABCD Put it all together

15 Think of a time you had a conversation with someone you didn't know, for example on a train, in a café, etc. Look at the **Questions** on >> p.131 and write notes.

16 Tell your partner about your encounter. Listen to your partner's story and be an interested listener.

I can report a conversation.
Tick ✓ the line.   with a lot of help   with some help   on my own   very easily

Writing A report

A Listen to a survey question

1 Which is the best way to do these things? Tick ✓ one or more boxes in each row. Compare your answers with a partner.

	face to face	phone	text	email	post
arrange to meet					
invite to a wedding					
apologize					
say 'happy birthday'					
say 'I love you'					
pass on a quick message					
give important information					

2 Sandra is doing a class survey and she has asked a question about communication habits. Read her notes. Which of the five forms of communication in exercise 1 could it be about?

> Why?
> – quick to send info: no conversation
> – convenient: if busy, can read later

3 **8E.1▶** Listen and check.

4 Listen again and answer the questions with a partner. Then check your answers in the audio script on **≫** p.155.
1 What four questions does Sandra ask?
2 What does the other person answer?

5 Imagine you are doing a survey on one of these topics. Choose a topic and think of three questions to ask.
1 What do people do when they receive a phone call from a company selling things?
2 When do people switch off their mobile phones?
3 When do people prefer to speak face to face?
4 What do people use email for?
5 Why do people still use the post?

B Read a report

6 Work with a partner. Complete Sandra's class report with these words and phrases.

so   however   if   because   such as

Why do people send text messages?

For me, writing a text message on a mobile phone isn't very easy. ¹_____, text messages are very popular these days. I decided to find out why.

I asked five people why they sent text messages. One person said she never sent them ²_____ they were too difficult. The other four said they often used them to send short pieces of information, ³_____ arranging a place to meet. One person said that text messages were convenient because the other person doesn't have to answer immediately. ⁴_____ they aren't able to answer now, they can answer later.

⁵_____ text messages are popular because they are convenient. Perhaps in the future, new technology will make them easier to write.

7 Match the words and phrases in exercise 6 with these uses.
1 to give a reason
2 to give an example
3 to introduce a conclusion
4 to introduce a contrasting fact
5 to introduce a possible situation

8 How is Sandra's text divided into paragraphs? Use the topics below to complete the description.

~~introduction to the topic~~   results
conclusion   the question

paragraph 1 = _introduction to the topic_
paragraph 2 = _____, _____
paragraph 3 = _____

AB Put it all together

9 Choose a topic and some questions to ask from exercise 5, or use your own survey ideas. Ask people around the class and take notes of their answers.

10 Write a report of your survey. Follow the same paragraph structure as Sandra's text in exercise 6.

11 Read other students' reports. Are any of the results surprising?

I can write a report.
Tick ✓ the line.   with a lot of help   with some help   on my own   very easily

Orientation

Context and Language

In this lesson, students use reported questions and answers to write a survey report.

Recycled language	words: *apologize, invite, message* phrases: *communication habits, switch off* grammar: *reported questions and answers*
Recognition language	words: *convenient, info, post, survey, text message* phrases: *contrasting fact, pass on*
Discourse	*because, however, if, so, such as*

End product

In *Put it all together*, students write a report of a class survey they conducted in exercise 9. Their report is based on a model in exercise 6.

Preparation

Write some possible questions in advance to give students ideas for exercise 5. Think about classroom organization so that students can conduct their class survey in exercise 9 and read each other's reports for exercise 11.

Warmer

Nominate various students to answer one or two questions from exercise 5. Ask students for reasons or to give an example when they answer the question. Encourage students with contrasting ideas to discuss their opinions. Make a note of different answers on the board and take a class vote for the most popular suggestion at the end.

Write *How to write a report* on the board.

A Listen to a survey question

In this section, students listen to a person being interviewed for a survey for detail.

1 Read the instructions and direct students to the table. Ask them to look at the information in the first column and across the top row and check vocabulary. Students tick the best ways of doing things and compare answers in pairs.

2 Direct students to the notes and go through each of the forms of communication in exercise 1 and take a class vote on each one. Ask students to explain their choice but do not comment on the answer at this stage as students will listen to check in the next exercise.

3 8E.1 Tell students they will listen to Sandra interviewing a person for her survey. Play the audio and elicit the answer *(text)*. Play the audio a second time if necessary.

4 Read the instructions and questions 1 and 2. Play the audio, pausing occasionally for students to make notes. Direct students to audio script 8E.1 on >> p.155–56 to check their answers.

5 Read the instructions and topics 1–5 with the class and check vocabulary as necessary. Monitor and help students with ideas. Check answers.

B Read a report

In this section, students analyse a survey report for the use of discourse markers and paragraph organization.

6 Go through the instructions and put students into pairs to do the activity. Remind students to read words before and after the blanks and to look at punctuation to help them find the correct word or phrase. To check answers, read the report and pause at the blanks for the class to say the answers.

> 1 However 2 because 3 such as 4 If 5 So

7 Go through uses 1–5 and check vocabulary as necessary. Ask students to match the words and phrases and uses individually, before comparing in pairs. Check answers.

> 1 because 2 such as 3 so 4 however 5 if

Extra activity

Ask students to underline reported questions and answers in the text and to change them into direct speech.

8 Read the instructions and example. Ask students for the first two words of each paragraph before they continue individually. Check answers.

> paragraph 2 = the question, the results
> paragraph 3 = conclusion

Extra help

Put students into pairs and ask them to find and underline any useful phrases and sentences to use in a report.

AB Put it all together

9 Go through the instructions and monitor and help as necessary. Ask students to interview five or more people in the class. Tell them to make notes of the answers like those in exercise 2.

10 Tell students to choose one or two questions with the most interesting answers. Encourage them to review their interview notes and to find and underline a reason, an example, and a contrasting fact before they write their report.

11 In small groups, students read and comment on each other's reports. Bring the class together and ask for volunteers to report any interesting or surprising survey results.

Student performance

Students should be able to write a report of a survey.

You can use this checklist to monitor and give feedback or to assess students' performance.

Content	Have students included the necessary information?
Organization	Have students organized their information logically?
Coherence	Have students used some discourse markers?

I can write a report.

Students tick *on my own* if they wrote their report following the structure in exercise 8. They can tick *with some help* if they looked at the model in exercise 6 occasionally.

Early finishers

Students choose a second topic and ask questions to the people in their group. They report each other's answers to the group.

Additional material

www.oup.com/elt/result for extra practice activities
www.oup.com/elt/teacher/result for extra teacher resources

Warmer

Remember the sentences

Write the following reporting verbs on the board: *advise, agree, ask, invite, offer, promise, refuse, say, tell, warn*. Say the following sentences for students to match with the reporting verbs:

1 What's the time? 2 Would you like to have dinner with me? 3 I think you should leave early. 4 Don't touch that pan. It's hot! 5 Yes, I think you're right. 6 I'll help you with that. 7 Good morning. 8 No, I don't want another cup of tea, thank you. 9 I'll pay you back next week. 10 I'm going to the north east of Brazil for my holiday.

> 1 ask   2 invite   3 advise   4 warn   5 agree   6 offer   7 say
> 8 refuse   9 promise   10 tell

A Grammar

1   Ability: *can, could, be able to, manage to* 8B exercise 6

Warm-up: Ask students what they can remember about Rico the collie, Alex the parrot, and Hans the horse. Direct students to *Intelligent Animals* on >> **p.78** to check.

Set-up: Remind students to look at the information before and after the blanks.

> 2 managed to   3 able to   4 can   5 able to   6 can
> 7 managed to   8 could

Follow-up: Ask students to write five sentences, some true and some false about Rico, Alex, and Hans using *can, could, be able to*, and *managed to*. Students read their sentences to a partner, who corrects the factually incorrect sentences.

2   Reported questions 8C exercise 6

Warm-up: Books closed. Write the following words on the board: *from, you, where, really, are, do, know, to, want*. Ask students to make two questions. Direct them to the example conversation to check.

Set-up: Go through the example and remind students to think about word order.

> 2 He asked me if I was married. She asked him why he was asking.   3 He asked her where she'd got her bag. She asked him if he liked it.   4 He asked her how she'd made the cake. She asked him if he'd like a piece.

Follow-up: In pairs, students write three strange interview questions similar to those in exercise 9 on >> **p.81**. They swap questions with another pair and write reported questions.

3   Reported imperatives and requests 8D exercise 4

Warm-up: Ask students to change direct speech to reported speech in these sentences: *Don't worry! Can you help me?* Direct students to exercise 4 on >> **p.83** to revise if necessary.

Set-up: Go through the instructions and remind students to think about the changes in pronouns.

> 2 He advised/asked me to fasten my seat belt.   3 He told me not to smoke in the taxi.   4 I asked him to go a bit slower.   5 He asked me to tell him the address again.   6 I told him to stop at the corner.

Follow-up: In pairs, students write similar sentences for cabin staff and passengers on an aeroplane. They write an answer key on a separate piece of paper. Pairs swap sentences and write the reported imperatives and requests. At the end of the activity, they swap answer keys and check.

B Vocabulary

4   Phrasal verbs 8A exercise 7

Warm-up: Books closed. Set a short time limit for students to write phrasal verbs they remember from the unit. Direct students to *Phrasal verbs* on >> **p.76** to check.

Set-up: Go through the example with the class.

> 2 g   3 e   4 a   5 d   6 b   7 h   8 c

Follow-up: In pairs, students take turns to read the sentences and monitor for correct stress of the particles.

5   Telephone words and phrases 8A exercise 6

Warm-up: Read items 1–8 in exercise 6 on >> **p.77** and ask students to write the telephone phrases. Direct students back to the exercise to check their answers.

Set up: Go through the example and point out that the first letter of each missing word is given.

> 2 Who's calling   3 line's busy   4 engaged signal
> 5 leave a message   6 let (her) know

Follow-up: Students look at the speech bubbles a–f on >> **p.76** and write similar gap-fill sentences for a partner.

6   Reporting verbs 8D exercise 11

Warm-up: Ask students which of the following verbs are used with a pronoun: *agree, advise, invite, offer, refuse, promise, warn*. Direct students to *Reporting verbs* on >> **p.82** to check their answers.

Set-up: Point out that students are given a choice of verbs in the first part of the text. In the second, they must choose from the three verbs above the text.

> 2 agreed   3 promised   4 warned   5 promised   6 advised
> 7 refused

Follow-up: In pairs, students review the unit and write an example direct speech sentence for each word in exercise 6. They swap with another pair and report the sentences using the correct verbs.

Early finishers

Ask students to look at their *can do* bars and to tell a partner or write sentences about their language ability using *can, could, be able to*, and *managed to*.

Unit 8 Review

A Grammar

1 Ability: can, could, be able to, manage to Complete the sentences with *can, could, able to* or *managed to*.

1 I _could_ swim when I was five.
2 Tom woke up late, but he _____ get to work on time.
3 I've never been _____ do calculations in my head.
4 These days, my son _____ run faster than I can.
5 Irene was _____ communicate with her parrot.
6 Some people _____ remember everything they see.
7 Hillary and Tenzing _____ reach the top of Mount Everest in 1953.
8 I _____ speak Arabic in the past, but I've forgotten it now.

2 Reported questions Report the questions in these short conversations.

1 **Man** Where are you from?
   He asked her where she was from.

   Woman Do you really want to know?
   She asked if he really wanted to know.

2 **Man** Are you married?
   _____

   Woman Why are you asking?
   _____

3 **Man** Where did you get your bag?
   _____

   Woman Do you like it?
   _____

4 **Man** How did you make the cake?
   _____

   Woman Would you like a piece?
   _____

3 Reported imperatives and requests You are in a taxi. Who said these sentences – you or the (male) taxi driver? Report the sentences.

1 Can you take me to 21 West Street?
   I asked him to take me to 21 West Street.
2 Can you fasten your seat belt, please?
   _____
3 Don't smoke in the taxi, please.
   _____
4 Go a bit slower, please.
   _____
5 Can you tell me the address again?
   _____
6 Stop at the corner, please.
   _____

B Vocabulary

4 Phrasal verbs Match 1–8 with a–h.

1 [f] A woman answered but she hung ...
2 [ ] Do you want to speak to Jo? I'll hand ...
3 [ ] I rang before, but I couldn't get ...
4 [ ] I'm in a meeting and I can't get ...
5 [ ] Sorry I'm late – the bus broke ...
6 [ ] Sorry, I'm busy – can you ring ...
7 [ ] Yes, he's in. Hang on and I'll put ...
8 [ ] Your new camera is here – call ...

a away at the moment.
b back in about half an hour?
c by and pick it up any time.
d down on the way here.
e through – all the lines were busy.
f ~~up as soon as I spoke.~~
g you over to her right now.
h you through to his office.

5 Telephone words and phrases Complete the phrases in this conversation.

A Hi, I'm [1]_calling_ from _____ ACM Insurance. Can I speak to Ms Soames, please?
S Yes. [2]W_____'s c_____, please?
A Mr Ackroyd.
S I'm sorry, Mr Ackroyd, the [3]l_____ b_____ at the moment – I'm just getting the [4]e_____ s_____. Would you like to [5]l_____ a m_____?
A Yes, can you tell her I called to [6]l_____ her k_____ about her claim. She's got my number.
S OK, Mr Ackroyd. I'll tell her to call you back. Goodbye.
A Bye.

6 Reporting verbs Complete the stories with the verbs in the correct form.

agree ~~invite~~ offer warn

Grandma [1]_invited_ Rose to go to her cottage for lunch. Rose [2]_____ to visit and [3]_____ to bring a basket of fruit. Grandma [4]_____ her not to take the path through the woods because it was dangerous. 'And you must promise not to talk to any strangers!' said Grandma.

advise promise refuse

Rose [5]_____ not to. On the way to Grandma's cottage, Rose met a stranger and he [6]_____ her to take the path through the woods because it was shorter. Fortunately, Rose remembered her promise to Grandma and she [7]_____ to listen to the stranger.

Weather

blowing boiling
cloud floods
freezing gales
heat wave lightning
mild pouring
shining showers
snowing soaking
stormy windy

Talk about the Weather

by Josh Elliot

'It's a lovely day, isn't it?'
'Yes, it's so mild for the time of year!'

Why do we talk so much about the weather? I mean, we don't really do it for practical reasons, do we? I can understand farmers or sailors being interested in the weather, but most of us live and work inside. And anyway, a lot of what we say are things that everybody knows already. On a cold day, why do I need somebody to say to me, 'It's freezing out there, isn't it?' I know that already! But there are some good reasons to talk about the weather.

Reason 1

It's a good way to start a conversation. Everybody knows something about it. Think of the alternatives. Try starting with something like, 'Picasso's early works are marvellous, aren't they?' It'll probably be a very short conversation! Everybody has different interests and opinions, but the weather is something which we share. We all have to live with the same weather. There's nothing we can do about it so we just celebrate it or complain about it together.

Reason 2

We all have lots to say about the weather. We have a lifetime of experience of it – or more. Ideas about the weather are given to us by our grandparents and great-grandparents. Think of old sayings like 'Red sky at night, sailor's delight'. In the days before weather forecasts, people had to predict what was coming by looking for clues around them. For example, there were clues in animal behaviour: 'If crows fly low, winds will blow'.

Reason 3

Weather is important to us. It can change our moods. We know that weeks without sunshine can cause winter blues, or seasonal affective disorder, as doctors call it. Statistics show that heat waves in New York cause more crimes. Also, it seems that many of us are fascinated by the weather. The weather forecast is one of the most popular programmes on TV. We don't just watch it for information, it's entertainment too – especially when it gets extreme, with snowstorms, gales, floods, and tornados.

Reason 4

We can talk about the weather to communicate other things. A character in an Oscar Wilde play says, 'Whenever people talk to me about the weather, I feel quite sure they mean something else.' It's true. When we say, 'Lovely day, isn't it?' perhaps we are really saying, 'I feel cheerful and I'd like a chat.' People enjoy chatting – it makes them feel part of a group. Monkeys pick insects from each other's hair for the same reason. But I'd prefer to talk about the weather!

Red sky at night, sailor's delight

If crows fly low, winds will blow

How to make small talk

Orientation

Context
In this lesson, students will practise using tag questions to start a conversation.

The illustrated magazine article, *Four good reasons to talk about the weather* on **>> p.86** takes a look at why many people use the topic as a conversation opener. The two photos below the article show well-known sayings about the English weather.

The picture accompanying *Weather* illustrates key words for the lesson.

Culture notes
Talking about the weather is often considered an exclusively British thing to do. In fact, talking about the weather is something that people of most cultures do as it is an easy topic of conversation to have with people you don't know.

Language

Focus grammar	tag questions: *isn't it?, is there?, aren't they?, do we?, don't we?*
Focus words	weather: *autumn, blowing, boiling, cloud, floods, freezing, gales, heat wave, lightning, mild, pouring, shining, showers, snowing, soaking, spring, stormy, summer, windy, winter*
Recognition vocabulary	words: *alternatives, cheerful, chatting, clues, farmers, floods, heat wave, lifetime, marvellous, mood, sailors, sayings, share, snowstorms, sociable, tornados* phrases: *conversation starter, cut off, seasonal affective disorder, winter blues*
Recycled language	words: *amazing, celebrate, chats, city, complain, entertainment, extreme, fascinated, forecast, forest, hills, insects, mountains, perhaps, probably, sea*
Pronunciation	tag questions 9A.3

Language note
There is a limited presentation of tag questions in this lesson. Tags using other verb forms will be dealt with later in the course.

End product
In *Put it all together*, students start and continue conversations with several people in the class. The conversations are based on audio script **9A.3**.

Preparation
Think about classroom organization for the mingle activity in exercise 15. Take dictionaries to class, if necessary.

Warmer
Write the following questions on the board: *When you're standing in a queue for something, do you talk to people next to you? What topics do you talk about?* Put students into small groups to discuss the questions. Monitor and join in the discussions. Ask for a student from each group to report back to the class. Take a vote on the most and least interesting topic.

Write *How to make small talk* on the board.

A Vocabulary weather

1 Direct students to *Weather* on **>> p.86** and read the instructions. Elicit or explain how to recognize nouns, verbs, and adjectives. *(Nouns might end in -s and they can be made plural; verbs might end in -s, -ing, or -ed; adjectives might end in -y or -ing.)*

Do one or two examples as a class to check students understand before they continue in pairs. Monitor and help as necessary. Draw three columns on the board and elicit answers around the class. Go through each one and check students understand meaning.

> **nouns:** heat wave, showers, cloud, gales, floods, lightning
> **verbs:** shining, snowing, pouring, blowing
> **adjectives:** mild, stormy, windy, boiling, soaking, freezing

2 9A.1 Go through the example together. Monitor and help as necessary as students continue individually. Elicit one or two answers before playing the audio for students to listen and check. Play the audio a second time, pausing after each item for students to repeat.

> 2 c   3 b   4 a   5 d   6 f

3 Read the instructions and ask students to read sentences 1–5, ignoring the blanks. Check vocabulary as necessary.
Go through the first item as a class, and demonstrate that if they decide on the type of word, e.g. a noun, verb, or adjective, it will be easier to find the answer. Monitor and help as necessary as students continue individually.

Nominate students to read the complete sentence to check answers. See if everyone in the class agrees, before confirming the answer. Give extra pronunciation practice as necessary.

> 1 showers   2 pouring, soaking   3 boiling, freezing
> 4 stormy, lightning   5 blowing, shining

4 Direct students to the picture in *Weather* on **>> p.86** and ask them to name the different places *(sea, city, hills, mountains, forest)*. Go through the example and ask students to use words in *Weather* to describe parts of the picture. Set a short time limit before putting students in pairs to compare. Elicit suggestions around the class.

> **Suggested answers**
> It's boiling hot over the sea.
> There are a few clouds over the city.
> It's pouring down in the hills.
> It's stormy in the mountains.
> It's freezing cold in the mountains.
> It's snowing in the forest.

Extra help
Make true or false sentences about the weather in the picture. The class repeats the sentences which are factually correct.

5 Read the questions and check students understand *mood (how you feel, happy, sad, etc.)*. Students discuss the questions in pairs. Monitor and give positive feedback for detail in answers. Students tell the class about themselves and their partner.

Extra activity
Put students into small groups to talk about the current weather. Ask the following questions: *Do they like it? Why? Why not? How does it make them feel? How important is a weather forecast? Is it always right?*

B Read and understand reasons

In this section, students read for gist, and scan an article for general information and detail.

6 Direct students to *Talk about the Weather* on >> **p.86**. Ask them to read the introduction and say what the article will be about.

Ask students to look at summary sentences a–d and check vocabulary. Do the first item together to demonstrate the activity. Point out or elicit that students should identify key words and ideas in the summary sentences before looking for the reason in the article. Tell students to ignore any new vocabulary for the moment. Monitor and help as students continue individually. Check answers.

> a 3   b 4   c 2   d 1

7 Read the instructions and point out that students answer the questions according to what the writer said in the text. Ask students to read questions 1–5 and check vocabulary. Remind students to use key words in the questions to find information and then to read carefully. Monitor and help as students continue individually.

Ask for volunteers to answer the questions. At the end of the activity, help increase students' confidence by pointing out that they have understood the main points in a difficult text.

> 1 Sailors and farmer are interested in the weather because they work outside.   2 Not everybody knows about art.
> 3 Sayings passed knowledge based on previous experiences before there were weather forecasts.   4 The weather is important because it can change our moods, it can cause crimes, it's fascinating and can be entertaining.   5 We say things like that to tell somebody that we'd like to talk to them.

C Listen to conversations about the weather

In this section, students identify key phrases and functions in short conversations.

8 9A.2 Read the instructions and check understanding. Elicit or give the names of the four seasons and write them on the board. Ask students about what typical weather they associate with each season in Britain and their own country.

Go through the example and advise students to listen for key words or phrases. Play the audio and pause after the first conversation. Elicit more phrases to add to those in the example *(snowstorms, heaviest snow)*.

Continue with the audio, pausing after each conversation to give students time to complete their notes. Play the audio a second time if necessary. Ask around the class for answers.

> 2 spring: lovely day, mild, showers   3 summer: hot, hottest August, no wind, heat wave, over 45 degrees   4 autumn: clear (not cloudy), cold already, nice and sunny tomorrow

9 Read the instructions and items a–g with the class. Check vocabulary, making sure that students understand the activity. Go through the example and explain that there might be more than one answer for each item.

Play the audio, pausing after each one to give students time to note their answers. Ask students to compare answers and play the audio again if necessary. Direct students to audio script 9A.2 on >> **p.156** and go through answers as a class.

> b 2   c 1, 2, 3, 4   d 1, 3, 4   e 2   f 1, 2, 3, 4   g 1, 2, 3

Extra help
Put students into pairs to underline one example for each of the items a–g in audio script **9A.2**.

D Grammar tag questions

10 Do the exercise as a class. Write *It's a lovely day, isn't it?* on the board and ask the class to say *true* or *false* for items 1–3. If there is disagreement, encourage students to explain their answers. Direct students to the title of the section and tell them that these types of questions are called *tag questions*.

> 1 True.   2 False.   3 True.

11 9A.3 Read the instructions and information to draw students' attention to the intonation in tag questions. Play the audio, and pause after each item for students to repeat. Trace the rise-fall intonation pattern by moving your finger in the air as students repeat. Mark the intonation pattern on the sentence on the board. Give more practice as necessary.

12 Direct students' attention to the sentence on the board. Ask what they notice about the verb *to be* in the question. Read sentences 1–5 and check meaning. Monitor and help as students continue. Nominate students to give answers and monitor for pronunciation. Ask a volunteer to add a reply.

> 2 aren't they?   3 don't we?   4 is there?   5 do we?

Extra help
In pairs, students take turns to say the first part of the tag. A partner continues the tag.

13 Go through the exercise with the class, eliciting answers.

> 1 If the sentence is positive, the tag is negative. If the sentence is negative, the tag is positive.   2 If the sentence contains *be*, the tag is *do*. If the sentence contains other main verbs, the tag is *do*.

14 Ask students to read sentences 1–5. Check vocabulary. Monitor and help as students continue individually. Check answers.

> 2 isn't it?   3 is it?   4 do you?   5 don't you?

ABCD Put it all together

15 Go through the instructions and point out that students should think about the type of weather before they start their conversations. Remind them to use appropriate vocabulary for that season. Put students into small groups or ask them to mingle and have conversations like Susan and Tom.

Student performance

Students should be able to start and continue a short conversation with a stranger.

You can use this checklist to monitor and give feedback or to assess students' performance.

Grammar	Do students use three different tag questions? exercise 12
Vocabulary	Do students use different weather words and phrases? exercise 4 Do students use weather words appropriately? exercise 8

I can make small talk.

Students tick *on my own* if they have had two or three conversations without looking at exercise 12. They tick *with some help* if they have looked at exercise 12 once or twice.

Early finishers
Volunteers act their conversations for the class, books closed.

Additional material

www.oup.com/elt/result for extra practice activities
www.oup.com/elt/teacher/result for extra teacher resources

How to make small talk

A Vocabulary weather

1 Look at the words in **Weather** opposite. Decide if they are nouns, verbs, or adjectives. You can use a dictionary. Work with a partner and think of other weather words.

2 **9A.1▶** Guess which words normally go together. Match the words in the two columns, then listen, check, and repeat.

1	[e] heavy	a	cold
2	[ ] blowing	b	hot
3	[ ] boiling	c	a gale
4	[ ] freezing	d	rain
5	[ ] pouring	e	~~showers~~
6	[ ] soaking	f	wet

3 Complete the sentences with words from **Weather**.
1 The day will start quite _mild_ and dry, but heavy _____ are expected in the afternoon.
2 We walked home in the _____ rain and got _____ wet.
3 We have an extreme climate, with _____ hot summers and _____ cold winters.
4 As a child, I hated _____ nights because I was afraid of thunder and _____.
5 It was _____ a gale last night but when I woke up, the sun was _____.

4 Describe the weather in different parts of the picture in **Weather**.
Example The sun's shining in the city.

5 What's your favourite weather? Does the weather change your mood? Why? Tell your partner.

B Read and understand reasons

6 Read **Talk about the Weather** opposite. Match summary sentences a–d with reasons 1–4.
a [ ] Most people are interested in the weather, and it can change how we feel.
b [ ] We sometimes talk about the weather just to be sociable, not because we're interested in it.
c [ ] Weather has always been a popular topic.
d [ ] Weather is a good conversation starter because it's a subject we all have in common.

7 Answer the questions with a partner.
According to the writer ...
1 why would sailors and farmers be interested in the weather?
2 why is talking about art not a good conversation starter?
3 why did our great-grandparents have a lot of sayings about the weather?
4 why is the weather important to us?
5 why do we say things like 'Lovely day, isn't it?'

C Listen to conversations about the weather

8 **9A.2▶** Listen to four conversations between Susan and Tom. What is the weather like in each conversation?
Example winter – cold wind; freezing

9 Listen again and tick ✓ the things they do in each conversation. Write the number of the conversation.
a Talk about extreme weather in other places. ✓ *1, 3*
b Say how nice the weather is.
c Complain about the weather.
d Talk about the weather forecast.
e Say what the weather will be like at the weekend.
f Agree with each other.
g Say how typical the weather is for the time of year.

D Grammar tag questions

10 Read Susan's sentence and say if 1–3 are *true* or *false*.
Susan It's a lovely day, isn't it?
1 Susan thinks it's a lovely day.
2 She isn't sure if it's a lovely day.
3 She invites Tom to agree with her.

11 **9A.3▶ Pronunciation** Listen and repeat the sentences from Susan and Tom's conversation. Notice that although *isn't it?* has a question mark, it isn't really a question, so you pronounce it like a statement.

12 Match the sentences with their tag questions.
aren't they? do we? is there? ~~isn't it?~~ don't we?

1 It's amazing, *isn't it?*
2 The days are getting shorter,
3 I guess we need it,
4 There's no wind at all,
5 We don't want floods,

13 Answer the questions with a partner.
1 When is the tag question positive or negative?
2 When do we use *be* or *do*?

14 Add tag questions to these sentences.
1 The nights aren't very long, *are they?*
2 It's a beautiful evening,
3 It isn't very warm,
4 You don't like hot weather,
5 You like cold weather,

More practice? **Grammar Bank** >> p.144.

ABCD Put it all together

15 Work with different partners. Start a conversation about the weather, and continue making small talk for as long as possible. Who did you have the longest conversation with?
Example Hi. It's freezing cold today, isn't it?

I can make small talk.

Tick ✓ the line. with a lot of help with some help on my own very easily

My Body in Five Years

1 I was at a job interview recently and they asked, 'Where will you be five years from now?' I didn't know what to say. Where will I be in five years' time? Perhaps I'll have a new job or maybe I'll be in another country, I've no idea. But one thing I DO know is – my body will have changed. How? Well, let's start from the top. All the hair which I have today will have gone and I'll have a completely new head of hair. It takes about five years from when a new hair starts growing to when it falls out.

2 Five years from now, my eyebrows and eyelashes will have changed between 15 and 20 times. My eyelashes are there to help me blink and keep my eyes clean, and over the next five years I'll blink about 30 million times. What about my nails, which are made from the same stuff as my hair? Well, in five years' time, I will have grown about ten new sets of fingernails – but only five sets of toenails. That's because fingernails grow twice as fast as toenails. Did you know your fastest-growing fingernail is on your ring finger?

3 Then there's the skin, which is the body's largest organ. My skin will have changed too, and during the next five years, I will lose about 10 kilograms of the stuff. The human body grows a new outer layer of skin every month.

4 I'll need to work to maintain my body over the next five years. For example, I'll probably eat about 2,500 kilograms of food, I'll breathe about 40 million times, and my heart will beat about 175 million times. The body never stops working and renewing itself. But it's not all good news. Unfortunately, some parts of my body won't get replaced. Hopefully, I'll still have the same teeth in five years' time, because I definitely won't grow any new ones. And my brain will get lighter by one gram each year as a small part dies, never to be replaced.

5 So next time I'm in a job interview and they ask, 'Where will you be in five years' time?' I'll know what to say!

My future

a Five years from now, I'll be sixty-six, but I'm not going to retire until I have to.

b In five years' time, I'll be 14. Hopefully, I'll have my own room by then.

c I've no idea where I'll be in five years, but I hope I'll have bought my own place to live.

d In five years' time, I'll have found a job. I'd like to be a fashion designer.

How to talk about your future

Orientation

Context

In this lesson, students will practise using the future perfect to exchange ideas about how they imagine themselves at some point in the future.

In the illustrated popular science article *My Body in Five Years* on **>> p.88**, the writer talks about changes in our bodies which happen over five years.

In *My future*, the four speech bubbles contain statements made by the people in photos 1–4.

Language

Focus grammar	future perfect: *My hair will have grown.*, *Things won't have changed much.*
Focus words	attitude adverbs: *definitely, hopefully, probably, unfortunately* parts of the body: *brain, eyebrows, eyelashes, fingernails, nails, ring finger, skin, teeth, toenails* others: *beat, blink, breathe*
Focus phrases	*By this time tomorrow ..., In five years' time, ..., five years from now*
Recognition vocabulary	words: *maintain, medical, organ, outer layer, renew, replace, retire, stuff* phrases: *a new head of hair, from the top, my own place, popular science*
Recycled language	words: *beauty, body, fashion, head, hair, heart, maybe, perhaps* phrases: *science fiction*
Pronunciation	sentence stress: *My **hair** will have **grown**.* 9B.1 word stress: ***defi**nitely, **hope**fully, **pro**bably, unfor**tu**nately*

End product

In *Put it all together*, students work in pairs and use their notes to describe what they think they will be like in five years' time. The activity is based on audio script 9B.2.

Warmer

Choose a time of day and ask students around the class what they were doing yesterday. Refer to the same time for tomorrow and ask for information. Monitor students' use of future tenses but do not overcorrect for accuracy at this stage. Repeat the activity, use the same time but refer to next week or next month. Listen out for opportunities to rephrase what students say to bring in the *future perfect* form. Ask the class to say who they think has the most exciting life.

Write *How to talk about your future* on the board.

A Read for detail

In this section, students read a popular science article for gist and detail.

1 Direct students to the photos on **>> p.88**. Put students into pairs and set a short time limit for them to write a list of the names for parts of the body. Elicit vocabulary around the class. Write any new words on the board and give pronunciation practice as necessary.

2 Read the instructions and items a–d and check vocabulary. Ask students how they are going to read the text. *Quickly or carefully? (Quickly.)* Set a short time limit for students to do the activity. Go through each item in turn and ask if it is an appropriate answer. Encourage students to say why or why not.

> c (chatty, non-technical vocabulary, an everyday topic)

Extra activity

Ask students about the purpose of the text: *Was it written to inform, advise, or entertain? (Entertain.)*

3 Go through the instructions and items 1–3. Check vocabulary and make sure students understand that there is more than one piece of information for each item. Monitor and encourage students to use what they understand and to ignore unknown vocabulary. Ask for volunteers to give answers and check the class agrees. Give pronunciation practice as necessary.

> 1 hair, eyebrows, eyelashes, nails, skin 2 blinks, breathes, heart beats 3 teeth, brain

4 Read the instructions and ask students how they are going to read the first paragraph. *Quickly or carefully? (Carefully.)* Monitor and help with vocabulary. Elicit answers around the class. Write the answers on the board for section B.

> **sure:** body will have changed, will have grown new hair
unsure: perhaps have a new job, maybe be in another country

Extra activity

In pairs, students find five new words in the text and guess the meaning. If they don't know the meaning by the end of the lesson, they should check in a dictionary for homework.

B Grammar future perfect

5 Write the sentence *In five years' time, my body will have changed.* on the board. Underline the verb form and elicit or explain that it's called the *future perfect*. Copy the time line onto the board and go through the exercise together.

Read rules a–c, directing students to the sentence and time line to help them understand the differences.

> Rule: b

6 Ask students to underline more examples of the future perfect in *My Body in Five Years*. Monitor and help as necessary. Elicit examples around the class and complete the rule together.

> **Rule:** *will* (or *won't*) + ***have*** + past participle

7 Read the instructions and copy the phrase *By this time tomorrow* onto the board. Check understanding by asking students what time tomorrow the phrase refers to. Go through the example with the class. Remind students that they can look at *Irregular verbs* on **>> p.148** or check in their dictionaries to find or check past participles. Monitor and help as students continue individually.

Nominate several students to give their answers and encourage them to begin with *By this time tomorrow*. Respond to students' statements using phrases like *Oh really?* or *Me too!*

> 2 I'll have slept for ...   3 I'll have had ... cups of coffee.
> 4 I'll have watched TV for ... hours.

8 9B.1 Go through the instructions and read sentences 1–4. Play the audio for students to underline the stressed words. Do not go over answers at this stage.

9 Play the audio for students to check their answers. Elicit or point out that only the nouns and past participle of the *future perfect* are stressed, we use the short form of will (*'ll*), and *have* is pronounced /həv/. Play the audio again, pausing for students to repeat.

Teaching tip

Direct students to *Pronunciation* **>> p.149** for rules on which kinds of words are stressed or unstressed.

Extra help

Chain drill. Choose a sentence from exercise 7 and nominate a student to make a new sentence. Monitor for pronunciation and give extra practice as necessary.

10 Read the instructions and check students understand the activity. Give students a couple of minutes to think of answers and monitor and help with ideas if necessary. Monitor as students continue in pairs and give positive feedback for pronunciation of *'ll have*.

Extra activity

Repeat exercise 10 as an open pair activity. Nominate two students to compare things they will have done before they go to bed. The class decides who they are most similar to.

C Vocabulary attitude adverbs

11 Go through the instructions and direct students back to *My Body in Five Years* to find the sentences in paragraph 4 which include the adverbs. Point out or elicit that these adverbs add *attitude* (they show how someone feels about something).

Read questions 1–3 and ask students to look at the sentences in the text to answer the questions. Put students into pairs to compare before going over answers as a class. Monitor for pronunciation and give extra practice as necessary.

> **Sentences:** I'll probably ...   Unfortunately, some parts ...
> Hopefully, I'll still ...   because I definitely won't ...
>
> 1 a hopefully   b unfortunately   c definitely   d probably
> 2 unfortunately, hopefully   3 before

12 Ask students to read sentences 1–5 and check vocabulary. Go through the example to demonstrate the activity. Put students into pairs or small groups to share their opinions on the topics. Monitor and join in conversations. Ask for volunteers to share their ideas with the class.

D Listen to people talking about their future

In this section, students listen to short monologues for key words and detail.

13 Direct students to the photos in *My future* on **>> p.88**. Ask students to read speech bubbles a–d and to look at photos 1–4. Check vocabulary as necessary and do the first item as a class to demonstrate (*a–4*). Ask students how they guessed who made the statement.

> b 1   c 3   d 2

14 9B.2 Read the instructions and ask students to look at photos 1–4 in *My future*. Play the audio. Ask students to compare their answers in pairs. Play the audio a second time if necessary. Ask for volunteers to give answers and reasons. See if the class agrees before giving feedback.

> **Speaker 1:** photo 4. She mentions her age, that she doesn't want to retire, and what others of retiring age will be doing.
> **Speaker 2:** photo 2. She talks about her age in five years' time, her studies, and plans for the future.

15 Direct students to the table and the key words. Play the audio while students listen and tick the topics they hear. Students compare answers in pairs. Play the audio a second time if necessary before checking answers as a class.

> **Speaker 1:** family, health, people at work
> **Speaker 2:** home, marriage, studies, transport, work

16 In pairs, students discuss what they can remember about what the speakers said about the topics. Monitor and give positive feedback where possible. Direct students to audio script 9B.2 on **>> p.156** to check.

ABCD Put it all together

17 Go through the instructions and give students time to make notes. Remind them to add attitude adverbs from exercise 11.

18 Put students into pairs to talk about what they imagine they will have done in five years' time. Ask for volunteers to tell the class about any similarities they have.

Student performance

Students should be able to give short personal descriptions.

You can use this checklist to monitor and give feedback or to assess students' performance.

Coherence	Do students use attitude adverbs to show how they feel? exercise 12
Vocabulary	Do students have enough vocabulary to talk about three or more topics? exercise 16
Pronunciation	Do students usually say *'ll have* without stress? exercise 10

I can talk about my future.

Students tick *on my own* if they have talked about three or more topics using their notes. They tick *with some help* if they looked at section B once or twice for help.

Early finishers

Students repeat the activity, talking about three things they think will have happened in the world five years from now.

Additional material

www.oup.com/elt/result for extra practice activities
www.oup.com/elt/teacher/result for extra teacher resources

How to talk about your future

G future perfect   **V** parts of the body; attitude adverbs   **P** stressed and unstressed words

A Read for detail

1 Work with a partner. Look at the photos opposite. How many body parts can you name?

2 Read **My Body in Five Years**. What kind of text is it?
   a medical text   c popular science
   b fashion and beauty   d science fiction

3 Read the text again and find the following things.
   1 five things that grow
   2 three other things the body does automatically
   3 two parts of the body that don't get replaced

4 In the first paragraph, underline two predictions which the writer is sure about and two which the writer isn't sure about. Compare with a partner.

B Grammar future perfect

5 Read the sentence and decide when the change happens – A, B, or C. Then choose the best ending for the rule.
   In five years' time, my body will have changed.

   A Between now   **B** 5 years   **C** More than 5
   and 5 years' time   from now   years in the future

   now

   Rule Use the future perfect to show that something …
   a will start at a certain time in the future.
   b will be finished by a certain time in the future.
   c will happen at a certain time in the future.

6 Underline five examples of the future perfect in the text and compare with a partner. Complete the rule.
   Rule The future perfect = will (or won't) + _____ + past participle

7 Use these words to make true sentences for you.
   By this time tomorrow,
   1 I/have/meals   *I'll have had three meals.*
   2 I/sleep/for/hours
   3 I/have/cups of coffee
   4 I/watch TV/for/hours

8 **9B.1▶ Pronunciation** Listen to these sentences and underline the stressed words.
   1 My hair will have grown.
   2 I'll have cut my nails.
   3 Things won't have changed much.
   4 I'll have passed the exam.

9 Listen again and check. Practise saying the sentences. Which kinds of words are *not* stressed?

10 Tell your partner the following.
   1 Three things you will/won't have done by the time you go to bed tonight.
   2 Three things you think will have happened in the world five years from now.

   More practice? **Grammar Bank** >> p.144.

C Vocabulary attitude adverbs

11 Look in paragraph four of **My Body in Five Years**. Find sentences with these adverbs and answer the questions.
   probably   un**fort**unately   **hope**fully   **def**initely
   1 Which sentences tell you something which the writer …
      a wants to happen?   c is very sure about?
      b isn't happy about?   d is not 100% sure about?
   2 Which adverbs go at the beginning of the sentence?
   3 In negative sentences, do *probably* and *definitely* come before or after *won't*?

12 Add adverbs to the sentences to give your attitude. Compare with a partner.
   One year from now …
   1 I'll be older.   *I'll definitely be older.*
   2 I will have learnt a lot more English.
   3 I will have grown a new set of toenails.
   4 there will be more people in the world.
   5 there will be less ice at the North Pole.

D Listen to people talking about their future

13 Look at the photos in **My future** opposite and match the sentences and the people.

14 **9B.2▶** You will hear two of the people giving more details. Who's talking? How do you know?

15 Listen again and tick ✓ the topics they talk about.

	age	family	health	home	marriage	people at work	studies	transport	work
1	✓								
2	✓								

16 Can you remember what they said? Tell a partner.

ABCD Put it all together

17 Imagine yourself in five years' time. What will you have done by then? Make notes about the topics in exercise 15.

18 Work with a partner. Tell your partner about your future. Find at least three things you have in common.
   Example In five years' time I'll have left home …

I can talk about my future.

Tick ✓ the line.   with a lot of help   with some help   on my own   very easily

Direction of movement

along   backwards   downhill   downwards   forwards
inside   outside   towards you   uphill   upwards

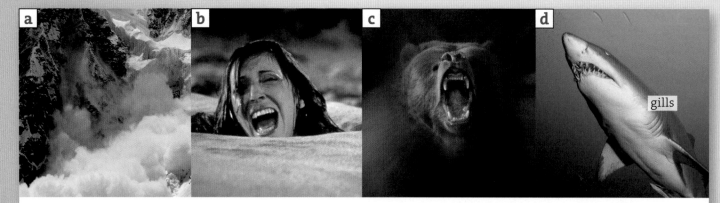

gills

NATURE'S NIGHTMARES
WHAT'S THE *WORST* THING YOU CAN DO …?

1 if a bear comes towards you?
a Make a noise.
b Turn and run.
c Climb a tree.
d Walk slowly backwards.

2 if you're stuck in quicksand?
a Lie down.
b Move a lot.
c Stay calm and wait.
d Hold a tree root.

3 if you're caught in an avalanche?
a Open your mouth.
b Drop your pack.
c Hold on to a tree.
d 'Swim' upwards through the snow.

4 if a current pulls you out to sea?
a Float with it.
b Swim parallel to the beach.
c Swim directly to the beach.
d Swim under the waves.

5 if you see a tornado coming towards you?
a Lie in a bath with a mattress over you.
b Get in a car and drive fast.
c Go into a basement and sit under a table.
d Lie in a ditch.

6 when you're in a lightning storm?
a Sit inside a car.
b Get out of the swimming pool.
c Stand under a single tall tree.
d Go inside.

7 if you're attacked by a shark?
a Play dead.
b Hit it in the eye.
c Take hold of its gills.
d Fight it.

8 if you're near a volcano and it erupts?
a Go inside and close the windows.
b Drive out of the area.
c Lie on the ground near a stream.
d Move uphill away from a stream.

lava

DANGER
STRONG
CURRENT

How to give advice

Orientation

Context

In this lesson, students will practise using *if clauses* to give advice for dangerous situations.

The illustrated quiz, *Nature's Nightmares*, on >> **p.90**, invites a reader to identify the worst things people can do in various dangerous situations.

Diagrams a–j illustrate the meaning of the words in *Direction of movement*.

Language

Focus grammar	1st conditional; *if* clauses: *If you run, the bear will probably run after you.*, *If you're not a good swimmer, you should stay near the beach.*
Focus words	direction of movement: *along, backwards, downhill, downwards, forwards, inside, outside, towards you, uphill, upwards*
Focus phrases	*Don't ..., walk slowly ..., you should ..., you shouldn't*
Recognition vocabulary	*aggressive, avalanche, basement, bear, bell, blocked, current, ditch, encounters, float, flow, gills, lie, mattress, noise, pack, parallel, paraphrase, paws, pipes, quicksand, ranger, root, single, spray, stream, stuck, volcano*
Recycled language	*corridor, door, exhausted, floor, lift, probably, school, should, shouldn't, tornado, workplace, window*

End product

In *Put it all together*, students work in small groups and use their notes to give advice to people who might find themselves in a dangerous situation. Students have practised this activity in exercise 13.

Preparation

Read *Saftey Leaflets A* and *B* on >> **p.131** and >> **p.135** so you can help students with exercise 13 if necessary. Think about classroom organization for the group work activity in exercise 16. Take dictionaries to class.

Warmer

Write the following weather conditions on the board: *It's ... freezing cold, boiling hot, pouring down, blowing a gale.* Put students into pairs to say what advice they would give to a person who was about to go out in these weather conditions. Ask for suggestions around the class and take a vote on the best idea. Monitor for students' use of the first conditional, but do not overcorrect for accuracy at this stage.

Write *How to give advice* on the board.

A Vocabulary direction of movement

1 Direct students to *Direction of movement* on >> **p.90**. Ask them to match pictures a–j with the words in the vocabulary panel. Ask students to compare with a partner before nominating students to give answers. See if the class agrees before giving feedback. Monitor for pronunciation of the final *s* and give extra practice as necessary.

> a forwards   b towards you   c backwards
> d upwards   e downwards   f inside   g outside
> h uphill   i downhill   j along

2 Read the instructions and questions 1–3, checking vocabulary as necessary. Students discuss the questions in pairs. Monitor and join in where you can. Elicit suggestions around the class and encourage students to explain why.

Extra help

In pairs, students take turns to point to a picture a–j, for a partner to say the word or phrase.

B Read and respond

In this section, students use clues to guess the meaning of new vocabulary before reading for detail.

3 Direct students to *Nature's Nightmares* on >> **p.90** and photos a–h. Ask students what they think the title means and help them express their ideas. Read the two questions and ask for opinions around the class. Do not explain new vocabulary at this stage, as students will focus on this in the next activity.

4 Direct students to the quiz questions. Read the first one and ask students to guess the corresponding photo number. Students work individually and compare in pairs. Nominate students to give answers and see if the class agrees.

> 1c   2b   3a   4h   5e   6f   7d   8g

5 Read the instructions and ask students to underline any new words in *Nature's Nightmares*. Ask students to guess the meanings of the words and to compare guesses with a partner.

Direct students to question 1 and options a–d. Ask students to choose four words and to tell each other how they guessed. Monitor and make a note of different strategies. Ask students if they thought their strategy was a good one or if they would choose another.

Encourage students to check the meanings of words they still don't know or are unsure of.

Teaching tip

Exercise 5 presents students with three ways of guessing meaning, which should help increase their confidence when dealing with new language. If students suggested different strategies, make a note of them on the board and suggest they try a different strategy next time they need to guess the meaning of a word.

6 Go through the instructions and put students into pairs to do the quiz. Monitor and help them express their ideas.

Go through each question in turn and elicit suggestions around the class. Encourage other students to add their comments. Do not comment on correctness at this point.

7 9C.1 Ask students to listen and check their answers. Play the audio, pausing after each one as necessary.

> 1 b   2 b   3 a   4 c   5 b   6 c   7 a   8 c

8 Read through the instructions and check vocabulary in sentences 1–5 if necessary. Do not explain the form of the first conditional at this stage as this is the focus of section C. Play the audio and pause after the first item to check students understand. Remind students to listen for key words and continue with the listening. Ask students to compare answers in pairs and play the audio a second time if necessary.

Nominate students to give answers and ask them to read the complete sentence. Monitor for the use of the 1st conditional, but do not correct for accuracy at this stage.

> 2 ... pull you downwards.   3 ... filled with snow.
> 4 ... get exhausted.   5 ... downwards.

C Grammar 1st conditional; *if* clauses

9 Direct students to the grammar box and the headings in the two columns. Copy the sentence onto the board and underline the verbs in both clauses. Put students into pairs to match questions 1–3 with answers a–c. Go over answers as a class.

> 1 present tense / *will* future
> 2 the main clause
> 3 c to warn of a danger

10 Ask students to read sentences 1–4, ignoring the blanks and check vocabulary as necessary. Go through the example to demonstrate the activity. Remind students about the use of *do* to make negatives for most verbs in the present tense. Monitor and make a note of any problems to go over as a class at the end of the exercise. Ask for volunteers to give answers and monitor for accuracy.

> 2 isn't careful; 'll hurt   3 gets; won't be able
> 4 don't hurry up; it'll get

11 Read the instructions and direct students to the grammar box to match the sentence halves. Check answers, pointing out that we can use *not* in either the *if* clause or the main clause. Go through questions 1 and 2 as a class.

> 1 b   2 d   3 c   4 a
> 1 1 present simple, present simple
> 2 present simple, *shouldn't* + infinitive
> 3 present simple, *should* + infinitive
> 4 present simple, imperative
> 2 a give advice

12 Go through the instructions and check any new vocabulary in situations 1–5. Point out that in situation 5, *when* can be used in place of *if*. Give students time to think of at least two ideas for each situation and remind them that they can make positive and negative main clauses. Monitor and help as necessary.

Put students into pairs to exchange advice. Ask students to choose the best piece of advice for each situation. At the end of the activity, ask each student to tell the class the best piece of advice they were given. The class guesses the situation.

Extra help
Students choose three situations from exercise 12 and write the sentences.

D Read and paraphrase

In this section, students read and summarize the main points in an explanation.

13 Put students into A/B pairs to read *Safety Leaflets A* and *B* in *Pairwork*. Read through the questions and check students understand the activity. Ask students how they are going to read to answer the questions *(look for key words)* and direct them to the section heading and elicit or explain the meaning of *paraphrase*. Explain that students will use their notes to give their partner advice in the situation, so they should write key words only.

Encourage students to use their dictionaries only when they can't guess. Monitor and help as necessary.

14 Remind students to use different ways of giving advice, e.g. *don't, you should, you shouldn't*. Give students some rehearsal time before you put them into pairs to do the activity. Monitor and give positive feedback when students use different ways of giving advice. Ask for volunteers to tell the class the situation and the advice they were given. Encourage students to make other suggestions. The class votes on the best piece of advice for each situation.

Extra activity
Put students into pairs or small groups. Students write two other dangerous situations and swap with another pair or group. Students give each other one piece of advice for each situation. They can use dictionaries.

ABCD Put it all together

15 Read the instructions. Ask students to choose one of the activities from the list and make notes to answer the questions in *Safety Leaflet A* on >> p.131. Remind students that they can make positive and negative statements and use different verb forms like those in the grammar box in exercise 11. Give students time to rehearse.

16 Put students into small groups to give each other advice for their dangerous situations.

Student performance
Students should be able to offer advice.

You can use this checklist to monitor and give feedback or to assess students' performance.

Vocabulary	Do students use direction of movement appropriately? exercise 2
Grammar	Do students use *if* clauses correctly? exercise 12 Do students use different forms to give advice? exercise 14

I can give advice.

Students tick *on my own* if they have given advice for dangerous situations using their notes. They tick *with some help* if they have looked at the grammar box in exercise 11 once or twice for help.

Early finishers
Students can repeat the activity, choosing different situations from the list in exercise 15.

Additional material

www.oup.com/elt/result for extra practice activities
www.oup.com/elt/teacher/result for extra teacher resources

How to give advice

G 1st conditional; *if* clauses   v direction of movement

A Vocabulary direction of movement

1 Look at **Direction of movement** opposite. Match the words and pictures.

2 Discuss these questions with a partner.
   1 Which is more tiring – walking uphill or downhill?
   2 Which is more fun – having meals inside or outside?
   3 Which is more difficult – walking backwards or walking along a rope?

B Read and respond

3 Look at the photos in **Nature's Nightmares** opposite. Answer these questions with a partner.
   1 Have you ever been near any of these things?
   2 Which ones do you think are the most frightening?

4 Read quiz questions 1–8 and match them with photos a–h.

5 Underline new words in the quiz and try to guess their meanings. Discuss with a partner.
   1 How did you guess the meaning? Choose one option.
      a From the photo.   c It's similar in my language.
      b From the context.   d other …
   2 Are there any you can't guess or you are not sure about? Check them in a dictionary.

6 Do the **Nature's Nightmares** quiz with a partner. Circle the worst option for each situation and say why.

7 **9C.1▶** Listen and check your answers.

8 Listen again and complete these sentences.
   1 If you run, the bear will probably …   *run after you.*
   2 If you disturb the quicksand a lot, it'll …
   3 If your mouth is open, it'll get …
   4 If you try to swim against the current, you'll probably …
   5 If any lava comes from the volcano, it will flow …

C Grammar 1st conditional; *if* clauses

9 Look at the grammar box and answer the questions with a partner.

1st conditional	
if clause	main clause
If you run,	the bear will probably run after you.

   1 What tenses are used in the *if* clause and main clause?
   2 Which part of the sentence makes a prediction?
   3 What is the sentence being used for?
      a to invite
      b to give advice
      c to warn of a danger

10 Put the verbs in the correct tense in these 1st conditional sentences.
   1 If you _don't take_ (not take) your coat, you _'ll get_ (get) wet.
   2 If he _____ (not be) careful, he _____ (hurt) himself.
   3 If it _____ (get) foggy, I _____ (not be able) to find my way down.
   4 If we _____ (not hurry up), it _____ (get) dark.

11 Match the beginnings and endings of the sentences in the grammar box and answer the questions.

other *if* clauses	
if clause	main clause
1 ☐ If you meet a bear,	a don't stand under a tall tree.
2 ☐ If it's foggy,	b walk slowly backwards.
3 ☐ If you're not a good swimmer,	c you should stay near the beach.
4 ☐ If there's lightning,	d you shouldn't drive fast.

   1 What verb forms are used in the *if* clause and main clause?
   2 What are these sentences being used for?
      a to give advice
      b to predict
      c to ask a question

12 Work with a partner. Give advice for these situations.
   1 If you drive your car into a river, …
      you should open the windows to get out.
   2 … if you can't swim.
   3 If you meet an aggressive dog, …
   4 … if you don't have a good map and some warm clothes.
   5 When it's dark, …

   More practice? **Grammar Bank >>** p.144.

D Read and paraphrase

13 Work in pairs.
   Student A Read **Safety Leaflet A** on **>>** p.131.
   Student B Read **Safety Leaflet B** on **>>** p.135.

14 Use your notes. In your own words, give your partner advice about what to do in your dangerous situation.

ABCD Put it all together

15 Think of a dangerous situation. Look at these examples.
   cycling in the city   driving on the motorway
   skiing   swimming in the sea   walking home at night
   walking in the mountains

16 Work in small groups. Give advice about what to do in your dangerous situation. Was all the advice good?

I can give advice.

HIGH-TECH

For this edition of *High-Tech*, Marion Brent travelled around the country and visited three technology fairs. She describes six of the most interesting devices she saw on display, and reports the reactions of some of the visitors.

Personal Helicopter

This personal helicopter will take off and land vertically, like a normal helicopter, and it will be able to fly for over two hours at around 100 km per hour. It has been available on eBay for several years already.

Inflatable Computer

This computer weighs less than a loaf of bread and it can fit in your pocket, but when you inflate it, it's the size of a normal laptop computer. It's waterproof too, so now you can surf the Internet in the swimming pool.

Memory Recorder

This is the prototype of a device to help you remember names. It continually monitors your conversation. When it hears the words 'Nice to meet you', it permanently saves the previous and next 10 seconds of the conversation. Later on, if you can't remember the names of the people you have spoken to, you can listen to the recording again.

Walking Chair

This is a robot with legs and a seat on top, and it is able to carry people. It can walk along level ground, but it can also go up and down stairs. This prototype has been developed at Waseda University in Japan.

Dream Programmer

This is a device designed to help you to choose your own dreams. Before sleeping, you look at a picture of what you want to dream about and record yourself talking about it. During the night, when you start a period of rapid eye movement (REM) sleep, the machine plays the recording along with music, lights, and smells.

Brain Keyboard

This is a prototype of a cap designed to read electrical signals from your brain and translate them into commands for a computer. With this cap, you will be able to control your computer without moving any part of your body.

GLOSSARY
prototype *n* the first design which other models are copied from
device *n* an object or machine designed for a particular purpose
rapid *adj* very quick

VISITOR COMMENTS

1 This would be fantastic for disabled people in wheelchairs. If they had one of these, they would be able to go to places where they can't go now. They could even go for a walk in the country. I wouldn't mind having one myself, actually – it would be great for walking the dog!

2 I think this would be really interesting. I'd love to know how it feels to look completely different. If you wore it on your face, your friends wouldn't recognize you, so you could hear what they talk about when you aren't there. I would wear it at parties!

3 If you had one of these, you'd have to be careful what you think! For example, what would happen if I was writing an email to Fred and I secretly think that he's an idiot? How would it begin? 'Hi Fred, you idiot'? I think you'd have to practise a lot to use this device, but it would probably be good for disabled people.

4 It would be nice to have one of these, but if we all had one, there would be traffic chaos. There would be people flying in all directions, bumping into each other and crashing into buildings. The traffic on our streets is bad enough already – imagine it in three dimensions!

5 This is like something from a James Bond film. If I had one of these, I'd go somewhere hot so I could see all the tropical fish and the coral. I'd be able to see the sharks and if they attacked, I'd be safe inside it. But where would I keep it? I don't live near the sea, and there isn't enough space in my garage – so it's not a very practical idea!

6 If I had one of these, I'd sleep for entertainment. It would be like going to the cinema, but better. However, there's a problem. I never remember my dreams, so I wouldn't know if the machine was working.

How to talk about unreal situations

Orientation

Context

In this lesson, students will practise using the 2nd conditional to talk about things they would like to have.

The illustrated regular website or magazine feature, *High-Tech*, on >> **p.92** describes various devices on show at three technology fairs. *Visitor Comments* give the reactions some visitors have sent to the website. Two of the reports do not relate to the devices described in the article.

Glossary gives the meaning of some key vocabulary.

Language

Focus grammar	2nd conditional: *if we all had a personal helicopter, there would be traffic chaos.*, *What would happen if we all had a personal helicopter?*
Focus words	compound nouns: *alarm + nouns, adjectives + alarm; book + nouns, nouns + book; computer + nouns, adjectives + computer; phone + nouns, adjectives + phone; service + nouns, adjectives + service; science + nouns, adjectives + science*
Focus phrases	*What would you do?, Which one would you choose?, Where would you go?*
Recognition vocabulary	words: *chaos, coral, device, dimensions, disabled, edition, fair, idiot, reactions, wheelchair* phrases: *bumping into each other*
Recycled language	words: *careful, crashing, entertainment, fantastic, interesting, president, recognize, rich, secretly, shark* grammar: *wh-questions*
Pronunciation	linking in questions: *would you* /wʊdʒju:/ **9D.2**

Language notes

Some grammar references suggest that *were* is used in the 2nd conditional *if* clause. In everyday speech, it is at least equally common to say *was*.

When a main clause comes before an *if* clause in a conditional sentence, it is not necessary to use a comma.

End product

In *Put it all together*, students have a conversations in pairs about what they would do if they had three different things. The conversation is based on audio script **9D.2**.

Preparation

Take dictionaries to class, if necessary.

Warmer

Ask students if anybody has ever been to a technology fair and what happens there. Elicit or explain that they are usually very big exhibitions which people visit to find out about the latest inventions. Put students into groups to discuss whether or not they would go to one of these events and to exchange ideas. Ask for opinions around the class and encourage students who have been to a technology fair to tell the class about their experiences. Help students express their ideas as necessary.

Write *How to talk about unreal situations* on the board.

A Vocabulary compound nouns

1 Read the questions and check vocabulary. Ask students to put the items in order, starting with the most important first. Put students into pairs to compare and explain their order. Monitor and give positive feedback. Invite volunteers to tell the class about the most and least important devices in the list. Encourage students with different opinions to respond.

2 Read the instructions and direct students to the example to demonstrate the activity. Write *phone book* on the board and elicit or explain that these types of words are called *compound nouns*. Ask questions to guide students to understand how compound nouns are formed. Ask *Which word answers the question 'What is it?' (The second word.) Which word answers the question 'What kind of ... is it?' (The first word.)*

Monitor and help as necessary as students continue individually. To go over answers, ask students to call out the answer for each item as a class. Give extra pronunciation practice. (Note: *cell phone* is American English.)

> phone box, phone call, car phone, phone card, cell phone, mobile phone, phone number, public phone

3 Read the instructions and check students understand the first words in items 1–5. Monitor and help students find the compounds in their dictionaries as necessary.

> 1 **computer** + technology, programmer, keyboard, graphics   laptop, desktop, personal + **computer**
> 2 **alarm** + clock, bell   fire, burglar, smoke + **alarm**
> 3 **science** + fiction, teacher, faculty   computer, medical + **science**
> 4 **service** + charge, station   room, health + **service**
> 5 **book** + shop, fair, club   address, exercise, text, phrase + **book**

Teaching tip

This section teaches students how compound nouns are formed. It's useful for students to be aware of this as it demonstrates that they need to look across word boundaries to identify meaning. This is also a useful reading strategy. Tell students that it will help them become better readers.

B Read for general meaning

In this section, students use pictures, sub-headings, and key words to identify general meaning, before reading for detail.

4 Direct students to the pictures which accompany the article *High-Tech* on >> **p. 92** and elicit or explain what the title means. *(The latest in technology.)* Ask them to read the first paragraph and check vocabulary as necessary. Ask students where they might find this information. *(On a website or in a magazine.)*

Go through the instructions and check students understand *joke*. Ask them how they can find the answer. *(By looking at the titles, pictures, and focusing on key words in the text.)* Point out the glossary and advise students to use the pictures and to guess or ignore other new vocabulary. Set a time limit of about three or four minutes to encourage them to scan the texts to find the answer *(inflatable computer).*

Extra activity

In pairs, students choose five new key vocabulary items and use different strategies from lesson 9C to guess the meaning. They check in their dictionaries.

5 Go through the instructions and direct students to *Visitor Comments* on >> **p.92**. Tell students that two of the texts are not connected with devices on display at this particular fair. Ask students how they will match the comments and the devices. *(By looking for similar key words and phrases in both.)* Monitor and help as students continue individually.

Check answers as a class and encourage students to explain.

> 1 Walking Chair   3 Brain Keyboard
> 4 Personal Helicopter   6 Dream Programmer
> The two devices not on display at the fair:
> 2 a kind of mask   5 a type of mini submarine

6 Put students into pairs to tell a partner which device they would like to have and why. Monitor and respond to students' ideas. Ask for volunteers to tell the class.

Teaching tip
At the end of the activity give positive feedback and build students' confidence at having understood the most important points in a difficult text.

C Grammar 2nd conditional

7 Go through the activity as a class. Read the instructions and direct students to the grammar boxes and example sentences. Copy the sentence in the first box onto the board and check vocabulary. Ask students to read options a–c and to choose the best one to describe what the sentences mean (c). Ask questions to check students understand. *Have we all got personal helicopters now? (No.) Will we all have personal helicopters in the future? (No.)*

Direct students to the second box and point out how the order of the clauses changes in the question form.

8 Ask the class about the *if* and main clauses in 2nd conditional sentences. Elicit or explain that when the verb in the *if* clause is in the past simple, the verb in the main clause is *would* + infinitive. Highlight the comma after the *if* clause.

9 Direct students back to *Visitor Comments* to find seven more examples. Monitor and help as students continue individually. Check answers.

> 1 If they had one of these, they would be able to …
> 2 If you wore it on your face, your friends wouldn't …
> 3 If you had one of these, you'd have to be …
> 4 … what would happen if I was …?
> 5 … if we all had one, there would be …
> 6 If I had one of these, I'd go …
> 7 If I had one of these, I'd sleep …

Extra help
Chain drill. Using one of the pictures, ask *If you had one of these, what would you do?* and name a student to answer. Encourage students to reply in full sentences. That student then asks about another picture and nominates a different student to reply.

10 Ask students to read sentences 1–4 and check vocabulary. Go through the example as a class and remind students to look at the grammar boxes in exercise 7 if necessary. Monitor and help while students continue individually.

To check answers, ask for volunteers to read the whole sentence and see if the class agrees before confirming answers.

> 2 would be, didn't have   3 would you do, attacked
> 4 could have, would you choose

11 Ask students to read sentences 1–4. Elicit one or two other examples for the first item before putting them into pairs to exchange ideas. Monitor and comment on interesting ideas. Nominate students to share their ideas with the class.

D Pronunciation linking in questions

12 9D.1 Go through the instructions and check students understand. Play the audio and ask students to compare their idea with a partner. Play the audio a second time if necessary. Check answers and point out that using fillers like *I don't know* and *ehm* is a good strategy to keep your turn in a conversation.

> Nicola sounds more sure. She hesitates less and doesn't use fillers like *Oh I don't know*, and *ehm* to give her time to think.

13 9D.2 Read through the instructions and point out how *would you* is linked with /dʒ/ and sounds like one word. Play the audio and pause after each item for students to repeat. Tap out the stress on a table to help students maintain rhythm and link the words. Give extra practice as necessary.

14 Read the instructions and ask students to say the verse together at normal speed. Ask them to say it a couple of times, encouraging them to say it faster each time.

Extra help
Students practise the conversation with audio script 9D.1 on >> p.156.

Extra activities
Students say the rhyme in exercise 14 with *did* instead of *would*, e.g. *Where did you go?* etc.
Students ask and answer in pairs about the topics in exercise 11.

ABCD Put it all together

15 Go through the instructions and check vocabulary as necessary. Ask students to think about their answers to the questions in exercise 14. Students could work in pairs.

16 Remind students to use *I don't know.* and *ehm* to keep their turn. In pairs, students ask and answer about the things they would like to have. They repeat the activity with another partner. At the end, ask students if they spoke to anybody who chose the same thing and if their ideas were similar.

Student performance
Students should be able to ask and answer about hypothetical situations.

You can use this checklist to monitor and give feedback or to assess students' performance.

Content	Do students use a variety of questions? exercises 13, 14
Fluency	Do students use fillers like *I don't know* and *ehm* to keep their turn? exercise 12
Pronunciation	Do students usually run *would* and *you* together? exercise 14

I can talk about unreal situations.

Students tick *on my own* if they have asked and answered without a lot of hesitation. They tick *with some help* if they have looked at the grammar box in exercise 7 once or twice.

Early finishers
Students repeat the activity using items in exercise 3.

Additional material

www.oup.com/elt/result for extra practice activities
www.oup.com/elt/teacher/result for extra teacher resources

How to talk about unreal situations

G 2nd conditional   **V** compound nouns   **P** linking in questions

A Vocabulary compound nouns

1 Which of the following things do you have? How important are they to you? Tell a partner.

an alarm clock   a DVD player   an Internet connection
a mobile phone   an MP3 player

2 Make compound nouns by putting the words below before or after *phone*.

book box call car card cell mobile number public

Example   phone book

3 Work with a partner. Make compound nouns using the words in **bold**. Check in your dictionary.

Example   laptop computer, computer technology …

1 **computer**   laptop, technology, programmer, desktop, keyboard, personal, graphics
2 **alarm**   fire, clock, burglar, smoke, bell
3 **science**   fiction, computer, teacher, faculty, medical
4 **service**   room, charge, station, health
5 **book**   shop, address, exercise, fair, text, phrase, club

B Read for general meaning

4 Read **High-Tech** opposite. Which device is a joke?

5 Read **Visitor Comments** opposite and match four of them with the objects in **High-Tech**. Can you guess what the other two devices in **Visitor Comments** are?

6 Which device would you like to have? Tell a partner.

C Grammar 2nd conditional

7 Read the 2nd conditional sentences in the grammar boxes. Then choose the best option to describe their meaning.

if clause	main clause
If we all had a personal helicopter,	there would be traffic chaos.

main clause	*if* clause
What would happen	if we all had a personal helicopter?

a They are about situations which will happen in the future.
b They are about situations which are true now.
c They are about situations which are not true now and probably won't be true in the future.

8 What tenses are used in the *if* clause and main clause of 2nd conditional sentences?

9 <u>Underline</u> seven more examples of 2nd conditionals in **Visitor Comments**.

10 Put the verbs in the correct tense.
1 If I _didn't have_ (not have) a TV, I _would be_ (be) very bored in the evenings.
2 Public transport _____ (be) much better if people _____ (not have) cars.
3 What _____ you _____ (do) if a shark _____ (attack) you?
4 If you _____ (can have) one of the devices, which one _____ you _____ (choose)?

11 Complete the sentences with true information and tell a partner.
1 If I had more free time,   *I'd learn the piano.*
2 If I was rich,
3 If I was the president,
4 If I could live anywhere in the world,

More practice? **Grammar Bank** >> p.144.

D Pronunciation linking in questions

12 **9D.1▶** Listen to Kurt and Nicola talking about the devices in **High-Tech**. Who sounds more sure about what they say? Compare with a partner and say why.

13 **9D.2▶** Listen and repeat these questions. Notice how *would you* is linked with a /dʒ/ sound.

would‿you = /wʊdʒjuː/
Which one would‿you **choose**?
What would‿you **do** with it?
Where would‿you **go**?
What would‿you **do** if you had **that**?

14 Say this rhyme a few times. Start slow, then go faster and faster. Remember to link *would* and *you*.

Where would you go?
Who would you meet?
What would you do?
What would you eat?

ABCD Put it all together

15 Think of three things which you would like to have. Choose from this list or think of something else.

a famous work of art   a good quality camera
a massive diamond   a private jet   an unusual pet
a very powerful computer   a year-long holiday

16 Ask your partner questions about the things he or she would like to have. Then change partners and ask again. Has anybody chosen the same things as you?

I can talk about unreal situations.

Tick ✓ the line.   with a lot of help   with some help   on my own   very easily

Writing An opinion

A Read opinions on an Internet page

1 How much do you use the Internet? Tell a partner.

2 Read these opinions from an Internet page. Do you agree with any of the points of view?

If you want to stop global warming, ban private cars!	
green_star	🗐 June 1st
	If you want to stop global warming, ban private cars! Obviously, private cars are convenient, but they also destroy the planet. Only the owners of cars enjoy the benefits, but everybody has to suffer the consequences, including people without cars. In global terms, that's a lot of people. Clearly, this is unfair.
Add a comment	
mickey says:	🗐 June 3rd 9.30 p.m.
	That's just crazy – how would I get from A to B if I didn't have my car? Unfortunately, public transport is not an option for me because I live outside the city. There are no buses where I live. What should I do – buy a horse?
green_star says:	🗐 June 3rd 9.55 p.m.
	If we banned private cars, public transport would get better. There would be more trains and buses because more people would want them. Also, buses would be faster because there would be less traffic. But also I think the government would have to pay for public transport in rural areas.
easy_rider says:	🗐 June 4th 3.05 a.m.
	Global warming? I love my big car, and I'm looking forward to surfing in Greenland!
peggy_sue says:	🗐 June 4th 7.15 a.m.
	I agree with green star that cars are a problem, but I don't think we should ban them. Unfortunately, the solution is not so simple. What about people who need to move around a lot for work, or people who need to transport heavy equipment? What about disabled people? What do you do if you need to travel in the middle of the night, when there are no buses? I think we should find other solutions such as tax benefits for cleaner cars.

3 Discuss these questions with a partner.
   1 Why do you think people often use false names on the Internet?
   2 Which comment is probably not serious? Why? Why do you think the writer sent it?

B Organize information in a paragraph

4 Read this description of how to write an opinion paragraph. Find examples on the Internet page.
   1 Start with a topic sentence which gives a brief summary of your point of view.
      Example If you want to stop global warming, ban private cars!

   2 Add two or three more sentences to do one or more of these things:
      a support your point of view
      b give examples
      c ask questions to the writer who you are addressing

5 Write a comment to add to the Internet discussion in exercise 2. Use the structure in exercise 4.

6 Read your partner's comment. Is the point of view clear?

C Use adverbs of attitude

7 <u>Underline</u> examples of *clearly*, *obviously*, and *unfortunately* on the Internet page. What do these adverbs mean? Choose the best answer for each one.
   a it is not difficult to see or understand
   b this is a fact which I'm not very happy about

8 Add attitude to this passage using the adverbs in exercise 7.

> Plane fares are much cheaper these days. This is good for travellers. But it's bad for the environment. We can't continue enjoying so many holidays abroad. We must fly less and use cleaner forms of transport such as the train.

ABC Put it all together

9 Work in small groups. Choose a different issue related to science and nature and write, briefly, what you think we should do about it. Start with a topic sentence and use adverbs of attitude. Here are some ideas.
   A healthy life is a boring life.
   There are some things which science can't explain.
   It's too late to stop global warming.
   Technology controls us.
   Nature is our enemy.

10 Give your page to another student. Read the problem and opinion and add your comment. Use a new name.

11 Continue passing around the pages. Add a comment to each problem, until everyone in the group has written one comment for each topic.

12 Find your comments and check your writing. Take turns to read out the discussions to the group. Which points of view are the clearest?

I can write about my opinion. ▬▬▬▬▬▬▬
Tick ✓ the line. with a lot of help with some help on my own very easily

Orientation

Context and Language

In this lesson, students follow a paragraph structure to express their opinion.

Recycled language	words: *buses, disabled, enemy, fares, government, nature, plane, surfing, technology, traffic, trains, transport, travel* grammar: *1st and 2nd conditionals* discourse: *also, and, as, because, but, such*
Recognition language	words: *banned, benefits, boring, consequences, convenient, destroy, equipment, healthy, planet, probably, rural, simple, solution, suffer, tax* phrases: *global warming*
Discourse	signalling opinion: *clearly, obviously, option, unfortunately*

End product

In *Put it all together*, students add comments to those of other students. They follow a paragraph structure they have practised in exercise 5. The group comments on the clarity of their opinions.

Warmer

Write *Technology is making the world a better place*. Give students two minutes to decide if they agree or not with the topic and to make a note of two reasons why. Ask for volunteers to say if they agree or not and to give reasons.

Write *How to write about my opinion* on the board.

A Read opinions on an Internet page

In this section, students read short opinion paragraphs for gist.

1 Put students into pairs to talk about how much they use the Internet. Bring the class together and nominate students to tell the class how much they use it and what they use it for.

2 Direct students to the title and check vocabulary. Tell students that the texts are part of a discussion on the Internet.

Set a short time limit of about two minutes for students to decide if they agree with any of the points of view. Tell students to guess the meaning of any new vocabulary.

Go through each of the comments in turn. Ask for a volunteer to summarize what each point says and see whose opinion is the most popular.

3 Read questions 1 and 2 and check vocabulary as necessary. Put students into pairs to discuss the questions and monitor and help them express their ideas. Bring the class together and ask volunteers to suggest answers.

> **Suggested answers**
> 1 People use false names to protect their identity, maybe from friends, family and people at work.
> 2 easy rider's comment probably isn't serious. He/She makes an extreme statement and gives an example of an extreme situation to show he/she doesn't think the topic is important or to make the discussion group angry.

B Organize information in a paragraph

In this section, students analyse opinion paragraphs, identifying a topic sentence and the functions of following sentences.

4 Read the descriptions and check students understand each of the points. Students choose an opinion text and find examples of the points. Monitor and help as necessary as students continue individually. Check answers.

> green star June 1st : a, b   mickey June 3rd : c, b   green star June 3rd: a, b   peggy sue June 4th: a, c

5 Ask students to write a comment for the discussion list.

6 Put students into pairs to read each other's comment and decide if they followed the structure in exercise 4. Volunteers can read their paragraph to the class. Who has similar ideas?

C Use adverbs of attitude

7 Read the instructions with the class. Monitor and help as students continue individually. Elicit answers and ask students about any similarities between the adverbs. *(They start a sentence and are followed by a comma.)*

> clearly a   obviously a   unfortunately b

8 Tell students to read the paragraph and say if the writer thinks travelling by plane is good or bad. Students rewrite the paragraph using adverbs of attitude. Point out that there is more than one way of writing the paragraph and monitor and help as necessary. In pairs, students compare paragraphs. Ask for volunteers to read different versions to the class.

ABC Put it all together

9 Put students into groups, read the instructions and check they understand the different topics. Each student chooses a different topic writes their opinion on it.

10 Students give their page to another student in the group and add their comment. Remind them to choose a different name.

11 Monitor and check students pass their pages around.

12 Read the instructions and ask students to review their own writing. Ask them to read the discussion to the group and to decide which points of view are the clearest. Bring the class together and ask for a volunteer from each group to read one of the discussions to the class.

Student performance

Students should be able to write an opinion paragraph, starting with a topic sentence.

You can use this checklist to monitor and give feedback or to assess students' performance.

Content	Have students supported their point of view and given examples?
Organization	Have students used a topic sentence?
Cohesion	Have students used adverbs of attitude appropriately?

I can write about my opinion.

Students *tick on my own* if they written one or two paragraphs without looking at exercise 4 again. They can tick *with some help* if they have looked at exercise 4 once or twice.

Early finishers

Students choose another topic from the list in exercise 9 and write an opinion paragraph. They read their opinions to the group, who decides which one they would reply to.

Additional material

www.oup.com/elt/result for extra practice activities
www.oup.com/elt/teacher/result for extra teacher resources

Warmer

Remember the situation

Write lessons A–D *How to* titles on the board: *A ... make small talk, B ... talk about your future, C ...give advice, D talk about unreal situations.* Say sentences 1–10 below for students to say the lesson letter.

1 By this time tomorrow, I'll have had four cups of coffee.
2 If you had more free time, what would you do with it?
3 If there's lightning, don't stand under a tree.
4 It's a lovely day, isn't it?
5 What would you do if a shark attacked you?
6 If it's foggy, you shouldn't drive fast.
7 If you see a tornado, you shouldn't try to escape in your car.
8 The days are getting shorter, aren't they?
9 If we all had a personal helicopter, there would be traffic chaos.
10 By this time next year, there'll be less ice at the North Pole.

> 1 B   2 D   3 C   4 A   5 C   6 C   7 C   8 A   9 D   10 B

A Grammar

1   Tag questions   9A exercises 12, 13, 14

Warm-up: Write these words on the board for students to make a sentence which includes a question tag: *no, is, wind, there's, all, at, there.* Direct students to **>> p.87**, exercise 12 to check their answer.

Set-up: Go through the example and remind students to think about *not* in the tag.

> 2 aren't you?   3 is it?   4 are you?   5 don't you?   6 do you?

Follow-up: Students write five sentences for a partner to finish with a tag question. They check answers together.

2   Future perfect   9B exercise 5

Warm-up: Write *By this time next week* on the board, and ask each student to say one true sentence about themselves. Direct students to **>> p.89**, section B to revise if necessary.

Set-up: Go through the example and remind students to use the past participle of the verbs.

> 2 won't have finished
> 3 'll have gone
> 4 'll have left; 'll have found
> 5 'll have used; 'll have found
> 6 'll have missed

Follow-up: Students write four sentences for the people in *My future* on **>> p.88**. They swap with another student, who guesses who said the sentence.

3   1st and 2nd conditional; if clauses   9C exercise 9

Warm-up: Ask around the class for students to give you advice about what to do when you miss the last bus home. Direct students to **>> p.91** and **>> p.93** section C to revise if necessary.

Set-up: Do the example with the class. Remind students to think carefully about the verb tense in the *if* clause and main clause.

> 2 meet   3 'd stop   4 see   5 lost   6 'd learn   7 'll miss
> 8 don't forget   9 wasn't /weren't

Follow-up: Students write four jumbled conditional sentences for a partner to write out in full. Students check each other's answers.

B Vocabulary

4   Weather   9A exercise 2

Warm-up: Set a short time limit for students to write words connected with vocabulary. Direct students to *Weather* on **>> p. 86** to check.

Set-up: Ask students to read the clues and check vocabulary.

> **Across** 4 boiling   5 showers   6 snowing   8 dry   9 freezing
> **Down** 1 clouds   2 blowing   3 lightning   5 stormy   7 gale

Follow-up: In pairs, students write five sentences with one gap for another pair to complete. They use the words in exercise 2 on **>> p.87**.

5   Attitude adverbs   9B exercise 11

Warm-up: Say the following sentence *By the time I go to bed, I probably won't have finished reading my book.* Ask students how you feel about it. *You want it to happen, you're very sure it will happen, you're unhappy about it, you're not 100% sure about it?* (You're not 100% sure about it.)

Set-up: Direct students to the example and remind them to think about the position of the adverbs in the sentences.

> 2 It will probably rain on Saturday.
> 3 Unfortunately, I left my umbrella on the bus.
> 4 It definitely won't be dark at five o'clock.
> 5 Hopefully, the train won't be late.

Follow-up: Students write sentences like those in exercise 7 on **>> p.89** and swap with a partner. Each student guesses how their partner feels about the facts and writes full sentences using attitude adverbs. Students read their sentences to each other and say whether they agree with the 'attitude'.

6   Direction of movement   9C exercise 1

Warm-up: Write these letters on the board and set a short time for students to write words for *direction of movement: a b c d f g h i k l n o p r s t u w.* They can use the letters more than once. Direct students to *Direction of movement* on **>> p.90** to check answers.

Set-up: Ask students to look at the pictures. Ask what they can see.

> 2 downwards   3 downhill   4 uphill   5 along   6 backwards
> 7 forwards   8 towards you

Follow-up: In pairs, students write gap-fill sentences to describe five of the pictures. They swap with another pair and complete the sentences from memory with books closed.

7   Compound nouns   9D exercises 1, 2

Warm-up: Choose two first parts of compound nouns from exercise 3 on **>> p.93** and elicit examples of compound nouns around the class.

Set-up: Check students understand that they use a word from each line. They use each word once.

> 2 credit card   3 DVD player   4 mobile phone   5 room service
> 6 computer programmer   7 text book

Follow-up: Students write a similar exercise for a partner.

Early finishers

Students review the unit and make list of the different strategies they can use to guess the meaning of words they don't know. They put the strategies in order, starting with the one they use the most.

Unit 9 Review

A Grammar

1 Tag questions Write the tag questions at the end of the sentences.

are you? aren't you? do you? don't you? is it? ~~isn't it?~~

1 Your name's Laslo, _isn't it?_
2 You're Italian, _____
3 Your name isn't Italian, _____
4 You're not from Venice, _____
5 You work in a car factory, _____
6 You don't work on Saturdays, _____

2 Future perfect Put the verbs in the future perfect.

1 Hi Gina! Listen, we're having dinner right now. Can you call back in half an hour? We _'ll have finished_ by then.   finish
2 The house isn't really ours yet. We borrowed all the money from the bank. I _____ paying until I'm 65!   not finish
3 I guess by the time I'm 50 I _____ bald, like my dad.   go
4 I'm still a student, but in five years' time I _____ university and hopefully I _____ a good job.   leave/find
5 A few years from now we _____ all the oil reserves. Hopefully, by then the scientists _____ a new, clean source of energy.   use/find
6 There's no point going to the cinema now. We _____ the start of the film.   miss

3 1st and 2nd conditional; *if* **clauses** Put the verbs in the correct form.

1 If we don't hurry, we _'ll be_ late.   be
2 If you _____ a bear, you shouldn't run away.   meet
3 If I won a lot of money, I _____ working.   stop
4 If you _____ Jeremy, tell him to call me.   see
5 What would you do if you _____ your passport?   lose
6 If I had more free time, I _____ to play an instrument.   learn
7 If the plane is delayed, we _____ our connection.   miss
8 If you go to the beach, _____ to use some sun cream.   not forget
9 I would go to the shops with you if I _____ so busy.   not be

B Vocabulary

4 Weather Do the crossword.

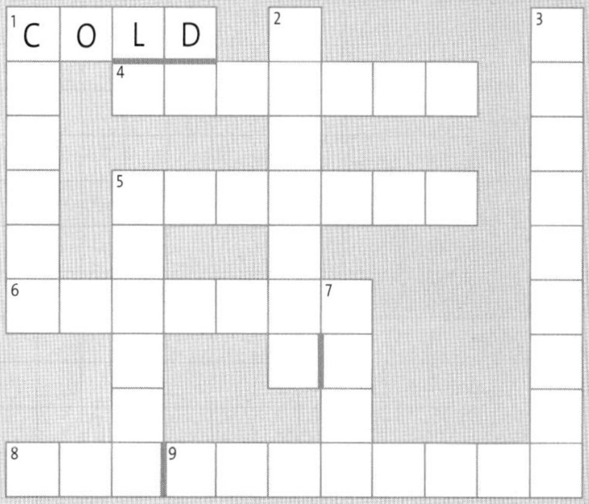

¹C	O	L	D		²				³	
		⁴								

(crossword grid)
- 1 C O L D
- 4
- 5
- 6   7
- 8   9

Across
1 Opposite of *hot*.
4 Very hot. _____ hot.
5 Short periods of rain.
6 Winter weather: it's _____.
8 Opposite of *wet*.
9 Very cold. _____ cold.

Down
1 White things in the sky.
2 The wind is _____.
3 Thunder and _____.
5 Weather with 3 down.
7 Very strong wind.

5 Attitude adverbs Order the words to make sentences.

1 be good Hopefully the tomorrow weather will
Hopefully, the weather will be good tomorrow.
2 It on probably rain Saturday will
3 bus I my left on the umbrella Unfortunately
4 be at dark definitely It five o'clock won't
5 won't the Hopefully late train be

6 Direction of movement Match the words and pictures.

along backwards downhill downwards
forwards towards you uphill ~~upwards~~

1 _upwards_   3 _____   5 _____   7 _____

2 _____   4 _____   6 _____   8 _____

7 Compound nouns Make compound nouns by matching one word from each line.

~~alarm~~ credit DVD mobile room computer text
book card ~~clock~~ programmer phone player service

1 _alarm_ _clock_   5 _____
2 _____   6 _____
3 _____   7 _____
4 _____

Death of the High Street

The butcher on the high street
Listens with alarm
They say that Farmer Jones
Is going to sell the farm
05 The greengrocer was driving past
And saw the land for sale
The cashier in the bank thinks
They're going to build a jail

The chemist tells the optician
10 The optician tells the nurse
The people on the high street
Say there's nothing worse
The newsagent saw an engineer
Walking on the land
15 The grocer on the corner
Saw a lorry full of sand

The baker saw a bulldozer
Driving through the town
'Did you hear about the farm house?
20 They've knocked the old place down!
They're building roads and walls
A big new shopping mall
We're going to lose our customers
The mall will take them all!'

25 **The mall kills the high street**

Have your say!

More and more big shopping malls are being built outside Britain's towns and cities, and traditional town-centre shopping streets are losing business. The old high-street shops are closing as shoppers abandon town centres and go to the malls instead. Is this a bad thing or is it modernization and progress? **What do you think? Opinions please!**

Amrita 25

I think big shopping centres are much more convenient than high-street shops. You can get everything in one place, so it's much quicker. I've got a full-time job, so I don't have time to go around lots of little shops. It's much easier to park the car, and it's all indoors so you don't have to walk around in the rain. Shopping centres have more up-to-date stuff and more to choose from, and I think they're cheaper, too. So yes, for me, shopping centres are definitely progress.

Jerry 31

In my opinion, high-street shops are much better than big shopping malls. The shopkeepers are friendlier and they give you better service. You can get fresh produce in small shops – local fruit and vegetables, and it's different from season to season. It's not all imported stuff from all around the world. Also, shopping malls are usually a long way outside town – that's no good for people who don't have cars, like me. I think local shops are the heart of our communities and if the shops close, our town centres will die.

How to exchange opinions

Orientation

Context

In this lesson, students practise using phrases to introduce their opinion in a discussion.

Death of the High Street on **>> p.96** is a verse which describes what local shopkeepers think when they hear rumours that nearby land is being sold and developed. The illustrations show the different shopkeepers on the high street. *Glossary* explains some key words.

Have your say! is a discussion forum. The pictures show how things might change and readers are invited to share their opinions on the topic. Two opposing opinions are printed.

Culture note

Expressing disagreement might cause offence and so English speakers use a fall-rise intonation pattern to sound more polite. If this isn't used, a person might sound rude or aggressive. (See *Pronunciation* below.)

Language

Focus grammar	articles: *the, a, an*
Preview grammar	quantifiers: *little, lots of, some*
Focus words	*baker, butcher, cashier, chemist, engineer, greengrocer, grocer, news-stand, optician*
Focus phrases	agreeing and disagreeing: *I think ..., In my opinion ..., Yes. maybe, but ...*
Recognition vocabulary	*alarm, abandon, bulldozer, checkout, convenient, jail, modernization, produce (n), progress, sand, shopping mall, truth*
Recycled language	words: *definitely, department store, fruit, library, lorry, market, milk, newsagent's, supermarket, vegetables, vehicle* grammar: *comparatives*
Pronunciation	agreeing and disagreeing intonation 10A.2
Discourse	pronouns, determiners, and ellipsis: *The people on the high street say there's nothing worse.*

Language notes

In Britain, High Street is a street where most of the shops are concentrated in a town. It may not have that name officially. In the USA, the equivalent is Main Street.

In American English, *store* is used instead of *shop*.

End product

In *Put it all together*, students choose a topic and have a group discussion. They can use their notes.

Preparation

Think about classroom organization for the final group work activity in *Put it all together*, exercise 15. Take dictionaries to class.

Warmer

Write the following topic on the board *Shopping: a necessary evil?* Nominate a couple of students to answer these questions: *Do you enjoy shopping? Why? Why not? Can you avoid shopping? How can you make it easy?* Put students into small groups to exchange their opinions. Bring the class together and ask for one spokesperson from each group to report their discussion to the class.

Write *How to exchange opinions* on the board.

A Read and infer

In this section, students read a verse and work out information which is not directly stated.

1 Read the questions and check vocabulary. Put students into pairs to discuss. Monitor and join in with students' conversations. Bring the class together and ask for volunteers to share their opinions with the class. Encourage students to respond to each other's opinions.

2 10A.1 Read the instructions and ask students what they think the title *Death of the High Street* means. Do not confirm students' suggestions at this point. Remind them that they will consider the topic from the point of view of shopkeepers.

Direct students to the verse on **>> p.96**. Play the audio. Elicit suggestions, encouraging students to explain their opinions.

> The shopkeepers fear it because they expect to lose all their customers.

3 Ask students to read questions 1–8 and check vocabulary. Direct students to the section title and remind them that they will need to think about information that is not clearly stated in the text. Do the first two questions as a class, pointing out the line numbers to help students find the information quickly. Monitor and help as students continue in pairs. Ask for volunteers to give answers and see if the class agrees before confirming. Encourage students to give reasons.

> 1 Shopkeepers on the High Street.　2 The farm.
> 3 They're going to build a jail.　4 Building a jail.
> 5 Farmer Jones' land.　6 To show these are the words actually spoken (direct speech is used to make the text more dramatic).
> 7 No.　8 Because shopkeepers lose their customers.

B Vocabulary shops

4 Go through the instructions and items a–c, eliciting another example for each category. Put students into pairs to continue. Monitor and help. Draw three columns on the board and copy the examples into each. Ask for suggestions and add them to the appropriate column. Elicit other words and phrases for each column and check vocabulary as you go along.

> a bread shop, clothes shop, etc.
> b grocer's, chemist's, optician's, newsagent's, baker's
> c bank

5 Read the instructions and go through the example. Ask students to read items 2–5 and check vocabulary. Nominate students to give answers and see if the class agrees.

> 2 **supermarket** You pay for things at different places in a market.　3 **news-stand** A newsagent's is a shop but a newsstand is in the street.　4 **library** A bookshop sells books.
> 5 **shopping mall** A department store is one big shop owned by one company.

Extra activity

Students write the heading *shops* and draw a table with three columns. They use headings a–c in exercise 4 and record examples in each column. Ask for suggestions of other information that could be added to the table, e.g. translation, marking pronunciation. Ask students to choose a focus for a fourth column and complete this for homework.

C Grammar articles *the*, *a*, *an*

6 Direct students to conversations a and b and ask if the speakers know each other. *(a Yes. b No.)* Ask for two volunteers to read the conversations. Go through questions 1 and 2 as a class. Elicit or explain that deciding which article to use (*the* or *a/an*) often depends on context rather than a grammatical rule.

Direct students to look at conversation b again, and ask why speaker B says *on the corner*. Elicit or explain that there might only be one corner near where the speakers are. Alternatively, speaker B might be pointing as he/she says *over there*. In this case, both speakers know which corner they are talking about.

> 1 a 2 In conversation a, the reference is specific, to one only. In conversation b, the first speaker asks about no particular shop.

Extra help

In pairs, students ask and answer about places in their local environment. They role play being friends and a visitor asking for information about local places.

7 Ask students to read the summary of *Death of the High Street* and check vocabulary. Do the example and one or two items together before putting students into pairs to complete the activity. To check answers, read the text aloud and pause at a blank for the class to say the missing word. Refer to questions 1 and 2 in exercise 6 again if necessary.

> 2 the 3 the 4 the 5 an 6 a 7 a 8 The 9 the 10 a 11 a

Extra help

Ask students to underline the articles in *Death of the High Street*. Check understanding.

Extra activity

Play audio script 10A.1 again for students to read along.

D Listen to people exchanging opinions

In this section, students listen to a conversation for key words and phrases for agreeing and disagreeing.

8 Direct students to *Have your say!* on >> **p.96**. Ask students to read the first paragraph and check vocabulary. Ask where they would find this text. *(On a website or in a magazine.)*

Read the instructions and ask students how they are going to read the texts. *Quickly or very carefully? (Quickly, and ignoring new vocabulary.)* Set a short time limit of about three minutes to encourage students to read for gist. Put students into pairs to exchange opinions. Monitor and join in with the discussions. Ask for volunteers to say who they agree with and why and encourage others to respond.

9 Read the instructions and go through the example to check students understand the activity. Monitor and help as students continue individually. Elicit examples of key points and check vocabulary as necessary.

> **Amrita:** shopping centres: get everything in one place, quicker, easier to park the car, more up-date-stuff, more to choose from, cheaper
> **Jerry:** high-street shops: better, shopkeepers friendlier, better service, fresh produce, different from season to season, not imported, near, keep town centres alive

10 10A.2 Read the instructions and play the audio. Play the audio a second time if necessary. Elicit answers around the class, helping students to get their ideas across.

> shopping centres are a long way out of town, it's easy to park the car, it doesn't help people without a car, better service in smaller shops,

11 Read phrases 1–8. Play the audio and check answers as a class.

> 2 Amrita 3 Jerry 4 Amrita 5 Jerry 6 Amrita 7 Jerry
> 8 Amrita

12 Read the instructions and items a–c. Do one or two examples to demonstrate the activity. Monitor and help as students continue individually. Put students into pairs to compare their answers. Play the audio again and pause after each phrase and elicit the answer.

> a 6 b 2, 4, 5, 8 c 3, 7

13 10A.3 Explain that English speakers use intonation to sound polite, especially when they disagree with somebody. Play the audio, pausing for students to repeat. Trace the pattern in the air, along with the phrases on the audio, to make it clearer for students to hear and copy. Give extra practice as necessary.

Extra help

Divide the class in half, for the As to read Amrita's part and the Bs to read Jerry's using audio script 10A.2 on >> **p.156–57**.

Extra activity

Students listen again and mark the intonation patterns on the phrases in exercise 11. They say a number, for a partner to say the phrase.

ABCD Put it all together

14 Read topics 1–3 and check vocabulary. Put students into pairs to make a note of *for* and *against* for each topic. Monitor and help with ideas if necessary.

15 Put students into small groups to choose and discuss one of the topics. At the end of the activity, ask a spokesperson to report back to the class.

Student performance

Students should be able to participate in a short discussion.

You can use this checklist to monitor and give feedback or to assess students' performance.

Interaction	Do students use a variety of agreeing and disagreeing phrases? exercise 13
Vocabulary	Do students use a variety of shopping vocabulary? exercise 5
Pronunciation	Do students usually use opinion intonation? exercise 13

I can exchange opinions.

Students tick *on my own* if they have had the conversation without looking at the phrases in exercise 11 or the vocabulary in exercise 4. They tick *with some help* if they have looked at the lesson notes a couple of times.

Early finishers

Students repeat the activity with a different topic from exercise 14.

Additional material

www.oup.com/elt/result for extra practice activities
www.oup.com/elt/teacher/result for extra teacher resources

How to exchange opinions

G articles *the, a, an*   V shops; agreeing and disagreeing   P agreeing and disagreeing intonation

A Read and infer

1 Do you like small, local shops or big shopping malls? Why? Think of two or three reasons and tell a partner.

2 **10A.1▶** Read and listen to **Death of the High Street** opposite. What opinion of the shopping mall do the shopkeepers have?

3 Answer the questions with a partner.
1 Line 3: Who are 'they'?
2 Line 5: 'The greengrocer was driving past' ... past what?
3 Line 7: What does the cashier think?
4 Line 12: 'Say there's nothing worse' ... worse than what?
5 Line 14: 'Walking on the land' ... what land?
6 Lines 19–24: Why are these lines in 'quotation marks'?
7 Was the cashier right? Did they build a jail?
8 How does the mall 'kill' the high street?

B Vocabulary shops

4 Work with a partner. Add more words to the lists of shops. Use **Death of the High Street** to help you.
a object + shop   *shoe shop; clothes shop ...*
b job + *'s* (shop)   *butcher's ...*
c other   *supermarket ...*

5 Work with a partner. Underline the correct word and explain why the other is not correct. You can use a dictionary.
1 You can buy milk at a grocer's/greengrocer's. *A greengrocer's sells fruit and vegetables.*
2 You pay at the checkout in a market/supermarket.
3 You don't have to go inside to buy a paper at a news-stand/newsagent's.
4 You don't pay to take books from a bookshop/library.
5 There are lots of shops with different owners inside a shopping mall/department store.

C Grammar articles *the, a, an*

6 Read these two conversations and answer the questions.
a **A** I'm going to the greengrocer's. Do you want anything?
   B Yes, can you get some apples, please?
b **A** Excuse me, is there a greengrocer's near here?
   B Yes, over there on the corner.

1 In which conversation do both people know the shop they're talking about?
2 Why does one speaker say *the greengrocer's* and the other *a greengrocer's*?

7 Work with a partner. Complete this summary of **Death of the High Street** with *the, a,* or *an*.
¹ *The* people on ²_____ high street all know each other. Everybody knows who ³_____ butcher is and who ⁴_____ greengrocer is. But there are some strange people and vehicles in town – ⁵_____ engineer, ⁶_____ lorry and ⁷_____ bulldozer. Nobody knows what they're doing here. ⁸_____ cashier in ⁹_____ bank thinks they're building ¹⁰_____ jail. But finally, everybody discovers the truth: they're building ¹¹_____ shopping mall.

More practice? **Grammar Bank** >> p.145.

D Listen to people exchanging opinions

8 Read **Have your say!** opposite. Who do you agree more with, Amrita or Jerry? Tell a partner.

9 Underline five or six key points in each opinion text.
Example I think big shopping centres are much more convenient than high-street shops.

10 **10A.2▶** Listen to Amrita and Jerry's conversation. Which of your underlined key points do they mention?

11 Listen again. Who uses these phrases, Amrita or Jerry?
1 I don't think so.   *Jerry*
2 Yes, maybe, but ...
3 Not really, no.
4 OK, that's true, but ...
5 Alright, but ...
6 Well, OK, you're right, I suppose.
7 I'm not so sure about that.
8 Yes, I agree, but ...

12 Match the phrases from exercise 11 with a–c.
a agree
b agree, but not completely
c disagree   *1*

13 **10A.3▶** Pronunciation Listen and repeat the parts of the conversation. Copy the intonation.

ABCD Put it all together

14 Work with a partner. Make a list of *for* and *against* points for each topic.
1 'Shopping with friends is better than shopping alone.'
2 'Internet shopping will kill traditional shopping.'
3 'Life in a small town is better than life in a big city.'

15 Work in groups. Choose one of the topics and exchange your opinions. Are your opinions similar?
Example **A** I think shopping with friends is more fun.
         B I'm not so sure about that ...

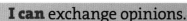

I can exchange opinions.

Tick ✓ the line.   with a lot of help   with some help   on my own   very easily

The RUBBISH Revolution

The average person in Britain produces seven times their own weight in rubbish every year. But perhaps this is not surprising when you look at the amount of packaging on supermarket food. And most of it is unnecessary. Think, for example, of four plastic pots of yogurt sold in a cardboard packet. The cardboard packet goes straight in the bin. Think of six plastic bottles of water packaged together in plastic packaging and carried home in a plastic bag. That's a lot of plastic. Only a few years ago we drank water out of the tap, and how much rubbish did that produce? None at all!

A lot of the rubbish we produce can be recycled of course, but that uses valuable resources too. It's better to buy food with as little packaging as possible. Some of the biggest supermarket chains in the country

have agreed to cut unnecessary packaging. However, government minister Ben Bradshaw says this is not enough and he is advising consumers to take direct action. He suggests that we take unnecessary packaging off our food at the supermarket checkout tills and leave it there.

Well, perhaps there are few people who are brave enough to leave rubbish at the till, but there are plenty of other things we can do to reduce waste:

- Say no to supermarket plastic bags. Take a few bags with you when you go shopping.
- If there is a choice, choose a product with less packaging.
- Buy a bigger packet if you think you will use it all. One big packet is better than lots of smaller ones.
- Try not to use plastic cups and plates.
- Choose food sold in environment-friendly packaging.
- If you find a product with too much packaging, complain to the manager.

But perhaps consumer action is not enough, and in fact some governments are taking stronger action. In 2002, Bangladesh became the first country to ban the plastic bag. Taiwan has gone a step further and banned plastic plates and cutlery as well as bags. But would consumers in Britain accept such a ban? The answer is yes. In the town of Modbury in Devon, they decided to ban the plastic bag for six months as an experiment. The ban was so popular that they have decided to keep it, and other towns are planning to follow their example.

How to **talk about your shopping habits**

Orientation

Context

In this lesson, students practise using quantifiers to talk about things they buy.

The Rubbish Revolution article on >> **p.98** is about the amount of waste produced by packaging and how consumers can take direct action to tell supermarkets that they don't want it. The article also mentions action which has been taken in Bangladesh. The photos show various types of packaged goods found on supermarket shelves.

Packaging lists vocabulary to describe shopping items in the photos.

Language

Focus grammar	quantifiers: *a few, a little, a lot of, any, hardly any, too much, too many, too little*
Focus words	*bag, bottle, box, can, carton, jar, ketchup, lid, margarine, packet, plastic, pot, recycled, rubbish, tin, toothpaste, tub, tube*
Focus phrases	*a jar of coffee, a packet of biscuits, a tube of toothpaste, etc.*
Recognition vocabulary	words: *ban, brave, cardboard, consumer, environmentally-friendly, recycled, revolution, rubbish, tills, unnecessary, valuable, waste* phrases: *Best before end … see lid, Store in a cool, dry place, etc.*
Recycled language	words: *advise, bin, biscuits, coffee, complain, cutlery, eggs, experiment, milk, perhaps, potatoes, tap, tomatoes, weight, yogurt* phrases: *go a step further, government minister* grammar: *comparatives and superlatives*
Pronunciation	*of* /əv/ rhythm 10B.1

End product

In *Put it all together*, students have a conversation about their shopping habits. It is based on audio script **10B.2** and students can use their notes to help.

Preparation

Take real examples or photos of different packaging to class for the *Warmer* (optional). Read the *Extra activity* which reviews *countable* and *uncountable* quantifiers at the start of section C.

Warmer

Ask students to imagine they are going to the supermarket and to write a shopping list. If you have any photos or examples of real items, elicit vocabulary connected to packaging. Put students into pairs or groups to compare their lists and see who plans to buy the most and the least.

Write *How to talk about your shopping habits* on the board.

A Vocabulary packaging

1 Direct students to *Packaging* on >> **p.98** and the photos in *The Rubbish Revolution*. Put students into pairs to find examples in the photos. Monitor and help as necessary. Check vocabulary as necessary as you elicit examples around the class.

2 10.B.1 Ask students to read phrases 1–10 and check vocabulary as necessary. Do the example, pointing out that the first letter of the word is given. Monitor and help if necessary.

Play the audio, pausing after each item for students to check their answers. Nominate students to say the item and give pronunciation practice if necessary.

> 2 packet   3 box   4 carton   5 pot   6 tin   7 bottle   8 bag
> 9 tube   10 tub

3 Read the instructions and elicit one or two items before students continue in pairs. Ask for examples around the class and write any new words on the board.

> 1 jar: jam, mayonnaise, etc.   6 tin: beans, fruit
> 2 packet: nuts, cigarettes, etc.   7 bottle: water, beer
> 3 box: cereal, soap powder, etc.   8 bag: apples, crisps
> 4 carton: fruit juice, tomato   9 tube: tomato puree
>   juice, etc   10 tub: cream, ice cream
> 5 pot: cottage cheese

4 Read the instructions and say one or two phrases from exercise 3 to illustrate the short form of *of* /əv/. Play audio script 10B.1 again, pausing for students to repeat. Give extra practice as necessary.

Extra practice

In pairs, students test a partner. They take turns to point to items in the photos on >> **p.98** for a partner to name them.

5 Read the instructions and ask students to look at the short pieces of information. Ask *Where would you find them and what do they mean?* Go over the example and one or two more items as a class and help students express their ideas. Put students into pairs to continue. Monitor and help as necessary. Go through each item in turn, eliciting answers.

> **Best before end … see lid:** You can't use this after the date.
> on food
> **Store in a cool place:** Keep in the fridge.   fresh food, vitamins
> **Keep out of reach of children:** Don't keep them where children can get them.   medicines
> **May contain nuts:** It's possible that there are nuts.
> pre-prepared meals
> **Suitable for vegetarians:** There's no meat.   pre-prepared meals
> **Smoking kills:** Smoking is deadly.   cigarette packets, tobacco
> **Do not exceed stated dose:** Do not take more than the instructions say.   medicines
> **Avoid contact with eyes:** Do not let any get in your eyes.
> cleaning products

B Read for general meaning

In this section, students read a magazine article for gist and detail.

6 Go through the instructions and ask students to read items a–d, checking vocabulary as necessary. Direct students to *The Rubbish Revolution* on >> **p.98** and ask them how they are going to read the text. *(Quickly, for the main idea.)* Set a short time limit of about three minutes to encourage students to

skim the text. Read each option and ask for a show of hands, encouraging students to give reasons for their choice (b The environment).

7   Go through the instructions and ask students to read sentences 1–8. Check vocabulary. Do the example as a class to demonstrate that students should look for key words in the item and the text. Tell students to guess the meaning of new words as they read.

Monitor and help as students continue the activity in pairs. Go over answers as a class and give positive feedback at the end as students will have understood the general meaning of a difficult text. Suggest they check the meaning of any words they guessed in a dictionary for homework.

2 True.   3 False. (A lot of the rubbish we produce …)
4 True.   5 True.   6 False. (One big packet is better …)
7 True.   8 False. (… they have decided to keep it …)

C Grammar quantifiers

Extra activity
Guessing game. Draw two columns on the board: A and B. Begin by saying the following quantifier words and phrases: *much, many, there is, there are*. Write words used with countable nouns in column A, and those used with uncountable nouns in column B. Continue with the following words and ask the class which column you should write them in: *a lot of, a little, a few, too much, too many, too little, some, any*. At the end, ask students for titles of the columns and elicit the terms *countable* and *uncountable*.

8   Go through the instructions and check students understand. Set a time limit of about two minutes for students to work individually. Monitor and help by suggesting students imagine the words with a plural -s. Ask *Do you often see this word in the plural?* Tell them that if they do, then it's countable. Go over answers as a class.

countable: bottle, cardboard packet, jar, plastic bag, rubbish bin, yogurt pot
uncountable: packaging, plastic, rubbish, water, yogurt

9   Read the instructions and do the examples as a class before students continue individually. Monitor and help as necessary before checking answers. Direct students to the quantifiers in blue, and encourage them to use the sentences to decide what types of nouns they can be used with.

3 d   4 h   5 g   6 b   7 e   8 c
countable: a few, many   uncountable: a little, much
both: any, a lot of

10 Ask students to read sentences 1–6 and check vocabulary. Go through the example with the class, and check students understand the different between *a little* and *very little*. Direct students to find the sentence in *The Rubbish Revolution* and to check their answer. Monitor and help as necessary as students continue individually before checking answers as a class.

2 too much   3 A lot of   4 too little   5 hardly any   6 too many

Extra help
Say the following words and phrases for students to say *countable*, *uncountable*, or *both*: *very little, enough, not much, too little, too much, hardly any, too few*. Point out that you can put *very* or *too* before *few* and *little* to amplify its meaning.

11 Put students into pairs. Go through the instructions and example as a class. Monitor and help as students continue.

Extra help
Ask students to give examples of world problems today. Write them on the board. Students add quantifiers as they discuss in pairs.

Extra plus
Students can give explanations for some of the world problems there are, e.g. *too many cars = more pollution*.

D Listen for specific information

In this section, students predict the answers to interview questions before listening to check.

12 Read the instructions and questions 1–5. Tell students they will listen to the interview. Ask them to predict what the shoppers say. Draw two columns on the board and elicit suggestions around the class. Write key words on the board.

13 10B.2 Play the audio for students to listen and check, pausing occasionally for students to add to their notes. Play the audio a second time, pausing to elicit answers around the class. Point out that the person answering gives informative answers.

Mark: 1 packet of pasta, a loaf of bread, a couple of toilet rolls, a tin of tomatoes, a bag of carrots, a jar of honey, a bottle of wine, some fresh fruit and veg   2 Martin normally buys these items.   3 two or three times a week   4 sometimes   5 cash
Linda: 1 a two-litre bottle of milk, eight cartons of yogurt, a box of cereal, some packets of kitchen paper, a bottle of olive oil, two big bottles of water, some boxes of tissues
2 Linda normally buys these items (but fresh fruit in the greengrocer's)   3 once a week   4 yes   5 debit card

Extra activity
Direct students to audio script 10B.2 on >> p.157. Ask students who they (or the shopper in their family) are most like.

ABCD Put it all together

14 Read the instructions and give students time to make notes to answer questions 2–5 in exercise 12.

15 Tell students to interview three or four others to see if anyone has the same shopping habits.

Student performance
Students should be able to respond to survey-type questions.

You can use this checklist to monitor and give feedback or to assess students' performance.

Content	Do students answer the questions in an informative way? exercise 13
Vocabulary	Do students have enough vocabulary to do the task? exercise 2
Pronunciation	Do students mostly pronounce /əʊ/ correctly? exercise 3

I can **talk about my shopping habits.**

Students tick *on my own* if they have answered the questions without a lot of hesitation. They tick *with some help* if they have given some answers with several pauses to think.

Early finishers
Students write questions for a survey on *The Rubbish Revolution* and ask three or four others.

Additional material

www.oup.com/elt/result for extra practice activities
www.oup.com/elt/teacher/result for extra teacher resources

How to talk about your shopping habits

G quantifiers V packaging P *of*

A Vocabulary packaging

1 Work with a partner. How many things in **Packaging** opposite can you find in the photos?

2 **10B.1▶** Complete the phrases with some of the words from **Packaging**. Listen and check.

1 a j*ar*____ of coffee   6 a t_____ of tomatoes
2 a p_____ of biscuits   7 a b_____ of ketchup
3 a b_____ of eggs   8 a b_____ of potatoes
4 a c_____ of milk   9 a t_____ of toothpaste
5 a p_____ of yogurt   10 a t_____ of margarine

3 Work with a partner. Think of other products which could complete the phrases in exercise 2.
Example a jar of baby food

4 **Pronunciation** Listen again and repeat. Notice that *of* is always unstressed and is pronounced /əv/.

5 Read the small pieces of text. Where do you think you would find them and what do they mean? Tell a partner.

Best before end ... see lid   Store in cool dry place
Keep out of reach of children   May contain nuts
Suitable for vegetarians   Smoking kills
Do not exceed stated dose   Avoid contact with eyes

Example Best before end ... see lid   *On a pot of yogurt.*

B Read for general meaning

6 Read **The Rubbish Revolution** opposite. What do you think the author is worried about?
a unhealthy eating habits
b the environment
c supermarkets killing the small shops
d high prices

7 Work with a partner. Write *true* or *false*. If the sentence is false, say why.
1 Food wrapping isn't necessary.
   False. Most of it, but not all of it, is unnecessary.
2 Drinking bottled water produces more rubbish.
3 All rubbish can be recycled.
4 Some supermarkets have agreed to use less food wrapping.
5 Consumers can take action to produce less rubbish.
6 You shouldn't buy bigger packets because they produce more rubbish.
7 Plastic bags have been banned in some places.
8 Plastic bags are so popular in Modbury that they've decided to keep them.

C Grammar quantifiers

8 Are these words countable or uncountable?
bottle cardboard packet jar packaging
plastic plastic bag rubbish rubbish bin
water yogurt yogurt pot

9 Match 1–8 with a–h. Do the quantifiers in blue go with countable nouns, uncountable nouns, or both?

1 [f] There's   a ~~a few~~ ~~bottles~~.
2 [a] There are   b many bags.
3 [ ] There's   c any rubbish bins?
4 [ ] There are   d a little yogurt.
5 [ ] There isn't   e any rubbish?
6 [ ] There aren't   f ~~a lot of~~ ~~packaging~~.
7 [ ] Is there   g much water.
8 [ ] Are there   h a lot of jars.

10 Underline the best answer, according to **The Rubbish Revolution**.
1 Britain produces a lot of/a little/very little rubbish.
2 Supermarkets use enough/too much/a lot of packaging on food.
3 A lot of/Not much/No packaging is unnecessary.
4 Supermarkets are doing too little/too much/enough to reduce packaging.
5 Bottled water produces lots of rubbish but tap water produces some/no/hardly any rubbish.
6 We take home a few/too few/too many plastic bags from supermarkets.

11 Tell your partner about problems in the world today, using quantifiers.
Example There are too many cars on the road.

More practice? **Grammar Bank >>** p.145.

D Listen for specific information

12 Look at Linda's shopping (photo 1) and Mark's shopping (photo 2) opposite. Guess their answers to these questions.
1 What's in your shopping basket today?
2 What do you normally buy?
3 How often do you go shopping?
4 Do you write a shopping list?
5 Do you pay by card or in cash?

13 **10B.2▶** Listen. Were your guesses correct?

ABCD Put it all together

14 What are your shopping habits? Write notes to answer questions 2–5 in exercise 12.

15 Ask other students about their shopping habits. Whose shopping habits are most similar to yours?

I can talk about my shopping habits.

Tick ✓ the line. with a lot of help with some help on my own very easily

THE SALESPEOPLE

1

Ms SAYLES We haven't been selling many of these sunshades lately. I want you to try harder. The one who sells the most over the next month or so will get a bonus.

2

ONE MONTH LATER

Ms S Right. What have you been doing to sell more sunshades, Winston?

WINSTON I've been offering two for the price of one, Ms Sayles.

3

Ms S And how many have you sold?

W I haven't sold many recently. People don't want sunshades with pink rabbits on.

Ms S How many, Winston?

W Well, none, in fact.

Ms S None. And how long have you been working here?

W Almost six months.

Ms S Nearly six months and you haven't learnt anything. It's not good enough!

4

Ms S What about you, Janet?

JANET I've been advertising in the daily paper, Ms Sayles. I've also been phoning people at home.

Ms S And how many have you sold?

J About five. It's been raining for weeks. Nobody wants a sunshade.

Ms S You're a saleswoman, Janet. It's your job to sell things that nobody wants.

5

Ms S And you, Charlie? How many have you sold?

CHARLIE Two thousand, more or less. People have been queuing to buy them.

Ms S That's amazing! What have you been doing?

6

C I've been selling them outside the station as umbrellas.

How to talk about recent activities

Orientation

Context

In this lesson, students practise using the present perfect continuous to talk about recent activities.

In the sketch, *The Salespeople* on >> **p.100**, the boss (Ms Sayles) wants her employees to explain what they have been doing to sell the sunshades. She offers a bonus to the salesperson who can sell the most in the next month. The team meet one month later and explain their selling strategies.

Language

Focus grammar	present perfect continuous: *It's been raining., It hasn't been raining., Have I been sleeping?*
Focus words	approximate times and amounts: *about, almost, lately, more or less, nearly, or so, recently*
Recognition vocabulary	words: *bonus, cheap, counter, out of contact, queuing, salespeople, sunshades* phrases: *wasting time*
Recycled language	words: *advertising, already, customer, flatmate, piano, product, the coast, trumpet, quality, umbrellas, windsurfing* phrases: *amazing* grammar: *time phrases: for ten years, nine months ago, one month later, since four o'clock; present perfect; comparatives*
Pronunciation	when to stress *have/has* 10C.2

End product

In *Put it all together*, students role play a conversation about their recent activities. Their conversation is based on audio script 10C.3.

Preparation

Take dictionaries to class.

Warmer

Write *What?*, *Where?*, and *How?* on the board. In groups, students talk about how many times people have tried to sell them things in the past month and what they were doing at the time.

Ask for volunteers to tell the class *what, where,* and *how*. They should say if and why they bought or didn't buy the item. Do not overcorrect for accuracy, but help students express their ideas.

Write *How to talk about recent activities* on the board.

A Read and follow an explanation

In this section, students read and follow a conversation for specific information and detail.

1 Read the question and statements a–d. Check vocabulary as necessary before putting students into pairs to discuss the best ways of selling. Monitor and encourage students to talk about different types of products, e.g. a raincoat or a bank-loan. Ask for volunteers to share their opinions with the class and encourage others to respond.

   Extra activity
   Students decide which techniques are most effective in their own countries.

2 10C.1 Read the instructions and direct students to *The Salespeople* on >> **p.100**. Tell students to listen and read carefully as the salespeople don't use exactly the same words as in a–d. Play the audio.

   To check answers, say the names of the people for students to call out a letter. Ask students to explain their answers and help them express their ideas.

   > Winston: c   Janet: d   Charlie: a

3 Ask students to read questions 1–6 and check vocabulary as necessary. Do the example to demonstrate the activity, and ask students what Janet has done *(advertised in the daily paper and phoned people at home)*. Monitor and guide students to the answers as necessary while students continue individually.

   Ask for volunteers to give answers and check the class agrees before confirming. Ask students to explain their answers using the information in *The Salespeople*.

   > 2 Charlie He's sold 2,000.
   > 3 Winston He hasn't sold any sunshades.
   > 4 Winston He's been selling two for the price of one.
   > 5 Ms Sayles, the boss.
   > 6 Janet She's done a lot of work but not sold any sunshades.

4 Put students into pairs to discuss their reasons. Monitor and help students express their ideas. Elicit suggestions around the class and note students' use of the present perfect and present perfect continuous. Do not overcorrect for accuracy as this is the focus of the grammar section.

   > **Winston:** He hasn't been successful. He says people don't like the design of the sunshades and he hasn't tried any of the techniques in exercise 1.
   > **Janet:** She hasn't been successful, even though she's been contacting lots of people. She hasn't been using the right strategies.
   > **Charlie:** He's been very successful. He's been selling the sunshades outside the station when it's been raining.

   Extra help
   Students role play the conversation in groups of four.

   Extra activity
   In pairs or small groups, students discuss what they would do if they worked for Ms Sayles.

T100

B Vocabulary approximate times and amounts

5 Read the section heading and copy the table onto the board. Go through the instructions and check that students understand the column titles. Ask students to underline the words and phrases in *The Salespeople* and to write them in the appropriate columns. Encourage them to check meaning in their dictionaries. Monitor and help as students continue individually. Elicit answers and write them in the table on the board.

Complete sentences 1–3 as a class, checking students understand the concept as you go through each one, e.g. for item 1, ask *Do we know when the action happened?*; for item 2 *Are we interested in when you bought the CDs? Is the sentence about the past, the past up to now, now or the future?*; for item 3 *Do you think the person still works at the same place. Is ten years a long time?* Do not focus on the form of the present perfect at this point as it will be covered in the next section.

> **a little less than:** nearly
> **in recent times:** lately, recently
> **approximately:** about, more or less, or so
> 1 about   2 recently   3 or so

6 Ask students to read items 1–4 and check vocabulary. Monitor for accuracy and offer help as students continue individually. Ask students to choose a statement to make to the class.

Extra help
Review *for* and *since*, if necessary.

Extra plus
Direct students to the text to find another phrase which refers to approximate time, e.g. *It's been raining for weeks.* Point out that the using plurals, e.g. days, weeks, months, etc. is another way of referring to approximate time.

C Grammar present perfect continuous

7 Write *It's been raining.* on the board. Direct students to the grammar box and ask them to name the tense used in the sentences in the three columns *(present perfect continuous)*. Underline the *-ing* on the board.

Ask students to complete the sentences in the grammar box. Monitor for accuracy and make a note of any problems to deal with at the end. Check answers and elicit and write an example of a negative and a question form on the board. Remind students of the form of the present perfect *(have + been)* if necessary.

> + I've been waiting.   – I haven't been sleeping.   You haven't been waiting.   ? Has it been raining?

8 10C.2 Direct students to the stress patterns at the top of the columns in the grammar box in exercise 7. Ask students to underline the stressed syllables in the sentences. Play the audio, pausing after each sentence for students to check. Play the audio a second time, pausing for students to repeat.

9 Write both sentences on the board. Ask students to read questions 1–4 and check vocabulary as necessary. Students answer the questions in pairs. Point to each sentence on the board as you go over answers with the class.

> 1 present perfect continuous   2 present perfect simple
> 3 present perfect simple   4 present perfect continuous

10 Ask students to read sentences 1–7 and check vocabulary. Do the first two items with the class. Ask students to underline the *time* and *amount* words and phrases before they decide on

the correct answer. Monitor and help. Ask for volunteers to read out the complete sentence when you check answers.

> 1 sold   2 been selling   3 been sitting   4 phoned
> 5 been raining   6 seen   7 been waiting

Extra activity
Students tell a partner about five things they've done or been doing this week, using the time and amount phrases in exercise 5.

D Listen for detail

In this section, students listen to a conversation for detail.

11 10C.3 Read the information about Simon and Teresa and check students understand that they are friends who haven't seen each other lately. Play the audio for students to make notes. Ask students to compare answers in pairs and play the audio a second time if necessary. Nominate students to give answers.

> **Simon:** 's been working at a travel agent's, hasn't been going out much
> **Teresa:** 's been learning to play the trumpet, 's been living on her own for nearly a year, 's been going away most weekends, 's been windsurfing

12 Direct students to audio script 10C.3 on >> p.157. Ask for two volunteers to have the conversation for the class. The class listens to decide if they sound pleased to see each other.

Put students into pairs to practise the conversation using their notes. Monitor and encourage them to look up from the page occasionally and make eye contact. Give positive feedback when they sound reasonably fluent. Check students swap roles.

ABCD Put it all together

13 Students read through the list and add to it using their own ideas. Monitor and help with ideas if necessary.

14 Go through the instructions and ask for two volunteers to read the example conversation. Encourage them to smile and sound pleased to see each other and to add another turn each. Put students into pairs to continue the activity.

Student performance
Students should be able to have a short, informal conversation.

You can use this checklist to monitor and give feedback or to assess students' performance.

Interaction	Do students sound pleased to see their 'friend'? exercise 12
Fluency	Do students use the present perfect continuous without a lot of hesitation? exercise 8
Vocabulary	Do students use approximate time phrases appropriately? exercise 6

I can **talk about recent activities.**
Students tick *on my own* if they have had the conversation looking at their notes occasionally. They tick *with some help* if they need to look at the grammar box in exercise 7 once or twice.

Early finishers
Books closed. Students stand up and role play the conversation.

Additional material

www.oup.com/elt/result for extra practice activities
www.oup.com/elt/teacher/result for extra teacher resources

How to talk about recent activities

G present perfect continuous   **V** approximate times and amounts   **P** when to stress *have/has*

A Read and follow an explanation

1 What's the best way to sell something? Discuss with a partner.
   a Offer your product to the customer at just the moment they need it.
   b Tell your customer that your product is the best quality.
   c Offer your product at a price which seems cheaper than normal.
   d Give information about your product to as many people as possible.

2 **10C.1▶** Listen and read **The Salespeople** opposite. Match *Winston*, *Janet*, and *Charlie* with a–d in exercise 1.

3 Answer the questions.
   Who has been …
   1 contacting lots of people?   *Janet*
   2 selling lots of sunshades?
   3 wasting his time?
   4 trying to sell sunshades cheap?
   5 waiting to see who sold most sunshades?
   6 working hard with poor results?

4 Work with a partner. Explain why each salesperson was or wasn't successful.

B Vocabulary approximate times and amounts

5 Underline these words and phrases in **The Salespeople**. Write them in the correct box. Then decide which of them can complete sentences 1–3.

lately   or so   recently   ~~almost~~
nearly   about   more or less

a little less than	in recent times	approximately
almost		

   1 I bought this computer _____ nine months ago.
   2 Have you bought any music CDs _____?
   3 I've been working here for ten years _____.

6 Complete these sentences to give true information about yourself. Compare with a partner.
   1 I've been studying this page for *15 minutes or so./ almost 15 minutes.*
   2 I've been sitting in this room since _____.
   3 I've been awake since _____.
   4 I haven't _____ lately.

C Grammar present perfect continuous

7 Complete the sentences in the grammar box.

+ ●●●●●	− ●●●●●●	? ●●●●●
It's been raining.	It hasn't been raining.	
I've been sleeping.		Have I been sleeping?
		Have you been waiting?

8 **10C.2▶** Pronunciation Listen, check, and repeat the sentences in exercise 7. Copy the stress pattern. When do we stress *have/has*?

9 Compare the sentences and answer the questions.
   present perfect simple   I've sold two thousand.
   present perfect continuous   I've been selling them for a month.

   1 Which sentence answers the question *How long*?
   2 Which sentence answers the question *How many*?
   3 Which sentence focuses on a completed achievement?
   4 Which sentence focuses on continuing actions?

10 Underline the best form of the verb. Compare with a partner.
   1 I've sold/been selling five umbrellas today.
   2 I've sold/been selling them outside the station all day.
   3 Winston's sat/been sitting behind the counter in his shop all morning.
   4 Janet's phoned/been phoning about 50 people.
   5 It's rained/been raining for three hours.
   6 I've seen/been seeing this advert three times already.
   7 Have you waited/been waiting for long?

   More practice? **Grammar Bank** >> p.145.

D Listen for detail

11 **10C.3▶** Two friends, Simon and Teresa, have been out of contact. Listen to their conversation. What have they been doing recently? Make notes.
   Example   Simon's been saving money.

12 Practise the conversation with a partner. Use your notes.

ABCD Put it all together

13 Write a list of activities you've been doing recently.
   Example   reading books; going to the gym; travelling for work …

14 Work with a partner and do a role play. Have a conversation about what you've been doing lately.
   Example   **A** I haven't seen you for ages! What have you been doing lately?
   B Oh, I've been travelling a lot for work …

I can talk about recent activities.

Tick ✓ the line.   with a lot of help   with some help   on my own   very easily

Personality Quiz!
What kind of shopper are you?

Which of the options best describes what you do in these situations? If you can't decide, choose two – or none!

1 You see a nice pair of shoes in a sale. They're good value and they're the last pair available. What do you think?

a 'I'll buy them as long as there's no queue in the shop.'
b 'I'll buy them if they're good quality.'
c 'I won't buy them unless I really need them.'
d 'I'll buy them quickly before someone else decides to buy them.'

2 You need a new printer. What do you do?

a I won't buy one unless I know it's one of the best available.
b I won't buy one until I've compared the prices in five different shops.
c Buy the first one I see, as long as it can print!
d Look around the shops until I see one which looks nice.

3 You decide to learn the guitar. How do you get your first instrument?

a Borrow one from a friend until he or she wants it back.
b Buy a guitar and perhaps buy a few other things while I'm in the shop.
c Find out what the professionals use before I buy one.
d Get the cheapest and upgrade when I know I'm going to continue.

4 You get a €15 book voucher for your birthday. What do you think?

a 'I'll check if there's anything I want in the bargain section.'
b 'I'll go to the shops and take my credit card in case I want to buy something else, too.'
c 'I'll read the book reviews in the paper before I go to the bookshop.'
d 'I'll wait until someone else's birthday comes round and I'll give it to them.'

5 You buy a fridge. When they deliver it, you notice it isn't the same colour as the one in the shop. What do you do?

a Ask them to replace it – unless it matches the colour scheme of my kitchen.
b Nothing. I don't mind as long as the fridge works.
c Complain even if I like the colour because I might get some money back!
d I go to the shops as soon as I can to buy more things which match the colour.

> **GLOSSARY**
> **sale** *n* an occasion when a shop sells things for a lower price
> **available** *adj* something you can get, buy, or find
> **upgrade** *vb* to get a better version of something you've already got
> **voucher** *n* a printed piece of paper which you can use like money
> **bargain** *n* a thing bought for less than the usual price
> **deliver** *vb* to take goods, letters, etc. to someone's home
> **replace** *vb* to change something which is damaged or not right for a new one

Buying a camera

Tina Oops, I've taken a photo of my foot!
Dan It's all right. We can delete it unless ...

A
D Yes, all included. And there's a six-month guarantee. If you have any problems with it, we'll repair it free of charge. Here, try it ...
T Mmm. Oops, I've taken a photo of my foot!

B
D A digital camera? OK. How much do you want to spend?
T £100 or so ...

C
D Sorry, we don't sell batteries, but you can buy them at any supermarket.
T How much do they cost?

D
D Well, this one is normally £120, but it's reduced at the moment to £99.99.
T Does that include the batteries, the memory card, and everything?

E
D Can you enter your PIN number, please ... Thanks. And here's your receipt. Keep it in case you need to bring the camera back.
T OK. Thanks. Goodbye.
D Bye.

F
1
D Can I help you?
T Yes, I'm looking for a cheap digital camera.

G
D £2.50, more or less. Would you like to buy a leather case for your camera? Brown, to match your shoes!
T Ha ha. No, thanks. That's all, thanks.

H
D OK. How would you like to pay – by cash or card?
T I'll pay by credit card, please.

I
D It's all right. We can delete it unless you want to keep it!
T No, thanks. I hate these shoes! OK, I think I'll take the camera. And I'll buy some spare batteries while I'm here.

Orientation

Context

In this lesson, students role play asking questions about products as a customer in a shop.

Personality Quiz! invites the reader to answer questions about what they do when they are buying the items in the pictures. The answers determine what kind of shopper a person is. The reader can calculate their score using the information in *Pairwork* on >> **p.131**.

Glossary gives the meaning of some key vocabulary in the text.

Buying a camera has the conversation between Tina (the customer) and Dan (shop assistant). Students will sequence the parts of the conversation.

Language

Focus grammar	time and conditional clauses: *as long as, as soon as, if, when, until, unless*
Focus words	*available, bargain, buy, cash, cheap, cost, credit card, deliver, guarantee, included, pay, PIN number, queue, receipt, reduced, repair, replace, sale, spare, spend, voucher*
Focus phrases	*bring back, Does that include ...?, free of charge, keep it in case, pay by cash, while I'm here ...*
Recognition vocabulary	words: *book voucher, browse, competitive, discount, match (v), options, professionals, upgrade* phrases: *bargain hunting, best deal, cheap rubbish, even if, get money off, good tastes, in case, kind of, quality products, read the small print, well-known makes*
Recycled language	words: *borrow, definitely, delete, fridge, guitar, instrument, maybe, perhaps, printer, queue, reviews* phrases: *colour scheme, more or less* grammar: *1st conditional*

Language note

As soon as is a partial synonym for *when*. It contains an added emphasis on *immediately*.

End product

In *Put it all together*, students take turns to be a customer and shop assistant.

Preparation

Look at *Personality Quiz!* on >> **p.131** in *Pairwork* so you are prepared to help students calculate their scores and plan their conversations in exercise 14. Take dictionaries to class.

Warmer

Write the following question and statements on the board: *What kind of shopper are you? a) You don't like spending time shopping. b) You only buy good quality things. c) You only buy things when you need them. d) You always compare prices in different shops before you buy. e) You always buy more than you plan to. f) You only buy things which look good together.*

In pairs, students discuss how they shop. Put pairs together to make small groups and ask for a spokesperson from each group to tell the class any interesting facts they found out about each other.

Write *How to ask about products in a shop* on the board.

A Read and respond

In this section, students read for detail and answer questions in a personality quiz.

1 Read the instructions and check vocabulary. Elicit a few suggestions for the first item around the class and put students into pairs to continue. Monitor and help students get their ideas across. Ask the class for suggestions for each item.

2 Direct students to read *Personality Quiz!* on >> **p.102**. Point out the glossary and encourage students to use their dictionaries to help with vocabulary if necessary. Remind them to make a note of their answers as they do the quiz.

3 Direct students to >> **p.131** to calculate their score and read about their shopping personality. Encourage students to guess the meaning of new words before checking in a dictionary. Monitor and help as necessary.

Ask for volunteers to tell the class about their shopping personality. Do not overcorrect for accuracy but help students express their ideas. Encourage students to add examples of things they do and don't do. Ask them if they agree with the results of the quiz.

B Grammar time and conditional clauses

4 Direct students to the sentences and go through the two questions as a class. Check students understand the difference in meaning between *if* and *when*.

> 1 b Maybe.
> 2 c Yes, definitely. (She's expecting to have the money in the future. She uses *when* to show she is confident that this will happen.)

Extra help

Use the sentences in exercise 4 to do a backchain drill. As a class, students repeat from the last word, adding one word at a time until they say the whole question, e.g. *T good SS good T they're good SS they're good T if they're good SS if they're good*, etc.

Extra activity

Direct students to look at the pictures in *Personality Quiz!* Ask students to write two sentences similar to Anne and Beth's using *if/when* for each of the items in the pictures. Monitor and help as necessary. Focus on each picture in turn and nominate students to say what they would do. Monitor for accuracy.

5 Read the instructions and example sentences before directing students to the grammar box. Check students understand the meaning of *synonym* and *opposite*. Elicit or explain that the time phrases relate to the condition not the result. Go through the activity as a class.

> **if:** opposite = unless
> **when:** synonym = as soon as; opposite = until

6 Read the instructions and the example to check students understand the activity. Monitor and help as students continue individually. Ask students about the tense of the verb in the condition clauses (*present simple tense*).

Extra activity

Ask students to highlight the conditional phrases in their answers to the questionnaire.

7 Read the instructions and direct students to the language box. Check vocabulary as necessary. Ask for two volunteers to read the example conversation to demonstrate the activity. Put students into pairs to continue the activity. Monitor and give positive feedback for accurate use of time phrases.

Nominate students to make statements about themselves and remind them to use time phrases. Encourage others to respond.

Extra help
Transformation drill. Nominate a student to make a sentence. The class reports what he or she said, e.g. *A I won't buy a jacket unless it's cheap. SS She/He won't buy a jacket ...*, etc.

Extra activity
Ask students to write sentences about their shopping personalities for each of the time clauses.

C Vocabulary words connected with buying and selling

8 Direct students to the photo in *Buying a camera* on >> **p.102**. Ask *Who's the customer? (Tina.) Who's the shop assistant? (Dan.)* and check students understand their conversation. Elicit the kinds of things customers and shop assistants say.

Put students into pairs and direct them to the start of the conversation (*F*). Ask students to ignore new vocabulary for the moment and to find the next part (*B*). Monitor and help as students continue the activity. Encourage them to read the conversation together to check their order makes sense.

9 10D.1 Play the audio, pausing after each part to elicit the next part. Encourage students to say why one part follows another. Play the audio a second time for students to follow the whole conversation.

2 B   3 D   4 A   5 I   6 C   7 G   8 H   9 E

Extra activity
Students say the conversation in pairs, taking turns to be the customer and shop assistant.

10 Read the instructions and ask students to guess and compare their ideas with a partner, before checking in a dictionary. Monitor and help as necessary. Go over answers as a class, helping students express their ideas. Monitor for pronunciation of the key vocabulary and give extra help as necessary.

11 Read the instructions and the words and phrases. Ask students to read questions 1–7 and ask who says each one, a customer or shop assistant? Check vocabulary as necessary. Students complete the exercise.

To check answers, ask for volunteers to say the complete question. See if the class agrees before giving feedback and give additional pronunciation practice as necessary.

2 cost   3 free of charge   4 spend   5 pay   6 guarantee 7 price

Extra activity
Students work in pairs. They choose an item to talk about, e.g. one of the things in the pictures on >> **p.102**. They take turns to be a customer and a shop assistant, asking and answering using the questions in exercise 11.

12 Direct students to the conversation grid and read the instructions to the class. Direct students to *Buying a camera* and the *Start* box. Elicit the words a shop assistant uses to offer help. Ask students about the next step in the conversation (*customer – say what you want*) and elicit what the customer says in *Buying a camera*. Tell students that they can move horizontally or vertically to find the next step in the conversation. Monitor and help as students continue in pairs. Go over answers as a class.

C say what you want   **S** ask how much C wants to spend **C** say how much you want to spend   **S** offer product **C** ask what's included   **S** say what's included **C** accept product,   ask for spares   **S** explain about spares, offer extra goods   **C** refuse extra goods   **S** ask about way of paying **C** choose a way of paying   **S** take payment, give receipt **C** say goodbye

Teaching tip
When checking the answers, elicit phrases for asking and answering for each of the turns. Write the key words for each stage of the conversation on the board as student support for the next exercise.

13 Go through the instructions and put students in pairs to role play the conversation. Monitor and encourage them to make eye contact and sound friendly. Check students swap roles. Give positive feedback.

ABC Put it all together

14 Go through the instructions and direct students to the pictures on >> **p.131**. Elicit the names of the different items in the pictures to check vocabulary. Ask for two volunteers to have the example conversation. Put students into pairs to continue and check they swap roles. At the end of the activity, ask students if their shop assistants sounded friendly.

Student performance
Students should be able to have a short transactional conversation.

You can use this checklist to monitor and give feedback or to assess students' performance.

Coherence	Do students ask and answer appropriately? exercise 13
Interaction	Do students sound friendly? exercise 13
Vocabulary	Do students use a variety of shopping words? exercises 10, 11

I can ask about products in a shop.

Students tick *on my own* if they have had the conversation using the grid in exercise 12 occasionally. They tick *with some help* if they have looked at the board or *Buying a camera* once or twice.

Early finishers
Students have a conversation about another item from the photos on >> **p.102** without looking at their books.

Additional material

www.oup.com/elt/result for extra practice activities
www.oup.com/elt/teacher/result for extra teacher resources

How to ask about products in a shop

G time and conditional clauses   V words connected with buying and selling

A Read and respond

1 You're buying one of these things. What do you do before you buy? Tell a partner.

a camera a car a flat a jacket a package holiday shoes

Example Try it on ...

2 Read **Personality Quiz!** opposite with a partner. Choose your answers for yourself.

3 Look on >> p.131 to calculate your score and read your shopping personality. Do you agree with the description?

B Grammar time and conditional clauses

4 Look at the sentences and choose the correct answer to the questions.

Anne I'll buy the shoes if they're good.
Beth I'll buy the shoes when I've got the money.

1 Will Anne buy the shoes in the future?
  a No. b Maybe. c Yes, definitely.
2 Will Beth buy the shoes in the future?
  a No. b Maybe. c Yes, definitely.

5 These sentences mean the same as the sentences in exercise 4. Put the words and phrases in blue in the box.

Anne I'll buy them as long as they're good. I *won't* buy them unless they're good.
Beth I'll buy them as soon as I've got the money. I *won't* buy them until I've got the money.

	if	when
synonym	as long as	
opposite		

6 Underline clauses in **Personality Quiz!** beginning with the words and phrases in exercise 5. What tense is the verb in the clause?

Example as long as there's no queue in the shop
present simple tense

7 Make true sentences from the box and tell your partner. Say if you agree with your partner's sentences.

Example A I won't buy a jacket unless it's cheap.
           B Oh, really? I don't mind paying more as long as it looks nice.

I'll	buy	a jacket	as long as	it's cheap.
I won't		a computer	as soon as	there's a guarantee.
		other	unless	I think it looks nice.
			until	*other*

More practice? **Grammar Bank** >> p.145.

C Vocabulary words connected with buying and selling

8 Read **Buying a camera** opposite and put the conversation in order. Compare with a partner.

9 **10D.1▶** Listen and check.

10 What is the difference between these pairs of words from the conversation? Use your dictionary.

buy – pay   spend – cost   reduced – included
guarantee – receipt /rɪˈsiːt/

11 Complete the questions with these words and phrases.

cost   free of charge   guarantee
~~included~~   pay   price   spend

1 Is the software _included_?
2 How much does it _____?
3 Do you deliver _____?
4 How much do you want to _____?
5 How would you like to _____?
6 Does it come with a _____?
7 What's the reduced _____?

12 What are the steps of the conversation in **Buying a camera**? Work with a partner and find the path from *Start* to *Finish*.

salesperson   customer

START offer to help	say what you want	offer extra goods	refuse extra goods
say how much you want to spend	ask how much customer wants to spend	explain about spares	ask about way of paying
offer product	accept product	ask for spares	choose way of paying
ask what's included	say what's included	say goodbye **FINISH**	take payment + give receipt

13 Practise the conversation with a partner. Don't read it – use the conversation map in exercise 12.

ABC Put it all together

14 Work with a partner. Role play shop conversations. The customer is buying the products in the pictures on >> p.131.

Example A Can I help you?
           B Yes, I'm looking for a camera.
           A What make are you looking for?
           B I don't mind as long as it's good quality ...

I can ask about products in a shop. ▬▬▬▬▬

Tick ✓ the line.   with a lot of help   with some help   on my own   very easily   103

Writing A letter of complaint

A Read a letter of complaint

1 Do you ever buy things from catalogues, from the Internet, or over the phone? What are the possible problems? Tell a partner.

2 Read the letter of complaint. Why do you think the company sent the wrong book?

3 Answer the questions with a partner.
   1 How does Marcus know the name of the person he's writing to?
   2 What's the name of the company he's writing to?
   3 Why doesn't he want to keep the book?
   4 Why didn't Marcus return the book immediately?

B Think about the reader

4 What do you think about Marcus Page from his letter? Choose the best description.
   a He seems aggressive and negative.
   b He seems angry and impatient.
   c He seems firm but friendly.

5 Read the tips for writing a letter of complaint. Do you agree? Do you think it is better to be more aggressive? Tell a partner.

6 Work with a partner and <u>underline</u> examples of the four tips in the letter of complaint.

7 Marcus divides his letter into paragraphs to make it clearer for the reader. What information does he give in each paragraph?

C Get ideas to write about

8 Brainstorm with a partner and write possible answers.
   You ordered a product:
   1 What did you order?
   2 What was the problem with the product?
   3 Have you contacted anybody about the problem yet? What did they say?
   4 How did you order (e.g. over the phone)?
   5 When did you place the order and when did it arrive?
   6 What would you like them to do about the problem?

9 Use Marcus's letter to put the information in order.

ABC Put it all together

10 Write a letter of complaint using some of your ideas from exercise 8. Follow the tips.

11 Check your writing and then pass it to a partner.

12 Read your partner's letter and imagine it is addressed to you. Does it make you want to help the person?

Oxford
April 1st 2010

Dear Ms Parchment

I'm writing to explain a problem I have had with your telephone ordering service. I recently ordered a book called "Lords of Things" – a history of modern Thailand by Maurizio Peleggi, but your company sent a different book.

I placed the order on February 29th and I received the package from your company about two weeks ago. I was away at the time, so I wasn't able to open it until this morning. Unfortunately, it was the wrong book; it was "The Lord of the Rings" by JRR Tolkien. It's a good book, but I've already read it! I rang your telephone service to explain the problem, but they said it was too late to change the book. Then they suggested I wrote to you.

I have ordered books from Paperbooks Express in the past and I have always found the service to be excellent. I'm sure this misunderstanding can be easily solved. Please could you send me the book I originally ordered? I will be happy to return the Tolkien book as long as you refund the postage costs.

I look forward to hearing from you.

Yours sincerely

Marcus Page

Marcus Page

TIPS FOR WRITING A LETTER OF COMPLAINT

How do you feel when you spend money but don't get what you want? Most of us feel angry and we want to shout at the people who sold us the goods or services. However, being aggressive is not usually the best way to get a positive response. If you really want to solve the problem, calm down and think about what you are going to say – or write. Try to give a firm but friendly impression:

1 Explain your problem **briefly**. Let your reader know quickly why they're reading your letter.

2 Give detailed **facts**. This will give the reader a chance to check their records.

3 Say what you'd like the reader to do. This will show the reader **a way forwards**.

4 Be **friendly**. A compliment or a touch of humour helps to create a positive feeling.

I can write a letter of complaint.

Tick ✓ the line. with a lot of help with some help on my own very easily

Orientation

Context and Language

In this lesson, students practise writing a formal letter based on a model. In the letter, Marcus Page has written to Ms Parchment in Paperbooks Express, to explain a problem. Both names add a humourous touch to the situation.

In *Tips for writing a letter of complaint* students are encouraged to consider the letter from the receiver's point of view.

New language	words: *complaint, package, refund* phrases: *place an order, telephone service*
Recycled language	words: *angry, catalogue, excellent, immediately, misunderstanding, recently, tips, unfortunately* phrases: *as long as, yours sincerely* grammar: *1st conditional; reported speech* discourse: *but, so, then*
Recognition language	words: *aggressive, briefly, compliment, impatient, impression, negative, parchment* phrases: *calm down, firm but friendly, touch of humour, way forwards*

End product

In *Put it all together*, students write a letter of complaint about an imaginary product or service.

Warmer

Put students into groups to discuss the types of things they complain to others about and how they complain.

Write *How to write a letter of complaint* on the board.

A Read a letter of complaint

In this section, students read a letter of complaint for specific information.

1 Put students into groups to discuss the questions. Monitor and help with vocabulary as necessary. Ask for a volunteer from each group to summarize the group's answers for the class.

2 Direct students to the letter of complaint. Ask students to read it quickly, ignoring new vocabulary, to answer the question.

> The titles are very similar: *Lord of the Rings* and *Lords of Things*.

3 Ask students to read questions 1–4. Check answers. Students continue the activity in pairs. Monitor and help, encouraging students to guess new vocabulary.

> 1 The person he spoke to at the company's telephone service probably told him.   2 Paperbooks Express   3 He's already read it.   4 He's been away for two weeks, and the book arrived while he was away.

B Think about the reader

In this section, students analyse the letter to see if it follows the writing tips.

4 Read descriptions a–c and check vocabulary. Elicit or explain the meaning of each description. Ask students to read the letter again to find the best description for Marcus Page. Take a class vote on the best description, encouraging students to explain.

> c Firm but friendly. He states clearly what he expects to happen and says nice things about the company *Paperbooks Express*.

5 Direct students to *Tips for writing a letter of complaint* and ask them to read and underline any new vocabulary. In pairs, students help each other with new vocabulary and answer the question. Elicit suggestions around the class.

> Being more aggressive might upset the reader. They might not solve the problem quickly or effectively.

6 Read the instructions and put students into pairs to underline the four tips. Check answers as a class.

7 Read the instructions and point out there are three paragraphs in the letter. Students compare in pairs. Check answers.

> **paragraph 1:** He explains the problem.
> **paragraph 2:** He gives detailed facts.
> **paragraph 3:** He compliments the company and states what he would like Ms Parchment to do.

C Get ideas to write about

8 Ask students to read questions 1–6 and check vocabulary. Put students into pairs to discuss the facts of a possible situation.

9 Elicit or explain that the answers to questions 1–6 describe the situation. Monitor and guide students to find similar information in the letter. Put students into pairs to compare. Check answers. Ask students why they should think about organizing the order of their information before they start writing. *(It's difficult to make changes once a letter has been written.)* Ask what other information they can find *(date, greeting, and closing)*. Elicit or explain that students should follow this format for a formal letter.

ABC Put it all together

10 Go through the instructions and remind students to follow their order in exercise 9 and to write in paragraphs.

11 Ask students what types of things they will check in their writing (grammar, spelling, capital letters, and punctuation).

12 Ask students to imagine that they work for the company that has been responsible for their partner's problem, and they received their partner's letter.

Student performance

Students should be able to write a letter of complaint which will have a positive effect on their intended reader.

You can use this checklist to monitor and give feedback or to assess students' performance.

Content	Have students included all the information a reader would expect?
Organization	Have students used paragraphs appropriately? Have students followed the letter format?

I can write a letter of complaint.

Students tick *on my own* if their letter would have a positive effect on their reader. They can tick *with some help* if they have looked at Marcus Page's letter or *Tips for writing …* occasionally.

Early finishers

Students write a second draft of their letter, including any changes suggested by their partner.

Additional material

www.oup.com/elt/result for extra practice activities
www.oup.com/elt/teacher/result for extra teacher resources

Warmer

Remember the places

Write the place names from lessons A–D on the board: *A The High Street, B A supermarket, C Ms Sayles' company, D The camera shop.* Say sentences 1–10 below for students to call out where people were when they said them, or which place they are about.

1 If there's a choice, choose a product with less packaging.
2 We'll repair it free of charge. 3 What have you been doing to sell more sunshades, Winston? 4 Farmer Jones is going to sell the farm.
5 How much do you want to spend? 6 How long have you been working here? 7 People have been queuing to buy them. 8 We're going to lose our customers. 9 Does that include the batteries?
10 Buy a bigger packet if you think you will use it all.

1 B	2 D	3 C	4 A	5 D	6 C	7 C	8 A	9 D	10 B

A Grammar

1 Articles *the, a, an* 10A exercise 7

Warm-up: Ask students for directions to different places near your school. Monitor for the use of articles and direct students to >> **p.97** exercise 6 if necessary.

Set-up: Students read the conversation and say where B's map is.

2 the	3 a	4 an	5 a	6 the	7 the

Follow-up: Students write two short conversations about directions to places from where they are now. They remove the articles and swap with a partner to complete the texts.

2 Quantifiers 10B exercises 9, 10

Warm-up: Write the following words on the board: *food, packaging, packets, people, rain, rubbish, shops, water.* Students decide if they are countable or uncountable.

Set-up: Ask students to read sentences 1–7. Check vocabulary.

2 much	3 little	4 a few	5 many	6 few	7 A lot of

Follow-up: Students prepare a similar exercise and swap with a partner.

3 Present perfect continuous 10C exercise 9

Warm-up: Direct students to A's first two sentences and ask why the present perfect simple is used in the first one, and the present perfect continuous is used in the second one. Direct students to >> **p.101** exercise 9 to revise if necessary.

Set-up: Point out the negative in item 2 and remind students to think about where to put it.

2 've not been going out much	3 've been trying
4 Have (you) been watching	5 've been reading
6 have (you) been doing	7 've been looking

Follow-up: Students talk to three or four other students to find the person who has been the busiest recently.

4 Time and conditional clauses 10D exercise 5

Warm-up: Write the following words on the board: *as, I'll, it, cheap, as, it's, long, buy.* Ask students to make a sentence using all the words. Ask students to rephrase the sentence using *if* and *unless*.

Set-up: Do the example. Remind students that *unless* means *if not.*

2 I won't buy it until I get paid.	3 Start as soon as you're ready.
4 Don't buy it unless you like it.	5 You can leave as soon as it's finished.

Follow-up: In pairs, students write another question for the *Personality Quiz!* on >> **p.102.** They swap with two other pairs.

B Vocabulary

5 Shops 10A exercise 4

Warm-up: Call out the following words from 10B for students to give you the packaging words associated with them: *coffee, biscuits, eggs, milk, yogurt, tomatoes, ketchup, potatoes, toothpaste, margarine.*

Set-up: Go through the instructions and ask students to read clues 1–10. Check vocabulary as necessary.

2 butcher's	3 shopping mall	4 news-stand	5 library
6 market	7 newsagent's	8 bank	9 greengrocer's
10 department store			

Follow-up: Students make anagrams of the names of six types of shops and swap with a partner.

6 Packaging 10B exercises 1, 2

Warm-up: Ask students to find an example of *Packaging words* in the pictures on >> **p.98.**

Set-up: Go through the instructions with the class.

horizontal: packet, bottle, pot   **vertical:** bag, carton, lid, tube, tub
diagonal: can, tin

Follow-up: In pairs, students prepare a similar exercise for another pair. They write five sentences to describe some of the things they can see in one of the pictures on >> **p.98.**

7 Approximate times and amounts 10C exercise 5

Warm-up: Write the words *almost, about,* and *nearly* on the board. Ask *What's the time?* and ask students to say it in three ways, using the words on the board. Elicit other words for approximate times and amounts.

Set-up: Ask students to read sentences 1–5 and say if they are about times or amounts.

2 recently	3 or so	4 nearly	5 about

Follow-up: Students prepare five similar sentences about things they have been doing recently. Four sentences should be true, one false. They swap with a partner and complete the sentences. They ask and answer together to find the false fact.

8 Words connected with buying and selling 10D exercises 10, 11

Warm-up: Put students into pairs to write questions they would ask a shop assistant if they were buying a digital camera. Direct them to audio script 10D.1 on >> **p.157** to check.

Set-up: Ask students to read the tips and check vocabulary.

2 prices	3 guarantee	4 included	5 cost	6 receipt

Follow-up: Direct students to exercises 10 and 11 on >> **p.103** to write three more tips using different vocabulary. Books closed. Students swap sentences and complete them from memory.

Early finishers

Students copy the names of the grammar and vocabulary points in Unit 10 from the *Contents* page. They give themselves a mark out of five for how well they think they can use each one.

Unit 10 Review

A Grammar

1 Articles *the*, *a*, *an* Write *the*, *a*, or *an* in each gap.

A Have you got ¹*a* road map?
B Yes, but it's in ²____ car.
A Oh. I didn't know you had ³____ car.
B Yes – I've got ⁴____ Opel.
A Where do you keep it? Have you got ⁵____ garage?
B No. I park it in ⁶____ street, in front of ⁷____ flat.

2 Quantifiers Complete the sentences with these quantifiers.

a few   ~~a little~~   a lot of   few   little   many   much

1 I always keep *a little* water in a glass by the bed.
2 There's too _____ packaging on supermarket food, and most of it isn't necessary.
3 There's been very _____ rain this year and the river's dried up.
4 There are _____ packets of nuts in the kitchen – help yourself!
5 There are too _____ people in the world and not enough food to feed them.
6 Unfortunately, there are very _____ places to buy fresh fish in my town.
7 _____ the rubbish we produce ends up in the sea.

3 Present perfect continuous Put the verbs in the present perfect continuous.

A I haven't seen you for ages. What ¹*have you been doing* (do) recently?
B Oh, I ²_____ (not go) out much.
  I ³_____ (try) to save money.
A ⁴_____ you _____ (watch) a lot of TV, then?
B Yes, TV and DVDs. And I ⁵_____ (read) a lot, too. And you – ⁶_____ you _____ (do) anything interesting?
A No, not really. Mum's not been very well so I ⁷_____ (look) after her.

4 Time and conditional clauses Write a sentence with the same meaning.

1 I'll buy it as long as it's cheap.   unless
  I won't *buy it unless it's cheap* .
2 I'll buy it as soon as I get paid.   until
  I won't _____ .
3 Start when you're ready.   as soon as
  Start _____ .
4 Buy it if you like it.   unless
  Don't _____ .
5 You can't leave until it finishes.   as soon as
  You can _____ .

B Vocabulary

5 Shops Write the words for these definitions.

1 b*o o k s h o p* You buy books here.
2 b_____'_ You buy meat here.
3 s_____ m_____ An enormous building full of shops.
4 n_____-s_____ You can buy a newspaper here without going inside.
5 l_____ You borrow books here.
6 m_____ People sell things in the street here.
7 n_____a_____'_ You can go inside and buy a newspaper.
8 b_____ You get money here.
9 g_____g_____'_ You can buy fruit and veg here.
10 d_____ s_____ An enormous shop with different departments.

6 Packaging Find the words for these items of packaging.

```
P A C K E T
T R A A Y U
U P R U N B
B O T T L E
A T O P I R
G E N I D N
```

7 Approximate times and amounts Underline the correct time expression in these sentences.

1 Fifty-five minutes is almost /or so /lately an hour.
2 Have you seen the news more or less /recently /about?
3 I've been waiting for half an hour about /or so /lately.
4 It's nearly /recently /or so three o'clock.
5 It takes lately /about /or so an hour to get to the station.

8 Words connected with buying and selling Complete the text with these words.

cost   guarantee   included   prices   receipt   ~~spend~~

Tips for shoppers
– Decide how much you want to ¹*spend* before you begin.
– Compare the ²_____ in at least three different shops.
– Check that the product comes with a ³_____.
– Check if batteries are ⁴_____ in the price.
– Find out how much the extras ⁵_____, e.g. ink for printers.
– Keep your ⁶_____ in case you need to return the product.

The Shakespeare Trail

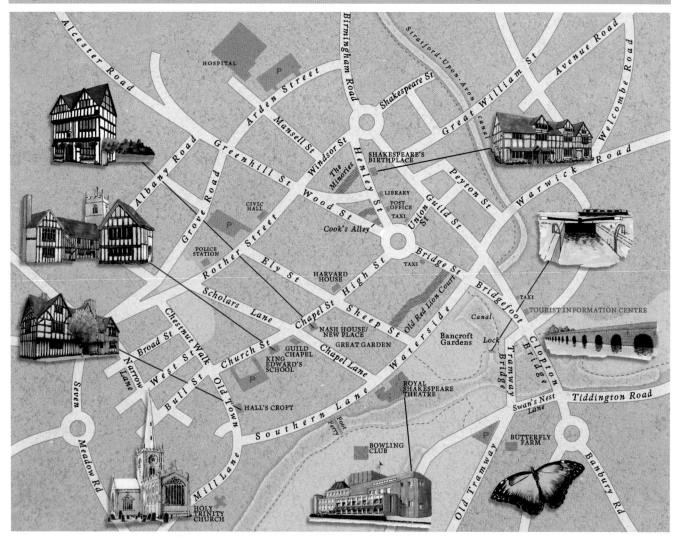

The town made famous as the birthplace of the great playwright, William Shakespeare, Stratford-upon-Avon is one of Britain's most popular tourist destinations. Here you can visit the house where the great poet was born, his old school, the place where he got married, and the house where he died. The best way to see everything is on foot, and on this two-hour walking tour, our expert guides will show you all the points of interest.

The tour will take us past the various homes where Shakespeare and his family lived in Stratford-upon-Avon. The route begins at Shakespeare's parents' home in Henley Street. Shakespeare was born in this house on April 23rd, 1564, and he spent his childhood years here.

From Shakespeare's birthplace, we go down Henley Street, turn right at the roundabout, and go along High Street. At the crossroads, we go straight across and then along Chapel Street, and we come to Nash's House on the left. This was the home of Shakespeare's granddaughter Elizabeth, and it is built next to the site of Shakespeare's own house, New Place. The house is no longer here, but we can still see the Great Garden which belonged to it. Shakespeare bought New Place when he got married and left his parents' house. He died here on April 23rd, 1616.

After visiting Nash's house, we continue along Chapel Street to the crossroads and then go along Church Street. We pass the Guild Chapel and the old grammar school. At the end of Church Street, we turn left and go along Old Town, and we come to Hall's Croft on the left. This was the home of Shakespeare's daughter Susanna.

From Hall's Croft, we continue down the road to Mill Lane and carry on until we reach the Holy Trinity Church. Shakespeare was baptized and also buried at this church. The end point of the Shakespeare trail is our visit to his grave.

How to give and ask about directions

Orientation

Context

In this lesson, students practise using indirect questions to ask politely for travel information.

The tour guide leaflet, *The Shakespeare Trail*, gives historical information about the various places connected with Shakespeare, his family, and his life. Students will mark the route of a tour on the illustrated map of central Stratford-upon-Avon.

Culture note

Indirect questions begin with a polite expression and are followed by a question which has no subject-verb inversion. An English speaker would tend to ask *Can you tell me where the station is?* rather than the more direct *Where's the station?*, especially when speaking to strangers.

Language

Focus grammar	open and closed indirect questions: *Can you tell me/Do you know if (or whether) there's a taxi rank near here?*, *Can you tell me/Do you know where Chapel Street is?*
Focus words	*alley, bridge, canal, dead-end street, ferry, monument, pedestrian street, T-junction, zebra crossing*
Focus phrases	directions: *carry on, continue along, go across, go along, go straight across, keep left, pass, the other side of, turn right,* etc.
Recognition vocabulary	*band stand, baptised, birthplace, bowling club, chapel, coach terminal, grave, guide, lock (canal), memorial, playwright, putting green, route, trail, town council, various*
Recycled language	*bridge, buried, bus stop, car park, chemist, church, coffee shop, crossroads, destination, garden, hall, library, market, museum, post office, restaurant, river, roundabout, school, shopping centre, site, taxi rank, theatre*

Language note

Indirect questions can be either *closed* or *open*. A *closed question*, e.g. *Is there a taxi rank near here?* is one which can be answered in a few words (*yes, no,* or a short phrase). The answer to an open question, e.g. *Where's Chapel Street?* is likely to contain more detail.

End product

In *Put it all together*, students use two versions of the same map to find information about various places.

Preparation

Check the location of the places in exercise 2 so you can help students with the activity. Take pencils and rubbers for students to use for exercise 4. Alternatively, you can copy the map and route onto a transparency to give answers. Take dictionaries to class.

Warmer

Say the names of places near your school. Put students into pairs to decide which direction phrases they would use to help someone find the place.

Write *How to give and ask about directions* on the board.

A Vocabulary the street

1 Put students into pairs, read the instructions, and direct them to pictures 1–5. Check students understand the following vocabulary by asking in which picture they can see *crossroads (3)* and a *zebra crossing (4)*. Do the example as a class and monitor and help as students complete the activity. Ask for answers to pictures 2–5 around the class. Elicit other phrases and check understanding as necessary.

> 2 turn left 3 go straight across at the crossroads
> 4 cross at the zebra crossing 5 go along the street
> **others:** down, up, over, turn right, etc.

2 Go through the instruction and put students into pairs. Say the names of a few streets to familiarize students with the map and do one or two examples as a class. Monitor and help as necessary, encouraging students to dictionaries to check new vocabulary. Give pronunciation practice as necessary.

Extra help

As you go over answers, elicit direction phrases that can be used with each one, e.g. *an alley – along, down, up; a bridge – over, across; a canal – along.* Students say a word and test a partner.

Extra plus

Practise using stress in names of places. Ask *Which of these words is **not** stressed when you say street names? Road, Street, or Lane?* (*Street* isn't stressed; *Lane* and Road *are*.) Model some examples to demonstrate: *Chapel Street, Chapel Lane, Warwick Road, Henley Street, Birmingham Road, Bridge Street, Mill Lane.*

B Read and follow directions

In this section, students read information about a guided tour for gist and detail.

3 Read the question and set a short time limit of about three minutes to encourage students to read for gist.

> People who want to know more about the route of a tour of famous places associated with William Shakespeare.

4 Go through the instructions and direct students to *The Shakespeare Trail* on **>> p.106**. Ask students which words they will focus on to do the activity (*names of streets, places, and direction phrases*). Monitor and help as necessary as students continue the activity. Encourage students to use the pictures on the map to help them guess new vocabulary.

Put students into pairs to compare. Show the route on a transparency, if you have prepared one earlier (see *Preparation*) or go through the tour information with the class.

5 Read the instructions and check students understand the activity. Ask students to find the Holy Trinity Church on the map. Read the first part of the directions and ask students to follow the route. Elicit the next instruction before putting students into pairs to continue. Monitor and help as necessary before putting students together with another pair to compare their answers.

Extra plus

Ask students to find words and phrases with these meanings: *way or path* (trail); *another word for church* (chapel); *the place where a building was or will be* (site); *continue* (carry on); *a place where a body is buried* (grave). Students check answers in their dictionaries.

C Listen and follow directions

In this section, students listen for key words in directions conversations.

6 Go through the instructions and ask students where they start from and where they want to get to. *(Tourist Information Centre, Shakespeare's Birthplace.)*

In pairs, students underline key words which helped them find the place. Monitor and help as necessary. Check answers.

> **key words:** door, right, keep left, Bridgefoot, crossroads, straight across, straight along, Bridge Street, roundabout, straight across, two streets, left, Henley Street, right, up Henley Street, past post office, library, house, right

7 11A.1 Read the instructions and items 1–3. Ask students to listen and find out where the people want to go. Elicit or remind students to focus their listening on key words only and play the audio. Pause the audio after each speaker to give students time to mark the place. Ask them to compare in pairs and play the audio a second time, if necessary. Do not check answers at this point as this will be done in exercise 8.

Teaching tip
Listening to directions is particularly difficult for language learners as there is usually little redundancy in the text. You could pause the audio at points during each conversation. Chunking the text to allow students to process the information bit by bit can help maintain students' motivation.

8 Direct students to audio script 11A.1 on >> p.157 to check their answers. Point out how both speakers repeat place names to check understanding, and give information piece by piece.

> 1 the police station   2 Butterfly Farm   3 the hospital

Extra help
Play the audio again for students to read and listen. They take turns and use the audio script to practise the conversations.

D Grammar indirect questions

9 Point out the section heading and elicit or explain that these are a more polite way of asking somebody to do something.

Direct students to the grammar box and elicit or explain the difference between open and closed questions (see *Language note*). Read both types of open and closed questions, direct and indirect questions, and focus on the difference in word order. For closed questions, point out that *Can you tell me* and *Do you know* can be used interchangeably, and the use of *if* and *whether* (*whether* is used when the expected answer might be *no*). Read the rules and elicit answers.

> 1 closed   2 indirect

10 Read through the instructions and point out or elicit that questions 1–4 are all direct questions. Direct students to look again at the grammar box in exercise 9 and elicit the answer to the first question.

Monitor for accuracy as students continue the activity individually. Ask for volunteers to give answers and the class to say if they agree or not before you give feedback.

> 1 Can you tell me … / Do you know where the Royal Shakespeare Theatre is?   2 Can you tell me if/where … / Do you know if/whether there's a bus stop near here?   3 Can you tell me … / Do you know where the town hall is?   4 Can you tell me if/where … / Do you know if/whether there's a shopping centre near here?

Extra help
Use the indirect questions to do a backchain drill. As a class, students repeat each word starting from the last one and adding one word at a time until they say the whole question, e.g. *T* is *SS* is *T* Street is *SS* Street is *T* Chapel Street is *SS* Chapel Street is, etc.

Extra activity
Books closed. Ask the class direct open and closed questions like those in exercise 10, for students to make them more polite.

11 Read the instructions and ask for two volunteers to read the example conversation. Remind the class that we use *Excuse me, …?* to attract attention. Ask students what they would do if they didn't understand the name of the place their partner wants to go to. *(Ask for repetition or repeat what they think the speaker said to ask for confirmation.)*

Students continue in pairs. Monitor and check that students' instructions are clear and that both students understand each other. Give positive feedback where possible. Ask each pair to choose one of their conversations to act out for the class.

Extra plus
Ask students to make eye contact when they have their conversations, and encourage them to try to do them without looking at the examples.

ABCD Put it all together

12 Go through the instructions and put students into A/B pairs to look at their maps. Check students understand that, for each turn, they choose a number on the map as a starting point and give students time to decide where they will start from for each one.

Student performance
Students should be able to ask for and give explanations.

You can use this checklist to monitor and give feedback or to assess students' performance.

Interaction	Do students use indirect questions to sound polite? exercise 11 Do students check and confirm information when necessary? exercise 11
Vocabulary	Do students use directions phrases accurately? exercise 1

I can give and ask about directions.

Students tick *on my own* if they have asked about and given directions to one or two places without looking at the example conversation in exercise 11 for help. They tick *with some help* if they looked at exercise 11 for help on two or more occasions.

Early finishers
Students take turns to role play being a tourist asking for directions to places in their area. Alternatively, they can repeat the activity starting from different places.

Additional material

www.oup.com/elt/result for extra practice activities
www.oup.com/elt/teacher/result for extra teacher resources

How to give and ask about directions

G indirect questions   V the street

A Vocabulary the street

1 Work with a partner and decide how to give these directions. What other words and phrases do you know for giving directions?

Example   1 turn right

2 Work with a partner. Look at the map opposite and find these things.

an alley   a bridge   a canal   a car park   a crossroads
a dead-end street   a path   a pedestrian street
a roundabout   a taxi rank   a T-junction

B Read and follow directions

3 Read **The Shakespeare Trail** opposite. Who do you think the text was written for?

4 Read **The Shakespeare Trail** again and draw the route on the map. Compare with a partner.

5 Work with a partner. Explain the route in the opposite direction – from the Holy Trinity Church to Shakespeare's birthplace. Compare with another pair.
   Example   Go along Mill lane. Then continue along Old Town, past Hall's Croft ...

C Listen and follow directions

6 Follow these directions from the tourist information centre. Where do they take you? Underline the key words with a partner.

Go out of the door and turn right. Keep left, along Bridgefoot until you come to a crossroads. Go straight across, and straight along Bridge Street and you'll come to a roundabout. If you go straight across, there are two streets – one on the left and Henley Street on the right. Go up Henley Street, past the post office and the library and you'll see the house on the right.

7 **11A.1▶** Three tourists have asked for directions. Listen and find out where they want to go.
   1 Paola's at the Royal Shakespeare Theatre. She wants to go to ...
   2 Ignacio's at Harvard House. He wants to go to ...
   3 Laura's at the Bowling Club. She wants to go to ...

8 Read the audio script on ≫ p.157 and check your answers.

D Grammar indirect questions

9 Complete the grammar box and underline the correct words in the rules.

	direct question	indirect question (more polite)
open	Where's Chapel street?	Can you tell me where Chapel Street is?
		Do you know where Mill Lane is?
closed	Is there a taxi rank near here?	Can you tell me if (or whether) there's a taxi rank near here?
		Do you know if there's a shopping centre near here?

Rules
1 Use *if* in open/closed questions.
2 To be more polite, use direct/indirect questions.

10 Make these questions more polite with *Can you tell me* or *Do you know*.
   1 Where's the Royal Shakespeare Theatre?
   2 Is there a bus stop near here?
   3 Where's the town hall?
   4 Is there a shopping centre near here?

11 Work with a partner. Ask about places on **The Shakespeare Trail** map.
   Student A   Ask politely where a street or place is.
   Student B   Answer and point to it on the map.
   Examples   A Excuse me, can you tell me where Chapel Street is?
               B Yes, it's here.
               A Excuse me, do you know if there's a taxi rank near here?
               B Yes, there's one here.

More practice? **Grammar Bank** ≫ p.146.

ABCD Put it all together

12 Work with a partner. Above your map, there is a list of six places you want to find. Ask your partner for directions. For each turn, start from a different number on the map.
   Student A   Look at the map on ≫ p.132.
   Student B   Look at the map on ≫ p.135.

I can give and ask about directions.

Tick ✓ the line.   with a lot of help   with some help   on my own   very easily

Accommodation adjectives

comfortable /ˈkʌmftəbl/   delicious /dɪˈlɪʃəs/   delightful /dɪˈlaɪtfl/   efficient /ɪˈfɪʃnt/
elegant /ˈelɪgənt/   friendly /ˈfrendli/   magnificent /mægˈnɪfɪsnt/   secluded /sɪˈkluːdɪd/

Punta Paloma
Resort

1 *Punta Paloma* is a luxury nature resort, located on Honduras's Caribbean coast only one hour from La Ceiba International Airport. It is set in the magnificent rainforest of the Punta Paloma National Park. At *Punta Paloma* we offer service with a smile from the moment you arrive. You will be greeted with a welcome cocktail while your luggage is collected from your car. Then you will be taken to your secluded guest cabin hidden among the coffee and cacao trees.

2 In *Punta Paloma*, **you** decide. Enjoy delicious Central-American cuisine in our elegant restaurant with views of the Bay Islands, or have your dinner served in the garden. Relax in our comfortable terrace bar, or have your drinks served by the pool. Choose from a delightful selection of fresh food at our breakfast buffet, or have breakfast brought to your room.

3 There's plenty to do during your stay at *Punta Paloma*. Follow forest paths through the hotel grounds and into the national park. Our guides will help you identify the exotic local birds and wildlife. Go riding, whitewater rafting, or snorkelling on the coral reefs. Take a day trip to the ancient ruins of Copán and have your photo taken beside a Mayan temple. Or simply relax by the pool!

4 At *Punta Paloma*, you will find the hotel staff friendly, efficient, and ready to help in any way. You only have to ask! Have your hair cut and styled by a qualified hairdresser. Have your clothes washed and ironed overnight. Have international newspapers brought to your room. Or simply hang out the 'Do not disturb' sign and enjoy the peace and quiet.

5 *Whether you're looking for sport, nature, peace, or comfort, Punta Paloma is your ideal holiday choice.*

Fish Head Inn

The **Fish Head Inn** is a run-down old guest house, located on the coast of Cumbria in north-west England, only four hours from Manchester International Airport. It is set in a desolate seaside resort only a couple of miles from the Sellafield Nuclear Power Station. When you arrive at the **Fish Head Inn**, you will have to ring five times at reception before anybody notices you. Then you will be given a key and you will have to carry your own bags up the narrow stairs to a room in the attic.

At the **Fish Head Inn**, you eat what you're given. Usually, it's a slice of pork with cold mashed potato. If you don't like it, there is a fish and chip shop just down the road. Breakfast is served from 7.30 until 8.00, and don't be late or you'll get nothing. You can have it in your room, but you'll have to fetch it yourself.

There's very little to do during your stay at the **Fish Head Inn**. Walk on the windy beach, visit the abandoned church, or have your photo taken in front of the nuclear power station. Or simply stay in bed and wait till it's time to leave!

At the **Fish Head Inn**, don't expect any help from the hotel staff. If you want anything, you'll have to do it yourself. We don't employ any cleaning staff, so we ask guests to wash their own sheets before leaving. And if anyone can fix the dripping taps, that would be much appreciated!

Whether you're looking for bad weather, desolate scenery, greasy food, or polite self-service, the *Fish Head Inn* is your perfect choice.

How to talk about holiday accommodation

Orientation

Context

In this lesson, students practise using *have something done* to talk about hotel services.

The two advertisements describe the location, meals, activities, and services available at two different hotels. The second advertisement, *Fish Head Inn*, is a joke.

In *Accommodation adjectives*, the phonetic transcriptions show pronunciation which is not always obvious from the spelling.

Language

Focus grammar	*to have something done*
Preview grammar	*have to – obligation*
Focus words	*chefs, comfortable, delicious, delightful, documents, efficient, elegant, finest, friendly, luxury, magnificent, perfect, qualified, safe, service, secluded, valuables*
Recognition vocabulary	words: *abandoned, appreciated, buffet, coral reefs, desolate, greeted, ideal, nuclear power station, rainforest, selection, snorkelling, temple, terrace* phrases: *dripping taps, hang out, hotel grounds, run-down, service with a smile, welcome cocktail, white water rafting*
Recycled language	words: *ancient ruins, attic, bring, church, cuisine, day-trip, fetch, forest paths, guide, luggage, narrow, national park, riding, pool, seaside resort, sightseeing, wildlife, youth hostel* phrases: *greasy food* grammar: *comparatives; conditionals*

Language note

Many words show people's emotions or feeling towards what the word refers to. The vocabulary items in *Accommodation adjectives* all have a positive connotation.

End product

In *Put it all together*, students describe accommodation to others in their group. They can use their notes. They decide which hotel they would like to visit.

Preparation

Read the *Teaching tip* before exercise 3 and decide if you would like to use the texts on >> **p.108** for a jigsaw reading activity. Think about classroom organization for the group work in exercises 2 and 16. Take dictionaries to class.

Warmer

Write the words *holidays* and *tourism* on the board. Elicit the difference and put students into groups to talk about the types of places they stay in and the things they do on holiday or when they visit foreign places. Ask for volunteers to tell others about any interesting or different holiday or travel experiences.

Write *How to talk about holiday accommodation* on the board.

A Vocabulary describing holiday accommodation

1 Put students into pairs. Go through the example vocabulary and check meaning. Set a time limit of about three minutes for students to brainstorm vocabulary. Elicit suggestions around the class and write any new vocabulary on the board.

2 Read through the instructions. Direct students to *Accommodation adjectives* on >> **p.108**. Ask if the words are positive or negative. *(Positive.)* Students continue in pairs.

Put students into groups of four to compare suggestions. Elicit suggestions for each word and check students understand the general meaning of the adjectives. Use the phonetic transcriptions on >> **p.108** and give extra pronunciation practice as necessary.

> **comfortable** (a good, physical feeling): chair, bathroom, sofa **delicious** (a great taste or smell): food, coffee **delightful** (a feeling of happiness or enjoyment): food, people, room **efficient** (quickly, organized): service, staff **elegant** (attractive appearance): furniture, room, restaurant **friendly:** guests, staff **magnificent** (beautiful, to be admired): gardens, hotel building **secluded** (quiet, away from people): hotel, building

Extra help

Check students understand the adjectives by using the brief definitions given above.

Teaching tip

If students are keeping vocabulary notebooks, suggest they write several examples of noun phrases in which the same adjective is used to describe similar things.

B Read holiday accommodation adverts

In this section, students read two holiday adverts for gist and detail.

Teaching tip

You can use the two texts as a jigsaw reading. Ask A students to read *Punta Paloma* and Bs to read *Fish Head Inn*. Ask students to make notes about the service, activities, and meals, using their dictionaries to help with vocabulary. Monitor and help as necessary. Put students into A/B pairs to do exercise 7.

3 Direct students to *Punta Paloma Resort* on >> **p.108**. Read the introduction and check vocabulary. Ask students to underline words which helped them decide on the title. Check answers

> 2 meals   3 activities   4 service   5 summary

4 Do questions 1–2 as a class. Guide students to the answer, if necessary, by giving different options, e.g. question 1, suggest *a worker or a guest*; question 2, suggest *entertain or inform*.

Read question 3 and elicit one or two examples to check students understand. Put students into pairs and monitor and help as students continue. Nominate different students to give examples, encouraging them to use the vocabulary in *Accommodation adjectives*.

> 1 a guest   2 to inform   3 magnificent, service with a smile, welcome cocktail, secluded, delicious, elegant, delightful, exotic, friendly, efficient, ready to help in any way, enjoy, ideal

5 Direct students to *Fish Head Inn* on **» p.108** and set a short time limit for students to read for gist. Elicit suggestions.

> The location in the photo doesn't look attractive, nobody would choose to stay here for a holiday. The place doesn't sound attractive, it sounds difficult to get to, the location is not nice, the food is boring, the service doesn't sound friendly, there's nothing to do, the weather doesn't sound good.

6 Go through the instructions and the example. Make sure students understand why *only four hours from Manchester* is bad. *(The hotel isn't within easy reach of the airport.)* Monitor and help, encouraging students to guess the meaning of unknown words and phrases. To check answers, go through each paragraph and ask for volunteers to read phrases or sentences.

> **Example answers**
> **paragraph 1:** You'll have to carry your own bags up …
> **paragraph 2:** If you don't like it, there's a fish and chip shop just down the road.   **paragraph 3:** There's very little to do during your stay …   **paragraph 4:** … don't expect any help from the hotel staff.

7 Put students into pairs and read the example. Encourage them to use vocabulary in *Accommodation adjectives*. Monitor and give positive feedback for interesting comparisons. Ask each pair to give one comparison.

C Grammar *to have something done*

8 Direct students to the pictures and ask them to match them with sentences 1 and 2. Go through the rule as a class. Copy the sentence *I had my photo taken.* onto the board, and elicit the names for the following parts of the structure: the infinitive *have*, the noun, and the past participle. Point out that the subject of the sentence is *I* and the sentence contains no information about who did the activity.

> 1 b   2 a   **Rule:** subject + *have* + object + **past participle**

9 Read the instructions and elicit or explain that *sth* is the dictionary abbreviation for *something*. Direct students to *Punta Paloma Resort* to complete the activity. Monitor and help as students complete the activity individually, directing them to the *Irregular verbs* on **» p.148** and information in their dictionaries if they need to check past participles.

Students compare in pairs before you check answers.

> have your dinner/drinks served; have breakfast brought; have your photo taken; have your hair cut and styled; have your clothes washed and ironed; have international newspapers brought

10 Direct students to look at the advert for *The Hotel Paris* and check vocabulary. Ask them to look at the nouns in each line and the verbs which follow. Elicit or point out that the sentence halves are mixed up.

Do one or two examples to demonstrate that students must think about the nouns and verbs to do the activity. Monitor and help as students continue individually. To check answers, say a number for students to say the whole sentence.

> 2 h   3 a   4 f   5 g   6 d   7 e   8 b

Extra help
Test a partner. Student A says a number, Students B says the sentence. Students then swap roles.

11 Ask students to read sentences 1–5 and check vocabulary. Go through the example and elicit or explain that the subject of the verb *(builders)* is omitted from the *have something done* sentence. Monitor and check for accuracy as students continue individually. Nominate students to give answers.

> 2 I have my car serviced once a year.   3 I had my back teeth taken out when I was a child.   4 I had my breakfast brought to my room. 5 I'm going to have my computer repaired.

Extra help
Students say sentences 1–5 in the past and with *going to* future.

D Listen for detail

In this section, students listen to a conversation for gist and detail.

12 11B.1 Read the instructions and play the audio. Ask a volunteer for the answer and check the class agrees. Play the audio a second time if necessary.

> Because she stayed there last year.

13 Put students into pairs and read questions 1–3. Tell students to look at the text to underline words and phrases as they hear them. Play the audio. Students compare answers in pairs. Play the audio again if necessary. Direct students to audio script 11B.1 on **» p.158** to check parts of the text they have underlined and ask for volunteers to answer questions 2 and 3.

> 1 Caribbean coast, rainforest, national park, secluded cabins, cuisine, garden, breakfast, the pool, the staff, having clothes washed   2 There's nothing to do during the day.   3 Probably not.

14 Read the instructions and put students into pairs to plan a similar conversation for the *Fish Head Inn*. They can use the topics from *The Hotel Paris* in exercise 10. Monitor and give positive feedback as students have their conversations. Ask for volunteers to have their conversations for the class.

ABCD Put it all together

15 Go through the instructions and monitor and help students with ideas if necessary. Remind students to use the vocabulary in *Accommodation adjectives*. Give them time to rehearse.

16 Put students into small groups to describe their accommodation. At the end of the activity, ask for volunteers to tell the class about the best and worst place.

Student performance
Students should be able to give a short description.

You can use this checklist to monitor and give feedback or to assess students' performance.

Content	Do students talk about all the topics? exercise 14
Grammar	Do students use *to have something done* appropriately? exercise 14
Vocabulary	Do students use a variety of adjectives? exercise 2

I can talk about holiday accommodation.

Students tick *on my own* if they have done the activity using their notes. They tick *with some help* if they looked at *Accommodation adjectives* once or twice.

Early finishers
In pairs, students give their descriptions without using their notes. Their partner ticks the topics in exercise 10 they talk about.

Additional material

www.oup.com/elt/result for extra practice activities
www.oup.com/elt/teacher/result for extra teacher resources

How to talk about holiday accommodation

G *to have something done*   V describing holiday accommodation

A **Vocabulary** describing holiday accommodation

1 Work with a partner. Make a list of words connected with holidays and tourism.
Example   seaside resort; sightseeing; youth hostel ...

2 Look at **Accommodation adjectives** opposite. What things could these adjectives describe? You can use a dictionary. Compare ideas with another pair.
Example   comfortable – room, lounge, bed ...

B Read holiday accommodation adverts

3 Read **Punta Paloma Resort** opposite. Match the paragraphs with these titles.
- [ ] activities
- [ ] service
- [1] introduction
- [ ] meals
- [ ] summary

4 Answer the questions with a partner.
1 Who is the text written for?
2 What is the purpose of the text?
3 How does the writer make the place sound attractive? Underline positive words and phrases.

5 Read **Fish Head Inn** opposite. How do you know it's a joke? Compare with a partner.

6 How does the writer make the place sound bad? Find one or more phrases in each paragraph.
Example   They say 'it's only four hours from Manchester'.

7 Talk to a partner. Compare the **Punta Paloma Resort** and the **Fish Head Inn**.
Example   The Punta Paloma Resort is in a rainforest, but the Fish Head Inn is in a seaside resort.

C **Grammar** *to have something done*

8 Match these pictures with the sentences. Underline the correct word in the rule.

1 [ ] I took my photo.
2 [ ] I had my photo taken.

Rule to have something done = subject + *have* + object + infinitive/past/past participle

9 Underline seven examples of the *to have sth done* form in **Punta Paloma Resort**. Compare with a partner.

10 In this advert, the text is mixed up. Match beginnings 1–8 with endings a–h.
Example   1 – c

THE HOTEL PARIS

WE OFFER THE BEST SERVICE

[1]Have your meals	[a]put in the hotel safe.
[2]Have your breakfast	[b]parked by our driver.
[3]Have your valuables	[c]cooked by Paris's finest chefs.
[4]Have your hair	[d]translated into perfect French.
[5]Have your clothes	[e]taken on top of the Eiffel Tower.
[6]Have your documents	[f]cut by a qualified hairdresser.
[7]Have your photograph	[g]washed and ironed overnight.
[8]Have your car	[h]brought to your room.

ENJOY YOUR STAY!

11 Rewrite these sentences using the *to have sth done* form. Keep the same tense as the original sentence.
1 My parents are paying some builders to decorate their house.   *My parents are having their house decorated.*
2 I pay a mechanic to service my car once a year.
3 A dentist took out my back teeth when I was a child.
4 Ask room service to bring breakfast to your room.
5 I'm going to pay a technician to repair my computer.

More practice? **Grammar Bank** >> p.146.

D Listen for detail

12 11B.1▶ Listen to a conversation between Claire and Ian. Why does she mention the Punta Paloma Resort?

13 Listen again and answer the questions with a partner.
1 What things in the **Punta Paloma Resort** text does Claire mention? Underline them.
2 What thing in the text does she disagree with?
3 Do you think Ian will go to the hotel?

14 Work with a partner. Look at the audio script on >> p.158. Have a similar conversation about the **Fish Head Inn**.

ABCD Put it all together

15 Choose a hotel or other holiday accommodation where you have stayed – good or bad. Make notes about the location, the meals, the activities, and the service.

16 Work in groups. Describe your accommodation and the services offered to the others. Listen to the others in the group. Which hotel would you like to visit?

I can talk about holiday accommodation.

Tick ✓ the line.   with a lot of help   with some help   on my own   very easily

109

Health Precautions

THINK BEFORE YOU TRAVEL!

- Are there any **injections** that you need to have?
- Will you have to show any **vaccination certificates**?
- Are there any **pills** that you need to take?
- Do you need to take out **medical insurance**?
- Should you drink the **tap water**?
- Are there any **local foods** that you ought to avoid?
- Do you need to take **sun block**?
- Should you carry a **first aid kit**?
- Will you need to take **insect repellent**?
- Should you carry a **mosquito net**?
- What should you do in an **emergency**?

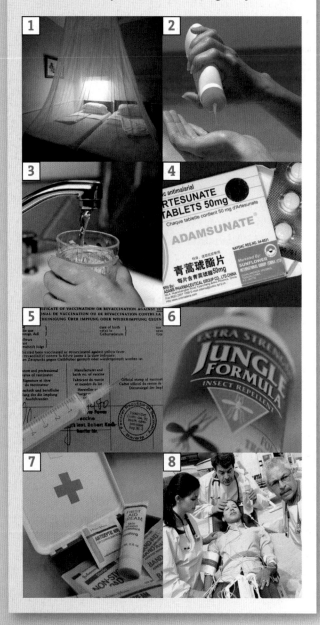

Ask the doctor

Dear Dr Sharma

I've just been to Ibiza for a week. I'd been very busy at work and I really needed to relax. But when I was there, I had a really bad cold. I had to stay in bed and my boyfriend had to look after me! I think I caught my cold on the flight. I've heard that people often catch colds on planes. Is that true, and if so, what can we do about it?

Tracey Williams

Dear Tracey

Yes, it's true. You have 100 times more chance of catching a cold on a plane than in your normal life. We're not sure why, but it's probably because the air is very dry on board. You can catch a cold more easily when your nose and throat are dry. And of course, there are a lot of people in a small space so germs don't have to travel far from one person to the next. But don't worry, you don't need to cancel your next holiday. Here are some simple things you can do to avoid aeroplane colds:

- DRINK WATER. In dry air, your body loses water so you need to replace it. You don't have to drink a lot, but you should drink little and often to keep your throat wet. Tea is also good because the steam goes up your nose and makes it less dry. But you shouldn't drink coffee or alcohol because these make your body drier.

- WASH YOUR HANDS. You catch more colds from touching than breathing. A cold or flu virus can live for several hours on an aeroplane seat or tray table. From there, the virus can pass to your hand and then your mouth. So ideally, you ought to wash your hands before eating snacks and meals. If you can't get out from your seat, you should clean your hands with disinfectant tissues.

- CLEAN YOUR MOUTH. Ideally, you ought to use a mouthwash to kill the germs before they act. However, you will need to go to the bathroom to use the mouthwash – not very convenient if you're in a window seat. Also, you'll need to check the rules for hand luggage – you won't be allowed to take a large bottle of mouthwash onto the plane.

- WEAR A FACE MASK. If you are really worried, you should think about wearing a mask. These can stop germs reaching your mouth and nose – but of course, people may look at you strangely!

Finally, remember that if you are travelling with a cold, you shouldn't pass on your germs to the other passengers. Cover your mouth when you cough and don't touch people – by shaking hands, for example. But hopefully, you won't have a cold the next time you fly!

How to give health advice

Orientation

Context

In this lesson, students practise using modal verbs to give advice.

The leaflet, *Health Precautions* on >> p.110, lists the types of health-related questions people should think about before they travel. These are illustrated in photos 1–8.

Ask the doctor is a website advice page. Dr Sharma answers Tracey's questions and gives detailed advice. He uses the generic *you*, which is typical in tips and advice. The doctor does not mean that these things apply only to Tracey, but to people in general.

Language

Focus grammar	*have to, need to, should, ought to*
Focus words	*certificates, emergency, first aid kit, injections, insect repellent, medical insurance, mosquito net, pills, sun block, tap water, vaccination*
Recognition vocabulary	words: *cough, disinfectant, flu, germs, ideally, mouthwash, precautions, steam, tissues, throat, travellers' cheques, tray table* phrases: *in advance, catch a cold, get up and go, health risk, loses water, 100 times more chance* grammar: *conditionals*
Recycled language	words: *busy, cancel, cash, documents, face, flight, guide books, luggage, mask, meals, passengers, passport, rules, snacks, virus* phrases: *a lot of, less, little, probably*
Pronunciation	main sentence stress 11C.1
Discourse	linkers: *also, and, because, but, finally, however, so*

End product

In *Put it all together*, students discuss statements about different attitudes and ways of preparing to travel. They work with a different partner or group, describing the type of holiday they have planned, and ask for advice.

Preparation

Familiarize yourself with the two stages of *Travel advice* on >> p.132 so you can help students as necessary in exercise 16. Think about classroom organization for both stages of the activity for *Put it all together*. Take dictionaries to class.

Warmer

Write *What kind of traveller are you?* on the board. Ask students to put the following descriptions of types of travellers in order: *I don't prepare for holidays in advance. I always get travel insurance before I travel. I always visit a health centre before I go to exotic countries.* Put students into pairs or small groups to compare their list and ask for volunteers to explain their order to the class. Encourage students to respond to each other's statements, saying if they agree or disagree and why and why not.

Write *How to give health advice* on the board.

A Vocabulary health and travel

1   Read questions 1 and 2 and check vocabulary. Monitor and join in students' conversations as they discuss in pairs, encouraging them to give details. Bring the class together and ask for volunteers to report their answers.

2   Direct students to *Health Precautions* on >> p.110. Ask students what type of document it is. *A letter, an information leaflet, or a newspaper article? (An information leaflet.)* Read the questions and set a short time limit for students to read quickly for gist, ignoring new vocabulary at this stage. Ask for a volunteer to suggest an answer and see if the class agrees. Do not correct for accuracy at this stage, but help students get their ideas across.

> Ways to avoid future problems and dangers.

Extra help

If students are finding this difficult, write these alternatives on the board: *ways to avoid future problems and dangers; problems you have when you travel; things you should do if you get ill* and ask them to choose the most appropriate answer.

3   Direct students to photos 1–8 on >> p.110 and ask them to find the names for the items. Use the example to show that the words they need are in bold in *Health Precautions*. To check answers, say the photo number for the class to say the answers.

> 2 sun block   3 tap water   4 (malaria) pills   5 injections;
> vaccination certificates   6 insect repellent   7 first aid kit
> 8 emergency

4   Read the instructions and put students into pairs to exchange information. Tell students to give details about the type of place, e.g. seaside, mountains, and the season of travel. Monitor and encourage students to say why. Ask for examples.

Extra help

Test a partner. Student A says a photo number, Student B says what it is. Students swap roles.

Extra plus

Students use the photos to test each other on the vocabulary from memory.

B Pronunciation the main stress in a sentence

5   11C.1 Direct students to the questions in *Health Precautions* and read the instructions. Play the audio and pause for students to repeat the questions. Give extra practice as necessary.

Teaching tip

The whole word or compound noun is in bold rather than just the stressed syllable. This is because analysing syllable stress here would distract attention from main sentence stress.

6   Read items 1–3 and check understanding. Ask students to look at photo 1 and the corresponding precaution in *Health Precautions*. Guide students to the answer items 1–3 for *Should you carry a **mosquito net**?* Monitor and help as students continue answering the questions for each precaution. Check answers. Play audio script 11C.1 again if necessary.

> 1 False.   2 True.   3 True.

7 **11C.2** Read the instructions and questions 1–4. Check vocabulary. Monitor and help as students continue individually, before playing the audio to check answers. Play the audio a second time for students to repeat. Give extra practice if necessary.

> 1 passport   2 documents   3 guide books   4 travellers' cheques

8 Put students into pairs to do the activity. Monitor for accurate sentence stress and give positive feedback.

C Read for the main points

In this section, students read a website article for the main points and detail.

9 Read the questions and put students into pairs to discuss. Monitor and encourage students to give examples. Ask volunteers to tell the class.

10 Direct students to *Ask the doctor* on **>> p.110**. Ask *Who's writing? (Tracey Williams.) Who's she writing to? (Dr Sharma.) Why? (She wants advice.)*

Read the instructions and set a short time limit for students to scan the doctor's answer to find the two reasons. Encourage students to guess the meaning of new vocabulary as they read. Elicit answers around the class.

> The air is very dry and you can catch a cold more easily. There are lots of people sitting close together.

11 Read summaries a–c. Direct students to *Ask the doctor* and ask them to read it again to choose the best summary. Ask about each alternative and elicit some examples of what people can do to make flying more healthy.

> b You can drink water, wash your hands, clean your mouth, wear a face mask.

12 Direct students to the table and go through the information in each column to check vocabulary. Students continue the activity individually. Encourage them to use their dictionaries. Monitor and help as necessary. Put students into pairs to compare before checking answers as a class.

> **washing your hands:** catch cold from touching, getting out of your seat   **using a mouthwash:** kill germs, going to the bathroom, hand luggage rules   **wearing a mask:** stop germs, look funny

Extra activity

Ask for volunteers to tell the class about a time they or someone they know was ill after a flight.

D Grammar *have to, need to, should, ought to*

13 Read the instructions and ask students to read sentences 1–8. Check vocabulary. Go through the example with the class to demonstrate the activity, pointing out the verbs in the heading. Monitor and help as necessary. Ask for volunteers to give answers and see if the class agrees.

> 2 I needed to relax.   3 You don't need to cancel your next holiday.   4 ... you should drink ...   5 ... you shouldn't drink coffee ...   6 ... you ought to wash ...   7 you will need to go ... 8 you shouldn't pass on ...

14 Go through the instructions and put students into pairs to answer the questions. Go over the answers to each of the questions as you work through the activities.

For question 1, item a, guide students to the answers to item 2 and 6 in exercise 13. Ask them to find other examples of *need*

to and *ought to* and other examples in *Ask the doctor*. For item b, guide students to item 1 and 5 in exercise 13 and repeat the activity. Monitor and help as students continue the activity. For question 2, go through the example and ask students to continue in pairs. For question 3, check students understand the question and monitor and help as necessary.

> 1 a *need to* is used to talk about something you want or you think is necessary; *ought to* is used when we want to explain the correct or best thing to do, what is right or appropriate.
> 1 b *have to* is used to express an obligation (or not) to do something; *shouldn't* is used to give strong advice or talk about strong obligation.
> 2 b You don't need to ...   c You shouldn't ...
> 3 need – needed (*need* can be a full or modal verb)

15 Ask students to read items 1–6 and check vocabulary. Go through the example to demonstrate the activity. Monitor and check for accuracy as students continue individually. Nominate students to give answers and monitor for correct sentence stress. Elicit reasons as you check answers.

> 2 You don't need to print your ticket.   3 You ought to buy a guide book.   4 You shouldn't carry lots of cash.   5 You have to take your passport.   6 You don't have to take a lot of luggage.

Extra help

Put students into pairs to decide a country or place to travel to. They ask and give each other advice using the words in bold in *Health Precautions* and the travel tips in exercise 15.

Extra plus

Put students into pairs to think about advice they would give to a person who is going climbing in the Alps; to be a volunteer in Africa; camping in Scotland; who thinks they're getting 'flu.

ABCD Put it all together

16 Direct students to *Travel advice* on **>> p.132** and go through statements 1–5 to check vocabulary. Ask students to tick the statements they agree with before discussing in small groups.

Read the instructions for the second part of the activity and tell students to choose two holidays. Students work with a different partner or group to ask for and give advice.

Student performance

Students should be able to make short statements and support them with reasons.

You can use this checklist to monitor and give feedback or to assess students' performance.

Grammar	Do students use a variety of modal verbs? exercise 15
Vocabulary	Do students use a variety of health and travel words? exercise 4
Pronunciation	Do students try to use main sentence stress? exercise 8

I can **give health advice.**

Students tick *on my own* if they have given two or three pieces of advice without looking at *Health Precautions*. They tick *with some help* if they have looked at *Health Precautions* once or twice.

Early finishers

Students repeat the activity for a different holiday.

Additional material

www.oup.com/elt/result for extra practice activities
www.oup.com/elt/teacher/result for extra teacher resources

How to give health advice

have to, need to, should, ought to   **v** health and travel   **P** the main stress in a sentence

A Vocabulary health and travel

1 Answer the questions with a partner.
   1 What are the main health risks when you travel?
   2 Have you ever been ill on holiday?

2 Read **Health Precautions** opposite. What do you think *precautions* are? Discuss with a partner.

3 Find the words for photos 1–8.
   Example 1 = mosquito net

4 Which of the precautions should visitors to your country follow? Compare your answers with a partner.

B Pronunciation the main stress in a sentence

5 **11C.1▶** Listen and repeat the questions in **Health Precautions**. Remember to put stress on the word or phrase in **bold**.

6 Look at **Health Precautions** again. Read 1–3 and write *true* or *false*.
   The main stress in the sentence is …
   1 always at the end of the sentence.
   2 usually at the end of the sentence.
   3 on the most important word or phrase in the sentence.

7 **11C.2▶** Where do you think the main stress will be in these questions? Underline the word or phrase. Then listen, check, and repeat.
   1 Do you need to carry your passport?
   2 Are there any documents that you need?
   3 Are there any guide books I should buy?
   4 Should you take travellers' cheques?

8 Work with a partner. Take turns to read the sentences in **Health Precautions**. Does your partner use main sentence stress?

C Read for the main points

9 Do you often travel by plane, and do you enjoy it? Why/Why not? Tell a partner.

10 Read **Ask the doctor** opposite and find two reasons why flying is unhealthy.

11 Choose the best summary of the doctor's reply to Tracey.
   a Yes, there is a problem, and there's nothing you can do about it.
   b Yes, there is a problem, but there are things you can do about it.
   c No, there's no problem, and you shouldn't worry about it.

12 Write notes to complete the table. Compare with a partner.

action	Why?	problems and difficulties
drinking	keeps nose, throat wet	alcohol, coffee – dry out body
washing your hands		
using a mouthwash		
wearing a mask		

D Grammar *have to, need to, should, ought to*

13 Find sentences or phrases in **Ask the doctor** with the same meaning as these.
   1 It was necessary for me to stay in bed.
      I had to stay in bed.
   2 It was necessary for me to relax.
   3 It isn't necessary to cancel.
   4 It's a good idea to drink.
   5 It isn't a good idea to drink coffee.
   6 It's a good idea to wash your hands.
   7 It'll be necessary to go to the bathroom.
   8 It isn't a good idea to pass on your germs.

14 Work with a partner. Answer the questions.
   1 What's the difference between these pairs of sentences? (Clue: look at the phrases in green in exercise 13.)
      a You need to wash your hands./You ought to wash your hands.
      b You don't have to drink a lot./You shouldn't drink a lot.
   2 What are the negative forms of these verbs?
      a You have to   *You don't have to*
      b You need to
      c You should
   3 Look at your answers to exercise 13. Which of the verbs have past tense forms and what are they?

15 Write travel tips with these words.
   1 not/have/get a visa   *You don't have to get a visa.*
   2 not/need/print your ticket
   3 ought/buy/guide book
   4 should/not/carry lots of cash
   5 have/take/passport
   6 not/have/take a lot of luggage

   More practice? **Grammar Bank** » p.146.

ABCD Put it all together

16 Look at **Travel advice** on » p.132. Work in pairs or small groups and give each other holiday advice.

I can give health advice.

Tick ✓ the line.   with a lot of help   with some help   on my own   very easily

Travel problems

run out	of petrol	of money	
miss	your plane	your stop	your turning
lose	your wallet	your way	your ticket
get	lost	stuck	stopped for speeding
have	a flat tyre	a breakdown	an accident

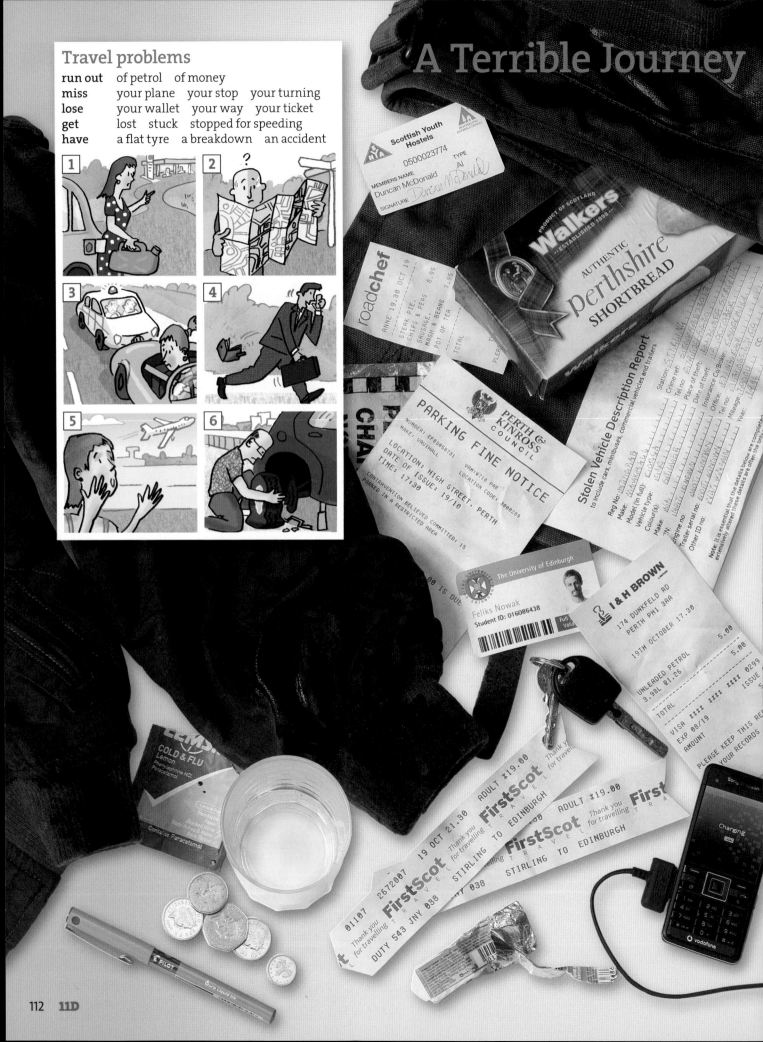

How to give extra information

Orientation

Context

In this lesson, students practise talking about journeys using non-defining relative clauses.

Travel problems gives common verb phrases using *run out, miss, lose, get,* and *have*. The phrases related to car journeys are illustrated in pictures 1–6.

The photos in *A Terrible Journey* tell the story of a difficult journey and provide additional information about the people, the places, the weather, and the problems.

Language

Focus grammar	*non-defining relative clauses*
Focus phrases	*get lost, get stopped for speeding, get stuck, have an accident, have a breakdown, have a flat tyre, lose your way, miss your turning, run out of petrol, etc.*
Recognition vocabulary	words: *shortbread (biscuits), spare (extra), unfair* phrases: *in the middle of nowhere, stolen vehicle report, no-parking zone*
Recycled language	*annoying, bus tickets, cold, flatmate, ID card, membership card, mobile phone, receipt, set off, youth hostel*
Pronunciation	*non-defining relative clauses* 11D.2

End product

In *Put it all together*, students use their notes to tell others in a group about a bad journey they have had. They can ask for help with words they can't remember, based on audio script 11D.1.

Preparation

Read the *Teaching tip* and familiarize yourself with audio script 11D.1 if you want to do the alternative activity for exercise 3. Think about classroom organization for the group work in *Put it all together*, exercise 15.

Warmer

Put students into small groups and set a short time limit of about three minutes for them to brainstorm the types of problems people can have when they travel by car. Elicit suggestions and write them on the board.

Write *who, where, what, when, why,* and *how* on the board and ask students to tell each other if they or someone they know has had any of the problems.

Write *How to give extra information* on the board.

A Vocabulary travel problems

1 Direct students to pictures 1–6 in *Travel problems* on **» p.112**. Ask them to describe them using the verbs and nouns in the vocabulary panel. Go through the example to demonstrate the activity and monitor and help as necessary. Ask for volunteers to give answers and check the class agrees.

> 2 get lost   3 get stopped for speeding   4 lose wallet
> 5 miss your plane   6 have a breakdown

2 Read the questions and direct students to *Travel problems* to decide which phrases are connected with car travel. Monitor and help with vocabulary as necessary.

Ask students to tell their partners about their car travel experiences. Monitor and comment on students' anecdotes. Nominate students or ask for volunteers to tell their stories to the class.

> **car travel problems:** run out of petrol, miss your turning, lose your way, get lost, get stuck, get stopped for speeding, have a flat tyre, have a breakdown, have an accident

Extra activity

Test a partner. Student A says a noun and Student B says the complete phrase.

B Listen for factual information

In this section, students listen to a conversation for specific information and detail.

Teaching tip

As an alternative to exercise 3, ask students to look at the pictures and ask you questions to find out about the story using the topic words in exercise 3. You can only answer *yes* or *no*, e.g. *S Was Duncan the driver? T Yes, he was.*

3 Direct students to *A Terrible Journey* on **» p.112** and the four topics. Demonstrate the activity by asking students to use the pictures to find out the places involved (*Edinburgh, Perth, Stirling*).

Put students into pairs to continue writing notes for the remaining topics. Monitor and help as necessary. Nominate students to give answers and ask them to say the number of the picture in which they found the information.

> **people:** Duncan McDonald, Feliks Nowak   **weather:** wet
> **problems:** ran out of petrol, petrol on coat, parking ticket, mobile phone flat, car stolen, cold

4 11D.1 Tell students that they will listen to Feliks telling his friend Fiona about what happened. Ask them to tick the words they hear in their notes in exercise 3. Play the audio, pausing occasionally to give students time to remember what they heard and tick the words.

5 Read the instructions and play the audio, pausing occasionally to give students time to make notes. Play the audio a second time if necessary. Elicit answers around the class.

Edinburgh: lived there, with friend   **The Highlands:** drove there, stayed in youth hostel, it rained, decided to go home   **Perth:** ran out of petrol, walked to the petrol station, got wet, got petrol on coat, got a parking fine   **Stirling:** stopped at a service station, had something to eat, car stolen, walked to phone box to call the police, filled in a report, caught the bus home

6 Go through the instructions and direct students to audio script 11D.1 on **>> p.158**. Do the first item together to demonstrate the activity. Elicit answers around the class and write them on the board. Elicit or point out that although Feliks doesn't know the words, he doesn't stop speaking. He finds another way of explaining what he means and asks for help by asking *How do you say …?* Point out how Fiona helps Feliks, and Feliks repeats the phrase to show he's understood.

1 how do you say … the petrol finished   2 how do you say … not there   3 had no power … ehm

7 Read the instructions and ask for or nominate a volunteer to do the first item with you to demonstrate the activity. Ask students to read sentences 2–4 and check vocabulary. Put students into pairs to continue the activity and monitor and check students ask and give help. Give positive feedback.

C Grammar non-defining relative clauses

8 Direct students to the grammar box, and say each of the sentences in turn. Ask *Which sentence describes the time by explaining what was happening?* (a … when I was living in Scotland.), and *Which sentence gives the exact time?* (b four years ago). Read questions 1–3 and elicit or explain answers as a class.

1 a when (that) I was living in Scotland; b   2 b
3 non-defining

Language note
If a non-defining clause is in the middle of a sentence, use commas before and after it.

9 Direct students to the relative pronouns and ask what they are used to describe *(where = place, which = thing, whose = what a person owns, when = time, who = person)*. Point out that these are the types of things that people often need to define by giving extra information. Go through the example to demonstrate that the pronoun usually relates to the type of information before it *(Edinburgh = place = where)*.

Ask students to read sentences 2–5 and check vocabulary as necessary. Monitor and help as students continue individually. Ask for volunteers to give answers and to read out the complete sentence. Check the class agrees before giving feedback.

2 when   3 who   4 which   5 whose

10 11D.2 Direct students to the pairs of sentences in the pronunciation box and check vocabulary as necessary. Go through the first pair and elicit or explain the difference between A and B. *(In A, the tyre which was flat identifies which of the four tyres was changed. In B, the tyre, which was flat gives extra information about the tyre (why it was changed.)*

Ask students to listen to the first two sentences and say what difference they hear. Play the audio and elicit or explain that there is a pause after the comma in a non-defining relative clause. Play the audio from the beginning, pausing at the end of each sentence for students to repeat. Give extra pronunciation practice as necessary.

Extra help
Say the sentences in the audio script, leaving a slightly longer pause before the comma preceding the non-defining clause, to help students hear the difference. Repeat exercise 10.

Extra activity
Direct students to audio script 11D.2 on **>> p.158** and put them into pairs to test a partner.

11 Ask students to read the information about Feliks and check vocabulary as necessary. Ask students to read sentences 1–5 and say who the writer is. *(Duncan.)*

Go through the example to demonstrate the activity. Monitor and help as necessary as students continue individually. Ask for volunteers to give answers and check the class agrees before giving feedback.

2 … where he works as a nurse.   3 … when he comes to Edinburgh.   4 … which he bought last month.   5 … who live by the seaside.

12 Go through the instructions and direct students to *A Terrible Journey*. Students continue the activity in pairs. Remind them to help each other with vocabulary if they can't remember a word or phrase. Monitor and give positive feedback.

ABC Put it all together

13 Read the instructions and suggest students invent a story relating to some of the pictures in *Travel problems* and the notes from the *Warmer* if they can't think of one. Monitor and check they make notes on all the topics.

14 Go through the instructions and example to demonstrate the activity. Direct students to exercise 9 for further help if necessary.

15 Put students into small groups to tell their story. Remind them to ask for help when they can't think of a word.

Student performance
Students should be able to tell a detailed narrative.

You can use this checklist to monitor and give feedback or to assess students' performance.

Content	Do students give extra information? exercise 11
Interaction	Do students ask for and give help when necessary? exercise 7
Vocabulary	Do students use a variety of phrases for travel problems? exercise 2

I can give extra information.
Students tick *on my own* if they have told their story using their notes. They tick *with some help* if they have looked at the grammar box in exercise 8 occasionally for help.

Early finishers
Students tell their stories again without using their notes.

Additional material

www.oup.com/elt/result for extra practice activities
www.oup.com/elt/teacher/result for extra teacher resources

How to give extra information

A Vocabulary travel problems

1 Describe the pictures in **Travel problems** opposite. Use phrases from the box.

Example 1 = She's run out of petrol.

2 Which problems are connected with car travel? Have you ever had any of these problems? Tell your partner.

B Listen for factual information

3 Look at **A Terrible Journey** opposite and guess what happened in the story. Work with a partner and write notes about these topics.

places   people   weather   problems

4 11D.1▶ Feliks tells Fiona about his terrible journey. Listen and tick ✓ the words and phrases you wrote in exercise 3.

5 Listen again. What happened in each of these places? Make notes and compare with a partner.

The Highlands → Perth → Stirling → Edinburgh

6 Feliks doesn't know how to say the sentences below in English. What does he say instead? Check the audio script on ≫ p.158.
1 We ran out of petrol.
2 The car was missing.
3 His batteries were flat.

7 Imagine you are telling your partner the things below but you don't know the words in green. Use other words with a similar meaning and ask for help like Feliks did.
1 I got stopped by the police for speeding.
2 I had a breakdown while I was driving to London.
3 I took the wrong turning off the motorway and got lost.
4 I got stuck in traffic on my way to work.

C Grammar non-defining relative clauses

8 Look at the grammar box and answer questions 1–3.

	question	When was it?
a	defining	It was during the time when (or that) I was living in Scotland.
b	non-defining	It was four years ago, when I was living in Scotland.

Note: you can't use 'that' for non-defining relative clauses.
1 In which sentence is the clause in blue very important for the meaning of the sentence? In which sentence is it simply extra information?
2 If you remove the clause in blue, which sentence still answers the question *When was it?*
3 Which relative clause has a comma before it?

9 Complete the sentences with these words. Compare with a partner.

~~where~~ which whose when who

1 It was in Edinburgh, *where* I was a student.
2 It was four years ago, _____ I was studying at university.
3 It was with Duncan, _____ was my flatmate.
4 I got petrol on my coat, _____ was new.
5 It was worse for Duncan, _____ car it was, because he never got it back.

10 11D.2▶ Pronunciation Listen and say *A* or *B*.

A defining	B non-defining
I changed the tyre which was flat.	I changed the tyre, which was flat.
They stopped the driver who was speeding.	They stopped the driver, who was speeding.
The man who was lost asked for help.	The man, who was lost, asked for help.

11 Read the information about Feliks. Add non-defining relative clauses to the sentences to give extra details.

Feliks is from Katowice. He's a nurse in London. He's coming to Edinburgh next weekend. He bought a new car last month. I once stayed with Feliks's parents – their house is by the seaside.

1 When I was at university, I shared a flat with Feliks, *who's from Katowice.*
2 Feliks moved to London,
3 I'm going to see him next weekend,
4 He's coming in his new car,
5 I once stayed with Feliks's parents,

12 Work with a partner. Look again at **A Terrible Journey**. Take turns telling the story from memory and ask your partner questions if they miss any details.

More practice? **Grammar Bank** ≫ p.146.

ABC Put it all together

13 Think of a bad journey you've made. Write notes about the times, places, people, and objects in the journey.

Example times   *four years ago ...*

14 Think of extra details which you could give about some of your notes. Write the end of the sentence.

Example ... four years ago, when I was living in Scotland.

15 Work in small groups. Tell the others about your bad journey. If you don't know how to say something in English, explain in other words and ask the others for help. Whose journey was the worst?

I can give extra information.

Tick ✓ the line.   with a lot of help   with some help   on my own   very easily   113

Writing   A website recommendation

A   Read for general information

1 How do you decide which places to visit while you're on holiday? Choose from the list and discuss your answers with a partner.

guide books   recommendations from friends
organized tours   the Internet   asking local people   other ...

2 Read the travel recommendation. Match the paragraphs with these questions.

a ☐ What do I need to take?
b ☐ Where is it and what is it?
c ☐ Are there any problems?
d ☐ What will I be able to see and do?

3 Look at the words and phases below with a partner. Which paragraph would you use them in? Which words and phrases tell us the order of events? Which introduce a contrasting idea?

group 1 first, then, after that, finally
group 2 unfortunately, however

B   Brainstorm ideas

4 The writer of the travel recommendation brainstormed ideas by drawing a mind map. Tick the ideas on the mind map which were used in the final text.

5 Read these tips for drawing a mind map. Which two are probably not good ideas?

1 Put the main topic in a circle in the middle.
2 Think of words connected with the topic and write them around it.
3 Make a list of words, and then copy them in the correct place in the mind map.
4 Try to put words which are connected with each other in the same area of the map.
5 Use your best handwriting.

6 Work with a partner. Think of a good place for an excursion which you both know. Draw a mind map.

AB   Put it all together

7 Your friend is going to visit an area you know. Write a website recommendation about an excursion in that area. Use your mind map from exercise 6, or draw a new one. Use the paragraph and text building ideas from exercises 2 and 3.

8 Read your partner's recommendation. Can you find the answers to the questions in exercise 2 easily?

A travel recommendation

1 If you're going to Crete, you ought to see the Samariá Gorge, which is in the west of the island. It's a really spectacular gorge and it passes through some enormous mountains.

2 It's a 16-kilometre walk from the head of the gorge to the sea, and it takes about five to seven hours. You need to wear some strong walking shoes and a sun hat. You don't need to carry a lot of water because there are springs along the path, but you need to carry enough food for the day.

3 First of all, you take a bus to the head of the gorge. You have to pay €5 to enter, and then you just follow the path, which is clearly marked. About halfway along, you pass an abandoned village, and after that you pass through a narrow gap between massive walls of rock. This is the most spectacular part of the walk. Finally you reach a village on the coast called Agía Rouméli, where you can have a swim and a snack. There are no roads, so you have to catch a ferry out.

4 Unfortunately, hundreds of tourists visit the gorge and it gets quite crowded. However, I think it's worth it, because it's so spectacular.

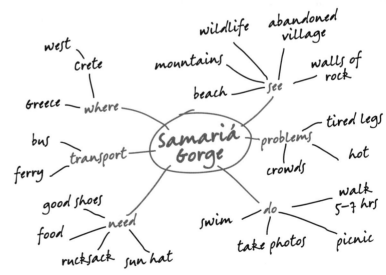

I can write a website recommendation.

Tick ✓ the line.   with a lot of help   with some help   on my own   very easily

Orientation

Context and Language

In this lesson, students analyse paragraph organization and text building words to order events and contrast ideas.

A travel recommendation is an illustrated website about the Greek island of Crete.

Recycled language	words: *beach, coast, crowded, enormous, ferry, guide books, island, mountains, path, picnics, sun hat, transport, village, walking shoes, west, wildlife* grammar: *modals (need to, don't need to, ought to); non-defining relative clauses*
Recognition language	words: *excursion, recommendation, rucksack, spectacular, springs* phrases: *abandoned village, clearly marked, halfway along, head of the gorge, massive walls of rock, narrow gap, organized tours, tired legs*
Discourse	*first of all, then, after that, finally, unfortunately, however*

End product

In *Put it all together*, students write a recommendation following logical paragraph organization and using a mind map. They swap writing and check how easy the recommendation is to follow.

Warmer

Tell students to imagine that they are on holiday but they don't know what there is to do. In pairs, students decide how they could get more information. Pairs of students compare ideas.

Write *How to write a website recommendation* on the board.

A Read for general information

In this section, students study paragraph organization and detail in a website article.

1 Go through the instructions and check vocabulary as necessary. Put students into pairs to discuss the question. Ask for volunteers to tell the class about the ways they decide on holiday places to visit.

2 Read the instructions and questions a–d and check vocabulary. Ask students how they are going to read to find the answers. *(Use the key words in questions a–d and each of the paragraphs.)* Do the first item as a class, asking students to guess the meanings of important new vocabulary.

Students continue individually. Ask for volunteers to give answers and check students agree before giving feedback.

a 2 b 1 c 4 d 3

3 Read the instructions and questions and check vocabulary. Direct students back to exercise 2. In pairs, students continue. Elicit answers as a class and check students agree before giving feedback. Ask students to underline the words in the paragraphs.

group 1: What will I be able to see and do? (d)
group 2: Are there any problems (c)

B Brainstorm ideas

4 Read the instructions and direct students to the mind map. Students read *A travel recommendation* carefully and do the activity. Put students into pairs to compare answers. To check answers as a class, go through each of the words radiating from the topic, in a clockwise direction.

Ask students why the writer didn't include all the information.

where: Crete, west **transport:** bus, ferry **need:** good shoes, sun hat, food **do:** swim, picnic **problems:** crowded **see:** abandoned village, walls of rock

5 Go through the instructions and tips 1–5 with the class. Students do the activity individually. Monitor and help by directing students to different parts of the mind map as necessary. Put students into pairs to compare ideas and to explain why they think the tips are not good. Check answers as a class.

3 If you write a list of ideas first you might forget some things you want to include.   5 Good handwriting isn't necessary as the map if only for the writer to use.

Extra activity

Ask students to match the main words in the mind map to the paragraphs in *A travel recommendation*.

6 Read the instructions and check students understand *excursion*. Put students into pairs to draw their mind maps and remind them to follow the tips in exercise 5.

Extra activity

Put pairs of students together to compare mind maps.

AB Put it all together

7 Read the instructions and check students understand. Remind them to think about topics and paragraphs. They don't have to use all the information in their mind maps.

8 Go through the instructions and ask students to swap their recommendations with a different partner. Students read each other's recommendation and tell their partner if it was easy to read and gave them sufficient information.

Student performance

Students should be able to produce a logically-organized recommendation.

You can use this checklist to monitor and give feedback or to assess students' performance.

Content	Have students included sufficient information for their reader?
Organization	Have students organized their paragraphs logically?
Discourse	Have students used text-building ideas to help their reader?

I can write a website recommendation.

Students tick *on my own* if their recommendation follows the paragraph order in exercise 2, and they have used text-building ideas. They can tick *with some help* if they have looked occasionally at exercises 2 and 3.

Early finishers

Students review their recommendations and underline any information they would add or cut.

Additional material

www.oup.com/elt/result for extra practice activities
www.oup.com/elt/teacher/result for extra teacher resources

Warmer

Remember the situations

Write lessons A–D *How to* titles on the board: *A ... give and ask about directions, B ... talk about holiday accommodation, C ... give health advice, D ... give extra information. Say* sentences 1–10 below for students to call out the lesson letter.

1 You shouldn't drink a lot of coffee. 2 Can you tell me where Chapel Street is? 3 Have your breakfast brought to your room. 4 You ought to wash your hands before eating meals. 5 Do you know where Mill Lane is? 6 It was five years ago, when I was living in Scotland. 7 Have your valuables put in the hotel safe. 8 They stopped the driver, who was speeding. 9 Have your clothes washed and ironed overnight. 10 Can you tell me whether there's a taxi rank near here?

1 C	2 A	3 B	4 C	5 A	6 D	7 B	8 D	9 B	10 A

A Grammar

1 Indirect questions 11A exercise 9

Warm-up: Books closed. Copy the words for item 1 onto the board for students to do in pairs.

Set-up: Remind students to add the question mark at the end of each question.

2 Do you know where platform four is?
3 Can you tell me if there's a bank near here?
4 Do you know whether the shops are open tomorrow?

Follow-up: Students write four more jumbled sentences for questions about places near their school. They swap with another student. They write the questions and answers and return papers.

2 to have something done 11B exercise 8

Warm-up: Books closed. Ask students to write down the things that they remember about what you can have done at the Hotel Paris. Students compare in pairs before checking on >> **p.109** exercise 10.

Set-up: Do the example as a class and check students understand why the verb form *(haven't + had)* is in the past tense.

2 have my hair cut 3 having my photograph taken
4 to have my nails cut 5 had my breakfast served

Follow-up: Students change the sentences which are true for them They read their sentences in small groups for the others to guess the false sentence.

3 have to, need to, should, ought to 11C exercise 13

Warm-up: Ask students to think about the type of things they *have to, need to, should,* and *ought to* do before making a trip to Ethiopia.

Set-up: Go through the example as a class.

2 have 3 have 4 should 5 need 6 should 7 ought

Follow-up: Students write five things people *have to, need to, should,* and *ought to* do when travelling to their country.

4 Non-defining relative clauses 11D exercise 8

Warm-up: Write the following words on the board: *Turkey, was, as, I, where, working, a, in met, Annie, teacher.* Students put the words in order to make a sentence.

Set-up: Ask students to check their answer to the jumbled sentence activity.

2 I shared a flat with John, who was from Portsmouth.
3 We lived in Izmir, which is on the west coast of Turkey.
4 I left Turkey two years later, when my contract finished.

Follow-up: Students write four sentences about themselves and swap with a partner. They ask each other for more information and then rewrite the sentences using non-defining relative clauses.

B Vocabulary

5 The street 11A exercise 2

Warm-up: Draw a simple plan of a place near to where you are now on the board. Elicit directions from the class.

Set-up: Check students understand the symbols on the map.

2 bridge 3 canal 4 path 5 park 6 rank
7 roads 8 street 9 roundabout

Follow-up: Ask students, in pairs, to draw an imaginary plan of a very small town. They should mark the tourist information office, and the names of five other places. They swap with another pair and ask for and give directions to the places marked on their maps.

6 Describing holiday accommodation 11B exercise 2

Warm-up: Tell students to imagine that they stayed in a fantastic hotel last month. Set a short time limit for them to write adjectives they could use to describe it to a friend. Direct them to *Accommodation adjectives* on >> p.108 to check.

Set-up: Ask students to read the nouns in the second column and check vocabulary as necessary.

3 b 4 h 5 a 6 c 7 f 8 e

Follow-up: In pairs, students make a similar exercise for another pair, based on *Fish Head Inn* on >> p.108.

7 Health and travel 11C exercise 3

Warm-up: Students write a list of all the things they have to do before they go on holiday to an exotic place.

Set-up: Do the example with the class.

medical insurance tap water local foods sun block first aid kit insect repellent mosquito net

Follow-up: Students write five pieces of advice as True/False sentences for a place they know. Their partner reads them and guesses the false fact.

8 Travel problems 11D exercise 1

Warm-up: Write the following verbs on the board: *run out, miss, lose, get,* and *have.* Set a short time limit for students to write phrases associated with travel problems. Direct them to >> **p.112** to compare.

Set-up: Ask students to read the passage and say what tense the verbs should be in. *(The past.)*

2 missed 3 ran out 4 got 5 missed 6 lost

Follow-up: In pairs, students write a similar gap-fill exercise and swap with another pair.

Early finishers

Students write five sentences using the verb phrases associated with travel problems on >> p.112. They write a translation of each sentence.

Unit 11 Review

R11

A Grammar

1 **Indirect questions** Put the words in order to make questions.

1 Can is me office tell the ticket where you
   Can you tell me where the ticket office is ?

2 Do four is know platform where you
   _____?

3 a bank Can here if me near tell there's you
   _____?

4 Do know open shops the tomorrow whether you are
   _____?

2 *to have something done* Complete the sentences with the *to have something done* form of the verb. Then change the sentences to make them true for you.

1 I *haven't had my teeth checked* for nearly two years.
   my teeth/not check

2 I _____ about once a month.   my hair/cut

3 I don't like _____.   my photograph/take

4 I'd like _____ by a professional.   my nails/cut

5 I've never _____ to me in bed. my breakfast/serve

3 *have to, need to, should, ought to* Complete the text with these words. Note that *have* and *need* are both possible in some of the gaps.

have   have   ~~need~~   need   ought   should   should

If you're planning to go to Ethiopia, you ¹ *need* to get a visa. You'll ² _____ to take your passport to the nearest consulate to get one. You'll ³ _____ to have some injections too – you ⁴ _____ ask about this at your health centre. You don't ⁵ _____ to take malaria pills in the mountains, but you ⁶ _____ carry some pills in case you decide to go to the lowlands. You ⁷ _____ to take some water purification tablets too.

4 **Non-defining relative clauses** Copy the sentences and add the extra information in the brackets as a non-defining relative clause.

1 I met Annie in Turkey (I was working there as a teacher).
   I met Annie in Turkey, where I was working as a teacher.

2 I shared a flat with John (he was from Portsmouth).
   _____

3 We lived in Izmir (it's on the west coast of Turkey).
   _____

4 I left Turkey two years later (my contract finished then).
   _____

B Vocabulary

5 **The street** Look at the map and complete the missing words in the directions.

Go straight on to the ¹T-*junction*. Then walk across the ²b_____ over the ³c_____. Walk along the ⁴p_____ to the car ⁵p_____. Go along the street, past the taxi ⁶r_____. Go straight over the ⁷cross_____ and along the pedestrian ⁸s_____, past the town hall. Finally, go straight across at the ⁹r_____.

6 **Describing holiday accommodation** Match 1–8 with a–h.

1 g an elegant   a rooms
2 d some delightful   b meal
3 ☐ a delicious   c waiters
4 ☐ a secluded   d ~~views~~
5 ☐ comfortable   e service
6 ☐ efficient   f countryside
7 ☐ magnificent   g ~~building~~
8 ☐ some friendly   h location

7 **Health and travel** Circle the words that go together to make compound nouns.

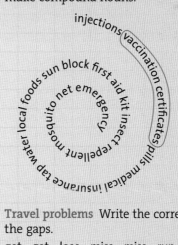

injections vaccination certificates sun block first aid kit insect repellent pills medical insurance local foods mosquito net emergency tap water

8 **Travel problems** Write the correct form of these verbs in the gaps.

~~get~~   get   lose   miss   miss   run out

What a terrible journey! First of all, we ¹*got* lost. Then we ² _____ our turning off the motorway and had to turn back. Then we ³ _____ of petrol and had a flat tyre. After that, we ⁴ _____ stopped for speeding. In the end, we arrived at the airport too late and we ⁵ _____ our plane. And just to complete the disaster, when we got back to the car, I discovered that I'd ⁶ _____ my keys!

African Stories

The Bread Seller's Trick

Once upon a time, there was a dishonest bread seller at the village market. She arrived early to get a good place and put her basket of bread under the market tree. Then she went to hide in the bushes.

A little while later, a meat seller arrived and sat down. She was hungry because she hadn't had time to eat that morning. She noticed the basket of bread and wondered who it belonged to. 'Whose bread is this?' she shouted. Nobody answered, so she repeated the question a few times. Finally, she decided that there was no owner so she took some of the bread to eat.

After seeing this, the bread seller came out of her hiding place. She said, 'You've taken some of my bread so you must give me some meat to pay for it.' The meat seller refused so the bread seller called the other sellers to support her.

The other sellers came and stood by the two women. They listened to their stories in order to decide who was right and who was wrong. Finally they decided that the bread seller had left the bread there to trick the meat seller. She didn't deserve to be paid because she had wanted the meat seller to take some bread.

The Smell of Soup

Once upon a time, there were two neighbours. One of the neighbours was a poor woman. She couldn't afford to make soup, so she had to eat just dry bread. One day, her richer neighbour was cooking soup. It smelt delicious, so the poor woman went to ask for a little. The richer woman refused. She sent the poor woman away with nothing because she thought she was lazy and didn't deserve any soup. However, the poor woman didn't go away. She sat outside the richer woman's house in order to enjoy the smell of the soup. Even the smell was better than nothing.

After that, the poor woman sat outside her neighbour's house every day because she liked smelling the soup. The richer woman became angry, so she went to the chief to complain. She explained the problem to him. 'My neighbour is stealing the smell of my soup,' she said. 'She is a thief so she must be punished!'

The chief said, 'I agree. She must be punished, and you must punish her. Take this stick and beat her shadow.' The richer woman did this and felt really stupid. From that day on, she gave her poor neighbour some soup to go with her bread.

How to explain your point of view

Orientation

Context

In this lesson, students practise using linkers to express causes, results, and purposes of actions.

The two illustrated stories were both written by Nigerian authors. They tell the tales of how one person was judged to have been unnecessarily wronged by another. Both stories end with a moral.

Culture note

English speakers tend to stretch sounds in words to keep the floor when they speak. Doing this gives them time to think and signals that they haven't finished speaking. Everyone involved in the same conversation respects this convention, and they would be unlikely to interrupt the speaker. This convention might be different for speakers of other languages. (See *Pronunciation* below.)

Language

Focus grammar	*because, (in order) to, so*
Focus phrases	opinion phrases: *I think ..., I don't think ..., To me ... , In my opinion ....*
Recognition vocabulary	words: *afford, basket, belong, bushes, deserve, dishonest, hiding, moral, place, punish, selfish, seller, shadow, stick, support* phrases: *identification collar, wondered*
Recycled language	words: *angry, check, complain, download, email, hungry, lazy, market, neighbours, pavement, private, rubbish bin, smell, steal, stupid, tap water, trick, valuable, video camera, village* phrases: *wireless internet connection* linkers: *after that, finally, however*
Pronunciation	keeping your turn 12A.3

End product

In *Put it all together*, students discuss their points of view on different situations in pairs or small groups. They indicate when they need time to think to avoid being interrupted or losing their turn in the conversation.

Preparation

Read both stories on >> **p.116** so you can monitor and help students as they do the jigsaw reading activities in exercises 2–4. Familiarize yourself with *Is it stealing?* on >> **p.132** for *Put it all together*. Take dictionaries to class.

Warmer

Choose one of the situations in *Is it stealing?* or think of another contemporary discussion point. Write the situation on the board and draw two columns, one for points in agreement and the other for points against. Put students into pairs and set a short time limit for them to think of arguments for and against. Elicit ideas around the class.

Write *How to explain your point of view* on the board.

A Read and follow

In this section, students use key words to focus on the actions of the main characters in a story.

1 Direct students to the photos on >> **p.116** and elicit suggestions of what the stories might be about. Write ideas on the board and check any new vocabulary as necessary. Do not comment on answers at this stage.

2 Put students into A/B pairs. Read the instructions and check vocabulary in the story titles. Monitor and help as necessary. Check answers as a class.

> **The Bread Seller's Trick:** bread seller, meat seller, other sellers
> **The Smell of Soup:** poor woman, rich woman, chief

3 Direct students to the box and check vocabulary. Go through the instructions and direct students to the box to complete the information about the story they read. Encourage students to check important vocabulary in their dictionaries and monitor and help as necessary.

Extra help

Put students who have read the same stories into pairs to compare answers.

4 Ask students to use their notes to tell their partner about the story they read. Remind them that they can ask for clarification or spelling before they write the notes in the box. Ask students to compare their information at the end of the activity before you go over answers.

> **The Bread Seller's Trick**
> 2nd woman: meat seller   2nd woman's action: took some bread
> 1st woman's response: asked for some meat   final result: other sellers decided bread seller didn't deserve to be paid
> **The Smell of Soup**
> 2nd woman: rich   1st woman's action: asked for some soup
> 1st woman's response: stayed to enjoy the smell of the soup
> 2nd woman's response: went to the chief to complain

5 Ask students to read questions 1–3 and check vocabulary. Put them into pairs to discuss the questions and monitor and help students express their ideas as necessary. Ask for volunteers to give their opinions and give reasons. Monitor and listen to see if students use *so, because,* and *in order to.* Do not overcorrect for accuracy at this point as using linkers is the focus of the next section.

Bring the class together and ask for volunteers to give answers. Encourage students to comment on each other's opinions.

> Students' own answers.

Extra activity

Ask students to read the other story again and to guess the meaning of three new words. They compare with a partner and can check in a dictionary if they have different ideas.

Extra plus

Ask students to tell the class about similar stories in their culture or country. Ask them to say why they think stories with morals were written. *(To entertain or to teach people.)* Do not overcorrect for accuracy, but help students get their ideas across.

B Grammar *so, because, (in order) to*

6 Go through the activity as a class. Direct students to the two boxes and the titles of the columns. Read the sentences and elicit or point out that the *cause* and *result* clauses can vary in position. Check students understand that *in order* is often omitted if it is easily understood in the context.

Read the rules, pausing at each blank to elicit answers.

> 2 so 3 (in order) to

7 Read the instructions and go through the first few sentences in the first story with the class. Monitor and help as necessary. Go through the remainder of the stories to check students have noticed the clauses. Help with new vocabulary as necessary.

8 Read the instructions and go through the example to demonstrate the activity. Elicit one or two more examples from the information in item 1, e.g. *I didn't sleep well so I'm going home. I want to go home because I need to rest.* Monitor and help as necessary as students continue individually. Ask for volunteers to give answers.

> 2 I passed the exams so I'm happy. I'm happy because I passed the exams. I'm happy so I'm going out. I'm going out (in order) to celebrate. etc.
> 3 I'm running because I'm late. I'm late so I'm running. I'm running to catch the bus. etc.

Extra help

Write these sentence stems on the board for students to complete: *I'm studying English ...; I've got a ...; I don't like ...; I've never been to ...; I want to go to ...*

Extra activity

Ask students to write sentences about two or three things they did yesterday and why they did them (similar to the ones in exercise 8). Put students into pairs to swap sentences and to write longer sentences using *so, because,* and *(in order) to.* Students swap sentences again for their partner to check.

C Listen for points of view

In this section, students listen to conversations for gist and to identify strategies for keeping their turn.

9 12A.1 Read the instructions and check vocabulary as necessary. Ask students what words they will listen for. *(The names of the people, and if Serge uses agreeing or disagreeing phrases.)* Play the audio, pausing occasionally for students to make notes. Play the audio a second time if necessary. Elicit answers around the class and help students express their ideas. Direct students to read the audio script and check vocabulary as necessary.

> Lucia thinks the rich woman is selfish; the chief is very clever; stealing a smell is stupid. Serge agrees with her.

10 12A.2 Read the instructions and play the audio. Elicit the topic of conversation *(using other people's Internet connections)* and help students express their ideas. Play the audio a second time for students to follow the conversation.

11 Put students into pairs to discuss Serge and Lucia's opinions. Monitor and help students get their ideas across if necessary. Ask the class if the speakers agree *(Yes, they do.)* and elicit reasons they give to explain their point of view. Ask students to say what they think and to give their reasons.

Extra activity

Students take turns to read the parts of Serge and Lucia in conversations in audio scripts 12A.1 and 12A.2. Monitor and give positive feedback.

12 12A.3 Read the instructions, the example sentences, and rules a and b to check students understand the activity. Play the audio. Put students into pairs to compare ideas before going over the answer *(a)* with the class. Play the audio a second time if necessary, and ask students if they do this in their language.

13 Play the audio, pausing after each sentence for students to repeat the phrases. Give extra practice if necessary.

Extra help

Put these simple sentence halves in jumbled order on the board: *I think she's very / very beautiful; I think he's very / very clever; She saw the / the basket; It's like ehm / reading someone else's book; She should pay or / or at least apologize.* Nominate students to match the halves, encouraging them to make the sound of the last word in the first part longer to give themselves time to think.

14 Read the instructions and direct students to audio scripts 12A.1 and 12A.2 on >> p.158 to find and underline the sentences which give opinions. Check answers as a class.

Extra activity

Put students into pairs and ask them to talk about the stories using their notes in exercise 3. Encourage them to use each opinion phrase once.

ABC Put it all together

15 Direct students to *Is it stealing?* on >> p.132. Ask them to read situations 1–10 and check vocabulary. Tell students to decide their answers to the questions. Monitor and help as necessary.

Put students into pairs or small groups to discuss each situation and explain the reasons for their points of view.

Student performance

Students should be able to express their opinions.

You can use this checklist to monitor and give feedback or to assess students' performance.

Coherence	Do students give logical reasons for their opinions? exercise 11
Interaction	Do students use strategies to keep their turn when necessary? exercise 13
Grammar	Do students use a variety of connectors to explain reasons? exercise 8

I can explain my point of view.

Students tick *on my own* if they have given an explanation for each point of view. They tick *with some help* if they explained their point of view for some of the situations.

Early finishers

Students rank the situations in terms of their seriousness and compare with a partner.

Additional material

www.oup.com/elt/result for extra practice activities
www.oup.com/elt/teacher/result for extra teacher resources

How to explain your point of view

G *so, because, (in order) to* P keeping your turn

A Read and follow

1 Look at the photos opposite. What are the stories about?

2 Work in pairs. Look at **African Stories** opposite. Write a list of the characters in your story.
   Student A Read **The Bread Seller's Trick**.
   Student B Read **The Smell of Soup**.

3 Read your story again and complete the notes in the box.

structure	The Bread Seller's Trick	The Smell of Soup
1st woman	bread seller	poor neighbour
2nd woman		
1st woman's action	left basket of bread under tree and hid in bushes	
2nd woman's action		refused to give soup
1st woman's response		
2nd woman's response	asked other sellers to support her	
final result		rich neighbour allowed to beat poor neighbour's shadow

4 Tell your story to your partner from your notes. Listen to your partner's story and complete the notes in the box.

5 Work with a partner. Answer the questions.
   1 The moral of **The Bread Seller's Trick** is *If you trick someone into taking something, you don't deserve to be paid for it.* What do you think is the moral of **The Smell of Soup**?
   2 Do you completely agree with the morals?
   3 Do you think both stories could be true?

B Grammar *so, because, (in order) to*

6 Read the grammar boxes and complete the rules.

result	cause	result
She was hungry	because she hadn't eaten.	
	She hadn't eaten	so she was hungry.

action	purpose
She arrived early	(in order) to find a good place.

Rules
1 Use *because* to give a cause.
2 Use _____ to give a result.
3 Use _____ to give a purpose.

7 Underline examples of *so, because,* and *(in order) to* in **African Stories**.

8 Work with a partner. Make sentences with *so, because,* and *(in order) to* from the information.
   1 I'm tired. I didn't sleep well. I want to go home. I need to rest.
      Example I'm tired because I didn't sleep well.
      I didn't sleep well so I'm tired.
      I want to go home to rest.
   2 I passed the exams. I'm happy. I'm going out. I want to celebrate.
   3 I'm running. I'm late. I want to catch the bus.

More practice? **Grammar Bank** >> p.147.

C Listen for points of view

9 **12A.1**▶ Listen. Serge and Lucia are discussing **The Smell of Soup** story. What are Lucia's opinions about the rich woman, the chief, and the idea of stealing a smell? Does Serge agree?

10 **12A.2**▶ Listen. What is the next part of Serge and Lucia's conversation about?

11 Do Serge and Lucia have the same point of view on the topic? Do you agree with them? Tell a partner.

12 **12A.3**▶ Pronunciation Listen and read these phrases from the conversation. Why do the speakers make the words in blue long? Choose the best option.
   ... the chief's very clever, b-e-c-a-u-s-e e-h he shows her ...
   ... stealing a smell is l-i-k-e like hitting a shadow ...
   ... you know s-o e-h-m so it's like the smell of soup ...
   ... people use your Internet connection in order t-o to get free Internet ...

   They pronounce the words longer ...
   a to give themselves time to think what to say.
   b to make their opinion stronger.

13 Listen again and repeat the phrases, including the long pronunciation.

14 Look at audio scripts **12A.1** and **12A.2** on >> p.158. Underline sentences with these phrases to give opinions.
   I think ...   I don't think ...   To me, ...   In my opinion, ...

ABC Put it all together

15 Read **Is it stealing?** on >> p.132 and decide your answers to the questions. Then discuss your point of view in pairs or small groups. Do you agree or disagree?

I can explain my point of view.

Tick ✓ the line.   with a lot of help   with some help   on my own   very easily

Three Wishes

a

b

c

1 I wish people would stop fighting and I wish there were no more wars. I hope there will be peace in the world one day in the future.
David, 7

2 I wish I had a genie. I would call him Aladdin. If I wanted anything, I could just call for Aladdin and make a wish.
Timothy, 5

3 This is me and my best friend Zoë. I wish she lived in my house. Then we could play together all day. I'm glad she's coming to my birthday party. I can't wait!
Grace, 6

Desert Island Joke

How to talk about hopes and wishes

Orientation

Context

In this lesson, students practise using *wish, hope,* and *be glad* to talk about and compare their feelings.

The three children's drawings in *Three Wishes* illustrate wishes 1–3. The cartoon story, *Desert Island Joke,* tells the tale of two shipwrecked men, *Lofty* and *Shorty.* They find a bottle containing a genie, who grants them three wishes.

Language

Focus grammar	*wish*
Focus words	*wish, hope, be glad*
Focus phrases	*I wish I didn't ..., I wish she ...*
Recognition vocabulary	words: *coconut, desert island, delighted, disappeared, fighting, genie, monkey, peace, signal, stuck, upset, war* phrases: *a million dollars, drive (sbd) crazy*
Recycled language	words: *borrowed, bottle, probably* grammar: *can, could, be able to; have to, had to; conditionals*
Pronunciation	contrastive stress 12B.4–5

Language note

This lesson deals with present wishes rather than regrets about things in the past. It is not necessary to discuss tense changes, e.g. *I wish I hadn't done that,* as this will be studied in the next level.

Wish, hope, and *be glad* share similar meanings but are used differently. The tense change with *wish* doesn't occur with *hope* or *be glad. Hope* is normally used with *will* future or present tenses. *Glad* is an adjective.

End product

In *Put it all together,* students ask and answer about their hopes, wishes, and feelings about possessions and actions. They have previously prepared a grid of topics to talk about.

Preparation

Look at *Wish box* on >> **p.133** so you are familiar with exercise 17.

Warmer

Write *Unhappy?* on the board. Put students into small groups to make a list of things people tend to want to change, now, or in the future.

Bring the class together and brainstorm a list of topics on the board. Check vocabulary as necessary.

Write *How to talk about hopes and wishes* on the board.

A Vocabulary *wish, hope, be glad*

1   Direct students to *Three Wishes* on >> **p.118** to match the pictures and the text. Ask students to compare in pairs and to say which words helped them choose a picture. Nominate students to give answers and explain which words helped them guess. Check vocabulary as necessary.

Ask students if they think these are typical children's wishes. Encourage them to respond to other students' comments and help them express their ideas.

> a 3   b 1   c 2

2   Go through the exercise as a class. Ask students to read definitions 1–3 and check vocabulary. Go through the first item as a class and ask students about the other definitions.

> 2 wish   3 glad

3   Direct students to the box and check vocabulary. Give students time to think before putting them into pairs to tell a partner. Monitor and comment on interesting ideas, or hopes and wishes you share. Ask for volunteers to tell the class about a partner and listen for the use of the past tense after *wish.* Do not overcorrect for accuracy at this stage, as this will be the focus of the grammar section.

Extra activity

Students make more sentences about the topics on the board from the *Warmer.*

B Listen and predict

In this section, students are guided, stage by stage, to predict the content of a joke.

4   Direct students to *Desert Island Joke* on >> **p.118**. Ask them to look at the pictures and say what they think the story is about. Point out the names of the characters in the first picture. Put students into pairs to compare ideas. Elicit suggestions around the class but do not comment at this stage.

5   Read the instructions and ask students to read sentences 1–7 and check vocabulary. Go through the example to demonstrate the activity. Ask students why Lofty probably said this. *(Because he doesn't like Shorty's guitar playing.)* Monitor and help as necessary as students continue individually. Put students into pairs to compare answers before asking around the class. Do not comment at this stage as students will listen to check.

Teaching tip

Students often understand individual words in a listening text, but not the overall meaning. Focusing on what the characters might say before listening helps students understand the bigger picture.

6   12B.1 Tell students that they will listen to the joke in three parts and not to worry about words they don't understand. Play the audio with the first part of the joke, pausing for students to check their answers to exercise 5.

Direct students to look at the picture again and elicit predictions for the next part. Write notes on the board and take a vote on the different predictions.

> 2 S (he looks happy playing his guitar) 3 L (he's unhappy and wants to leave the island) 4 both 5 S 6 L 7 S

7 12B.2 Play part 2 of the joke for students to check their predictions. Pause occasionally for students to look at the suggestions on the board. Ask students to predict how the joke ends, but do not comment at this stage.

8 12B.3 Play the audio for students to check their predictions. Give positive feedback by pointing out that understanding jokes in another language is a difficult task. Ask for a show of hands to see who thinks the joke is funny. Ask *why/why not* and help students express their ideas as necessary.

C Grammar *wish*

9 Read the instructions and direct students to audio scripts 12B.1–3 on >> p.158–59 and underline examples of *wish*.

> I wish I was somewhere far away. (verb)
> I'll give you three wishes. (noun)

10 Do the exercise as a class. Write *I wish I had a new guitar.* on the board and go through items 1–3 to establish the meaning and use of *wish*.

> 1 hasn't   2 now   3 present

11 Direct students to the grammar box, and the first sentence in both columns. Point out that after *wish* we can use *was* or *were* but that most speakers use *was*. Students complete the sentences in pairs. Monitor and help as necessary. As you go over answers with the class, draw students' attention to the use of the past tense for *wish* in positive and negative sentences, and the change in the modal *can* and *will*.

> **real situation:** I work in a shop. They won't/don't listen to me.
> **wish:** I wish I had a car. I wish I could speak German.

12 Ask students to read conversations 1–5 and check vocabulary. Go through the example with the class to demonstrate the activity. Monitor and help as students continue individually. Ask students to compare in pairs before going over answers as a class. To check answers, ask for pairs to volunteer to read their conversations. The class listens to decide if the conversations make sense. Give extra practice if necessary.

Direct students to the sentences in exercise 2 and elicit or point out that there is no change in tense after *hope* and *be glad*.

> 2 had/didn't have   3 could/could
> 4 was (were)/wasn't (weren't)   5 would/would

Extra help
Ask students to write a true sentence for themselves about each of the topics in exercise 12. They tell a partner and see if they share any of the same wishes (positive or negative).

D Pronunciation *contrastive stress*

13 12B.4 Read the instructions and the example conversation. Play the audio and elicit or explain that B stresses *I* and *didn't* to show that she thinks the opposite. Point out the title of the section heading. Ask students to read B's parts and play the audio a second time.

14 Go through the instructions and direct students back to B's lines in exercise 12. Do the first one as a class to demonstrate the activity. Explain that students look first at what A said, so they can find the contrast. Ask students to compare in pairs.

15 12B.5 Direct students to audio script 12B.5 on >> p.159 and play the audio for students to listen and check. Play the audio a second time, pausing as necessary for students to repeat. Give extra practice as necessary.

Extra help
Say the first line of each conversation for students to read B's lines as a class.

Extra activity
Put students into pairs to practise the conversations. Students swap roles.

16 Read the instructions and ask for two volunteers to read the example to demonstrate the activity. Remind students to use *wish, hope,* and *be glad*. Monitor and give positive feedback when students use contrastive stress clearly.

Extra help
Students change partners and repeat the activity.

Extra plus
Students change partners and talk about three hopes and wishes from memory.

ABCD Put it all together

17 Direct students to *Wish box* on >> p.133 and read the instructions to check students understand the activity. Ask students to complete the sentences about themselves and transfer the key words into the box. Monitor and help with ideas as necessary.

18 Write or elicit an example conversation, e.g. *A Oh, have you got a motorbike? B No, but I wish I had one. A Really? I'm glad I haven't got one! B Why?* ... Put students into pairs to continue the activity.

Student performance
Students should be able have a short conversation expressing contrast.

You can use this checklist to monitor and give feedback or to assess students' performance.

Content	Do students talk about most of the topics? exercise 3
Vocabulary	Do students use a variety of words for wishes? exercise 16
Pronunciation	Do students try to use contrastive stress? exercise 16

I can **talk about hopes and wishes.**

Students tick *on my own* if they have talked about some of the topics without looking at the grammar box in exercise 11. They tick *with some help* if they have looked at the grammar box occasionally.

Early finishers
Students have a imaginary conversation between Lofty and Shorty using the pictures on >> p.118.

Additional material

www.oup.com/elt/result for extra practice activities
www.oup.com/elt/teacher/result for extra teacher resources

How to talk about hopes and wishes

G *wish*   V *wish, hope, be glad*   P *contrastive stress*

A   Vocabulary *wish, hope, be glad*

1   Work with a partner. Read **Three Wishes** opposite. Match pictures a–c with texts 1–3.

2   Match the blue words with the definitions.

I'm glad she's coming ...

I hope there will be peace ...

I wish she lived in my house ...

1   to want something which is possible for the future (vb)   *hope*
2   to want something which is impossible for now or the past (vb)
3   happy about a situation (adj)

3   Make true sentences from the box. Tell a partner.

I wish I had a	million dollars car mobile phone
I'm glad I've got a	child dog new computer
I hope one day I'll have a	home of my own friend like you! *other*

B   Listen and predict

4   Look at **Desert Island Joke** opposite. What can you guess from the pictures about the story?

5   Guess who says these sentences with a partner.
1   I wish I was somewhere far away from here.   *Lofty*
2   Oh, it's not so bad.
3   I hope a passing ship rescues us.
4   I hope I never see another coconut again in my life!
5   I'm glad I've got my guitar.
6   I wish you hadn't saved the guitar. It's driving me crazy.
7   Look what I've found.

6   **12B.1▶** Listen to part 1 of the joke and check your answers. Then predict what will happen next.

7   **12B.2▶** Listen to part 2 of the joke and check your predictions. Then predict the end of the joke.

8   **12B.3▶** Listen and check. Do you think the joke is funny?

C   Grammar *wish*

9   Underline sentences with *wish* in audio scripts **12B.1▶** – **12B.3▶** on **>>** p.158–159. Is *wish* a noun or a verb?

10   What is the meaning of this sentence? Underline the correct word in the explanations.

Shorty   'I wish I had a new guitar.'
1   Shorty has/hasn't got a new guitar.
2   Shorty wants a new guitar now/in the past.
3   The verb *had* is in the past tense but the meaning is past/present/future.

11   Complete the grammar box. What are the rules for the tense of the verb after *wish*?

real situation	wish
I'm not rich.	I wish I was* rich.
I don't have a car.	
	I wish I didn't work in a shop.
I can't speak German.	
	I wish they would listen to me.

*or *were*

12   Fill the gaps in these short conversations with positive ⊞ or negative ⊟ forms of verbs. Compare with a partner.
1   **A** I wish I ⊞ *lived* in a big city.
   B Really? I wish I ⊟ *didn't live* in a big city.
2   **A** I wish I ⊞ _____ an office job.
   B Really? I wish I ⊟ _____ an office job.
3   **A** I wish I ⊞ _____ speak Arabic.
   B Really? I wish I ⊞ _____ speak Chinese.
4   **A** I wish I ⊞ _____ older.
   B Really? I wish I ⊟ _____ so old!
5   **A** I wish people ⊞ _____ drive more carefully on the motorway.
   B Really? I wish people ⊞ _____ drive more carefully everywhere!

More practice? **Grammar Bank >>** p.147.

D   Pronunciation *contrastive stress*

13   **12B.4▶** Listen. Explain why B stresses the words in **bold**.
   A I wish I lived in a big city.
   B Really? **I** wish I **did**n't live in a big city.

14   Which words make a contrast? Underline the two stressed words in each of B's lines in exercise 12.

15   **12B.5▶** Listen, check, and repeat.

16   Work with a partner. Say your sentences from exercise 3 again. Respond with a contrasting sentence.
   Example   **A** I wish I had a dog.
                     B Really? I'm glad I haven't got a dog.

ABCD   Put it all together

17   Look at **Wish box** on **>>** p.133 and complete the sentences about yourself.

18   Show your **Wish box** to your partner. Ask and answer about the words and names.

I can talk about hopes and wishes.

Tick ✓ the line.   with a lot of help   with some help   on my own   very easily

///||THE BOOKSHELF DETECTIVE||\\\

What can you learn about people from their book collections? Here are some questions to consider …

1 How many books are there?
2 Is there a wide variety, or are all the books similar?
3 What genres of fiction are there?
4 Are there any textbooks? What subjects are they?
5 Are there other kinds of books – cookery, computer manuals, and so on?
6 How 'used' do they look?
7 Have they been bought as sets, or one by one?
8 What languages are they in?
9 Are there a lot of best-sellers?
10 How are they kept and organized?

Antique Book Covers

1 What will people read in history textbooks in the year 2106? Dr Phillip Raven sees the book in his dreams and writes down all that he can remember. First of all, there is a world war which lasts nearly 30 years. Civilization is almost destroyed by a killer virus, and after that, the world is controlled by a dictatorship. This book, written in 1933, is full of predictions, and many of them have already turned out to be true. Perhaps the pages contain the shape of more things to come?

2 Two wagons leave Kansas heading along the Oregon Trail for a new life in the west. One of the wagons is driven by Sam, a violent man, and the other is driven by a charming captain called Will. Both men compete for the love of the same woman. She is a pretty passenger called Molly. Their journey is full of difficulty and dangers, including dry deserts and high mountains. They are also attacked by Indians. But who will Molly choose to be with when they reach their journey's end?

a b c d

3 Eighteenth-century London; in a dark, narrow alley off Fleet Street there is a barber's shop. The owner is a man called Sweeney Todd, and nobody is more skilful with a razor. Todd's closest friend is the baker, Mrs Lovett. Her bakery is famous for its tasty meat pies. When men in the neighbourhood begin to disappear, people suspect that Sweeney Todd is responsible. They see customers going into his shop, but nobody can remember seeing them come out. But if Sweeney Todd is a murderer, what has he done with the bodies?

4 Allan Quartermain is an English hunter living in Africa. One day, a man called Henry Curtis approaches him asking for help. Henry's brother has gone into the heart of Africa to look for King Solomon's mines and hasn't returned. Henry wants to rescue him – and perhaps find the mines, which contain a treasure of gold, diamonds, and ivory. He offers Allan a share of the treasure … if they can reach the mines. But first they must get past the fierce Kukuana warriors and their king.

How to describe the plot of a story

Orientation

Context

In this lesson, students will practise using *-ing* and *-ed* clauses to talk about stories they have read or seen in films.

The Bookshelf Detective lists questions we could ask about people's bookshelves in order to find out a little about the person.

The book covers, a–d, in *Antique Book Covers* are well-known or famous genres. Texts 1–4 contain the back cover blurb for each of the books.

Language

Focus grammar	*-ing* and *-ed* clauses: *The man was a hunter living in Africa.*, *The passenger was a woman called Molly.*
Focus words	*action, adventure, best-sellers, bookshelf, character, collections, covers, fantasy, fiction, genre, horror, mystery, manuals, organized, plot, romance, setting, sets, western*
Recognition vocabulary	words: *alley, antique, approach, attacked, charming, civilization, compete, demon, diamonds, dictatorship, expert, fierce, hunter, Indians, ivory, mines, neighbourhood, razor, rescue, similar, skilful, suspect, trail, treasure, violent, wagons, warriors* phrases: *code message, heart of Africa, killer virus, shape of things to come, wide variety*
Recycled language	*attractive, barber's, baker, clues, desert, dreams, journey, king, mountains, murderer, owner, passenger, perhaps, predictions, tasty*
Pronunciation	*well* and *anyway* 12C.2

End product

In *Put it all together*, students describe the genre, setting, character, and plot of a story they know. Their description is based on audio script 12C.1.

Preparation

Read the *Extra activity* after exercise 13. Think about classroom organization if you'd like students to do the *Put it all together* activity in groups. Take dictionaries to class.

Warmer

Write a list of the following types of books on the board: *autobiography, cookery book, encyclopaedia, computer manual,* and *novel*. Ask students to choose one to take with them on a long train journey. Elicit suggestions around the class, encouraging students to explain why they chose that particular book. If students chose a novel, ask them about the types of stories they prefer to read.

Write *How to describe the plot of a story* on the board.

A Read plot descriptions

In this section, students use illustrations and their general knowledge to guess what novels might be about before they read for detail.

1   Direct students to *The Bookshelf Detective* on **>> p.120**. Ask them to read the first sentence and questions 1–10 and say where they think they would find this text. *In a dictionary, an encyclopaedia, or a magazine? (Magazine.)* Ask students to answer questions 1–10 with the help of their dictionary.

    Put students into pairs to ask and answer. Monitor and encourage them to give examples and join in their conversations.

2   Read the instructions and the example to demonstrate the activity. Ask students to say what they think their partner's books say about them. Ask for volunteers or nominate students to tell the class about their partner.

3   Go through the instructions with the class. Direct students to *Antique Book Covers* on **>> p.120** and elicit or explain the meaning of *antique*. Ask around the class for suggestions about each of the stories and help with vocabulary as necessary.

    Ask students to read questions 1–3. Students continue the activity in pairs. Monitor and help as necessary. Go through each of the books in turns, eliciting answers to questions 1–3. Do not comment on answers at this stage but help students with pronunciation.

    The Covered Wagon: Indian, love, wagon, western
    Sweeney Todd: barber, murderer, murder mystery, razor
    King Solomon's Mines: adventure, diamonds, hunter, ivory, treasure, war, warriors
    The Shape of Things to Come: dictatorship, killer, science fiction, virus

4   Set a short time limit of about three or four minutes for students to match the books and covers to check their guesses in exercise 3. Tell students to use their dictionaries to help with vocabulary, but only if they can't guess the meanings of words.

    1 c   2 b   3 d   4 a

5   Ask students to read sentences 1–8 and check vocabulary as necessary. Go through the example together and remind students to use key words in the question to help them locate the story and information in texts 1–4. Monitor and help as students continue individually, checking that they use *doesn't say* if there is no information in the text..

    Ask volunteers for answers and see if the class agrees before giving feedback. Encourage students to give reasons for their answers.

    2 Doesn't say.   3 True.   4 True.   5 True.   6 Doesn't say.
    7 False.   8 Doesn't say.

6   Put students into pairs to tell a partner which one they would like to read and why. Ask for a show of hands to see which book is most and least popular with the class.

B Grammar -ing and -ed clauses

7 Direct students to sentences 1–5 and check vocabulary. Read the instructions and go through the first item to demonstrate the activity. Monitor and help as necessary. Ask for volunteers to read out the complete sentences to check answers.

> 2 They see customers going into his shop, but nobody can remember seeing them come out. 3 This book, written in 1933, is full of predictions ... 4 She is a pretty passenger called Molly. 5 Allan Quartermain is an English hunter living in Africa.

8 Direct students to the grammar box and read the example sentences column by column. Elicit or explain that the subject of each clause must be the same before we can join the clauses to make a longer sentence.

Ask students to look at sentences 1–5 below the box and check vocabulary. Go through item 1 together to check they understand the activity. Remind students that an -ed clause includes any past participle, e.g. taken. Monitor and help as students continue individually. Ask students to compare in pairs before nominating individuals to give answers.

> 2 He sees a thief stealing the diamonds. 3 He finds a box covered in gold. 4 It's about a civilization destroyed by war. 5 It's about two men fighting for survival.

Extra plus

Ask students to make one sentence for each of these pairs of sentences from *Antique Book Covers: 1 Two wagons leave Kansas. They are heading west. 2 The charming captain drives a wagon. He is called Sam. 3 Their journey is dangerous. It includes lots of dangers. 4 Allan Quartermain is approached by a man. He is called Henry Curtis.*

Extra activity

Students write five sentences about books they have read or songs they like, starting with *It's about ...* . Monitor and help as necessary. Put students into pairs to tell a partner.

C Listen to a plot description

In this section, students listen to a description of a plot for gist and detail.

9 12C.1 Read the instructions and play the audio. Put students into pairs to answer the questions. Ask if anybody knows the title and who has read it (or seen it – it was made into a film by the same name).

> *The Da Vinci Code* by Dan Brown.

10 Go through the instructions and ask students to write notes to see what they can remember. Play the audio a second time, pausing occasionally for students to check their notes. Elicit answers around the class.

> **genre:** murder mystery, adventure story **set in:** mainly Paris **characters:** Robert Langdon, language expert and Sophie, the daughter of the dead man **start of the story:** a dead body is found in a museum, he has a message in code on his back

11 Put students into pairs to talk about what else they can remember. Remind students that they can make words sound longer to show that they haven't finished speaking and to give them a little more time to think. Ask for volunteers to tell the class and give positive feedback in general.

D Pronunciation *well* and *anyway*

12 Direct students to audio script 12C.1 on **>> p.159** to underline examples of *well* and *anyway*. Read meanings a and b to the class and go through the examples in the audio script to guide students to the use of each word in a conversation. Play the audio again for students to focus on the use of the two words.

> a anyway   b well

13 12C.2 Read the instructions and explain that *well* and *anyway* are said in a high voice so the listener can tell what the speaker is going to do. Play the audio, pausing after each sentence for students to repeat. Encourage students to use a high voice by pointing upwards. Give extra practice as necessary.

Extra activity

Get students to produce a class *do-it-yourself* murder mystery. Ask them to take a piece of paper and to write the information you ask them to (see below). After they have written each answer, they fold the paper and pass it on. When they have finished, they open the paper, read the whole story and give it a title. They then read it to the class, using *well* and *anyway*. The class votes on the best story.

Information: *a murder mystery set in ...; a body is found lying ...; there's a message nearby which says ...; clues lead the detective to ...; the detective meets an attractive ...; the killer is ...*

ABCD Put it all together

14 Read the instructions and tell students that the story can be a book or a film. Ask them to make notes and remind them to use -ing or -ed clauses in their notes. Give students some time to rehearse by whispering or mumbling to themselves.

15 Put students into pairs or small groups to tell their stories. Ask them to say if they knew the story and if they would like to see the film or read the book.

Student performance

Students should be able to give a short description using compound sentences.

You can use this checklist to monitor and give feedback or to assess students' performance.

Content	Do students talk about all the topics? exercise 11
Interaction	Do students use *well* or *anyway* appropriately? exercise 13
Grammar	Do students use -ed and -ing clauses appropriately? exercise 8

I can describe the plot of a story.

Students tick *on my own* if they have told their story without a lot of pauses. They can tick *with some help* if they have paused a lot of times while they have thought about what to say next.

Early finishers

Students tell their stories again without using their notes.

Additional material

www.oup.com/elt/result for extra practice activities
www.oup.com/elt/teacher/result for extra teacher resources

How to describe the plot of a story

G -ing and -ed clauses   V stories, books, fiction   P well and anyway

A Read plot descriptions

1 Answer the questions in **The Bookshelf Detective** opposite about your book collection. You can use a dictionary. Ask the questions to your partner.

2 Say what you think your partner's book collection shows about him or her.

   Example You've got a lot of old textbooks – perhaps you used to be a student.

3 Look at the pictures in **Antique Book Covers** opposite, but don't read the texts. What can you guess about the stories? Answer the questions with a partner.

   1 Which genre does the story belong to? Choose one or more for each book.
   adventure fantasy horror murder mystery
   romance science fiction western

   2 Which story do you think you will find these things in? Use your dictionary if necessary.
   barber diamonds dictatorship hunter Indian
   ivory killer virus love murderer razor treasure
   wagon war warriors

   3 What can you guess about the setting, characters, and plot?

4 Read texts 1–4 and match them with covers a–d. Check your guesses in exercise 3.

5 Write *true*, *false*, or *doesn't say*.

   1 Mrs Lovett's bakery sells pies. *True*
   2 Sweeney Todd is definitely a murderer.
   3 Phillip Raven often sees books in his dreams.
   4 *The Shape of Things to Come* was written over 70 years ago.
   5 Sam, Will, and Molly are travelling west.
   6 Molly prefers Will to Sam.
   7 Allan travels to the heart of Africa to rescue Henry.
   8 Henry's brother is inside the mines.

6 Which of these books would you most like to read? Why? Tell your partner.

B Grammar -ing and -ed clauses

7 Look at **Antique Book Covers** again. Underline sentences with the same meaning as the pairs of sentences below.

   1 The owner is a man. He is called Sweeney Todd.
   The owner is a man called Sweeney Todd.
   2 They see customers. They are going into his shop.
   3 This book is full of predictions. It was written in 1933.
   4 She is a pretty passenger. She is called Molly.
   5 Allan Quartermain is an English hunter. He's living in Africa.

8 Look at the grammar box. Make one sentence with an -ing or -ed clause from the pairs of sentences below.

-ing clause	-ed clause
He's a hunter.	The passenger was a woman.
+ He's living in Africa.	She was called Molly.
= He's a hunter living in Africa.	The passenger was a woman called Molly.

   1 He found a painting. It was stolen from the Louvre.
   He found a painting stolen from the Louvre.
   2 They see a thief. He's stealing the diamonds.
   3 He finds a box. It was covered in gold.
   4 It's about a civilization. It was destroyed by war.
   5 It's about two men. They're fighting for survival.

   More practice? **Grammar Bank** >> p.147.

C Listen to a plot description

9 **12C.1▶** Listen to a description of a best-seller. Do you know the title? Have you read it? Tell a partner.

10 Write notes on these topics then listen again to check.
   genre set in characters start of story

11 What can you remember about the story? Tell a partner.

D Pronunciation *well* and *anyway*

12 Read audio script **12C.1▶** on >> p.159. Underline the words *well* and *anyway*. Match them with these meanings.
   We use this word to show ...
   a that we're moving on to the next part of the story.
   b that we're starting our description of the story.

13 **12C.2▶** Listen and repeat these sentences. *Well* and *anyway* are said in a high voice so that the listener notices.
   Well, it's a murder mystery.
   Anyway, it starts when they find a body.
   Well, it's a romance.
   Anyway, she meets an attractive stranger.
   Well, it's an adventure story.
   Anyway, they start their journey.

ABCD Put it all together

14 Think of a story you've read or seen. Make notes about the genre, setting, characters, and plot.

15 Work in pairs or small groups. Tell the others about your story. Listen to the other stories. Do you know them?
   Example Well, I read a story called ...

I can describe the plot of a story.

Tick ✓ the line.   with a lot of help   with some help   on my own   very easily

Extreme Decisions

1 Monica was putting up a shelf when she dropped a piece of wood from the window of her flat by mistake. It fell on a man's head. He fell into the road and a car hit him and killed him. The driver thought he was responsible. Nobody had seen the piece of wood fall, so Monica didn't tell the police.

2 Fernando was a prisoner of war. The enemy captain told him to shoot another prisoner. 'If you don't kill one, I will kill two,' he said. Fernando refused and the captain shot two prisoners.

3 Basia was travelling with her teenage daughter in a country where the penalties for smuggling are very severe. The customs officers found prohibited goods in her daughter's bag and asked, 'Whose bag is this?' Basia said it was hers so she was arrested.

4 A group of passengers were stuck on a high mountain after a plane crash. Many of the passengers had died in the crash and their bodies were lying around in the snow. It was impossible for the survivors to walk to safety, and there was no food. After a few days, they decided to eat the frozen bodies in the snow.

5 Jim and Neil's car broke down in the desert. They started to walk but Jim fell and broke his leg. He couldn't walk without help from Neil. The nearest water was two days' walk away but with Jim's broken leg it would take a week, and they couldn't survive that long without water. Jim told Neil to go alone. Neil did this and Jim died.

6 There was a cruel landlord who everybody feared and hated. One day, Ernesto was in a fight with the landlord and killed him, but nobody saw the crime. Ernesto told his best friend Toni about it and Toni promised to keep the secret. Some time later, an innocent man was wrongly accused of the crime and sentenced to death. Toni told the police what Ernesto had told him.

Karen's Life Map

leave school

study French at university

move to Los Angeles

get job as secretary in film company

travel to America

meet Martin

get married

be offered a part in a movie

return to Britain

become a French teacher

stay in New York

become an actor

How to talk about important decisions

Orientation

Context

In this lesson, students use the 3rd conditional to talk about actions and decisions in the past.

The article, *Extreme Decisions*, describes six different situations in which people have been forced to make very difficult decisions. The photo reflects the seriousness of the situation in the first story.

The illustrated maze, *Karen's Life Map*, shows various things she might have done in her life had she made a different decision at each point.

Language

Focus grammar	3rd conditional: *If Neil had stayed with him, he would have died too.*
Recognition vocabulary	words: *decide, innocent, prisoner* phrases: *break a promise, done the same, go straight to university, keep quiet about sth, method of survival, movie business, play a part, take a year off*
Recycled language	words: *arrested, appearance, daughter, happened, husband, parent, prison, probably, secretary, shot, whether* phrases: *be in a lot of trouble*
Pronunciation	*would have* /wʊ dəv/ **12D.1**

Language note

I would have can also be said *I'd have* /aɪ dəv/.

End product

In *Put it all together*, students talk about decisions they have made in their lives, and what would have happened if they had made a different decision. The activity is based on audio script 12D.2.

Preparation

Think about classroom organization if you want students to do the *Put it all together* activity in exercise 15 in groups. Take dictionaries to class.

Warmer

Put students into small groups to think about the decisions they have made so far today, e.g. what to wear, how to walk, what to eat. Elicit examples around the class.

Ask students to choose a decision and to make notes on the following: the situation, their decision, whether or not they'd made the right decision and why/why not. Put students into pairs to tell their partner about their decision. Ask for volunteers to tell the class about their partner.

Write *How to talk about important decisions* on the board.

A Read for detail

In this section, students read short stories for gist and detail.

1   Read the decisions with the class and check vocabulary. Ask students to order the decisions from easy to difficult. Monitor and elicit reasons. Put students into pairs to compare and ask for volunteers to tell the class about their partner.

2   Direct students to *Extreme Decisions* on >> **p.122** and the illustration next to the title. Elicit or give one or two examples of extreme decisions and point to the picture in the article.

Ask students to read sentences a–f and check vocabulary. Set a time limit of about three or four minutes for students to do the matching activity. Monitor and help as necessary, encouraging students to guess new vocabulary and to scan for key words in the statements and stories. Ask for volunteers to give answers and see if the class agrees before giving feedback.

```
b 2   c 6   d 4   e 1   f 5
```

3   Read sentences a–f with the class, checking vocabulary as necessary. Go through the first item with the class to demonstrate the activity. Monitor and help as students continue individually. Ask students to compare their answers in pairs before eliciting answers around the class. Do not focus on the form of the 3rd conditional at this stage as this will be done in the next section.

```
b 6   c 5   d 1   e 4   f 3
```

4   Put students into pairs to discuss the questions. Monitor and help them get their ideas across. Encourage students to use phrases for giving an opinion from lesson 12A. Bring the class together for volunteers to share their opinions with the class.

Extra activity

Tell students to choose one new word in each story and to guess the meaning. They compare ideas with a partner before checking in a dictionary.

B Grammar 3rd conditional

5   Direct students to the sentence in the grammar box and write it on the board. Go through questions 1–5 as a class. Use the sentence on the board to highlight the verb tenses in *if* and main clause.

```
1 No.   2 Yes.   3 The past.   4 An imagined result.
5 a if + past perfect   b would + present perfect
```

6   Ask students to read sentences 1–6 and check vocabulary as necessary. Go through the first example with the class and put students into pairs to continue the activity. Remind students they can use their dictionaries or *Irregular verbs* on >> **p.148**. Monitor and help as necessary.

To check answers, ask for volunteers to read the full sentences and check the class agrees before giving feedback.

```
2 had, been   3 said, have   4 would, hadn't
5 have, had   6 hadn't, would
```

7 Ask students to read sentences 1–3 and check vocabulary. Monitor and encourage students to ask for help if necessary as they continue the exercise. Ask different volunteers to tell the class about their school days and see if anyone had similar experiences.

8 Read the instructions and go through the example to check students understand the activity. Elicit a second example for the opposite situation, e.g. *If I had been good at maths, I would have passed the exams.* Monitor and check for accurate use of the negative.

Extra activity

Students swap sentences and check each other's work for accuracy.

9 12D.1 Read the instructions and play the audio, pausing after each item for students to repeat. Monitor and check students run the words together, and give extra practice as necessary.

Extra help

Backchain drill. Use the sentence *I would have done the same.* to help students practise pronouncing saying *would have* /wʊ dəv/ in context. *T same SS same T the same SS the same T done the same SS done the same T would have /wʊ dəv/ done the same SS would have done the same T I would have done the same. SS I would have done the same.* Repeat the activity, using another sentence from exercise 9, if necessary.

10 Read the instructions and put students into pairs to talk about *Extreme Decisions*. Monitor and help with for pronunciation if necessary. Ask for volunteers to share their ideas with the class.

C Listen for detail

In this section, students listen to a description and identify a route in a diagram.

Teaching tip

Going through as many of the possibilities as possible, before students listen to the audio, will help familiarize them with some of the content of the text. This will give students a greater sense of achievement and help with overall listening motivation.

11 Direct students to *Karen's Life Map* on ›› **p.122** and go through the example. Set a short time limit to maintain pace as students continue the activity in pairs. Elicit suggestions around the class and ask students to explain their answers.

> **suggestions:** was a successful actress, left her job in the film company, married Martin, etc.

12 12D.2 Read the instructions and check students understand the activity. Play the audio, pausing occasionally to give students time to mark Karen's route Ask students to compare in pairs and play the audio a second time if necessary.

Elicit answers around the class, using sequencing adverbs, e.g. *first, next, then, after that.* Check students agree before giving feedback and ask students to make corrections to their route if necessary.

> travelled to America, met Martin, got married, moved to Los Angeles, got a job in a film company, offered a part in a movie, became an actor

13 Go through the instructions and read the example sentence. Do the activity as a class, eliciting sentences about her decisions. Monitor for accurate use of the 3rd conditional.

Extra activity

Put students into pairs to test a partner. Student A points to a picture. Student B makes a sentence about what would have happened if she'd done something differently. Students swap roles.

ABC Put it all together

14 Go through the instructions and ask students to note three or four important decisions or moments in their life. Give some examples if necessary *(a difficult exam, an accident, a relationship).*

Ask students to make a note of key words and to rehearse using these to make sentences about how their life might have been different.

15 Read the instructions and put students into pairs or small groups to talk what would have happened if they'd made the opposite decision.

Student performance

Students should be able to hypothesize about the past.

You can use this checklist to monitor and give feedback or to assess students' performance.

Content	Do students talks about a variety of decisions? exercise 13
Grammar	Do students talk about positive and negative conditions? exercise 13
Pronunciation	Do students try to pronounce *would have* and *wouldn't have* as one word when appropriate? exercise 9

I can talk about important decisions.

Students tick *on my own* if they have talked about two or three decisions without looking at the grammar box in exercise 5. They tick *with some help* if they looked at the grammar box more than once.

Early finishers

Students look through the book and exchange ideas about how things would be different if they hadn't learnt certain grammar, vocabulary or pronunciation, or read certain articles, etc.

Additional material

www.oup.com/elt/result for extra practice activities
www.oup.com/elt/teacher/result for extra teacher resources

How to talk about important decisions

G 3rd conditional   P *would have*

A Read for detail

1 Put these decisions in order from easy to difficult.

☐ what to have for lunch ☐ what career to choose
☐ whether to get married ☐ whether to have children
☐ where to live ☐ where to go on holiday

2 Read **Extreme Decisions** opposite. Say which story.

a [3] A parent saved her daughter from prison.
b ☐ A person refused to kill someone.
c ☐ A person broke a promise.
d ☐ People found an extreme method of survival.
e ☐ A person kept quiet about what happened.
f ☐ A person left a friend to die.

3 Match each story with the final sentences below.

a [2] If Fernando had shot a prisoner, the captain would probably have shot another one anyway.
b ☐ If he hadn't, the innocent man would have died.
c ☐ If Neil had stayed with Jim, he would have died too.
d ☐ If she'd told them, she'd have been in a lot of trouble.
e ☐ If they hadn't, they would have died.
f ☐ If they'd known it was her daughter's bag, her daughter would have been arrested.

4 Discuss with a partner. Which decision was the most difficult? Did any of the people make the wrong decision?

B Grammar 3rd conditional

5 Read the sentence and answer the questions.

if clause	main clause
If Neil had stayed with Jim,	he would have died, too.

1 Did Neil stay with Jim?
2 Did Jim die?
3 Is the sentence about the past or present?
4 Is the sentence about a real or imagined result?
5 How do you form the verb ...
  a in the *if* clause?   b in the main clause?

6 Complete these sentences with a partner.

1 If Monica *had* told the police, they *would* have arrested her.
2 If Fernando _____ shot a prisoner, the result would probably have _____ the same.
3 If Basia hadn't _____ the bag was hers, her daughter would _____ been in trouble.
4 The survivors _____ have died if they _____ eaten the bodies in the snow.
5 Neil wouldn't _____ gone if Jim _____ asked him to stay.
6 If the police _____ arrested an innocent man, Toni _____ have stayed silent.

7 Underline the correct words to make these sentences true about your school days.

1 I was/wasn't good at maths so I passed/didn't pass the exams.
2 I lived/didn't live near school so I walked/didn't walk there.
3 I liked/didn't like music so I wanted/didn't want to learn an instrument.

8 Write a conditional sentence about the *opposite* situation from your sentences in exercise 7.

Example I was/wasn't good at maths so I passed/didn't pass the exams.
If I hadn't been good at maths, I wouldn't have passed the exams.

9 **12D.1▶ Pronunciation** Listen and repeat the sentences. Notice the pronunciation of *would have* and *wouldn't have*.

I would have /wʊ dəv/ (done the same/waited/said something/kept quiet/tried to escape)
I wouldn't have /wʊdn təv/ (done that/said that/made that choice)

10 What would or wouldn't you have done in the situations in **Extreme Decisions**? Tell your partner.
More practice? **Grammar Bank** >> p.147.

C Listen for detail

11 Look at **Karen's Life Map** opposite. Guess some of the things she has done in her life. Tell a partner.
Example I guess she's been to university.

12 **12D.2** Listen to Karen describing the important decisions she has made in her life. Draw her route through the life map from leaving school to becoming an actor.

13 What were Karen's important decisions and what would have happened if she'd decided differently?
Example Her decision to travel to America was important. If she hadn't gone, she wouldn't have met Martin.

ABC Put it all together

14 Make a list of three or four important decisions or moments in your or your family's life.
Example When I was young, my family moved to ...

15 Work in pairs or small groups. Tell the others about your decisions. Say what would have happened if you'd made the opposite decision.

I can talk about important decisions.

Tick ✓ the line.   with a lot of help   with some help   on my own   very easily

Writing A story with a moral

A Read a story with a moral

1 Work with a partner. Complete the sayings with these nouns.

baby ~~bird~~ book eggs hand houses

1 A _bird_ in the hand is worth two in the bush.
2 Don't bite the _____ that feeds you.
3 Don't put all of your _____ in one basket.
4 People who live in glass _____ shouldn't throw stones.
5 Don't throw the _____ out with the bathwater.
6 Never judge a _____ by its cover.

2 Work with a partner and answer the questions about the sayings in exercise 1.

1 What do you think the sayings mean? Match them with these meanings.
   a ☐ Don't choose things just because they look nice.
   b ☐ Don't keep all of your valuables in one place.
   c ☐ Don't say bad things about a person who's helping you.
   d ☐ *1* It's better to have one thing for certain, than just a possibility of having two.
   e ☐ People who have done bad things shouldn't talk about other people doing bad things.
   f ☐ When you are changing old things for new, be careful not to lose good things too.

2 Are there similar sayings in your country?

3 Read this story and add a saying from exercise 1.

A Heart of Gold

Mrs Goodwill lived alone in a big old house. She wasn't strong enough to do a lot of cleaning so the place was filthy. The paint was falling off the window frames because she couldn't afford to keep the house in good condition. She wanted to sell the place and move somewhere smaller, but nobody would buy it.

Mrs Goodwill never used the upstairs, so she decided to rent it out in order to earn some extra cash. She advertised in the paper and rented the rooms to the first person who called. He was a young man called Mick, with a shaved head, a torn leather jacket, and a broken nose. One day, Mrs Goodwill's daughter Hillary came to visit, and when she saw Mick, she was horrified. 'Mother, he looks like a criminal,' she said, 'If I'd been here, I wouldn't have let him through the door!'

Hillary didn't visit again until three months later, and when she arrived, she couldn't believe her eyes. The house was beautifully clean, all the window frames were newly painted, and Mick was in the garden cutting the grass. 'Mick's been helping me a lot,' Mrs Goodwill explained, 'That boy's got a heart of gold!'

Moral: _____

4 Complete these sentences.

1 Mrs Goodwill's house was filthy because ... *she wasn't strong enough to clean it.*
2 She couldn't afford to keep the house in good condition so ...
3 She put an advert in the paper in order to ...
4 Hillary was horrified because ...
5 Hillary couldn't believe her eyes because ...

B Think about paragraph structure

5 Cover the story in exercise 3. What extra information can you remember from paragraphs 1–3? Note key words and phrases with a partner.

Paragraph structure

para 1 – **situation**	old woman lived in house in bad condition *filthy, paint falling* ...
para 2 – **action**	rented rooms to man called Mick; daughter didn't like him
para 3 – **result**	Mick helped old woman a lot; daughter surprised
para 4 – **moral**	Never judge a book by its cover.

6 Work with a partner. Decide how to finish these story outlines. Write notes for the missing parts.

1 **situation** woman won lottery
   action she invested all her money in an Internet company
   result _____
   moral Don't put all of your eggs in one basket.

2 **situation** politician said another politician was corrupt
   action the police investigated
   result _____
   moral People who live in glass houses shouldn't throw stones.

3 **situation** a man looking for work got a good job offer
   action he refused because he thought he could get a better offer
   result _____
   moral A bird in the hand is worth two in the bush.

AB Put it all together

7 Work with a partner. Choose one of the story outlines in exercise 6, or think of another. Add more notes to the situation, action, and result paragraphs.

8 Write your story. Don't include the moral at the end.

9 Work in groups. Read out your story to the others. Listen to the other stories. What is the moral? Does the story fit the moral well?

I can write a story with a moral.

Tick ✓ the line.   with a lot of help   with some help   on my own   very easily

Orientation

Context and Language

In this lesson, students practise using paragraph structure to write a story with a moral. Story morals are often well-known sayings or proverbs which have been passed on from generation to generation and give some kind of advice about how people should behave, e.g. *Don't bite the hand that feeds you.* Sayings and proverbs are usually based on collective folk-wisdom, e.g. *An apple a day keeps the doctor away., A watched pot never boils.*

Recycled language	words: *baby, bite, bed, bird, book, broken, cover, criminal, egg, enough, hand, houses, judge, lottery, nose, politician, rooms, shaved, surprised, upstairs, valuables* grammar: *because, so, (in order) to; 3rd conditional*
Recognition language	words: *bathwater, basket, corrupt, daughter, filthy, horrified, invest, stones, torn, window frames* phrases: *afford to, couldn't believe her eyes, cutting the grass, for certain, good condition, rent (it) out*

End product

In *Put it all together*, students write a story with a moral. They read their stories to the group for others to guess the moral. Their writing is based the paragraph structure in exercise 5.

Warmer

Elicit or remind students of weather sayings from lesson 9A, e.g. *Red sky at night, sailor's delight.* In pairs, students discuss other sayings in their own language. Ask for volunteers to tell the class about the sayings and what they mean.

Write *How to write a story with a moral* on the board.

A Read a story with a moral

In this section, students read for gist and detail in sayings and a short story.

1   Ask students to read sayings 1–6 and check vocabulary. Go through the instructions and the first example. Elicit or explain that they should choose a word which is connected to the topic of the sentence. Tell students they will think about the meaning in the next exercise.

Put students into pairs and monitor and help as necessary. Ask for volunteers to give answers and see if the class agrees.

> 2 hand   3 eggs   4 houses   5 baby   6 book

2   Read through questions 1 and 2 before asking students to read meanings a–f. Check vocabulary and go through the example. Monitor and help as students continue in pairs. Check answers before asking students to tell the class about sayings with similar meanings in their language.

> a 6   b 3   c 2   e 4   f 5

3   Go through the instruction and direct students to *A Heart of Gold.* Ask students to read the story, ignoring new vocabulary. Students compare answers in pairs before checking as a class. Encourage them to explain why the moral matches the story and help them get their ideas across.

> **Moral:** 6 Never judge a book by its cover.

4   Read sentences 1–5 with the class and check vocabulary. Do the example with the class. Monitor and help, encouraging students to use their dictionaries only when they need to. Students compare answers in pairs before checking as a class.

> 2 ... she decided to rent it out to somebody.   3 ... find somebody.
> 4 ... she thought Mick looked like a criminal.   5 ... the next time she visited, lots of work had been done to the house and garden.

B Think about paragraph structure

5   Ask students to cover the story in exercise 3. Set a short time limit for students, in pairs, to add any key words and phrases from the story. Give students time to look again at the story before eliciting answers around the class.

> **para 1:** not strong, window frames, couldn't afford to, wanted to sell, wanted to move
> **para 2:** upstairs not used, decided to rent, earn cash, advertised, shaved head, torn leather jacket, broken nose, like a criminal
> **para 3:** three months later, Hilary visited, house beautiful, window frames painted, Mick cutting grass

6   Read the instructions and check vocabulary in the stories. Go through the first story with the class to demonstrate the activity. Elicit or point out that the paragraph order is the same as that in *A Heart of Gold.* Students continue in pairs, using dictionaries as necessary. Elicit answers around the class.

Monitor and help as students continue with the other story outlines. Ask for volunteers to tell their ideas to the class.

> **Suggested answers**
> 1 The woman lost everything.   2 The police found that the politician who had complained was corrupt.   3 He couldn't find another job.

AB Put it all together

7   Go through the instructions. Students complete the activity in pairs. Remind them they can use the story outlines in exercise 6, write a story for another moral in exercise 1, or think of another story to end with a moral from their own language.

8   Ask students to write their stories but remind them not to include the moral at the end. Remind students to use *because, so,* and *(in order) to* to join clauses, and *-ing* and *-ed* clauses when the subject of two short sentences is the same.

9   Put students into groups to read and guess the moral.

Student performance

Students should be able to write a detailed narrative with a moral.

You can use this checklist to monitor and give feedback or to assess students' performance.

Content	Have students given sufficient detail to explain the events of the story?
Organization	Have students followed the paragraph structure?
Discourse	Have students used *because, so,* and *(in order) to* to link clauses?

I can write a story with a moral.

Students tick *on my own* if they can write their story without looking at the grammar areas in lessons 12A and C before joining clauses. They can tick *with some help* if they need to look at 12A or 12C again before joining clauses.

Early finishers

Students read their text again and check grammar and vocabulary.

Additional material

www.oup.com/elt/result for extra practice activities
www.oup.com/elt/teacher/result for extra teacher resources

Warmer

Remember the story

Write the following story titles on the board: *A Desert Island Joke; B Sweeney Todd; C The Shape of Things to Come; D The Covered Wagon; E King Solomon's Mines; F The Bread Seller's trick; G The Smell of Soup; H Basia and her daughter; I The cruel landlord; J Karen's life.*

Say sentences 1–10 below for students to call out the story letter.

1 This book was written in 1933 and is full of predictions. 2 One of the characters in this story finds a bottle. 3 This murder story takes place in a barber's shop. 4 This story is about a woman who wanted some meat. 5 In this life story, the woman became an actress. 6 In this romance, Molly leaves Kansas to find a new life in the west. 7 This story involves the murder of a cruel landlord. 8 In this story, a woman saves her daughter from prison. 9 This is an adventure about an English hunter living in Africa. 10 This story is about a woman who beat a person's shadow.

| 1 C | 2 A | 3 B | 4 F | 5 J | 6 D | 7 I | 8 H | 9 E | 10 G |

A Grammar

1 so, because, (in order) to 12A exercise 6

Warm-up: Write the words *tired, sleep well,* and *rest* on the board. Ask students to write three sentences, using the words *so, because,* and *in order to.*

Set-up: Ask students to read items 1–6 and check vocabulary.

2 so 3 because 4 (in order) to 5 (in order) to 6 so

Follow-up: Students look again at *African Stories* and write five gap-fill sentences for *so, because,* and *in order to.* They swap with a partner and complete the sentences.

2 wish 12B exercise 11

Warm-up: Set a short time limit of about two minutes for students to write sentences about Shorty and Lofty using *wish.*

Set-up: Ask students to read the text and find four topics (*place to live, money, speak languages, world peace*).

2 didn't live 3 was/were 4 didn't have 5 could speak
6 would communicate

Follow-up: Students look at >> p.133 and write their own desert island *Wish box.* They tell a partner about their wishes and explain why.

3 -ing and -ed clauses 12C exercise 8

Warm-up: Write the following words on the board for students to make a sentence with two clauses: *owner, man, the, is, called, Sweeney, he, a, is, Todd.* Tell them there are two words that they don't need. (*The owner is a man called Sweeney Todd.*)

Set-up: Go through the example and point out that the verb at the end is used twice.

2 called, calling 3 written, writing 4 covering, covered

Follow-up: In pairs, students write a short text about a book or a film they know. Each sentence includes an *-ed* or *-ing* clause. They swap with another pair and check.

4 3rd conditional 12D exercise 5

Warm-up: Write *I ate the fish.* on the board. Elicit examples of sentences about the opposite situation beginning with *If I hadn't eaten the fish ... .*

Set-up: Remind students to think about positive and negative clauses.

2 ... I wouldn't have bought it.
3 ... raining, we wouldn't have gone out.
4 If I hadn't heard a noise, I wouldn't have phoned the police.
5 If they had studied, they wouldn't have failed the test.

Follow-up: Student write five statements about something they have done. They swap with a partner, who writes or talks about the opposite situation, before swapping back and deciding if they agree with what their partner says.

B Vocabulary

5 wish, hope, be glad 12B exercise 2

Warm-up: Use the cues in exercise 3, >> p.119 to ask students about their feelings, hopes, and wishes.

Set-up: Point out that item 2 is a dialogue.

2 I hope 3 I wish 4 I wish 5 I hope 6 I'm glad

Follow-up: Students write a similar exercise for a partner.

6 Stories, books, fiction 12C exercise 3

Warm-up: Set a short time limit for students to remember vocabulary to describe the books covers on >> p.120. Direct students to exercise 3 on >> p.121 to check.

Set up: Ask students to read the clues and check vocabulary as necessary.

Across 4 plot 6 adventure 8 set 9 character 10 story
11 romance 12 bestseller
Down 1 collection 2 murderer 3 science 5 western 7 treasure

Follow-up: In pairs, students write sentences to describe a famous book or film. They tell another pair, who guess the name.

Early finishers

Students find ten words connected with stories, books, and fiction that they want to remember. They write a sentence with each one.

Unit 12 Review

A Grammar

1 *so, because, (in order) to* Complete the sentences with *so*, *because*, or *(in order) to*.

1 The grass is wet *because* it's been raining.
2 It's been raining _____ the grass is wet.
3 She went to bed _____ she was tired.
4 She went home _____ rest.
5 I went to the market _____ buy some food.
6 I needed some food _____ I went to the market.

2 *wish* Complete the text with the correct form of the verbs in brackets.

Three wishes
OK, first – I wish I ¹ *lived* (live) somewhere nice. I wish I ² _____ (not live) in a noisy city with terrible weather. Second – I wish I ³ _____ (be) rich. I wish I ⁴ _____ (not have) to work every day. And my third wish – I wish I ⁵ _____ (can speak) lots of languages. I wish people around the world ⁶ _____ (will communicate) with each other instead of fighting.

3 *-ing* and *-ed* clauses Complete the sentences with the verbs in the correct form to make *-ing* and *-ed* clauses.

1 The baby was in a bag *left* on the step. Nobody saw the mother *leaving* it.   leave
2 Harry was in a pub _____ the Red Lion. He was on the phone _____ the police.   call
3 There was a message on the wall _____ in red paint. No one was seen _____ it.   write
4 There was a hole and there were dry leaves _____ it. Jim fell into it and came out _____ in mud.   cover

4 3rd conditional Write sentences in the third conditional to give the opposite situation.

1 I ate the fish and I felt sick.
   If I hadn't eaten the fish, *I wouldn't have felt sick.*
2 The CD was good so I bought it.
   If the CD hadn't been good, _____
3 It wasn't raining so we went out.
   If it had been _____
4 I heard a noise so I phoned the police.
   _____
5 They didn't study so they failed the test.
   _____

B Vocabulary

5 *wish, hope, be glad* Complete the sentences with these phrases.

   I wish   I hope   I'm glad

1 Here's a little present for you. *I hope* you like it.
2 **A** Thanks for the present. I love it.
   B You're welcome. _____ you like it!
3 _____ it would stop raining! I've got to go out to the shops.
4 _____ my flat wasn't so small. I haven't got enough space for my books.
5 _____ I'll have a job by this time next year.
6 _____ I've got a book to read, otherwise I'd be bored to death.

6 Stories, books, fiction Do the crossword.

Across
2 A genre: murder _____.
4 What happens in a story.
6 A genre with a lot of action.
8 The story happened in London. It is _____ in London.
9 A person in a story.
10 Something which happened, real or fiction.
11 A love story.
12 A book that thousands of people buy.

Down
1 A group of objects of the same sort, e.g. a book _____.
2 The person who kills in 2 across.
3 A genre: _____ fiction.
5 A story about cowboys and Indians.
7 A collection of gold, diamonds, jewellery, and other valuables.

Pairwork

1B Put it all together
Student A Two countries

Make notes to answer these questions.
1 How do people greet each other?
2 How do they address each other?
3 What do people say when they meet?

1 China

The Chinese bow slightly when they greet each other, and they often shake hands when they meet people for the first time. The handshake is not very strong, and it lasts quite a long time. People address each other by their surname and a title such as Mr or Mrs, Doctor or Teacher. They never use the surname without a title. The most common greeting in formal situations is 'How are you?' while in informal situations they often ask, 'Have you eaten?' People often reply, 'Yes, I have' to this question to be polite, so the other person doesn't have to offer food.

2 Jamaica

When Jamaicans meet for the first time, it is normal to shake hands, smile, and look each other in the eye. When people know each other better, women usually hug each other and kiss each other on both cheeks, starting with the right. Men often touch each other on the arm while greeting. To begin with, people address each other by their surname and a title such as Mr, Mrs, or Miss. Common greetings include 'Good morning', 'Good afternoon', and 'Good evening'. When people know each other, they use first names or nicknames.

1D Put it all together
Misunderstandings

In a shop ...
A Can I have some pears, please?
B Some pairs of what?

At home ...
A Where's the flour?
B The flower? It's in the vase on the table.

On holiday ...
A How did you get here?
B Road.
A Rode what? A bike?

A stressed parent ...
A I just want a little peace.
B A little piece of what?

Planning a meeting ...
A Does anybody know when the meeting is?
B Mr Long knows.
A Who's Mr Long Nose?

2C Exercise 14
Object A

This is a kind of bag from Scotland, and it's called a *sporran*. Men wear it with the traditional Scottish Highland clothing. This sporran is made of fur and it has a metal part to close the top of the bag. It's used for carrying money or other things, which is useful because traditional Highland clothes don't have any pockets.

1C Put it all together
Student A Family photo

Ask and say who the people are.
Example A Who's the woman in the green T-shirt? She's sitting and talking to two other women.
B That's Clara. She's Billy's aunt. She's a graphic designer.

1 Billy. Aged 13. Loves sports. Wants to be a footballer.
3 Grace. Aged 14. Wants to be a singer.
5 Laura. Aged 15. Likes clothes. Wants to be a model.
7 Jean. Billy's mum. Works in a bank.
9 Raymond. Billy's grandfather. Retired.
11 Nina. Friend of the family. Lives in California.
13 Uncle Joe. Jean's brother. Taxi driver.
15 Belinda. Joe's girlfriend. Hairdresser.

2C Put it all together
Guess the objects

corkscrew	saw	ice cube tray	razor
nail clippers	paint brush	paper clip	drill
orange juicer	scissors	plaster	hairdryer
hole punch	tape measure	teaspoon	can-opener

3C Put it all together
Hospitality role play

Role play 1

A host	B visitor
– your visitor's coat is wet	– you've been out in the rain
– your visitor looks hungry	– you had dinner half an hour ago
– the radio is very loud	– you've got a headache
– your visitor looks bored	– you'd like to watch the news on TV
– your visitor looks thirsty	– you'd like a cup of tea

Role play 2

B host	A visitor
– your visitor looks very hot	– you've been playing tennis
– your dog is jumping on your visitor	– you love dogs
– your visitor must catch an early train tomorrow morning	– you left your alarm clock at home
– your visitor looks hungry	– you are very hungry
– your visitor goes to wash the dishes	– you want to help by washing up

4A Put it all together
Student A Feelings

Write one or two words in each shape.
1 Something you do when you're bored.
2 An amazing place you've visited.
3 An amusing film you've seen.
4 Something you're interested in.
5 Music you find exciting.
6 Something that makes you feel worried.
7 The most terrifying moment in your life.

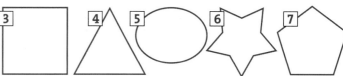

Now look at the words in your partner's shapes and ask about them.

Example **A** Draw – what's that?
B It's something I do when I'm bored. I draw little pictures on my notebook.
A So when do you feel bored?
B In meetings ...

4B Exercise 3
Are you into music? Answer Key

Calculate your partner's score.

1 Score 1 point for each tick and 1 point for the correct order: radio–records–tapes–CDs–MP3 player
2 Score 1 point for matching all three:
   a 3 **c** 2 **d** 1
3 Score 1 point for each tick.
4 Score 1 point each for **a**, **b**, **c**, and **d**. Score 3 points for **e**!
5 Score 1 point for each correct answer.
   a a grand piano is bigger than a keyboard
   b an electric guitar is louder than a Spanish guitar
   c a saxophone is heavier than a recorder
   d the violin is the smallest, the double bass is the biggest
6 Score 1 point each if you ticked **a** and **b**. Score 2 points if you ticked **c**. Score 3 points if you ticked **d**.
7 Score 1 point for getting all the correct answers and 1 point for the question.
   1 rap **2** rock **3** opera **4** country **5** jazz **6** reggae
   Opera is the oldest.
8 Score 1 point for each tick.
9 Score 1 point if you ticked **c**, and 2 points if you ticked **d**.

------

35 or more points You are a real music fan, maybe even obsessed! I don't think I'd like to share a flat with you.

Between 25 and 34 points You seem to be into music. We know what to get you for your birthday!

Between 15 and 24 points You're not especially into music. You don't mind what you listen to. Let somebody else make the party mix!

Fewer than 15 points I guess you're not too keen on music, then?

Pairwork

4B Put it all together
Music

Make notes in the table about the music, venues, and entertainment you prefer and why. Then discuss your ideas.

	I prefer ...	because ...
music	classical ...	most relaxing ...
venues	stadium ...	
entertainment	theatre ...	

4D Exercise 4
Types of film Research results

Order of preference		
	male	female
1	drama	drama
2	action	romance
3	science fiction	action
4	comedy	comedy
5	fantasy	fantasy
6	romance	musical
7	musical	science fiction

5A Put it all together
Politics

1 Who is the head of state and what is his/her title (president/prime minister/king ...)?
2 How often are there elections? Who can and can't vote?
3 What are the main parties? Which are more left wing and which are more right wing?
4 Where are the government buildings and what are they called?
5 What international organizations does the country belong to?
6 What does the flag look like? What does it represent?
7 Are there any animals, trees, or flowers which are used as symbols of the country?

5C Put it all together
Headlines

WOMAN ARRESTED IN HOUSES OF PARLIAMENT **MAN ATTACKED BY CROCODILE**

PRESIDENT'S SON KIDNAPPED **FIVE HURT IN TRAIN CRASH**

Write notes to answer these questions.
1 When and where did it happen?
2 Who were the people involved?
3 How/Why did it happen?
4 What are the details?

5E Exercise 10
Narrating a story

I was walking back to the hotel when I noticed that someone was following me. It was late at night and I was alone. This was in Barcelona. I'd been to a concert and I'd taken a taxi back to the hotel. The taxi couldn't take me to the door of the hotel because it was in a pedestrian area, so I had to walk the last 500 metres.

When I heard the footsteps behind me, I was scared and I walked faster. The person behind me walked faster too, so I started to run. The person behind me shouted, 'Stop!' but I didn't stop until I reached the hotel. At the hotel it was light and there was a night porter, so I felt safe. I had escaped from my attacker!

However, to my surprise, my attacker followed me into the hotel. But he wasn't a robber and he hadn't been trying to attack me. He was the taxi driver and he was returning my bag. I'd left it in the taxi!

6A Put it all together
Tell a story

Think of the best or worst ...
   film you've seen or book you've read.
   hotel or holiday place you've stayed at.
   experience you've had while travelling.
   experience you've had at school or work.

What happened? Why was it good or bad?

What extreme adjectives could you use to describe ...
   the experience?
   your feelings about it?

6B Put it all together
Student A Picture story

You are the person in the story. For each of the four pictures in the story, imagine some extra details – for example, when and where was it? How did you feel? Write notes.

6C Put it all together
Are you a good neighbour?

Interview your partner and tick ✓ the answers which are true for him/her.

1 Who do you know in your neighbourhood?
I know the next-door neighbours.
I know the upstairs/downstairs neighbours.
I know some people in the building/street.
I know some shopkeepers.
Other ...

2 How well do you know your neighbours?
We say hello.
I know their names.
We often stop for a chat.
I often socialize with them.
I never see them, and I'm happier that way.
Other ...

3 What kinds of problems have you had with people in your neighbourhood?
They're nosy.
They're noisy.
Their children are naughty.
Their dog barks all day.
They park their car in my space.
They always complain.
Other ...

4 How much do you help each other?
We look after each other's pets or water each other's plants while we're away.
We keep a key for each other in case of emergency.
We help each other with shopping or housework.
I go to community meetings.
Other ...

6D Put it all together
Student A The Violin Story Part A

Sebastian, dressed in cheap clothes and carrying a violin, went into the Ritz Restaurant and had a meal. At the end, he said to the owner, 'I'm sorry. I've left my wallet at home. I'll go home and collect it. I'll leave my violin with you as security.'

Sebastian returned to the restaurant with his wallet and paid for his meal. The restaurant owner said, 'I like your violin. I'll give you $5,000 for it.' Sebastian agreed, took the money, and left.

Tell your part of the story to your partner, using reported speech. Then answer these questions with your partner.
1 How are the two parts of the story connected?
2 How much is the violin really worth?
3 Did John know Sebastian?
4 Who is telling a lie?
5 Who is the victim?

Now read the solution on ➤➤ p.133.

7A Put it all together
Portraits of men

Student A Choose a photo, but keep it secret.

The others Ask closed questions to guess which photo it is. Don't say the number until you are sure.

Example **B** Has he got long dark hair?
A No, **short** dark hair.
C Does he look happy?
A No, he looks **worried**.

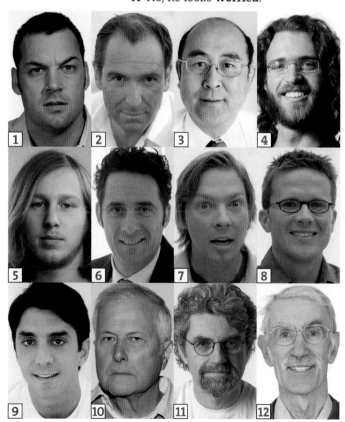

Pairwork

7D Exercise 4
The Bedroom in Arles

The picture is called 'The Bedroom' and it was painted by Vincent van Gogh (born 1853, died 1890). The room is in Arles, in the south of France. One of the portraits we see on the wall is this self-portrait by the artist.

Vincent moved to Arles from Paris in 1888 and rented this room and a couple of others. He had very little money and survived with help from his brother, Theo.

Vincent suffered from mental health problems and killed himself in 1890. The house in Arles was destroyed in the Second World War.

7D Put it all together
Two rooms – the photos

Tell your partner your guesses about the photos. Do you agree?

Example   **A** I think this must be a man's room.
       B Are you sure? It might be a woman's room.
       A I think it's a man's room because …

Then read about the people who live in these rooms on » p.134. Were any of your guesses correct?

Room 1

Room 2

8A Put it all together
Phoning Frank

Choose roles, plan what you are going to say, and then do the role play.

Example   **A** This is the ABC Tyre Company. Can I help you?
       B Yes, I'd like to speak to Frank Jones on extension 123, please.

Caller
You are Mary Smith and you urgently need to speak to Frank Jones at the ABC Tyre Company. You phone the company and speak to his secretary. Ask for Mr Jones on extension 123. If he's busy, say you'll wait or call back again. You want to speak to him personally and you don't want to leave a message. You could ask for his mobile number. If you get cut off, call again. If you think the secretary is trying to stop you getting through to Mr Jones, say that you're calling about a *very* important business deal which could earn Mr Jones many thousands of euros, but you must speak to him today.

Answerer
You are Frank Jones's secretary at the ABC Tyre Company. Mr Jones has taken the afternoon off to go and play golf, but he doesn't want anybody to know. He has asked you to make excuses for him, saying he's busy in a meeting or speaking on the phone or his car's broken down or something. You could take a message or offer to put callers through to his colleague, Mrs Sandra Summers. You *mustn't* give his mobile phone number to anybody! If callers insist on speaking to Mr Jones, you could hang up and pretend that you got cut off.

8B Put it all together
Ideas

Look at these ideas. Write notes about your story in the box.
1 The first time you did something (went abroad; rode a bike; spoke in public …)
2 A time when you lost something (a key; a passport; money …)
3 A time when you wanted to do something but couldn't (start a car; find the way; remember a name …)
4 *Your ideas* …

When and where did it happen?	
Who is it about?	
What was the problem?	
What did the people do to solve the problem?	
What was the result?	

8D Put it all together
Questions

Look at these questions and write notes.

1 Where and when was it?
2 Why did you speak to him/her?
3 Was it a nice encounter or an unfortunate one?
4 Who spoke first – you or the other person?
5 Which of these things did you or the other person do?
   advise agree ask invite offer
   promise refuse tell warn
6 What did you or the other person actually say? Write it down. If it was in another language, translate it into English.

9C Exercise 13
Student A Safety Leaflet A

Write notes to answer these questions.

1 Where could you face this danger?
2 What shouldn't you do, and why?
3 What *should* you do, and in what situation?
4 What can you do to protect yourself?

NATIONAL PARK GUIDELINES
BEAR SAFETY

What should I do if I meet a grizzly bear?

If a grizzly bear sees or hears you, it will probably run away. Most bears don't like contact with humans. For this reason, it is a good idea to make some noise while you're walking. You could carry a bell, or clap your hands and shout every few minutes.

However, if you get too close and surprise a bear, it might get aggressive. If the bear is angry, it will hit the ground with its paws, show its teeth and rush towards you. If this happens, stay calm. Do not turn and run. If you run, the bear will run after you – and bears can run up to 50 km per hour! Make yourself look big by putting your arms up. If you are in a group, stay close together. Don't take off your backpack – if the bear attacks, it will give you protection. Talk to the bear, and walk slowly backwards. You could climb a tree if you have time, but remember that bears can climb the lower part of a tree, so you will need to go up high.

If the bear attacks, you can use a bear spray. Wait until the bear is very near and direct the spray at its face. This will often stop an attacking bear. However, if it continues attacking, fall to the ground, protect your head and play dead. When the bear moves away, don't move immediately or it will come back again.

Please report all encounters with aggressive bears to the park ranger.

10D Exercise 3 and Put it all together
Personality Quiz!

Calculate your score to find your shopping personality. Circle your answers for each question and then count how many W, X, Y, and Z you've got.

Are you mostly W, X, Y, or Z? Most people will have a little of all four, but you're probably more of one than the rest. Read your shopping personality below.

	a	b	c	d
1	Z	X	W	Y
2	X	W	Z	Y
3	Z	Y	X	W
4	W	Y	X	Z
5	X	Z	W	Y

W You're an **organized shopper**. You plan what you're going to buy and shop around for the best deal. You like bargain hunting in discount shops. You do a lot of research about products and make notes. You always ask the shop assistant about what's included in the price. You read the small print of the guarantee. If the product is not perfect, you'll ask for a discount. It's a competitive world out there, and everybody's trying to get your money off you – but you won't let them!

X You're a **good-taste shopper**. You look for quality products and well-known makes. You often read about products in magazines or on the Internet so you know which is best and most up-to-date. You don't mind paying more for something good. There are lots of people out there trying to sell you cheap rubbish, but you know better!

Y You're a **pleasure shopper**. Shopping is one of the things you like doing in your free time. You like browsing in the shops to see what there is, and you quite often buy things you never planned to buy. How can you know what you want until you've seen what's available? You'll wander around the shops even if you haven't got any money – dreaming is free!

Z You're an **anti-shopper**. You buy what you need, when you need it. You go for the easiest option – you don't waste time shopping around. You sometimes surprise shop assistants by saying, 'I'll take it' immediately, with no questions asked. Maybe you could get a better deal if you spent more time looking, but life's too short and you've got better things to do!

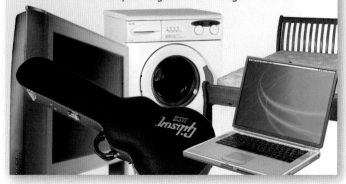

Pairwork

11A Put it all together
Student A Map

You want to find:

Luigi's Restaurant   Stanton's Chemist   Public Library
Chaucer Monument   Post Office   Clancy's Coffee Shop

Example   **A** (I'm at number 1) Excuse me, can you tell me the way to Luigi's Restaurant?
B Yes. Go straight along …

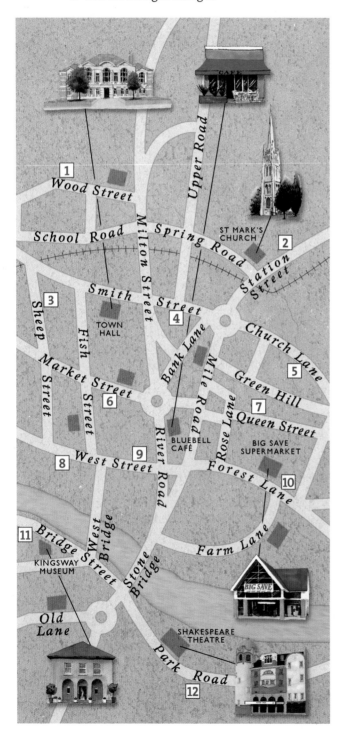

11C Put it all together
Travel advice

1 Tick ✓ the statements you agree with.
   1 You don't need to prepare for holidays in advance.
   2 You need to get travel insurance.
   3 You ought to take all possible health precautions.
   4 You should just get up and go.
   5 Travel is more fun when you're not too well prepared.

2 Work in pairs or small groups. Choose two of these holidays and tell the others where you're going and what you plan to do. Listen and give the others travel advice.
   – Backpacking in Asia
   – Camping in Central Europe
   – Carnival in Brazil
   – Safari in East Africa
   – Working holiday in the USA

   Example   **A** I'm going backpacking in Asia. What should I do before I go?
   B You should have some injections.
   C You ought to …

12A Put it all together
Is it stealing?

Look at these situations. Do you think the person has done anything wrong? Is it stealing?

1 Adam takes an apple from a tree. The tree is in a private garden but the apple was hanging over the pavement.
2 Barbara sits in the park working on her laptop. She notices that somebody's wireless Internet connection is available, so she checks her email.
3 Colin finds a valuable antique in a rubbish bin, so he takes it.
4 Diana takes a video camera into the cinema and records the whole film to watch again later.
5 Eddy downloads a film from the Internet. He records it onto DVDs to sell around the college.
6 Fiona makes a copy of her new CD to give to a friend.
7 Gemma finds somebody's cat in her house. It doesn't have an identification collar, so she decides to keep it.
8 Harry finds a €20 note in the street. Nobody has seen him pick it up, so he keeps it.
9 Ian finds a €20 note on the floor of the bank and keeps it.
10 Jenny drinks the mineral water from the hotel mini-bar. Then she discovers that it's much more expensive than normal, so she fills the bottle with tap water and puts it back.

12B Put it all together
Wish box

Complete these sentences with a word or phrase. Write your word or phrase in one of the squares in the wish box below. For example, if your first sentence is *I wish I was rich*, write the word *rich* in one of the squares in the wish box.

I wish I was …	I wish I could …
I hope I'll be able to …	I hope I'll get …
I'm glad I've got a …	I wish I could travel to …
I'm glad I'm not …	I wish I had a …
I hope I won't meet …	I wish I didn't have to …
I'm glad I can …	I hope I'll never have to …

6D Put it all together
The Violin Story solution

Sebastian and John were working together to trick the restaurant owner. Sebastian ate at the restaurant, went home to collect his wallet, and left the violin as security. John went into the restaurant after Sebastian had left to collect his wallet. He convinced the owner that the violin was valuable, but in fact it was a very cheap violin. He offered to buy it and left his phone number. When Sebastian returned, the restaurant owner decided to buy the violin from him so that he could sell it to John. Sebastian and John earned $5,000 in the deal, minus the cost of the cheap violin and two meals.

1B Put it all together
Student B Two countries

Make notes to answer these questions.
1. How do people greet each other?
2. How do they address each other?
3. What do people say when they meet?

1 France
The French shake hands in formal situations, but with friends and family, they kiss on the cheeks. This can happen between two women or between a man and a woman. Two men sometimes hug or touch each other on the shoulder. The number of kisses in a greeting is different in different parts of the country – in some places it's two kisses, in other places three, and in Paris it's four. In formal situations, people address each other by a title – Mr, Mrs, or Miss and a surname. They use first names when they know each other well. Common greetings include 'Good day' and 'How are you?'

2 Indonesia
Indonesians usually shake hands with each other and say the word 'Selamat' when they meet. After shaking hands, they often bow slightly or put their hand over their heart. When they meet a few people at the same time, they greet the oldest first. People greet each other using a title such as Mr or Doctor and the person's name. Many Indonesians have only one name, and often it is very long, so when they know each other better, they use a nickname.

2C Exercise 14
Object B

This is a kind of water heater from Russia, and it's called a *samovar*. The hot water is used for making tea, and there is a teapot on the top of the samovar. The samovar is made of metal and looks like a vase. It stands on one leg, and it has handles on the sides for carrying it. It has a tap in the front for pouring the hot water out.

1C Put it all together
Student B Family photo

Ask and say who the people are.

Example **B** Who's the boy in the yellow T-shirt? He's catching a ball …

A Well, that's Billy. He's 13, and he loves sports. He wants to be a footballer.

2 Clara. Aunt of the boy with the ball. Graphic designer.
4 Ellen. Aged 12. Interested in animals. Has a pet spider.
6 Kylie. Aged 9. Top in her class at school.
8 Frank. Jean's husband. Doctor. Owner of the house.
10 Jeff. Clara's husband. Comes from Puerto Rico.
12 Martin. Friend of the family. Actor.
14 Maya. Clara's sister. Works in a supermarket.
16 Lisa. Aged 18. Plays the guitar. Studying at university.

Pairwork

4A Put it all together
Student B Feelings

Write one or two words in each shape.

1 An exciting film you've seen.
2 A game you find entertaining.
3 Something that would make you feel embarrassed.
4 Something that fascinated you as a child.
5 Something that makes you worried.
6 Something that makes you feel annoyed.
7 The most amazing thing you've done.

Now look at the words in your partner's shapes and ask about them.

Example A Draw – what's that?
B It's something I do when I'm bored. I draw little pictures on my notebook.
A So when do you feel bored?
B In meetings …

6B Put it all together
Student B Picture story

You are the person in the story. For each of the four pictures in the story, imagine some extra details – for example, when and where was it? How did you feel? Write notes.

6D Put it all together
Student B The Violin Story Part B

John, dressed in expensive clothes, went into the Ritz Restaurant for a meal. He noticed a violin lying on the bar and said to the restaurant owner, 'I like the violin. I'm a collector. It's a very fine instrument. I'll give you $50,000 for it.'

The restaurant owner said, 'I don't know. I'll think about it.' John gave the restaurant owner his phone number and left.

Tell your part of the story to your partner, using reported speech. Then answer these questions with your partner.

1 How are the two parts of the story connected?
2 How much is the violin really worth?
3 Did John know Sebastian?
4 Who is telling a lie?
5 Who is the victim?

Now read the solution on >> p.133.

7D Exercise 7
Mystery person

The mystery person is Nicole Kidman.

7D Put it all together
Two rooms – the people

Room 1

This room belongs to Jimmy Eberhard, from Bremen. He's in his late twenties and he's single. He lives in a rented flat with two friends. He's a sound engineer, and he sometimes works from home. He doesn't earn a lot of money and he doesn't save much from month to month. He plays the electric guitar in a heavy rock group.

Room 2

This room belongs to Aurora Gonzalez, from Valencia. She's in her sixties and she's a retired government worker. She never married. Her main interest is history – she has a lot of books and magazines about it, and she has studied the history of her own family tree. She has quite a lot of money saved in the bank as well as her pension, but she doesn't spend a lot.

9C Exercise 13
Student B Safety Leaflet B

Write notes to answer these questions.
1 Where could you face this danger?
2 What shouldn't you do, and why?
3 What *should* you do, and in what situation?
4 What can you do to protect yourself?

Citizens Advice
What to do in a tornado

A tornado can lift a person off the ground and carry them up to a mile away. However, this is very rare. The biggest danger is being hit by flying rubbish.

If you see a tornado, you shouldn't try to escape in your car. A tornado can move faster than a car, and cars are often lifted by tornados. In any case, the road may be blocked.

If you're in a house, you should go into the basement. If you haven't got a basement, find a place away from the windows – an inner room or cupboard perhaps. Bathrooms are often the best place. If you lie in the bath with something over you, you will be well protected. The bath is fixed to the ground by the water pipes, and sometimes it's the only thing left after a tornado has passed!

If you're in a mobile home, you should get out fast and find a safer place. Most tornado deaths happen in mobile homes.

If you are out in the open, the best thing to do is lie in a ditch. Try to find something to cover you to protect you from flying rubbish.

If you're in a school or workplace, go to an interior room or corridor on the lowest floor. Don't go into very large open rooms – corridors are better. Don't use the lift. Stay away from windows and doors. Sit on the floor, cover your head, and try to make yourself as small as possible!

11A Put it all together
Student B Map

You want to find:

St Mark's Church   Town Hall   Big Save Supermarket
Shakespeare Theatre   Bluebell Café   Kingsway Museum

Example **B** (I'm at number 2) Excuse me, can you tell me the way to St Mark's Church?
         A Yes. Go straight along ...

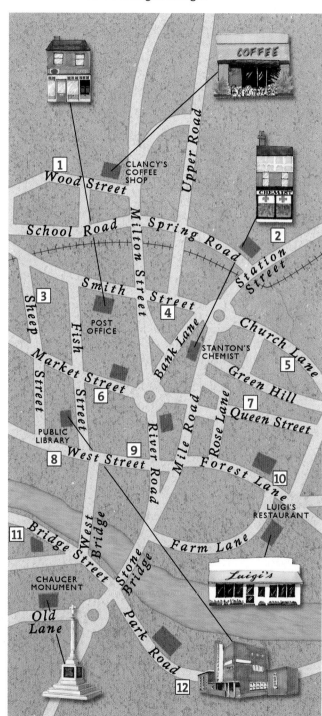

Grammar Bank

1A subject and object questions

Use a subject question to ask about the subject, who or what does an action.

Use an object question to ask about the object, who or what receives an action.

subject questions	object questions
Who lives **here**? Julie.	Who did you call? My sister.
Who lives **with Wanda**? Fatima.	Who was Jim talking to? His brother-in-law.

- Change the word order in an object question, e.g. *He works in an office. Where does he work?*
- Don't change the word order in a subject question, e.g. *Julie lives here. Who lives here?*
- Don't use the auxiliary verb *do* in subject questions. ~~What did happen?~~

>> Now go to **exercise 1.1** to practise.

1A *wh-* / *how* questions

Use *wh-* and *how* questions to ask for information.

Who's your boss?   What's your name?
Which is their flat? Number 6 or number 7?   Where does he live?
When did she call?   Why are we waiting?

>> Now go to **exercise 1.2** to practise.

1B reflexive pronouns

Use reflexive pronouns when the subject and object are the same.

Use *by* + a reflexive pronoun to mean *alone*, e.g. *I did my homework by myself.* (without any help)

subject pronouns	possessive adjectives	object pronouns	reflexive pronouns	
I	my	me	myself	I introduced myself to the rest of the group.
you	your	you	yourself	Why don't you get yourself a drink?
he	his	him	himself	He lives by himself.
she	her	her	herself	Ellen taught herself to paint.
we	our	us	ourselves	We enjoyed ourselves at the party.
they	their	them	themselves	Julie and Dave did everything by themselves.

>> Now go to **exercise 1.3** to practise.

1C present simple and continuous

Use the present simple for verbs which describe states, an action which happens often, and permanent or long-term facts.

Use the present continuous for actions happening at this moment and actions happening these days, but perhaps not at this moment.

present simple	present continuous
I sometimes visit art galleries.	I'm wearing my new shoes.
You're often late for lessons.	You're looking at a painting by Goya.
He doesn't live in Paris.	My computer isn't working.
Does she like modern art?	Is Simon enjoying his course?
How do we get to the museum?	Where are they sitting?

- Use the present simple with state verbs, e.g. *believe, know, see, understand, want,* etc.

>> Now go to **exercise 1.4** to practise.

1.1 Are the questions subject questions or object questions?
Example Who works in a bank?   *subject*

1   Who did you see at the party?
2   Who married Tom Cruise?
3   Who is learning to play a musical instrument?
4   Who divorced Brad Pitt in 2005?
5   Who does he work with?
6   Who did they meet in London?
7   Who left this message for me?
8   Who lives in this house?

1.2 Underline the correct question word.
Example Who/What is Tina's flatmate?

1   Where/When do your parents live?
2   Who/Why does your neighbour complain?
3   What/When do you do?
4   When/Which building does he work in?
5   What/When did they get married?
6   Who/What lives in that house?

1.3 Right or wrong? Tick ✓ or correct the underlined words.
Example I taught himself to play the guitar. ✗ *myself*

1   They cooked the meal themselves.
2   I cleaned the house herself.
3   He introduced herself to the class.
4   We did the homework by each other.
5   Have you known each other for a long time?
6   Julie, I want you to do this by myself.
7   She doesn't live by yourself.
8   We said 'Hello' to ourselves.

1.4 Underline the correct tense – present continuous or present simple.

A   My mum sent me some old family photos. Do you want/Are you wanting to see them?
B   Yes, please. I ¹love/'m loving old photos.
A   This is my friend Josie. She ²studies/'s studying maths at Oxford University now so we ³don't see/aren't seeing each other very often.
B   Oh, right!
A   Her brother ⁴has/'s having a house in Spain and we ⁵sometimes spend/'re sometimes spending our holidays there.
B   This is my family – we ⁶have/'re having a picnic at my cousins' house. I ⁷sit/'m sitting on the ground and my cousins ⁸stand/are standing behind me.
A   Where ⁹do your cousins live/are your cousins living?
B   In London. Oh, here's another picture of me.
A   The sun ¹⁰shines/is shining! Why ¹¹are you wearing/do you wear a winter coat?
B   I ¹²don't know/'m not knowing. I was only three years old!

2A the before geographical names

names with the	mountain ranges, rivers, oceans and seas, island groups, deserts, some countries, some regions	We visited the Andes. The River Seine flows through Paris. I worked in the Middle East.
names without the	most regions, single mountains, most countries, continents, single islands, cities, lakes	She lives in Western Australia. They climbed Mount Everest. France is in Europe.

>> Now go to **exercise 2.1** to practise.

2B adverbs of frequency

Use adverbs of frequency to say how often something happens.

100%   0%

always   often   sometimes   never
    usually   quite often   hardly ever / rarely

use an adverb of frequency before the main verb	Janet usually goes abroad on her holidays.
use an adverb of frequency after the verb be	She's rarely late.

- Put an adverb of frequency between an auxiliary verb and a main verb, e.g. *I've never been on a plane.*

>> Now go to **exercise 2.2** to practise.

2C phrases + prepositions / adverbs

use *made of* + a material or substance	The desk is made of wood.
use *use for / use as* + a purpose	This machine is used for making coffee. Vegetable oil can be used as fuel for cars.
use *covered with* + a material or substance	Baseballs are covered with leather.
use *a kind of* + a classifying noun	A sporran is a kind of bag.
use *look like* + a noun to compare two things	The fishing floats look like balls.

>> Now go to **exercise 2.3** to practise.

2D past simple and past continuous

Use the past continuous for longer actions / to describe the context of a story.

Use the past simple for shorter actions / to describe the events of a story.

past continuous	past simple
While I was sitting on the train,	my mobile phone rang.
They were having dinner	when we arrived.

>> Now go to **exercise 2.4** to practise.

2E time expressions

period of time	relate two times	put events in order
in / during / for a moment / for a while	before / after / (a couple of years) ago / later / when	first / second / then / next / in the end / finally
We met in the evening. I lost my watch during the first week of term.	Put your coat on before you go out. I saw him a few days ago.	It was our first time in Japan. I got up, then I had a shower.

>> Now go to **exercise 2.5** to practise.

2.1 Right or wrong? Tick ✓ or correct the sentences.
Example Washington is in ˏthe USA.

1 The highest mountain in Africa is the Mount Kilimanjaro.
2 United Arab Emirates and India are countries in Asia.
3 They crossed Sahara on foot.
4 We went sailing on Lake Windermere last year.
5 There are some beautiful beaches in California.
6 The Paris is on the River Seine.
7 My sister is working in Far East.
8 Cuba and the Bay Islands are in Caribbean.

2.2 Rewrite the sentences using the adverbs of frequency.
Example I buy souvenirs when I go to a new place.   always
       I always buy souvenirs when I go to a new place.

1 They go to Spain on their holidays.   often
2 I've been to South America.   never
3 He enjoys sightseeing.   rarely
4 We visit museums when we go abroad.   hardly ever
5 Tourists say that Britain is expensive.   sometimes
6 The trains to London are late.   quite often
7 The weather is good in July and August.   usually

2.3 Complete the sentences with these phrases.
made of   used for   ~~used for~~   used as
covered with   a kind of   look like

Example Chopsticks are _used for_ eating Chinese and Japanese food.

1 A kilt is _____ skirt that is sometimes worn by Scottish men.
2 The floors in the house are _____ carpet to keep the rooms warm.
3 DVDs _____ CDs, but you can store more information on a DVD.
4 These books are _____ teaching English.
5 I only wear shoes that are _____ leather.
6 Nowadays, the Internet is often _____ a way of sending messages to people.

2.4 Underline the correct verb form.

I was having/had lots of interesting experiences while I was [1] living/lived in Hong Kong. One evening my boss, Lin, [2] was inviting/invited me to a dinner party in a very expensive Chinese restaurant. When I [3] was arriving/arrived at the restaurant, Lin and her family [4] were waiting/waited at the table. Everyone [5] was wearing/wore traditional Chinese clothes. We [6] were starting/started to eat our meal. It [7] was being/was a bit difficult because I [8] wasn't knowing/didn't know how to use chopsticks. I [9] was sitting/sat opposite Lin's parents and halfway through the meal I [10] was noticing/noticed that they [11] were looking/looked at me. They [12] were trying/tried not to laugh. Lin [13] was explaining/explained that I [14] was holding/held my chopsticks upside down!

2.5 Complete the text using the time expressions.
after   ~~ago~~   before   during   first   for a while
in the end   in the morning   then   when

Four years _ago_ I went to Syria. I had a few problems [1]_____ the first few days because I didn't speak Arabic. I decided to buy a phrase book and every morning, [2]_____ I left the hotel, I practised a few new phrases. At [3]_____ I found the language difficult, but gradually I learnt enough words to say 'Hello' and ask for things in the shops.

I spent a few days in Damascus, [4]_____ I travelled to Palmyra to see the old Roman city. [5]_____ Palmyra, I took a bus to Aleppo. It was so nice that I decided to stay [6]_____ and enrol on an Arabic course. I had lessons [7]_____ and [8]_____ they were over, I explored the city and applied for teaching jobs. [9]_____, I got a job in a language school and stayed for a year.

3A used to

Use *used to* to talk about repeated actions in the past or states in the past that aren't true now.

+	I/You/He/She/It/We/They	used to	get good grades.
			be shy.
−	I/You/He/She/It/We/They	didn't use to	get good grades.
			be shy.
?	Did I/you/he/she/it/we/they	use to	get good grades?
			be shy?

short answers	
Yes, I/you/he/she/it/we/they did.	No, I/you/he/she/it/we/they didn't.

>> Now go to **exercises 3.1 and 3.2** to practise.

3B present perfect and past simple

Use the past simple to talk about past actions which happened in a finished time.

Use the present perfect to talk about past actions which happened in an unfinished time.

past simple	present perfect
I took an exam a few days ago.	She's taken several exams in the last few days.
We didn't have a maths test last term.	They haven't had a maths test this term.
Did you learn any new words last week?	Have you learnt any new words this week?
What did he do yesterday?	What have you done today?

>> Now go to **exercise 3.3** to practise.

3B time expressions

Use expressions of finished time with the past simple.
Use expressions of unfinished time with the present perfect.

expressions of finished time	expressions of unfinished time
yesterday/last week/last year/ in 2002/(a few minutes) ago/ when (you started)	today/this week/this year/ in the last few (minutes)/ since (you started)/in (my) life

>> Now go to **exercise 3.4** to practise.

3C phrasal verbs (1)

A phrasal verb is a verb used with an adverb. Together, they have a particular meaning, e.g. *make up = invent*.

Phrasal verbs can have more than one meaning, e.g. *Take your coat off. The plane took off on time.*

non-separable phrasal verbs without an object (intransitive)	Come on, Jim! I grew up in Italy.
non-separable phrasal verbs with an object (transitive)	Who's looking after the children?
separable phrasal verbs with an object (transitive)	Turn the TV on. He turned it on.

- Phrasal verbs have two parts: a verb + an adverb particle.
- Intransitive phrasal verbs do not have an object. The verb and adverb cannot be separated.
- Transitive phrasal verbs have an object that can be a noun or a pronoun. Sometimes it is possible to put the object between the verb and adverb.
- If the object of a separable transitive verb is a pronoun (*me, you, him, it*, etc.), it must come before the particle. Nouns can go before or after the particle.

>> Now go to **exercise 3.5** to practise.

3.1 Complete the sentences using the correct form of *used to*.
Example **A** Do you ever think about Park School?
B No, I *used to hate* going to school. hate

A We ¹_____ those blue uniforms. wear
B And the boys from Don School ²_____ at us! laugh
A Our teachers were OK though.
B They ³_____ all the time. shout
A Mr Hinchley was nice.
B Did ⁴_____ history? he/teach
A That's right. Did ⁵_____ to his lessons? you/go
B Yes, but I ⁶_____ good grades. not/get

3.2 Tick ✓ the correct sentence in each pair. In some cases both sentences are correct.
Example a We did sport on Wednesdays. ✓
b We used to do sport on Wednesdays. ✓

1 a They had lunch in the school dining room.
  b They used to have lunch in the school dining room.
2 a We had our school disco in the hall yesterday.
  b We used to have our school disco in the hall yesterday.
3 a One year there was a fire in the science classroom.
  b One year there used to be a fire in the science classroom.
4 a Did you have a lot of homework?
  b Did you use to have a lot of homework?
5 a My son went to Park School for four years.
  b My son used to go to Park School for four years.

3.3 Complete the text using the present perfect or the past simple.
8.15 a.m.
Today is Maria's first day at school. Last week we *visited* (visit) the school together and ¹_____ (meet) her new teacher. Maria ²_____ (not/talk) about anything but school since then. A few minutes ago she ³_____ (put on) her new uniform and Jim ⁴_____ (take) a photo of her. I can't believe how much she ⁵_____ (grow) this year.

11.30 a.m.
Jim and I ⁶_____ (be) really busy since we ⁷_____ (leave) Maria at school and we ⁸_____ (not/have) any time to miss her. I ⁹_____ (clean) the house, and Jim ¹⁰_____ (do) the washing and it's only half past eleven! I think we ¹¹_____ (achieve) quite a lot. I wonder if Maria ¹²_____ (enjoy) herself this morning.

3.4 Order the words to make sentences.
Example didn't Spanish when was school I at I study .
I didn't study Spanish when I was at school.

1 week We test didn't this a have .
2 exams passed of He's year all his this .
3 few finished lesson a ago The minutes .
4 you Have started learnt course lot the a since ?
5 school week The closed last was .
6 Have a had they today lesson maths ?

3.5 Underline the correct phrase.
Example The story wasn't true. The journalist made it up/ made up it.

1 Hurry up!/Hurry you up! We're late.
2 Will you turn up the radio/turn up? I want to listen to the news.
3 Why did you wake up me/wake me up? It's only 5 a.m.
4 Shall I put on/on put the new DVD?
5 I'm going to take off/take them off these shoes when I get home.
6 If you've got a mobile phone, please turn off it/turn it off.

4A -ed and -ing adjectives

Use -ed adjectives to talk about how someone feels.
Use -ing adjectives to talk about the cause of a feeling.

-ed adjectives	I'm bored, there's nothing to do here. Mike is interested in art.
-ing adjectives	I think football is boring. Have you got an interesting hobby?

>> Now go to **exercise 4.1** to practise.

4B comparatives and superlatives

Use a comparative adjective or adverb + *than* to compare two things.

We use *slightly / a bit* before comparative adjectives and adverbs to show that two things are not very different, e.g. *The Spanish guitars are a bit cheaper than the electric guitars.*

We use *much, far, a lot* before comparative adjectives and adverbs to show that two things are very different, e.g. *Madonna is much more famous than Rhianna.*

to make comparative adjectives and adverbs		
one-syllable adjectives and adverbs	+ er	Keyboards are cheaper than pianos. Henry sings louder than anyone else.
adjectives and adverbs with more than one syllable	more + adjective or adverb	Are the *Spice Girls* more famous than *Madonna*? You can hear the notes on a piano more clearly than the notes on a guitar.
irregular adjectives and adverbs	change their form	Rap is good but I think reggae is better. Sheila sang badly but Maria sang worse.

Use a superlative adjective or adverb to compare more than two things.

to make superlative adjectives and adverbs		
one-syllable adjectives and adverbs	+ est	He bought the cheapest guitar in the shop. This MP3 player sounds the clearest.
adjectives and adverbs with more than one syllable	the most + adjective or adverb	They're the most popular band in the UK. Mandy practised the most frequently.
irregular adjectives and adverbs	change their form	My brother is the worst singer in the world. Of all the CD players, this one is the best.

>> Now go to **exercises 4.2 and 4.3** to practise.

4C comparing with *as*

Use *as ... as* to say that two things are equal or unequal.

as + adjective or adverb + as	I've never had a meal as nice as this. She can cook as well as a professional chef.
not as + adjective or adverb + as	My cooking isn't as good as my mother's cooking. We don't eat out as often as we used to.

>> Now go to **exercise 4.4** to practise.

4D defining relative clauses

Use defining relative clauses to identify the person, thing, or place you are talking about.

people	who/ that	Bridget Jones is a woman who is looking for love. Renée Zellweger is the actress that played the part of Bridget.
things	which/ that	A comedy is a film or a play which is funny. *Nemesis* is one of the stories that Agatha Christie wrote.
places	where	This is the town where *Mr Bean* was filmed.

- We don't need to use a subject or object pronoun (*he / they / it*, etc.) when we use a relative pronoun.
- We can leave out *who, which,* or *that* when they are the object of a relative clause, e.g. *He's an actor (that) I like.*

>> Now go to **exercise 4.5** to practise.

4.1 Underline the correct word.
Example She doesn't enjoy watersports because she's terrified/terrifying of water.

1 I'm a bit worried/worrying about my exam tomorrow.
2 Mark's stamp collection is fascinated/fascinating.
3 The view as we climbed to the top of the mountain was amazed/amazing.
4 They were annoyed/annoying because their football team didn't win the match.
5 Body building? That's disgusted/disgusting!
6 They're excited/exciting because it's the first time they've been skiing.

4.2 Complete the sentences with the comparative or superlative form of the adjective. Add any extra words you need.
Example Is flamenco music _more popular_ than opera in Spain? popular

1 This band is _____ the other one. noisy
2 Wembley Arena is one of _____ concert venues in Britain. big
3 Can you be a bit _____? I'm trying to practise for my music exam. quiet
4 I think this is _____ song Elton John has recorded. bad
5 What's _____ concert venue you've been to? unusual
6 Which is _____ club in town? good

4.3 Complete the sentences with these adjectives and adverbs.
earlier   harder   worst   loudest   carefully   ~~better~~

Example Do you think that Coldplay's music sounds _better_ than the Beatles'?

1 All of my family dance badly, but my dad dances the _____.
2 You will need to practise _____ than the others to succeed.
3 Look after that violin more _____ or you'll break it.
4 I arrived late – the concert started _____ than I thought.
5 You can always hear Sam – he plays the _____.

4.4 Rewrite the sentences using (not) as ... as and the words in red.
Example The Crown and the Red Lion have both been open for three years.
The Crown has been open _for as long as_ the Red Lion. long

1 Tom ate a lot of food and Mike ate a lot of food.
Tom ate _____ Mike. much
2 A meal in the cafeteria is €8. A meal in the restaurant is €15.
The cafeteria _____ the restaurant. expensive
3 The Italian restaurant and the Chinese restaurant both have 20 customers.
The Italian restaurant _____ the Chinese restaurant. busy
4 I bought the melons today and the strawberries last week.
The strawberries _____ the melons. fresh
5 Thai curries are hot. Indian curries are hotter.
Thai curries _____ Indian curries. hot

4.5 Underline the correct relative pronoun.
When I was a Singer is a love story which/where takes place in France. Alain is a middle-aged man [1] which/who sings in a local nightclub. He meets Marion in the club [2] that/where he sings and falls in love with her. The next day he visits the office [3] where/who she works but she isn't interested in him. Marion is trying to get over a marriage [4] which/who failed. She wants to find a place [5] which/where she can build a new life with her young son. There are some scenes in the film [6] where/which are very sad, but it's a story [7] that/who I enjoyed very much.

5A the or no article in names of institutions

institutions with *the*	positions	the president of France the managing director
	organizations	the World Health Organization
institutions with no article	the names of individual people	King Juan Carlos President Sarkozy

- Don't use an article with *Mr, Mrs, Miss*, or *Ms*, e.g. *Has Mrs Smith arrived?*

>> Now go to **exercise 5.1** to practise.

5B modals of obligation

Use *can* to say what is allowed.
Use *can't* and *mustn't* to say that something is forbidden.
Use *must* and *have to* to say that it's important to do something.
Use *don't have to* to say that it's not necessary to do something.

can + verb	You can take photos in the museum.
can't + verb	You can't take dogs into restaurants in Britain.
must + verb	You must have a licence to drive a car.
mustn't + verb	You mustn't smoke in the classroom.
don't / doesn't have to + verb	You don't have to pass a test to ride a bicycle.

>> Now go to **exercise 5.2** to practise.

5C active or passive?

Use the passive when you don't know who does an action, or when the action is more important than the person who does it.
Use the active when you know who does an action, or when the person is more important than the action.
We can use the passive with *by* to show who did the action. *A man was bitten by a crocodile.*

active	passive
The police arrest criminals.	Criminals are arrested.
The police are arresting the murderer.	The murderer is being arrested.
The police arrested the criminals.	The criminals were arrested.
The police have arrested the burglars.	The burglars have been arrested.

>> Now go to **exercises 5.3 and 5.4** to practise.

5D past perfect

Use the past perfect when you are talking about the past and want to say that an action happened at an earlier time in the past.

+	I/You/He/She/It/We/They	'd been to a concert.
−		hadn't been to a party.
?	Had I/you/he/she/it/we/they	been to a party?

>> Now go to **exercise 5.5** to practise.

5E linkers

Use *and then / after / while* to say when something happened.
Use *and then* to show the sequence that things happen in.
Use *after* to show that one thing was completed before another started.
Use *while* to say that one thing was happening when another happened.

and then	I wrote the email and then I left the office.
after	After I'd written the email, I left the office. I left the office after I'd written the email.
while	Liz arrived while I was writing the email. While I was writing the email, Liz arrived.

>> Now go to **exercise 5.6** to practise.

5.1 Right or wrong? Tick ✓ or correct the sentences.
Example Do you think ⟨*the* Socialist Party will win the next election?
1 Head of state is Queen.
2 Do you know where headquarters of UN are?
3 Government is worried about the rate of inflation.
4 George Washington was first president of USA.
5 Britain, Republic of Ireland, and Denmark joined European Union in 1973.
6 Grace Kelly was married to Prince Rainier III of Monaco.

5.2 Underline the best modal verb.
Example All passengers must/don't have to wear a seatbelt.
1 You can't/don't have to pass a test to ride a bike.
2 Cyclists under 14 years old must/mustn't wear a helmet.
3 You can/have to pay to drive in London.
4 You mustn't/don't have to switch your bicycle lights on to see during the day.
5 You can't/must ride a horse on a motorway.
6 Drivers can/mustn't use mobile phones while driving. It's forbidden.

5.3 Put the words in order to make sentences.
Example was bank A yesterday robbed .
   A bank was robbed yesterday.
1 robbers Guns the used were by .
2 tied customers up were The .
3 One hurt was woman .
4 filled with The bags cashiers money .
5 bags money robbers with The of escaped the .
6 The arrested been have robbers .

5.4 Underline the correct verb form.
A young student attacked/was attacked in the park this morning. Lee Yin was on his way to his language school when two men ¹stopped/were stopped him. One of the men ²hit/was hit Lee Yin and the other ³stole/was stolen his bag. A passer-by ⁴called/was called an ambulance and Lee Yin ⁵took/was taken to hospital, where a doctor ⁶examined/was examined him. Luckily Lee Yin ⁷didn't badly injure/wasn't badly injured. The police ⁸have sent/have been sent a description of the attackers to all the local language schools.

5.5 Complete the sentences using the past simple and the past perfect.
Example Before he _died_, King Edward _had asked_ his brother Richard to look after his two sons. die/ask
1 No one _____ the princes – Richard _____ them into the Tower of London. see/put
2 Richard finally _____ the king of England – he _____ to be king for a long time. become/want
3 Henry Tudor, Richard's enemy, _____ to England in 1485 – he _____ the previous two years in France. return/spent
4 Henry _____ the title of King of England after he _____ Richard in battle. took/kill
5 People _____ to talk about the princes. They said Richard _____ them. continue/murder
6 In 1502, James Tyrell _____ to the murder of the two princes. Richard _____ him to kill them. confess/order

5.6 Complete the sentences with *and then, after*, or *while*.
Example The phone usually rings _while_ I'm having a shower.
1 I didn't see Mike. He arrived _____ I'd left.
2 Our house was burgled _____ we were on holiday.
3 We watched a film _____ we'd finished dinner.
4 Sally bought a dress _____ she went home.
5 I read a book _____ I was waiting for you.
6 They had a party _____ they'd decorated the house.

6A so and such

Use *so* to make an adjective or adverb more extreme.
Use *such* to make a noun more extreme.

so + adjective	The children were so tired that they fell asleep immediately. Why are you so happy?
such + article + noun	It was such a bad experience that I just want to forget it. Why is he such a fool?

>> Now go to **exercise 6.1** to practise.

6B infinitives and gerunds

to + an infinitive	I decided to visit my sister.
verb + gerund	Do you fancy going for a walk?
preposition + gerund	They arrived after travelling for two hours.

• Use *to* + an infinitive after verbs such as *decide, expect, forget, hope, phone, want, refuse*, etc.
• Use a gerund after verbs such as *enjoy, fancy, finish, mind*, etc.
• Use a gerund after a preposition (e.g. *after, before, for*, etc.).

>> Now go to **exercise 6.2** to practise.

6C pronouns in reported speech

direct speech	reported speech
She says, 'I'm tired.'	She says she's tired.
He says, 'You can't play in the hall.'	He says I/we can't play in the hall.
She says, 'He/She/It's noisy.'	She says he/she/it's noisy.
He says, 'We don't play loud music.'	He says they don't play loud music.
She says, 'They shout a lot.'	She says they shout a lot.

• Pronouns sometimes change in reported speech, depending on the situation.
• We don't need to change the tense of the reporting verb, i.e. *say*, when it is in the present tense.

>> Now go to **exercise 6.3** to practise.

6D tenses in reported speech

	direct speech	reported speech
present simple	I play the violin. I don't like the music.	He said (that) he played the violin. She said (that) she didn't like the music.
past simple	We played tennis. They didn't win the game.	They said (that) they had played tennis. They said (that) they hadn't won the game.
future simple	He'll get better soon. She won't need a doctor.	She said he would get better soon. He said that she wouldn't need a doctor.

• We can shorten *had* and *would* to *'d*.

>> Now go to **exercise 6.4** to practise.

6E connectors

Use connectors to join ideas.
Use *anyway* to mean *also* or *and*.
Use *by the way* to introduce an unconnected topic.
Use *however* and *although* to mean *but*.

anyway	I don't really want to go out. Anyway, I've got too much homework to do.
by the way	Well, I think I've told you all my news. By the way, did you know that Sam and Alice have split up?
however/although	We haven't finished painting the house. However, we've done the most important rooms. He likes his job, although he has to travel a lot.

• Use a comma after *by the way*, *however*, and *anyway*.

>> Now go to **exercise 6.5** to practise.

6.1 Complete the sentences with *so* or *such*.
Example Joanne is __such__ a horrible woman!

1 Why are you _____ angry?
2 Her son behaves _____ badly!
3 This is _____ a brilliant CD!
4 We had _____ an amazing time in Japan!
5 It's _____ a lovely surprise to see you again!
6 He speaks _____ quickly that I can't understand him!

6.2 Complete the text with the gerund or infinitive form of the verbs.

My friend Annie phoned to _ask_ (ask) me if I fancied ¹_____ (spend) a weekend in Paris. She wanted me ²_____ (feed) her cat while she was in New York. Of course I said yes. I always enjoy ³_____ (visit) Paris and, after ⁴_____ (finish) my exams, I was ready for a break. And I didn't mind ⁵_____ (look after) her cat either. Before ⁶_____ (set off) on my journey, I checked that I had everything I needed.

After ⁷_____ (drive) for three hours and ⁸_____ (get) lost twice, I finally arrived. I was hoping ⁹_____ (see) Annie but she'd already left. There was a note on the door thanking me for ¹⁰_____ (look after) the cat, but Annie had forgotten ¹¹_____ (leave) her key. Luckily, I found the cat in the garden so we spent the weekend in a hotel!

6.3 Rewrite the sentences as reported speech. Use the pronouns.
Example Mrs Smith says, 'My neighbours are horrible.'   her
  She says her neighbours are horrible.

1 He says, 'Your children are badly behaved.'   our
  He says _____
2 She says, 'I don't like them.'   she
  She says _____
3 He says, 'You should move.'   we
  He says _____
4 She says, 'Your music is too loud.'   my
  She says _____
5 He says, 'I can hear them arguing.'   he
  He says _____
6 She says, 'We can't sleep at night.'   they
  She says _____

6.4 Underline the correct form of the verb.
Example 'My birthday is in July.'
  Sally said her birthday will be/was in July.

1 'We'll give you some money.'
  They said they would give/had given me some money.
2 'I bought a new dress.'
  Jill tells/told me she'd bought a new dress.
3 'She lost her purse.'
  He said that she lost/she'd lost her purse.
4 'I don't know him.'
  She said that she didn't know/hadn't known him.
5 'They won't invite you to the party.'
  He says/said that they wouldn't invite me to the party.
6 'We live in Prague now.'
  Linda told me that they would live/lived in Prague now.

6.5 Put the connecting word in the correct place. Add any necessary punctuation.
Example I don't like my new job it's very well paid.   although
  I don't like my new job, although it's very well paid.

1 My new neighbours are friendly. They've got a big dog.   however
2 We've just moved house. Did I tell you I met Susan last week?   by the way
3 I've joined a gym. I've only been twice.   however
4 He plays his music very loudly. I can't really say anything because I practise my trumpet every day.   anyway
5 We bought a new car. We couldn't really afford it.   although

7B wh- clauses

Use wh- clauses like nouns to refer to things, people, etc.

	clause begins:	
things	which / what	She can't decide which outfit looks best. They don't know what they want.
people	who	Do you know who designed this skirt?
places	where	This is where we buy most of our clothes.
times	when	I can't remember when I bought this suit.
reasons	why	He doesn't understand why his wife buys so many shoes.
methods/ conditions/ quantities	how	Does she know how to sew? I know how you feel about dressing up. I don't mind how much you spend.

• We often use a wh- clause after know.

>> Now go to **exercises 7.1 and 7.2** to practise.

7C future intentions

Use the present continuous to talk about arrangements and appointments.
Use going to to talk about plans you've had for a while.
Use will to talk about plans you've just decided.

present continuous	going to	will
I'm having a haircut on Friday. They aren't doing anything tomorrow. Are you meeting Jim later? What are we having for dinner tonight?	He's going to do more exercise. I'm not going to go abroad this year. Are you going to learn Thai? Where are you going to stay?	Maybe we'll have a big party after the exams. I won't study tonight. Will you give me a lift to work today? What shall we do at the weekend?

• Use shall instead of will in questions with I and we.

>> Now go to **exercises 7.3 and 7.4** to practise.

7D modals of deduction must, might, can't

Use must to say what you are sure is true.
Use might to say what you think is possibly true.
Use can't to say what you are sure is not true.

must + verb	He must be very rich if he's got a Rolls-Royce.
might + verb	The shutters are closed. She might be asleep.
can't + verb	They can't be poor if they live in the most expensive part of town.

• Use an infinitive without to after a modal verb.

>> Now go to **exercise 7.5** to practise.

7.1 Order the words to make sentences and questions.
Example what likes She she knows .
    She knows what she likes.

1 when Does know she the close shops ?
2 clothes cheap where They to know buy .
3 know how you this is much dress Do ?
4 why suit I know this don't bought I .
5 fashionable are which know Do colours you ?
6 well dress know to how We .

7.2 Complete the sentences with the wh- words.
how how ~~what~~ when where which

Example I like _what_ you're wearing today.

1 When he saw _____ cheap the shirts were, he bought six.
2 I can't remember _____ I bought this tie – maybe in Japan.
3 I'm not sure _____ the sales start – probably in June or July.
4 I can't believe _____ many clothes you've got.
5 She liked all the shoes and didn't know _____ ones to buy.

7.3 Complete each sentence by adding one word.
Example I'm tired, I think I'll _go_ to bed.

1 Paul and Terry _____ visiting their parents tomorrow.
2 I think I _____ stay in and watch this film.
3 _____ Tom coming to the party?
4 What _____ you going to do during the holidays?
5 Who _____ Italy playing tonight?
6 We _____ going out. We're too tired.

7.4 Underline the correct verb form.
Example **A** Do you fancy a game of tennis?
        B Sorry, I 'm meeting/'ll meet Javi.

1 **A** Have you made any plans for the weekend?
  B Yes, I 'll/'m going to relax.
2 **A** Did you phone the doctor?
  B Yes, I 'm seeing/'ll see him on Thursday.
3 **A** Are you doing/Will you do anything interesting tonight?
  B No. I'm studying/going to study for the test.
4 **A** Have you booked your holiday?
  B No, we aren't going to go/won't go away this year.
5 **A** What time are you meeting/will you meet Mandy?
  B We won't meet/aren't meeting her. She's cancelled her trip.
6 **A** Oh no! I've left my wallet at home.
  B Don't worry. I 'll pay/'m paying with my credit card.

7.5 Choose the best sentence.
Example There's a lot of cat food in the cupboard.
        a ☐ They can't have a cat.
        b ☑ They must have a cat.

1 I don't know what time the bank closes.
  a ☐ It can't be open now.
  b ☐ It might be open now.
2 They argue all the time.
  a ☐ They can't be happy.
  b ☐ They must be happy.
3 He speaks English.
  a ☐ He might be from Canada.
  b ☐ He can't be from England.
4 The lights are out and the doors are locked.
  a ☐ The party must be over.
  b ☐ The party might be over.
5 They've been walking for six hours.
  a ☐ They can't be tired.
  b ☐ They must be tired.

8A phrasal verbs (2)

phrasal verbs which can't be separated	The car broke down. We called by the garage on the way home.
phrasal verbs which can be separated	You can pick up your messages later. You can pick your messages up later. I'll put you though.

- If the object of a separable verb is a pronoun (*me, you, him, it,* etc.), it must come before the particle, e.g. *Pick it up.*
- Nouns can go before or after the particle, e.g. *Pick up a message. Pick a message up.*

>> Now go to **exercise 8.1** to practise.

8B ability *can, could, be able to, manage to*

general ability in the present	I can speak French. Many dogs are able to swim.
general ability in the past	She could swim when she was a child. He had a car so he was able to travel a lot.
general ability on one occasion in the past	They were able to book the flights on the Internet. We all managed to pass the English test.
other tenses or modals	We've been able to save enough money for a holiday.

- Put the infinitive form of the verb after *can, could, be able to, managed to.*

>> Now go to **exercises 8.2 and 8.3** to practise.

8C reported questions

Use *ask* when you want to report a question.

	direct questions	reported questions
present simple	Where is he from? Where does he work?	They asked him where he was from. She asked him where he worked.
past simple	How was your interview? When did your course start?	She asked me how my interview had been. He asked us when our course had started.
future tenses	Where will you be? What will you do?	She asked me where I would be. We asked him what he would do.

>> Now go to **exercise 8.4** to practise.

8C reported questions: open and closed questions

	direct questions	reported questions
open questions (*Who, Where,* etc.)	Why are you looking for a new job?	She asked him why he was looking for a new job.
closed questions (*Are, Do, Can,* etc.)	Can you speak any foreign languages?	They asked her if she could speak any foreign languages.

- Open questions are questions with many possible answers.
- Closed questions have only two possible answers.
- We use *if* when we report a closed question.

>> Now go to **exercise 8.5** to practise.

8D reported imperatives and requests

Use *told* + person + infinitive with *to* to report imperatives.
Use *asked* + person + infinitive with *to* to report requests.

	direct speech	reported speech
imperatives	Be careful! Don't move!	She told the children to be careful. I told him not to move.
requests	Can you tell me the time?	She asked me to tell her the time.

>> Now go to **exercise 8.6** to practise.

8.1 Underline the correct words.
Example He can't <u>get through</u>/get him through to the manager's office.
1 Pete said he'd call back/call back you later.
2 Why did you hang me up/hang up on me?
3 I'll have to hand you over/you hand over to my manager.
4 She was cut off/cut her off in the middle of her call.
5 Could you put through/put me through to the office, please?
6 Can you hang on/hang on you while I go and find Terry?

8.2 Order the words to make sentences.
Example able are birds Most fly to .
       Most birds are able to fly.
1 was was when able walk he old ten to Toby months .
2 can My walk his dog legs back on .
3 to able We the be competition win might .
4 next go year to be I'll to university able .
5 meeting the managed She for time to arrive on .
6 were We our able to night homework last finish .

8.3 Complete each sentence by adding one word.
Example Luckily, I _was_ able to find a parking space near the office.
1 She _____ to complete the marathon in four hours.
2 We might _____ able to come to the party.
3 My mum _____ dance very well when she was young.
4 He _____ been able to learn Greek, even though he's tried.
5 Holland managed _____ score three goals against Italy.
6 She _____ cook very well – this food is delicious.

8.4 Report the direct questions.
Example What is your name?
       The officer asked _me what my name was_____.
1 What's your address?
   He wanted _____.
2 Where do you come from?
   He asked _____.
3 What is your profession?
   His colleague wanted to know _____.
4 When did you leave the USA?
   He asked me _____.
5 Why did you move to Australia?
   They wanted to know _____.

8.5 Complete the reported questions. Use *me* where it is appropriate.
Example How old are you?
       She asked _me how old I was_____.
1 Where do you go to school?
   She wanted to know _____.
2 Are you a good student?
   She asked _____.
3 What's your favourite subject?
   She asked _____.
4 Do you speak any foreign languages?
   She wanted to know _____.

8.6 Complete the sentences with the correct form of the verbs.
give   help   not leave   show   not smoke   ~~tell~~   turn off
Example He asked me to _tell_ him where the ticket office was.
1 She asked me _____ her a single ticket to Brighton.
2 The guard told us _____ him our tickets.
3 He advised us _____ our bags in the aisle.
4 The passenger refused _____ her mobile phone.
5 The guard told me _____ on the train.
6 A man offered _____ the old lady put her bags on the train.

9A tag questions

Use tag questions to check something that you think is true.
Use sentences with tag questions to start a conversation.

positive questions	negative questions
It's cold, isn't it?	It isn't a very nice day, is it?
The flowers are pretty, aren't they?	The days aren't very long, are they?
There's a lot of snow, isn't there?	There isn't a cloud in the sky, is there?
They live in Mexico, don't they?	They don't have a big garden, do they?
She enjoys the snow, doesn't she?	He doesn't like the rain, does he?

>> Now go to **exercise 9.1** to practise.

9B future perfect

Use the future perfect to talk about something that will be
finished by a certain time in the future.

+	I / You / He / She / It / We / They	'll have finished work by six o'clock.
−		won't have finished work by six o'clock.
?	Will I / you / he / she / it / we / they	have finished work by six o'clock?

>> Now go to **exercise 9.2** to practise.

9C 1st conditional

Use the first conditional to talk about possible future actions and
predict their results (e.g. to give advice or warn about danger).

if clause	main clause
If we make a noise,	the bear will run away.
If you stay in your car during a tornado,	you won't be safe.
If there's a tornado,	where will you go?

- Use the present simple in the *if* clause and *will* + verb in the main clause.
- The *if* clause can go before or after the main clause.
- When a conditional sentence begins with the *if* clause, use a comma to separate the two clauses.

>> Now go to **exercise 9.3** to practise.

9C other *if* clauses

Use an *if* clause followed by a main clause with an imperative or
should + a verb to give advice.

if clause	main clause
If there's an accident,	call the police.
If the road is flooded,	don't try to drive.
If you cycle on a busy road,	you should wear a helmet.
If you see a bear,	you shouldn't run after it.
If there's a fire,	what should we do?

>> Now go to **exercise 9.4** to practise.

9D 2nd conditional

Use the second conditional to talk about situations which are not
true now and probably won't be true in the future.

if clause	main clause
If I had a dream programmer,	I'd choose dreams about travelling.
If someone gave us a personal helicopter,	we would fly to Barbados.
If I didn't have a car,	I would walk to work.
If you could buy anything in the magazine,	what would you buy?

- Use the past simple in the *if* clause and *would* + verb in the main clause.
- The contraction of *would* is *'d*.
- The *if* clause can go before or after the main clause.

>> Now go to **exercise 9.5** to practise.

9.1 Complete the sentences with a tag question.

aren't they   do we   doesn't it
don't they   ~~don't we~~   is it   isn't it

Example We spend a lot of time talking about the weather,
don't we ?

1 The days are getting longer, _____?
2 It isn't snowing there, _____?
3 We don't need an umbrella, _____?
4 Sailors listen to the weather forecast every day, _____?
5 It rains a lot in Ireland, _____?
6 It's quite mild today, _____?

9.2 Complete the sentences with the future perfect form of the verbs.

Example I _won't have finished_ cleaning the house by
lunchtime.   not finish

1 I hope I _____ weight by the end of this diet.   lose
2 He _____ 42 kilometres when he finishes the marathon.   run
3 Sally's worried that she _____ her exams.   not pass
4 I _____ this essay by Friday.   not do
5 Next year we _____ married for 25 years.   be
6 By the end of their trip, they _____ almost 6,000 miles.   drive

9.3 Make 1st conditional sentences.

Example If/you/not/hurry up/we/leave/you/behind.
If you don't hurry up, we'll leave you behind.

1 If/you/not/give/us/a safety leaflet/we/not/know/what/to/do.
2 What/he/do/if/there/be/an emergency?
3 How/they/find/their way/to/the campsite/if/it/be/dark?
4 You/get/lost/if/you/not/take/a map.
5 She/make/a camp fire/if/it/be/very cold.
6 If/you/leave/food/near/the tent/it/attract/the bears.

9.4 Match 1–6 with a–f.

1 [a] You shouldn't play dead
2 [ ] You shouldn't stand under a single tree
3 [ ] Swim parallel to the beach
4 [ ] Don't move a lot
5 [ ] You shouldn't run
6 [ ] You should go into a basement and sit under a table

a if you're attacked by a shark.
b if you see a tornado coming towards you.
c if there's a lightning storm.
d if a bear comes towards you.
e if you are stuck in quicksand.
f if a current pulls you out to sea.

9.5 Complete the sentences with the correct form of the verb. Add
a pronoun where necessary.

Example Where _would you go_ if you _could go_ anywhere you
wanted?   go/can go

1 I _____ a house if I _____ more money.   buy/have
2 If we _____ so much homework, we _____.
   not have/can go out
3 My parents _____ happy if I _____ all my exams.
   be/passed
4 If he _____ his own computer, he _____ to use mine.
   had/not need
5 What _____ if you _____ a teacher?   do/not be
6 If you _____ a bit harder, you _____ better grades.
   work/get

10A articles *the, a, an*

Use *a/an* with singular countable nouns, e.g. *a shop, an engineer*.
Use *the* with singular or plural nouns, e.g. *the shop, the shops*.

a/an	the first time you mention someone/something	There's a lorry outside my house.
	to say what someone's job is	He's an engineer.
	to say what something is	It's a new shopping mall.
the	when there is only one of something	I saw him in the high street.
	when it's clear who/what you are talking about	Mr Jones is talking to the butcher.
	with places in a town	Have you been to the bank?

>> Now go to **exercise 10.1** to practise.

10B quantifiers

Use quantifiers to say and ask about how much or how many of something there is/are.

	plural countable nouns	uncountable nouns
+	There are a lot of shops. There are a few shops.	I've got a lot of money. I've got a little money.
–	There aren't many shops. There aren't any shops.	I haven't got much money. I haven't got any money.
?	Are there many shops? Are there any shops?	Have you got much money? Have you got any money?

- Use *a lot of* with plural countable and uncountable nouns. Only use *of* before a noun.
- Use *too* + an adjective, *too much* + an uncountable noun, and *too many* + a countable noun to say there is more than we want, e.g. *There is too much sugar in this coffee.*
- Use *not* + an adjective + *enough*, and *not enough* + a noun to say that there is less than we want, e.g. *There isn't enough sugar in this coffee.*

>> Now go to **exercises 10.2 and 10.3** to practise.

10C present perfect continuous

Use the present perfect continuous to talk about an activity which started in the past and has continued until now.

+	–	?
I/You/We/They've been learning English for a long time.	I/You/We/They haven't been learning English for a long time.	Have I/you/we/they been learning English for a long time?
He/She/It's been learning English for a long time.	He/She/It hasn't been learning English for a long time.	Has he/she/it been learning English for a long time?

- Don't use the present perfect continuous with state verbs (*be, believe,* etc.)

>> Now go to **exercises 10.4 and 10.5** to practise.

10D time and conditional clauses

if/as long as	I'll buy the camera if/as long as it's cheap.
unless	I won't buy the camera unless it's cheap.
when/as soon as	We'll buy a car when/as soon as we've saved enough money.
until	We won't buy a car until we've saved enough money.

- Time clauses and conditional clauses can go before or after the main clause.

>> Now go to **exercise 10.6** to practise.

10.1 Complete the text with *the, a,* or *an*.

Looking for _a_ nice place to spend ¹_____ afternoon? Come to Old Basing, ²_____ old-fashioned English village in Hampshire. During ³_____ summer you can visit ⁴_____ ruins of Basing House. ⁵_____ original house was destroyed in 1645 during ⁶_____ English Civil War. Today, you can walk around ⁷_____ gardens and enjoy ⁸_____ ice-cream or ⁹_____ cup of coffee in ¹⁰_____ café. If you're hungry after your walk, why not have dinner in ¹¹_____ pub next door? They have ¹²_____ award-winning chef and you are always sure of ¹³_____ warm welcome from ¹⁴_____ pub owner and his family.

10.2 Complete the sentences with *a little, a few, a lot of, much,* or *many*.

Example I've got _a little_ money so I can lend you some.

1 We haven't got _____ potatoes.
2 Hurry up! There's only _____ time before the shop closes.
3 There isn't _____ food in the house.
4 Don't buy any more eggs – there are _____ in the fridge.
5 There are _____ strawberries here. Too many for me to eat.
6 Are there _____ good restaurants in the town centre?

10.3 Underline the correct words.

Example How much/<u>many</u> plastic bags do you use when you go shopping?

1 We don't recycle enough/too many rubbish.
2 A few/lot countries have banned plastic bags.
3 Are there a few/little recycling centres near your house?
4 A lot of/lot this packaging is unnecessary.
5 Why do people buy so many/much bottled water?
6 We are producing too much/enough waste.

10.4 Complete the sentences using the present perfect continuous form of the verbs.

go out   play   not rain   read   ~~use~~   not work

Example Who _'s been using_ my mobile phone?

1 I _____ a book about sailing.
2 There's a problem with the computers. They _____ today.
3 How long _____ Tom _____ with Sue?
4 They _____ computer games all day.
5 It _____ for long. Maybe it will stop soon.

10.5 Underline the correct form of the verbs.

Example I 've tried/<u>'ve been trying</u> to finish this report all day.

1 We haven't waited/haven't been waiting for long.
2 I 've written/'ve been writing four emails today.
3 Has he passed/Has he been passing his English exam?
4 How long have you studied/have you been studying Russian?
5 I haven't seen/haven't been seeing Debbie for 20 years.

10.6 Write sentences with the same meaning using the word or phrase in red.

Example I won't buy it unless they reduce the price.
   as long as
   I'll _buy it as long as they reduce the price_

1 I won't leave until I find what I'm looking for.   as soon as
   I'll _____
2 Buy it if you're sure it's what you want.   unless
   Don't _____
3 You have to pay when you leave.   until
   You don't _____
4 They won't replace the camera unless you show the receipt.   as long as
   They'll _____
5 She won't order those shoes until she gets paid.   when
   She'll _____

11A indirect questions

Use an indirect question when you want to be more polite.

	direct question	indirect question
closed questions with *be*	Is there a newsagent's near here?	Can / Could you tell me if there's a newsagent's near here?
closed questions with an auxiliary verb and a main verb	Can I buy a map here?	Do you know if I can buy a map here?
open questions with *be*	Where is the town hall?	Do you know where the town hall is?
open questions with an auxiliary verb	When does the shop open?	Can / Could you tell me when the shop opens?

>> Now go to **exercise 11.1** to practise.

11B *to have something done*

> I have my hair styled every week.
> My sister's having her house painted.
> They've had a new garage built.

- Make the causative (*to have something done*) with subject + *have* + object + past participle.

>> Now go to **exercise 11.2** to practise.

11C have to, need to, should, ought to

Use *have to / need to* to say that it is necessary to do something.
Use *don't have to / needn't* + verb to say that it isn't necessary to do something.
Use *should / ought to / shouldn't* + verb to give advice.

have to / need to + verb	You have to take the pills three times a day. You'll need to show your passport at the hotel.
should / ought to / shouldn't + verb	You should make an appointment to see the doctor if you're ill. You ought to keep a first aid kit in your car. You shouldn't leave medicine where children can reach it.

>> Now go to **exercise 11.3** to practise.

11D non-defining relative clauses

Use defining relative clauses to identify the person, thing, or place you are talking about. See **4D**.
Use non-defining relative clauses to add extra information to a sentence.

people	My sister, who is from Barcelona, speaks Castellano and Catalan.
possessive	Sam, whose father is a doctor, is studying French.
things, places (subject)	Edinburgh, which is in the east of Scotland, is a beautiful city.
places (object)	Edinburgh, where we spent our holiday, is a beautiful city.
times	The accident happened on Tuesday, when I was driving home.

- We don't need to use a subject or object pronoun (*he / they / it*, etc.) when we use a relative pronoun.
- We can't leave the relative pronoun out of a non-defining relative clause.
- Use commas to separate a non-defining relative clause from the rest of a sentence.

>> Now go to **exercise 11.4** to practise.

11.1 Rewrite the questions as indirect questions. Add *me* where necessary.
Example Is the museum open today?   Do you know …
Do you know if the museum is open today?

1 Where is the tourist information office?   Could you tell …
2 Can we take photos inside the theatre?   Do you know …
3 Is this Bridge Street?   Could you tell …
4 How old is that building?   Do you know …
5 When does the library close?   Can you tell …

11.2 Rewrite the sentences using the correct form of *to have something done*.
Example They replaced the broken windows.
They had the broken windows replaced.

1 They redecorated the house.
2 They repaired the heating.
3 They've put an alarm system in the house.
4 They've built a new garage.
5 They're fitting the new carpets today.
6 They're making new curtains for all the rooms.

11.3 Put the words in order to complete the dialogues.
Example A I   money   change   the   Should   my   at   airport   ?
Should I change my money at the airport?
B No, you can change it at any bank.

1 **A** I don't know what to take.
  B need   pack   to   clothes   warm   some   You'll   .
2 **A** Is   anything   shouldn't   my   suitcase   there   in   which   I   put   ?
  B Yes, here's the list.
3 **A** Where's my hairdryer?
  B You   hairdryer   take   needn't   your   .
4 **A** Perhaps   taxi   order   I   a   should   .
  B It's OK, I've already ordered one.
5 **A** have   When   we   to   do   check   in   ?
  B At 1.30.
6 **A** I've never flown before.
  B You   relax   to   need   .

11.4 Complete each sentence with the correct non-defining relative clause. Add commas where necessary.
~~which is a small village in Spain~~
whose apartment I share
when she was working in Paris
who is teaching me Arabic
where I used to live
which meant I was late for work

Example Luis and Eva come from Belchite,   *which is a small village in Spain*   .

1 There was a long traffic jam _____.
2 She met her husband 17 years ago _____.
3 Anna _____ is coming to visit me.
4 I was on my way to Rome _____.
5 Alain _____ loves animals.

12A so, because, (in order) to

Use *so* to talk about the result of a situation.
Use *because* to talk about the cause of a situation.
Use *(in order) to* to talk about a purpose.

so	I got up late so I missed the bus.
because	I missed the bus because I got up late.
(in order) to	I got up early (in order) to catch the bus.

>> Now go to **exercise 12.1** to practise.

12B wish

Use *wish* to talk about unreal situations in the present.
Use *hope* to talk about things that we want to happen in the future.
Use *be glad* to say that you are happy about a situation.

real situation	wish / hope / be glad
I'm so tired.	I wish I wasn't / weren't so tired.
I'm not rich.	I hope I'll be rich soon.
I live in the city centre.	I wish I didn't live in the city centre.
I haven't got any problems.	I'm glad I haven't got any problems.
I can't drive.	I wish I could drive.
They won't speak to me today.	I hope they'll speak to me tomorrow.

• Change the tense in sentences with *wish* to show that the situation is unreal.

>> Now go to **exercise 12.2** to practise.

12C -ing and -ed clauses

Use *-ing* and *-ed* clauses to add extra information about the subject of a sentence.

-ing clauses	The story is about a man. + He's working in London.	The story is about a man working in London.
-ed clauses	The author was a man. + His name was Emerson Hough.	The author was a man called Emerson Hough.

• Form *-ed* clauses with any past participle, including irregular past participles, e.g. *written*, *seen*, *said*, etc.
• Use *-ed* and *-ing* clauses when both clauses in a sentence have the same subject.
• Use *-ed* for past tenses and *-ing* for continuous tenses.

>> Now go to **exercise 12.3** to practise.

12D 3rd conditional

Use the third conditional to talk about an imagined situation in the past (something that didn't happen) and its imagined result.

If we'd worked harder at school,	we'd have passed our exams.
If they'd invited me to the party,	I wouldn't have gone.
If he hadn't gone to Mexico,	he wouldn't have met his future wife.
If you'd won the lottery last week,	what would you have done with the money?

• Use the past perfect in the *if* clause and *would have* + past participle in the main clause.
• *'d* in the *if* clause is a contraction of *had*, but *'d* in the main clause is a contraction of *would*.
• The *if* clause can go before or after the main clause.
• When a conditional sentence begins with the *if* clause, use a comma to separate the two clauses.

>> Now go to **exercises 12.4 and 12.5** to practise.

12.1 Complete the sentences with *because*, *(in order) to*, or *so*.
Example He couldn't get a job _because_ he didn't have any qualifications.
1 I spent a year in Cuba _____ improve my Spanish.
2 He read the book _____ he wanted to learn more about the Internet.
3 I didn't want to pay for the DVD _____ I copied my friend's.
4 We grow our own vegetables _____ save money.
5 We bought a guide book _____ we could plan our trip.
6 She downloaded some music _____ she could listen to it.
7 I stayed up all night _____ finish the homework exercises.
8 My dad was angry _____ I crashed his car.

12.2 Rewrite the sentences. Use the words in blue.
Example My brother won't tidy up.   I wish
           I wish my brother would tidy up.
1 I don't share a room with my sister.   I'm glad
2 The football isn't over.   I wish
3 Her friends won't stop talking.   I wish
4 We didn't go out.   I'm glad
5 They might buy me a present.   I hope
6 It isn't raining.   I'm glad
7 I can't find a nice boyfriend.   I wish
8 Our kids might stop arguing soon.   I hope

12.3 Complete the sentences with the *-ing* or *-ed* form of the verbs.
talk   call   direct   injure   read   take   ~~wearing~~
Example Who is the woman _wearing_ the red coat?
1 It's an adventure film _____ by Steven Spielberg.
2 A man _____ Pete left these flowers for you.
3 The coach _____ us to the airport broke down.
4 This is a picture of Tom Cruise _____ to fans at the opening of his new film.
5 Everyone _____ in the train crash was taken to hospital.
6 The only person in the library was a man _____ a newspaper.

12.4 Match 1–6 with a–f to make 3rd conditional sentences.
1 [b] He wouldn't have broken his leg
2 [ ] If I'd driven any faster,
3 [ ] You would have hurt yourself
4 [ ] If he hadn't gone to the party,
5 [ ] What would we have done
6 [ ] Which language would you have learned

a if you'd had a choice?
b if he'd been more careful.
c he wouldn't have met his old school friend again.
d if we'd had an accident?
e I would have crashed.
f if you'd fallen down those stairs.

12.5 Rewrite the sentences using the 3rd conditional.
Example I didn't fail my exams so I was able to go to university.   *If I'd failed my exams, I wouldn't have been able to go to university.*
1 I studied and did well in my course.
2 I saved some money and spent a year travelling around Africa.
3 I stopped in Egypt and saw the pyramids.
4 I didn't go to Kenya so I didn't climb Mount Kilimanjaro.
5 I got a job in Botswana and I met my husband.
6 I wrote a book and I became famous.
7 I earned a lot of money and I bought a big house.
8 My wife wasn't happy so she left me.

Irregular verbs

verb	past simple	past participle
be	was	been
	were	
become	became	become
begin	began	begun
bite	bit	bitten /'bɪtn/
blow	blew	blown
break	broke	broken
bring	brought /brɔːt/	brought /brɔːt/
build /bɪld/	built /bɪlt/	built /bɪlt/
burn	burnt	burnt
	burned	burned
buy	bought /bɔːt/	bought /bɔːt/
catch	caught /kɔːt/	caught /kɔːt/
choose	chose /tʃəʊz/	chosen /'tʃəʊzn/
come	came	come
cost	cost	cost
cut	cut	cut
do	did	done
draw	drew	drawn
dream	dreamt /dremt/	dreamt /dremt/
	dreamed	dreamed
drink	drank	drunk
drive	drove	driven /'drɪvn/
eat	ate	eaten
fall	fell	fallen
feel	felt	felt
find	found	found
fly	flew	flown
forget	forgot	forgotten
forgive	forgave	forgiven /fə'gɪvn/
freeze	froze	frozen
get	got	got
give	gave	given
go	went	gone
		been
grow	grew	grown
hang	hung	hung
have	had	had
hear	heard /hɜːd/	heard /hɜːd/
hide	hid	hidden /'hɪdn/
hit	hit	hit
hold	held	held

verb	past simple	past participle
hurt	hurt	hurt
keep	kept	kept
know	knew /njuː/	known /nəʊn/
learn	learnt	learnt
	learned	learned
leave	left	left
lend	lent	lent
let	let	let
lie	lay	lain
lose	lost	lost
make	made	made
mean	meant /ment/	meant /ment/
meet	met	met
mistake	mistook /mɪ'stʊk/	mistaken
pay	paid	paid
put	put	put
read	read /red/	read /red/
ride	rode	ridden /'rɪdn/
ring	rang	rung
rise	rose	risen /'rɪzn/
run	ran	run
say	said /sed/	said /sed/
see	saw /sɔː/	seen
sell	sold	sold
send	sent	sent
set	set	set
shake	shook /ʃʊk/	shaken
shine	shone /ʃɒn/	shone /ʃɒn/
show	showed	shown
shut	shut	shut
sing	sang	sung
sink	sank	sunk
sit	sat	sat
sleep	slept	slept
smell	smelt	smelt
	smelled	smelled
speak	spoke	spoken
spell	spelt	spelt
	spelled	spelled
spend	spent	spent
split	split	split

verb	past simple	past participle
spoil	spoilt	spoilt
stand	stood /stʊd/	stood /stʊd/
steal	stole	stolen
stick	stuck	stuck
swear	swore	sworn
swim	swam	swum
take	took /tʊk/	taken
teach	taught /tɔːt/	taught /tɔːt/
tear	tore	torn
tell	told	told
think	thought /θɔːt/	thought /θɔːt/
throw	threw	throne
understand	understood	understood
wake up	woke up	woken up
wear	wore	worn
win	won /wʌn/	won /wʌn/
write	wrote	written /'rɪtn/

≪ **Look at the verb column. Cover the past simple and past participle columns and test yourself.**

Pronunciation

Vowel sounds

/æ/ apple /ˈæpl/	/e/ egg /eg/	/ɪ/ fish /fɪʃ/	/ɒ/ office /ˈɒfɪs/	/ʌ/ uncle /ˈʌnkl/	/ʊ/ book /bʊk/
/ɑː/ car /kɑː(r)/	/ɜː/ girl /gɜː(r)l/	/iː/ eat /iːt/	/ɔː/ four /fɔː(r)/	/uː/ two /tuː/	
/eə/ hair /heə(r)/	/ɪə/ ear /ɪə(r)/	/ʊə/ newer /njʊə(r)/	/əʊ/ phone /fəʊn/	/aʊ/ mouth /maʊθ/	
/aɪ/ ice /aɪs/	/eɪ/ eight /eɪt/	/ɔɪ/ boy /bɔɪ/	/ə/ cinema /ˈsɪnəmə/		

Consonant sounds

/p/ pen /pen/	/b/ bed /bed/	/t/ table /teɪbl/	/d/ door /dɔː(r)/	/tʃ/ chair /tʃeə(r)/	/dʒ/ jeans /dʒiːnz/
/f/ food /fuːd/	/v/ visit /ˈvɪzɪt/	/θ/ thing /θɪŋ/	/ð/ father /ˈfɑːðə(r)/	/k/ cup /kʌp/	/g/ garden /ˈgɑːdən/
/s/ sister /ˈsɪstə(r)/	/z/ zoo /zuː/	/ʃ/ shoe /ʃuː/	/ʒ/ television /ˈtelɪvɪʒn/	/h/ house /haʊs/	/l/ lunch /lʌntʃ/
/m/ man /mæn/	/n/ nine /naɪn/	/ŋ/ sing /sɪŋ/	/r/ red /red/	/w/ water /ˈwɔːtə(r)/	/j/ young /jʌŋ/

The alphabet

A	B	C	D	E	F	G	H	I	J	K	L	M	N
/eɪ/	/biː/	/siː/	/diː/	/iː/	/ef/	/dʒiː/	/eɪtʃ/	/aɪ/	/dʒeɪ/	/keɪ/	/el/	/em/	/en/

O	P	Q	R	S	T	U	V	W	X	Y	Z
/əʊ/	/piː/	/kjuː/	/ɑː(r)/	/es/	/tiː/	/juː/	/viː/	/ˈdʌbljuː/	/eks/	/waɪ/	/zed/, _American_ /ziː/

Stressed and unstressed words

Stress 'vocabulary' words ...	
nouns	_book, girl, time ..._
main verbs	_walk, speak, play ..._
adjectives	_big, green, old ..._
adverbs	_easily, fast, slow ..._
question words	_Who, What, How, ..._
negatives	_not, aren't, can't ..._

Don't stress 'grammar' words ...	
articles	_a, an, the ..._
prepositions	_in, on, of ..._
conjunctions	_and, but ..._
auxiliary verbs	_is, was, do ..._
pronouns	_you, we, them ..._
possessives	_me, your, their ..._
demonstratives	_this, that ..._

Example stress patterns

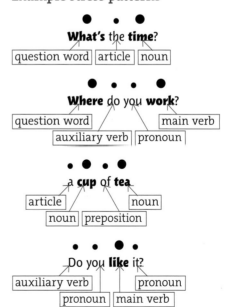

149

Audio scripts

1

1A.1

1 Oh, eh … hello, this is Margaret speaking. A young man visited today. He had a horrible red jumper and he frightened my cat! He knocked on your door for half an hour. Knock knock knock! What a noise! I couldn't sleep! Please could you tell your friends to be quieter. Thank you!

2 Hi, this is a message for Wanda. This is Mr Robbins from the office. Listen, we have a big job tomorrow and, ehm, well, I thought ehm … could you work a bit later tomorrow evening? Just an extra hour or something … and then, ehm … I'll buy you dinner, if you want … OK, well, we can talk about it in the morning. Ciao.

3 Hi Wanda, it's me. I called at your flat today but you were out. That horrible woman in the next flat came out and shouted at me. I was only knocking on the door! Anyway, let's meet up for a coffee some time. Or maybe we could go to the cinema … How about tomorrow? I'll call round at seven o'clock then, OK? Alright, see you tomorrow. Bye.

4 Wanda, it's me. Listen, can you come to our house and look after Grace tomorrow night? Me and Ray want to go to a concert. Could you come at seven o'clock? It's easy, just give Grace a bath, put her in bed, and watch TV. I'll leave some soup for you. Right, see you tomorrow then. Bye-bye.

5 Hi Fatima, it's your mother. Are you there? … Go on, pick up the phone … OK, you're not there … I'll call back later, OK? Bye.

6 Hello, Wanda, it's me. Listen, Roxette's coming to London tomorrow, and she's got quite a lot of baggage, so maybe you could help her? Could you meet her at the airport? It's flight 6254 from Malaga, and it arrives at seven o'clock. Thanks a lot darling. Love you. Bye for now. Bye.

7 Hi Wanda, are you there? … It's me, calling from Nottingham. Having a great time. Listen, I'm coming home tomorrow evening, but ehm … I forgot my keys when I left the flat yesterday, so, ehm could you let me in? I'm arriving back at about seven o'clock, so could you stay home and open the door for me? Cheers! See you tomorrow.

8 Hello Wanda, it's me. Why don't you come round for dinner one night this week? Me and Costas would love to see you. And could you bring my pink umbrella back? I left it at your flat last time I was there. So how about tomorrow evening? Seven o'clock? Give me a ring. Bye love.

1B.1

OK, number one, ehm … well in Britain, shaking hands is quite common, yeah, and sometimes you put your hand on the other person's shoulder, yeah, but ehm … we never bow – well, people bow when they meet the Queen I guess, but we don't normally bow.

Hugging is quite common in the family and with good friends. Some people kiss their friends on the cheeks. Kissing on the lips – well, I guess girlfriends and boyfriends do this – couples, or whatever, OK, and waving, well yeah, that's very common.

Number two … when I meet a good friend, well, with women we kiss each other on the cheeks and with men, we usually shake hands. An acquaintance, well, I guess I just say 'Hello' or something, and the same for an older neighbour – or maybe I'd say 'Good morning' or whatever. The same for my boss. If I meet one of my parents after a long time, we hug each other, and I kiss my mum on the cheeks. OK, and my nephew or niece – well, I hug them or just touch them on the head.

Question three … well, actually I address all of these people with their first name, but some people would use 'Mr' or 'Ms' and the surname when they talk to their boss, I think.

OK, number four … in this situation, in the café, my friend would introduce me to the other people I think, but they wouldn't all stand up or anything.

Number five … well, I never say 'Enchanted', I mean that's really old fashioned, nobody says that nowadays. I often say 'Pleased to meet you'. I would never ask 'How old are you?' – well, maybe to a child, but not to an adult. I never introduce myself with Mr and my surname, I just say 'Hi, I'm Greg'. Ehm … I would never say 'Peace be with you', very strange, that, and 'Greetings', I would never say that either.

OK, six … meeting my teacher in the street, I'd say 'Hello' and the first name, ehm … I guess children would say 'Mr' or 'Miss' and the surname.

And finally seven … to attract attention, I'd say 'Excuse me'. The other ones are rude, I think.

1B.2

This is Mrs Mirren.
Good afternoon, Mr Brown.
Please come in, Miss Jones.
He introduced me to Ms White.
I saw Mr Costas.
Are you Ms Phillips?
Pleased to meet you. I'm Mrs Smith.
Where are you from, Miss Wilson?

1C.1

Barbara Who are those two people?
Guide Which two?
B At the back of the room – I think they're in a mirror?
G Ah, well, that's the king and queen. King Phillip the fourth and Queen Mariana.
B So *is* it a mirror?
G Yes, it is.
B So that means the king and queen are in the room as well?
G That's right. They're probably standing where we are.
B So we're looking through their eyes?
G Yes. And in fact the princess and the other people are looking at the king and queen, not at us.
B Oh, OK.
G There's something else interesting in the picture, too. You see the painter Velázquez there on the left?
B Uh huh?
G Well, he's wearing a black jacket and there's a red cross on the front of it.
B Yes.
G Well, that's the symbol of the Order of Saint James. The king made him a member of that order.
B Oh, yeah?
G But that was three years *after* Velázquez painted the picture.
B Oh – so how is it in the picture?
G Well, some people say that the king painted it there himself.
B Oh, right.

1D.1

Nose, N-O-S-E, is pronounced the same as … knows, K-N-O-W-S.
Piece, P-I-E-C-E, is pronounced the same as …
Guest, G-U-E-S-T, is pronounced the same as …
Threw, T-H-R-E-W, is pronounced the same as …
Road, R-O-A-D, is pronounced the same as …
Meet, M-double E-T, is pronounced the same as …
Knew, K-N-E-W, is pronounced the same as …
Board, B-O-A-R-D, is pronounced the same as …

1D.2

A Can I have some bananas, please?
B Yes, of course. Which ones do you want?
A Oh, ehm … I'll take that pair.
B Pardon? Don't you want any bananas then?
A I'm sorry, I don't understand …
B You want a pear?
A Oh, I see! No, no, no. I meant pair, P-A-I-R! I'd like those two bananas, please.
B Oh, ha ha. OK. Sorry, I misunderstood. I thought you said pear, P-E-A-R!

1D.3

I don't understand.
No, I meant pair.
I thought you said pear.
Oh, I see!
Pardon?
Sorry, I misunderstood.

2

2A.1

This picture shows a woman standing beside Lake Titicaca in Bolivia. She's wearing a traditional black hat and carrying a brightly coloured cloth bag. The Aymara people have their own language, called Aymara.

2A.2

a This picture shows a young man from the Atlas Mountains in Morocco. His people are mostly Muslims. He's got a cloth tied around his head to protect him from the sun. The bright blue colour of his clothing is typical of the region.

b This is a photo of a young man with a black head cloth. He has white lines and spots painted on his face, and his lips are painted black. His people live in the Sahara Desert, in Niger. He's at a marriage festival and he wants to find a wife.

c This young man holding two birds is from Jordan. He's wearing the typical red headscarf of the region. The Bedouin people live all over the Middle East and they are Muslims. Behind him you can see a wall made of mud and stones.

d   This is a picture of a woman in the north of Tanzania. She's wearing the traditional red costume of her tribe and a wide necklace of coloured beads. She's got short hair and she's wearing earrings. She's standing in front of a wooden door.

e   This is a man from the island of Raiatea in French Polynesia. His skin is decorated with traditional tattoos. He's got a marker pen through a hole in his ear, and his long hair is tied up. You can see the sea behind him.

f   Here we see a young girl from Guatemala in Central America. She's wearing a blue shirt or dress and she's smiling at the camera. Behind her you can see some traditional blue handmade local cloth.

g   This girl with pieces of wood through her nose and lower lip is an Indian from Brazil. She's also wearing a necklace made of beads. Her hair is straight and black. Her people live in the Amazon rainforest in the north of the country.

h   This man with white paint in his beard is a tribesman from Papua New Guinea. Papua New Guinea is part of an island to the north of Australia. The man has lots of necklaces made from coloured beads, and he's carrying some spears. He has red spots painted on his face.

i   This picture shows a man from Baffin Island in the far north of Canada. He's wearing a thick fur coat to protect him from the cold arctic weather. He's got straight black hair. Behind him, you can see clouds and sky.

2A.3
My name's Gerry. I'm 19 and I work in a garage. I'm from a village near Galway in the west of Ireland. I speak English and Gaelic. I'm not religious but my parents are Catholic. I come from a working class family. I've got cousins in America because my aunt Celia married an American man and moved to the USA. They live in Georgia. I enjoy motor racing and I write articles for a car magazine.

2B.1
They always like the city lights
They usually go to see the sights
They often go to see Big Ben
They quite often visit 'Number Ten'
They sometimes take a photo there

They rarely miss Trafalgar Square
The action hardly ever stops
They never want to miss the shops

2B.2
Country one
First clue – When people think of this country, they usually think of mountains. There are a lot of mountains here and some of them are very famous, such as the Eiger and the Matterhorn.

The next clue is food. The country is quite famous for cheese and chocolate, and they often eat them in a fondue. People who visit this country often buy chocolate to take home.

OK, the last clue is about typical goods. People often buy watches from this country, for example Rolex watches, or Swatch. Other souvenirs include army penknives and coloured pencils.

Country two
First clue – When people think of this country, they often think of flowers. It's very flat, there aren't any mountains, and they grow a lot of flowers. It's also well-known for cheese.

Clue number two – People usually visit the most famous city, and there are a lot of canals; you can take a boat on the canals, and you see a lot of people on bicycles here.

Next clue – There are a lot of famous painters from this country, for example Rembrandt and Vincent Van Gogh.

Country three
First clue – People always think this country is very big and very cold, and there are a lot of forests. In fact, it's the biggest country in the world.

OK, next clue – There are a lot of very well-known writers from this country, for example, there's Tolstoy, who wrote War and Peace, and there's Dostoyevsky.

Last clue – When people visit the capital, they usually go to see Red Square and the Kremlin.

Country four
First clue – When people think of this country, they often think of Carnival and dancing in the street and samba, and tropical fruit and sunshine.

OK, next clue – People usually visit the beaches in the most famous city, and they go to the top of some of the mountains in the city such as Sugar Loaf.

Last clue – There are a lot of famous footballers from this country, including Pelé and Ronaldo.

2C.1
What's it used for?
It's used for cutting fruit.
It's used for opening tins.

What's it made of?
It's made of metal.
Where's it from?
It's from Africa.
What's it used as?
It's used as a stool.

2C.2
Elaine What's this?
Nilson It's a kind of cup.
E   Uh huh.
N   Ehm, it's used in the south of Brazil for drinking maté – that's a kind of tea. The cup's called a chimarrão in Portuguese.
E   Oh yeah? What's it made of? It looks like wood …
N   It's made of dried gourd – you know gourd? It's a kind of fruit.
E   Oh yeah, I know. And what's this metal thing for? Is it for mixing the sugar or something?
N   No, that's used as a straw for drinking the tea. It's called a bomba.
E   Why don't people just drink out of the cup?
N   Ah, I guess you've never seen maté! There are lots of leaves on the top, so if you drink it from the cup, you get leaves in your mouth.
E   Oh, OK. And how do you put the cup down? I mean, the bottom's round. Doesn't it just fall over when you put it on the table?
N   You don't put it down. Where I come from, people hold these things all day, and when they've finished, they just put more hot water in.
E   Wow, that's so strange. I've never heard of that.
N   Uh huh.

2D.1
Linda I lived in Spain a couple of years ago, and …
F   Oh yeah? What were you doing there?
L   I was studying Spanish.
F   Uh huh.
L   So anyway, in the first week I didn't go out because I had a cold, but in the second week I was feeling better …
F   Mmm.
L   And, ehm, some friends from the university invited me out to eat in the evening.
F   Uh huh.
L   So we met at ten and we went to a bar for a drink before dinner, you know.
F   Uh huh.
L   Anyway, my friends ate the 'tapas', you know, the bar snacks, while we had a drink, but I didn't have any tapas because I wanted to be hungry for dinner.
F   Oh yeah?
L   Anyway, after a while, we went to another bar and the same thing happened again.

More drinks and tapas. And again. And again.
F   So didn't you have any dinner?
L   Well, no. Finally, I asked, 'When are we going to have dinner?', and my friends laughed and said the tapas WERE the dinner!
F   Oh no!
L   Yeah, so in the end I went to bed hungry.

3

3A.1
The **first time** I **fell** in **love**
How could I for**get**?
She **used** to **sit** at the **front** of the **class**
And her **name** was **Berna**dette
She **nev**er **used** to **get** it **wrong**
A **real teacher's pet**
'**A**' in **Science**, '**A**' in **Maths**
I used to **love** her, **my** sweet **Berna**dette

She **used** to **sing** in **as**sembly
And **play** the **clarinet**
She **didn't** use to **make** mi**stakes**
And her **name** was **Berna**dette
She **ran** around the **play**ing **field**
And **didn't** use to **sweat**
The **cap**tain of the **hockey team**
I used to **love** her, **my** sweet **Berna**dette

She **didn't** use to **look** at **me**
Our **eyes nev**er **met**
She **used** to **be** too **good** for me
And her **name** was **Berna**dette
Last week I met her
I **found** her on the **Internet**
She's **mar**ried with two **kids** now
I used to **love** her, **my** sweet **Berna**dette

3A.2
first time
last week

used to **sit**
get it **wrong**
teacher's **pet**
make mi**stakes**

sit at the **front**
front of the **class**

3A.3
Antonia
Ehm, I remember I used to sit by the window, and there was a heater there so it was really warm, and I used to sit and look out of the window, and ehm, sometimes the teacher got really angry and she used to say 'Pay attention, Antonia!' … ehm …
I remember one teacher especially – his name was Mr Collins but we called him Collie, and he used to teach Maths, and he always used to wear really big ties, very wide ties, with pictures on them. Maths was my worst subject, I always used to get a D or E in Maths exams and Collie was angry and he gave me extra homework. I hated that.

Jeremy

OK, well, my first school ... ehm ... I think the place I remember most was the big room where we used to have assembly – a big dark hall and it had these pictures of old head teachers and things on the wall, and a piano, oh and I remember the playground – we used to go out there in the breaks and it was always raining ... Erm, another thing I remember is we used to have a uniform – it was a green jacket and grey shorts, and we had to wear these grey shorts, even in the freezing cold in winter. Then, there were the school trips – that was the best thing, because we didn't have to wear the uniform, and we used to sit on the bus and sing songs, and the teachers were always more friendly on school trips, so it was quite good fun.

3C.1

Mum Daniel Peter Marston! Just look at the time! Where have you been? This isn't a hotel, you know!

Daniel I wish my mum understood me!

M You look tired, Danny. Don't get up. Shall I wake you up when the football starts?

D What? Eh ... yeah, thanks Mum.

Emma Mum – Danny's left the bathroom floor wet!

M I'm sure that's not true, Emma. Don't make stories up about your brother. Hurry up Danny, the football's about to start. Don't tidy up. I'll put your clothes away if you like.

M I'll turn the telly on for you. Just sit down, take off your trainers, and put your feet up. Help yourself to crisps.

M Lunch is on the table, Danny!

D Oh Mum! I'm watching The Simpsons!

M Oh sorry! Would you like me to bring your lunch on a tray?

D Yes, please.

M Don't worry about the dishes, Danny. I'll wash up today. Why don't you turn your music up – it's very nice! Is everything alright?

D No. I'm fed up!

M Why don't you try something new? Take up the electric guitar. Get a tattoo.

D Alright! I'll invite 30 friends for a party next Friday. We'll put heavy metal music on, turn it up really loud, and dance on the furniture. Is that OK?

M Oh, that sounds great! I'm looking forward to it already!

D Aargh! I can't stand it! You're too NICE! You're my mum – you're supposed to shout at me and tell me off! If you carry on like this, I'll grow up SPOILT!

M Daniel, it's nine o'clock! Get up at once!

D Oh! Good morning, Mum! I love you!

3C.2

Mrs Marston Hello, Jessica! Come in!

Jessica Hello, Mrs Marston. Thanks.

M I'll take your coat if you like.

J Thank you.

M Just leave your bag on the sofa.

J OK.

M Would you like me to make you a cup of tea?

J No, thanks. I'm fine.

M Danny isn't home yet. Why don't you watch TV for a bit?

J OK, thanks.

M Shall I change the channel for you? I'm not watching this programme.

J No, it's fine, thanks.

M Help yourself to some of these biscuits.

J Thanks, Mrs Marston.

M Don't worry about the dog. He won't bite.

J OK.

M Do you need anything, or is everything alright?

J I'm fine, thanks.

M OK, well, I'll leave you in peace then.

J OK, thanks.

3C.3

I'll take your coat if you like.
Just leave your bag on the sofa.
Would you like me to make you a cup of tea?
Why don't you watch TV for a bit?
Shall I change the channel for you?
Help yourself to some of these biscuits.
Don't worry about the dog.
Do you need anything, or is everything alright?

3D.1

educate	edu**ca**tion
qualify	qualifi**ca**tion
graduate	gradu**a**tion
apply	appli**ca**tion
technical	tech**no**logy
photograph	pho**to**graphy
public	pub**li**city

3D.2

Well, I left school after my GCSE exams when I was 16. I wanted to get a job and earn some money, you know, so I signed on at the job centre and, anyway, they offered me a job as an assistant in an old people's home, so I took the job, and ehm ... well, I quite liked the work, and I stayed there for a couple of years, but it was going nowhere, I couldn't move up in the job – I couldn't get promotion without qualifications, so in the end I decided to leave and go to night school. I studied marketing and publicity, I don't know why, but anyway, I did well, and I went on to do a master's. After that, I got a job in an international advertising agency. I worked hard and got promoted up and up, and now I'm the head of the design team. So that's where I am now. It's OK. The money's good, but it's not a secure job. You never know where you'll be tomorrow.

4

4A.1

/d/
amazed
bored

/t/
embarrassed

/ɪd/
excited
fascinated
disgusted
interested

4B.1

a nice venue
a nicer venue
an old song
an older song
a deeper sound
a deep sound
a bigger stage
a big stage
a small studio
a smaller studio

4B.2

Jan I don't buy CDs any more. I just download MP3s off the Internet.

Andrea Oh, I still buy CDs. I think the quality's better, you know, the sound's much clearer.

J Yeah, people say that, but I can't tell the difference myself. And you can find the songs you want much more easily on the Internet, especially if you're looking for a more unusual track, you know, there's a lot of stuff you can't find in the normal shops.

A Maybe I'm old-fashioned, but I like having the CD. I don't know ... I like looking at the picture on the box. If I can't find the CD in the shop, I'll order it, no problem.

J That's much slower.

A So what's the hurry?

J Well ... Anyway, MP3 music's much more convenient, too. You can put it on your iPod. They're much smaller than a CD walkman. And CDs jump if you're moving around. No, iPods are much better.

A Why do you want to move around? The best place to listen to music is on the stereo system at home. It's much more comfortable. And anyway, I hate listening to music through headphones. It gives me a headache, and I think two good quality speakers give a much better sound.

J Alright, but what about the family? They always ask you to play it more quietly, and you can't hear it properly.

A I live on my own, so I don't have that problem. You can have your MP3s, but I'm happier with my CDs.

4C.1

Sarah Shall we go out for a meal on Friday evening?

Tom Friday? Ehm ... **yes, OK, good idea**. Where shall we go?

S Let's look at the restaurant reviews and choose somewhere different. Let's see ... ehm ... OK, here we are ... well, there's the Café Paradiso, but we've been there before ...

T Yeah. I can't stand that place. It's always full of children. What about this one ... Old Peking ... 'The Old Peking is under new ownership, but it's just as good as ever'. That sounds good.

S **Well, I'm not too keen on Chinese food.** I prefer Indian food. How about the Bombay Palace?

T **Ehm, well, I don't know** ... How about this French place, for example? ... Chez Dominique ... I absolutely adore French cooking.

S It looks a bit expensive ...

T Alright. Why don't we try this place ... The Chestnut. It looks really good, and it isn't as expensive as the French place.

S It's vegetarian.

T Yeah. Why not? Do you want a place that serves meat?

S No, it's alright. I don't mind vegetarian food. **OK then, let's try it**. We'd better book – it says book as early as you can.

T OK. I'll do that now.

4C.2

Yes, OK, good idea.
Well, I'm not too keen on Chinese food.
OK then, let's try it.
Ehm, well, I don't know.

4C.3

Sarah Shall we go for a pizza?
Tom Mmm mmm mmm.

S Let's go for an Indian meal.
T Mmm mmm mmm.

S Why don't we go to a French restaurant?
T Mmm mmm mmm.

S How about going out for a Chinese meal?
T Mmm mmm mmm.

4D.1

Interviewer On today's programme, we're going to talk about women's films, and here to talk to us is Janet Shaw, professor of Media Studies at Midland University.

Professor Hello.

I First of all, Professor Shaw, what ARE women's films? Are they all about romance and relationships?

P Well, they aren't just one

kind of film, in fact, there are lots of different kinds of women's films. Yes, a lot of them are about romance and relationships. Women's films focus more on the people and dialogue, and men's films often focus more on the action.

I So action films are men's films.
P Well, not necessarily. Some women's films are action films too – but they take a woman's point of view, and the main characters are often women – characters that a female audience can identify with. For example, there was the film *Thelma and Louise*, about two female criminals, or the science fiction film *Alien*, with Sigourney Weaver.
I Ah. Are the main characters always female?
P No – a lot of women's films have lead actors like Nicolas Cage or Hugh Grant or Mel Gibson – male actors who a lot of women find attractive.
I Uh huh. Are women's films actually made for women? I mean, do the film makers sit down and say 'We're going to make a women's film here'?
P Yes, they often make a story which they think women will like. But often it's the other way round. For example, films from classic literature, such as *Pride and Prejudice* – these could be called women's films.
I Because they focus on characters …
P Yes, characters and relationships – more dialogue, less action.
I OK, and finally – do women watch only women's films?
P No – that would be impossible! There are far fewer women's films than men's films, so women have to watch men's films, too. And of course, people aren't just stereotypes. There are a lot of men who like women's films, and a lot of women who actually prefer men's films.
I OK … and what about you?
P Ooh, now that's a difficult question! Actually, I prefer reading books!
I Ah ha, yes, I see. OK, well, thank you very much for joining us today.
P You're welcome.
I Goodbye.

5

5A.1
Question 1. An election is a system in which the people choose their political leaders. In the past, only men were allowed to vote. Which country, in 1893, became the first nation to allow women to vote in elections?

a The United Kingdom
b Indonesia
c New Zealand

5A.2
Question 2. We often think of kings and queens as historical figures, but many countries today still have them – for example the United Kingdom and Spain. Which of the following countries does NOT have a king or queen?
a Norway
b The Czech Republic
c Saudi Arabia

Question 3. Many countries have a president as the head of state. Which of these countries does NOT have a president?
a The United Kingdom
b Brazil
c France

Question 4. In most countries, the main centre of government is in the capital city. For example, the United States congress is in the capital, Washington DC. Which of these capital cities is NOT the centre of government of the country?
a Amsterdam
b Buenos Aires
c Tokyo

Question 5. The world is divided into nations, and nearly all of them are members of an international organisation called the United Nations, or UN. The UN was formed in 1945 and has over 190 member states. Where is the headquarters of the UN?
a Geneva
b Beijing
c New York

Question 6. In Europe, many countries have joined together to form the European Union. Which of the following countries is NOT in the European Union?
a Switzerland
b Bulgaria
c Finland

Question 7. We sometimes use the name of a famous government building to refer to the government of that country. For example, people often say 'The White House' to refer to the United States government. What famous building is used to refer to the government of Russia?
a The Bundestag
b The Kremlin
c The Winter Palace

Question 8. Many of the world's flags have three stripes of different colours. For example, the French flag has one stripe of red, one of white, and one of blue. Which of these countries does NOT have a flag with stripes of three different colours?
a Germany
b Italy
c Australia

5A.3
Question 1 – the answer is c, New Zealand.

Question 2 – the answer is b, the Czech Republic doesn't have a king or queen.

Question 3 – the answer is a, the United Kingdom doesn't have a president.

Question 4 – the answer is a, Amsterdam is the capital, but the centre of government isn't Amsterdam – it's The Hague.

Question 5 – the answer is c, the headquarters of the UN is in New York.

Question 6 – the answer is a, Switzerland is not in the European Union.

Question 7 – the answer is b, the Kremlin.

Question 8 – the answer is c, the Australian flag doesn't have stripes of three different colours.

5A.4
the emperor of Japan
the US president
the Australian prime minister
the head of state
the European Union
the United Nations
the Irish government
the Liberal party

5B.1
Jeff What are you going to do with your old one?
Sally Oh, I don't know. I hadn't thought about that. I'll put it out with the rubbish bins, I guess.
J But you can't do that, I mean, it isn't allowed, is it?
S Oh?
J Yeah, it's got some dangerous chemical in it, apparently, so …
S So what do I have to do with it?
J I'm not sure. I suppose you have to phone somebody to come and take it away.
S What, for free?
J No, you have to pay, I think. I don't really know. When I got my new one, the people from the shop took the old one away.
S Oh, that was good.
J Yeah.

5C.1
baseball bat
birthday party
cash machine
earrings
headline
sports car
steering wheel
taxi driver

5C.2
A Renoir painting worth three million euros has been stolen from the National Gallery. Police believe it was done with the help of someone who works in the gallery. Apparently, a door of the gallery was left open and the alarms were switched off. The security guards were drugged and all the film from the security cameras was deleted. The thieves knew exactly what they were looking for, and less valuable paintings were not taken.

Hold on, some news is just coming in. We've just been informed that the painting has been found in Hong Kong and three men have been arrested. We'll get back to you as soon as we have any more news on that story.

5D.1
Part 1
Interviewer Welcome to Mysteries from History, and on today's programme, Dr Andrew Griffiths is going to talk to us about one of the most famous murder mysteries in British history – the murder of the princes in the Tower of London in 1483. Good morning Andrew!
Dr Griffiths Morning.
I So … did Richard the Third kill the princes in the Tower?
D Well, it's a good question. Most people think they were murdered by Richard the Third, but I'm not so sure. I think somebody *wanted* people to think he was the murderer. You have to remember that the people who first wrote about the princes in the tower wrote about it when Henry the Seventh was in power.
I And Henry was Richard's enemy.
D Exactly. So these writers wanted to please Henry. Very dangerous to make the king angry in those days!
I So they had to write the story Henry wanted to hear.
D That's right. And Henry wanted people to think Richard had murdered the princes.

Part 2
D Now, remember that in 1502, Richard's friend Sir James Tyrell confessed to the murder. Well, we know that he confessed under torture. He was *forced* to confess. But he didn't say where the bodies were. I don't think he knew. I don't think he *had* killed the boys at all.
I Oh, right. And what about the bones – the children's bones they found in 1674?
D Well, it's not clear that they were the princes' bones. They were examined in 1933, and guess what? Some of them were animal bones! I don't think it's clear at all. And then there's the painting of Richard the Third.

I Uh huh.
D Well, the painting has been examined with X-rays, and we know that it was changed later. Somebody had made one shoulder bigger than the other – someone tried to make Richard look ugly afterwards. Remember, in those days, a deformed body was a sign of an evil mind.
I Interesting.

Part 3
I So who do *you* think did it?
D Well, I don't know of course, but I think possibly Henry the Seventh. I think the princes had still been alive when Henry won the Battle of Bosworth Field. Now, remember that Prince Edward's father had been king; Prince Edward was next in line.
I So Henry wanted him out of the way?
D Exactly. I think Henry murdered the princes and told everybody that Richard had murdered them. Maybe Richard was framed after he had been killed – in other words, Henry made it look like Richard was guilty.
I Oh, I see. Hmm, interesting. Well, thanks for coming to talk to us today.
D Thank you.

6

6A.1
Paul Look what you've done to my car! Women! They're absolutely awful drivers! Suzi! Is that you Suzi? I can't believe it! It's me, Paul!
Suzi Paul. What a surprise.
P This is absolutely amazing! It's such a strange coincidence! Are you hurt?
S No, I'll be fine.
P This is unbelievable. It's so wonderful to see you again!
S So … How's your super-model girlfriend, Mercedes?
P We've split up. Look, I'm so sorry about what happened. You and I were so good together. I was such a fool to leave you for Mercedes.
P And don't worry about the car. We'll have to tell the police it was your fault, of course – you were driving so badly. You always were such a terrible driver! But I don't mind about the car – I'm just so happy I've found you again!
S Oh, Paul, you're so kind! Listen, I've got a bottle of champagne in the car – let's have a drink to celebrate.
P Whew, I needed that. More?
S No, I'm fine for now, thanks. Help yourself.
P You haven't touched your cup. Aren't you going to have any?

S No, thanks. You go ahead and drink. I'll just wait for the police.

6A.2
I'm **so** ex**haust**ed!
It's **such** a **bri**lliant **film**!
It's **such** an e**nor**mous **car**!
It's **absolutely aw**ful!
She's **so fur**ious!
It's **absolutely** a**maz**ing!
It's **absolutely te**rrible!
I was **absolutely te**rrified!
It's **absolutely won**derful!

6A.3
1
A I thought it was quite good.
B Yeah! I thought it was **absolutely bri**lliant!
A Yeah – it had a good ending.
B Yeah I know. It was **such** an a**maz**ing story.
A Great music, too.
B Yeah. It was **so good**. I could see it again tomorrow.
A Really?
B Yeah, absolutely!
2
A How was it?
B It was **absolutely won**derful!
A Oh, really? Great!
B Yeah, we had **such** a **bri**lliant time!
A So you liked the place, then?
B Yeah, it's **so** a**maz**ing we've decided to go again next year!
A Wow! Sounds good. Maybe I'll go there, too!
B Yeah, you should! You'll love it!
3
A Have you got them yet?
B Yeah.
A So how are they?
B **Absolutely aw**ful!
A Oh no!
B My parents are **so fur**ious that they won't let me go to the camp.
A What – were they so terrible then?
B Yeah. I'll have to do them again. I'll have to spend all summer preparing!
A Oh no! Poor you!

6B.1
Ben Did you read the story about that man who lost his wallet?
Julia Yeah, yeah, and he got it back after 39 years. Amazing, eh?
B Yeah, I bet he didn't expect to see that again!
J I know. I hate losing things. I lost my handbag last year, it was awful, because I had all my documents in there, you know – bank cards, ID card and all of that …
B What a pain!
J Yeah. I forgot to pick it up when I was getting off a train.
B Uh huh.
J And my mobile phone was in there too, so I lost everybody's phone number …
B Oh no! And was there much money in there?

J There was a bit of money, yeah, but the worst thing was the ID card … and the phone.
B Mmm … yeah … And did you get it back?
J No, no, no. So I cancelled all the bank cards and everything.
B Mmm.
J And it took months to get a new ID card …
B Yeah, all the paperwork and everything …
J Ha ha – maybe I'll get it back in 39 years, like that man in the story, no …
B It'll be a bit late by then!
J Yeah, right.

6C.1
OK, well top of the list is noise. Noise is the biggest problem for neighbours in the UK, according to our survey. The second in the list is rough behaviour, and after that, in third place – naughty children. The fourth place is problems with walls and fences. After that in fifth place are problems to do with car parking. In sixth place are animal problems, for example dogs barking. And finally, in seventh position are problems to do with rubbish.

6C.2
Love Your Neighbours

Mrs Dickson thinks the Lanes
Are noisy and rough
She says the kids are naughty
She says she's had enough
Mr Dickson says they leave
Their rubbish by the door
'You can't complain', says Mrs Lane
'It's not against the law'
Love Your Neighbours …

Mrs Dickson says their children
Play their music loud
She says she hears them swearing
It shouldn't be allowed
Mr Dickson says he hears them
Fighting all night long
'You can't complain', says Mrs Lane
'We're doing nothing wrong'
Love Your Neighbours …

Mrs Dickson says they kick
Their ball along the hall
She says she saw their daughter
Writing on the wall
Mr Dickson says he hears them
Talking on the phone
'Don't complain', says Mrs Lane
'Leave us all alone'
Love Your Neighbours …

6D.1
he tried to
he'd tried to

she needed
she'd needed

6D.2
He said he'd tried to help.
He said he tried to help.
He said he'd try to help.

She said she'd need money.
She said she needed money.
She said she'd needed money.

7

7A.1
This man's in his early twenties, and he's got straight dark hair … ehm … it's quite long. He's got quite a long face, and his nose is long and thin too. His eyes are wide open – he looks a bit surprised. He looks a bit shy, nervous perhaps, I don't know.

7A.2
a This woman's in her early fifties, and she's got wavy light brown hair … ehm … it's quite short and parted on the side. She's got quite a long nose, and she looks like an ambitious character. She looks very confident, serious maybe, like a school headmistress or something.
b This girl's in her late teens or early twenties, and she's got very long ginger hair, and it's straight. It's parted in the middle and she hasn't got a fringe. She looks like an outgoing character, she's got a friendly smile. She looks imaginative and artistic.
c I guess this man's in his mid thirties. He's got short dark hair and he's clean-shaven. He's got a round face with a high forehead and a short nose. He looks unfriendly – he looks aggressive, in fact.
d This woman's in her late sixties and she's got short, curly grey hair. She looks like a happy grandmother. Ehm … she looks kind – she's probably quite a generous woman, and she looks lively and active.
e This man's in his seventies, and he's got shoulder-length white hair and a beard and moustache. He's got bushy eyebrows as well. He looks quite lively and intelligent – he looks like he wants to ask you a question.

7A.3
A Is it a man or a woman?
B A man.
A A man, OK. Has he got long dark hair?
B No, he's got long **white** hair.
A Long **white** hair. OK, I know who it is …

7A.4
No, long **fair** hair.
No, **long** fair hair.

No, curly **ging**er hair.
No, **curly** ginger hair.

No, **late** twenties.
No, late **twen**ties.

No, **big** brown eyes.
No, big **brown** eyes.

7B.1

Wang Li
I'm not fashion-conscious. I wear what I'm expected to wear for work. After that, I don't mind what I wear as long as it's comfortable. I don't understand what's so special about designer clothes – I never look at labels. I don't like clothes shopping – I don't know what to look for.

Heather
I dress how I want, and I don't care what people think! I know what I like and I don't just follow everybody else. I don't spend a lot on clothes – I wear what I can afford. I don't think it's important how much your clothes are worth. The cheapest things can look cool.

Marcela
How I look is very important to me. My outfit changes how I feel, so I spend a lot on clothes. I think people notice what you're wearing, and if you're well dressed, they treat you differently. I love how it feels when I go out in a new outfit and I know everybody's looking at me.

7B.2

1 I don't mind what I wear.
2 I don't care what people think!
3 I never look at labels.
4 If you're well-dressed, they treat you differently.
5 I wear what I'm expected to wear.
6 My outfit changes how I feel.

7C.1

A Are you doing anything interesting this week?
B No, not much. I'm doing my French exam on Monday, so I'm going to stay home and study.
A So you're not going out at the weekend?
B No. Maybe I'll go out to celebrate after the exam! What about you? Are you doing anything special?
A Well, I'm starting dance classes on Thursday.
B Really? What sort of dancing?
A We're going to study salsa, tango, rumba ... that sort of thing.
B Wow, sounds great.

7D.1

This is a young woman's bedroom. There's a big birthday card on the wall saying 'Happy Birthday Liz', so her name must be Liz and it must be her birthday. There are two party dresses hanging up, so she must be having a party and she's deciding which one to wear. It must be an important birthday because the dresses are expensive. Perhaps it's her 18th or 21st birthday. She might be American or British, because of her name, and the birthday card's in English.

There's a photo of a young woman on the wall, which might be her. It looks like a graduation photo. She's a white girl with long dark hair. She might be a student. There are lots of books in her room. It might be a student flat or maybe it's a room in her parents' house.

She probably isn't married. She must like babies because there are photos of babies and children on the wall. She probably plans to get married and have children in the future.

There's also a painting on the wall. Perhaps the girl likes painting. This might be a portrait of her sister or a friend.

7D.2

perhaps it's her 18th or 21st birthday
maybe it's a room in her parents' house
she probably isn't married
she probably plans to get married and have children
perhaps the girl likes painting

8

8A.1

1 Look, I'm with a client and I can't get away right now. Can I ring you back tomorrow?
2 Have you got her mobile number please? ... Great. Hang on, I'll just get a pen to write it down ... OK, go ahead.
3 Look, I've tried that number already, but I can't get through. I either get cut off or I just get the engaged signal. Is there another number I can call? Please don't hang up!! Hello?
4 Hi, Lucy. It's me. I'm calling from the hospital. Gloria has had the baby. It's a beautiful boy! Hang on, I'll hand you over to Gloria ...
5 Extension 483? Who's calling please? ... Hold on. I'll put you through ... I'm sorry, the line's busy right now. Would you like to leave a message or call back in five minutes?
6 Hello, can you put me through to the emergency rescue service, please. My car's broken down ... Thanks.
7 Hello, it's Mike calling from Bike World. I'm calling to let you know the spray paint you ordered has arrived, so you can call by and pick it up some time ...

8A.2

a I **called** by **pub**lic **phone**.
b I **called by** this **morn**ing.

8A.3

Stephanie Hello?
Voicemail Hello, this is Max Motors. I'm sorry, all our lines are busy. Please call back in five minutes.
Secretary Max Motors. Can I help you?

S Oh, ehm, hello, can you put me through to the emergency rescue service, please. My car's broken down. I'm on a main road near Stratford upon Avon.
Sec Hang on, I'll put you through.
Sec Max Motors. Can I help you?
S Hello, I called a minute ago but I got cut off.
Sec Oh yes, sorry about that. What was the problem again?
S My car's broken down. The engine won't start. I'm on the side of a road near Stratford upon Avon.
Sec OK, so you want to speak to a mechanic. If you hold the line, I'll put you through.
Mechanic 1 Hello?
S Hello. My car's broken down near Stratford upon Avon ...
M1 I'm sorry, I'm in the middle of something right now. I'll hand you over to my colleague.
Mechanic 2 Hello. Can I help you?
S Hello. There's a problem with my car – something's wrong with the engine, and I need someone to look at it.
M2 I see. Well, if you call by the garage, I'll check your car and we'll see what the problem is.
S I'm sorry, you don't understand. I can't call by. The car's broken down on the side of the road and the engine won't start.
M2 Ah well, I'm sorry, I can't help you then. We don't have a call out service. Goodbye.
S Wait – don't hang up! ... Oh no!

8B.1

able	a**bility**
popular	popu**lar**ity
active	ac**tiv**ity
curious	curi**os**ity
real	re**al**ity
possible	possi**bil**ity

8C.1

Ricardo Oh, hi Cath. How was the interview? Was it alright?
Cath Hmm, well. I don't think it went very well, actually.
R Oh, really? What happened?
C I don't think I gave very good answers to their questions.
R Oh. What did they ask?
C Well, they asked why I wanted to work for them, and I couldn't think of an answer.
R So what did you say?
C I said I needed the money. I couldn't think of anything else to say.
R Hmm. What else did they ask?
C They wanted to know what foreign languages I spoke.
R Uh huh.
C And in particular, they asked if I spoke German.
R So what did you say?
C What could I say? I told them I didn't speak any foreign languages.
R Oh. Is that a problem?
C Well, it's a German company. They need their staff to travel to Germany sometimes.
R Oh I see. So how did it end?
C Well, they asked me what salary I wanted. I said £30,000 a year.
R And what did they say about that?
C Nothing. They just thanked me for coming to the interview, and that was it. They said, 'Don't call us, we'll call you'.
R Hmm. It doesn't sound very good. Have you got any other interviews lined up?
C No.

8D.1

I asked her to wait.
She told me not to wait.
I told him not to go.
He asked me to go.

8D.2

Anita Hi, Vikram. When did you get back from Paris?
Vikram Last night.
A So how was the journey?
V Great, except I was tricked out of some money by a man at the station.
A Why? What happened?
V Well, when I arrived at the Gare du Nord, an English man approached me and asked me if I spoke English. So I said yes, and then he asked me to give him ten euros for his train ticket.
A So did you give it to him?
V Yes, and he promised to send it back to me when he got home, but I just told him to keep it.
A That was very nice of you.
V Well, it wasn't very much. I felt sorry for him – in fact, I invited him for a coffee.
A Uh huh.
V And he told me to be careful because there were thieves in the station.
A Mmm.
V So anyway, we said goodbye, and then the next day I was in the station again, and guess what: he was there again.
A So that story about the train ticket was a lie ...
V Exactly, **and** he was asking a woman to give him money. Another victim!
A Did you say anything?
V Yeah, I did. I went over and I warned the woman not to give him anything.
A Quite right too!

8E.1

Sandra Hi. I'm doing a survey about communication habits. Can I ask you a question?
B Uh huh, sure.
S Do you send a lot of text messages?
B Quite a lot, yeah.
S Uh huh. Why do you send them? I mean, why don't you just phone?
B Well, it's a quick way to send information, because you don't have to have a conversation.

And it's convenient. If the other person is busy and isn't able to answer right at that moment, they can read it later.
S Yes, right. OK, thank you very much.

9

9A.1
heavy showers
blowing a gale
boiling hot
freezing cold
pouring rain
soaking wet

9A.2
1 Winter
Susan Ooh, there's a cold wind out there!
Tom Yeah, I know. It's freezing, isn't it? It goes right through your coat.
S And they say it's going to rain later.
T Oh, yeah?
S Yeah. Still, it could be worse I suppose. They're having snowstorms in the north, aren't they?
T Yes, I saw that on the news. The heaviest snow in 50 years, they say.
S Yeah, it's amazing, isn't it? Some villages are completely cut off.

2 Spring
S It's a lovely day, isn't it?
T Yes. It's so mild for the time of year.
S Yeah, I know. Normally this time of year we have the heating on!
T Yeah, it's great, isn't it? Do you think it will last until the weekend?
S Probably not. I'm going away. It'll probably rain.
T Oh well, I guess we need it, don't we? You know what they say: April showers bring May flowers.
S Yeah, but the showers are always at the weekends, aren't they?

3 Summer
S It's hot, isn't it?
T Yeah, I know. It's terrible, isn't it? I prefer cold. At least you can put more clothes on. When it's hot, there's nothing you can do about it.
S Mmm. They say it's the hottest August since 1920.
T Really? And there's no wind at all, is there?
S No. I wonder how long it will go on for.
T I don't know. They say there's a heat wave all over Europe. In some parts of the Mediterranean it's over 45 degrees.
S Wow. I guess we shouldn't complain, then.

4 Autumn
S The days are getting shorter again, aren't they?
T Yeah. Dark at six thirty!
S It's a clear night though, isn't it? Look at that moon!
T Yeah, it's going to be a cold one. You know what they say: Clear moon, frost soon.
S It's cold already, isn't it? My ears are freezing.
T Yeah, but it'll be nice and sunny tomorrow.
S Mmm.

9A.3
It's freezing, isn't it?
It's amazing, isn't it?
It's a lovely day, isn't it?
It's great, isn't it?
It's terrible, isn't it?
It's a clear night though, isn't it?
It's cold already, isn't it?

9B.1
My **hair** will have **grown**.
I'll have **cut** my **nails**.
Things won't have **changed much**.
I'll have **passed** the exam.

9B.2
1
Five years from now I'll be 66. Hopefully, I'll be in good health, because I don't want to retire. I don't want to sit in front of the television all day. I want to be active and look after the business. My husband and I started this business from nothing and now it's listed in the best restaurant guides. Unfortunately, Luigi won't be here. That's Luigi behind me – he's the head chef. He's going to retire next year and go back to Italy. Hopefully, I'll have found a new chef by then, but it won't be easy to get someone as good as Luigi. Maybe one day my son will return and work with me. He's working in America at the moment, but I don't think he's happy. Hopefully, in five years' time he'll have moved back here and we'll be together again.

2
In five years' time, I'll be 24 and I'll have finished university. I'm going to study Art History. Hopefully, I'll get good final exam results. I'll probably have found a job. I'd like to be a fashion designer. I'll probably work for a company at first, and then maybe I'll start my own business. Hopefully, I'll have bought my own little flat, and maybe a cat called Toby. I probably won't be married – it's too soon, and I want to start my career first. Perhaps I'll never get married, I don't know. I don't think I want children, really. I won't have a car, because of pollution and all that – I think we'll have to take more care of the environment, so I'll still use my bicycle.

9C.1
1 The worst option is b. If you run, the bear will probably run after you. The other options are all recommended.
2 The worst option is b. If you disturb the quicksand a lot, it'll pull you downwards. The best option is to try to lie on your back on top of the quicksand and get your legs out little by little.
3 The worst option is a. If your mouth is open, it'll get filled with snow. Breathing is the biggest problem when you're trapped in the snow. The other options are all recommended.
4 The worst option is c. If you try to swim against the current, you'll probably just get exhausted. The best option is to swim parallel to the beach to get away from the current.
5 The worst option is b. A tornado can easily lift up a car. The other options are all recommended. Sometimes, the bath is the only part of the house which is left after a tornado has passed!
6 The worst option is c. The tree may attract the lightening. The other options are all recommended. If you are in a pool when lightening strikes, the electricity will pass through the water to you.
7 The worst option is a. Sharks won't get bored and go away like grizzly bears. The eyes and gills are the shark's weakest places.
8 The worst option is c. If any lava comes from the volcano, it will flow downwards in the valleys on the mountain side. Also, the worst of the gases are heavier than air and are close to the ground.

9D.1
Nicola If you could have one of these devices, which one **would you** choose?
Kurt Ehm ... I don't know ... ehm ... I think I'd have the personal helicopter. Yeah, that looks great fun.
N Uh huh, yeah. So what **would you** do with it? Where **would you** go?
K Oh, I don't know – I guess I'd fly over the town, see what it looks like from up there. Maybe go across the channel to France.
N Mmm. Very nice.
K So what about you. Which device would you choose?
N I'd quite like the brain keyboard.
K So what **would you** do if you had that?
N Well, I work at the computer all day long and I'm not very good at typing, so I waste a lot of time. If I had that, I could just think what I want to write

and that would be it.
K So you'd use it for work?
N Yeah, I'd use it for work.

9D.2
Which one would you **choose**?
What would you **do** with it?
Where would you **go**?
What would you **do** if you had **that**?

10

10A.1
Death of the High Street
The butcher on the high street
Listens with alarm
They say that Farmer Jones
Is going to sell the farm
The greengrocer was driving past
And saw the land for sale
The cashier in the bank thinks
They're going to build a jail

The chemist tells the optician
The optician tells the nurse
The people on the high street
Say there's nothing worse
The newsagent saw an engineer
Walking on the land
The grocer on the corner
Saw a lorry full of sand

The baker saw a bulldozer
Driving through the town
'Did you hear about the farm house?
They've knocked the old place down!
They're building roads and walls
A big new shopping mall
We're going to lose our customers
The mall will take them all!'

The mall kills the high street

10A.2
Jerry Hi Amrita. How are you?
Amrita Oh, hi Jerry. I'm fine, and you?
J Not too bad thanks. Hey, have you seen they're building a new shopping centre out near the motorway?
A Are they? That's great. We need a good shopping mall around here.
J I don't think so. I mean, there are lots of good shops on the high street, aren't there?
A Yes, maybe, but shopping centres are more convenient, don't you think?
J Not really, no. They're always a long way out of town.
A OK, that's true, but there's no traffic and it's always easy to park the car ...
J Alright, but that's no good if you haven't got a car – like me.
A Well, OK, you're right, I suppose. But you could get the bus. And things are always cheaper in malls ...
J I'm not so sure about that. They're cheap at first, and then when all the small shops close, they put up the prices! Anyway, you get much better service in smaller shops.

A Yes, I agree, but I haven't got time to go round lots of little shops. I think it's better to get everything in one place.

J OK, well you go to the new mall, but all the small shops will close, you'll see!

A Oh Jerry, you can't stop time, you know. You can't keep living in the past!

J Hmm.

10A.3

I don't think so.
Yes, maybe, but shopping centres are more convenient.
Not really, no.
OK, that's true, but there's no traffic.
Alright, but that's no good if you haven't got a car.
Well, OK, you're right, I suppose.
I'm not so sure about that.
Yes, I agree, but I haven't got time.

10B.1

a jar of coffee
a packet of biscuits
a box of eggs
a carton of milk
a pot of yogurt
a tin of tomatoes
a bottle of ketchup
a bag of potatoes
a tube of toothpaste
a tub of margarine

10B.2

Linda

Interviewer Hi, I'm doing a survey of shopping habits. Do you mind if I ask you a few questions?

Linda No, go ahead.

I OK, well, first of all, can you tell us what you're buying today?

L Let's see ... I've got a two-litre bottle of milk, ehm, eight cartons of yogurt, a box of cereal, ehm, some packets of kitchen paper, a bottle of olive oil, two big bottles of water, some boxes of tissues ...

I That's a lot of stuff. How are you going to get it all home?

L I've got the car in the car park.

I OK, that's good. Why are you buying so much?

L Well, I've got two children, and I haven't got time to go shopping during the week, so I just do one big weekly shop.

I OK. You've got lots of packets and bottles here, but there isn't much fresh stuff. Is this what you normally buy?

L Yes, but I buy fresh stuff from other shops, too. I normally buy my fruit in the greengrocer's across the road. I think it's better.

I I see. And do you write a shopping list?

L Yes, I need a shopping list, because if I forget something, I won't have time to come back.

I OK, last question. Do you pay in cash or by card?

L I usually pay with my debit

card. I don't like carrying too much cash, or I'll just spend it!

Mark

Interviewer Hi, I'm doing a survey of shopping habits. Do you mind if I ask you a few questions?

Mark No, go ahead.

I OK, well, first of all, can you tell us what you've got in your basket today?

M Let's see, there's a packet of pasta, a loaf of bread, a couple of toilet rolls, a tin of tomatoes, a bag of carrots, a jar of honey, a bottle of wine, some fresh fruit and veg ...

I And are these the kinds of things you normally buy?

M Yes, this is more or less normal. I like cooking so I buy quite a lot of fresh stuff.

I And how often do you shop for food?

M Oh, two or three times a week.

I Do you write a shopping list?

M Yeah, sometimes, especially if there's something I know I'll forget.

I OK, and last question – do you normally pay in cash or with a card?

M Cash. I usually get cash out of the cash machine. I don't like paying by card.

10C.1

Ms Sayles We haven't been selling many of these sunshades lately. I want you to try harder. The one who sells the most over the next month or so will get a bonus.

Ms S Right. What have you been doing to sell more sunshades, Winston?

Winston I've been offering two for the price of one, Ms Sayles.

Ms S And how many have you sold?

W I haven't sold many recently. People don't want sunshades with pink rabbits on.

Ms S How many, Winston?

W Well, none, in fact.

Ms S None. And how long have you been working here?

W Almost six months.

Ms S Nearly six months and you haven't learnt anything. It's not good enough!

Ms S What about you, Janet?

Janet I've been advertising in the daily paper, Ms Sayles. I've also been phoning people at home.

Ms S And how many have you sold?

J About five. It's been raining for weeks. Nobody wants a sunshade.

Ms S You're a saleswoman, Janet. It's your job to sell things that nobody wants.

Ms S And you, Charlie? How many have you sold?

Charlie Two thousand, more or less. People have been queuing

to buy them.

Ms S That's amazing! What have you been doing?

C I've been selling them outside the station as umbrellas.

10C.2

It's been **rain**ing.
I've been **sleep**ing.
You've been **wait**ing.
It **has**n't been **rain**ing.
I **have**n't been **sleep**ing.
You **have**n't been **wait**ing.
Has it been **rain**ing?
Have I been **sleep**ing?
Have you been **wait**ing?

10C.3

Teresa Hi Simon!

Simon Oh, hello Teresa.

T What have you been doing lately? I haven't seen you around for ages.

S Oh, I haven't been going out much. I'm trying to save some money for a trip to India.

T India? Oh, very nice. Are you still working at the sports shop?

S No, I've been working in a travel agent's for the last three months. What about you? Have you been doing anything interesting? Still playing the piano?

T Well, I've been learning to play the trumpet, actually.

S Oh really? That must be nice for your flatmate! What's her name? Sarah?

T Sarah. I don't live with Sarah any more. I've been living on my own for nearly a year.

S Oh yeah. Are you enjoying it?

T Yeah, it's great. I've been going away most weekends, to the coast.

S Oh yes, I remember – you go windsurfing, don't you?

T Yes, windsurfing. I'm still doing that.

S Listen, I've got to go, but I'll give you a ring. Have you still got the same phone number?

T Yeah, still the same.

S Yes, mine's the same too. I'll be in touch. Bye!

T See you!

10D.1

Dan Can I help you?

Tina Yes, I'm looking for a cheap digital camera.

D A digital camera? OK. How much do you want to spend?

T £100 or so.

D Well, this one is normally £120, but it's reduced at the moment to £99.99.

T Does that include the batteries, the memory card, and everything?

D Yes, all included. And there's a six-month guarantee. If you have any problems with it, we'll repair it free of charge. Here, try it ...

T Mmm. Oops, I've taken a photo of my foot!

D It's all right. We can delete it

unless you want to keep it!

T No, thanks. I hate these shoes! OK, I think I'll take the camera. And I'll buy some spare batteries while I'm here.

D Sorry, we don't sell batteries, but you can buy them at any supermarket.

T How much do they cost?

D £2.50, more or less. Would you like to buy a leather case for your camera? Brown, to match your shoes!

T Ha ha. No, thanks. That's all, thanks.

D OK. How would you like to pay – by cash or card?

T I'll pay by credit card, please.

D Can you enter your PIN number, please ... Thanks. And here's your receipt. Keep it in case you need to bring the camera back.

T OK. Thanks. Goodbye.

D Bye.

11

11A.1

Paola

Paola Excuse me, do you know the way to (*beeeeep!*)

M Yes, go out of the building and go straight across the road and up Chapel Lane, and you'll see a church on your left.

P OK, up Chapel Street and ...

M No, Chapel LANE, and you'll see a church on the left and the Great Garden on your right, OK? And at the crossroads, turn right along Chapel Street and then turn left up Ely Street.

P Ely Street, uh huh ...

M Yes, and at the top of Ely Street, you'll come to a T-junction, and you turn left on Rother Street. You'll find the place you're looking for on the right.

P On the right. OK, thanks.

Ignacio

Ignacio Excuse me, can you tell me how to get to (*beeeeep!*)

W OK, go out of the building and cross High Street, then go down Sheep Street.

I Ship Street, OK ...

W SHEEP Street.

I Sheep Street, OK.

W Ha ha, yeah, like the animal, and at the end of Sheep Street you'll come to Bancroft Gardens, take the path across the gardens until you come to the canal.

I A path to the canal, OK.

W Walk across the lock to the other side of the canal and you'll see the Tramway Bridge. Go over the bridge to the other side of the river and you'll come to Swan's Nest Lane.

I Swan's Nest Lane.

W Yeah, you'll see a car park there, and the place you're looking for is just the other side of the car park.

I OK, thanks very much.
W Hope you enjoy it!

Laura

Laura Excuse me, can you tell me the way to (*beeeeep!*)
M OK, so go across the river on the foot ferry and turn right on Southern Lane.
L The foot ferry?
M Yes. A boat across the river.
L Oh, I see. OK.
M OK, and take the second left.
L Second left ...
M And go straight up to the crossroads. Go straight across and along Ely Street.
L Along Ely Street, yes.
M Yes, go along Ely Street until you reach Rother Street, then turn right. Then take the second left, which is Mansell Street.
L Mansell Street.
M Yes, Go along Mansell Street and across Arden Street, and the entrance is right there.
L OK – sounds complicated!
M Yes, well maybe you can ask someone else when you're nearer.
L OK, well, thanks very much.

11B.1

Claire Oh, you're going to Honduras? We went there last year.
Ian Oh yeah? Where did you stay?
C We stayed in a place called Punta Paloma on the Caribbean coast. It's a great place, set in a national park with mountains and rainforests. The hotel rooms are all separate cabins in the forest and they're really quiet and secluded – the only noise is the birds.
I Oh, wow. Sounds lovely!
C Yeah, really nice. The food's delicious and you can eat in the restaurant or have it served in the garden. There's a nice bar. For breakfast, there's a buffet, or you can have it brought to your room.
I Great. And what's there to do, you know, during the day?
C Oh, there's nothing to do really, but it's such a beautiful place just to spend time. We just relaxed by the pool and read a few books.
I And what are the people like – the hotel staff and so on?
C They're really efficient and helpful, you know, and if you want to have your clothes washed for example, you just leave them in a basket by the bed and they're clean the next day. So yeah, it's really comfortable. I'd recommend it.
I Right, OK. The Playa Paloma, you say?
C Punta. Punta Paloma.
I OK. Is it expensive?
C Ah! That's the thing. It's not cheap!
I Hmm ... that could be a problem.

11C.1

Are there any **injections** that you need to have?
Will you have to show any **vaccination certificates**?
Are there any **pills** that you need to take?
Do you need to take out **medical insurance**?
Should you drink the **tap water**?
Are there any **local foods** that you ought to avoid?
Do you need to take **sun block**?
Should you carry a **first aid kit**?
Will you need to take **insect repellent**?
Should you carry a **mosquito net**?
What should you do in an **emergency**?

11C.2

Do you need to carry your **passport**?
Are there any **documents** that you need?
Are there any **guide books** I should buy?
Should you take **travellers' cheques**?

11D.1

Fiona What about you, Feliks?
Feliks My worst journey was about four years ago, when I was live ... eh living in Scotland.
Fi Oh, really? Did you live in Scotland?
Fel Yeah, it was in Edinburgh, where I was a student, and, ehm ... anyway, I went away one weekend with a Scottish friend called Duncan, who was my flatmate at the time, and eh ... we drove to the Highlands, which is a few hours away by car, and we stayed in a youth hostel, but the next day it rained a lot and in the end we decided to go home early.
Fi Uh huh.
Fel So anyway, we got in the car and set off, and then we ... eh ... how do you say ... the petrol finished.
Fi You ran out of petrol?
Fel Yes, we ran out of petrol.
Fi What, in the middle of nowhere?
Fel No, luckily. This was in a town called Perth, which was about half way home. But anyway, we had to take the spare petrol can and walk to a petrol station. We had to leave the car on the side of the road. We got completely wet 'cause it was raining hard, and eh ... and I got petrol on my coat, which was new. And then when we got back to the car, we had a parking ticket ... eh ... a parking fine.
Fi Oh no!
Fel Yeah, we had a parking fine 'cause it was a no-parking zone.
Fi How annoying! That's so unfair!

Fel Yeah, I know. But that's not the end of the story. Later on, we stopped at a service station in a town called Stirling, where we had something to eat, and then when we came out, the car was ... how do you say ... not there ... ehm ...
Fi Gone? Stolen?
Fel Yeah, stolen.
Fi Really? So what did you do? Did you call the police?
Fel Well, Duncan tried to phone them on his mobile, but his batteries were ... had no power, ehm ...
Fi Flat?
Fel Yeah, his batteries were flat and we had to walk to the nearest phone box, which was a kilometre away. Anyway, the police came and Duncan filled in a report, and then we had to catch a bus home.
Fi What a horrible trip!
Fel Yeah, but it was worse for Duncan. It was his car!

11D.2

I changed the tyre which was flat.
I changed the tyre, which was flat.

They stopped the driver, who was speeding.
They stopped the driver who was speeding.

The man, who was lost, asked for help.
The man who was lost asked for help.

12

12A.1

Serge S-o what do you think is the point of that story?
Lucia Well, I think it's that you can't e-h, you can't own the smell of your food, you know, e-h-m I mean, I think the richer woman's very selfish so she doesn't want to give anything away, not even the smell of her food, I mean, she thinks e-h ... she thinks the smell belongs to her.
S Yeah, so she thinks the poor woman i-s is stealing from her, stealing the smell. That's really stupid, isn't it?
L Yeah. And so I think the chief's very clever, b-e-c-a-u-s-e e-h he shows her how stupid it is, e-h stealing a smell is l-i-k-e like hitting a shadow, you know, what's the point of that?
S Uh huh, yeah.

12A.2

Lucia Yeah. And so I think the chief's very clever, b-e-c-a-u-s-e e-h he shows her how stupid it is, e-h stealing a smell is l-i-k-e like hitting a shadow, you know, what's the point of that?
Serge Uh huh, yeah. It reminds

me of that stuff with Internet, you know, t-h-e the wireless Internet connection thing ...
L Wireless?
S Yeah, you know – those people who use other people's wireless connections in order to get onto the Internet. I don't think that's stealing because e-h-m because if it's out in the street, it belongs to everybody. I think it's out in public space, so everybody can use it, you know s-o e-h-m so it's like the smell of soup ...
L I don't think it's the same, because you have t-o to pay for the Internet connection, so it's different. You don't have to pay for the smell of your soup.
S Yeah, but what difference does it make if somebody else uses your Internet connection? I mean, it doesn't take anything from you, so what's the problem? It's like this ... You're playing your car radio, and e-h-m the window is down so everybody can hear it – are they stealing your sound?
L No, of course they aren't. But they aren't out there in order to hear your radio, are they? So it's different. People use your Internet connection in order t-o to get free Internet. In my opinion, that's stealing.
S But you don't have to pay more if somebody uses your connection, I mean, e-h you probably won't even notice.
L E-h-m but it makes your Internet connection wor – e-h-m slower, doesn't it?
S No, I don't think so.
L And what if they use your Internet connection to do s-o-m-e-t-h-i-n-g e-h criminal?
S Ah yes, OK, but that's different. If you're worried about that, you should put a a password on your connection.

12A.3

... the chief's very clever, b-e-c-a-u-s-e e-h he shows her ...
... stealing a smell is l-i-k-e like hitting a shadow ...
... you know s-o e-h-m so it's like the smell of soup ...
... People use your Internet connection in order t-o to get free Internet ...

12B.1

There were two men – Lofty and Shorty, and they were stuck on a desert island.

'Oh, I wish I was somewhere far, far away from here', said Lofty, 'I can't stand this place!'

Shorty, on the other hand, said, 'Oh, it's not so bad!'

Lofty spent all his time trying to make a signal. 'I hope a passing ship rescues us soon', he said, 'And I hope I never see another coconut again in my life!' Shorty, on the other hand, said, 'I'm glad I've got my guitar.' He spent the whole day and half the night playing it, and badly.

'I wish you hadn't saved that guitar', said Lofty, 'It's driving me crazy. I wish it had gone down with the boat!' Shorty carried on playing happily. And badly.

One night, while Shorty was sleeping, Lofty threw the guitar into the sea. In the morning, Shorty was upset. 'Where's my guitar?' he asked. 'Erm, the monkeys probably borrowed it', suggested Lofty, so Shorty went off to search for it.

A little while later, he returned holding an old bottle. 'Look what I've found', said Shorty.

12B.2
'Let's see', said Lofty, taking the bottle. He took the top off and, to their surprise, a genie came out.

'Ah! I've been stuck in this bottle for 1001 years', said the genie. 'And now you've freed me. Thank you! As a reward, I'll give you three wishes.'

'Yes!!!' shouted Lofty. 'I've dreamed of this moment for so long! Me first!'

'What is your first wish?' asked the genie.

'I wish I was in Las Vegas with a beautiful girl and a million dollars', said Lofty.

'Abracadabra', said the genie, and Lofty disappeared.

Now Shorty was alone, and there were two wishes left.

'What is your second wish?' asked the genie.

'I wish I had a new guitar', said Shorty.

'Abracadabra', said the genie, and a new guitar appeared. Shorty was delighted.

'And what is your third and final wish?' asked the genie.

12B.3
Shorty thought about it for a moment and then said, 'I wish my friend Lofty was back on the island to hear my new guitar!'

12B.4
A I wish I lived in a big city.
B Really? I wish I **did**n't live in a big city.

12B.5
A I wish I had an office job.
B Really? I wish I **did**n't have an office job.
A I wish I could speak Arabic.
B Really? I wish I could speak Chin**ese**.
A I wish I was older.
B Really? I wish I **was**n't so old!
A I wish people would drive more carefully on the motorway.

B Really? I wish people would drive more carefully **ev**erywhere!

12C.1
Well, it's a murder mystery to begin with, but it's also an adventure story, and, ehm, it's set mainly in Paris. The main character is a professor called Robert Langdon, an expert in languages and codes, anyway, the story starts when they find a body lying on the floor in the Louvre Museum, and there's a coded message written on his body, so the police ask Robert Langdon to help, anyway, he meets Sophie, the attractive daughter of the dead man, and they try to solve the mystery together. The trail of clues leads them to a big secret connected with the history of the church, and there are some powerful men trying to stop them discovering this secret ... so, erm, anyway, there's lots of mystery and lots of action.

12C.2
Well, it's a murder mystery.
Anyway, it starts when they find a body.
Well, it's a romance.
Anyway, she meets an attractive stranger.
Well, it's an adventure story.
Anyway, they start their journey.

12D.1
I would have done the same.
I would have waited.
I would have said something.
I would have kept quiet.
I would have tried to escape.

I wouldn't have done that.
I wouldn't have said that.
I wouldn't have made that choice.

12D.2
Well, I didn't really decide to become an actor, it just kind of happened, ehm, when I finished school, I was planning to study French at university, but I decided to take a year off before that, and I travelled to America. I guess if I'd gone straight to university, I'd have become a French teacher or something. Anyway, so I went to America and I was planning to return to Britain to go to university, you know, that was the plan, and I would've done that if I hadn't met Martin – he's my husband. This was in New York. So yeah, I decided to stay in America and Martin and I got married, and we decided to move to Los Angeles. I guess that was lucky, because I wouldn't have got into the movie business if we'd stayed in New York. Anyway, in Los Angeles, I got a job as a secretary in a film production company, and one day I was at work and I was noticed by a director of casting, it was just lucky really, they were looking for somebody with exactly my appearance, so they asked me to play a part in a movie, and it all started from there, you know, and if I hadn't been noticed that day, I would never have got into acting at all, yeah, life's funny like that.

Grammar Bank Key

Unit 1

1.1 1 object 2 subject 3 subject
4 subject 5 object 6 object
7 subject 8 subject

1.2 1 Where 2 Why 3 What
4 Which 5 When 6 Who

1.3 1 ✓   5 ✓
2 myself   6 yourself
3 himself   7 herself
4 ourselves   8 each other

1.4 1 love 2 's studying 3 don't see
4 has 5 sometimes spend
6 're having 7 'm sitting
8 are standing 9 do your cousins live
10 is shining 11 are you wearing
12 don't know

Unit 2

2.1 1 The highest mountain in Africa is
Mount Kilimanjaro.
2 **The** United Arab Emirates and India
are countries in Asia.
3 They crossed **the** Sahara on foot.
4 ✓
5 ✓
6 Paris is on the River Seine.
7 My sister is working in **the** Far East.
8 Cuba and the Bay Islands are in **the**
Caribbean.

2.2 1 They often go to Spain on their
holidays.
2 I've never been to South America.
3 He rarely enjoys sightseeing.
4 We hardly ever visit museums when
we go abroad.
5 Tourists sometimes say that Britain
is expensive.
6 The trains to London are quite often
late.
7 The weather is usually good in July
and August.

2.3 1 A kilt is a kind of skirt which is
sometimes worn by Scottish men.
2 The floors in the house are covered
with carpet to keep the rooms
warm.
3 DVDs look like CDs, but you can
store more information on a DVD.
4 These books are used for teaching
English.
5 I only wear shoes that are made of
leather.
6 Nowadays, the Internet is often used
as a way of sending messages to
people.

2.4 1 living   8 didn't know
2 invited   9 was sitting
3 arrived   10 noticed
4 were waiting   11 were looking
5 was wearing   12 were trying
6 started   13 explained
7 was   14 was holding

2.5 1 during 2 before 3 first 4 then
5 After 6 for a while 7 in the
morning 8 when 9 In the end

Unit 3

3.1 1 used to wear
2 used to laugh
3 used to shout
4 Did he use to teach
5 Did you use to go
6 didn't use to get

3.2 1 a ✓ b ✓ 2 a ✓ b ✗ 3 a ✓ b ✗
4 a ✓ b ✓ 5 a ✓ b ✗

3.3 1 met   7 left
2 hasn't talked   8 haven't had
3 put on   9 've cleaned
4 took   10 's done
5 's grown   11 've achieved
6 have been   12 's enjoyed

3.4 1 We didn't have a test this week.
2 He's passed all of his exams this
year.
3 The lesson finished a few minutes
ago.
4 Have you learnt a lot since the
course started?
5 The school was closed last week.
6 Have they had a maths lesson today?

3.5 1 Hurry up! 2 turn up the radio
3 wake me up 4 put on
5 take off 6 turn it off

Unit 4

4.1 1 worried   4 annoyed
2 fascinating   5 disgusting
3 amazing   6 excited

4.2 1 noisier than 2 the biggest
3 quieter 4 the worst
5 the most unusual 6 the best

4.3 1 worst 2 harder 3 carefully
4 earlier 5 loudest

4.4 1 Tom ate as much as Mike.
2 The cafeteria isn't as expensive as
the restaurant.
3 The Italian restaurant is as busy as
the Chinese restaurant.
4 The strawberries aren't as fresh as
the melons.
5 Thai curries aren't as hot as Indian
curries.

4.5 1 who 2 where 3 where 4 which
5 where 6 which 7 that

Unit 5

5.1 1 ✗ **The** head of state is **the** Queen.
2 ✗ Do you know where **the**
headquarters of **the** UN are?
3 ✗ **The** government is worried about
the rate of inflation.
4 ✗ George Washington was **the** first
president of **the** USA.
5 ✗ Britain, **the** Republic of Ireland,
and Denmark joined **the** European
Union in 1973.
6 ✓

5.2 1 don't have to   4 don't have to
2 must   5 can't
3 have to   6 mustn't

5.3 1 Guns were used by the robbers.
2 The customers were tied up.
3 One woman was hurt.
4 The cashiers filled bags with money.
5 The robbers escaped with the bags of
money.
6 The robbers have been arrested.

5.4 1 stopped 2 hit 3 stole 4 called
5 was taken 6 examined
7 wasn't badly injured 8 have sent

5.5 1 had seen/had put
2 became/had wanted
3 returned/had spent
4 took/had killed
5 continued/had murdered
6 confessed/had ordered

5.6 1 after 2 while 3 after
4 and then 5 while 6 after

Unit 6

6.1 1 so 2 so 3 such 4 such
5 such 6 so

6.2 1 spending   7 driving
2 to feed   8 getting
3 visiting   9 to see
4 finishing   10 looking after
5 looking after   11 to leave
6 setting off

6.3 1 He says our children are badly
behaved.
2 She says she doesn't like them.
3 He says we should move.
4 She says my music is too loud.
5 He says he can hear them arguing.
6 She says they can't sleep at night.

6.4 1 would give 2 told 3 she'd lost
4 didn't know 5 said 6 lived

6.5 1 My new neighbours are friendly.
However, they've got a big dog.
2 We've just moved house. By the way,
did I tell you I met Susan last week?
3 I've joined a gym. However, I've only
been twice.
4 He plays his music very loudly.
Anyway, I can't really say anything
because I practise my trumpet every
day.
5 We bought a new car, although we
couldn't really afford it.

Unit 7

7.1 1 Does she know when the shops
close?
2 They know where to buy cheap
clothes.
3 Do you know how much this dress
is?
4 I don't know why I bought this suit.
5 Do you know which colours are
fashionable?
6 We know how to dress well.

7.2 1 how 2 where 3 when 4 how
5 which

7.3
1 Paul and Terry **are** visiting …
2 I think **I'll** stay in …
3 **Is** Tom coming to the party?
4 What **are** you going to do …?
5 Who **are** Italy playing tonight?
6 We **aren't** going out. We're too tired.

7.4
1 I'm going to
2 'm seeing
3 Are you doing/going to study
4 aren't going to go
5 are you meeting/aren't meeting
6 'll pay

7.5 1 b 2 a 3 a 4 a 5 b

Unit 8

8.1 1 call back   2 hang up
3 hand you over   4 cut off
5 put me through   6 you hang on

8.2 1 Toby was able to walk when he was
ten months old.
2 My dog can walk on his back legs.
3 We might be able to win the
competition.
4 I'll be able to go to university next
year.
5 She managed to arrive on time for
the meeting.
6 We were able to finish our
homework last night.

8.3 1 She **managed** to complete …
2 We might **be** able to come …
3 My mum **could** dance very well …
4 He's **never** been able to learn Greek, …
5 Holland managed **to** score three …
6 She **can** cook very well …

8.4 1 … to know my address.
2 … me where I came from.
3 … what my profession is/was.
4 … when I left the USA.
5 … why I moved to Australia.

8.5 1 … where I went to school.
2 … me if I was a good student.
3 … me what my favourite subject was.
4 … if I spoke any foreign languages.

8.6 1 to give   4 to turn off
2 to show   5 not to smoke
3 not to leave   6 to help

Unit 9

9.1 1 aren't they   4 don't they
2 is it   5 doesn't it
3 do we   6 isn't it

9.2 1 will have lost
2 will have run
3 won't have passed
4 won't have done
5 will have been
6 will have driven

9.3 1 If they don't give us a safety leaflet,
we won't know what to do.
2 What will he do if there's an
emergency?
3 How will they find their way to the
campsite if it's dark?
4 You'll get lost if you don't take a
map.
5 She'll make a camp fire if it's very
cold.
6 If you leave food near the tent, it
will attract the bears.

9.4 2 c 3 f 4 e 5 d 6 b

9.5 1 'd buy/had
2 didn't have/could go out
3 will be/pass
4 had/wouldn't need
5 would you do/weren't
6 worked/'d get

Unit 10

10.1 1 an 2 an 3 the 4 the 5 The
6 the 7 the 8 an 9 a 10 the
11 the 12 an 13 a 14 the

10.2 1 many   2 a little   3 much
4 a few   5 a lot of   6 many

10.3 1 enough   2 few   3 few
4 lot of   5 much   6 too much

10.4 1 've been reading
2 haven't been working
3 has Tom been going out
4 've been playing
5 hasn't been raining

10.5 1 haven't been waiting
2 've written
3 Has he passed
4 have you been studying
5 haven't seen

10.6 1 I'll leave as soon as I find …
2 Don't buy it unless you're sure …
3 You don't pay until you leave.
4 They'll replace the camera as long
as you show …
5 She'll order those shoes when she
gets paid.

Unit 11

11.1 1 Could you tell me where the tourist
information office is?
2 Do you know if we can take photos
inside the theatre?
3 Could you tell me if this is Bridge
Street?
4 Do you know how old that building
is?
5 Can you tell me when the library
closes?

11.2 1 They had the house redecorated.
2 They had the heating repaired.
3 They've had an alarm system put
in the house.
4 They've had a new garage built.
5 They're having the new carpets
fitted today.
6 They're having new curtains made
for all the rooms.

11.3 1 You'll need to pack some warm
clothes.
2 Is there anything which I shouldn't
put in my suitcase?
3 You needn't take your hairdryer.
4 Perhaps I should order a taxi.
5 When do we have to check in?
6 You need to relax.

11.4 1 There was a long traffic jam, which
meant I was late for work.
2 She met her husband 17 years ago,
when she was working in Paris.
3 Anna, who is teaching me Arabic, is
coming to visit me.
4 I was on my way to Rome, where I
used to live.
5 Alain, whose apartment I share,
loves animals.

Unit 12

12.1 1 in order to   5 so
2 because   6 so
3 so   7 in order to
4 in order to   8 because

12.2 1 I'm glad I don't share a room …
2 I wish the football wasn't over.
3 I wish her friends would stop …
4 I'm glad we didn't go out.
5 I hope they might buy …
6 I'm glad it isn't raining.
7 I wish I could find a nice boyfriend.
8 I hope our kids might stop …

12.3 1 directed   4 talking
2 called   5 injured
3 taking   6 reading

12.4 2 e 3 f 4 c 5 d 6 a

12.5 1 If I hadn't studied, I wouldn't have
done well in my course.
2 If I hadn't saved some/any money,
I wouldn't have spent a year
travelling around Africa.
3 If I hadn't stopped in Egypt, I
wouldn't have seen the pyramids.
4 If I'd gone to Kenya, I would have
climbed Mount Kilimanjaro.
5 If I hadn't got a job in Botswana, I
wouldn't have met my husband.
6 If I hadn't written a book, I
wouldn't have become famous.
7 If I hadn't earned a lot of money, I
wouldn't have bought a big house.
8 If my wife had been happy, she
wouldn't have left me.

Unit 1 Test People and communication Date: _____

Grammar

1 Subject and object questions Look at each statement. Complete the questions about Sally.

Example Sally married someone.
Who *did Sally marry* _____?

1 Sally loves someone.
Who _____?

2 Someone phoned Sally.
Who _____?

3 Sally visited someone.
Who _____?

4 Someone likes Sally.
Who _____?

5 Someone took Sally for a meal.
Who _____?

☐ **5**

2 Reflexive pronouns and *each other* Complete the dialogues with a reflexive pronoun or *each other*.

Example A Does your mother know a lot of people?
B Yes, she always introduces *herself* to people at parties!

myself   each   other   himself
~~herself~~   each other   yourself

1 My best friend and I speak to _____ every day.

2 I painted this _____. Do you like it?

3 My brother's talking to _____ again!

4 Sally and Joe never understand _____.

5 Do you go to your English class by _____?

☐ **5**

3 Present simple and present continuous Complete the email with the correct form of the verbs.

✉ ☐
Hi Jeremy,
Thanks for your email. Yes, I'd love to meet your friend from Mexico. Did you know that I *'m studying* (study) Spanish at the moment? It's a really good course. We ¹_____ (do) a lot of conversation practice every week, so my speaking ²_____ (get) much better. Every day, I understand a lot more when my teacher ³_____ (talk) to me. The teacher is great. She's British, but she ⁴_____ (speak) Spanish really well. I can't write any more now because I ⁵_____ (do) my Spanish homework!
See you soon,
Myra

☐ **5**

Vocabulary

4 Ways of greeting Complete the way of greeting in each sentence.

Example I always kiss my sister on the c *h e e k s* when I go home.

1 Only my girlfriend kisses me on the l_____.

2 When I meet someone for the first time I usually s_____ hands with them.

3 I w_____ to my friends when I see them.

4 My Japanese friends b____ to their teacher.

5 I h___ my parents when I come back from holiday.

☐ **5**

5 People in my life Choose the correct answer a, b, or c.

My family and friends
My *parents* divorced five years ago and my dad married again last year. His wife's name is Olga. She was one of Dad's ¹_____ when he worked at the bank. She's quite a nice ²_____ and I like living there. The ³_____ on Dad and Olga's street are all really friendly, too. Mr Robson is the best. His wife died a few years ago so he's a ⁴_____. He comes for dinner every week and he always tells interesting stories. My ⁵_____ is Emily. She doesn't live near me, but we talk on the phone or email every day. She's great!

Example a neighbours b cousins c ~~parents~~

1 a colleagues b cousins c widows
2 a neighbour b step-mother c aunt
3 a acquaintances b step-fathers c neighbours
4 a uncle b nephew c widower
5 a acquaintance b best friend c flatmate

☐ **5**

Pronunciation

6 The alphabet Think about the sound of these letters of the alphabet. Circle the letter which sounds different.

Example Ⓐ B C

1 I Y L   4 D E F
2 T H V   5 G K J
3 P Q U

☐ **5**

☐ GVP Total ▮ **30**

Reading and Writing
A self-introduction email

1 Read the text. Choose a title for each paragraph.
  a Advice for making friends ____
  b Other ways to meet people on the Internet ____
  c Making friends – the old way and the new way

  ____
  d Don't forget the real world ____
  e Using Internet websites to meet friends ____

[ ] **5**

Making friends in the 21st century

1 The traditional way to make new friends is by meeting people who are your friends'
05 friends. In the 21st century, we have another option – we can use the Internet.

2 Websites like *MySpace* and *Facebook* all work in the
10 same way. A friend emails you and invites you to join. You send a description of yourself, and then you can communicate with your friends.

3 There are also lots of discussion groups on the Internet. You can join one and communicate with
15 people who have similar interests to you.

4 Decide which type of website you want to use and follow these guidelines. Always read other members' comments before you write. You can see which topics they are interested in and what
20 style they write in. Don't give too much personal information about yourself, like your home address and telephone number.

5 The Internet is one way to make friends. Remember, you still need to go to real clubs and parties. You
25 never know where you'll meet your next friend!

2 Read the text again. Write T (true) or F (false) for sentences 1–6.

Example The article is about families. ___F___

1 The text was written to advertise. ____
2 Members introduce people on *Facebook*. ____
3 Discussion groups are a good way to find old friends. ____
4 'one' (line 14) refers to a discussion group. ____
5 'they' (line 20) refers to topics. ____
6 You can only make friends by going to clubs. ____

[ ] **6**

3 Read the emails of self-introduction on a friendship website and complete the table below.

> ✉ ▢
> Hi everyone,
> I'm Francesca. I'm 25, I'm single and I'm a music teacher in a big school. I really love my job and the students are great. The other teachers are nice too, but most of them are older than me. I'd really like to make new friends who are the same age as me.
> I live with my colleague Meg. She's from the north of London, but we live in a small flat in the middle of the city. We often go out to the cinema or to concerts. Music is my main hobby, but I also love running. I run in the city parks almost every night.
> I'm looking for friendship on this website – but who knows? Perhaps I will find someone special here. Is that you? Why not send me an email and introduce yourself?
> Francesca

> ✉ ▢
> Hi Francesca,
> My name's Anthony. I'm 28 and I'm single. I haven't got a job at the moment, but I'm studying Hotel Management. I live with my cousin Carlos in Brighton. Our house is behind the train station so it's quite noisy, but I like it!
> You're a music teacher and I'm learning to play the guitar at the moment. I'm teaching myself so I'm making slow progress! What musical instruments do you play? And what sort of films and music do you like?
> Write soon,
> Anthony

	Francesca	Anthony
age	25	5 _____
job or studies	1 music _____	6 studying _____ Management
lives with	2 her _____	7 his _____
lives in	3 flat in the _____ of London	8 house _____ the train station
hobbies	4 likes films and music; _____ in city parks	9 learning to play the _____

[ ] **9**

4 Write an email of self-introduction for a friendship website. Write 80–100 words.

[ ] **10**

Reading and Writing Total [**30**]

Unit 2 Test People, places and cultures Date: _____

Grammar

1 *the* **before geographical names** Write *the* or Ø (no article) in the gaps.

Example The Sahara Desert is in _Ø_ North Africa

1 The Chalk Mountains are in _____ United States.
2 _____ Easter Island is in the Pacific Ocean.
3 Mount Fuji is in _____ Japan.
4 _____ Canary Islands are north west of Africa.
5 _____ United Kingdom is in Europe.

☐ **5**

2 **Adverbs of frequency** Rewrite the sentences using the adverbs of frequency.

Example Boris reads guide books. (never)
Boris never reads guide books .

1 The waiters here are very friendly. (usually)
_____ .
2 We buy souvenirs on holiday. (rarely)
_____ .
3 Kevin takes photos on holiday. (hardly ever)
_____ .
4 I visit museums when I'm on holiday. (quite often)
_____ .
5 Jason's really interested in local food. (always)
_____ .

☐ **5**

3 **Past simple and past continuous** Complete the story with the correct form of the verb in (brackets).

The Rules of the Road

This happened to me when I _was working_ (work) in Hungary. One day I ¹_____ (walk) to work. It was very early and the city was quiet. I came to a street that I needed to cross. The traffic lights were on green, but I couldn't see any cars so I ²_____ (start) to cross the road. As I ³_____ (cross) the road, a police officer ⁴_____ (see) me.
He came and spoke to me. 'You crossed when the lights were on red,' he said, and he told me to pay him some money. 'But there weren't any cars on the road,' I said. He ⁵_____ (not agree) with me, so I paid the money and went to work.

☐ **5**

Vocabulary

4 **People and places** Match 1–6 with a–f.

1 Brazil, Tanzania, Canada   a part of continent/
2 man, woman   region
3 Muslim, Jewish, Christian   b ethnic background
4 The Middle East, Central   c country
    America, North Africa   d gender
5 mountain, desert, lake   e environment
6 Bedouin, Berber, Maori   f religion

☐ **5**

5 **Words and phrases for describing objects** Complete the description of an object with these words.

made of   used for   used as   kind of   ~~from~~   looks like

A 'kotatsu'

With a 'kotatsu' you can have dinner, play games, do your homework – and keep warm at the same time! What is it?

A 'kotatsu' is a piece of furniture *from* Japan. It's a
¹_____ table. When you first look at it, it
²_____ a normal table. It's a low and flat with
four legs, and it's usually ³_____ wood.

But this table is also ⁴_____ keeping the legs and feet warm. Under the top of the table there is an electric heater. A special 'kotatsu' blanket is used with the table for extra warmth. So a 'kotatsu' is a piece of furniture that is
⁵_____ a table and also a heater.

☐ **5**

Pronunciation

6 *c* **and** *g* Think about the sound of *c* and *g* underlined in these words. Tick ✓ the correct sound.

Example <u>c</u>ountry   /k/ ✓   /s/ ☐

1 Mon<u>g</u>olia   /g/ ☐   /dʒ/ ☐
2 <u>c</u>ity   /k/ ☐   /s/ ☐
3 religion   /g/ ☐   /dʒ/ ☐
4 Afri<u>c</u>a   /k/ ☐   /s/ ☐
5 <u>g</u>ender   /g/ ☐   /dʒ/ ☐

☐ **5**

☐ GVP Total ☐ **30**

Reading and Writing
An intercultural experience

1 Read the text and answer the questions.

🔄 🔄 ⬜ www.columbiatouristguide.com

The Gold Museum (*El Museo del Oro*)
Bogotá, Colombia

There are more than 33,000 pieces of pre-Hispanic things made of gold in the Gold Museum, Bogotá, Colombia. The Bank of the Republic bought the first piece of gold in 1939. The museum now contains the biggest collection in the world. Each piece is beautiful, and the museum is an unforgettable place to visit.

What to see

• The famous **Quimbaya** *poporo* was the first piece in the collection. Poporos are small containers which are used for holding things. The design of the Quimbaya poporo is simple and it looks like a modern object. However it is actually 2,300 years old. It is a national symbol in Colombia, and it's used on coins and bank notes.

• The **Muisca's Golden Raft** is a tiny boat made of gold with figures on it. This small and incredibly beautiful object comes from the Muisca culture of Colombia, which existed 600 years ago. It represents an important tradition in Indian culture. The famous story of El Dorado comes from this tradition.

• The **Salon Dorado** is a special room on the third floor of the museum. 8,000 of the most important works of gold in the museum are kept here. Two guards allow just a few visitors at a time to enter. You walk inside, the heavy doors close behind you, and then the lights come on. You are surrounded by spectacular shining gold.

Practical information

The museum is open every day except Monday, from 9.00 a.m. to 7.00 p.m. and 10.00 a.m. to 5.00 p.m. on Sundays.

Example   How many pieces of gold are on display in the museum? *more than 33,000* .

1   When did The Bank of Republic start the collection?
_____

2   How old is the Quimbaya *poporo*?
_____

3   Which famous story is connected to the Muisca Golden Raft? _____

4   Where in the museum is the Salon Dorado?
_____

5   How many pieces are in the Salon Dorado?
_____

6   Which day is the museum closed?
_____

⬜ **6**

2 Read the text. Write T (true), F (false), or DS (doesn't say) for sentences 1–7.

Water Mix-up by Robert Richardson

Last year I went to Malaysia on business. My hosts were very friendly and most evenings they took me to different restaurants and ordered food for me. However, one evening I went out alone. I wanted to try the local food. I found a
05 restaurant with a wonderful aroma of spicy food so I decided to try it. Of course, the menu was all written in Malaysian and I didn't understand anything.

The man at the next table was eating something interesting. I called the waiter, pointed, and made eating gestures to show
10 that I wanted the same thing. The waiter and the man at the next table laughed and I felt happy. The waiter brought me the food, a fruit juice and a bowl of water.

The meal was excellent. The man next to me was eating with his right hand, so I did the same. When I needed to
15 wash my fingers, I used the small bowl of water. Immediately the waiter came and brought me a new water bowl. This happened several times. When it happened for the fifth time, he put the bowl on my table with a bang.

I noticed that the man at the next table wasn't using the
20 water to wash his fingers – he was drinking it. I felt very stupid. I was sorry that the waiter was angry, but I didn't know how to say that. I gave him some extra money when I paid for my meal.

1   Robert went to the same restaurant. _____
2   His hosts usually chose his food. _____
3   When he went out alone he wanted European food.
_____
4   He went to the restaurant because it was cheap. ___
5   He was happy when he ordered his meal. _____
6   He washed his fingers in the wrong bowl. _____
7   He didn't go to the restaurant again. _____
⬜ **7**

3 Read the text again and answer the questions.
Example   When did Robert go to Malaysia? *last year* .

1   Why did Robert go to Malaysia? _____
2   Why didn't he understand the menu? _____.
3   What three things did the waiter take to his table?
_____
4   Which hand did he eat with? _____
5   How did he feel about his mistake? _____.
⬜ **7**

4 Imagine you are the waiter in 'Water Mix-up'. Write the same story from your point of view. Write 80–100 words.
⬜ **10**

⬛ Reading and Writing Total ⬜ **30**

Grammar

1 *Used to* Replace the bold words with phrases with *used to* where possible. If it is not possible, write ✗.
When I was a teenager …

used to ask
- my parents **asked** me to jobs around the house.
- my mother always ¹**cleaned** my bedroom.
- I ²**had** a big party when I was 16.
- I ³**didn't pay** for my clothes and shoes.
- my father only ⁴**got** very angry with me once.
- When you were a teenager … ⁵**were you** happy?

☐ **5**

2 **Present perfect and past simple** Read the text and underline the correct form of the verb.

More Homework for Vicky

Vicky Phillips is thirteen. In many ways she's a typical teenager. However, there's one thing about Vicky that's very different from her friends. She *never went* / *'s never been* to school. Vicky is a 'homeschool' student – her parents ¹*taught* / *have taught* her at home since she was five. When Vicky was young her parents didn't believe that the local school was the best place for her education. Instead, they chose to teach her themselves and Vicky ²*studied* / *has studied* happily at home for eight years.

So far, Vicky's parents ³*were* / *have been* her teachers for every subject, from Science to Physical Education. However, recently, they ⁴*decided* / *have decided* to employ a maths teacher. 'Vicky's maths is excellent. She ⁵*got* / *has got* 99% in an exam last month and now she needs a teacher who can really push her. We simply can't do that any more!' they said.

☐ **5**

3 **Phrasal verbs** Rewrite the sentences replacing the underlined words with it.

Example I made up the story. *I made it up.*

1 Put your book away.

_____ .

2 Can you turn on the TV?

_____ ?

3 He turned up the music.

_____ .

4 Take off your hat.

_____ .

5 Put your jacket on.

_____ .

☐ **5**

Vocabulary

4 **Education** Match 1–6 with a–f to complete the sentences.
1 ☐ *d* He teaches in the Geography _____.
2 ☐ I learnt French at evening _____.
3 ☐ I'm studying maths at night _____.
4 ☐ The Music department is in the Arts _____.
5 ☐ I really liked my first school _____.
6 ☐ She wants to be a university _____.

a teacher
b classes
c professor
d ~~department~~.
e school
f Faculty

☐ **5**

5 **Achievement** Complete the dialogue with these words and phrases. There is one extra phrase.

~~passed~~ succeeded failed managed to
achievement give up keep trying

Chris How is your Italian course going?
Rich Not bad thanks. I _passed_ my exam last week. How's your French course going?
Chris Terrible! I think I might ¹_____. It's very difficult for me.
Rich Really? I thought you were enjoying it.
Chris I don't know. I've got a big exam next week. I ²_____ the practice test last week, so I don't feel very good about it all.
Rich But exams aren't the only important thing. I ³_____ understand most of an Italian film last night. It was a great ⁴_____.
Chris Yes, I know you're right really. I'll ⁵_____ with my French.

☐ **5**

6 **Rhythm** Think about the rhythm of these phrases. Write the phrases in the correct column.

~~used to sit~~ get it wrong make mistakes
last week teacher's pet front of the class

● ●	● · ●	● · · ●
	used to sit	

☐ **5**

☐ GVP Total ☐ **30**

Reading and Writing A CV

1 Read the text and choose the correct answer a, b, or c.

'Learning for life' – what does it mean?

Learning used to be simple. You went to school and then you went to college or university. You learnt most of what you needed before the age of 21. Then you got a job for life or you stayed at home with the children. In recent years, society
05 and technology have developed rapidly. As our world keeps changing, we need to keep learning, at home and in the workplace. Learning just never stops!

Janice Eagles, 29, has worked for an international drinks company for three years. She enjoys her work, and says, 'I've
10 learnt so much in this job – more than I learnt at university! I've done a time management course and learnt to use two new computer systems. I've even had free Spanish lessons because I sometimes travel with my job.'

And it's not just people of working age who are learning for life.
15 73-year-old Russell Leach has been retired for eight years. He used to be a busy engineer, and now has a lot of spare time. He spends a lot of it studying with the U3A – The University of the Third Age. This isn't actually a university, but an international learning organization for people who no longer work.

20 U3A groups offer courses such as computing, science, art, history, and languages to older people. There are no exams, so people who follow these courses don't get qualifications. They are just for people's interest and personal development. 'It's never too late to learn' the U3A's website says. It seems that
25 for all of us, those words have never been more true!

Example What is this text?

a an advert (b) an article   c a story
1 Why does learning 'never stop' these days?
  a People study longer at school.
  b People need more skills.
  c More people go to university.
2 Where did Janice study time management?
  a at work   b at home   c at university
3 Why did Janice study Spanish?
  a for a holiday
  b for her job
  c for an exam
4 What does 'retired' (line 15) mean?
  a ill
  b looking for a job
  c stopped working
5 How was Russell's life different before he retired?
  a He taught with the U3A.
  b He studied with the U3A.
  c He didn't have much spare time.
6 What does 'They' in line 22 refer to?
  a exams   b courses   c qualifications

    6

2 Read the email. Write T (true), F (false), or DS (doesn't say) for sentences 1–7.

Hi Charlie,
I wonder if you could give me some advice? I'm trying to decide what to do with my career. When I was young I used to want to be a racing driver. Well, I've got my Advanced Driver's Licence now – but I'm still a taxi driver after six years.
It's not that I haven't enjoyed the job, but I'm getting bored now. I left school at sixteen and I didn't get good qualifications. The only subject I did well in was Art. I got C in History and Geography, but only a D in Maths.
Before working for City Cars I worked as a security guard in the Carlton Art Gallery. What an easy life! I still like drawing, and last week I sold one of my pictures – what a great a sense of achievement! So, I'll apply to art college.
However, yesterday I saw an advertisement for a job as a city tour guide. I think I've got the skills for it. I certainly know the city very well – I've driven on every street. I've learnt a lot about the history of Liverpool and I enjoy talking to people.
Well, you've known me since we were at school. What should I do – go to art college or try to be a tour guide? Thanks!
Nathan

Example Nathan is writing about his new job. ___F___

1 He wanted to be a racing driver. _____
2 He has always hated being a taxi driver. _____
3 He has done the same job for three years. _____
4 He wasn't a good Maths student. _____
5 His job in the Art Gallery was difficult. _____
6 He sold one of his pictures for £150. _____
7 He saw a job advert in the paper. _____

    7

3 Read the email again and complete Nathan's CV.

Personal Profile: Experienced _taxi_ driver with
1 _____ Driver's Licence
2 _____ and reliable

Education: 1994–1999 Gatacre Comprehensive School

GCSEs: Art A   History [3] _____
Geography C   [4] _____   D

Work experience: 2002 to present: Taxi driver, City Cars
1999–2002: [5] Security _____ : Carlton Art Gallery

Interests: [6] _____ and painting, local [7] _____

    7

4 Choose a job you would like and write your CV.
    10

  Reading and Writing Total   **30**

Unit 4 Test Free time activities

Date: _____

Grammar

1 **Subject and object relative clauses** Complete the sentences with the words below.

you   which   that   ~~who~~   where   who

Example   Tom is the man _who_ taught me French.

1 The review _____ I wrote is in today's paper.
2 That's the café _____ I met my friend earlier.
3 That's my friend _____ met Kate Winslet.
4 Is that the film _____ saw last week?
5 I like films _____ tell a true story.

[ ] **5**

2 **-ed and -ing adjectives** Underline the correct word to complete the conversation.

Carly I'm meeting James again tonight.
Ana Oh, that's *exciting / excited*! He seems really nice.
Carly I'm a bit [1] *worried / worrying* about it. We didn't have a very good time at the concert last week.
Ana Why not?
Carly It was [2] *boring / bored*. All the songs were the same.
Ana Oh, that's a pity.
Carly Then he wanted to dance. It was very [3] *embarrassing / embarrassed*!
Ana So what are you doing tonight?
Carly We're going to the Green Tree resturant.
Ana I don't think that's a good idea. I went there a few weeks ago. The food was [4] *disgusting / disgusted* and I couldn't get my money back. I was very [5] *annoying / annoyed*.

[ ] **5**

3 **Comparative and superlative adjectives; comparisons with as** Complete the text with the correct form of the adjectives in (brackets).

RESTAURANT REVIEW: PINNOCCHIO'S PIZZAS

A new Italian restaurant opened on South Street last week. We went to visit and here's what we thought.

At Pinnochio's Pizzas. The menu is _the longest_ (long) one I've ever seen! The pizzas aren't [1] _____ (big) as you get in other restaurants, but they are fresh and tasty.

What's [2] _____ (good) thing about Pinnocchio's Pizzas? Well, you can listen to live jazz music while you eat your pasta. It's [3] _____ (crowded) on Saturday than it is on Sunday, so go early if you want to get a table. There's always a great atmosphere at the weekend.

Pinocchio Pizzas is [4] _____ (expensive) than other Italian resturants in town.

It's certainly [5] _____ (entertaining) Italian restaurant in town.

$$$ Seats: 70   Opens 6.00 pm till midnight

[ ] **5**

Vocabulary

4 **Music** Complete the music word in each sentence.

Example   She's playing a Mozart s *y m p h o n y* with the orchestra.

1 I love listening to my M _ _ _ _ _ _ _ _ on the bus.
2 Last night's j _ _ _ concert was great.
3 The guitar s _ _ _ was excellent.
4 My favourite Beatles t _ _ _ is *Yesterday*.
5 More than 40,000 people went to the rock concert in the s _ _ _ _ _ _ last night.

[ ] **5**

5 **Expressing likes and dislikes** Complete the conversation with these words.

adore   stand   keen   mind   like   ~~love~~

Maria What do you in your free time?
Eric I _love_ being outdoors – swimming in the sea, walking in the mountains. How about you?
Maria Well, I read a lot of books, and I absolutely [1] _____ music and modern art
Eric I listen to music a lot, but I can't [2] _____ modern art. I just don't understand it! Tennis, skiing, football – they're my favourite activities.
Maria Oh, I'm not [3] _____ on sport really.
Eric But do you [4] _____ being outdoors?
Maria Oh yes, I don't [5] _____ walking in the park or on the beach.

[ ] **5**

Pronunciation

6 **-ed endings** Think about the sound of the *-ed* ending in these words. Write the words under the correct sound.

bored   disgusted   embarrassed
fascinated   amazed   ~~interested~~

-d	-t	-id
		interested

[ ] **5**

GVP Total [ ] **30**

Reading and Writing
A description of a film or book

1 Read the text and choose a title for each paragraph.

A 'It's not perfect but I'm in some films!' _____
B 'I can watch films while I work.' _____
C 'It's hard work but very exciting.' _____
D 'I don't even mind the cleaning!' _____

A future in film?

Many people love films and dream of working in the film industry one day. Two young people who dream of a future in films told us how they are starting out.

1 James (17) loves films and wants to be a film director. Every weekend he works as a cinema attendant. He checks people's tickets as they arrive and helps them find seats. 'After that, I sit at the back of the cinema and watch the film. Last weekend I watched the same science fiction film six times! My friends think that's really boring, but I find it fascinating! I like most kinds of films, but I'm not too keen on musicals or romances!'

2 'When everybody leaves at the end of the film I tidy the cinema. It's amazing how much rubbish people leave under their seats – sometimes it's really disgusting. But I don't mind. This job's just right for me at the moment.'

3 Annabel (20) works in a restaurant. In her free time she is a film extra – an actor who appears in the film, but doesn't usually speak. Most extras don't get much money, but Annabel is a dancer so she can earn slightly more. Sometimes extras speak a few lines in a film, and these are paid the most. 'I'm not famous, of course,' says Annabel, 'but I have appeared in a few films.'

4 'Some people do this work for the money, but for me it's a hobby. I adore films, and I'd love to act in a comedy one day. A day working as an extra is much longer than a day in the restaurant. It's very hard work and isn't well paid. I never get bored as I really like watching how the actors and director work together. It's fascinating.'

2 Write T (true) , F (false), or DS (doesn't say) for sentences 1–7.

Example James does Film Studies at college. *DS*

1 James's friends don't know why he likes his job. ____
2 James loves all kinds of films. ____
3 The cinema is usually dirty at the end of a film. ____
4 Annabel works three days a week. ____
5 Annabel was an extra in a fantasy film. ____
6 Annabel earns more money as an extra because she can also dance. ____
7 Annabel has met some famous actors. ____

[7]

3 Read the text and answer the questions.

www.moviereviews.co.uk

Two films, one love story

Before Sunrise (1995) and *Before Sunset* (2004) are two romantic dramas set in Europe. They star Ethan Hawke and Julie Delpy as Jesse and Celine. In *Before Sunrise*, the couple spend just one day and night together. In *Before Sunset*, they have just one day.

In *Before Sunrise*, Jesse and Celine meet on a train. Jesse is going to Vienna to fly home to the USA the next morning. Celine is returning to France after visiting Budapest. The couple start talking, and Jesse convinces Celine to get off the train in Vienna. They spend their time walking around the city exchanging their ideas and opinions about life. A romance develops between them.

Vienna is an amazing location for the film and Hawke and Delpy are both excellent actors. However, the best thing about *Before Sunrise* is the dialogue. The couple talk about everyday topics, but their conversation is never boring.

In *Before Sunset* Jesse and Celine meet again nine years later in a bookshop in Paris. Jesse (now an author) is talking about his book. *Before Sunset* is a good film, but it isn't as special as *Before Sunrise* and the dialogue isn't as interesting. *Before Sunrise* is a more unusual film and also much more magical. In fact, it's one of the most romantic films you can see.

Example What kind of films are *Before Sunrise* and *Before Sunset*? *romantic dramas*

1 How long are the couple together in *Before Sunrise*?
_____
2 How long are the couple together in *Before Sunset*?
_____
3 Where does Jesse live? _____
4 Where does Celine live? _____
5 In *Before Sunrise*, where do Celine and Jesse meet?
_____
6 In *Before Sunset*, where do the couple spend their day? _____
7 What does the writer like about *Before Sunrise*?
_____
8 In *Before Sunset*, where do Celine and Jesse meet in Paris? _____
9 Which film does the writer prefer? _____

[9]

4 Write a description of a film or book that you like. Include the information below. Write 80–100 words.

• the setting and main characters • how the story
begins • the best thing about the film or the book

[10]

Reading and Writing Total [30]

Unit 5 Test Power, law, and crime

Date: _____

Grammar

1 *the* or *no* **article in names of institutions** Write *the* or Ø (no article) in the gaps.

Example Sheikh Khalifa is __the__ President of __the__ United Arab Emirates.

1 _____ Indira Ghandi was the Prime Minister of India for fifteen years.
2 When will Prince William be _____ British King?
3 Who is the leader of _____ Liberal Party?
4 The King of Spain is _____ King Juan Carlos I.
5 Who is the Secretary General of _____ United Nations?

[ ] **5**

2 **Active and passive** Rewrite the news in the passive.

PAINTING FOUND

Police have found a famous painting in a house in Bristol. Someone stole the painting from the Carlton Museum three years ago. The police have arrested two women in connection with the crime.

A famous painting ¹ *has been found* in a house in Bristol. The painting ² _____ from the Carlton Museum three years ago. Two women ³ _____ in connection with the crime.

TOWN CENTRE ATTACK

Someone attacked two men in the city centre last night. A friend took one of the men to hospital. Someone has given a description of one of the attackers to the police.

Two men ⁴ _____ in the city centre last night. One of the men ⁵ _____ to hospital. A description of one of the men ⁶ _____ to the police.

[ ] **5**

3 **Modals of obligation** Underline the correct word or phrase to complete the text.

Why do laws exist?

All societies have laws – but why do different laws exist?

Most laws are made to keep people safe. For example, you *mustn't/don't have to/can* kill or hurt another person. On the road, you ¹*don't have to/can't* drive too fast.

There are also many laws to organize society. You ²*have to/mustn't/can* drive on the same side of the road. You ³*have to/mustn't/can* steal or damage another person's possessions.

Other laws educate people to do the right thing. In some countries, everybody ⁴*can/must/doesn't* have to vote in an election.

And finally, most countries give people 'freedom of speech' – people ⁵*must/have to/can* say or write their opinions freely.

[ ] **5**

Vocabulary

4 **Countries and government** Match the definitions 1–6 with words a–f.

1 Conservative
2 president
3 Socialist
4 elections
5 republic
6 capital

a The city where the main political buildings are.
b A country with no king or queen.
c A head of state who is not a king or queen.
d The event when people vote to choose people in government.
e A right-wing political party.
f A left-wing political party.

[ ] **5**

5 **Crime verbs** Choose the correct word to complete the text.

Yesterday two men __robbed__ a bank in the city centre. They ¹_____ the security guard and ²_____ one of the bank workers in the leg. The thieves ³_____ more than £10,000. Police have ⁴_____ one man who they believe is connected with the crime. One bank worker said afterwards, 'I was terrified. I thought they were going to ⁵_____ someone.'

Example a stole ⓑ robbed c attacked d shot

1 a stole   b hijacked   c arrested   d attacked
2 a kidnapped   b killed   c murdered   d shot
3 a robbed   b stole   c shot   d hijacked
4 a arrested   b attacked   c hijacked   d kidnapped
5 a steal   b arrest   c kill   d rob

[ ] **5**

Pronunciation

6 **Stress in two-syllable nouns and verbs** Think about the sound of these words. Underline the stressed syllable.

Example power

1 complete   4 happen
2 battle   5 return
3 shoulder

[ ] **5**

GVP Total [ ] 30

Reading and Writing Narrating a story

1 Read the webpage and choose the best answer.

FLAG FACTS

Flags are colourful, powerful, and symbolic objects. They represent countries, institutions, history, and organizations.

National flags

The most common colours used on national flags are blue, yellow, red, green, white, and black.

Most flags are rectangular. However, the Swiss and Vatican City flags are square. All the sides are the same length.

The Libyan flag is the only one with one colour, green.

The flags of Monaco and Indonesia are identical. They are red and white and have the same design.

When flags from different countries are flown together, they must be the same size and be flown at the same height.

International flags

The United Nations flag was designed about 50 years ago. It has a white map of the world on a light blue background. The colours and design of the flag are symbols of international peace.

The official flag of the Olympic Games was designed by Pierre de Coubertin in 1913. It has five coloured rings on a white background. The rings are blue, yellow, red, green, and black. With the white background, these form the six colours which are seen on most national flags.

Example This text is about _____.
a countries   b history   (c) flags

1 The writer wrote this text to _____.
a tell a story   b give information
c give an opinion
2 National flags DON'T often use the colour _____.
a yellow   b orange   c black
3 The Swiss and Vatican City flags are _____.
a square   b round   c rectangular
4 The Libyan flag is _____.
a green   b light and dark green
c green and white
5 The flags of Indonesia and Monaco are the same _____.
a colour   b design   c colour and design
6 When two national flags are flown together they must be the same _____.
a size   b colour   c design
7 The United Nations flag is _____.
a blue   b white   c blue and white
8 When was the Olympic flag designed?
a About 50 years ago.   b In 1913.   c In 1945.
9 How many colours has the Olympic flag?
a four   b five   c six

[ ] 9

2 Read the text and match the titles to the sections.
1 Check your car is locked when you park. [ ]
2 Never leave your keys in the car. [ ]
3 Know the history of a car when you buy it. [ ]
4 Don't leave things where people can see them. [ ]
5 Jenny's story [A]

[ ] 4

Car crime stories

A Jenny's car was stolen and she didn't have much money to buy a new one. Eventually, she found a cheap one and bought it. Three weeks later, the problems started. First it was the oil. Then, much more seriously, the brakes stopped working.

Jenny took it to a garage and was shocked when they told her she had been the victim of a serious crime. Her 'new' car had originally been two cars – parts of two old cars had been used to make a new one.

B Adrian bought a new car. He went to the post office to pay his car tax. The assistant checked on the computer and told Adrian there was a problem. His new car was a stolen car. She advised Adrian to contact the police. Just like Jenny, Adrian didn't know the true story about his car's past when he bought it.

C Karen got into her car and put her handbag on the passenger seat. It was a hot day so she opened the windows. When she stopped at some traffic lights, someone reached into the car and stole her handbag.

D Jim filled his car with petrol at the garage. When he went inside to pay, he left the keys in the car. Someone stole his car while he was paying for the petrol.

E Beverly parked her car outside her house one evening. It had been a hot day and Beverley had opened the sunroof. She checked the doors and windows were closed, but she forgot the sunroof. During the night thieves stole the car stereo.

---

3 Read the text again and answer the questions.
Example Whose car was stolen? *Jenny's*

1 Why did Jenny have to buy a new car? _____
2 What two problems did she have with her new car? _____ and _____
3 What was the problem with Adrian's car? _____
4 Where did Karen put her handbag? _____
5 What was Jim doing when someone stole his car?
_____
6 When did thieves steal Beverly's stereo? _____

[ ] 7

4 Choose one of the four stories, or another one. Tell it in a more exciting way. Write 80–100 words.

[ ] 10

Reading and Writing Total [ ] 30

Unit 6 Test Feelings and behaviour   Date: _____

Grammar

1 So and such Complete the sentences by putting *so* or *such* in the correct place.

Example I'm _*so*_ sorry about that. (so)

1 That is good news! (such)
2 That's a stupid idea! (such)
3 I'm a fool. (such)
4 I'm angry with her. (so)
5 He was driving badly! (so)

 5

2 Infinitive and gerund <u>Underline</u> the correct words to complete the conversation.

Judy I'm going now, Nick. It's been an excellent party. Thanks for *inviting* / *to invite* me.

Nick You're welcome. I'm glad you could come.

Judy It was great to meet your sister. I really enjoyed ¹*talking* / *to talk* to her.

Nick That's good. I didn't expect her ²*coming* / *to come* – she doesn't usually like parties.

Judy Really? She seemed very happy when I saw her ³*leaving* / *to leave*.

Nick Good. Now, how are you going to get home?

Judy It's too late ⁴*getting* / *to get* a bus. I'll walk.

Nick Are you sure? Why don't you take a taxi?

Judy No, it's not far. I don't mind ⁵*walking* / *to walk*.

 5

3 Tenses in reported speech Complete the reported speech sentences.

Example James took some flowers from the neighbour's garden. He said to his mother, 'I bought them in a shop.'
He told his mother he _*had bought*_ them in a shop.

1 I told the doctor I felt ill. She said, 'You'll be fine.'
She said I _____ fine.
2 I met a man on the train yesterday. He said, 'I'm a famous actor.'
He told me he _____ a famous actor.
3 Ryan said, 'I don't feel very well.'
Ryan told me he _____ very well.
4 'I'll help you paint the kitchen,' said Katy.
Katy said she _____ me paint the kitchen.
5 Mia said, 'I got the job!'
She told me she _____ the job.

☐ **5**

Vocabulary

4 Behaviour Order the letters to make words.

Example Miss Baxter is very ndriflye *friendly* . When I see her she always says 'Good morning'.

1 The people who live next door are very niyso _____. They shout all the time.
2 I think Mrs Veale asks too many personal questions. She's very syno _____.
3 The children at number 29 are terrible. They're really uynahtg _____.
4 Mr Robson? He's lovely. He's very flhupel _____ if you have a problem.
5 A lot of the neighbours have cats. They often igtfh _____ at night – it's horrible.

☐ **5**

5 Extreme adjectives Complete the dialogues with these words.

enormous   furious   exhausted
terrified   awful   ~~wonderful~~

Example A Davina told me you had a good holiday.
B It was _*wonderful*_ ! Great hotel, good food, perfect weather ...

1 A You seem tired.
B I'm _____. I've worked really hard today.
2 A Was the film good?
B No, it was _____. I left before it finished.
3 A Were you afraid when he shouted at you?
B Yes, I was _____.
4 A Otto's new house is _____!
B I know. Lots of really big rooms and a big garden.
5 A What's the matter?
B Someone's stolen my new bike. I'm _____!

☐ **5**

Pronunciation

6 Spelling and pronunciation *gh* Think about the sound of these words. Is *gh* not pronounced or is it pronounced as the consonant sound /f/? Write NP (not pronounced) or F.

Example nau<u>gh</u>ty *NP*

1 rough ____   4 daughter ____
2 neighbour ____   5 enough ____
3 fight ____

☐ **5**

| GVP Total | 30 |

Reading and Writing
Exchanging news in a personal letter

1 Read the article. Choose a title for each paragraph.
1 Take care of your home ____   3 Be friendly ____
2 Polite parking ____   4 Be quiet ____

How to be a good neighbour

Being a good neighbour helps make your life more peaceful. It can also make your area a safer place to live in. Follow this advice to avoid problems with your neighbours.

A When you move to a new home, introduce yourself
05 and ask questions to learn about the local area. Smile and say hello when you see your neighbours. Offer to help them if you can.

B Noise is a common reason for complaints by neighbours. If you listen to loud music, think carefully
10 about where you put your music system. Your neighbour probably won't be very happy if you put it against their bedroom wall. Tell them if you are going to have a party or invite them to come too.

C Your home belongs to you, but don't forget that you
15 are also part of a community. Try to keep the outside of your home tidy. Your neighbours may complain if you leave rubbish outside for too long. Fences and walls between houses can also be areas for disagreement. If a fence or wall near your home is broken, check if you are
20 responsible for it. If you are, repair it as soon as possible.

D Don't leave your car in front of someone else's house and park quietly if you arrive home early in the morning or late at night.

2 Read the article again and choose the best answer.

Example   This article ____ .
    a tells funny stories (b) gives advice
    c gives the results of a survey

1 Being a good neighbour is ____.
  a a good idea   b a problem   c safe
2 Ask about local things to ____.
  a offer help   b find information   c say hello
3 The article gives advice about noise from ____.
  a children   b animals   c music
4 Before having a party, ask if neighbours ____.
  a are happy about it   b would like to come
  c will be at home
5 A 'community' (line 15) is a group of ____ in a town or city.
  a people   b streets   c houses
6 If a wall or fence near you is broken, you should

  ____.
  a repair it   b see who owns it
  c ask a neighbour to fix it

  | 6

3 Read the emails. Write T (true), F (false), or DS (doesn't say) after sentences 1–10.

Dear Robin,

How are you? I'm OK, but I could be better!

Here's the good news. We've got a new dog! He's called Henry and he's great! He's full of energy and really sweet, although
05 he is a bit naughty too. He's already eaten my shoes and ruined the garden! We're getting lots of exercise taking him for walks every morning and evening.

And now the bad news – I've broken my foot. I was decorating the kitchen and stood on a chair to get
10 something. Henry came in the room and barked loudly. He surprised me and I fell off the chair!

It was such a stupid thing to happen and I couldn't believe it when the doctors said it was broken. It was painful so I knew I'd hurt it badly, but not so badly. Anyway, at least I don't
15 have to go to work for a month, so I've got time to write letters to my friends!

Of course, I can't take Henry out for walks at the moment. Fortunately, Paul's very happy to do that. The one thing he won't do, however, is finish decorating the kitchen. Did I
20 tell you Paul's got a new job? He was very unhappy in the old one – very boring, too much work, and not enough money. He actually enjoys going to work now!

So, what about your news? How's everyone in your family these days? Last time you wrote you were talking about
25 studying Chinese. Have you started classes yet? How's it going?

Love from Laura xx

PS My sister's going to have a baby next year. I'm going to be an aunt! It feels brilliant!

30 PPS Do you fancy coming to stay for a weekend? I need visitors

Example: Laura is writing a letter of complaint. __F__

1 Laura writes about good and bad news. ____
2 'We' (line 2) is Robin and Laura. ____
3 The dog is very young. ____
4 Laura doesn't like Henry. ____
5 Henry goes out for walks twice a day. ____
6 The kitchen chair's broken. ____
7 Laura's off work for a week. ____
8 Paul's taking Henry for walks. ____
9 Paul doesn't like his new job. ____
10 Laura's sister's having a baby in May. ____

  | 10

4 You are Robin. Write a reply to Laura. Add news about yourself and people you know. Write 80–100 words.

  | 10

Reading and Writing Total   30

Unit 7 Test Appearance and lifestyle   Date: _____

Grammar

1 wh clauses Add <u>three</u> words to the second sentence so that it means the same as the first two sentences.

Example How tall is he? I can't remember.
I can't remember how _tall he is_.

1 Where does he buy his shoes? I'd like to know.
I'd like to know _____ his shoes.

2 When's her birthday? Do you know?
Do you know when _____?

3 Why did she say that? I don't understand.
I don't understand _____ that.

4 Who gave me this ring? I've forgotten.
I've forgotten _____ this ring.

5 What colour does she want? I don't know.
I don't know what _____.

 5

2 Future intentions <u>Underline</u> the correct future forms in this conversation.

Mia Have you got any plans for tomorrow?
Tom Well, ¹*I'm having / I will have* a 'style makeover'.
Mia Really? I think ²*I'm going to come / I'll come* and watch. I'd like to see what they do to you!
Tom I've decided ³*I'm going to tell / I'm telling* them exactly what I want. I don't want a stupid hairstyle with strange colours in it.
I ⁴*'m meeting / I will meet* some important colleagues on Monday.
Mia So why ⁵*are you having / will you have* this makeover?
Tom It's a present from my girlfriend!

 5

3 Modals of deduction <u>Underline</u> the correct word to complete each conversation.

Example A Let's take a look at those designer t-shirts.
B They *might* / *must* / *can't* be really expensive. How much are they?

1 A Do you think that woman is a doctor?
B Maybe. Or she *might* / *must* / *can't* be a dentist.

2 A She's from Switzerland so she must speak Italian.
B Well, she *might* / *must* / *can't* speak French.

3 A I think Frank is about fifty.
B No, he *might* / *must* / *can't* be! He looks forty!

4 A She spends about €500 on clothes every month.
B Yes, she *might* / *must* / *can't* be really rich.

5 A That man wears sunglasses even when it's raining.
B He *might* / *must* / *can't* be someone famous.

 5

Vocabulary

4 Looks and character Complete the descriptions with the words below. There are two that you don't need.

bushy   round   nervous   imaginative
~~ginger~~   confident   active   ambitious

Example Amelia likes having _ginger_ hair, but her sister doesn't.

1 Eva hopes to do well in her exams. She's _____.

2 Alan never gets angry or worried. He looked very _____ and relaxed after the interview.

3 Stefan's got big _____ eyebrows and looks like his dog.

4 Bethany has lots of good ideas for stories and poems. She's very _____.

5 Nick loves playing football and cycling. He's always _____.

 5

5 Compound adjectives Complete the compound adjectives in the text with these words. There is one word you don't need to use.

fitting   looking   conscious   shaven
fashioned   ~~off~~   dressed

> **Me and Tom**
> Tom and I are good friends but we're completely different. Tom's a student and he doesn't have much money. I've got a good job and I'm quite well- *off*. People say Tom's very ¹good-____: he's tall, with dark hair and brown eyes. I'm short with blond hair. The biggest difference is our clothes. I feel comfortable in ²loose-____ clothes, and I don't mind wearing ³old-____ things. Tom hasn't got much money, but he is very ⁴fashion-____. What's his secret? He studies clothes in style magazines and buys things that look the same, but cost less. As he says, 'You don't have to be rich to be ⁵well-____.'

 5

Pronunciation

6 Contrastive stress Think about the sounds in each reply. Underline the stressed word in each reply.

Example Has she got short grey hair? No, <u>long</u> grey hair.

1 Is she in her early fifties? No, late fifties.
2 Has he got big blue eyes? No, big green eyes.
3 Has she got wavy fair hair? No, wavy dark hair.
4 Is he in his early twenties? No, early thirties.
5 Has he got curly hair? No, straight hair.

 5

GVP Total   30

7

Reading and Writing A letter of application

1 Read the advert. Choose a title for each paragraph.

1 What happens on the show _____
2 How to apply _____
3 Appear on TV and change your life _____
4 The prizes _____

| 4 |

CHANNEL T21: Want to appear on TV?

A CHANNEL T21 is looking for ten people to take part in a new makeover competition, *Look Good, Feel Good*. We need interesting candidates of different ages, appearance and personality. If you want to change the
05 way you look and feel then this is the show for you!

B The ten successful candidates will go to Scotland where they'll stay in a hotel in the country for six weeks. They'll be filmed every day as they complete exercises to improve physical health, fitness, and
10 ways of thinking. Candidates will learn Latin American dancing and practise yoga relaxation techniques.

C There is a £10,000 prize for the person who changes most in six weeks and there are some great smaller prizes for weekly winners too. These include mountain
15 bikes, clothes, and weekend holidays. Each week, viewers will decide who has made the most progress in seven days. At the end of the programme, they vote for an overall winner – the person who's changed the most.

20 **D** **Want to apply?** Send a handwritten letter telling us a bit about your lifestyle, appearance, and personality. Describe yourself in 80–100 words, and explain why you want to be on the show. Enclose three recent photos of you doing something typical in your free
25 time.

---

2 Read the advert again and choose the best answer.

Example How many people will appear on the show?
    a 6 (b) 10 c 21

1 What does 'take part in' (line 1) mean?
   a appear on the show b apply for the show
   c watch the show
2 What does 'where' (line 7) refer to?
   a a secret location b a hotel c Scotland
3 Who learns Latin American dancing and yoga?
   a all the candidates b the ten successful contestants c the winner
4 Who decides the winner of *Look Good, Feel Good*?
   a The experts b Channel T21 c TV viewers
5 What are 'These' (line 14)?
   a prizes b mountain bikes c clothes
6 How should you contact the organisers?
   a by letter b by phone c by email

| 6 |

3 Read the letters of application from Adam and Myra. Complete the table with one word in each gap.

Dear Sir or Madam,

I'm writing to apply to appear on your new show *Look Good, Feel Good*.

I'm Australian, but I've lived in England for twenty years. My wife is British and we have three children. I'm 51, tall, with very short hair. Some people say I look aggressive, but I'm actually very calm and quiet. I'm a self-employed architect.

I'm a bit shy at times and in my free time I prefer to do things alone, such as reading, listening to music, and jogging. I would really like to change the way I look and feel. Appearing on the programme would be a great chance to do this. It would help me to be more confident when I meet new people. I really hope you will offer me a place and I look forward to hearing from you soon.

Yours faithfully,

Adam Lewis

Dear Sir or Madam,

I saw your advertisement in *Time Off* magazine and would like to apply to be a contestant on the show.

I'm an art student from Dublin, 25 and single. Next year, I hope to start work as an interior designer. I look very artistic and I wear unusual clothes. I've got long curly hair. I'm lively and outgoing. I enjoy cooking, going to night clubs, and clothes shopping!

I think I'd be a great candidate for your programme. I need to get fit, and be more independent. I think your viewers would enjoy watching me.

Yours faithfully,

Myra Boden

	Adam	Myra
background	Australian, architect	Dublin, 6_____ student
marital status and age	married, three children, 1_____	single, 25
appearance	tall, 2_____ hair	long 7_____ hair
personality	calm, 3_____, shy	lively, 8_____
hobbies	reading, music, 4_____	cooking, nightclubs, buying 9_____
reasons for applying	be more 5_____	get 10_____, be more independent

| 10 |

4 Imagine you would like to appear on the programme. Write a letter of application of about 90–100 words.

| 10 |

| Reading and Writing Total | | 30 |

Unit 8 Test Communication

Date: _____

Grammar

1 Reported imperatives and requests Rewrite the sentences in reported speech.

Example I / her 'Don't worry.' *I told her not to worry* .

1 She / him 'Open the door!'

_____ .

2 I / you 'Don't call me at work!'

_____ .

3 He / them 'Please can you *not* shout?'

_____ .

4 She / me 'Could you close the window, please?'

_____ .

5 He / me 'Be careful!'

_____ .

[ ] **5**

2 Ability: *can, could, be able to, manage to* Underline the best word or phrase to complete each conversation.

Example I managed *to / could / 'll be able to* ski when I was younger, but I'm too old now.

1 I *can't / didn't manage to / couldn't* sing.
2 I'm sure we *can / could / 'll be able to* communicate with animals in the future.
3 My friend's got a dog and it *'ll be able to / could / can* dance to music!
4 I *was able to / will be able to / could* find the information for the report on the Internet.
5 I found a bag on the train last week. I gave it to the police and they *could / managed to / can* find the owner.

[ ] **5**

3 Reported questions Complete the conversations about job interviews with the words below.

would   him   ~~why~~   could   did   were   if

Example A Did they ask Anna about her current job?
B Yes, they asked her _why_ she wanted to leave.

1 A Did you feel nervous in the interview?
B Yes. I asked if I _____ have a glass of water.
2 A How did you begin the interview with Sarah?
B We asked her what her good points _____.
3 A Did the interview go well?
B Yes, they asked if I _____ be able to start soon.
4 A Did they ask John any strange questions?
B Yes, they asked _____ which star sign he was.

5 A What happened at the end of the interview?
B They wanted to know _____ I had any questions.

[ ] **5**

Vocabulary

4 Telephone words and phrases Use the words below to complete the phone verbs.

off   ~~through~~   over   up   through   back

Example 'I've tried to call David about six times this morning, but I just can't get _through_ .'

1 'Listen, I know you're angry, but we need to talk. Simon, don't hang _____, please! Hello?'
2 'Millie's got some exciting news for you! Just a minute, I'll hand her _____ to you.'
3 'Hello, can you help me? I was talking to someone called Anne, but I got cut _____.'
4 'Hello, could you put me _____ to the sales department please? Thank you.'
5 'I'm really sorry, but I'm busy at the moment. Can I ring you _____ in five minutes?'

[ ] **5**

5 Reporting verbs Match 1–6 with reported speech a–f.

1 'I'll go, I promise.' [*f*]
2 'I'll go, if you want.' [ ]
3 'You shouldn't go.' [ ]
4 'No, ok, I won't go.' [ ]
5 'No. I'm absolutely not going.' [ ]
6 'Would you like to go?' [ ]

a He **invited** me to go.
b I **refused** to go.
c She **offered** to go.
d We **advised** them **not** to go.
e He **agreed not** to go.
f She **promised** to go.

[ ] **5**

Pronunciation

6 Stress in words ending *-ity* Think about the sound of these words. Underline the stressed syllable.

Example *ability*

1 popularity   4 possibility
2 curiosity   5 activity
3 reality

[ ] **5**

GVP Total		30

8

Reading and Writing A report

1 Read the text. Choose the best title for each paragraph.
1 Becoming an inventor ____
2 Family life ____
3 Helping students to communicate ____
4 An early experiment in communication ____

[ ] 4

Alexander Graham Bell

A Alexander Graham Bell is famous for inventing the telephone. Bell was born on the 3rd of March, 1847. His mother, Eliza, was almost completely deaf and could only hear a few loud sounds. She hadn't been able to hear since
05 the age of four. Amazingly, despite being deaf, she could play the piano incredibly well. When he was thirty Bell married Mabel Hubbard, who was also deaf.

B Bell could read and write when he was very young, and he had a clear speaking voice. He first learnt to communicate
10 with his mother using his fingers. However, he really wanted to speak to her. He used to speak very close to her head in a deep voice and she was able to hear him. Bell understood that this was because of the vibrations of his voice.

C In 1863 Bell became a teacher. First he taught music and
15 language, then he started working in a school for deaf children. Bell's deaf students communicated with sign language. However, he believed that deaf people should speak like everybody else, using their voice. He taught his students a special alphabet called 'Visible Speech'.

20 **D** Bell started to become more interested in the science of the human ear, and between 1872 and 1874 he worked at different universities. In 1874 he first had the idea for the telephone. Two years later, on 10th March, 1876, Bell spoke to someone on the telephone for the first time. He phoned his
25 assistant, Thomas Watson, in the room next door. Another inventor, Gray, invented the telephone at about the same time as Bell. However, Bell registered his invention first. Bell invented many different things before his death in 1922, but he always remained fascinated by communication.

2 Read the text again and answer the questions.
Example Bell was born in _1847_.

1 Bell's wife had been deaf from the age of _____.
2 His mother was deaf, but could play the _____.
3 He got married when he was _____.
4 Bell first talked to his mother using his _____.
5 Bell taught language and _____.
6 Bell taught his students an alphabet called _____.
7 In 1872, Bell was interested in the science of the _____.
8 In 1876, Bell invented the _____.
9 Bell registered his invention before _____.

[ ] 9

3 Read the emails. Write T (true), F (false), or DS (doesn't say).

Hi everyone,
Can you help me with something? I have to write a short report for homework. I need you to answer the question: Which animal is the most intelligent? Why? Email your answer quickly. I have to hand it in tomorrow morning. Thanks!
Orla

Hi Orla,
That's easy! Dogs are the most intelligent animals because they can understand everything. When I tell my dog to get a ball, he always does it.
Bye, Jake

Dear Orla,
That's a difficult question! What does 'intelligent' mean? Animals are intelligent in different ways. Some monkeys can communicate with humans. There are also some birds which can talk – that's quite clever! Dogs are very intelligent too. Police dogs and farm dogs do jobs that humans can't. Yes, I think dogs are the most intelligent.
See you on Thursday, Sheryl

Hi Orla
I don't know. I read somewhere that cats are very clever and have good memories. Also, they like experimenting and enjoy finding solutions to problems.
All the best, Ben

Hi Orla,
Most people will answer 'dogs'. I believe that dolphins are more intelligent than all other animals. A dolphin brain is bigger than the human brain. Also, scientific tests show that they can understand complicated ideas. Good luck! Megan

Example Orla wants help with her homework. _T_

1 Jake's dog can understand instructions. ____
2 Sheryl says 'intelligent' has different meanings. ____
3 Police dogs have more abilities than farm dogs. ____
4 Ben has got a pet cat. ____
5 Cats can remember things and experiment. ____
6 Megan thinks dogs are the most intelligent. ____
7 A dolphin brain weighs about 2kg. ____

[ ] 7

4 Imagine you are Orla. Write a report called 'Animal intelligence' in about 90–110 words.

[ ] 10

Reading and Writing Total [ ] 30

Unit 9 Test Science and nature

Date: _____

Grammar

1 Tag questions Add the correct tag question to each sentence.

Example It's cold today, *isn't it* ?

1 There aren't any students today, _____?
2 You've got a mobile phone, _____?
3 They live in Mexico, _____?
4 The mountains are beautiful, _____?
5 He isn't very old, _____?

 5

2 1st conditional; *if* clauses Choose the correct words to complete the fire safety advice.

> ### FIRE!
>
> **In a fire**
> If you *are / were / will be* in a burning building, stay close to the floor.
>
> **Escape**
> If you leave a burning building, you ¹*should / will / would* close all doors behind you. If you close the doors, the fire ²*doesn't / wouldn't / won't* spread so quickly through the building.
>
> **Kitchen**
> If you have a fire in a cooking pan, you ³*will / wouldn't / don't* put water on it. Cover the fire with a wet cloth.
>
> **Clothes**
> If your clothes ⁴*catch / will catch / caught* fire, fall to the ground and roll. If you run, the fire ⁵*should / will / would* burn faster.

 5

3 2nd conditional Write the correct form of the verb in (brackets).

Example A I'd love to have a really big garden.
         B Really? It *would need* a lot of work. (need)

1 A Would you pay more than €80 for a meal in a restaurant?
   B Yes, if I _____ more money! (have)
2 A My friend has left her job to travel the world.
   B Lucky her! If I did that, I _____ to go back to work again. (not want)
3 A Would your life be different if you were rich?
   B Yes, I think I _____ happier. (be)
4 A Would you like to have a pet?
   B Yes, maybe – if I _____ children. (not have)
5 A Imagine if someone _____ you €50,000. (give)
   B I know... I could buy a house and a car.

 5

Vocabulary

4 Weather Choose the correct word to complete the weather forecast for the coming week.

> On Monday it will be *dry* in most parts of the country, with just a few ¹____ in the east. Tuesday will be wet everywhere in the morning, with some very heavy ²____ in the north. Overnight it will be stormy, with ³____ and lightning in many places. Wednesday will be a better day. The sun will shine in most places and it will be ⁴____ Unfortunately, the clouds return on Thursday and Friday, and also very strong winds. In fact, there will probably be ⁵____ everywhere at the end of the week, so stay at home if possible.

Example a heat wave b soaking ⓒ dry d gales

1 a floods   b showers   c shining   d windy
2 a rain   b blowing   c mild   d cold
3 a pouring   b cloud   c snow   d thunder
4 a lightning   b mild   c freezing   d wet
5 a sun   b hot   c gales   d blowing

5

5 Compound nouns Put the words in the correct place to complete each conversation. There are two extra words.

laptop   book   science   ~~computer~~
address   service   call   club

Example A What's Millie's job?
         B I think she's a *computer* programmer.

1 I'm going to join a book _____.
2 Could I have an alarm _____ in the morning?
3 Is Dean's phone number in the _____ book?
4 How much is the _____ charge?
5 I watch DVDs on my _____ when I'm travelling.

5

Pronunciation

6 Stressed and unstressed words Think about the stressed and unstressed words in these sentences. Underline one more stressed word in each sentence.

Example She'll have *passed* the *exam*.

1 My body will have changed a lot.
2 I'll have found a job.
3 Lucy will have cooked the dinner.
4 They won't have grown much.
5 He'll have cut his hair.

 5

| GVP Total | | 30 |

Reading and Writing An opinion

1 Read the safety leaflet. Choose the best heading for each paragraph.

1 Where not to stand in a thunderstorm _____
2 Beautiful but dangerous _____
3 Get your body in a safe position _____
4 The home can be dangerous too _____
5 The '30-30' rule _____

 5

WHAT TO DO IN A **THUNDERSTORM**

A Thunderstorms can be very exciting – the rain is heavy, the thunder is loud, and the lightning can be fascinating to watch. However, strong winds and floods can cause problems and lightning can be dangerous. It hurts and kills thousands of people every year. So, what should you do if you are outside in a thunderstorm?

B First of all, find out how near the storm is by counting the time between the lightning and thunder. If it is less than 30 seconds, the storm is very near you. You should find somewhere safe to wait until the storm passes. After the last flash of lightning, wait 30 minutes before leaving your safe place.

C If you are outside in a thunderstorm, don't stand in an open field or on top of a hill. Don't stand near a tower or a single tree. You should also stay away from lakes, rivers, and the beach. If the beach is wet and the lightning strikes the sea, the electricity will travel along the beach.

D Try and make yourself as small as possible, so there is less chance the lightning will hit you. Put your feet together, your head between your knees and your hands over your ears. Get your whole body as close to the ground as you can. If you are with a group of people, stay 6m apart from each other. Then, if lightning does strike a person, it won't be able to travel to others in the group.

E The best place to be in a thunderstorm is inside. However, if you are at home and a lightning storm is near here's some useful advice – don't use the phone, the computer, or the TV, and don't take a bath or have a shower. Most importantly, don't go outside to watch the lightning!

2 Read the text again. Write T (true), F (false), or DS (doesn't say) for sentences 1–5.

Example Lightning kills three people every year. _F_

1 Most thunderstorms occur in hot weather. _____
2 Thunder is more dangerous than lightning. _____
3 If you are in the sea, go to the beach for safety. _____
4 Lightning can hit more than one person if they stand together. _____
5 Lightning can hit you if you are in the bath. _____

 5

3 Read the article. Choose a heading for each paragraph.

1 Food modification _____   3 Design your family _____
2 Weather control _____   4 Body perfection? _____

 4

New technology and progress?

As technology advances, we find more ways to change the world we live in. For some people, development is progress. For others, using science and technology to change nature is wrong. In this article, Dr. Nolla gives some examples of new developments.

A We are making progress because doctors today can help babies, even before they are born. They can discover health problems and – sometimes – they can even resolve them. Parents can already choose to have a boy or a girl, and soon they'll be able to choose their baby's eye and hair colour. Some scientists think we might be able to choose a personality and level of intelligence for our children.

B Another way in which medical science is helping people is with cosmetic surgery. Doctors can change most parts of a person's face or body and this is very important for people who have been in accidents. People can also use cosmetic surgery to make them look exactly how they want to. In my opinion, this will make even more people unhappy.

C Scientists use chemicals to change the weather and we can now create rain in some areas, and stop it in others. Controlling the weather for sporting events is great. Making rain in countries without water can help millions of people with nothing to drink.

D GM technology makes rice and potatoes grow better. Many people believe that this will change the natural environment. However, this can also help people with no food.

4 Read the article and answer the questions.

Example What can doctors find out about babies before they are born? _health problems_

1 Which two things can people choose for their babies? _____ and _____
2 According to Dr Nolla, who is cosmetic surgery good for? _____
3 How does Dr Nolla think people who have cosmetic surgery will feel? _____
4 What do scientists use to change the weather? _____
5 What's the name of the way of making some plants grow better? _____

 6

5 Choose one of the topics (A–D) in the article. Write a paragraph giving your opinion in 90–110 words.

 10

Reading and Writing Total   30

Unit 10 Test Buying and selling

Date: _____

Grammar

1 Time and conditional clauses Complete each sentence with a word or phrase from below.

until   as long as   as soon as   won't   ~~unless~~   unless

Example   You won't have any money _unless_ you get a job.

1 I'll do the shopping _____ you pay for it.
2 I _____ go home until I find some new shoes.
3 People will stop using the local shops _____ the shopping mall opens.
4 I won't stop looking _____ I find a dress.
5 I won't buy that camera _____ it's reduced.

☐ 5

2 Articles *the, a, an* Complete the conversation with *the*, *a*, and *an*.

Tony How are you feeling?
Freda Not great. Are you going into _the_ town centre?
Tony No, I'm just going to ¹_____ post office.
Freda Oh, I'd really like ²_____ ice-cream.
Tony Well, I can go to ³_____ supermarket, if you want.
Freda Thanks! Can you get me the new book by Ted Olsen, too?
Tony I don't think I can get that in town.
Freda Yes, you can. There's ⁴_____ bookshop on the High Street near ⁵_____ bank.

☐ 5

3 Quantifiers Choose the correct word to complete each conversation.

Example   A How _much_ rubbish do you throw away each week?
            a little b few c ~~much~~ d many

1 I always take _____ bags with me when I go shopping.
  a a little b little c a few d few
2 A Do you drink bottled water?
  B Yes, but I don't buy _____ bottles.
  a many b much c any d a little
3 You can recycle _____ packaging now.
  a too much b a lot of c a few d hardly any
4 Very _____ people use the new supermarket.
  a a little b little c a few d few
5 A There's no milk for my coffee.
  B I think there's _____ milk in the fridge.
  a few b a few c little d a little

☐ 5

Vocabulary

4 Packaging Match 1–6 with a–f to make the names of things you buy.

1 a tin of———————a tomatoes
2 a jar of   b margarine
3 a tub of   c coffee
4 a tube of   d toothpaste
5 a pot of   e biscuits
6 a packet of   f yoghurt

☐ 5

5 Words connected with buying and selling Complete each sentence with a word or phrase from below.

buy price pay ~~spend~~ reduced receipt

Do you _spend_ too much money when you go shopping? Here is some advice to help you stop.

– Make a list before you go. Decide how much you want to ¹_____ for each item on the list.

– When you are at the shops, only ²_____ things that are on your shopping list.

– If you like something, check the ³_____ before you decide that you absolutely love and must have it!

– For bigger items, visit different shops. You might find it in a sale at a ⁴_____ price.

– Remember, you can always take something back if you change your mind. When you buy something, put the ⁵_____ in a safe place.

☐ 5

Pronunciation

6 When to stress the auxiliary *have / has* Think about the sound of *have / has* in these sentences. If it is stressed write S. If it is unstressed, write U.

Example   We've been working. _U_

1 They haven't been sleeping. _____
2 Has she been waiting? _____
3 I've been thinking. _____
4 It hasn't been raining. _____
5 Have they been talking? _____

☐ 5

GVP Total ☐ 30

Reading and Writing A letter of complaint

1 Read the text. Write T (true), F (false), or DS (doesn't say) for sentences 1–6.

Packaging rage

You bought a new toy for your child and you've been trying to open it for twenty minutes. You've used your teeth and a knife, but it's too strong. You get angry. Your child starts to cry.

05 You are experiencing 'packaging rage' – the anger created by packaging that seems impossible to open. Over the last ten years, manufacturers have been using increasing amounts of packaging on all products. Many people also feel angry about the effects of this on the environment.

10 So, what kinds of products cause packaging rage? CD cases wrapped in plastic are one example. In the bathroom, it's bottles of medicines and boxes of washing powder. In the kitchen, it's cartons of milk, tins of food and packets of biscuits. Even little labels on apples can make people angry.

15 This may all seem seem like a joke to some people, but packaging rage does have a serious side. Older people can have real problems trying to open food and medicines. Trying to open strong packaging with your teeth can be dangerous too. If you use a knife and it slips on the

20 packaging, it can cause serious cuts or other injuries. Around 60,000 British people a year need hospital treatment for injuries caused when they were trying to open things.

Example The writer bought a toy for his child. _T_

1 The writer tried different ways to open the toy. ____
2 Manufacturers use more packaging now than ten years ago. ____
3 Some people find jars of jam difficult to open. ____
4 It's safe to open packaging with your teeth. ____
5 50,000 people in Britain hurt themselves on packaging every year. ____
6 Some manufacturers have promised to make changes to their packaging. ____

☐ 6

2 Read the article again. Choose the best answer.
Example What does 'it' refer to (line 3)?
a the knife b the scissors ⓒ the packaging

1 People feel angry because packaging is ____.
a difficult to throw away
b bad for the environment   c expensive
2 What does 'it' (line 13) refer to?
a products b cartons of milk   c packaging rage
3 'This' (line 15) refers to ____.
a an apple b packaging rage   c a joke
4 'they' (line 22) refers to ____.
a old people   b children   c British people

☐ 4

3 Read the emails and answer the questions below.

> ✉   ☐
> Hi Vernon,
>
> You know those shoes I ordered on the Internet? I've been having some problems and I'd like your advice.
>
> I ordered size 39 and they arrived a few days later. I wore them to work and they seemed a bit small. I checked the size – they were size 38, not 39.
>
> First, I sent an email to the company, but they didn't answer. Then I phoned the company. I explained the situation and asked them to exchange the shoes for the correct size. They say they can't because I've worn them. I'm so angry. It's their mistake, but they say it's my fault. I've spent £60 on a pair of shoes I can't wear!
>
> What do you think I should do? Should I make a complaint?
>
> Bye for now,
>
> Tess
>
> PS I'm going to local shops from now on!

> ✉   ☐
> Hi Tess,
>
> Yes, you should definitely complain! The company made a mistake when they sent you the wrong size. If I were you, I'd write a letter. It's more formal than an email.
>
> I know what you mean about using the local shops. But then I had a bad experience in the local bookshop. Seems like you can't win wherever you shop these days! Good luck!
>
> Vernon

Example Where did Tess buy the shoes?
on the Internet

1 What size shoes did she order? _____
2 What size shoes did she receive? _____
3 Where did she wear the shoes? _____
4 Why did she think the shoes felt small? _____
5 What did she do before phoning the company? ____
6 Why won't the company change the shoes? _____
7 How much did Tess pay for the shoes? _____
8 Where will Tess shop in the future? _____
9 What does Vernon think Tess should do? _____
10 In which shop did Vernon have a problem? _____

☐ 10

4 Imagine you are Tess. Write a letter of complaint to the shoe company in 90–110 words.

☐ 10

Reading and Writing Total ☐ 30

Unit 11 Test Travel and holidays

Date: _____

Grammar

1 ***Have something done*** Add <u>three</u> words to the second sentence so that it means the same as the first.

Example Someone washes our clothes every day.
We _have our clothes_ washed every day.

1 Let's ask reception to bring dinner outside!
Let's _____ _____ _____ outside!
2 Someone cleaned our house yesterday.
We had _____ _____ _____ yesterday.
3 Pay someone to cut your hair!
_____ _____ _____ cut!
4 Someone is translating our documents.
We're _____ _____ _____ translated.
5 My neighbour's repairing my car tomorrow.
I'm _____ _____ _____ repaired tomorrow.

▢ **5**

2 ***Have to, need to, should, ought to*** Choose the correct word or phrase to complete each conversation.

Example A I'm only going to drink bottled water when I'm on holiday.
B Yes, and you *need to / don't need to / shouldn't* have any ice in your drinks.

1 You *should / shouldn't / don't need to* take a bus. The hotel's only 100 metres from here.
2 A I've got a really bad stomach ache.
B You *ought to / have to / don't need to* stay in bed.
3 A What time shall we go to the airport tomorrow?
B I think we *have to / don't have to / shouldn't* check in three hours before the flight leaves.
4 A I cut my leg when I was swimming on holiday.
B Oh no! Was it a very bad?
A Yes. I *ought to / had to / should* go to hospital.
5 A Will I be safe in the city centre?
B Yes, but you *shouldn't / don't need to / don't have to* walk near the station at night.

▢ **5**

3 **Non-defining relative clauses** Choose the correct word below to complete each conversation.

where when ~~which~~ which whose who

Example A I heard about your trip to China!
B Yes, it was an amazing experience, _which_ I'll never forget.

1 A Are you going on holiday this summer?
B Yes, to the village in France, _____ we usually go.
2 A Did you go to India alone?
B No, I went with Billy, _____ I've known for many years.

3 A Did you stay in a flat in New York?
B Yes. But I didn't see Gina, _____ flat it is.
4 A When do you usually go on holiday?
B In June, _____ the weather isn't too hot.
5 A Did you have a good trip?
B No. I lost my suitcase, _____ was full of presents.

▢ **5**

Vocabulary

4 **Travel problems** Match 1–6 with a–f.

1 get   a your plane
2 run out of b stopped for speeding
3 miss c your way
4 lose d an accident
5 have e petrol
6 have f a flat tyre

▢ **5**

5 **The street** Complete the words in each conversation.

Example A We'll never get across this road!
B There's a b *r i d g e* over there. Let's use that.

1 A The city is built on water, isn't it?
B Yes. Our hotel was on a c _ _ _ _.
2 A Is there much traffic in the city centre?
B Yes, but there are lots of p _ _ _ _ _ _ _ _ streets.
3 A Oh, the last bus has gone. Shall we get a taxi?
B There's a taxi r _ _ _ over there. Come on.
4 A What do I do when I get to the c _ _ _ _ _ _ _ _ ?
B Just go straight on. Don't turn left or right.
5 A Excuse me! Is this the road to the station?
B Yes, but there's a quicker way for bicycles. Take that p _ _ _. It goes straight to the station.

▢ **5**

Pronunciation

6 **The main stress in a sentence** Think about the sound of these sentences. Where is the main stress? <u>Underline</u> the word in each sentence.

Example Can I drink the <u>water</u> here?

1 What do we do in an emergency?
2 Have you had your injections yet?
3 Have you got your passport?
4 What pills do I need to take?
5 How much is the insurance?

▢ **5**

GVP Total ▢ **30**

Photocopiable © Oxford University Press 2009

11

Reading and Writing
A website recommendation

1 Read the text. Choose the best title for each problem.

  1 Too much sun ____   3 Insects bit me ____

  2 Not enough money ____ 4 A bad cold ____

 4

Holiday Headaches

Are your friends going on holiday while you're still working? Don't worry, life isn't always easy when you're on holiday! Here are some holiday stories to make you feel better.

A **Hannah (19)** My friend and I went to Venice, Italy for a week. It's a magnificent city, and we loved the canals and enjoyed getting lost in all the beautiful back streets.

However, we ran out of money after three days. We had to leave our elegant hotel and stay in a really cheap one. It was so frustrating not to be able to go shopping or eat in the nice restaurants. We just ate pizza outside every day!

B **James (30)** I went to Malta for a week. The first day was great. I went to the beach and in the evening I ate some delicious food in a seafront restaurant. The next morning I woke up covered in mosquito bites! They were so uncomfortable, and they were all over my face. I bought some insect repellent for the next night. I'll take a mosquito net if I go again!

C **Hugh (25)** I did a really stupid thing when I was on holiday in Spain. I found a small, secluded beach near the hotel, so I took my clothes off. I fell asleep without any sun block on. Of course, I got really bad sunburn. My back and legs were incredibly red and sore. I had to spend the first few days inside until my skin was better.

D **Alice (33)** I hadn't had a holiday for ages, so I was really excited about this holiday in Egypt. My friend and I had planned lots of diving trips in the Red Sea. On the second day, I had a blocked nose. I realized I was probably getting a bad cold. The next day I couldn't do any diving because I couldn't swim underwater with my cold. I just lay on the beach rest of the week. I guess I caught it on the plane.

2 Read the text again and answer questions 1–7.

Example How long did Hannah go to Venice for? *a week*

  1 What did Hannah eat in Venice every day? _____

  2 Where was James bitten? _____

  3 What did James use on the second night? _____

  4 What should Hugh have used on the beach? _____

  5 Which word in Hugh's story means 'painful'? _____

  6 What did Alice have on the second day? _____

  7 Where does Alice think she got her cold? _____

  7

2 Read the email. Write T (true), F (false), or DS (doesn't say) for sentences 2–10.

Dear Lee,

I've just come back from a luxury cruise in the Adriatic Sea. The ship was delightful. Our room – I mean cabin! – was very comfortable and the staff were friendly and efficient. We had breakfast served in our cabin every morning. I had my hair cut and John had his feet massaged!

There were several day excursions to the Croatian islands and mainland. The best one was to Krka National Park, which is an area of lakes and waterfalls. We each paid 45 kunas (about €6) to go in, but there is lots to see once you're inside. First, we went to Lake Visovac in the middle of the park. There's a small island on the lake which you can visit by boat. At the end of the day we swam in the lake. It was beautiful. Unfortunately, lots of other people were swimming there too, but it was still a good experience.

Anyway, it's back to work tomorrow. College begins again and the new students are arriving. I'm planning to take a group on a trip to your part of the country next summer. I need to plan some excursions in the area. Can you recommend any places we could visit? It could be somewhere in the countryside, or a town, or city. I want to put the information on the college website for students to read in advance.

I look forward to your reply!

Harriet

PS We're having the house decorated at the moment. I thought the painters would finish the job while we were on holiday. But no – they're still here. I need another holiday!

  1 Harriet went on a cruise in the Mediterranean Sea. *F*

  2 Harriet was pleased with the service on the cruise. ____

  3 The Krka National Park is about 100km². ____

  4 It costs about €6 to visit the National Park. ____

  5 You have to swim to get to the island on Lake Visovac. ____

  6 Harriet and John were the only people in the lake. ____

  7 Harriet works at an art school. ____

  8 Harriet wants suggestions for excursions near where Lee lives. ____

  9 She'll put the information on a noticeboard. ____

  10 The painters haven't finished decorating Harriet's house. ____

  9

4 Imagine someone is planning a holiday in your country. Write a letter, suggesting places for them to visit. Write 90–110 words.

  10

Reading and Writing Total	**30**

Unit 12 Test Books and stories

Date: _____

Grammar

1 *so, because, (in order) to* Choose the correct answer.

Example I'm sad _____ my friend is in hospital.
a so b in order to ⓒ because

1 I needed a book _____ to the library.
a in order to go b so I went c because I went

2 Denise worked hard _____ a lot of money.
a in order to make b because she had
c so she needed

3 James went to the city _____ look for a job.
a because b to c so

4 They were thirsty _____ there was no water.
a so b to c because

5 The bread smelt very good _____ it.
a so I ate b in order to eat c because I ate

 5

2 *-ing and -ed clauses* Underline the correct word to complete the story.

The House in the Woods

A boy *called / calling* Ralph is walking in the woods. He finds the ruins of house ¹*destroyed / destroying* by fire. He hears a child ²*cried / crying*. He decides to go inside. He sees a young boy with black hair ³*worn / wearing* strange clothes. Ralph speaks but the boy doesn't answer.

Later, Ralph meets an old woman ⁴*walked / walking* in the woods. He tells her about the house and the boy. She says, 'Come to my house. I want to show you something.'

She says, 'Look at this picture ⁵*painted / painting* by my father. Is this the boy in the house?'

'Yes,' said Ralph. 'That's him.'

'Frances was my brother. He died 70 years ago today.'

5

3 **3rd conditional** Choose the correct word to complete each sentence.

have   you'd   had   hadn't   ~~would~~   wouldn't

Example A My friend found £100 in the street.
She took it to the police.
B Really? I _would_ have kept it.

1 If I _____ studied French, I wouldn't be a French teacher now.

2 What would you _____ done if you'd seen it?

3 If she'd seen you _____ have been in trouble.

4 If he _____ stayed in London, he would have missed the party.

5 If I'd known she was rich, I _____ have given her that money.

5

Vocabulary

4 **Stories, books, fiction** Read the descriptions and match them with books a–f.

a romance b fantasy c western
~~d adventure~~ e science fiction f murder mystery

Example ☐ *d* Carl Heller is hunting for an ancient city in the jungle, when his plane crashes.

1 ☐ Three woman are dead. Detective Pearson must find the killer fast.

2 ☐ In a universe far away, an evil ruler plans to destroy other worlds from his spaceship.

3 ☐ It's 1876. Ned and his young wife face many difficulties as their wagon travels through the deserts of Arizona, USA.

4 ☐ A new doctor has just arrived at the hospital. Nina thinks she's falling in love again.

5 ☐ A family spend a week in a remote house. Tim meets a mysterious man who takes him to a magical world.

 5

5 *Wish, hope, be glad* Complete the sentences with the correct form of *wish*, *hope*, or *be glad*.

Example I _'m glad_ I work in a shop. I really like it.

1 It's raining! I _____ I had a car to drive you home.

2 Seth's worried. He _____ he'll find a job soon.

3 I _____ you enjoy the book. I thought it was great.

4 Now she _____ she'd moved to the city.

5 I _____ I bought that new computer. My old one was so slow!

 5

Pronunciation

6 **Contrastive stress** Think about sentence stress in speaker B's replies. Which word has the main stress? Underline it.

Example A I wish I was younger.
B Really? I wish I *wasn't* so young!

1 A I wish he would talk more.
B Really? I wish he would listen more!

2 A I hope one day I have a lot of money.
B I wish I had a lot of money now!

3 A I'm glad I've got a mobile phone.
B Really? I wish I didn't have a mobile phone!

4 A I wish I could speak Italian.
B Really? I wish I could speak Spanish.

5 A I wish I had a dog.
B Really? I'm glad I haven't got a dog!

 5

GVP Total	**30**

12

Reading and Writing A story with a moral

1 Read the book reviews and choose the best answer.

True Adventures

This week we review two bestselling stories of real-life adventure and drama.

The extreme situations experienced by the men and women in these two books are described in vivid detail. The
05 authors take you inside the minds of people making life or death decisions. These stories leave you thankful to be alive.

INTO THIN AIR by Jon Krakauer (1999)
This is an account of a disaster on Mount Everest, written by one of the people involved. Krakauer is a journalist working
10 for Outside magazine. He wants to write a story about the tour companies working on Mount Everest. He joins a climbing tour with a company so he can find out about how they operate.

Krakauer is an experienced climber. However, many of other
15 people in the group have little or no experience. The climb to the top of Everest is successful. However, on the descent, they are hit by a storm and eight of the climbers die. Some of those who died had been climbing for many years.

The book describes the horror of the experience. At the
20 same time it considers the decisions and mistakes made by the climbers and and the tour company.

ADA BLACKJACK by Jennifer Niven (2003)
This is the true story of a woman who survived for two years on an Arctic island in the 1920's.

25 Four Canadian and American men living in Nome, Alaska, plan a trip to Wrangel Island, Russia. They are going to live there for a year to show that it's possible to survive in the Arctic. They can't cook or make clothes, so they advertise for someone to accompany them. Ada Blackjack, a 23-year-old
30 Inuit Eskimo woman, is the only person who applies. She is hired to cook for the men and to repair their clothes.

After several months on the island, the group face serious problems so three of the men leave the island to find help. They never return. The man left with Ada dies, so she is left
35 to survive alone.

Example Krakauer goes to Mount Everest ____.
a for work   b to learn how to climb
ⓒ for a holiday

1 Eight climbers die on Everest because they have ____.
a no experience   b bad weather
c the wrong clothes

2 In Alaska, four men make a difficult journey ____.
a for work   b for survival   c to write a story

3 Ada Blackjack goes on the trip ____.
a to work   b to write   c for adventure

4 Three of the men leave the island because ____.
a they need help   b Ada is ill   c one dies

☐ **4**

2 Read the reviews again and answer the questions.
Example Which word means 'popular'? _bestselling_

1 Which word means 'a true story'? _____
2 Which word means 'how things work'? _____
3 Which word means 'the journey down'? _____
4 What does 'they' (line 17) refer to? _____
5 What does 'it' (line 20) refer to? _____
6 What does 'there' (line 27) refer to? _____
7 Which word means 'go with'? _____
8 Which word means 'bright, strong, and clear'? _____
9 Which word means 'happy'? _____

☐ **9**

3 Read the text and complete the summary below.

The Chief's Party

It had been a successful year in his village. The weather had been good, the wheat and corn had grown well, and the cows and the animals were fat. The village chief decided to have a party to celebrate and invited everyone. He said he would provide meat, bread, and cakes, and asked each guest to bring some wine to put into the big pot.

One man wanted to go to the party but he had no wine. He thought, 'Why spend money on wine in order to go to a party which is free? It would be better to buy new clothes for the party.' Then he had an idea. He would take a jar of water because nobody would notice a little bit of water in such a lot of wine.

On the day of the party, everybody put on their best clothes and went to the chief's home. On tables were the bread, meat, and cakes that the chief had promised. Each guest poured the contents of their jar into the big pot as they arrived.

The chief ordered his servants to give everyone some wine and, when he signalled, everybody took their cups and drank. To their surprise, it was ... WATER!

MORAL: Do what's best for the group, and not what's best for you.

situation: A *village chief* decides to have a party to celebrate the good ¹_____ of his village. He says he'll provide meat, bread, and ²_____.
He asks the guests to bring the ³_____.
One man doesn't want to spend ⁴_____ on wine for the party

action: He decides to buy new ⁵_____ for the party instead and takes ⁶_____ to put in the wine pot.

result: When the servants fill the cups from the wine pot, it is water.

moral: Do what is best for ⁷_____.

☐ **7**

4 Write a short story of a book or film you know, or invent your own. Write 90–110 words.

☐ **10**

Reading and Writing Total ☐ **30**

Tests key

Unit 1

Grammar

1
1 does Sally love
2 phoned Sally
3 did Sally visit
4 likes Sally
5 took Sally for a meal

2
1 each other
2 myself
3 himself
4 each other
5 yourself

3
1 do
2 's / is getting
3 talks
4 speaks
5 'm / am doing

Vocabulary

4
1 lips 2 shake 3 wave
4 bow 5 hug

5 1 a 2 b 3 c 4 c 5 b

Pronunciation

6 1 L 2 H 3 P 4 F 5 G

Reading and Writing

1 1 c 2 e 3 b 4 a 5 d

2
1 False 2 True 3 False 4 True
5 False 6 False

3
1 teacher 2 colleague 3 middle
4 run(s) / running 5 28 6 Hotel
7 cousin 8 behind 9 guitar

4 Students' own answers.

Marking guidelines		marks
Task	Have students included all the information? Have students organized their ideas logically?	4
Grammar	Have students used the present simple and continuous accurately? Have students joined simple sentences accurately?	4
Vocabulary	Have students spelt words for hobbies accurately? Have students used capital letters accurately?	2

Unit 2

Grammar

1 1 the 2 Ø 3 Ø 4 The 5 The

2
1 ... are usually very friendly.
2 We rarely buy ...
3 ... hardly ever takes ...
4 I quite often visit ...
5 ... 's always really interested ...

3
1 was walking
2 started
3 was crossing
4 saw
5 didn't agree

Vocabulary

4 2 d 3 f 4 a 5 e 6 b

5 1 kind of 2 looks like 3 made of
4 used for 5 used as

Pronunciation

6 1 /g/ 2 /s/ 3 /dʒ/ 4 /k/ 5 /dʒ/

Reading and Writing

1
1 1939
2 2,300 (years)
3 (the story of) El Dorado
4 (on the) third / 3rd floor
5 8,000
6 Monday(s)

2 1 False 2 True 3 False 4 Doesn't say
5 True 6 True 7 Doesn't say

3
1 work or business
2 written in Malaysian
3 food, fruit juice, bowl of water
4 right
5 stupid

4 Students' own answers.

Marking guidelines		marks
Task	Have students included all the information? Have students organized their ideas logically?	4
Grammar	Have students used the past simple and past continuous appropriately?	4
Vocabulary	Have students got enough vocabulary to express their ideas clearly?	2

Unit 3

Grammar

1
1 used to clean
2 ✗
3 didn't use to pay
4 ✗
5 Did you use to be

2
1 have taught
2 has studied
3 have been
4 have decided
5 got

3
1 Put it away.
2 Can you turn it on?
3 He turned it up.
4 Take it off.
5 Put it on.

Vocabulary

4 2 b 3 e 4 f 5 a 6 c

5 1 give up 2 failed 3 managed to
4 achievement 5 keep trying

Pronunciation

6 ● ● last week
● ● ● get it wrong, make mistakes, teacher's pet
● ● ● ● front of the class

Reading and Writing

1 1 b 2 a 3 b 4 c 5 c 6 b

2 1 True 2 False 3 False
4 True 5 False 6 Doesn't say
7 Doesn't say

3 1 Advanced 2 Hard-working 3 C
4 Maths 5 guard 6 Drawing
7 history

4 Student's own answers.

Marking guidelines		marks
Task	Have students included all the sections? Have they written relevant information?	4
Grammar	Have students used capital letters correctly?	4
Vocabulary	Have students used a variety of words to describe themselves and their interests? Have students spelt words correctly?	2

Unit 4

Grammar

1 1 that 2 where 3 who
4 you 5 which

2 1 worried 2 boring
3 embarrassing 4 disgusting
5 annoyed

3 1 as big
2 the best
3 more crowded
4 more expensive
5 the most entertaining

Vocabulary

4 1 MP3 player 2 jazz 3 solo
4 track 5 stadium

5 1 adore 2 stand 3 keen
4 like 5 mind

Pronunciation

6

-d	-t	-id
amazed bored	embarrassed	disgusted fascinated

Reading and Writing

1 1 B 2 D 3 A 4 C

2 1 True 2 False 3 True
4 Doesn't say 5 Doesn't say
6 True 7 Doesn't say

3 1 a day and night 2 a day
3 (the) US(A) 4 France
5 (on) (a) train 6 in a bookshop in Paris
7 more unusual and magical
8 (in) (a) bookshop 9 *Before Sunrise*

5 Students' own answers.

Marking guidelines		marks
Task	Have students included the main points?	4
Grammar	Have students used present tenses appropriately? Have students used present tenses accurately?	4
Vocabulary	Have students used a variety of adjectives?	2

Unit 5

Grammar

1 1 Ø 2 the 3 the 4 Ø 5 the

2 2 was stolen 3 have been arrested
4 were attacked 5 was taken
6 has been given

3 1 can't 2 have to 3 mustn't
4 must 5 can

Vocabulary

4 2 c 3 f 4 d 5 b 6 a

5 1 d 2 d 3 b 4 a 5 c

Pronunciation

6 1 complete
2 battle
3 shoulder
4 happen
5 return

Reading and Writing

1 1 b 2 b 3 a 4 a 5 c
6 a 7 c 8 b 9 c

2 1 E 2 D 3 B 4 C

3 1 (her) last car was / had been stolen
2 (the) oil (and) (the) brakes
3 it was / had been stolen
4 on the passenger seat
5 (he was) paying for petrol
6 (in the / at / during the) night

4 Students' own answers.

Marking guidelines		marks
Task	Have students included all the information? Have students organized their ideas to keep their reader interested?	4
Grammar	Have students used a variety of past tenses appropriately?	4
Vocabulary	Have students got enough vocabulary to express their ideas? Have students spell irregular past tenses correctly?	2

Unit 6

Grammar

1 1 That is such good news!
2 That's such a stupid idea!
3 I'm such a fool.
4 I'm so angry with her.
5 He was driving so badly!

2 1 talking 2 to come 3 leaving
4 to get 5 walking

3 1 would / 'd be 2 was 3 didn't feel
4 would / 'd help 5 had / 'd got

Vocabulary

4 1 noisy 2 nosy 3 naughty
4 helpful 5 fight

5 1 exhausted 2 awful 3 terrified
4 enormous 5 furious

Pronunciation

6 1 F 2 NP 3 NP 4 NP 5 F

Reading and Writing

1 1 C 2 D 3 A 4 B

2 1 a 2 b 3 c 4 b 5 a 6 b

3 1 True 2 False 3 Doesn't say
4 False 5 True 6 Doesn't say
7 False 8 True 9 False
10 Doesn't say

4 Students' own answers.

Marking guidelines		marks
Task	Have students responded to Laura's news? Have students connected ideas accurately?	4
Grammar	Have students used question forms accurately? Have students used adjectives in the correct position?	4
Vocabulary	Have students used conversational phrases correctly?	2

Tests key

Unit 7

Grammar

1 1 where he buys 2 her birthday is
3 why she said 4 who gave me
5 colour she wants

2 1 I'm having 2 I'll come
3 I'm going to tell 4 I'm meeting
5 are you having

3 1 might 2 might 3 can't
4 must 5 might

Vocabulary

4 1 ambitious 2 confident 3 bushy
4 imaginative 5 active

5 1 looking 2 fitting 3 fashioned
4 conscious 5 dressed

Pronunciation

6 1 No, <u>late</u> fifties.
2 No, big <u>green</u> eyes.
3 No, wavy <u>dark</u> hair.
4 No, early <u>thirties</u>.
5 No, <u>straight</u> hair.

Reading and Writing

1 A Appear on TV and change your life
B What happens on the show
C The prizes
D How to apply

2 1 a 2 c 3 a 4 c 5 a 6 a

3 1 51 2 short 3 quiet 4 jogging
5 confident 6 art 7 curly
8 outgoing 9 clothes 10 fit

4 Students' own answers.

Marking guidelines		marks
Task	Have students included appropriate information? Have students used appropriate openings and closings?	4
Grammar	Have students used a variety of tenses?	4
Vocabulary	Have students used a variety of *looks* and *character* adjectives appropriately?	2

Unit 8

Grammar

1 1 She told him to open the door.
2 I told you not to call me at work.
3 He asked them not to shout.
4 She asked me to close the window.
5 He told me to be careful.

2 1 can't 2 'll be able to 3 can
4 was able to 5 managed to

3 1 could 2 were 3 would
4 him 5 if

Vocabulary

4 1 up 2 over 3 off
4 through 5 back

5 2 c 3 d 4 e 5 b 6 a

Pronunciation

6 1 popul<u>ar</u>ity 2 curi<u>os</u>ity 3 re<u>al</u>ity
4 poss<u>ib</u>ility 5 ac<u>tiv</u>ity

Reading and Writing

1 1 D 2 A 3 C 4 B

2 1 four (4)
2 piano
3 thirty (30)
4 fingers
5 music
6 Visible Speech
7 human ear
8 telephone
9 Gray

3 1 True 2 True 3 Doesn't say
4 Doesn't say 5 True 6 False
7 Doesn't say

4 Students' own answers.

Marking guidelines		marks
Task	Have students included all the necessary information?	4
Grammar	Have students used a variety of tenses? Have students used reported speech accurately?	4
Vocabulary	Have students used a variety of words to talk about ability?	2

Unit 9

Grammar

1 1 are there 2 haven't you
3 don't they 4 aren't they 5 is he

2 1 should 2 won't 3 don't
4 catch 5 will

3 1 had 2 wouldn't want
3 'd / would be 4 didn't have
5 gave

Vocabulary

4 1 b 2 a 3 d 4 b 5 c

5 1 club 2 call 3 address
4 service 5 laptop

Pronunciation

6 1 body 2 job 3 Lucy
4 won't 5 cut

Reading and Writing

1 1 C 2 A 3 D 4 E 5 B

2 1 Doesn't say 2 False 3 False
4 True 5 True

3 1 D 2 C 3 A 4 B

4 1 boy or girl and eye and hair colour
2 people (who have been) in accidents
3 unhappy
4 chemicals
5 GM technology

5 Students' own answers.

Marking guidelines		marks
Task	Have students use paragraphs accurately? Have students supported their point of view?	4
Grammar	Have students linked simple sentences appropriately? Have students used a variety of verb tenses?	4
Vocabulary	Have students used adverbs of attitude appropriately? Have students used a variety of topic-related vocabulary?	2

Unit 10

Grammar

1 1 as long as 2 won't
3 as soon as 4 until 5 unless

2 1 the 2 an 3 the 4 a 5 the

3 1 c 2 a 3 b 4 d 5 d

Vocabulary

4 2 c 3 b 4 d 5 f 6 e

5 1 pay 2 buy 3 price
4 reduced 5 receipt

Pronunciation

6 1 S 2 U 3 U 4 S 5 U

Reading and Writing

1 1 True 2 True 3 Doesn't say
4 False 5 False 6 Doesn't say

2 1 b 2 a 3 b 4 c

3 1 39
2 38
3 to work
4 (because) they were new
5 (sent an) email
6 She / Tess has worn them
7 £60
8 (the) local shops
9 write a letter (to complain / of complaint)
10 bookshop

4 Students' own answers.

Marking guidelines		marks
Task	Have students included the information a reader would expect? Have students organized paragraphs appropriately?	4
Grammar	Have students used past tenses accurately?	4
Vocabulary	Have students spelt vocabulary correctly?	2

Unit 11

Grammar

1 1 have dinner brought
2 our house cleaned
3 Have your hair
4 having our documents
5 having my car

2 1 don't need to 2 ought to
3 have to 4 had to 5 shouldn't

3 1 where 2 who 3 whose
4 when 5 which

Vocabulary

4 2 e 3 a 4 c 5 f 6 d

5 1 canal 2 pedestrian 3 rank
4 crossroads 5 path

Pronunciation

6 1 What do we do in an emergency?
2 Have you had your injections yet?
3 Have you got your passport?
4 What pills do I need to take?
5 How much is the insurance?

Reading and Writing

1 1 C 2 A 3 B 4 D

2 1 pizza 2 face 3 insect repellent
4 sun block 5 sore 6 blocked nose
7 (on the) plane

3 2 True 3 Doesn't say 4 True
5 False 6 Doesn't say 7 False
8 True 9 False 10 True

4 Students' own answers.

Marking guidelines		marks
Task	Have students given their reader enough information? Have students organized their letter into paragraphs?	4
Grammar	Have students used verb tenses accurately?	4
Vocabulary	Have students a variety of words for places to visit?	2

Unit 12

Grammar

1 1 b 2 a 3 b 4 c 5 a

2 1 destroyed 2 crying 3 wearing
4 walking 5 painted

3 1 hadn't 2 have 3 you'd
4 had 5 wouldn't

Vocabulary

4 1 f 2 e 3 c 4 a 5 b

5 1 wish 2 hopes 3 hope
4 wishes 5 'm glad

Pronunciation

6 1 listen 2 now 3 didn't
4 Spanish 5 haven't

Reading and Writing

1 1 b 2 b 3 a 4 a

2 1 (an) account
2 operate
3 (the) descent
4 the group / the climbers
5 the book
6 Wrangel Island (Russia)
7 (to) accompany
8 vivid
9 thankful

3 1 fortune 2 cakes 3 wine
4 money 5 clothes 6 water
7 (the) group

4 Students' own answers.

Marking guidelines		marks
Task	Have students used paragraphs logically? Have students given enough information?	4
Grammar	Have students linked clauses using *because, so,* and (*in order*) to accurately? Have students used a variety of tenses?	4
Vocabulary	Have students got enough vocabulary to express their ideas?	2

OXFORD
UNIVERSITY PRESS

Great Clarendon Street, Oxford OX2 6DP

Oxford University Press is a department of the
University of Oxford. It furthers the University's
objective of excellence in research, scholarship,
and education by publishing worldwide in

Oxford New York

Auckland Cape Town Dar es Salaam
Hong Kong Karachi Kuala Lumpur Madrid
Melbourne Mexico-City Nairobi New Delhi
Shanghai Taipei Toronto

With offices in

Argentina Austria Brazil Chile Czech Republic
France Greece Guatemala Hungary Italy Japan
Poland Portugal Singapore South Korea
Switzerland Thailand Turkey Ukraine Vietnam

OXFORD and OXFORD ENGLISH are registered
trade marks of Oxford University Press in the
UK and in certain other countries

ACKNOWLEDGEMENTS

*The authors and publisher are grateful to those who have given permission
to reproduce the following extracts and adaptations of copyright material:*
p18 Extract from 'Chinese tourists flock to UK in search of Clarks,
fog and the big stupid clock' by Richard Jinman and Hsiao-Hung
Pai, 27 June, 2005, from *The Guardian* © Guardian News and Media
Ltd. 2005. Reproduced by permission. p78 Extract from 'That damn
bird: A talk with Irene Pepperberg' first published by Edge on the
website www.edge.org Copyright © 2003 Edge Foundation, Inc.
Reproduced by permission.
Sources: www.bbc.co.uk /news

Illustrations by: David Atkinson pp106, 107, 132, 135; Derek Bacon
pp26, 96; Jeremy Banx p12; Gill Button p50; Cyrille Berger p122;
Mark Duffin pp55, 105; Glyn Goodwin pp25, 112, 129, 134; Andy
Hammond pp37, 109; Joanna Kerr p38 (musical instruments), 75;
NAF-represented by Meiklejohn Agency (Desert Island Joke) p118;
Gavin Reece pp56; Mark Ruffle pp 43, 95.

*The Publishers and Authors would also like to thank the following for kind
permission to reproduce photographs:* Alamy Images pp8 (mother &
daughter greeting, Turkey/Janine Wiedel Photolibrary), 8 (students
bowing/Christian Kober), 15 (Fifer 1866/The Print Collector), 16
(Masai woman/J Marshall – Tribaleye Images), 18 (tourists/PS/DW),
18 (Karl Marx tomb/Charlie Newham), 20 (stools/blickwinkel), 20
(boxing glove/Judith Collins), 20 (fishing net float/High Threlfall),
20 (bottles/Gabe Palmer), 20 (headrest/Simon Colmer and Abby
Rex), 20 (antique potato masher/Kari Marttila), 20 (vase/ImageClick,
Inc.), 20 (carved wooden drum/Eric Nathan), 22 (Indian black tea
in white bowl/Radek Detinsky), 28 (school children/Eye Ubiquitous),
34 (Girl portrait/Nick Emm), 36 (Multi BASE jumper/Christophe
Diesel Michot), 36 (karaoke singer/PYMCA), 36 (male bodybuilder/
CoverSpot), 38 (listening to music/Jupiter Images), 38 (Kanye West/
DEK C), 38 (Dave Grohl onstage/Content Mine International),
38 (singer/Redferns Music Picture Library), 40 (restaurant/
Directphoto), 40 (pub sign/picturesbyrob), 40 (Indian restaurant/
Directphoto.org), 46 (Ghana voting/Julian Nieman), 46 (Road signs),
46 (UN Peacekeeper/Adrian Bradshaw), 46 (vote green sign/David
Robertson), 46 (The Parthenon in Athens Greece/David Levenson),
46 (Poland Warsaw Palace of Culture/Tibor Bognar), 46 (Pentagon
star army jeep/Brian Elliott), 46 (South Bank Lion London/Hugh
Threlfall), 46 (Emblem of Austrian flag/imagebroker), 48 (Judges
hammer/Jan Tadeusz), 48 (Do not feed seagulls sign/Chris Howes/
Wild Places Photography), 48 (alligator sign/Darren Baker), 48
(sign board/Pixoi Ltd), 48 (dog in barber chair/Colin Hawkins), 48
(Cat sitting on car roof/IML Image Group Ltd), 48 (raccoon/Holger
Ehlers), 50 (blackberry brambles/Andrea Jones), 52 (The Tower of
London/Andrew Carruth), 52 (Richard III slain/Mary Evans Picture
Library), 52 (bones/Phil Cawley), 54 (woman leaning against wall/
Peter Glass), 60 (boy with ball/imagebroker), 60 (teenage girl/
[apply pictures]), 60 (rubbish sign/Streets Ahead/Den Reader),
62 (Scrap/Michael Foyle), 66 (woman with long hair/Fashion
Beauty), 66 (Afghan Hound/Juniors Bildarchiv), 66 (Chihuahua/
Annette Shaff), Alamy Images p66 (man with white hair/Pencho
Tiho); 66 (Elderly woman/blickwinkel), 66 (English Bulldog/Andrew
Rubtsov), 66 (poodle/Eliane SULLE), 66 (miniature schnauzer terrier/
Isobel Flynn), 66 (Surprised man/Poligons Photo Index), 68
(businesswoman/UberFoto), 68 (Asian woman/Blend Images),
70 (couch potato/Lourens Smak), 70 (hairdresser/Lourens Smak),
70 (man at hairdressers/Lourens Smak), 70 (man/Lourens Smak), 70
(Pilates/IML Image Group Ltd), 70 (dance class/Oliver Knight),
70 (Thai boxing lesson/Thomas Boehm), 70 (Man in Turkish bath/
LOOK Die Bildagentur der Fotografen GmbH), 76 (shop assistant/
Steve Skjold), 78 (parrot on laptop/Juniors Bildarchiv), 78 (dog agility/
Arco Images GmbH), 82 (50 euro note/Photostock – Burkhard Katz),
82 (crumpled 10 euro note/kolvenbach), 82 (travel ticket/Wolf
Kettler), 82 (Espresso cups/Marco Secchi), 82 (Eurostar passengers/
Brotch Images), 84 (girls talking/Don Smetzer), 84 (Posting a Letter/
mediablitzimages (UK) Limited), 90 (Creepshow film 1982/Photos
12), 90 (bear/SCPhotos), 90 (shark/Wolfgang Pölzer), 90 (tornado
over farm/Jim Zuckerman), 90 (Puu Oo volcano/Greg Vaughn),
90 (danger sign/Giles Bracher), 92 (soft sculpture computer/Steve
Cavalier), 96 (Rye High Street/PCL), 98 (checkout/Rob Walls), 102
(vintage dance shoes/Tony Rusecki), 102 (Inkjet printer/D. Hurst),
102 (acoustic guitar/music Alan King), 102 (Prestcold Fridge/Ian
Cartwright still-life), 106 (William Shakespeare portrait/Pictorial
Press Ltd), 108 (Cumbria seafront/travelibUK), 110 (glass of water
from tap/David R. Frazier Photolibrary, Inc.), 110 (tablets/PHOTOTAKE
Inc.), 110 (travel Inoculation/WoodyStock), 110 (mosquito spray/
Niall McOnegal), 110 (first aid kit/PHOTOTAKE Inc.), 114 (Samaria
Gorge Greece/LOOK Die Bildagentur der Fotografen GmbH), 116
(African market/Sun Cunningham Photographic), 116 (Woman
preparing food/Robert Estall photo agency), 118 (child's drawing/
Tallulah Tormey), 118 (child's drawing/Purestock), 120 (Western
artwork/Mary Evans Picture Library), 120 (Sweeney Todd cover/Mary
Evans Picture Library), 120 (Joyle Solomon's Mines/Mary Evans
Picture Library), 120 (H.G Wells cover/Mary Evans Picture Library),
127 (nail clippers/Mode Images Limited), 127 (Cordless electric
drill/David J. Green – studio), 127 (tape measure/Mode Images
Limited), 127 (can opener/Gabe Palmer), 127 (scissors/D.Hurst),
127 (glass lemon squeezer/Andrew Twort), 127 (paintbrush/Jon
Helgason), 127 (disposable razor/Andrew Paterson), 127 (Ice cubes
in tray/Carol and Mike Werner), 129 (Portrait of man/avatra
images), 129 (Businessman/Mode Images Limited), 129 (Happy
old man/Andres Rodriguez), 130 (Messy teenager's room/Janine
Wiedel Photolibrary), 133 (Traditional Russian samovar/Clive
Tully), 134 (Nicole Kidman/Lou-Foto); BBC stills p80 (Guy Goma
being interviewed) Bridgeman Art Library Ltd p52 (The Princes
Edward and Richard in the Tower, 1878 (oil on canvas), Millais,
Sir John Everett (1829–96)/Royal Holloway, University of London);
Corbis pp12 (Man and woman talking/M Thomsen/zefa), 12
(Cheerful man/Pinto/Zefa), 36 (Smiling man with backpack/Jason
Hosking/zefa), 38 (Opera singer/Robbie Jack), 38 (George Strait/
Reuters), 40 (Cooks preparing pizzas/Owen Franken), 40 (Restaurant/
Dan Forer/Beateworks), 62 (Counterfeiter Victor Lustig/Bettman),
62 (Deputies escorting Victor Lustig/Bettman), 62 (Alcatraz/
Bettmann), 62 (Avalanche/Galen Rowell); Getty Images pp6 (girl
with cup/LWA/The Image Bank), 6 (woman/Pam Francis/Riser), 6
(man with mug/Michael Cogliantry/The Image Bank), 6 (couple/Seth
Kushner/The Image Bank), 6 (boy with trumpet/Russell Underwood/
Riser), 6 (man in red sweater/Diana Koenigsberg), 6 (couple with car/
Nick Dolding/Photographer's Choice), 8 (business/David Woolley/
Stone+), 9 (woman in vineyard/Christopher Robbins), 10 (Las
Meninas, detail of the lower half depicting the family of Philip IV
(1605–65) of Spain, 1656 (oil on canvas) Diego Rodriguez de Silva
y Velasquez/The Bridgeman Art Library), 12 (crossword puzzle/Lisa
Spindler Photography Inc.), 16 (Bedouin boy/Nevada Wier/Riser),
16 (Berber male/Hugh Sitton/Riser), 16 (Aymara Indian woman/
Angelo Cavalli/Riser), 16 (Wodaabe man/Jason Dewey/Stone), 16
(Guatemalan girl/Raul Touzon/National Geographic), 16 (Yanomamo
Indian/Ed George/National Geographic), 16 (Inuit hunter/Gordon
Wiltsie/National Geographic), 16 (Huli man/Stefano Scata/Riser),
20 (baseball mitt/Davies and Starr/Stone), 24 (young businesswoman/
Tony Anderson), 28 (Kenyan student Kimani Ng'ang'a/Stan Honda),
30 (Teenagers at house party/Lisa Peardon), 32 (students walking/
West Rock), 33 (young businessman/Seth Joel), 36 (sudoku
competition/Nico Casamassima), 38 (singer Ky-mani Marley/AFP),
40 (waiter carrying dishes/Keren Su), 49 (Dogs in prison costumes/
Pam Francis), 59 (open handbag/Mark Weiss), 66 (senior couple at
window/Dan Kenyon), 66 (portrait mature woman/Roger Wright),
66 (Border collie puppy/Ronald Wittek), 72 (Van Gogh's Bedroom
at Arles 1889/Vincent van Gogh/The Bridgeman Art Library), 72
(bedroom/Rosanne Olson/Stone), 76 (man in car/Antonio Mo/Taxi),
76 (parents with new born/Hans Neleman), 76 (woman with headset/
Charles Thatcher/Stone), 78 (Irene Pepperberg/Time & Life Pictures),
82 (train station/Panoramic Images), 86 (weather/Shape&Content/
Stock Illustration Source), 86 (scarecrow/James Nelson/Stone), 86
(sunset/Pat Fridell/Illustration Works), 88 (woman morphing into
mother's image/Kent Mathews), 88 (girl/Eric McNatt/Stone+), 88
(teen girl/Karan Kapoor/Stone), 92 (personal helicopter/Millennium
Jet), 92 (memory prototype/Accenture Technology Labs), 92 (mobility
robot/Yoshikazu Tsuno/AFP), 92 ('Dream Factory'/Yoshikazu Tsuno/
AFP), 92 (EEG invention/John MacDougall/AFP), 97 (young woman
writing/Erik Dreyer), 98 (shopping basket/Roy Botterell/Stone),
110 (hotel room/Wonderlust Industries), 110 (sunscreen/Dougal
Waters), 122 (life/death buttons/Christian Michaels/Photographer's
Choice), 122 (chalk outline/Laurence Dutton/Stone), 126 (family
reunion/Yellow Dog Productions), 129 (young man wearing flannel
shirt/Catherine Ledner), 130 (Self portrait, 1889/Vincent Van Gogh),
130 (Bedroom/Robert Warren); Jupiter Images pp20 (wine flask/
Hemera Technologies), 69 (teen girl/Polka Dot Images); Kobal
Collection pp42 (*The Lord of the Rings*/New Line/Saul Zaentz/Wing
Nut), 42 (*The Matrix*/Warner Brothers), 42 (Bridget Jones's Diary/
Miramax/Universal), 42 (The Queen/Miramax), 42 (*Mission: Impossible
3*/Paramount Pictures), 42 (*Mamma Mia!*/Universal), 42 (*Jaws*, 1975/
Universal), (*Arachnophobia*/Hollywood Pictures/Amblin; Mary Evans
Picture Library p62 (Eiffel Tower c1908); NI syndication p80 (Guy
Goma outside BBC studios); OUP pp15 (cardboard box/Ingram), 15
(Toy bus/Photodisc), 35 (girl at keyboard/OJO Images), 44 (spider/
Photodisc), 46 (EU flag/EyeWire), 72 (boy with magnifying glass/
Ingram), 74 (Portrait of a young woman/Photodisc), 85 (telephonist/
Photodisc), OUP p96 (Lakeside Retail Park/Hufton + Crow); OUP
p127 (teaspoon/Stockbyte); PA Photos pp58 (Ray Heliwagen with
WWII wallet/Amanda Stratford/AP), 58 (soldier photo/Amanda
Stratford/AP); Photolibrary pp8 (Woman greeting each other/Kim
Steele), 8 (Business people shaking hands/Radius Images), 9 (couple
with barbecue/Ale Ventura), 12 (classroom/Blend Images), 12 (Fruit
market stall/Stella), 14 (woman holding camera/Photodisc), 36
(Friends doing karaoke/Image Source), 36 (woman smiling/
Medioimages), 36 (smiling businessman/Adrian Weinbrecht),
40 (Home Sweet Home Painting/Steve Taylor), 48 (skunk/Corbis),
64 (Moving boxes in living room/Photodisc), 66 (man shouting/
Charlie Schuck), 77 (car mechanic/Juice Images), 84 (student using
mobile phone/i love images), 84 (girl with mobile phone), 84
(young woman with laptop), 93 (college students in library/Sigrid
Olsson), 102 (salesman/Radius Images), 108 (tourist resort/Glow
Images), 110 (medical team/Creatas), 110 (doctor/Image Source),
126 (Sporran/Photodisc), 127 (handsaw/Photodisc), 127 (Adhesive
bandage/Photodisc), 127 (Paperclip/Corbis), 127 (Corkscrew/
Iconotec), 127 (Hairdryer/Photodisc), 127 (Hole punch/Photodisc),
129 (Portrait of man/Radius Images), 129 (portrait of man sitting/
Image Source), 129 (middle aged man/moodboard), 129 (mature
man smiling/Digital Vision); Picturetank pp68 (The Congolese
Sape/Héctor Mediavilla), 68 (The Congolese Sape/Héctor Mediavilla);
PunchStock pp (man with cup/Stockbyte), 6 (barber/Stockbyte),
6 (woman/Photodisc), 6 (mother with baby/Valueline), 6 (woman
with bunny ears/Valueline), 8 (couple hugging each other/
BananaStock), 8 (Asian woman/DAJ), 9 (Smiling kids hugging/
BananaStock), 16 (Maori/Melba Photo Agency), 20 (net/Alaska
Stock), 20 (mate & bombilla/Valueline), 22 (Asian man/Dex Image),
22 (man with cold/fStop), 22 (ice/foodcollection), 38 (woman
listening to music/Brand X Pictures), 38 (man doing air guitar/
image100), 48 (puppy/MIXA), 48 (chick/Stockbyte), 76 (couple/
Digital Vision), 76 (man by car/Digital Vision), 76 (broken down car/
Comstock), 82 (man with glasses/Digital Vision), 86 (man with
umbrella hat/Creatas), 88 (man with guitar/Digital Vision), 88
(hotel owner/Digital Vision), 90 (lightning/Comstock), 129 (young
man making face/Digital Vision), 129 (Young man with blonde
hair/Photodisc), 129 (Portrait of man/Photodisc); Reuters Pictures
pp50 (Upholstered taxi/Ivan Alvarado), 78 (Border collie with toy/
Manuela Hartling); Rex Features pp40 (Angus Steak House
restaurant/Alex Segre), 42 (*Mr Bean's Holiday* film/Universal/
Everett); StockFood UK p22 (Finger bowls with lemon/Jan-Peter
Westermann); The Royal Collection Picture Library p52 (Richard
III/The Royal Collection © 2008 Her Majesty Queen Elizabeth II)
OUP pp163 (working with laptop/Photodisc), 164 (tram in city
street/Photodisc), 166 (College students/Somos), 168 (Girl with
MP3 player/PhotosIndia.com LLC), 172 (Tulips/Photodisc), 178
(fire extinguisher/Ingram), 180 (Jewellery shop window/Corbis),
182 (Doctor with syringe/Photodisc).

Commissioned photography by: Gareth Boden pp30, 31, 100;
MM Studios (Graham Alder) p112

*The Publishers and Authors are very grateful to the following for providing
personal photographs:* Doug and Vickie Schmitt and Natalie Edwards
p58 (university ID card and photo of couple)

*The Publishers and Authors would particularly like to thank the following
readers and teachers for their help with the initial research and piloting:*
Sandra Maria Andrin, Maggie Baigent, Jo Cooke, Rachel Godfrey,
Amanda Jeffries, Marisa Perazzo, Graham Rumbelow, Enda Scott,
Joanna Sosnowska, Carol Tabor, Michael Terry.

Recordings directed by: Leon Chambers
Engineered by: Wilfredo Acosta
Words and music in songs by: Mark Hancock
Musical arrangements by: Phil Chambon
Vocals in songs by: Gina Murray and Jo Servi